# Censored Books II

## *Critical Viewpoints, 1985–2000*

Edited by

## Nicholas J. Karolides

The Scarecrow Press, Inc.
Lanham, Maryland, and London
2002

## SCARECROW PRESS, INC.

Published in the United States of America
by Scarecrow Press, Inc.
4501 Forbes Boulevard, Suite 200, Lanham, Maryland 20706
www.scarecrowpress.com

4 Pleydell Gardens, Folkestone
Kent CT20 2DN, England

Copyright © 2002 by Nicholas J. Karolides

British Library Cataloguing-in-Publication Information Available

**Library of Congress Cataloging-in-Publication Data**

Censored books II : critical viewpoints, 1985–2000 / [edited by] Nicholas Karolides.
   p. cm.
  Includes bibliographical references and index.
  ISBN 0-8108-4147-9 (cloth : alk. paper)
   1. American literature—History and criticism. 2. Censorship—United
States. 3. Young adult literature, American—History and criticism. 4.
Children's literature, American—History and criticism. 5. Young adult
literature, American—Study and teaching. 6. Children's literature,
American—Study and teaching. 7. American literature—Study and teaching. I. Title:
Censored books 2. II. Title: Censored books two. III. Karolides, Nicholas J.

PS65.C46 C45 2002
810.9—dc21                            2001045871

To Nikolas Joshua Karolides and
Sage Michael Karolides

# Contents

Contents vii

# Foreword

## Nat Hentoff

If the First Amendment guarantee of freedom of speech and press is to mean anything ... it must allow protests even against the moral code that the standard of the day sets for the community.

Supreme Court Justice William O. Douglas, dissenting.<br>
Roth v. United States, 1957.

One afternoon, at a public school in Brooklyn, I was talking to students who had been reading a novel of mine for young readers, *The Day They Came to Arrest the Book*. All these students were black, and they had been intrigued by all the people in my novel who had so fiercely desired to ban *The Adventures of Huckleberry Finn* from the school.

And I told them about other censors through the years who believed that Mark Twain's story was unfit for children. Many black parents are still indignant about the book's profuse use of the word "niggers." Fundamentalist Christians have objected to Huck's profane language and his disinclination to go to church. And feminists have complained that all the women in the book are dumb and subservient to men.

Since these Brooklyn students had read my novel, I asked whether they thought *Huckleberry Finn* should be on a public school reading list. I had told them that in 1905, the book had been thrown out of the Brooklyn Public Library as "a bad example for ingenuous youth."

"Well," a young woman said, "I learned something from reading it. I learned that what 'nigger' means depends on how it's used in the conversation." Another student told me he had bought a paperback copy of that embattled novel, liked it, and now some of his schoolmates were curious to read it. As for whether it should be banned, there was general laughter in the classroom.

"How are you going to learn anything that way?" one of them said.

During Banned Books Week in September 2000, the American Library Association reported that *The Adventures of Huckleberry Finn* was high on the list of those who would remove it from the schools; of the ten most frequently challenged books of the past decade, *Huckleberry Finn* came in at number five.

J. K. Rowling's *Harry Potter* series is coming up fast. When its huge sales became front-page news, as well as the focus of television features, there was widespread rejoicing that kids were actually clamoring to get copies of the books. They were reading again! But censors scented witchcraft and other dark powers in those books that might ensorcell ingenuous youth.

*Huckleberry Finn*, meanwhile, has also been the center of a federal court decision that is the clearest, most forceful explanation in American judicial history of why the First Amendment must protect the right to read—very much including in public schools.

Kathy Monteiro, a black woman and a teacher in the Phoenix, Arizona, public schools, had charged that her fourteen-year-old daughter had suffered psychological damage as a result of the Twain novel having been assigned as mandatory reading in her classroom. The word "nigger" appears in that novel 215 times, and her daughter, as a result, had become a captive of a hostile educational environment.

In ruling against this teacher and mother, Judge Stephen Reinhardt wrote: "The fact that a student is required to read a book does not mean that he is being asked to agree with what is in it. It cannot be disputed that a necessary component of any education is learning to think critically about offensive ideas. Without that ability, one can do little to respond to them.

"Second, it is important for young people to learn about the past and to discover both the good and bad in our history. Third, if all books with messages that might be deemed harmful were removed, the number of 'acceptable' works would be highly limited. . . . It would be folly to think that there is a certain 'safe' set of books written by particular authors that all will find acceptable."

Then Judge Reinhardt focused on the ceaseless lawsuits brought to "protect" readers from insidiously infectious books:

> Courts cannot ban books or other literary works from school curricula on the basis of their content. . . . Even when the works are accused of being racist. . . . We reject the option that putting books on trial is the proper way to determine the appropriateness of their use in the classroom.
> Kathy Monteiro v. The Tempe Union High School District,
> No. 97-15511. October 19, 1998.

Nor is it appropriate, under the First Amendment, to put books on trial outside the classroom. In the American Library Association's comprehensive *Banned Books 2000*, novelist Milan Kundera is quoted: "The first step in liquidating a people is to erase its memory. Destroy its books, its culture, its history. Then have somebody write new books, manufacture a new culture, invent a new history. Before long the nation will begin to forget what it is, and what it was. The world around it will forget even faster."

In a Maryland schoolroom, Erika Stokes explains to her sixth-grade class why it's necessary to have Banned Books Week every year.

"Before the class meets," she told me, "I put children's books that were banned or challenged somewhere sometimes (from the ALA list) into brown paper bags. I xerox the description from the resource book about why they were banned or challenged and tape it to the outside of the bag."

At that point, the children do not know the titles of the books.

After Erika Stokes talks about censorship and about how a man, Hitler, burned books, she hands out the 'bagged' books. "Students," she continues, "read the descriptions and tell me why the book they have in their hands was banned. We keep a tally of how many books were banned for the various reasons we discussed.

"Then we open the bags, and I see the amazement on the children's faces as they take out books like *The Great Gilly Hopkins, James and the Giant Peach, My Brother Sam Is Dead*. The look on their faces is priceless!

"'But that's my favorite book! Why would they ban it!' It never fails."

One year, Erika Stokes "set up an empty bookcase with a sign that read, 'These books don't offend anyone.' That sparked quite a bit of discussion." The children realized that "if we took every book off the shelf that offended somebody, we wouldn't have any left."

There once was a store in Orem, Utah, the Book Rack. The town of about 35,000 had no bookstores, so Carole Grant, a middle-aged woman, decided to open one. Five months later, she was served with a criminal summons. The charge: she had violated the town's Ordinance 210, which had established a Commission of Decency. The commissioners had discovered four publications in the Book Rack that were so indecent as to be, they said, obscene: *A Clockwork Orange, The Symbol, Last Tango in Paris*, and *The Idolaters*. Criminal charges were also brought against four superstores that sold everything from furniture to groceries. Their criminal activity involved selling such magazines as *Penthouse, Playboy*, and *Viva*.

As I wrote in my book, *The First Freedom* (Delacorte Press): "All the merchants in Orem who sold magazines and other publications held a meeting. . . . Each publicly swore to remove from their places of business all 'obscene' or 'doubtful' material." And they earnestly asked the Commission of Decency "to help them identify whatever obscene materials might still be in their stores."

Three book publishers—Random House, Dell, and Pocket Books—sent lawyers to help Carole Grant. Meanwhile she refused to pledge future "good behavior" to the Commission of Decency. Her pledge, she said, was to the First Amendment.

After months of negotiations, all charges against Carole Grant were dropped. Seven days later she closed the Book Rack. She had been worn down by all the pressures. As the National Ad Hoc Committee on Censorship said in an obituary for the Book Rack: "As is often the case, there had been no need to prosecute, intimidation had finally sufficed."

These pressures have not abated in the least. In 1999, the First Amendment Center—part of the Freedom Forum—after asking 1,001 Americans eighteen years of age or older what they thought of the First Amendment guarantees of free speech and free press, published its *State of the First Amendment Survey*.

A thumping 67 percent of those asked said that public remarks that racial groups might find offensive should not be prohibited. Such disapproval extends, of course, to "offensive"—however broadly described—books and other forms of expression.

Louis Brandeis, a Supreme Court Justice who often emphasized that all our liberties flow from our right to speak, write, and read freely, said:

> Experience teaches us to be most on our guard to protect liberty when the government's purpose is beneficent. The greatest dangers to liberty lurk in insidious encroachments by men of zeal, well-meaning but without understanding.

*Censored Books II: Critical Viewpoints, 1985–2000* makes vivid the continuing history of those forces that do not understand that a nation cannot remain free if censors, governmental and private, have the power to become the guardians of our minds.

"If large numbers of people believe in freedom of speech," George Orwell wrote, "there will be freedom of speech, even if the law forbids it. But if public opinion is sluggish, inconvenient minorities will be persecuted even if law exist to protect them."

And any of us can become an inconvenient minority of one.

# Introduction

## Nicholas J. Karolides

### *Legacies*

A pair of legacies, at once intertwined and confrontational, emerging out of the distant past, have been embedded in the American consciousness. The first pages of our history give striking evidence of these forces. Among the first European settlers on North American shores, the Puritans—beleaguered in England for their religious militance (and also prompted by economic motives)—sailed to New England seeking religions freedom. Yet their practices, rigid and authoritarian, insisted on particular interpretations of the Bible; also, church and state were not separate, religious leaders wielding much unofficial influence.

Legacy one: Puritan leaders, intolerant of dissenters, insisted on uniformity. Non–church members were not permitted to vote; Quakers "were persecuted with fines, flogging, and banishments" (Bailey 27). Legacy two: Resistance to intolerance, that is, the Puritans' religious stringencies, emerged. Roger Williams was a primary, though not a solitary, dissenter.

A clergyman, Roger Williams was a chief architect of dissent. He argued for religious tolerance and a separation of church and state. His radical ideas and . . . unrestrained tongue" led to a trial by the general court which found him "guilty of disseminating 'newe and dangerous opinions' and ordered [him to be] banished" (Bailey 27). (Another dangerous opinion: he defended Indian claims to their land.) Williams fled to Rhode Island where, having purchased the land from the Indians, he founded a new colony on the basis of complete religious tolerance.

In 1791, the framers of the Bill of Rights, amendments to the 1787 Constitution of the United States, established the underlying protections that have shaped American life. In the context of censorship, Article 1 sets the "rights" standard:

> Congress shall make no law respecting the establishment of religion, or prohibiting the free exercise thereof; or abridging the freedom of speech, or of the press, or right of the people to peaceably assemble, and to petition the government for a redress of grievances.

Two seemingly synonymous guarantees are activated in the practice of freedom of speech and the press: the right to protect and the right to protest. Thus, we can resist the infringement of these rights by individuals or groups and governments at all levels, at once protecting and protesting. Yet these forces seem to have become oppositional: on the one hand, individuals or groups challenge the reading/teaching of certain books in classrooms and the availability of certain books and materials in libraries; on the other hand, individuals or groups protest the infringement of the right to read, protected by the First Amendment. Both insist they are protecting children, the former from ideas and information perceived to be deleterious—even dangerous, the latter from the absence of ideas and information perceived to be valuable and necessary for meaningful intellectual and emotional development. These ideas and information, the center of censorship controversies, are the focus of this *Censored Books II: Critical Viewpoints, 1985–2000* collection through the interpretation and valuation of challenged literary works and the concomitant responses to the censorship challenges.

## The Collection

The present volume is similar to the preceding collection, *Censored Books: Critical Viewpoints*, issued in 1993, in its primary purpose: to provide rationales for teachers and other citizens in defense of frequently censored/challenged books for the period between 1985 and 2000. (The earlier volume surveyed the 1950 to 1985 period.) The identified works are primarily an array of fiction for early childhood readers through literature for adolescents and adults. Included also are volumes of poetry for children and nonfiction, such as autobiography and sexuality education texts. In addition to the frequency factor, several books whose challenges resulted in federal and state lawsuits are selected based on this criterion. For example, *In the Spirit of Crazy Horse*, by Peter Matthiessen, faced both federal and state court action; the censoring of *I Am the Cheese*, by Robert Cormier, was challenged in federal court in Florida. The first was challenged to ban its sale and distribution, the second to reinstate it in a middle school curriculum.

How was frequency determined? Essentially, the publications of the

American Library Association and People For the American Way, respectively the *Newsletter on Intellectual Freedom* and *Attacks on the Freedom to Learn*, were carefully examined to identify a basic list of censored books. Other sources were *SLATE*, a newsletter of the National Council of Teachers of English, and *Censorship News*, the newsletter of the National Coalition Against Censorship. These data were tabulated to establish frequency. Also examined were annual lists of most frequently censored books published by these organizations and authors.

A substantial number of titles have a long censorship history, spanning the 1950 to 1999 years. Those that were included in the 1993 volume of *Censored Books: Critical Viewpoints* were excluded from Volume II. High on the American Library Associations "Top 100 Banned or Challenged Books" from 1990-1999, which were thus excluded, are: *I Know Why the Caged Bird Sings*, by Maya Angelou; *Adventures of Huckleberry Finn*, by Mark Twain; *The Chocolate War*, by Robert Cormier; *Of Mice and Men*, by John Steinbeck; *Forever*, by Judy Blume; *Catcher in the Rye*, by J. D. Salinger; and *The Color Purple*, by Alice Walker.

Rationales for sixty-five works, including five series, are in this collection. The essayists—authors of children's, adolescent, and adult literature, college and secondary school teachers of literature, librarians, and curriculum specialists—were charged to write a defense of the particular work or works they had chosen. In short: Why should anyone read this book? Why should it be recommended? They were asked to express their impressions and interpretations of the text, of the concepts and emotions the readers might experience. A corresponding concern addressed the censorship issues surrounding the book: Why is this book being challenged? The reviewers were asked to consider the censorial challenges to the text in relation to its perceived merits.

The essays are organized alphabetically by the book's title. They provide a varied perspective. Some are oriented toward personal transactions with the text, reflecting aspects that have been challenged; others are concerned with social issues; while some also provide suggestions for classroom application. Altogether, these reviews provide diverse approaches, thoughtful and enlightening in their defense of each text and emphatic in their opposition to censorship. Given this diversity, it is evident that there is more than one way to prepare a rationale for a particular book.

## Censorship Update

The challenging and banning of books, fiction and nonfiction, has thrived in the United States over this 1985-2000 time period. The data of the

American Library Association (ALA) and People For the American Way (PFAW) attest to this observation. The lists of type of challenges are also parallel: ALA names nine (in order of frequency)—sexually explicit, offensive language, unsuited to age group, occult/satanism, violence, homosexuality, religious viewpoints, and racism (see the rationale written by Michael Angelotti defending *The Martian Chronicles*); PFAW lists only the top three—sexual content, objectionable language, and religion—but particularly identifies antigay challenges and those focused on racism, and witches/demons/devils/Halloween.

The analysis provided by People For the American Way in several of its annual summaries, *Attacks on the Freedom to Learn*, argues that the attacks on public education have broadened, encompassing—beyond individual books—entire curricular programs, education reforms, and legislative initiatives. Among these are health and sexuality programs, including AIDS education; guidance, personal self-esteem, and self-discovery programs; student expression—newspapers, literary magazines, dramatic productions, student art displays; and materials perceived not to be firmly grounded in the objector's religious faith, including science textbooks. PFAW also points to the promotion of the Parental Rights Amendment (PRA) in state legislatures. This amendment is based on the concept: "The right of parents to direct the upbringing and education of their children shall not be infringed" (Attacks 24). The implication of this amendment is that it will establish the power of veto for individual parents over public school curricula so that they will more easily succeed, not merely in limiting what their own children read but in controlling the curriculum and library selections for other parents' children.

Some significant court decisions in recent decades—with a few exceptions—have supported the rights of freedom of speech, indeed, have expanded the "definition" of this freedom.

• In the *Minarcini v. Strongsville City District* (1976) decision (five students had brought suit to have Kurt Vonnegut's *Cat's Cradle* and Joseph Heller's *Catch 22* returned to the school library), the Sixth Circuit's Court of Appeals ruled that the removal of books from a library by a school board required a legally defensible and constitutionally valid reason rather than "plac[ing] conditions on the use of the library related solely to the social or political tastes of school board members" (Karolides 88). The court signaled the distinction between content-based versus content-neutral censorship, barring the suppression of ideas.

Within the text of this ruling, another significant feature emerges within the context of a school library's function:

> A public school library is also a valuable adjunct to classroom discussion. If one
> of the English teachers considered Joseph Heller's *Catch 22* to be one of the
> most important modern American novels (as, indeed, at least one did), we
> assume that no one would dispute that the First Amendment's protection of
> academic freedom would protect both his right to say so in class and his
> students' right to hear him and find and read the book. (O'Neil 146)

In his discussion of the evolution of this appellate court's ruling, Robert
O'Neil calls attention to an "emerging doctrine," an outgrowth of cases
adjudicated by the Supreme Court in the early 1970s, that is, cases involving
the interests of listeners and viewers. The outcome: "[T]he Supreme Court
acknowledged the importance of 'a First Amendment right to receive
information and ideas' and observed that 'freedom of speech necessarily
protects the right to receive'" (147).

• The majority opinion of the Supreme Court in the landmark case *Board of
Education, Island Trees Union Free School District v. Pico* (1982) reiterated these critical positions. (Five students had filed suit in 1977 to have
nine books, including *Black Boy*, by Richard Wright, and *Slaughterhouse
Five*, by Kurt Vonnegut, returned to the library.) "The majority relied on the
concept that the 'right to receive ideas' is a 'necessary predicate' to the
meaningful exercise of freedom of speech . . ." (Karolides 49-50). Justice
William Brennan wrote for the majority:

> [W]e hold that local school boards may not remove books from school library
> shelves simply because they dislike the ideas contained in those books and seek
> by their removal to "prescribe what shall be orthodox in politics, nationalism,
> religion, or other matters of opinion . . . ." Such purposes stand inescapably
> condemned by our precedents. (Supreme 173)

• During the same year, 1982, U.S. District Court Judge Conrad Cyr struck
another chord advancing this concept. Responding to the banning of Ronald
J. Glasser's *365 Days* for its excessive use of four-letter words (rather than
its theme of death and dying and, perhaps, its antiwar message), Judge Cyr
enjoined the Baileyville School Committee from banning the book. Citing
the right-to-receive-information-and-ideas doctrine of the Supreme Court
and noting that "Public schools are major marketing places of ideas, and
First Amendment rights must be accorded to all 'persons' in the market for
ideas, including secondary school students . . ." (365 Days 67), he wrote:

How anomalous and dangerous to presume that state action banning an entire book, when the social value of its content is roundly praised and stands unchallenged by the state, does not directly and sharply implicate First Amendment rights because the ban was not intended to suppress ideas.

The social value of the conceptual and emotive content of censored expression is not to be sacrificed to arbitrary official standards of vocabular taste . . . . As long as words convey ideas, federal courts must remain on First Amendment alert in book banning cases, even those ostensibly based strictly on vocabular considerations (365 Days 68)

- Students' rights to receive ideas were undermined in the *Hazelwood School District v. Kuhlmeier* (1988) decision. The Supreme Court ruled in favor of the district's right to stop the publication in school-sanctioned newspapers of articles (in this instance on teen pregnancy and divorce) that are deemed to be "related to legitimate pedagogical concerns."

Since this ruling, according to the Student Press Law Center, requests for assistance from high schools had risen from 548 in 1988 to almost 1,500 in 1995 (Goodman n. pag.). People For the American Way documented the increased number of these challenges to student expression, noting that objectors "attempted to eliminate discussion of controversial issues or soften criticism of school officials or community establishments. But increasingly these actions are direct attempts to suppress efforts by students to raise awareness of a particular idea or theory" (Attacks 16).

- In 2001, the *Hazelwood* decision was judged to be inapplicable to a university situation in the *Kincaid v. Gibson* lawsuit. (The 1994 student yearbook had been confiscated by a Kentucky State University official.) The entire judicial body of the U.S. Court of Appeals for the Sixth Circuit, overturning rulings of both the District Court and its own three-member panel, found that there was "no justification for suppressing the yearbook on the grounds that it might be unsuitable for immature audiences." Judge R. Guy Cole, Jr., in his majority opinion wrote:

Confiscation ranks with forced government speech as amongst the purest forms of content alteration. There is little if any difference between hiding from public view the words and pictures students use to portray their college experience and forcing students to publish state-sponsored script. In either case, the government alters student expression by obliterating it. We will not sanction a reading of a First Amendment that permits government officials to censor expression in a limited forum in order to coerce speech that pleases the government. (Student 65)

• As far as Internet access is concerned, the 1994 Communications Decency Act was invalidated by the Supreme Court in 1997, following a successful challenge by the American Civil Liberties Union, the American Library Association, the National Council of Teachers of English and other groups. The court reasoned that in an effort to protect children the law had the effect of denying adults access to what they are legally entitled to receive. The Supreme Court has agreed to review the Children's Internet Protection Act passed by Congress in 1998; the ACLU and ALA have filed lawsuits to overturn this act.

## Setting Our Sights

These decisions of the U.S. Supreme Court—this heartening support of access to ideas, of the freedom of speech, encompassing the freedom both to read and to receive, should not make us sanguine. The gauntlet is still down. While the suppression of ideas, books, and school programs is the puritanical aim of today's relentless challengers, promoters of First Amendment rights must take on the steadfast commitment of Roger Williams. Through such commitment, ideological conformity and thought control will be resisted; the teaching of how to think, rather than what to think, will be encouraged and critical reasoning embraced.

## Acknowledgements

The essays in this volume convey the expertise, the expressive thoughts, and the commitment of their authors. I am indebted to them for that commitment, and for their willingness to participate in this collection, as well as for their clear, meaningful, and persuasive defenses of these challenged books. I am also indebted to several colleagues: Michael Norman for his knowledge and advice regarding censorship court cases; Ruth Wood, Marshall Toman, Steven Luebke, and Laura Zlogar for their help in locating potential authors and for their editorial advice; and Inga Karolides for her acuity and finesse with language. I acknowledge with much appreciation as well the dedication and efficiency of Doreen Cegielski, who prepared this manuscript, and Robin Boles, who contacted contributors and also prepared the "About the Contributors" section.

## Works Cited

*Attacks on the Freedom to Learn.* Washington, D.C.: People For the American Way, 1996.

Bailey, Thomas G. *The American Pageant: A History of the Republic.* Heath, 1956.

*Board of Education, Island Trees Union Free School District #26 v. Pico et al.*, 457 U.S. 853, 102 S.Ct. 2799, 73 L.Ed. 25 435 (1982).

Goodman, Mark. "Student Journalism after Hazelwood." Student Press Law Center. www.asne.org/kiosk/editor/julyaugust/goodman.

Karolides, Nicholas J. *Banned Books: Literature Suppressed on Political Grounds.* New York: Facts on File, 1998.

*Minarcini v. Strongsville City District*, 541 F. 2d 577 (6th Circuit 1976).

O'Neil, Robert M. *Classrooms in the Crossfire: The Rights and Interests of Students, Parents, Teachers, Administrators, Librarians and the Community.* Bloomington: Indiana University Press, 1981.

"Student Press." *Newsletter on Intellectual Freedom* 50 (2001): 65-66.

"The Supreme Court's Decision in *Island Trees*." *Newsletter on Intellectual Freedom* 31 (1982): 149, 173-181.

"*365 Days* Returned to Maine School Library." *Newsletter on Intellectual Freedom* 31 (1982): 33, 67-69.

# Banned by Neglect: *Tom Sawyer*, Teaching the Conflicts

## Tim Hirsch

I have to tell you in this first sentence: I consider much of *The Adventures of Tom Sawyer* offensive. I am offended that someone like Tom could be the hero of the book. I don't like the ways he bullies other kids and how he tortures animals. I don't like the way he lies to and cons both other children and adults. I don't like the way he treats women and girls. I object vehemently to the blatant anti–American Indian racism in the book, and to the more sly but equally offensive anti–African American racism. I also am troubled by the violence in the book, and by its idealization of child neglect and rebellion against "civilization." So I have no trouble at all understanding why some folks would like to ban the book. But I do not advocate censoring the book in any way. Absolutely not!

I also find most of *Tom Sawyer* absolutely delightful. I laugh out loud at his ability to con his friends into paying him for the right to paint the fence. I shudder with delicious fear when Huck and Jim witness the murder in the graveyard. I smile when Tom's invitation to become engaged to Becky backfires. I laugh again when Tom uses his fence profits to buy coupons to win a prize for learning Bible verses, and then I groan when he is forced to reveal his total ignorance of the Bible. The book moves adroitly between scenes of adolescent shenanigans and real terror. Like life in most of the United States before the Civil War, the book balances pleasure and pain, rustic good fun and the ominous presence of brutality. Although Twain called it "a hymn to a boy's life," it is really an astute and satirical treatment of the unique conflicts of American culture, not only in 1845, but now. By definition, of course, satire points out tensions between the conventional view of things and how things really are.

Without doubt, teachers should use the book in class and librarians should recommend the book to students. I first used *Tom Sawyer* with ninth graders in 1966. Since then, even though I have included *The Adventures of*

1

*Huck Finn* on my reading lists innumerable times, only recently, when I began teaching a course devoted entirely to Samuel Clemens, have I begun to include *Tom Sawyer* as a primary text. Now I am wondering why I was so late coming back to it as a classroom text. In many ways, it is even richer in teachable conflicts than *Huck Finn*. I agree with Gerald Graff, Professor of English at the University of Chicago, who argues that educators have a responsibility to "teach the conflicts." The presence of controversial materials in *Tom Sawyer* makes it an excellent candidate for "teaching." In his landmark book, *Beyond the Culture Wars: How Teaching the Conflicts Can Revitalize American Education*, Graff shows educators how to organize the classroom examination of texts around the conflicts they reflect. Is *Tom Sawyer* a racist text? What are our criteria for reaching an answer to that question? What can we learn from an examination of the contexts that constitute a racist community? Was it possible for Twain to depict Hannibal, Missouri, circa 1840, as anything but racist? What do we gain if we ignore and/or ban books that depict racist behavior? What do we lose?

Every American young person needs to read *Tom Sawyer* because it is an important work of literature, the all-time best-seller of Twain's works by a good bit. It has never been out of print since the first edition in 1876. Today it is possible to select from among more than 200 English language editions, and an additional 72 dozen films. Jim Zwick, a Twain scholar who built and maintains the best website/clearinghouse for Twain web resources, points out that a "Tom Sawyer" search on any major search engine will bring up more than a thousand sites. Perhaps it is the amazing success of *Tom Sawyer* that irritates folks who do not like it; commercially successful books seem to be more vulnerable to banning than little-known works. Or, as Twain was fond of suggesting, perhaps it was the attempts to ban the book that contributed to the popularity. Tom Sawyer is among the nation's best-known literary characters. It is no exaggeration to call him an icon for the likable young male mischief-maker so common in American popular culture.

Ironically, although many more young people (and adults) have read *Tom Sawyer* and/or seen him in a film version, it has been my impression that the book is not included in English classes nearly as often as *Huck Finn*. To check that impression, I recently asked the members of the Twain Forum, an on-line discussion site for Twain scholars, how many of them either used *Tom Sawyer* in class themselves or knew of a teacher who did. The responses came from middle school, high school, and college teachers. Although most regularly teach *Huck Finn*, very few have ever taught *Tom Sawyer*—even in courses devoted entirely to Twain.

When I asked these Twain scholars why *Tom Sawyer* is rarely taught in

English classes, none of them identified the hazards of a challenge as a factor. Instead, they suggest that *Tom Sawyer*, the book, and Tom Sawyer, the character, are less serious than *Huck Finn*, the book, and Huck Finn, the character. Only a few Twain scholars have defended Twain's creation of Tom. Bernard DeVoto was among them a half-century ago. In his introduction to *The Portable Mark Twain*, DeVoto suggested that Tom is one "exploration" of the depravity of the backwoods mind (32-33). Today, Bruce Michelson, in *Mark Twain on the Loose: A Comic Writer and the American Self*, also attempts to show both Tom and his namesake book as complex and worthy of more critical attention. Michelson summarizes, "Tom gets a lot of bad press, and persuasive readings of Huck's own narrative have made much of Tom as Huck's bad angel, a spirit of malignant childishness haunting the world his friend must pass through" (102). That description of Tom' behavior— "malignant childishness"—is my response, too, until I read more carefully and try to understand the conflicts Clemens builds into the narrative. Following Graff's lead, I encourage every teacher to look again at *Tom Sawyer* and think about how the conflicts in the book might produce more fruitful discussion and significant learning for their students.

Some of the earliest challenges to *Tom Sawyer* suggested that it might be an acceptable book for adults, but that children should not read it because they might be encouraged by Tom's success with pranks and rebellious behavior to emulate him. Ironically, Twain began *Tom Sawyer* with an adult audience in mind, but his wife, Livy, and his friend William Dean Howells Twain writes, "Although my book is intended mainly for the entertainment of boys and girls, I hope it will not be shunned by men and women on that account. . . ." Your students might be interested in the tension Twain felt about the intended audience. When we read through the book, where do we see the residual evidence of that tension? For example, my students always wonder about Tom's age. In some scenes—carrying junk and dead animals around—he appears to be at least fourteen. Students enjoy trying to fix Tom's age for each of his scenes.

These early challenges to *Tom Sawyer* opposed it because the book glorifies and seems to approve of Tom's "bad" behavior. I feel that way myself about some parts of the book. It is helpful to me, however, and it might be to students, to know that Tom is simply a new member of a long line of literary "bad boys," including some created earlier by Twain himself. In the 1850s a humorist named Benjamin Penhallow Shillaber was writing stories about Ike Partington, who did things like hang cats from trees ("The Life and Ways of Mrs. Partington and Others of the Family," New York: J. C. Derby, 1854). Shillaber's Ike was one of Twain's favorites. Another favorite was a bad boy named Tom, created by Thomas Bailey Aldrich, whose best-known work, *The Story of a Bad Boy*, first appeared serially, in 1869, in *Our Young Folks*, a humor magazine for young adults. Aldrich's Tom enjoys brawling, vandalism, and general mischief-making. Twain's own contribution to this genre included "The Story of the Bad Little Boy That Led a Charmed Life," first published in the *Californian Magazine* in 1865. Jim, the bad boy in this story, commits several cruel and nasty deeds. He is never caught nor punished, and he never repents. The story ends:

> And he grew up, and married, and raised a family, and brained them all with an ax one night, and got wealthy by all manner of cheating and rascality; and now he is the infernalist wickedest scoundrel in his native village, and is universally respected, and belongs to the Legislature.

Twain followed his story about the bad boy with a story, also first published in the *Californian*, entitled, "The Story of the Good Little Boy Who Did Not Prosper." This little boy is as good as the other bad, but he ends up getting blown to bits while attempting to do a good deed.

Clearly these stories show that Mark Twain was struggling with the questions, "Why do bad things happen to good people?" and "Why do bad people sometimes seem to prosper?" These are questions humans have asked for thousands of years.

Young people especially appear adept at seeing "unfairness" all around them. In *Tom Sawyer*, Twain addresses these questions with more subtlety than he had in his earlier "bad boy/good boy" stories. Although Tom does get away with some "bad" boy stuff, he also sometimes gets punished for things he has not done. While the book does not present a picture of moral inevitability, it does show that characters are usually regarded and/or punished for the general trend of their behavior. I could not think of a more horrible punishment for Injun Joe than his death in the cave. On the other hand, while it's probably true that Tom does not deserve to win both the girl and the treasure, he and Huck discover that the treasure does not improve the quality of their lives. Justice is not certain, but on average it works out. *Tom Sawyer* is an excellent book to use for young people who are often having trouble coming to grips with the tension between how life ought to be ideally and how they experience it.

The many scenes in *Tom Sawyer* that focus on innocent people accused of wrongdoing provide teachers an opportunity to address issues of justice and fairness: In chapter 2, Tom is thumped for breaking the sugar bowl though Sid did it; in chapter 4, Tom gets the Bible Prize though he knows not even one verse; in chapter 18, Tom gets punished for spilling ink on his spelling book though Albert Temple did it; in chapter 20, Tom takes the blame for tearing the page out of Dobbins's book though Becky did it. These little injustices set the stage for and surround the most important one: Muff Potter is accused of a murder he has not committed. All the other rascally things Tom does are mediated by his empathy for the unjustly accused Muff and by his courageous decision to testify in Muff's defense.

My favorite scene in the book is the one in chapter 23 when Tom and Huck go to see Muff in jail and talk with him through the barred window. Muff asks to shake Tom's hand:

> "Get up on one another's back, and let me touch 'em. That's it. Shake hands—yourn'll come through the bars, but mine's too big. Little hands—and weak—but they've helped Muff Potter a power, and they'd help him more if they could." (190)

Tom reaches across this barrier, touches Muff's hand, and feels an empathy that stimulates his conscience to testify on Muff's behalf, to tell the truth when it most matters. In that simple scene, Twain reveals to his readers the moral heart of everything he ever wrote: when good human beings reach across barriers and touch each other's hearts, it is no longer possible to be cruel or indifferent. Once that essential electricity of empathy crosses from Muff's hand to Tom's, he knows he must do the right thing—he must testify. Tom may be a "bad" boy in small ways, but in the most important way of all—the ability to feel empathy for even the town drunk locked in jail—Tom has a "good heart."

This scene helps us understand and teach the conflict Twain feels between "model" behavior, which is based on following rules and obeying conventions, and "good-hearted" behavior, which is based on empathy and respect for the essential sister/brotherhood of all humans. In the first chapter, Tom admits that "he was not the Model Boy of the village. He knew the model boy well enough—and loathed him." Twain cinches the point by showing us Albert Temple two paragraphs later: "He was well dressed, too—well dressed on a weekday. This was simply astounding." For Tom, Albert represents pretension and snobbery, and Tom's greeting to him is "I can lick you." Tom is always ready to combat snobbery and convention. He cannot be indifferent to Albert because Albert's clothes and condescension make him feel shabby. He has to confront this stimulus of his shame. People of all ages, but especially young people, understand Tom's impulse, but with guidance they might also see how Tom's response to Albert is entirely superficial—based on nothing but clothes. Albert is new to town; he cannot be expected to know how to dress in this new place. If Tom had been able to show the same kind of empathy for Albert as he shows later for Muff, he might have taken him aside and given him advice on how to dress in St.

Petersburg instead of challenging him to fight. Even very young readers can see how Twain is using Tom's cruel treatment of this new kid in town to satirize "dressing up" for status and acceptance. They can see, too, that Tom's response to Albert's clothes reveals that he is not immune to the power of clothes.

Crafting his satire, Twain often gives Tom the dual role of pointing out injustices and incongruities by doing something slightly cruel. Tom gives his Aunt Polly's cat, Peter, medicine she intended for him to point out that people do things to children they would never do to pets. But the cat suffers. Tom uses a cat again to lift Dobbins's wig to reveal the schoolmaster's gilded bald head and his drinking problem, but the poor cat, dangling at the end of a rope, clearly suffers. He allows his family and the townspeople to think he is dead to point out the irony that the dead are often more loved than the living, but we also see that Aunt Polly suffers deep grief unnecessarily.

Many young readers find it difficult to appreciate satire, but I have seen them respond to the satire in *Tom Sawyer*. I believe that Mark Twain delineates teachable conflicts better than any other American writer, and I think that *Tom Sawyer* is especially good for this purpose. Every day American high school and middle school students confront attempts at humor that may seem funny to the perpetrators but, in fact, are more cruel than funny. *Tom Sawyer* is a book that we can use to address this conflict and help students negotiate the boundaries between funny and cruel.

Samuel Clemens was a writer who lived his life in boundaries, not only between cruel and funny, but between most of the major conflicts in American cultural history. No wonder he even feels conflict between his given name, Samuel Clemens, and his public persona, Mark Twain. He grew up on the edges between the North and the South at a time when the tensions between them were at their peak—a slaveholding South and an abolitionist North; an honor-bound South and a pragmatic North. It is inevitable that race and racial relationships are among the most important conflicts in his writing. Strangely, he deals only in subtle ways with African Americans in *Tom Sawyer*. The boy, Jim, whom he first tries to con into painting the fence would have been a slave, although Twain describes him much like any free boy. Beyond that, African Americans are specifically referred to only as sources of information about such things as how to whistle or how to use or protect yourself from superstitions. Why are African Americans almost invisible in *Tom Sawyer*? This question can be a window into other related questions: Why are there no black characters in the television programs of the 1950s and 60s? Why are the sports teams of fifty years ago all white?

For me, the most troubling and interesting racial conflict in *Tom Sawyer* centers on Injun Joe. Most Twain scholars agree that his attitudes about

American Indians are much more racist than his attitudes about any other group. The selection of a mixed-blood American Indian for his deeply evil antagonist in *Tom Sawyer* seems to confirm it. Twain claimed that he named Injun Joe after the only Indian living in Hannibal, an Osage who had been scalped by Pawnees as a child. He had survived and was brought to Hannibal by a crew of cowboys. Twain did not suggest that he also based the character of Injun Joe on this unfortunate orphan. More likely, the evil character of Injun Joe grew out of Twain's bitter disappointment that the Indians he saw on his journeys west did not match the pictures of "Noble Savages" he had read in works by writers like James Fenimore Cooper. Again and again in his life, Samuel Clemens's reading and imagination enabled him to create impossibly idealized stereotypes, only to be disappointed when he encountered the real thing. Chapter 19 of *Roughing It* provides a clear and sad glimpse into Twain's proclivity to be disappointed by reality. Though we cannot approve of Twain's racism, it is possible to understand it in this context. I address this issue in class by reading a passage or two from Cooper's *The Deerslayer*, and then Twain's description of the Gosiute people whose arid territory on the edge of the Great Salt Lake Desert combined with pressure from other tribes and the westward movement of whites had forced them to eat insects. Though Twain had an amazing capacity to transcend—through empathy—the limitations of his time and place, it took him many more years to get over his disappointment with real American Indians. Such issues need to be addressed in school. As teachers, we should not ignore conflict. We need to make conflict the center of our curriculum.

Yes, *Tom Sawyer* is a troubling book. It forces us to address innumerable unsavory features of American history. It forces us to examine our attitudes about "model" behavior, and the possibility that what makes us laugh might make others suffer. The book shows us that attitudes change, and it provides a case study of several—treatment of animals, race relations, gender relations. Through a guided reading of *Tom Sawyer*, our students can consider points of tension and grow in their understanding of how empathy can be a key to unraveling many conflicts. Though *Tom Sawyer* is not challenged or banned nearly as often as *Huck Finn*, it is also not taught nearly as often in schools. I think that's a shame. Neglect can be a more effective vehicle for dismissing a book than banning. Young people need to read *Tom Sawyer* with the guidance of a teacher who can help them frame the tensions in the book in the context of time and place. *Tom Sawyer* is an exciting and engaging story full of delightful characters and scenes. That's why it has continued to be a success even though teachers have neglected it. *Tom Sawyer* is also a great book for teaching the conflicts that have engaged

American people for several hundred years.

## Works Cited

DeVoto, Bernard (ed). *The Portable Mark Twain*. New York: Viking Press, 1946.
   With this anthology of Twain's work, DeVoto reintroduced for critical discussion several issues and texts that had been essentially cut off from examination by Albert Bigelow Paine and Clara Clemens. DeVoto is among the earliest writers about Clemens to focus on the distinctions between Mark Twain and Samuel Clemens.

Graff, Gerald. *Beyond the Culture Wars: How Teaching the Conflicts Can Revitalize American Education*. New York: W.W. Norton & Company, 1992.
   Graff's classic work on how to negotiate conflict in American classrooms is an excellent starting point for anyone interested in teaching banned books. His suggestion that we "teach the conflicts" provides an excellent framework for addressing different points of view.

Hoffman, Andrew. *Inventing Mark Twain: The Lives of Samuel Langhorne Clemens*. New York: William Morrow, 1997.
   This is my favorite new biography of Samuel Clemens. I like it because Hoffman, like Graff, believes that a frank, dispassionate examination of conflicts is one of the most important ways to learn. He does an excellent job of addressing the many points of tension in Clemens's life.

Michelson, Bruce. *Mark Twain on the Loose: A Comic Writer and the American Self*. Boston: University of Massachusetts Press, 1995.
   Michelson does an excellent job of positioning the comic writing of Samuel Clemens, both among other comic texts and the evolving sense of what it means to be an "American."

Rasmussen, R. Kent. *Mark Twain A-Z: The Essential Reference to His Life and Writings*. New York: Oxford University Press, 1995.
   Rasmussen's book is an extremely valuable reference for anyone reading or teaching a work by Samuel Clemens. Everything you'll probably ever want to know about Clemens, about his work, and about his world, are in *A-Z*. If you want to know even more, he provides a comprehensive bibliography for you to continue.

Twain, Mark. *The Adventures of Tom Sawyer*. New York: Heritage Press, 1936.

Zwick, Jim. *Mark Twain*. http://marktwain.about.com/arts/marktwain/.
Jim Zwick maintains by far the most useful website available on Samuel Clemens. The site includes access to the Twain Forum, to Twain chat rooms, and many other resources. It includes links to other sites, including e-text sources for almost everything Clemens wrote, e-text sources of critical writings about Clemens's work, and innumerable sources of teaching materials.

# Growing up with the *Alice* Series by Phyllis Reynolds Naylor

## Katherine T. Bucher and M. Lee Manning

Select one of the following groups of words and phrases to describe the books in the *Alice* series written by Newbery Medal–winning author Phyllis Reynolds Naylor:

A) Too explicit—graphic—sarcastic—mentions underwear—contains offensive language—unsuited to age group condoning sex with dead people and drunk girls—inappropriate for any age group.
B) Preachy—didactic—contrived.
C) Full of vitality—readable—laughable—lighthearted—sensitive—true to life—compassionate—reassuring—deftly written—contains substantial themes—sweet and witty—strongly characterized—age appropriate—cheerful, upbeat writing with a positive emphasis.
D) All of the above.

As you probably guessed, D is the correct answer. It is, however, the description in answer A that has placed the *Alice* series in the number 2 spot behind the Harry Potter series in the top ten challenged books for 1999 (Chansanchai 1E) and in the fourteenth spot in the top 100 challenged books from 1990 to 1999 ("The 100 Most"). To explain this placement, it is necessary to look, first, at the books in the series, and, then, at the objections to the books and the rationale for rejecting attempts to censor them.

Phyllis Reynolds Naylor begins her saga as Alice McKinley is ready to start sixth grade in Silver Springs, Maryland. Since Alice's mother died when she was four, her Dad and brother, Lester, have been raising Alice with occasional help from Aunt Sally, who lives in Chicago. In *The Agony of Alice*, Alice tracks her progress through the normal trials and tribulations of growing up by keeping a journal of the things she does that show she is moving forward in life and the things that show she is moving backward. The "backward" list includes opening the wrong dressing room door at a store and seeing a boy in blue underpants, kicking a teacher accidentally while dressed as a horse for Halloween, and pulling her friend Pamela's hair during the annual school pageant.

Then, suddenly, sixth grade is over. *Alice in Rapture, Sort of* finds Alice and her close friends Pamela and Elizabeth getting ready for junior high in what her dad calls the summer of the first boyfriend. The three girls must cope with Alice getting her first perm and learning to babysit, Pamela's boyfriend Mark stealing her Up-Lift Spandex Ahh-Bra, and Elizabeth refusing to eat in front of boys. Patrick, the boy in the blue underpants, is now Alice's boyfriend; but Alice often wonders if things were not better when they were just good friends.

*Reluctantly Alice*, *All But Alice*, and *Alice in April* follow Alice through seventh grade as she tries to match her dad with Miss Summers, her new English teacher; teach Elizabeth about the human body through the photographs in *National Geographic*; and "help" twenty-year-old Lester cope with his two girlfriends. When she attempts to become one of the "in" group, Alice finds that kindness to your friends is the most important thing after all. As the year ends and her birthday approaches, Alice tries to assume more responsibility at home while coping with the boys at school, who are giving the girls nicknames of states based on the geography of the state and the contours of the girls' chests. Absorbed in her own problems, Alice does not realize that abuse at home is driving one of her classmates toward suicide.

In the summer between seventh and eighth grade, Alice finds she still has a lot of growing up to do and some difficult situations to get through in *Alice In-Between*. In addition to the train trip where Pamela pretends she is a college student and winds up hiding from an amorous businessman, Alice has to eat dinner at Patrick's house, find out if she has to wear a bra, and help Pamela cut her long blonde hair after the boys put gum in it.

The book title may be *Alice the Brave*, but Alice feels anything but brave when she thinks about the deep end of a swimming pool. It is summer and everyone is having fun at the pool. Everyone, that is, except Alice, who is deathly afraid of being thrown in the deep water.

Eighth grade is full of surprises. *Alice in Lace* finds Alice and Patrick planning their wedding. Although it is not an actual wedding and is just part of a "critical choices" unit in Mr. Everett's class, Alice and her friends find themselves facing a variety of problems. Thus, Pamela copes with a pregnancy and Elizabeth buys a car while they both help Alice plan the big event. In *Outrageously Alice*, Alice is tired of being the same old Alice and vows to be different. Dying her hair green only gets her in trouble with her dad, and dressing up as a showgirl for Halloween leads to an unexpected and unwelcome kiss in the school's broom closet. When Alice tries to devise a plan to help her dad's romance in *Achingly Alice*, she finds that life is full of unpleasant surprises. She also has to help Elizabeth have a pelvic exam, and has to choose between two boys that she likes.

*Alice on the Outside* has Alice waiting for the visit of Carol, Aunt Sally's divorced daughter. Alice thinks this will be her chance to ask if sex is really like what you see in the movies. To her surprise, she finds out that everything is more complex than she believed, even the attitudes of her classmates. When the school participates in Consciousness Raising Week, Alice learns what prejudice is really like and that some students do not remember its lessons very long.

Finally eighth grade is over, and Alice and her friends are going to get in shape before high school. In *The Grooming of Alice*, Alice, Pamela, and Elizabeth plan on an exciting summer; and Alice is looking forward to some time alone with Patrick when her dad visits Miss Summers in England. But things change when Alice lies to her dad and is placed on restriction, Elizabeth begins to starve herself in an effort to become thin, and Pamela is sent to Colorado to live with her mom.

Naylor expects to continue the series until Alice is eighteen, with the next book, *Alice Alone*, published in 2001. Among the many awards and accolades received by the series are a *School Library Journal* Best Book for *All But Alice*; an International Reading Association Children's Choice Selection for *All But Alice* and *The Agony of Alice*; an ALA Quick Pick for *Alice in April*; and several starred or pointered reviews in *School Library Journal*, *Kirkus Reviews*, and *Booklist*.

A number of reviewers have praised the *Alice* books. Speaking of *Reluctantly Alice*, Pamela K. Bomboy found the characters "realistic and full of vitality" with a "cheerful, upbeat writing and positive emphasis" (193). Diane Roback and Richard Donahue called the same book an "honest and funny portrayal of the ups and downs of seventh grade" (58). In a review of *All But Alice*, Deborah Stevenson noted that the book is "a smart and funny paean to the pleasures and trials of the herd instinct as well as the rewards and pains of moving beyond it" (244). Noting that Naylor has the ability to use humor to treat serious problems, Betsy Hearne found *Alice In-Between* full of "energetic dialogue" as well as "sprightly episodes" (296). Hazel Rochman summed up the feelings of many reviewers when she wrote, in her review of *Alice the Brave*, "Alice's wry, funny, vulnerable voice expresses every girl's fears about what is 'normal' in an imperfect world" (Brave 1575). In addition, Kitty Flynn called Alice a "refreshingly honest character with poignantly realistic adolescent highs and lows" and praised the "funny and reassuring stories about growing up" (Achingly 348). Reviewing *The Grooming of Alice*, Dina Sherman pointed out that Naylor "includes candid information on topics such as sex, physical development in adolescence, and eating disorders in a way that makes it completely accessible to readers" (175). She concluded that this is an "engaging story with strong, three-dimensional characters" (175). Finally, Kitty Flynn noted the growing number of "self-esteem-boosting nonfiction books for girls" (Grooming 463) and summed up the entire *Alice* series when she wrote,

> the twelve-book Alice series . . . offers a similar message: if you're happy with who you are on the inside, you'll be happy with how you look on the outside. But hearing it from Alice . . . carries more weight than the advice of experts and the testimonial of strangers." (Grooming 463)

Indeed, Naylor's series has been referred to as a "novelized handbook on adolescence" (Vasilakis 372). The books have also been seen as ones that "make Judy Blume's *Forever* (1975) seem old-fashioned" (Rochman, Still 1586). Thus, because of the frankness of her characters and the situations in which she places them, Phyllis Reynolds Naylor has found her *Alice* series in second place on the list of most challenged books of 1999 because of "offensive language" and "being unsuited to age group" (Chansanchai 1E). Several cases illustrate the controversy that has surrounded these works.

In 1997, although a committee of educators and parents had voted to keep *All But Alice*, the Rosemount-Apple Valley-Eagen School Board in Minnesota removed the book from all of its elementary school libraries because of "a passage on one page about rock lyrics that mentions having sex with drunk girls" ("District Pulls Book" 03B). There was also a feeling that the book "condone[s] sex with dead people or drunk girls" (Endler 9A). A parent had raised the initial objection to the book but had indicated that she thought the book would be more suitable for older students.

*The Agony of Alice* was challenged in Fairfax, Virginia, in 1999 when two parents objected after it was assigned to their fifth-grade daughter. Calling the book "too explicit and graphic for elementary students," the parents also objected to the book's tone and the use of "sarcastic humor" (Benning 8B). The parents involved had also not enrolled their daughter in the Family Life Education curriculum in the school. Although the teacher allowed the daughter to read an alternative book, the parents "still wanted the book removed from school libraries and the district's list of approved reading materials" (Benning 8B). Agreeing with several school and district committees, the School Board voted to retain the book with the stipulation that it not be used for required reading for fifth graders or younger students and that it be used for small group discussions only with groups of girls.

On the other side of this controversy are the thousands of avid readers, adults as well as children and adolescents, who have made the *Alice* series so popular. As one teenager wrote about *Alice in Lace*, "it really made me think about how problems like these could really mess up your life" (Bellhouse 43). "A story makes you think about what's up ahead" (Bellhouse 44). Naylor herself recounts the actions of a group of boys who bought some of the Alice books because they could "learn about girls this way" (Rochman, Still 1586). Undoubtedly, children and young adults can relate to Alice and her experiences.

Another appeal of the *Alice* series is the ability of adults to use them as a starting point for discussions. When their daughters were getting ready to enter junior high school, a group of mothers in Silver Springs, Maryland, started a mother-daughter book club to discuss important issues. Selecting *The Agony of Alice* because Alice has feelings of inadequacy as well as her first boyfriend, first kiss, and first menstrual period, the mothers were surprised to find that the daughters focused on the complex issues in the books (Jacobsen 5B). In one junior high school, the teacher of a Family Life/Health class read the *Alice* books aloud to her coed class, finding that students felt comfortable discussing the issues that are raised in the books (Rochman, Still, 1586). As these adults found out, having a fictional story or character to talk about makes it easier for many children and adolescents to talk about serious problems and difficult situations. To her credit, Naylor keeps up with the changing world of teenagers by listening to them, reading "their graffiti in school restrooms" (Rochman, Still 1586), and reading their letters and e-mails.

But what about the concerns and challenges that have been raised about the books in the series? Somehow the concern about sixth-grade Alice seeing a boy in his underwear seems strange in an age where the Victoria's Secret catalog shows what used to be seen only in *Playboy*. In deciding what goes in her books, Naylor sets two criteria. First, the subject must be viewed from a child's perspective. In addition, the topic must be dealt with honestly (Merina 9).

All of the books in the series are told from the point of view of Alice McKinley, a warm, caring girl in a single-parent household, a trait typical of many modern families. Her father, Ben McKinley, has kept the family together while dealing with the problems of both Alice and her older brother, Lester, a college student. The broad spectrum of children and young adolescents is seen in Alice and her friends; especially her best friends Pamela, the typical "fast" girl in the crowd, and prudish Elizabeth. As Alice grows up, she does things wrong; worries about the unknown; speculates about relationships and what happens in them; and questions her dad, her friends, and her brother. The supportive family environment of the McKinley household comes through in each book as Alice realizes the importance of family relationships, being truthful, and helping each other. For example, in *Outrageously Alice*, after Alice goes to school with green eye shadow and green spiked hair, she realizes that, even though she disappointed her father, he still loves her.

> I sat watching Dad sew on his button and realized that maybe when you love someone, it isn't always the same. You could be disappointed in him one day and go right back to loving him the next. Maybe you could even be disappointed in him and go on loving him, both at the same time. (71-72)

While many parents do not want their children to read about sex, this does not stop children from thinking about it, or from learning about it on the school bus, over the television, on the Internet, or through other things that they see, read, and hear every day. Children today have more freedom and more choices than ever before. The books in the *Alice* series allow children to see the problems and pitfalls that this freedom brings. The questions that Alice and her friends have are those that most children and young adults would like to ask if only they could find someone they felt comfortable asking. Through Alice and her friends, girls have an opportunity to confront many of the problems they will face as they mature, not only the problems of physical development, but psychological and social problems as well. Alice is placed in a number of situations that force her to make decisions. While her decisions are not always right, she learns and grows from them. These are the same situations that happen in real life. However, the fact that they happen in a book does not mean that the author condones or endorses them. What Naylor does is give Alice the opportunity to react to the situation. Sometimes Alice or her friends make the right choice, sometimes the wrong one. But, unlike real life, the readers can learn from the results without suffering the real-life consequences. Naturally, as Alice matures, her concerns and the problems that she faces become more serious. In *The Grooming of Alice*, Alice kisses Patrick and feels "a *zing*" go through her. Then she wonders "what would happen if I ever *was* in the house alone with Patrick and we knew for sure Dad wouldn't be there" (27).

According to Naylor, "the people most vehement about my books haven't read them" (Merina 9). It is true that in *All But Alice* there are rock lyrics that mention "sex with zombie girls" (40), but when Alice hears the lyrics she blushes and is embarrassed that she wrote a fan letter to a member of the group without really knowing much about the group or their music. In *The Agony of Alice*, a younger Alice remembers sticking crayons up her nose in third grade. Instead of sanctioning this practice, Naylor mentions the incident to point out how most people have done things they would prefer to forget.

As Judith Saltman comments, "our libraries, schools, and bookstores exist . . . in a pluralistic society serving communities which contain families and cultural and social groups with a vast range of beliefs and values" (11). In her opinion, this diversity demands a parallel diversity of "viewpoints, values, and options in our children's books" (11). Books like those in the *Alice* series have emotional realism that helps children develop the skills to make informed decisions, develop personal value systems, and build "empathetic relationships" (12) with others.

Naylor's belief that there is a strong moral element in the *Alice* books (Rochman, Still 1586) is confirmed by several examples from *Alice in Lace*. Thinking about how things just happen, Alice compares life to "an obstacle course, with detours, yield signs, stop signs and cautions"(3). When she wishes she had been born with a built-in buzzer to warn her before she does anything stupid, her father calmly reminds her that she does have a buzzer—her conscience. Later in the same novel, as she learns from her experiences, Alice also sees that life is about "setting priorities, figuring out what was really important and what wasn't" (98). Life is also thinking "about things *before* they happen so you can make the best choices" (130).

Naylor believes that it is important for authors to address social, racial, and political issues that concern them in their books. While she cautions against preaching a sermon, she believes that the topics should be woven into the book. Thus readers find Alice dealing with serious issues including racial prejudice, the treatment of homosexual classmates, and anorexia. When Alice finds that two of her classmates are lesbians, she wonders "why people seem so afraid that someone who's gay or lesbian might make a pass at them. All you have to say is no, just like you'd tell a guy who was hitting on you" (*Alice on the Outside* 103). Although some parents object to the inclusion of these topics in the books, others see these same topics as excellent starting points for thoughtful, mature conversations with their children. Alice herself wonders why adults "think that if we hear or read about something, we'll rush right out and do it" (*Alice in Lace* 12). A lot of adults wonder the same thing.

Why should adults recommend the *Alice* series to children and adolescents? In addition to providing factual answers to many of the questions that children have about the physical changes that occur as they grow up, the *Alice* books help students deal with the moral dilemmas they encounter. "In my Alice series . . . I promised myself that I would write about everything that a girl would wonder about, and I am sticking to that promise. . . . I refuse to back away just because it's controversial" (West 181).

A key word in the use of the *Alice* series with children is "appropriate." Parents and teachers throughout the country have questioned whether the books are appropriate for a fifth grader? a fourth grader? a third grader? Even Alice and her friends Pamela and Elizabeth would have different reactions to that question. Pamela, who is physically mature enough as a seventh grader to pass for a college student, and whose father leaves his copy of *Playboy* in the living room, would be reading the entire series. However, Elizabeth probably would not begin the series until she is in high school. According to Alice, Elizabeth would have felt right at home in the Victorian age.

Is the *Alice* series appropriate for every child? As Bruce D. Endler, the only member of the Rosemount-Apple Valley-Eagan School Board who voted to keep *All But Alice* in the libraries of the district's elementary schools, said, "many fourth- and fifth-grade students possess sufficient intellectual and emotional maturity to make this book an appropriate choice for them. . . . Removing *All But Alice*. . . . protects one group's values at the expense of another group's rights" (9A). But anyone considering the use of the *Alice* series should remember that Alice grows up and matures throughout the series. A fifth grader may feel very comfortable with the problems, issues, and concerns in *Alice in Rapture, Sort of,* but may not be ready for the situations encountered by eighth-grade Alice in *The Grooming of Alice*. As Maeve Visser Knoth noted, the later books in the series may be "better suited to the older middle-school readers who have themselves been growing up along with Alice" (461). However, as Naylor says, it is "important that parents understand that they have the right to approve or disapprove of what their own children are reading, but they have no right at all to censor what children or other parents might find interesting" (West 182).

## Works Cited

"The 100 Most Frequently Challenged Books of 1990-1999." *American Library Association. Office of Intellectual Freedom.* (2 December 2000.) http://www.ala.org/alaorg/oif/top100bannedbooks.html.

Bellhouse, Lauren. "Alice in Lace" [book review]. *Stone Soup* (September-October, 1997): 43+.

Benning, Victoria. "Fairfax to Keep Book in School Libraries: Novel on Puberty Upset Girl's Parents." *The Washington Post* (22 December 1999), Final ed. 8B. 5 January 2001. http://ptg.djnr.com/ccroot/asp/publib/story.asp.

Bomboy, Pamela K. "Reluctantly Alice" [book review]. *School Library Journal* (March 1991): 193.

Chansanchai, Athima. "Most-loved Books Often Most-banned Literature." *The Baltimore Sun* (29 September 2000), Final ed.: 1E.

"District Pulls Book from School Libraries." *Star-Tribune Newspaper of the Twin Cities Minneapolis-St Paul* (30 July 1997). Metro ed. 3B. 5 (January 2001) http://ptgo.djnr.com/ccroot/asp/publib/story.asp.

Endler, Bruce D. "Voting Against a School Book Ban; Let Parents Decide for Their Own Kids, Not Others'." *Star-Tribune Newspaper of the Twin Cities Minneapolis-St. Paul* (4 August 1997). Metro 9A. (1 January 2001) http://ptg.djnr.com/ccroot/asp/publib/story/asp.

Flynn, Kitty. "Achingly Alice" [book review]. *Horn Book Magazine* 74.3 (1998): 348.

———. "The Grooming of Alice" [book review]. *Horn Book Magazine* 76.4 (2000): 463.

Hearne, Betsy. "Alice In-Between" [book review]. *Bulletin of the Center for Children's Books* (May 1994): 296.

Jacobsen, Mary Jeanne. "Families; Members of the Club; Mothers & Daughters Making a Connection With Books." *The Washington Post* (7 May 1993). Final ed.: 5B. 5 January 2001 http://ptg.djnr.com/ccroot/asp/publib/story.asp.

Knoth, Maeve Visser. "Outrageously Alice" [book review]. *The Horn Book Magazine* 73.4 (1997): 460-461.

Merina, Anita. "Write from the Heart." *NEA Today* (May 1992): 9.

Naylor, Phyllis. *Achingly Alice*. New York: Atheneum, 1998.

———. *The Agony of Alice*. New York: Atheneum, 1985.

———. *Alice in April*. New York: Atheneum, 1993.

————. *Alice In-Between*. New York: Atheneum, 1994.

————. *Alice in Lace*. New York: Atheneum, 1996.

————. *Alice in Rapture, Sort Of.* New York: Atheneum, 1989.

————. *Alice on the Outside*. New York: Atheneum, 1999.

————. *Alice the Brave*. New York: Atheneum, 1995.

————. *All But Alice*. New York: Atheneum, 1992.

————. *The Grooming of Alice*. New York: Atheneum, 2000.

————. *Outrageously Alice*. New York: Atheneum, 1997.

————. *Reluctantly Alice*. New York: Atheneum, 1991.

Roback, Diane, and Richard Donahue. "Reluctantly Alice" [book review]. *Publishers Weekly* (12 April 1991): 58.

Rochman, Hazel. "Alice, Still Outrageous." *Booklist* 95.7 (1999): 1586.

————."Alice the Brave" [book review]. *Booklist* 91.17 (1995): 1575.

Saltman, Judith. "Censoring the Imagination; Challenges to Children's Books." *Emergency Librarian* (January/February 1998): 8-12.

Sherman, Dina. "The Grooming of Alice" [book review]. *School Library Journal* (May 2000): 175.

Stevenson, Deborah. "All But Alice" [book review]. *Bulletin of the Center for Children's Books* (May 1992): 244.

West, Mark I. "Speaking of Censorship: An Interview with Phyllis Reynolds Naylor." *Journal of Youth Services in Libraries* (Winter 1997): 177-182.

Vasilakis, Nancy. "Alice in Rapture, Sort Of" [book review]. *The Horn Book*. (May/June 1989): 372.

# Facing Intolerance: *All-American Boys* by Frank Mosca

## Sharon M. Scapple

At the very least, the subject of homosexuality is disconcerting to many readers in society, particularly adults, the consequent censors, who hold that texts bearing gay characters or themes are immoral, even damaging to the young reader. It is hard to get past this condemnation and move on to the reading itself. But move past it we must if we are to give heterosexual adolescents stories that realistically portray lives different from their own, that enable them to know the struggles gay teens face and to know that gays are people, too. And, move past it we must if we are going to give homosexual adolescents stories that will validate their struggles growing up gay. If such a text did not strike a note of compassion within the reader, if the text did not draw the audience into a sympathetic and understanding relationship with the characters, then it would suffer for lack of credibility. Neither scenario is true of Frank Mosca's *All-American Boys*.

As did many of the books written in the 1980s that featured gay characters and focused on gay bashing—violence against homosexual characters was "rampant" in these novels (Cuseo 3-4)—*All American Boys* illuminates the idea that homosexual behavior can be hazardous to those involved. It would be simplistic, however, to leave the description of this text to gay-bashing and the bitter consequences of living the gay life. And, though it is true that the main characters, Neil and Paul, are terrorized and punished for being gay, that Neil finds revenge when attacked, that the perpetrators are sentenced lightly, the promise in Mosca's *All-American Boys* is the positive and, at times, tender depiction of two high school seniors coming out and then finding love. It is not an easy road, but Neil and Paul are honest with each other; they are in discovery of themselves individually as gay teens as well as partners in a life together. Most important, they communicate their fears and delights, and they lay a foundation where trust exists between them. Because the text emphasizes the acceptance of self and does so in a believable way, *All-American Boys* holds credibility as a novel to be read by young adults.

As the story begins, Neil speaks after the fact about the coming out story he is going to tell. Forthrightly, he announces he is gay, that he has known since age thirteen—nearly five years previous to the time of his story—and that until he discovered that queer bashing meant pounding on guys that weren't macho *enough*, he regarded his sexual identity as the "most natural thing in the world" (7). It was Paul who drew him away from a possible life of doom, living secretively in the closet.

It is here too, in this introductory chapter, that Neil identifies himself as an all-around guy, an All-American boy by the book's title. He is athletic, smart, witty; he races pigeon flyers, plays fullback on the soccer team, aspires to be famous in molecular genetics, and has earned a black belt in kung fu. An ideal characterization perhaps, but not necessarily for Claremont, California, and for the image-making around manliness that occurs during adolescence. Aside from his achievements, Neil behaves as a soon-to-be eighteen-year-old. Like many adolescents, Neil is concerned with his appearance; he believes his nose is too big, and he jokes about how the sun distresses him rather than tans him. He sees himself as a klutz, especially regarding things mechanical and his father's skills as a mechanic. Neil's emotions are strong and at times explosive: in matters of love, he is quick to respond with angry words when attacked; yet, he is compassionate and can appreciate the flight of a bird, as well as tell his father that he loves him.

At first sight of Paul, Neil describes him as good looking, pleasant, a bit skinny, and a "kook." New to California and from Illinois, Paul had never experienced burritos and sushi (Neil's favorite food), but he was willing to have a try. Paul is also athletic, probably running and biking, Neil notes, and he is bright, interested in too many subjects to settle on one, but willing to admit what he does not know. Although Paul has difficulty making friends, his humor is attractive, and he respects himself. Because Paul has come out to others and has had more experience with other gay folks than Neil has had, he is more settled than Neil about his sexual orientation. His response to words and acts of homophobia is to remain calm; he is not physical but strikes with retorts that comically turn the bigotry back onto the aggressor.

Through Neil's and Paul's characterizations, Frank Mosca asserts that men who are gay are "real" men, contrary to stereotyping of gay men as effeminate, passive, and only interested in, even only capable of, "women's work." Although both boys are cast as manly and All-American to break stereotypes, Mosca's theme goes deeper to emphasize that homosexuals are human beings, part of the whole of humanity. He tells readers how fear and ignorance of *difference* and acts of violence force gay people to hide their identity, to live a split life—a lie, and then hate themselves for doing so. At one point, Neil questions his father as to why people are afraid of gays, why his loving Paul threatens others. After all, he says, as a gay person, he sleeps, eats, cries, even hates schoolwork just like everyone else. It is Paul's belief in himself as a valuable human being that gives Neil courage to trust himself and to understand that being gay does not diminish his worthiness as a person.

Although the censor may strenuously object to writing that describes how a love relationship develops between boys, Mosca's telling is not graphic. In fact, Neil says that what happened after their first kiss, a gentle kiss: "well, there are parts of everyone's life that are not open for public inspection" (44). As the text is a first-person point of view, readers hear how Neil feels about Paul, that he is attracted to him, his legs particularly and his smile, that he loves Paul, yearns for him, and for many reasons is joyous to be with him.

Their love is mutual. Paul, too, is well-grounded in his identity, and he tells Neil that when he first came out to his sister he was in a state of ecstasy for he had finally found himself, and it was thrilling to know who he was. From the beginning of their relationship, Paul articulates his needs, feelings, fears, and love. He establishes his need for friendships to be based on truth with a clear absence of word games, of telling lies. Neil, of course, agrees. The idea communicated here that relationships begin in friendship is a positive one for any reader to behold, and it further validates the positive messaging that Mosca includes in his storytelling. For Neil and Paul, it is first love, though it doesn't seem to be a love obsessed; more so it is a love embraced, enjoyed, and explored with respect and with an endurance to survive the pangs of adolescence and the ill-conceived acts of violence.

When their intolerant classmate, Brian Newton, the unsavory character whose body odor would require persons near him to pack a "can or two of *Raid* and maybe some *Lysol*" (35), drops off unsigned letters to the boys' homes exclaiming that Neil and Paul are gay—fags and fruits—, the budding romance needs to stand strong against the disbelief, guilt, disassociation, and brutality of others who are driven by ignorance and fear. Pressured by a family showdown in response to Brian's letters, Paul and then Neil admit to their parents they are gay. Mr. Carrington, Paul's father, reacts by verbally erupting; he accuses his son of making a pass at his own brother and then strikes him so hard he falls half out of the chair. He yells his disgust at having a son who is a *frigging faggot*, not fit to live under his roof and not fit to be his son any longer. Only his mother's threat to leave with the other children keeps Paul at home. Mr. Carrington carries out his sentencing of Paul by ignoring his son, refusing to talk to him. As Paul puts it to Neil, he feels as though he were a ghost in the house.

Later, at the hospital, after Mr. Carrington tries to boot Neil out of Paul's room, he apologizes for his behavior and tells Neil he can visit Paul anytime, especially if it will help Paul recover. Carrington is sincere as he extends his hand and acknowledges that he understands Neil's anger toward him; especially, at this moment, he is a father truly affected by the sight of his son's injuries; he is a father who loves his son.

Neil doesn't accept Carrington's gesture; instead he confronts him with harsh words about his treatment of Paul, all the while noting that Mr. Carrington flinches "with every word" (90). Still caught in his pain, Neil admits he is glad he has hurt the man and has caused him a "smidgeon" of Paul's misery. Once again Carrington admits he deserves Neil's criticism, but he does have a reason for rejecting his son, and he believes that his actions were done in an attempt to protect his son from a miserable and tragically short-lived life. Though his tone is sarcastic in the beginning and of the "I-am-an-adult-who-knows-from-experience" variety, Carrington's tale of how his college roommate had hanged himself after making a pass at Carrington and was rejected and perhaps humiliated causes Neil to feel his hatred toward Paul's father fall away. For Neil, Paul's father is a pathetic character, one for whom he feels sorry, just as he now feels sorry for those who oppress gay people and whose hatred turns to violence; they are blind to the person inhabiting the homosexual body.

Neil's father cries when he realizes his son is gay, but through an accepting gesture shortly after, he expresses his love for Neil. Wearily he nods his head in understanding that Neil needed to leave the house and be with Paul rather than stay and talk with him. This father-son relationship in the absence of a mother lost to cancer when Neil was eleven is a good one to see unfold. Before he is told of his son's homosexuality and in response to a TV news clip of a Gay Pride parade, Mr. Meislich comments that he doesn't hate gay people, he just didn't like them. After the boys' coming out, he questions his own actions, fears he should have remarried, and wonders whether Neil is going through a phase or that Neil will be friendless in life. Because he loves his son, though, he is able to support Neil and even rushes to the hospital after finding his son's pigeons mutilated and a hastily written note from Neil. Father and son have their battles and outbursts, but they always come around to acknowledging their behavior, apologizing, and expressing their love for each other.

It is not only love for Paul that enrages Neil when the violence against them occurs, but also need for self-respect, the book's central message. Paul is the first to state firmly that he likes himself, and he will allow no one to take that away—not his parents, not Brian, not even Neil. This message is reiterated, perhaps to a fault in its repetition, but clearly stated, and it demonstrates to the reader the struggle gay people endure when others do not understand that the choice homosexuals have is not one of *should I be gay*, but rather *should I come out*. As Paul says it: "there was no choice involved except when I decided to live my life in the light instead of skulking around corners like I was something dirty instead of a person" (80).

Throughout the narrative Neil questions why people respond so hatefully knowing a person is gay; after all, he exclaims, he is the same person after he comes out as he was before he reveals his secret. This is perhaps the greatest struggle for gay teens and the greatest test to any love relationship. To maintain self-worth and not allow others to degrade the discovery of self is central to growing up homosexual.

I don't believe Mosca is advocating that the maintenance of self-respect necessarily requires violence. Paul tends to dismiss homophobic taunts, but it is Neil who possesses a fighting spirit and who quickly rises with threats of harm should any one interfere with him or his love for Paul. Mosca gives Neil a black belt in kung fu and an attitude that sometimes fighting is needed for protection. After Paul is beaten to near death, Neil is so enraged that he swears to Paul on his dead mother's soul that he would kill if Paul were ever harmed again. Though his words are angry ones, he speaks through tears at the sight of Paul's battered body. The reader, too, is forewarned in the first chapter that Neil surprises himself that he could become so angry.

Neil also takes pleasure in tangling with the gang that attacked Paul, for he is well trained, and he is bent on administering the pain that he and Paul have suffered. His pleasure during the fight, though, is more about skill in martial arts, of being able to make his body do what he wants it to do (21), than it is of rage. Unmistakably, he is angry, but he assumes a "coldly calculating" stance as he assesses his position in relation to the five boys encircling him. In self-defense, his kicks are brutal, and he literally strikes down all five who attack him, breaking their noses, legs, ribs. Neil verbally jabs Danny with words of triumph, even as Danny is being loaded into the ambulance; Neil has to be pulled away.

Several events precipitate the gang's attack on Neil, events that fuel both Brian's homophobia and Neil's anger and confusion about why gay people are beaten. No doubt Brian's anger toward Neil and Paul is ignited when Neil, unable to tolerate Brian and his negativity toward gays, traps him in a hammerlock and tells him how obnoxious he is and that he should never come back. Brian, who came to warn Neil about being associated with a known gay person (Paul), leaves with homophobic epithets spewing from his mouth. Later, Brian appears in the school lunchroom accompanied by three seniors, masquerading as effeminate boys; moving in single file, one hand upon another's shoulder, they swish and sashay, speak with a lisp, carry baskets of fairy dust (glitter) to spread over Neil and Paul and hum the Sugar Plum Fairy (78).

Shortly after this display, all of Neil's birds are slaughtered and the word *faggot* is scrawled in blood on the shed's wall. Paul is severely beaten; an ear has nearly been severed and half his body is held in a cast. When Neil's father finds his son at the hospital, he points out that Neil could have been harmed had he been at home with the birds. With this realization, Neil literally grows cold; his tears cease and he vows not to cry again. He rather "relishes" the idea of revenge and even prays that Paul's assailants would approach him. Alarmed by his son's cold stare, Mr. Meislich warns Neil that his look was one he had seen before during the war, when someone set out to kill another. Neil rails about gay bashing and the injustice of it all; he is in a defense mode, ready to protect Paul and defend himself. Hours later, his rage resurfaces when he watches a boy and girl on campus, walking and laughing; his impulse is to do them harm, for he cannot cope with their joy while Paul was lying in the hospital.

When Brian and his buddies do approach Neil on the street, forming a semicircle around him, he tries to walk around and away from them, shouting at them to "bug off." Hungry for blood, they taunt him with homophobic slurs and gloat over their beating of Paul, how they slashed his "pretty pansy face" and tortured Neil's pigeons (105). The fight begins when one boy challenges Neil's skill in kung fu. Neil is victorious; he finds revenge as he fights in self-defense. He is trained to protect himself; this he does skillfully, but his kicks carry the force of his anger. In this he is vindicated. Even his father and brother, when they hear of the fray, rush off to boast about his rising from the fight unscathed.

In the end the perpetrators are brought to justice, though their punishment does not fully fit their crime, as it often does not in real life. For what Paul perceives as attempted murder, the five are placed on one year's probation and agree to pay all of Paul's medical expenses. Neil has found connection with the gay policeman who was called to the fight; this leads both teens to find mentors, especially other gays in long-term relationships, and entrance into the larger gay community. The happy ending may be saccharin for some readers, especially the points that Paul is better-looking than ever after reconstructive surgery and Mr. Carrington calls Neil his son-in-law; however, the writing needs to reveal to adolescent readers that there is hope and that some conflicts can be resolved; and if not resolved, at least there are ways to approach difficulties in life.

In epilogue, Neil reports that Paul has healed, and, after waiting for Paul to make up his senior year, they have gone off to college together, committed to making their relationship work and in pursuit of their dreams—Neil in biology and Paul in business. Neither boy holds any illusions about what lay ahead of them, for they lost their innocence in the streets and in the courtroom.

Mosca's views of gay teen love are expressed clearly, directly, and realistically. "Respect yourself" strikes the loudest chord, followed by speaking proudly about who you are. His storytelling is conversationally that of a teen voice and his rendering is done respectfully, honestly, and with compassion. Rather than condoning violence or even sensationalizing it, Mosca demonstrates in *All-American Boys* that gays are assaulted in this society; some have been killed. It can be an ugly and dangerous world for anyone who may be different. To read the book is to know that living life as a gay person is risky but that strong relationships can be built on caring, trust, and open communication, be it a love between homosexual teens or heterosexual teens. On these accounts, Mosca serves his adolescent readership well.

And, it is to these accounts that readers will respond. They will not be able to disregard Mosca's descriptions of the barbs and violence leveled against gays and the rage that consumes Neil. Heavy-handed as these may be in their depiction, they do echo society's homophobia. Readers will know that coming out as a gay person is part of the process of self-acceptance and being whole in the world. Being gay is who a person may be, and not to acknowledge and accept this part of oneself is to deny, even obstruct, personal fulfillment and a life fully lived. Each boy rejoices in knowing his gay identity, all the while fearing the rejection and abuse perpetrated by others who take it upon themselves to rid their world of a perceived evil.

Neil and Paul are real enough as teenagers: they are male friends, regular guys; they are manly and physical. Both are sensitively portrayed, not because they fulfill any stereotype of a gay man being sissified, but because they are good human beings who have learned compassion and who must struggle to maintain their own self-worth, a struggle that is more formidable than that of a heterosexual adolescent. They are sons of fathers who need to adjust to the boys' gayness, who need to release their fears regarding any personal blame, as does Neil's father, and their fears that somehow their sons are corrupted, as does Paul's father.

At the very least, *All-American Boys* delivers the message that being gay is a hard life to live. Rather than being damaging to the reader, the text asks readers to question their own actions and attitudes toward gay people and those they may witness in others.

Though the boys suffer great consequences for coming out and pursuing their love for each other, Mosca does not leave them in crisis. For gay readers there is hope and support and an abiding belief that they are not less than other people because they are homosexual.

## Work Cited

Cuseo, Allan A. *Homosexual Characters in YA Novels: A Literary Analysis, 1969-1982*. Metuchen, N. J.: Scarecrow Press, Inc., 1992.
Mosca, Frank. *All-American Boys*. Boston: Alyson Publications, 1983.

# *Always Running* from the Real Issues:
# Why Kids *Should* Read about Gangs and Drugs

## Peter E. Morgan

When *Always Running, La Vida Loca: Gang Days in LA* was first published by Curbstone Press in 1993, Luis Rodriguez, by his own estimate, reached some seventy million people through interviews with, among others, National Public Radio, *Good Morning America,* and the *Oprah Winfrey Show,* and in readings, book signings, and community presentations nationwide. With more than 100,000 copies in print in both English and Spanish language editions, teachers and librarians across the country still recommend this dramatic and profoundly moving account of the early life of the ex-gangbanger-turned-poet-and-social-activist. At the same time, Rodriguez's work helping troubled teens escape the gang lifestyle and generally make smart choices in life continues to gain ever-greater national recognition.

Ten years before Curbstone Press accepted his manuscript, Rodriguez tried to publish a fictional account of his gang days (*Mi Vida Loca*) but received rejections from twenty-two major publishers; as one company explained to him rather bluntly, "they had published an 'Hispanic' novel ten years before—and they felt they had done enough as far as 'Hispanic' literature was concerned" (Rodriguez, *Contemporary Authors* 229). By the time *Always Running* was accepted, however, Rodriguez had become a nationally acclaimed poet and widely read columnist, a voice it was much harder to ignore, writing the book as he had originally envisioned it—as a nonfiction memoir. Recognition came quickly. *Always Running* won the Carl Sandburg Literary Arts Award (1993) and the *Chicago Sun-Times* First Prose Award (1994). It was acclaimed by reviewers in the *New York Times,* the *National Catholic Reporter,* and the *Washington Post,* in which Paul Ruffins said, "As America becomes truly multi-cultural, Rodriguez's book will be a useful tool for understanding the Chicano rights movement as a response to racism and social segregation that rivaled that of the deep South.

Ultimately this is a very political book, but. . . [t]hroughout, most of the language is hauntingly lyrical." (x1).

Perhaps Ruffins's assessment reveals why the book became, in one school district at least, the catalyst for a new and sweeping policy of censorship—why those who fought so fervently to ban *Always Running* did so with such unrelenting bitterness. Certainly, as its opponents continue to point out, *Always Running* deals graphically in places with sex, drug use, and violence. Yet the fundamental message of the memoir is the message Rodriguez has devoted his life to promoting: that young people have the power to organize and to be heard—that they can make sweeping and dramatic changes in their schools, in their communities, and in their lives if they take responsibility for their actions and unite against those who strive to maintain a vision of the American dream that papers over inequalities rooted in race and class.

Of course, this is a message that many would rather not hear. It challenges the popular assumption that it is some sort of moral decline leading to fatherless families that is the root cause of delinquency. In this real-life autobiography, the truth is that Rodriguez had a father, a former high school principal in Mexico who could find work in Los Angeles only as a laborer (Ruffins x1). Furthermore, it challenges the widespread belief that schools and boards of education always create policy based on students' best interests; and it shows how today's so-called zero-tolerance policies, so much a part of entrenched school law-enforcement thinking, are unlikely to succeed if they fail to address the systemic social and economic causes of youth violence. The models Rodriguez provides for change are therefore based in empowerment rather than repression, education rather than control—and "empowerment" is the last thing, as Rodriguez shows, that school authorities generally want to share with "troubled" teens.

Rodriguez dedicates *Always Running* to his twenty-five friends who were "killed by rival gangs, police, drugs, car crashes and suicides" (4) by the time he had turned eighteen years old, but he writes for his own son, Ramiro, for whom staying out of gang life in Chicago was, at the time he wrote, a choice to be made one day at a time. Beginning with his own journey from Mexico in the mid-1950s, Rodriguez paints the daily struggle of Mexicans and Chicanos in Los Angeles and of inner-city youth everywhere. His early memories, he writes, remain with him "like a foul odor" (19), memories of "a strange world, most of it spiteful to us, spitting and stepping on us," (19) where his parents worked in factories and sweatshops, cleaning houses, or as manual laborers. He describes how the *clicas, or clubs,* that evolved into today's gangs began, most of them quite innocently, as groups of kids with a common interest or neighborhood. *Clicas* that

survived grew and became more organized—and invariably more
dangerous—adopted jackets and colors, and gave themselves names like
"Thee Imitations," carefully drawn in old English script. Teens joined for
protection against other clubs and as a way to belong to something, to
develop an identity in a country that denied their legitimacy and seemed
committed to excluding them from every legal opportunity. With numbers
came the courage to defy authority and the power to do so with greater
impunity. "I was . . . intrigued," Rodriguez says. "I wanted this power. . . .
All my life until then had been poised against me: telling me what to be,
what to say, how to say it. I was a broken boy, shy and fearful. I wanted what
'Thee Mystics' had; I wanted the power to hurt somebody" (42). As Luis
and his friends negotiate their embattled adolescence, they get into trouble,
they fight, they begin carrying weapons and experimenting with sex and
drugs, they are harassed by police, and they adorn their young bodies with
homemade tattoos, drawn in India ink with sewing needles. The young Luis
pays $5 for his first tattoo, a tragically prophetic "outline of a cross beneath
the words '*Mi Vida Loca*'" (45).

Of course, by the time the six-year-old Rodriguez enrolls in school, he
already has several strikes against him. Teachers want little to do with kids
who have a "language problem" (26). Some respond to the presence of the
bewildered kindergartner with anger: one complains about "kids who didn't
even speak English. And how was she supposed to teach anything under
these conditions" (26). Others are simply disengaged: "'Okay, why don't
you sit here in the back of the class. . . . Play with some blocks until we
figure out how to get you more involved.' It took her most of that year to
figure this out. I just sat in the back of the room, building blocks" (26).
Luis's brother, later to become an academic leader, is shoved into a class
with mentally disabled students. Meanwhile, in a sinister precursor to the
more recent "English Only" legislation a number of states have enacted,
fearing somehow that they will not be able to control students who might be
talking about them in a language they cannot understand, school administrators enforce rules making it "a crime to speak anything but English. If a
Spanish word sneaked out in the playground, kids were often sent to the
office to get swatted or to get detention" (27).

It is little wonder that schools in which there are rarely pencils, paper,
or books for students to use and where the dropout rate among Mexican
students reaches 50% *before high school* become for the youthful Luis little
more than a place for gangs to recruit—a place where he learns to follow
Cholo fashion and wage psychological warfare against teachers, many of
whom leave with nervous breakdowns or worse. In the late 1960s, as
Rodriguez describes them, the mounting years of racial tension were leading

more and more frequently to serious outbursts of violence, as school corridors became rivers of anger forcing dispossessed Mexican and Chicano kids with nothing to lose together with angry Anglos supported by a brutal police force and a school administration willfully blind to the institutionalized racism on which it based its policy decisions.

Under the tutorial guidance of Chente Ramírez—a social worker and activist who comes to work in the Bienvenidos Community Center in 1970 as the gang violence flourishes, police response escalates, and the fight for better schools for barrio kids intensifies—the young gang warrior slowly comes to see beyond the day-to-day battles to the broader causes of the conflict. Chente, a founding member of United Mexican American Students (UMAS) and Movimiento Estudiantil Chicano de Aztlan (MEChA), leads study groups in politics, philosophy, and economics and becomes an intellectual role model to a young Luis sorely in need of guidance: "He was someone who could influence me without judging me morally or telling me what to do. He was just there. He listened, and when he knew you were wrong, before he would say anything, he would get you to think" (114). Most important, perhaps, Chente teaches Luis that everything one does in life is a choice: "[Y]ou have to make a choice now. Either the craziness and violence—or here, learning and preparing for a world in which none of this is necessary" (159). As Luis becomes increasingly conflicted—feeling sympathy for the victims of his actions, grief for the family whose home he is ordered to firebomb, and gut-wrenching nausea at the sight of a homeboy raping a drugged-out teenage girl—he learns that individual change does not come from a simple decision to take one path instead of another; it is a matter of making difficult choices "not just once, but every time they come up" (132).

Despite the fact that school "guidance" authorities relegate him to industrial arts classes like auto shop and printing, Luis slowly begins to feed his growing consciousness with library books about the struggles of black Americans. From here, he discovers Puerto Rican and Chicano writers and finally storms out of his English Literature class (the only nonapplied class he has been permitted to take) when he is humiliated by the teacher for reading Beatrice Griffith's *American Me* in place of the assigned text, Wordsworth's *Prelude*. Although he ends up once again back on the streets, this is a turning point for Rodriguez, a discovery of the power of knowledge and the ability of books to deliver it: "A power pulsed in those books I learned to savor, in the magical hours I spent in the library—and it called me back to them" (139). And when a new principal at Keppel High announces his willingness to meet with the community and then agrees to provide a Chicano Student Center, a full-time Youth Advisor, and a club for Chicano students, Luis is poised for a life-changing role.

Until now, despite the fact that Keppel High is forty percent Chicano, it has been the Anglo students who run everything from the newspaper to the pep rallies. Even the school mascots "Joe and Josephine Aztec," white students draped in "Indian-like garb" (172), are sad parodies of Indian people; yet when Esme, a student activist from the largely female Chicano leadership set, persuades Luis to partner her in learning an authentic *folklorico* dance and trying out successfully for the mascot position, the long process of dismantling cultural stereotypes and reestablishing pride in and recognition for their heritage has for them begun. This success generates a permanent *folklorico* group at the school, followed by a drama group, an urban twist on the rural Teatro Campesino of Cesar Chávez's farm workers' union, performing plays and leading subsequent discussions about police brutality on the one hand and ways to end barrio warfare on the other.

The struggle Rodriguez describes is difficult and painful. Following a number of organized mass student walkouts and setbacks, such as the vandalism of the Chicano Student Center, Luis is successful, with his fellow activists, in gaining a Chicano Studies class, a full-time Chicano teacher at the school, and for himself a position in student government and a column in the school newspaper; but these improvements are too little too late for many—certainly for the 25 fallen friends to whom he dedicates his book. Rodriguez writes compelling, frequently poetic prose, starkly real, yet tinged, when the reality becomes too absurd, with occasional flights into a magical realism reminiscent of Gabriel Garcia Marquez. His story never strays far from its twofold message: first that gang membership, popularity, and loyalty are a function of the economic and racial dynamics of this country, and that American society requires not a series of Band-Aid solutions but a thorough reorganization through which education, health care, food, clothing, housing, and personal safety are available not simply to those who can afford them but to all; and second, that adolescents (and adults, too) must be educated to understand their position in society, the serious consequences of the choices that they make in life, and their ability to determine their own pathways to a better future through self-improvement and community action.

Whether it is to the message or the medium that critics object, *Always Running* has become a focus of controversy across the country, from Rockford, Illinois, where in 1996 it formed the nucleus of a collection of seventeen banned books, to Santa Rosa, Fremont, San Jose, and San Diego, California, where school boards alternately restricted access to the book or struggled with the issue of whether or not to keep it on the library shelves. The Rockford case became the focus of a local columnist and member of the far-right organization Citizens for Excellence in Education (CEE), a group founded in 1983 to stamp out "the atheist dominated ideology of secular humanism" and which is described by People For the American Way as "easily the most destructive censorship organization active in the schools today" (Chatelle). Robert L. Simonds, CEE President, denounced *Always Running* as "a dirty and sexually explicit library book . . . by Linda [sic] Rodriguez (an Hispanic author)," and went further in condemning such organizations as the American Library Association and People For the American Way as liberal, anti-Christian hate groups (Simonds). As often in such cases, the debate moved between the book under consideration and the broader objectives of the would-be censors: justifying his position on the 4-3 vote to have the book removed from the school libraries, Rockford school board member David Strommer called the book "irreligious, anti-family, left-wing, Anti-American and radical," saying "what's in the book is harmful, ungodly and wrong." Another board member challenged "anyone who knows how the mind works, after reading this book, not to be more likely to assume the lifestyle of a gang person and not to be more likely to have sex in the back of a car" ("Shameful Book Banning").

Meanwhile, Dennis Wolfe, in the *San Jose Mercury News*, argued that *Always Running* is typical of the sort of "'literature'" which is being taught in place of "basic skills" and traditional "values," a "perfect example of what's wrong with our schools." He claims Rodriguez has produced a book which "condones rape and the degradation of girls and women as sexual objects and portrays cops as nothing more than another gang on the streets" and argues that the book is a failure because Rodriguez wrote it to keep his son out of gangs but ultimately could not do so. Wolfe offers the incendiary and sensationalist analogy, "Suppose a teacher, seeking to teach that rape is evil, assigns three high school boys to rape a female student. The lesson might achieve its goal of discouraging rape by exposing children to the trauma and pain. But surely we would all agree such an extreme lesson is not worth the cost." Such books remain in schools, he argues, only as a result of "distorted reasoning by 'educrats' and a well crafted strategy [by the California Teachers Association, among others] to defend schools from any parental concerns," and he calls for parents to unite and promote legislation that brings the pendulum back to the "center" (1C).

School board members who hold out against pressure from such well-organized pressure groups often do so at considerable risk to their jobs. Members of the Parents' Rights Organization mounted a sustained effort to recall three members of the San Jose Unified School Board for their handling of the book, which, they claim, "violates certain provisions of the education code" in promoting obscenity (Aratani, "Parents" 1B). The Board voted to retain the text for classroom use after considering extensive input from several public hearings and the district's book committee (which included parents, teachers, and district staff). Teachers, they said, should continue notifying parents about the book's content and allowing individual parents to decide whether or not they wanted their children to read the book (Aratani, "Parents" 1B).

Several critics wince at a particular scene—Rodriguez's initiation into gang life when, drunk, he plunges a screwdriver into the flesh of one of his gang's victims. While Reuben Sosa Villegas accepts that Rodriguez has reformed his own life, Villegas cannot empathize: "He did bad. He transformed. He does good. Now, the subplot of his problem. His son" (Villegas 3). He acknowledges Rodriguez's insights as to why gangs exist but claims that "Rodriguez is profiting from the misdeeds and suffering administered by the same hands that now describe love and hope. And that is not acceptable" (Villegas 3). Villegas and others worry that the book will become a source of comparison for gang members' misdeeds, a benchmark in a sort of macabre bragging contest. Most attacks indeed focus on Rodriguez's graphic depiction of violence and sex (as well as his use of strong language), although the book's treatment of poverty, racism, and police brutality are also frequently mentioned by opponents as reasons for banning the book from schools ("Censorship Comes to Santa Rosa Schools").

Rodriguez himself makes no apology for the explicit nature of his work: "It's a hard-core book. I'm the first to admit that. . . . There's a lot of graphic material. But that's done for a reason. There's no way you can write this kind of book without getting as close as possible to what these young people are going through" (Sullivan). Rodriguez notes that although his book may have been a *catalyst* for repressive action on the part of the Rockford School Board, "they went ahead and banned 16 other books, . . . so there seems to be more than just my book at stake. There's an agenda of keeping certain voices, certain experiences, certain kinds of literature out of the hands of our kids. It's bigger than just *Always Running*" (Sullivan). To the claim that the book glorifies gang violence, Rodriguez counters that while it doesn't glorify it, neither does it demonize gang involvement: "Both views distort reality. I work with gang kids today, and I realize that these kids have rational reasons for joining gangs, and I also realize that it can be very destructive and against their own dignity and value as human beings. It's a complicated thing, and we should spend time looking at it" (Sullivan). Rodriguez claims that the graphic nature of the book is necessary to establish not only authenticity but authority: he knows from experience that kids—especially those he really wants to reach—will seldom listen to someone who doesn't appear to know the reality of street life. And if the sex, the drugs, and the violence are explicit in the book, Rodriguez recognizes that his depictions are more often than not mild compared to the experiences many kids today are facing (Sullivan).

Interestingly, Rodriguez notes, all of those who spoke against the book at the Santa Rosa School Board meeting were white, while a number of the book's defenders were Latino youths. He sees this as a pattern across the country resulting from our "highly polarized" racial climate; yet he sounds a cautionary note that it is white suburban kids who, as a group, are today experiencing the fastest rise in gang membership, and he describes the fear some in middle-class America have of his book as a dangerous blend of ignorance and denial (Sullivan).

Margarita Rosenthal, an intergroup education specialist in the 1970s with the Alhambra, California, school district (where Rodriguez went to school), remembers how she was then attending four or five funerals a year for kids killed in gang warfare in Rodriguez's community. "[H]owever 'graphic' or disturbing this truth about gang culture may appear to parents," she contends, "it is a reality young people are already aware of," a menace to youth that "can only be dealt with by comprehending its adverse nature. Reading the book is the first step to achieve that necessary comprehension." Students and teachers tend to agree. Curbstone Press publisher Sandy Taylor claimed when the book was banned by Rockford that it had been used by 40 high schools nationwide: "We've received more letters from young people thanking us for this book than for any other book we've ever done" (Kinsella 12).

Many teachers describe the effectiveness of *Always Running* in helping to promote frank and honest classroom discussion about racism and the choices students make (Aratani, "Memoir" 1); moreover, it seems that in reality most parents do *not* object to the book and agree with teachers that the impact the book has on students is primarily a positive one. One student, speaking in front of a heated board meeting in San Jose at which the book's supporters were heckled with shouts of "Heathen," said, "We are here because of two pages. Yeah, they are graphic pages, but that wasn't the whole message" (Wallace).

Sadly, while most schools are more than willing to assign alternate readings to students whose parents object to a particular text, strident opponents of a particular book seldom rest until they have prevented everyone from reading it. In the words of Rockford school board member Edward Sharp, "To really do some good the book should be kept from the public altogether." Similarly, when the ACLU branch in Sonoma County, California, following a school board vote *not* to ban the book from libraries under its jurisdiction, purchased and donated copies of *Always Running* to each high school library in the district, these books promptly vanished from a number of the school libraries. Subsequently, investigating claims that the books were disappearing, the ACLU discovered that certain board members who had voted unsuccessfully to remove the book had secretly ordered its removal from individual libraries without returning to the Board for permission to do so (Grabill).

Such opposition is not only unconstitutional, it undermines the very population at risk as those most in need of a salutary warning against the potential destructiveness of gang life are denied free access to this important resource. While conservative groups may seek to challenge the judgment of the ACLU and other purportedly liberal groups, a report issued by the United States Department of Justice appeals very specifically for the wisdom and involvement of those with the experience that Rodriguez has. Most kids who enter and become active in gangs do so only for a relatively short period of time, usually between 14 and 18 years of age (10). "Outside expertise should be brought in," the Justice Department urges, "to educate personnel in such gang-related topics as gang-member drug abuse and trafficking, the influence of street and prison gangs . . . , gang-related social investigation . . . , crisis intervention and mediation skills . . . , and community mobilization techniques," especially in areas where gang activity is relatively new and local institutions have little experience in recognizing and understanding the issues at stake (13).

The report goes on to recommend that "a combined social opportunities and social intervention strategy should make use of volunteer mentors who can assist as tutors or supportive mentors to remind youth gang members of what they are supposed to do" (16). This is exactly the sort of project to which Rodriguez dedicates his time and energy, traveling the country to promote the message of *Always Running* (as well as his other books) by participating in events such as Multicultural Events for Youth, and leading poetry and performance groups for inner-city kids with organizations such as *El Centro de la Raza* (Rodriguez, "Gang Youth"). At times, ironically, the Justice Department report sounds as if Rodriguez himself were the author, particularly when discussing ways to empower inner-city youth: "A key concern of training should be the development of ways to enhance the self-esteem and self-discipline of youth gang members" (16). The report goes on to discuss programs in schools that aim to accomplish many of the effects Rodriguez describes in *Always Running* and which he credits as having helped to pave his own steep path out of gang life. The study ends with a call to involve grassroots organizations, parents, and former gang members, "to mobilize local energy . . . [and] compel outside interest and concern" (24). It also recognizes, however, that such organizations "may also need to challenge public and nonprofit agencies over issues of racism, agency corruption, staff incompetence, and lack of resources, which contribute to the failure to resolve the gang problem" (25). Such challenges may occur in calls for community policing and increased accountability on the part of law enforcement organizations. They may surface in advocacy for job training and urban development for at-risk areas. But we must also be alert and ready to raise such challenges when naive representatives of special interest groups seek to compel school boards not only to abridge their students' right to read (as the National Council for Teachers of English has defined it) but to take from those students the very materials that are often so important in helping them make the right choices for the future.

As Rodriguez says, "I actually hope that my book will lose its validity some day, that there isn't a need for a book like *Always Running* . . . that we don't have gangs, and kids killing each other, and drugs in the communities. I hope that someday it becomes obsolete. But right now that's not the case. The book is very relevant, and as long as that's the case, then we should make sure that people can get access to it" (Sullivan).

## Works Cited

Aratani, Lori. "Memoir on Gangs Captures Support/Schools' Boss OKs Book; S.J. Board Will Decide." *San Jose Mercury News* (20 May 1998), morning final ed.: 1B.

Aratani, Lori. "Parents Prepare to Launch Recall/Furor Over Gang Book Prompts Bid to Oust Three from S.J. Board." *San Jose Mercury News* (23 July 1998), morning final ed.: 1B.

"Censorship Comes to Santa Rosa Schools." *Sonoma Civil Liberties* 34 (fall 1998). 5 December 2000 users.ap.net/%7Eaclu/newsletterarchive/ SCL34Fall98.html.

Chatelle, Bob. Personal letter to Richard Vargas of the *Rock River Times*. n.d. (11 January 2001) www.ultranet.com/~kyp/cee.html.

Grabill, David. "Censorship in the Schools was This Year's Leading Issue." *Year in Review*. ACLU of Sonoma County, Calif. (14 November 1999). 12 December 2000 www.aclusonoma.org/yearinreview_1999. html.

Kinsella, Bridget. "School Board Bans Acclaimed Gang-Life Memoir." *Publishers Weekly* 39:243 (23 September 1996): 12.

"Luis J. Rodriguez." *Contemporary Authors Autobiography Series* 29. Ed. Joyce Nakamura. Detroit: Gale, 1988. 223-236.

Rodriguez, Luis J. *Always Running, La Vida Loca: Gang Days in L.A.*

Willimantic, Conn.: Curbstone; New York: Touchstone-Simon and Schuster, 1994.

———. "Gang Youth, Art and Soul." Interview with Bert H. Hoff. *M.E.N. Magazine* (January 1997). 11 January 2001 www.vix.com/menmag/rod ruiiv.htm.

Rosenthal, Margarita. Letter. *San Jose Mercury News* (May 20, 1998), morning final ed.: 7B.

Ruffins, Paul. "West Coast Stories." Rev. of *Always Running: La Vida Loca: Gang Days in L.A.*, by Luis Rodriguez. *The Washington Post* (7 February 1993), Sunday final ed.

"Shameful Book Banning in Rockford, Illinois." 5 December 2000 www. ultranet.com/~kyp/rockbann.html.

Sharp, Edward. Personal letter to Sue Telingator, Chair, Chicago Local, National Writers' Union. (3 November 1994). 11 January 2001 www. ultranet. com/~kyp/sharp.html.

Simonds, Robert L. Letter to the Editor, *Rock River Times* (23 October 1996). 11 January 2001 www.ultranet.com/~kyp/simonds.html.

Sullivan, Patrick. "Class War: Luis Rodriguez Casts a Skeptical Eye on Attempts to Ban His Autobiography." *Sonoma County Independent* (4 February 1999). 25 October 2000 www.metroactive.com/papers /sonoma/02.04.99/rodriguezl-9905.html.

United States Dept. of Justice, Office of Juvenile Justice and Delinquency Prevention. *Gang Suppression and Intervention: Community Models: Research Summary*. Washington: GPO, 1994.

Villegas, Reuben Sosa. "In a Word, Gangster's Book Is Unacceptable." *Denver Rocky Mountain News* (9 January 1994), final ed.: 3N.

Wallace, Rebecca. "Board OKs Contentious Book's Use in Classes." *Willow Glen Resident* (27 May 1998). 5 December 2000 www. metroactive. com/papers/willow.glen.resident/05.27.98/Always Running.html.

Wolfe, Dennis J. "Parents, Not 'Educrats,' *Know What's Best for Kids*." *San Jose Mercury News* (14 June 1998), morning final ed.: 1C.

# The Amazing Bone:
# Any Book Can Offend Someone

## Jane Smiley

*The Amazing Bone* at first seems an unlikely target for censorship. Pearl, the child-figure, is happily enjoying a spring day; her idleness and her choice to take a long walk home through the woods aren't very cautious, but they are understandable, and the book can be read as a conventional cautionary tale about what happens when a child wanders off without telling any adults. Censorship, or attempted censorship, of *The Amazing Bone* by William Steig illustrates as much as anything that almost any book can give offense to someone or other, and that almost anyone can generate a rationale for attacking or defending any children's book.

Children's books are always first and foremost assertions about the nature of children, and since almost all of them are written by adults, they are adult projections of what children need to know or what might entertain children. They are, therefore, a subtle form of propaganda. Each book generally supports one of two ideas—either that children are innocent and need to develop the strength to resist temptation, as Pearl does, or that the moral nature of children is as variable as the moral nature of adults and that they need to understand themselves and their world in order to make moral choices. Almost no children's books promote amorality or immorality. The only choices are between different paths to the good and the true, to inclusion, collaboration, and love. This is undoubtedly a reflection of adult understanding of a child's need for care and nurturing, but nevertheless, it is propaganda, because it has a manipulative goal—to train the child to think in accordance with community norms.

*The Amazing Bone* shows Steig's loyalty to the world of fairy tale and folktale. While the characters of the story are dressed in modern fashion, the story itself makes use of "Little Red Riding Hood" and "Hansel and Gretel," tales that have such widespread appeal that Steig no doubt considered them part of the universal language of children's literature, ripe for creative variation. It can be said that the parents who objected to *The Amazing Bone* seem to not understand narrative themes that are among the most traditional we have, but it is also true that folktales and fairy tales are often more gruesome in their traditional versions than modern parents can tolerate—in one traditional version of "Snow White," for example, the evil queen is punished by being forced to dance to death in fiery shoes at Snow White's wedding to the Prince. Modern versions of the tale have gotten rid of this vengeful aspect of tradition because it doesn't fit in with our notions of justice. Parents who object to Steig's robbers and to Pearl's abduction, I think, are reading the story's fairy-tale elements literally, when standard fairy-tale literary theory suggests that they are more appropriately read as projections of wild thoughts and ideas that children generate themselves. However, standard theory, based in Freudian and Jungian psychology, and therefore Freudian and Jungian premises about childhood sexuality and so forth, is also controversial. It may be that the cruelty of universally told fairy tales and folktales reflects not the natural content of the childish mind, but the callousness of the traditional societies that originally composed the tales. To tell a tale like "Hansel and Gretel" or "Little Red Riding Hood" is to promote the second theory of childhood mentioned above—not that children are innocent, but that children have urges toward sexuality and violence that need to be expressed in order to be made sense of and controlled.

Of course, the world of children's literature is one in which all issues are more contentious because members of the community are alert to ways in which the children of the community might be led into disagreeing with or challenging prevailing norms, and the conflict over what children are and what their needs are cannot be resolved once and for all in a culture as diverse as ours. There can only be an ongoing discussion that sometimes rises to the level of argument. The attempts of various parents to exclude *The Amazing Bone* from school curricula and libraries have to be seen as the expression of a negotiating position. In every case, their positions have been overridden by other parents who agree with Steig's view of childhood or find it harmless, and people in authority, such as school boards. The negotiation has thus been decided in favor of the author's position. But have the dissenting parents no right to state a position? Even though I do not support censorship, and find nothing controversial in *The Amazing Bone*, and am glad that the authorities in question have not caved in to the parents' position, I would never challenge the right of these parents to state their position. Neither the rights of the author nor those of the community are absolute—the author has a right to express himself, but not to go unquestioned. The community has a right to criticize the author, but not to suppress access to his work by others. I would, in fact, say that these private citizens have benefited themselves and their communities by seriously engaging with the book, by reading it, and by formulating ideas about its content and weighting those against the institutional support that the book receives as a prizewinner and a staple of children's literature. Citizen objections to a book are not the same as government attempts to suppress freedom of speech or thought; they are disagreements, not oppression.

For the fact is that children inevitably grow toward freedom, and that literature of all kinds always serves their growth. For most readers, myself included, *The Amazing Bone* is more witty than frightening. The drawings of the robbers make them look like little more than bullies, the fox is rather rueful about the necessity for eating Pearl, Pearl is frightened but unharmed, and her parents receive her with love and gratitude, thereafter giving honor to something so humble as a bone. Steig's world is a benign one, where danger comes from likely quarters and miracles occur. One of the dilemmas of children's literature, indeed, of literature in general, is that the interest of the plot always demands jeopardy of some sort. Stories proceed by way of dramatic tension. Children, no matter what their parents think, know this. In addition, forbidden books that children read in secret mold their minds not only because of what they learn from them, or how they enjoy them, but also because they have to keep them secret. They help children define who they are by contrast to who their parents seem to be. A child's difference from his parents will inevitably express itself, and literature, as an attractive artifact of the world outside the family, will promote that growth. Censorship of children's literature is bound to fail.

Discourse in America is often contentious, not only because of diversity, but also because the roots of American life are philosophical and ideological. The thread of self-justification and ideology therefore runs through many aspects of American life, including literature, children's literature, and education. Each mini-culture is sometimes appalled at the attitudes and ideas of the mini-cultures around it. But as long as the discourse remains open and structured, as long as the government takes no position, but leaves it to the citizens to decide, then the individual author and the communal audience will have a good chance of finding where they can make a truce, or even find real peace, with one another.

## Work Cited

Steig, William. *The Amazing Bone*. New York: Puffin Books, 1976.

# Stock Phrases for All Occasions:
# The Lessons of *As I Lay Dying*

## Brian Fitch

No additional argument needs to be made for the enduring power of William Faulkner's work, in this case *As I Lay Dying*, nor for the influence of Faulkner on generations of writers to follow. However, the need for *As I Lay Dying* to be read, reflected upon, and discussed by the current generation of young people has never been greater for the very reasons that cause some people to question the book's suitability for the classroom and the library.

Over time, not everyone has agreed with this need. An entry in the May 1987 issue of the American Library Association's *Newsletter on Intellectual Freedom* refers to the parent of a high school sophomore in Sinking Valley, Kentucky, who "browsed through the book" and found that it "contains profanity and a segment about masturbation." On this basis she declared the book "pure filth" and said, "The man who wrote it must be a little off his gourd" (90). What this parent has conveniently missed in the passage that first intimates masturbation is the larger feeling that Darl is referring to, the cool silence in the darkness that connects him to his memories of drinking in the dark, the stars in the bucket and in the dipper, the amazing feeling of being a boy alive on the Earth (10-11). I am surprised that a reader astute enough to recognize masturbation in the poetic inner voicing of one of Faulkner's characters, after simply browsing through the book, could so completely miss the larger vision of the book. Perhaps this is not so surprising, however, if this parent closed her mind to the book, after "browsing" just eleven pages.

Admittedly, the seriocomic journey of the Bundrens to carry Addie's rotting corpse to Jefferson for burial with her "people" might be seen as offensive in terms of public health, civics, and even mainstream religion. As well, the fact that Addie's third son, Jewel, is a result of an adulterous affair with the preacher Whitfield may be construed as offensive, along with Dewey Dell being pregnant out of wedlock seeking an abortion, but refusing

42

to see this short novel as anything other than offensive is to commit the very sin Faulkner decries: self-interest and hypocrisy that both contribute to and arise from a narrow worldview. Indeed, the rotting corpse of Addie may be seen as the rotting corpse of a society that has produced the damaged characters of the novel. In *As I Lay Dying*, self-interest gives rise to isolation that, in turn, produces a fragmented and superficial society.

Certainly, a narrow worldview with its accompanying surface reading of human life, a quick and simple transaction with the complexities, joys, and pains of humanity is easy. Phrases such as "Make my day," "Just say no," "Read my lips," "Just do it," "Be like Mike," "The future is now," "If it ain't broke, don't fix it," "Pull yourself up by your bootstraps"—the list goes on and on—are too common as answers to pressing social concerns. These sorts of stock phrases, the offspring of platitudes such as "Rome wasn't built in a day," "It takes all kinds," "The lord helps those who help themselves," are the vocabulary of superficiality, the underpinning of self-interest that leads to isolation and decay of the body politic.

A nation of children raised on these sorts of stock phrases are positioned to easily be led away from active engagement toward passive isolation, away from becoming members of thoughtful, reflective communities who make decisions based not on self-interest, but on civic interest. This rush toward quick and easy engagement with complex and difficult social concerns quite naturally leads to a desire for quick and easy access to information that can then be used in a facile way. In fact, a path from platitudes to stock phrases to the oxymorons of information access (virtual reality, interactive software, user friendly, and so forth) is currently under way.

Without doubt, we are being pushed at from many directions these days to privilege this sort of access without the necessary attendant reflection. The mainstay of personal technology, the computer, has become a New Age shaman, touted to enlighten instantly a struggling student, transform a failing school district into a paradigm of education, bring joy and togetherness to families, open the secrets of the universe—but most important: *easily*. With just a switch on, a mouse click, a drag and drop, we are transformed.

I do not mean to demonize technology, however. Technology is essentially inert. The use to which we put technology should be our litmus test. Unfortunately, too often the path from platitudes to stock phrases to the superficial perception of and use of technology is unbroken, creating a circle back to empty language furthered by quick and easy access to information.

So how will *As I Lay Dying* help prevent this from happening? The first and most apparent way is that reading this novel is not easy. Reading *As I Lay Dying* will expose students to the language and structure of Faulkner in order to help them see and feel what happens when language is not used superficially. Faulkner prohibits a simple reading by his extraordinary manipulation of language: language both fails to capture human experience, and language is all we have to articulate human experience.

Nanci Kincaid, in an article in the summer 1994 issue of *Southern Review*, claims that this is the primary focus of the novel, that "it is the power and the uselessness of language that fuels *As I Lay Dying*" (593). Jerome Beaty, editor of *The Norton Introduction to the Short Novel*, refers to this manipulation of language as "double voicing." He says, "This 'double-voiced' language, this character's voice imbued with a second voice, that of the author, takes us deeper into the nature of this narrative." (458).

I agree with Beaty that a number of Faulkner's characters in *As I Lay Dying* are double-voiced, but I think Kincaid is closer to explaining Faulkner's genius here. Especially in the characters of Darl (Addie Bundren's second-oldest son) and Dewey Dell (Addie's fourth child and only daughter), we see the inability to articulate, or more accurately, we do not hear in conversation their deepest feelings, the sorts of feelings human beings have when looking out at a sometimes frighteningly beautiful and strange world. But Faulkner does not leave us with this lack of words to articulate, and he does not leave Darl and Dewey Dell without potential. Rather he uses language, with all of its shortcomings, to reveal the depths of Darl and Dewey Dell as human beings. Here language is the suddenly visible energy that surrounds, inhabits, and animates complex emotion. Predictably, these looks inside Darl and Dewey Dell are highly poetic.

In fact, this double-layered existence of Darl and Dewey Dell, the lack of articulation reflected against their complex inner sensibility, creates characters that defy understanding in a superficial way. Faulkner not only creates a narrative that requires concentration and thought, but also pulls us even closer by compelling us to untangle the narrative through understanding these human and appropriately complicated characters.

Unfortunately, the poetic inner voicings of Darl and Dewey Dell are not enough. Both characters, ultimately, are driven by self-interest, even though this self-interest emerges from more complex and understandable human conditions than is the case with, for example, Anse and Whitfield.

For Darl, this failure is at the hands of an unresponsive family and society that leave him unconnected. Donald Kartiganer makes the point that

> the most incisive vision in the novel—that of Darl—has nothing whatever to do with the controlling action. . . . *As I Lay Dying*, in other words, becomes a symbol of rigidity, of the imagination imprisoned in an action remote from its deepest motives. The quest has been carried out, but what has been won? (6)

The answer is nothing, unless we consider the reader. Over the course of the

Bundrens' journey, Faulkner provides us with a gallery of other characters—Cora, Tull, Anse, Peabody, Whitfield, and others—to show how members of society become blind to their inner potential when they engage the world through platitudes and stock phrases. These characters create the "rigid" world within which Darl and Dewey Dell find themselves (represented by their inner voicings) "imprisoned." Young people reading this book may discover how to avoid being imprisoned in this sort of rigid world.

From the outset, Faulkner allows us to see this tug-of-war between rich inner perception and superficial self-interest, as we look inside Darl's emotional engagement with his family and the surrounding landscape. In the first section, one of nineteen Darl sections, the cottonhouse appears "in empty and shimmering dilapidation." In this section we see Jewel, Addie's third-oldest son and the issue of her affair with Preacher Whitfield: "Still staring ahead, his pale eyes like wood set into his wooden face, he crosses the floor in four strides with the rigid gravity of a cigar store Indian. . . ." (4). In Darl's second section we see Jewel again, as we are dropped below surface articulation into the deeper poetic depths of human perception: "Then Jewel is enclosed by a glittering maze of hooves as by an illusion of wings. . . . They stand in rigid terrific hiatus. . . . Then Jewel is on the horse's back. He flows upward in a stooping swirl like the lash of a whip. . . . " (11-12). Another example of Darl's poetic inner perception is his description of Pa (Anse) in section 6: "It is as though upon a face carved by a savage caricaturist a monstrous burlesque of all bereavement flowed" (73-74).

Surely Darl does not know the words "shimmering dilapidation," "rigid gravity," "glittering maze," "rigid terrific hiatus," "caricaturist," nor even "burlesque," but his inner sense knows the feeling of these words, because he has not settled for the stock phrase or platitude to dismiss powerful human moments.

Dewey Dell, arguably the character next-best suited to break the bonds of self-interest due to her capacity for poetic inner vision, also succumbs to self-interest through her need for an abortion, a need that grows out of a narrow ("rigid") societal worldview. While her immediate need for an abortion clearly supersedes the ostensible reason for the journey to town—to bury her mother—Dewey Dell is also a victim of a society with a demeaning code of behavior for women. Jill Bergman comments that "when we take into account the historical setting of the novel, we realize that Dewey Dell's inability to articulate her condition stems in part from laws which forbade as indecent the dissemination of information about contraception" (402). Not only has Dewey Dell suffered from these written laws, but also from the unwritten laws of society that put her in the kitchen of the farmhouse, providing sustenance for the men.

Again, Faulkner lets us see the tension between Dewey Dell's inner voicing, even if failed, and her self-interest that is a result of her position in her family and society. In the first of her four sections, Dewey Dell sees her oldest brother Cash "sawing the long hot sad yellow days up into planks," and Darl "at the supper table with his eyes gone further than the food and the lamp, full of the land dug out of his skull and the holes filled with the distance beyond the land" (25). Unlike Darl, obscure words are not part of Dewey Dell's inner voice. Like Darl, she is capable of feeling powerful human moments expressed in complex phrases because she has not blinded herself to her inner vision.

Further on, in her second section, one of the sections that may have upset the parent in Sinking Valley, Kentucky, if she browsed past page eleven, Dewey Dell is in the barn to milk the cow:

> The cow breathes upon my hips and back, her breath warm, sweet, stertorous, moaning. The dead air shapes the dead earth in the dead darkness, further away than seeing shapes the dead earth. It lies dead and warm upon me, touching me naked through my clothes. I feel like a wet seed wild in the hot blind earth. (61)

If Dewey Dell were in the habit of speaking in platitudes and stock phrases, she would not be able to feel herself "like a wet seed wild in the hot blind earth."

Reflected against the poetic inner voicing of Darl and Dewey Dell are a number of characters who do view the world in surface terms voiced in platitudes. These are the characters who create the "rigid" world of the novel. The tension produced between the rich, reflective inner voicings of Darl and Dewey Dell and the characters who have embraced the platitudes of a decidedly classist, sexist, and racist society is remarkable. The most obvious of these latter characters are Cora, a neighbor who speaks in religious platitudes, her husband, Tull, whose platitudes are secular and more pragmatic, and Anse, Addie's husband and the father of four of her five children, who speaks in a gumbo of secular and religious platitudes and profane language.

The instances of platitudes and stock phrases are many and sprinkled throughout the novel. For example, in the first of Cora's three sections, when faced with cakes baked for Miss Lawington, a wealthy town lady who has decided she doesn't need them, Cora says, "Riches is nothing in the face of the Lord, for he can see into the heart" (7). Perhaps these sorts of phrases began as anodynes to an unfair world, but through a lifetime of repetition they have become a thoughtless way of ordering the complex and messy situations of life. Further on, in Cora's second section, we have another example of how words replace actions. She tells her husband, Tull, "I have tried to live right in the sight of God and man, for the honor and comfort of my Christian husband and the love and respect of my Christian children" (22). In Tull's second section Cora says, "It's [the heavy rain threatening the Bundrens' journey to Jefferson] a judgment on Anse Bundren. May it show him the path of sin he is a-trodding" (69). Both natural law and human law can be dispatched easily and quickly with a sufficient supply of stock phrases. Further on in that same section, she tells Tull,

> I have bore you what the Lord God sent me. I faced it without fear nor terror because my faith was strong in the Lord, a-bolstering and sustaining me. If you have no son, it's because the Lord has decreed otherwise in His wisdom. And my life is and ever has been a open book to ere a man or woman among his creatures because I trust in my God and my reward. (70)

In other words, don't bother me with issues we might have to talk through. Again, these stock phrases and platitudes may have begun as an anodyne to pain, but they have become a thoughtless approach to dispense with life.

That Cora has reduced the world to a series of stock phrases for all occasions, not without a tinge of superiority that often accompanies this superficial way of engaging life—commenting on Addie's death she says, "But the eternal and the everlasting salvation and grace is not upon her" (8)—has not escaped her husband. Tull thinks:

> I reckon if there's ere a man or woman anywhere that He could turn it all over to and go away with His mind at rest, it would be Cora. And I reckon she would make a few changes, no matter how He was running it. And I reckon they would be for man's good. Leastways we would have to like them. Leastways, we might as well go on and make like we did. (70)

The power of platitudes is evident here in Tull's resignation to the blunt instrument his wife has become.

In a similar way to Cora, Tull, and Anse, but more internalized, Cash Bundren, eldest child of Addie and Anse, has reduced the world to various lists and rules of carpentry. In the instance of his mother's death, Cash's first section is, in its entirety, a list of thirteen items including "4. In a house people are upright two thirds of the time. So the seams and joints are made up-and-down. Because the stress is up-and-down," and "7. A body is not square like a crosstie" (77). Even with the event of his mother's death, Cash's various lists and ultracareful work are directed primarily toward others perceiving him as an extraordinary carpenter. Jewel, Addie's son by Whitfield, knows this. In his only section, Jewel observes, "that goddamn adze going One [sic] lick less. One lick less. One lick less until everybody that passes in the road will have to stop and see it and say what a fine carpenter he is" (15).

That the world cannot be perceived and dealt with in this simplistic way should be apparent to readers, if not to Cash. His family puts Addie backward into the painstakingly crafted coffin Cash has made. His attempt to ford a raging river ends in disaster, including his broken leg. And above all of Cash's right angles, beveled surfaces, and plumbed lines hover the vultures—literally following the rotting body of Addie and symbolically following the body of Cash's rigid and narrow worldview as it disintegrates in the face of a complex, often unfair society and an indifferent natural world.

Leading the Bundrens on this flawed journey is Anse, Addie's husband and perhaps the most offensive member of the family. His unctuous speech betrays a nature so entirely self-centered that he has constructed elaborate schemes to explain away his dependence on others to do his work. For example, in the first of the Anse chapters, we hear his lengthy explanation of how a road running by the house has ruined his life, by carrying Cash and Darl away from him:

> Making me pay for Cash having to get them carpenter notions when if it hadn't been no road come there, he wouldn't a got them. . . .
>        And Darl too. It ain't that I am afraid of work . . . it's that they would short hand me. . . . It wasn't until that ere road come and switched the land around longways . . . that they begun to threaten me out of him. (35-36)

But the real reason for Anse's unhappiness becomes clear in the following paragraph when we discover his central concern is not Darl, Cash, Addie, the farm, nor anything else but getting new teeth. He thinks: "And now I got to pay for it, me without a tooth in my head, hoping to get ahead enough so I could get my mouth fixed . . . and her hale and well as ere a woman in the land until that day" (36).

Over the remaining sections of the book, we continue to hear Anse expound with stock phrases and platitudes on all the reasons why his life is difficult, without ever taking personal responsibility. At the center of this self-engrossed narrative remains his real quest—new teeth. In Anse's third section, after the journey to carry Addie's corpse to Jefferson has begun and before the Bundrens have come to the flooded river, we hear, arguably, the height of this ongoing gumbo of secular and religious platitudes and profane language.

> Nowhere in this sinful world can a honest, hardworking man profit. . . .
> Sometimes I wonder why we keep at it. It's because there is a reward for us

above. . . . Every man will be equal there and it will be taken from them that have and given to them that have not by the Lord.

But it's a long wait, seems like. . . . I am chosen of the Lord, for who He loveth, so doeth He chastiseth. But I be durn if He don't take some curious ways to show it, seems like.

But now I can get them teeth. That will be a comfort. It will. (104-05)

Of the nonfamily members, the preacher Whitfield is perhaps the most hypocritical and the most driven by platitudes. When he learns Addie is dying, he becomes both fearful that she will reveal their secret while at the same time transmuting her possible confession: "Let me not have also the sin of her broken vow upon my soul" (170). Before he discovers she has died, Whitfield informs us of his intent to confess the affair to Anse before Addie can. But when he rides up and learns that Addie has already died, we are reminded of Addie's earlier admonition about words: "How words go straight up in a thin line, quick and harmless, and how terribly doing goes along the earth. . . ." (165). Whitfield thinks:

He will accept the will for the deed. Who knew that when I framed the words of my confession it was to Anse I spoke them, even though he was not there. It was He in His infinite wisdom that restrained the tale from her dying lips. . . . Praise to Thee in Thy bounteous and omnipotent love; O praise. (171)

With Whitfield's empty praise, let me return to an earlier statement. *As I Lay Dying* illustrates how self-interest produces damaged humans and a fragmented and superficial society. Faulkner shows us a closed loop of self-interest that directs the characters away from consideration of others' needs, which in turn produces an even narrower worldview.

While the central vehicle for moving *As I Lay Dying* forward appears to be the journey to Jefferson to bury Addie with her people, Faulkner has created a much more complex narrative. By exposing the self-interest of the book's characters, he gives us a clear look at how doomed any journey and any society will be when constructed out of self-interest. In fact, even before the journey, Addie has viewed the world as a series of mercantile trades: her hatred of teaching for a life with Anse where love is dead, the birth of Dewey Dell "to negative Jewel," then "Vardaman to replace the child I had robbed him [Anse] of" (168).

What we are left with, ultimately, is the empty quest (earlier identified by Donald Kartiganer) spurred by Addie's request to be buried in Jefferson, which originates in the worst sort of self-interest—revenge. Addie thinks, "My revenge would be that he would never know I was taking revenge. And when Darl was born I asked Anse to promise to take me back to Jefferson when I died. . . ." (164-165).

After the storm and the deluge, after the halting journey to Jefferson, nothing has changed, except that Anse has new teeth at the expense of an unraveling family. His new bride is simply a substitution for Addie. We can easily see the same patterns of life repeating themselves again and again.

Faulkner certainly did not intend for readers to view the novel as a celebration of self-interest with its damaged lives and corrupt society. Rather he asks that we see where self-interest leads, reflected against a deeper poetic vision available to us all if we look toward one another. In this way, the circular structure of *As I Lay Dying* can be a springboard to other discussions of what happens when self-interest overtakes a society, including critical observations of our current information age. In other words, by not dismissing the book as a work that simply "contains profanity and a segment about masturbation," by not falling into the trap of quick and easy engagement with complex human issues, *As I Lay Dying* can provoke valuable discussions of current society and the family structures within this society.

## Works Cited

American Library Association. *Newsletter on Intellectual Freedom* (May 1987): 90.

Beaty, Jerome. Afterword to *As I Lay Dying* by William Faulkner. In *The Norton Introduction to the Short Novel*. 2nd ed. New York: Random House, 1987.

Bergman, Jill. "This Was the Answer to It: Sexuality and Maternity in *As I Lay Dying*." *The Mississippi Quarterly* 49 (1996): 393-407.

Faulkner, William. *As I Lay Dying*. Rev. ed. New York: Random House, 1964.

Kartiganer, Donald. *The Fragile Thread: The Meaning of Form in Faulkner's Novels*. Amherst: University of Massachusetts Press, 1979.

Kincaid, Nanci. "As Me and Addie Lay Dying." *Southern Review* 30 (1994): 582-96.

# Censors "Who Like to Watch" Curricula: Jerzy Kosinski and the Banning of *Being There*

## Dave Wood

When Nicholas Karolides asked me to contribute an essay on Jerzy Kosinski's *Being There* to this volume, I quickly agreed. I had never read the novel but had seen the movie starring Peter Sellers and had long ago read *The Painted Bird*, his picaresque novel about a little Polish boy buffeted from pillar to post in World War II Poland. I had only one personal encounter with Kosinski, but was much taken with his friendliness and generosity and later curious about the circumstances surrounding his 1991 suicide.

Ever since that day I've been interested in Kosinski. According to news reports his wife and friends had been encouraged by what seemed to be improving health and a lessening of depressive moods. On May 2 he attended a book party at the home of Gay and Nan Talese, dined with his mistress, excused himself and returned home, ingested sleeping pills and alcohol, got into a tub of warm water, tied a plastic bag around his head and asphyxiated himself, a suicide method approved by The Hemlock Society. What still troubles me is that just two days after the report, I received from him a check for $35, his membership dues in the National Book Critics Circle, of which I was membership chair at the time. The check bore the same date as his suicide.

The year before, I had met Kosinski in a reception line for him and George Plimpton during a party thrown for them at the Willard Hotel in Washington, D.C., site of that year's National Booksellers' Association convention. The party was opulent, in the manner of publishing parties in those days. Hundreds of critics, authors, and the media had shown up and the reception line was a long one. When I finally shook Kosinski's hand, he seemed eager to chat, which surprised me, a book review editor from "flyover land," the Upper Midwest. While we chatted, I told him that my wife, then a high school teacher, greatly admired *The Painted Bird* and was teaching it that term in one of her classes. Kosinski immediately snapped his fingers and a "gofer" appeared. "Get me a copy of *The Painted Bird*," he said in the trademark staccato I remembered from his riveting appearances on the "Tonight Show." The copy appeared and Kosinski quickly inscribed it to my wife.

This was not the sort of treatment I expected from this writer whose personality had drawn so much media attention, much of it negative, and whose person had become as important as his work. In fact, he had been swathed in controversy from the publication of his first non-fiction books to the end of his troubled life.

As early as the 1960s, the Communist elite took exception to his unflattering portrayal of Poland during World War II and his even less flattering portrayal of the Communist party at work behind the Iron Curtain. Prestigious critics like Peter Prescott and Elie Wiesel, novelists like James Leo Herlihy compared him to Joseph Conrad and Vladimir Nabokov, two other Russians who wrote so brilliantly in their second language. Yet American critics would finally come to bedevil and discredit Kosinski, near the end of his life, even though he had served brilliantly, and significantly, as president of PEN[1] and supported censored writers, not only on the left, but on the right as well.

In 1982, for instance, Geoffrey Stokes and Eliot Fremont-Smith wrote a story for the left-leaning *Village Voice* accusing Kosinski of employing ghostwriters in the composition of *The Painted Bird* and, further, making up the whole story, after he had suggested that it was taken from his own experiences as a refugee. (In point of fact, Kosinski was always enigmatic about the truth behind his fiction.) It was not secret that Kosinski was anti-Communist, but rumors spread he was an operative for the CIA, not really a novelist at all.

Even after his death, Kosinski's visibility is such that the controversy continues. Kosinski biographer James Park Sloan reports that Polish author Joanna Siedlecka in her 1994 biography of Kosinski, *Czarny Ptasior*, claimed that Christian Poles protected Kosinski's Jewish family at great risk, that Kosinski was never separated from his family as was the young boy in *The Painted Bird*, whom Kosinski had often implied was modeled on his own childhood. Communist intellectuals agreed with Siedlecka; anti-Communist Poles did not. At that juncture Slaon went to Poland to see for himself. He concluded that it was a literary tempest in a political teapot. But even Sloan, a Kosinski apologist, admitted that the author's most famous novel probably sprang from Kosinski's fertile imagination rather than from his own life experiences.

Sloan also asserts, with more than a touch of irony, that Siedlecka's book acts as a very strong rebuttal to the claims by Stokes and Fremont-Smith that Kosinski didn't even write *The Painted Bird*.

All this serves as a background to Kosinski's *Being There*, written in 1971, six years after *The Painted Bird*. The later novel also brought plagiarism charges against its author, even though its supposed source, *Nicoldem Dyzma*, was set in Poland and the new one in Washington, D.C. When Professor Karolides told me that *Being There* had been banned in several schools, I immediately jumped to the conclusion that the book must be much more sexually explicit than the movie starring Peter Sellers, because the movie was certainly not prurient, the brief sexual scenes being nothing more than amusing. Or might the censors be leftists, spiritual soulmates of the Stokes and Fremont-Smith variety? The far left has been known to censor books with as much vigor as the far right.

Well, it didn't turn out that way.

For those unacquainted with the movie or the novel, which are very similar, the story, briefly, goes like this:

The main character, Chance, works as a gardener for a wealthy man in Washington, D.C. Chance, imperially slim, handsome, and mentally retarded, had been dropped off at the rich man's house, an orphan. Since then into middle age he has never left the rich man's compound. He works in a vacuum, the garden, takes his meals in his room, and constantly watches television, his only connection with the outside world.

When his employer dies, it's obvious Chance doesn't even know what death is, because he just goes to his supper and turns on the TV. But then the estate lawyers come, ask for his birth certificate, ask for some evidence of his existence. Chance attempts to assert his existence, but without something in print, the lawyers say he doesn't exist and ask him to leave the house and garden without as much as severance pay.

Clad in his former employer's castoff clothing, which happens to have come back in style, Chance walks out into the street for the first time in his adult life, looking distinguished; he is almost immediately struck down by a limousine, in which is riding Elizabeth Eve Rand, the young wife of a fabulously wealthy financier, an adviser to presidents, a man who calls to mind a figure like Bernard Baruch or Averell Harriman.

Elizabeth Eve, concerned about a lawsuit, whisks Chance off to the Rand mansion, where a doctor is always in attendance because her aged husband is on the brink of death. There, his injuries are attended to, and he's asked to stay for dinner and overnight. He does so and in the course of his stay has conversations with the sick old man, who expresses concern about the current economic recession. Chance vaguely remembers such conversations from his television watching and blurts out a cliché about gardening and about how plants die and reappear again in their "proper season."

The rich old man takes this as a metaphor for economic recovery and figures Chance is an economic genius. (He calls him "Chauncey Gardiner.") Chance does nothing to dissuade him or encourage him because he hasn't a clue of what's going on. Soon, Chance meets with the President of the United States, who is also impressed with his "expertise," his easy platitudes taken from horticulture. TV appearances of Chance follow and soon he is a media personality, lionized by all of the Important People inside the Beltway. That includes a very important man, a homosexual who lures Chance into a bedroom and offers sexual favors. Chance, who is apparently impotent, declines, saying that he only "likes to watch" (meaning TV programs). So the homosexual, who misunderstands, obliges by masturbating in front of him.

Then Elizabeth Eve falls in love with Chance, encouraged by her own ailing husband, who wants her to have a suitable mate when he is gone and believes Chance would be a perfect match. She also tries to seduce Chance with the same results fostered by the homosexual suitor.

And so the novella goes. At story's end, Chance is bruited about by Washington's movers and shakers as a fine vice-presidential candidate.

So my suppositions about why the book was banned were both wrong. The sexual scenes, although slightly more explicit than they were in the movie, are most certainly not prurient. And Kosinski's main theme, the foolishness of the book's capitalists, who want to make a moron into a possible president, obviously wouldn't have been a suitable target for left-wing wannabe censors.

So why did some want the book banned? For all the old reasons.

A censorship case reported in the *New York Times* as recently as June 16, 1996, involved Southbury, Connecticut, where Pomeraug High School parents objected to *Being There* on grounds of language. But the superintendent of schools turned down the complaint, pointing out that the book was not required, but only on a recommended reading list (McDonald 13 CN, 3).

Dawn B. Sova, in her book *Banned Books: Literature Suppressed on Social Grounds*, writes that *Being There* has been challenged in high schools for containing "inappropriate images" and for its depiction of masturbation and the "homosexual near-experience" of Chance. Critics say the book is "sex-oriented" and contains "suggestive language" (39-40) unsuitable for high school students. Specifically:

•At Crete High School in Nebraska in 1989, *Being There* was an eleventh-grade reading assignment. Parents asked that the requirement be changed.

The high school said the requirement would stay, but ordered the teacher to provide alternate books for those who objected to reading it (Doyle 58).

•In the same year, parents in Mifflinburg, Pennsylvania, objected to Chance's homosexual encounter—rather "near" encounter. The book was first removed from the class but later reinstated as an alternative reading choice (Doyle 58).

•In 1993, in Davenport, Iowa, the book was removed from the high school's required reading list when parents complained that the description of masturbation was too graphic (Doyle 58).

What a shame! For here is a book that has most of the earmarks of a very teachable piece of literature for high school classes.

From a practical point of view, it's very short, 23,000 words, a book even slow readers could absorb in a short time. Besides that, Kosinski resorts to his "plain style," a bare bones accounting of the plot, accessible to anyone who can read and a model for exquisite, if simple, word choice. Listen to this from the opening of the novel:

> [Plants and people] needed care to live, to survive their diseases, and to die peacefully. Yet plants were different from people. No plant is able to think about itself or able to know itself; there is no mirror in which the plant can recognize its face; no plant can do anything intentionally; it cannot help growing, and its growth has no meaning, since a plant cannot reason or dream. (3)

I'd bet that most kids, after reading that, might say: "Just like Chance!"

I can't think of a better modern example if one wished to teach students the art of parable. In fact, the book reads like a Biblical parable, with Chance's Edenic existence at his employer's compound, after which he is sent "East" of Eden (along with someone who's middle name is Eve!) to the foolish hurly-burly of our nation's capital.

If I were a courageous high school teacher, which I'm not, and a school board wanted to knock *Being There* off my reading list or course syllabus I'd tell them this: Here's a book that takes on TV at its worst, one of literacy's and humanity's worst enemies, and knocks it into a cocked hat. If you want your children to know of its dangers, have them read *Being There*. Chance first finds out that he doesn't "exist" when the rich employer's lawyers ask him for a birth certificate, and he can't produce one.

And, as the book progresses, readers also find out that Chance doesn't exist, except in the insubstantial world of the television screen. Here is the narrator on that subject:

> As long as one didn't look at people, they did not exist. They began to exist as
> on TV, when one turned one's eyes on them. Only then could they stay in
> one's mind before being erased by new images. The same was true of him
> [Chance]. By looking at him, others could make him be clear, could open him
> up and unfold him; not to be seen was to blur and fade out. (12)

This, of course, gives Chance an advantage over "real" people because
everything he says is based on unrelated remarks he's heard on television,
ofttimes childish or outlandishly irrelevant to the topic of conversation.

For example, when he meets the Soviet ambassador at the United
Nations, the Russian says: "Mr. Gardiner, after all . . . shouldn't we, the
diplomats, and you, the businessman, get together more often? We are not
so far from each other, not so far!"

To which Chance replies: "We are not . . . our chairs are almost
touching."

The ambassador mistakes this for Chance's wry wit and stupidly
extends what he takes to be Chance's metaphor for peacemaking. Could
anything be more clear and penetrating to a high school student?

So I most certainly would rather teach it to modern high school
students than subject them to Christian in John Bunyan's *Pilgrim's
Progress*, or some other less accessible allegory.

And that brings us to the teaching of satire. *Being There* and its
absurdities have been compared to the works of Jonathan Swift, also a
proponent of the "plain style," but one less accessible than Kosinski's. In
fact, I've had college students fail to grasp Swift's point in "A Modest
Proposal," thinking instead that Swift is a psychotic and actually means to
suggest that Irish babies be butchered and eaten by the British middle class.
I believe that no one could miss the point of Kosinski's attack on the vacuity
of the wealthy and the powerful in modern America—and also in Soviet
Russia, judging from the Soviet ambassador's response when Chance visits
the United Nations with Elizabeth Eve.

I don't believe literature's main purpose is to act as a vehicle for
providing students with object lessons for living the good life. But let's not
look a gift horse in the mouth. *Being There* is a crystal clear indictment of
indiscriminate television viewing and its possible consequences. When a
student finishes it, he's bound to figure out if he spends his life in front of the
tube, he'll end up the cipher that Chance is—except he'll have no offer of a
cabinet post.

So the kids in Davenport and elsewhere missed a good bet, when their
parents objected to the sexual content of *Being There*, a book that is almost

as sexual as its hero, who only likes to watch—television, that is—a universally available medium much more graphic these days than Kosinski's creation. It's also a good bet that students old enough to read *Being There* wouldn't really need the sexual passages as an instruction book on self-abuse!

## Note

[1] An international association of poets, playwrights, screenwriters, essayists, editors, novelists, historians, and critics whose purpose is to foster a sense of community among writers to advance the freedom to write throughout the world. It combats the suppression of freedom of expression and opposes arbitrary censorship and the evils that often accompany a free press, such as deceptive publication and deliberate falsifications for political and personal gain.

## Works Cited

Corry, John. "The Most Considerate of Men," *American Spectator* (July 1991): 17 ff.

Doyle, Robert P. *Banned Books 1999 Resource Guide*. Chicago, Ill.: American Library Association, 1999.

Kosinski, Jerzy. *Being There*. New York: Harcourt, Brace, Jovanovich, 1971.

Lavers, Norman. *Jerzy Kosinski*. New York: Twayne, 1982.

McDonald, Thomas. "Janet Vaill Day: Fighting Censorship at the Town Library." *New York Times* (16 June 1996): Section 13 CN, 3.

Siedlecka, Joanna. *Czarny Ptasior*. Gdansk: Wydawn. Marabut, Poland, 1994.

Sloan, James Park. *"Jerzy Kosinski: A Biography"* New York: Dutton, 1996.

_____. "Kosinski's War," *New Yorker* (19 October 1994): 46 ff.

Sova, Dawn B. *Banned Books: Literature Suppressed on Social Grounds*. New York: Facts On File, 1998.

Stokes, Geoffrey, and Eliot Fremont-Smith. "Jerzy Kosinski's Tainted Words," *The Village Voice* (22 June 1982): 1ff.

Straus, Dorothea. "Remembering Jerzy Kosinski," *Partisan Review* (winter 1993): 138 ff.

# Un-*Beloved*?

## Marshall B. Toman

Our most recent Nobel Prize winner for literature, Toni Morrison is arguably the best living American writer. Her storytelling power, her meticulously crafted language, her scrutiny of American history and culture, and, above all, her tragic vision of what it means to be human established her in that position. Yet her 1987 novel *Beloved* is not beloved of all. It has met challenges as either required or supplementary reading in advanced placement English courses in high schools from Maine to Texas and Virginia to Washington.[1] Criticisms of Morrison's novel are often reported as blanket charges that encompass several other books by different authors, so dealing with specifics is difficult. A parent in Madawaska, Maine, for example, admitted that he had not read the whole novel but read a passage—not specified in the report—and was disturbed at "language for which students would be punished for using in school" ("Madawaska" 14). A composite indictment of the book, however, would contain the vague but repeated charges of "bad" language, sexual material, and violence.

From Virginia we also hear a protest against "bestiality" ("From the Front(Line)" 2). The *American Heritage Dictionary* defines the word as "sexual relations between a human being and an animal," of which relations there are none presented in the novel[2]; or "conduct or action marked by carnality or brutality," one or the other of which appears in just about every story of human life, from the Bible and fairy tales to prizewinning novels—such a charge would ban just about every book—or "the quality of being bestial; animal nature," a quality that, with reference to humans, is explicitly attacked in the novel when Paul D. tells Sethe that she has two legs, not four (165)—that she is most emphatically not an animal and thus responsible for all her actions.

Also, from Virginia we hear, from the same protester who feared bestiality, an objection to "Biblical references" ("From the Front(Line)" 2). As with most respected Western writers, Morrison knows the Bible well and uses her knowledge well. Often the use is subtle, as in the chapter that relates

Sethe's apocalyptic act, the killing that ends her world as she knows it and that brings judgment down on her. The chapter opens with an oblique reference to the four horsemen of the Apocalypse: "When the four horsemen came—schoolteacher, one nephew, one slave catcher and a sheriff—. . . they thought they were too late" (148). Sometimes the use of the Bible is prominent, as in the novel's epigraph, which is taken from Romans 9:25:

> I will call them my people,
> which were not my people;
> and her beloved,
> which was not beloved.

I will return to the epigraph later when it may be seen how the novel inculcates genuine and fundamental Christian values, such as concern for one's neighbor in matters both worldly and spiritual.

Those who have read the whole novel will understand the context of the violence and of some of the sexual material that is contained within that framework of violence. The most important context is slavery. Morrison's inspiration for this novel was her reading the true story upon which the novel is based. The story involved an enslaved woman, Margaret Garner, who had fled Kentucky to Ohio. She was resting in Ohio with what of her family she could gather about her—her four children and her mother-in-law, but not her husband.[3] It was after the Fugitive Slave Law had been passed. Slave catchers identified her. Before she could be prevented, she killed one of her children in her attempt to kill them all in order to stop their return to slavery. A dramatic lithograph appeared with her story in *Harper's Weekly* in 1867. A scholarly history of the Margaret Garner episode, Steven Weisenburger's *Modern Medea*, has been written since Morrison's novel focused our attention on the incident.

Morrison did not set out to tell a history of slavery. "I never thought I had the emotional resources to deal with slavery," she relates. "I thought I was writing a story about, a very contemporary story. I wanted to write about self murder—the ways in which we can sabotage ourselves with the best of all possible intentions. . . . I never liked books about slavery. They were always so big and so flat and you could just never get close to them" (*The Southbank Show*).

Rather, her task is always the same as that of one of her literary mentors, William Faulkner. Faulkner, about whose work Morrison wrote part of her master's thesis, always told the "truths of the human heart." Morrison asked herself what, ever, in the world, could bring a mother to attempt to kill her children. "For me [the killing of Beloved] was the ultimate gesture of the loving mother. . . . 'You [children] of all things cannot be dirtied, cannot be sullied. You [enslavers] can do it to me, but not to my children.' Because that is the best part of you; that's the immortality. That's the best thing you've ever done" (*The Southbank Show*). These sentiments are echoed in the novel when Denver ruminates on her mother's urgent arguments with Beloved.

> Sethe's greatest fear was the same one Denver had in the beginning—that Beloved might leave. That before Sethe could make her understand what it meant—what it took to drag the teeth of that saw under the little chin . . . to squeeze her so she could absorb, still, the death spasms that shot through that adored body, plump and sweet with life—Beloved might leave. Leave before Sethe could make her realize that worse than that—far worse—was what Baby Suggs died of, what Ella knew, what Stamp saw and what made Paul D tremble. That anybody white could take your whole self for anything that came to mind. Not just work, kill, or maim you, but dirty you. Dirty you so bad you couldn't like yourself anymore. Dirty you so bad you forgot who you were and couldn't think it up. And though she and others lived through and got over it, she could never let it happen to her own. The best thing she was, was her children. Whites might dirty *her* all right, but not her best thing, her beautiful, magical best thing. . . . (251)

Morrison's idea seems to complicate the problem. A mother who kills her child must now not only be understood but be seen as committing the act out of love. Really, this insight, however, is the only one that allows us to understand Morrison's "Margaret Garner," her Sethe—the only insight that allows for "understanding" other than the easy, automatic charge of insanity. In the court-handed-down opinion, Margaret Garner was "insane." That verdict allowed her to escape many of the traditional punishments of both the escaped slave and murderer. But Morrison asks what constitutes "sanity" in the brutalizing world of slavery.

In many places, the novel challenges complacent views of "sane" and "insane." Sethe's husband Halle can be driven permanently mad by witnessing from his hiding place the gang rape of his wife (68-69). The rape is presided over by "Schoolteacher," the plantation owner. The name of "Schoolteacher" should establish him as a figure of rule and order in any ordinary definition of a sane and rational world. Instead, Schoolteacher represents an inane pseudo-hyperrationality in his phrenological measure-ments of the heads of the Sweet Home slaves (191) that ultimately are an attempt to justify the power he holds over other human beings. His insistence on precisely passing on his obsession by having his pupils list the "human characteristics on the left; . . . animal ones on the right" (193) demonstrates the perversion of the teaching function that perpetuates his world of power rather than a rational and egalitarian world.

Another inversion of the sane-insane dichotomy is Sethe's regretting the fact that she could not permit herself to become insane (an easy way out for Halle, Sethe implies) because of her responsibility to her children: "Other people went crazy, why couldn't she? . . . What a relief to stop it right there. Close. Shut. Squeeze the butter [as Halle did all over himself in his insanity]. But her three children were chewing sugar teat under a blanket on their way to Ohio and no butter play would change that" (70-71). Paul D summarizes yet another inversion of the sane when he remembers his imprisonment in the Alfred, Georgia, ditch "with anything that crawled or scurried welcome to share that grave" (106). He thinks that that experience "drove him crazy so he would not lose his mind" (41). The novel invites us to see just how fluctuating "sane" behavior can be when perspectives shift. Schoolteacher's definitions can turn a human into a beast. Baby Suggs's perspective suggests that Schoolteacher's dehumanization of others creates a beast out of himself: "even when [white people] thought they were behaving, it was a far cry from what real humans did" (244). If we understand the context of slavery, our perspective on Sethe's act should shift also.

In order for the premise that Sethe killed out of love to be absorbed by readers, Morrison must make them feel the same insanity and horror of slavery that Sethe felt. Consequently, Morrison has the reader encounter—with Paul D's tactile wonder—Sethe's back, lacerated by the whip (17-18). She presents Schoolteacher's "correction" of Sixo, his murder by being burned alive and shot (226). She refers to the rapes and eventual mutilation and burning-alive murder of Sethe's mother (60-62). She describes Paul D's humiliation and obliteration of any worthy sense of self when he is subjected to the "three-spoke collar" (227-28) and the bit (69-72):

> how offended the tongue is, held down by iron, how the need to spit is so deep you cry for it[! Sethe] already knew about it, had seen it time after time in the place before Sweet Home. Men, boys, little girls, women. The wildness that shot up into the eye the moment the lips were yanked back. Days after it was taken out, goose fat was rubbed on the corners of the mouth but nothing to soothe the tongue or take the wildness out of the eye. (71)

Virtually every character is scarred deeply by slavery: the infidelity with her white master that Stamp Paid's wife was forced to undergo; Ella's rapes by "the lowest yet"; the nauseating sex enjoined by the white guards upon the prisoners of Alfred (107-08). Sethe's enigmatic line, "They took my milk" (16, 17), is eventually clarified in the narration of her rape where the plantation young men sport with Sethe, the lactating object of their violence.

This last-referred-to scene is not just another element in the well-documented atrocities of slavery. The "taking of Sethe's milk" is a symbol

of just how unable an enslaved woman was of protecting her children. Those
children could, of course, be sold away from her—as routinely happened to
Baby Suggs (25) until she was brought to the Garner plantation. But
potentially a mother might even have to starve her infant so that she can be
the object of unnatural license in some rapists. Not even so basic a function
as the giving of her mother's milk to her daughter was allowed her without
question. To such a condition Sethe refuses to return Beloved, the daughter
she does manage to kill.

Sethe's infanticide is, in these depictions, made intelligible to the
reader; her act, however, is not condoned. Paul D is one of the most
sympathetic characters of the novel. All the tremendous violence and
violation that he has suffered has not turned him incapacitatingly bitter or
vengeful. As Sethe tells Paul D,

> "People I saw as a child . . . who'd had the bit always looked wild after that.
> Whatever they used it on them for, it couldn't have worked, because it put a
> wildness where before there wasn't any. When I look at you, I don't see it.
> There ain't no wildness in your eye nowhere." (71)

Paul D is horrified when he finds out that Sethe killed her daughter, and,
though in sorrow, he leaves her. The African American community, too, is
appalled. Most of all, Sethe herself is haunted by her guilt.

Although the novel asks readers to accept the corporeal presence of an
autonomous Beloved, the ghostliness of Beloved raises the (literal)
specter—the shadow of an idea—that Beloved is the imagined projection of
Sethe's heavy guilt. The argumentative dialogue between Sethe and Beloved
near the beginning of part three can thus be viewed as Sethe's debate within
herself about her actions.

> Sethe began to talk, explain, describe how much she had suffered, been
> through, for her children. . . . None of which made the impression it was
> supposed to. Beloved accused her of leaving her behind. . . . She said they were
> the same, had the same face, how could she have left her? And Sethe cried,
> saying she never did, or meant to—that she had to get them out. . . . (241)

Sethe does not allow her psychological projection to accept the explanations;
in effect, Sethe does not forgive herself. In hindsight, Sethe recognizes "her
error of love."[4]

In this supernatural tale, however, the narrative's focus is not on Sethe's
guilt but on the concrete manifestation, on the character of Beloved. Some
readers interpret Beloved as the murdered daughter come back from the
dead. This daughter is intent upon gaining all Sethe's love, to the ruin of

Denver, Sethe's only child to remain with her, and to the ruin of Sethe herself. At least as plausible from the point of view of Beloved's physical realness is the idea that the devil has assumed a pleasing form in Beloved.[5] Morrison makes clear that Sethe has made one mistake in killing her daughter. Her way of atonement, the cutting of herself off from the community, is another. Evil is feeding on evil. The bad spirit who has assumed the shape of Sethe's daughter, who is known only as "Beloved," gains Sethe's love, excludes Denver from Sethe's attention, and begins to destroy Sethe, first by seducing Paul D, her one link to a world of hope for some happiness. "Beloved," after all, does not make "herself" known until Baby Suggs, the community's healer and preacher, dies.[6] Baby Suggs had commanded the people in her flock to love themselves:

> Love it. Love it hard. Yonder they do not love your flesh. They despise it. . . . Love your hands! Love them. Raise them up. . . , stroke them on your face 'cause they don't love that either. *You* got to love it, *you*!. . . No, they don't love your mouth. *You* got to love it. . . . And all your inside parts that they'd just as soon slop for hogs, you got to love them. The dark, dark liver—love it, love it, and the beat and beating heart, love that too. More than eyes or feet. More than lungs that have yet to draw free air. More than your life-holding womb and your life-giving private parts, hear me now, love your heart. For this is the prize. (88-89)

Such a community, based on African traditions, is doubly important in the face of slavery's degradations and destruction of the spirit. With the denial of self that the slave society imposes, only a community, constituted by such rituals of love as Baby Suggs directs, can provide a basis for self-affirmation. With Baby Suggs's death, such a ritual ceases. The community of love is weakened, and evil in the shape of Beloved finds an opportunity to enter and to attempt to imprison Sethe in the consequences of her actions, that is to say, in the indirect legacy of slavery.

Ultimately, then, the novel is about the healing of one who has sinned, about repentance, atonement, and finally redemption through the community's exorcism of "Beloved." When that community, led by Ella, assembles at 124, for "Sethe it was as though [Baby Suggs's ceremony in] the Clearing had come to her" (261). The community, reconstituted by their ritualistic chanting on behalf of one of its fallen members, can make an appropriate acceptance of Sethe. They enable Sethe to symbolically and publicly erase her killing of her daughter as a scene similar to the one of eighteen years previous transpires. This time Sethe leaves Beloved on the porch and attacks, ineffectually, the white passerby Edward Bodwin. Equally important the community enables Sethe's living daughter Denver to be reintegrated into its web of life.

Morrison does not approach her presentations of lived experience simply. Her artistic vision requires that she be faithful to the complexities that motivate human action within the system of slavery. Neither is her citation of Romans 9:25 without its ambiguity. The context is Paul's call to all peoples of the world to enjoy the community of Christianity. To read just the last lines, one tends to think of "beloved" as that daughter of Sethe, the little girl who seemed not to be loved but who in fact was deeply, if misguidedly, loved. However, the first lines emphasize an integration into a community, and the quotation in total suggests that the sinner, Sethe, and the outcast, Denver, can be assured of a call to mesh with their life-sustaining community if they will but heed it.

Such an interpretation of the novel, based on its entirety and upon the intention of the author as we can discover it in interviews as well as in the text itself, would seem consonant with the values of love and charity, even to those who object to the use of biblical references. Such a reading, then, while requiring a wise maturity and a careful, thorough understanding of the novel in the reader, is in harmony with a true Christian spirit, which emphasizes those genuinely fundamental Christian values, as the epigraph suggests.

Though the foregoing foregrounds Morrison's intention in emphasizing the human tragedy that was the story's inception and though Morrison "never liked books about slavery," *Beloved* at one level is such a book, and it may be perceived by some readers to have as its central message the fact of the past existence of slavery. For those who wish Americans—especially young Americans, for whose reading the book has been challenged—to have an unclouded conception of benevolence, confidence, and righteousness, negative and painful portrayals of the past are detrimental. Why write "about slavery"?

One response is that with slavery's being the context for Morrison's exploration of Sethe's tragedy, Morrison was uncovering from history some of the heroism of ordinary African American life. She had discovered the history of Margaret Garner while she was working on *The Black Book*, compiled by A. Harris Middleton in 1974.

> This collection of memorabilia represents 300 years of black history, and not only records the material conditions of black life from slavery to freedom, but also exhibits the black cultural production that grew out of and in spite of these conditions. Compiled in scrapbook fashion, it contains everything from bills of sale for slaves to jazz and poetry. Through diverse images of black life presented in such items as photos of lynchings, sharecropping families and slave-made quilts, and encoded in excerpts from such sources as slave narratives, folk

sayings, and black newspapers, *The Black Book* tells a complex story of oppression, resistance and survival. More importantly, it was published at a moment in American history when many feared that the Black Power movement of the 1960s and early 1970s would be reduced to faddish rhetoric and mere image rather than understood for its cultural and political implications. Morrison herself feared the movement propounded a kind of historical erasure or denial of those aspects of the past which could not be easily assimilated into its rhetorical discourse or into the collective consciousness of black people as a group. She feared, for example, that the rhetoric of the movement, in its desire to create a new version of history that would affirm the African past and the heroic deeds of a few great men, had inadvertently bypassed the equally heroic deeds of ordinary African-Americans who had resisted and survived the painful traumas of slavery. In other words, she questioned what she perceived to be a romanticization of both the African past and the American past that threatened to devalue 300 years of black life on American soil before it was fully recorded, examined or understood for its complexity and significance. Thus, *The Black Book* was a literary intervention in the historical dialogue of the period to attest to "Black life as lived" experience. (Mobley 189-190)

*Beloved* also creates African American life as lived experience for a wider audience than *The Black Book* would reach and in a more profound manner than the historical documents within *The Black Book* could attain. It provides vignettes of the heroic deeds of ordinary African Americans in Sixo's selfless rescuing of the Thirty-Mile Woman and their unborn child when he pushes her one way and runs the other way into the group of slave catchers looking for him (225) and in Stamp Paid's devotion to people:

> But sneaking was his job—his life; though always for a clear and holy purpose. Before the War all he did was sneak: runaways into hidden places, secret information to public places. Underneath his legal vegetables were the contraband humans that he ferried across the river. Even the pigs he worked in the spring served his purposes. Whole families lived on the bones and guts he distributed to them. (169)

In addition to celebrating strayed African American history as heroic, the novel also helps readers understand the legacy of systematic repression as well as some of the continuing gender-role tensions. As Valerie Smith points out, "retelling the story of slavery has allowed contemporary fiction writers such as David Bradley and Charles Johnson to explore the relationship between the commodification of black physical labor in the antebellum period and the commodification of black creative and intellectual labor in the late twentieth century. In their retellings of slavery, Bradley and Johnson, as well as Octavia Butler, Sherley Anne Williams, Gayl Jones, and Toni Morrison, all consider the construction of black male and female gender roles and sexuality" (343).

A third important reason for keeping the memory of enslavement alive, however, is to remember our capacity for personal and institutionalized evil in order to be vigilant against it. Stalin said that the death of a million people is a statistic; the death of one man is a tragedy. When the Holocaust Museum was opened, the problem that faced the directors was how not to make the experience of the museum, with its documentation of the deaths of more than six million, seem to visitors not to be a statistic. The solution was to give each visitor a card with the biography of one person involved in the Holocaust. At stations throughout the chronologically arranged exhibits, the visitor could receive information on that person's life at that moment in time. The visitor did not know when the person would die or whether the person might survive: a statistical immensity made comprehensible as human tragedy. *Beloved* accomplishes the same. In Sethe's tragedy we see and feel at a deeply personal level the capacity for our society to create institutionalized evil. We need to be aware of this potential, as Sinclair Lewis was, in order to combat it. In 1935, Lewis, our first writer to win the Nobel Prize for Literature, wrote a prescient novel called *It Can't Happen Here*. Based on what Lewis observed occurring in Nazi Germany, he showed in the ironically titled novel how easily institutionalized totalitarian evil might occur here, in America. What is important for readers to realize is that we need neither to imagine an evil that never in fact happened here nor to search elsewhere, in Europe or Asia or Africa; we need only to properly remember.

But while *Beloved* is "about slavery" in one sense and there are reasons to remember that history today, *Beloved*'s themes are universal. Trudier Harris, for example, has pointed out the extensive use of debt and exchange metaphors in pointing to the theme of possession in the novel. Slavery literalizes the ownership of one human being by another. Despite concepts of autonomy, a person can feel possessed by another under slavery. The character Stamp Paid is a meditation on this feeling. As the slave Joshua, he has been forced to allow his wife Vashti to become the mistress of his owner's son during the length of the son's pleasure. This causes Joshua to reflect on how extensively he is owned and how, in an exchange economy, he may "purchase" his freedom. He does "buy" his freedom by an act of will and reflection. He reflects that he has paid by acquiescing in this arrangement. "With that gift, he decided that he didn't owe anybody anything. Whatever his obligations were, that act paid them off" (185). His act of will is to declare a new identity, a change of name to "Stamp Paid" (185, 232-233). Exteriorly a member of the oppressed class, interiorly he has sounded forth the trumpet that demolishes the Jericho Wall of an enslaved state of mind.

But we all owe debts based upon a metaphorical possession to others[7]—self-imposed debts, debts imposed by others; most of these are socially and legally enforced within family relationships, and slavery becomes an extreme and concrete realization of an enduring human relationship that all readers, particularly secondary school young adults, must encounter. What is owed to whom? What is unjustly demanded? What must we pay to release ourselves and how shall we count the costs of those actions, psychological costs as well as economic. As Sethe fervently tells Paul D, "No more running—from nothing. I will never run from another thing on this earth. I took one journey and I paid for the ticket, but let me tell you something, Paul D Garner: it cost too much! Do you hear me? It cost too much" (15). As Harris points out, *Beloved* is about the price of our actions. *Beloved* emphasizes both a notion of possession by another person when Beloved seeks to possess Sethe and the notion of possession by an idea when Sethe acquiesces in that possession. As when slavery forces a person to refer all actions to a legalized owner (where one lives, how one lives and loves), so Sethe, possessed by the idea of her love for and guilt over her daughter, refers all her actions to that idea—until she can free herself from it.

*Beloved* shows that the attempted possession of another can spring from an overprotectiveness as well as selfishness. Sethe killed Beloved to save her from the future; Sethe raises Denver by "keeping her from her past" (42). Sethe has thus overprotected Denver to protect her from the past (Mobley 194), thereby denying Denver the right to confront that past and move forward in her life. As a shocked Paul D warns Sethe, "You can't protect [Denver] every minute" (45). For readers *Beloved* explores the boundaries of appropriate and inappropriate parental protection and of appropriate resistance to "possession."[8]

The biblical references, the sexual material, and the violence that are objected to are woven into an immensely moving portrait of human tragedy and heroism. The novel's themes of debt and guilt and love and possession and community healing are artistically presented in a narrative that circles its painful central episode, like a mind unwilling to confront a dark truth and that ultimately asks us to remember.

## Notes

[1]See "From the Front(Line)" for Washington; Suhor "Hit List" and "Update" for Virginia and Texas; and "Madawaska, Maine." *SLATE* ["Support for the Learning and Teaching of English"], from which the first three references are taken, is published by the National Council of Teachers of English.
[2]Allusions to bestiality in the first sense (10, 11, 26) suggest the unnatural-

ness of the slave system, which truncates natural sexual relations between enslaved men and women. Sixo's clandestine night journeys of over thirty miles to rendezvous with the Thirty-Mile Woman is another reference to the grotesque form that the system of slavery imposed on sexual relations. By including the sympathetically drawn character of Paul D in these allusions, Morrison places him in a similarly taboo situation to Sethe, whose transgression was to have killed her child. *Beloved* posits the cause of these aberrations to be the system of slavery. That these intensely driven young men of Sweet Home exercise complete restraint toward Sethe and respect her contrasts with her casual rape by Schoolteacher's "pupils."

[3]Morrison retains the name of "Garner" in the novel, perhaps suggesting Sethe's desperate attempt to gather her children to her.

[4]My colleague Nicholas Karolides in conversation expressed this inisght; the quoted words are his.

[5]The first interpretation could be called the Janey version. When Denver tells Janey of Beloved's presence, Janey concludes that "Sethe's dead daughter, the one whose throat she cut, had come back to fix her" (255). The second interpretation could be called Ella's version. "When Ella heard 124 was occupied by something-or-other beating up on Sethe, it infuriated her and gave her another opportunity to measure what could very well be the devil himself." (256). Ample references to Beloved as a devil rather than a reincarnated daughter are scattered throughout the novel.

[6]I would like to thank my colleague Jenny Brantley for her generous sharing of information on and interpretation of *Beloved* that shaped this paragraph.

[7]Three streams of consciousness cover 200 to 213. Each emphasis within the following quotations is my own. Sethe's long interior monologue begins "Beloved, she *my* daughter. *She mine*" (201). Denver's begins "Beloved is *my* sister" (205). Beloved's begins "I am Beloved and *she is mine*" (210). This theme of owning another person continues over 214-217 in a prose poem that merges the three meditations on possessing another:

> She is mine. . . .
> Your face is mine. . . .
> You are my sister
> You are my daughter
> You are my face; you are me
> I have found you again; you have come back to me
> You are my Beloved
> You are mine
> You are mine
> You are mine. . .

[8]If this novel were to be discussed by young adults, one prediscussion

writing prompt might be "On what occasions have you felt that a parent or grandparent was overly protective of you? Looking back, do you still feel the parent acted inappropriately or do you think the parent was ultimately justified?"

## Works Cited

*American Heritage Dictionary*, 2nd College ed. Boston: Houghton, 1991.

"From the Front(Line): Update on Help from SLATE." *SLATE* 22.3 (Nov. 1997): 1-2. [Washington]

Harris, Trudier. "Escaping Slavery but Not Its Images." In *Toni Morrison: Critical Perspectives Past and Present*. Ed. Henry Louis Gates, Jr. and K. A. Appiah. New York: Amistad, 1993. 330-341.

"Madawaska, Maine." *Newsletter on Intellectual Freedom* 47.1 (Jan. 1998): 14.

Middleton, A. Harris, comp. *The Black Book*. New York: Random House, 1974.

Mobley, Marilyn Sanders. "A Different Remembering: Memory, History and Meaning in Toni Morrison's *Beloved*." In *Modern Critical Views: Toni Morrison*. Ed. Harold Bloom. New York: Chelsea House, 1990. 189-199.

Morrison, Toni. *Beloved*. 1987. New York: Plume, 1988.

"Round Rock, Texas." *Newsletter on Intellectual Freedom* 45.3 (May 1996): 99.

Smith, Valerie. "'Circling the Subject': History and Narrative in *Beloved*." In *Toni Morrison: Critical Perspectives Past and Present*. Ed. Henry Louis Gates, Jr. and K. A. Appiah. New York: Amistad, 1993. 342-355.

*The Southbank Show*. Interview with Toni Morrison. 1987. Dir. Alan Benson. London Weekend Television. Bravo. 50 min. 1997.

Suhor, Charles. "From the Front(Line): Hit List Update—SLATE Responds to Censorship Calls." *SLATE* 22.3 (Nov. 1996): 1-2.

———. "From the Front (Line): Update on Help from SLATE." *SLATE* 23.1 (Apr. 1998): 1-3.

Texas. *Attacks on the Freedom to Learn: 1996 Report*. Washington, D.C.: People For the American Way, 1997. 276.

Weisenburger, Steven. *Modern Medea: A Family Story of Slavery and Child-Murder from the Old South*. New York: Hill and Wang, 1998.

# Censorship and *Bless Me, Ultima*:
# A Journey through Fear to Understanding

## Linda Varvel

When I first read an excerpt from Rudolfo Anaya's *Bless Me, Ultima* in *Braided Lives* in 1994, I was intrigued by several radical elements of the novel: the young protagonist has a healthy dose of feminine qualities; the novel acknowledges the spiritual life of children; and it reveals the Chicano American worldview of psychic power and witches as accepted and essential to the fabric of spirituality and community. I did question, however, if students in heartland Minnesota would find it too radical and threatening to mainstream Christian beliefs. Therefore, I initially put it on an optional reading list for extra-credit book reports.

Because reading is not always the first recreational choice for high school students in twenty-first-century America, English teachers are always on the lookout for novels that capture average or resistant readers and take particular note of a story that engrosses a student to the point of talking about the book or making an extra report. When a rather typical 10th-grade boy who had been shy and rather disengaged eagerly volunteered to speak about *Bless Me, Ultima* in his small group and write a book report on it, I was particularly pleased. Gradually, I worked the novel into the curriculum and found it to be an engaging and provocative book for the class as a whole.

Based on my observations of students' reading and reactions to the book as well as my own reader response and teaching notes, it seems clear that some of the aspects that distinguish this novel as unique are the elements that make it vulnerable to challenge. In fact, the very things that draw some young people to the book, when taken out of context and emphasized, may incite fear and directly cause it to be challenged in the public schools. Perhaps my insights on some of these key concepts may help other teachers navigate troubled waters with this book within the standard curricula.

*Bless Me, Ultima* is a "coming of age" novel with a difference. In many young adult novels, a boy is thrust out into the wider world and wages a "battle" to conquer all kinds of adversaries. Often, physical danger and death are at stake. By contrast, many female characters tend to suffer psychological dangers and interior wars for identity, confidence, and right moral action. Rudolfo Anaya's hero, Antonio (Tony) Marez, is not a typical boy. Although, like Huck Finn in Mark Twain's American classic, Antonio is exposed to the violence, greed, and manipulation in the larger adult world around him, he is not a tough, foul-mouthed, fisticuffs boy who leaps from one hair-raising danger to another. Whereas Huck must flee intense physical abuse by his father, survive floods, brawls, and the abuse of thieves, con artists, and slave traders, Antonio is not compelled to dominate people or events around him. He is primarily an empathetic witness to the conflicts raging within his own community. Until his schoolmate Horse attacks him outright, he refuses to fight and resists rowdy, physical games or confrontation. Antonio's instinctive reaction is to "fold" the dramatic events around him into his psychological and emotional being, sometimes collapsing into physical illness, dreaming, and reflection as he wars within himself. His "dangerous adventure" is a spiritual crisis—one that is inherently less rambunctious and more "feminine" in nature.

The young Antonio witnesses a killer being hunted down by an angry mob. Yet, when this man Lupito is given a name and begs the young boy's forgiveness the moment before his death, this killer becomes vulnerable and a needy human being. When Tenario's angry mob comes to drag Ultima to her death, the boy sees a reputedly inferior man stand up to the peer pressure of this mob. When the mob in effect "puts her on trial" by initiating a test for "witchcraft," he sees an owl protect Ultima through violent means. This same "curandera" who is accused of using potions and curses on one of Tenario's daughters later heals his Uncle Lucas back from death and cures the Agu Negra household of ghosts. Witnessing the violence of these conflicts within the adult world is profoundly disturbing to Antonio, and in each case, he withdraws to ponder and struggle with this new knowledge. His reaction takes the reader into the inner life of a child's thoughts and feelings and increasingly into his disturbed dreams. His involvement with the adult world evolves because Antonio is psychic and intuitive, typically feminine qualities, and the fact that this vulnerable child is not protected from this adult world but is drawn further and further into its mysteries and paradoxes may be one of the controversial aspects of the story. The style of this evolution of self is more characteristically feminine, and the fact that he does not fight or physically defend himself against terror and fear may be disturbing to the parents of student readers when he is perceived as a weak boy in a dangerous situation.

As the character of Antonio Marez unfolds, it becomes increasingly clear that Rudolfo Anaya believes that young children are not just physical and mental creatures. Embodied in this boy's intense, sober search is the author's belief that children are intuitive and spiritual beings from birth, looking for moral guides within a profoundly layered and mysterious society and universe. Antonio's compelling desire to distinguish good from evil resembles Scout's painful struggle in Harper Lee's classic, *To Kill a Mockingbird*. Both Antonio and Scout possess an intense curiosity about the terrors in the larger, "outside" adult world and a "psychic sense" of exactly where good and evil will meet. Scout discovers that Atticus and her father's black client possess inherent moral integrity. Boo Radley's courageous physical act proves that moral goodness is not necessarily where the community decides it is. Whereas Scout's training is in the realm of racial and gender politics ending in a court of law, Antonio's journey moves from social morality to inner spirituality ending in personal insight. Narciso's physical courage and defense of Ultima and Ultima's spiritual protection of Antonio provide a similar moral compass for the boy that is equally nonconformist.

The spiritual and psychic truth about children that Anaya tells in *Bless Me, Ultima* is firmly rooted in twentieth-century Chicano American culture. Standing at the center of this particular Chicano family are two strong women, a mother and a spiritual healer who becomes a "surrogate grandmother" to Tony; both strive to resist evils within their family as well as in the outside community. They do not remain silent, nor do they subjugate themselves to the will of men. Maria speaks her mind in her troubled marriage. Rather than give in to her husband Gabriel's despair and destructive drinking, Maria remains devoted to her Catholic faith and her family ties to Las Pasturas. She prays when Gabriel leaves to join the manhunt of Lupito but also offers celebratory prayers when her sons return from war. She argues convincingly not to abandon Ultima to poverty in the home village and lights candles for prayers regularly. Although there is much loss, she is determined to create a religious foundation in the home.

By contrast, the men in Antonio's family and community are restless and uprooted from themselves, both the victims and perpetrators of violence and revenge. When the three older Marez sons come home from a foreign war full of rage and grief, Gabriel alternates between uneasy discontent and dreaming with them about escape to California. Leon, Eugene, and Andrew hide from their pain in sexual and hedonistic indulgence with prostitutes and alcohol; they lose all sense of day, night, work, and ethics, destroying property and taking extreme physical risks. Because his elders provide no psychological insulation or moral guidance, Antonio's childhood cocoon is invaded by the destructive realities of male rage, violence, and revenge. In a conversation with David Johnson and David Apodaca in "Myth and the Writer: A Conversation with Rudolfo Anaya," Anaya talks about the influence of the male and female perspective in the boy's life: "Antonio, when we discover him, is both [male and female]. He's complete. He hasn't broken up that harmony. One of the things that happens during the novel is that he is taught more and more about the male character and imbued with that, so that eventually he acquires more of a sense of the male principle." He continues, "but the way we're taught to grow up, it's unbalanced" (qtd. in Dick 32-33). Anaya seems to be implying that the adult world for a Chicano man is cruel and hard.

Anaya very skillfully plants another important mentor in the story who is equally compelling to Antonio's mind and psyche. Burdened with the onus of "town drunk," over time, Narciso's actions reveal courage, compassion, and principled truth to Tony. In the scene with Lupito at the bridge, Tony hears Narciso reach out to Lupito with compassion about his war experience as he tries to negotiate less bloody resolution. Narciso gives Gabriel support against the mob at their door. Tony is profoundly disturbed by the death of Narciso at the hands of Tenorio, partly because his own brother will not leave his whore to help, which Tony sees as immoral, and also because Antonio senses the growing power of Tenorio. Narciso could definitely be seen as a Christ figure for readers who are searching for that kind of imagery and transformation. Narciso takes strong physical action in the face of injustice; the tragedy is that he must stand alone. Antonio sees that good men cannot always resist evil and survive.

Although Antonio's instinctive quest to find a true source and arbiter of moral good and evil opens his child mind and awareness up to the larger philosophical and spiritual meanings of life, he feels compelled to find an identity as a man. As the youngest son in his family, Antonio is offered two choices—to live in the image of his mother and become a priest in a farming town like Las Pasturas or to live in the image of his father and find a land or dream to conquer with physical prowess. Maria holds Antonio close to her and, as he matures, guides him into the safety of the Catholic priesthood; Tony feels drawn to realize her dreams. Yet, he is also sensitive to his father's desire for him to be a man and show outward courage and strength because "a man from the llano does not run from a fight" (37). Maria equates manhood with sinfulness: "Ay, but life destroys the pureness God gives— . . . if only he could become a priest. That would save him. He would be always with God" (31). His father, Gabriel, however, believes that priests are weak and too "feminine," and that Tony must be allowed to experience the physical and mental trials of becoming a man. He argues "It [life] does not destroy, it builds up. Everything he sees and does makes him a man" (31). What Maria does not see is that Antonio cannot hide from the brutalities of life; what Gabriel does not see is that a boy needs compassion-ate dialogue and spiritual food to cope with the trials he undergoes as he enters into manhood.

The timing of Ultima's arrival in Antonio's home is critical to his spiritual survival and moral growth. For the first time, his whole being, including his soulfulness, is visible to another adult human being. Tony finds Ultima irresistible because she provides the spiritual mothering that the boy craves. Magically by his side with herbs and potions whenever he is suffering and in turmoil, she invites him to watch her work, to talk about his visions, and to rest and recover from inner turmoil. She ministers to him rather than tries to control him. Central to their relationship is the asking and answering of questions from a wise adult to a hungry child. She provides the fertile place for this "tender" boy to take root and grow. Ultima does not close her eyes to the forces of evil around her, nor does she revile them and seek revenge against them; she and Tony have this in common.

Why, then, is Ultima potentially a controversial character? The real trouble stems from the words "witch" and "witchcraft." Historically, in America and also in Western Europe, "witchcraft" has evoked images of Satanic worship and Walpurgisnacht rites of depraved sexuality and devil worship. These were carried to the New World in the form of the ever-present Christian dichotomy of absolute Good and Evil—God and Satan, the spirit and the flesh, sanctioned religious ecstasy directed by ministers and men of God as opposed to chaotic and lewd ecstatic rituals enacted in the woods at midnight. The implication that evolves out of the strictness of this dichotomy is that a person is either one or the other, which leaves little room for the experiential reality of the great majority of human beings who live and strive to do good in the midst of evil.

Anaya takes his character Antonio into the "belly of the whale" —into the "space" of the spiritual vision quest—where the psychological mind experiences death in the absence of control. One truth that becomes visible in that space is that violence and religion both erupt out of intense fear and a desire to protect from perceived 'death'—one is a physical, animal response and the other is a mental, spiritual response. In Anaya's world, devil worship and black magic are Catholic doctrine and practice turned upside down out of a need to gain control over those who are seen as the projected "enemy." Out of personal suffering, the Trementina sisters turn toward "the devil as rebel" within the Christian traditions and perform Black Masses and black magic; in the Chicano worldview, they are brujas. Their father, Tenorio, projects his pain and sorrow about their illness upon La Grande, the pagan curandera, to get revenge and gain control over his daughters' fate—daughters whom he believes to be right and good. Tenorio murders Narciso because Narciso defends Ultima; the revenge cycle continues. In a human competition for control, one loves what one can control and hates what cannot be controlled.

Antonio's father, Gabriel, has also been going through a spiritual crisis, although outside the traditional Catholic Church, around the loss of his elder sons and his dream of the llano. Both Gabriel and Antonio are ready to let go of the past and search for new answers about the meaning of life. After a summer with Ultima's healing hand and patient example, Tony has the courage to ask his father, "Papa, can a new religion be made?" and his father is now willing and able to answer him with love and compassion:

> I think most of the things we call evil are not evil at all; it is just that we don't understand those things and so we call them evil. And we fear evil only because we do not understand it. . . . In the end understanding simply means having a sympathy for people. Ultima has sympathy for people, and it is so complete that with it she can touch their souls and cure them. (248)

Father and son agree that it is magic and that it is unexplainable. Gabriel's words echo Anaya's thoughts about the child's journey from the female to male principle being something that runs deeper than categories of gender or religious doctrine. "That is why it is magic. To the child it is natural, but for the grown man it loses its naturalness—so as old men we see a different reality. And when we dream it is usually for a lost childhood, or trying to change someone, and that is not good. So, in the end, I accept reality" (248).

Antonio merges both worlds within the creative spirituality that is his own life. As his mother wishes, he is always with God, but it is a God that is evolving, learning, and constantly embracing all life around him with an open and loving heart. However, moving intimately inside and breaking up that traditional Christian dichotomy is radical. Showing a Chicano sense of positive and negative psychic power in which Ultima is a "good" witch whose power brings healing and life and Tenario's daughters are brujas because they project evil onto others and create violence is potentially controversial to readers who wish to confine all spiritual evil to the work of the "devil."

After Narciso's death, Tony throws himself fully into the Catholic catechisms and consecration. However, it does not provide the kinds of answers and solace that he desires; he has seen too much. When he is forced into the 'Confession Game' with his peers, they rightfully give him the position of priest. He listens attentively as the game comes around to the poorest boy, Florence. When Florence proclaims "I have no sin!" and "It is

God who has sinned against me," Antonio decides to forgive him. The children are so outraged at his version of his sacred duty that they violently attack him for his defiance of the patented hierarchy of sin: those who are disadvantaged and children of sin are not forgiven. In the game of life, Tony suffers the fate of a Catholic "martyr," especially when he does not require a penance of this child of sinful parents, again breaking the boundary between child and adult knowledge and moral action.

Readers—whether parents or students—who wish to censor this book may very well be trying to reject this story and thinking out of the very fear and desire to control life (i.e., protect one's children) that Anaya is talking about. Perhaps the parents who would censor this book are just as fearful as Maria and Gabriel are about their child's future. They need to be shown that this book argues for compassion and moral goodness, not chaotic violence and self-destruction before God. Encouraging them to see this deeply layered and subtle message is crucial at this point. Gaining control, whether physical, moral, or spiritual, is not strength; understanding and compassion create strength. Ultima knows this and is trying to teach it. A strong, active female "curandera" and emotional, angry male fighters are part of the paradox. Each time Tony sees men do evil things to each other, he returns to the sacred womb of Ultima's love. Trusting in her loving presence, he falls into subconscious dreaming where disturbing paradoxes appear and war with each other. Very gradually, Antonio begins to integrate this dangerous knowledge of the adult world into his own, unique meaning.

Anaya creates, however, a very distinct children's space within this conflicted world, with Samuel and Cico by the lake. Cico teaches Antonio about the truth of good and evil. The story of the Golden Carp is a metaphor that is huge, yet concrete and tangibly beautiful. Cico's teaching verifies what Antonio has experienced in his Catholic schooling: "The god of the church is a jealous god; he cannot live in peace with other gods. He would instruct his priests to kill the golden carp—" (237). Tony is considering whether this God would be peaceful and all-encompassing enough for him to be *its* priest. The crucial test comes in the midst of Antonio's vision of the Golden Carp. Florence's death by drowning in the river just as Tony and Samuel decide to open the sacred circle to this disadvantaged boy is a psychic and spiritual violence only Ultima can help him swallow and survive. Perhaps the death of peers is so devastating to young people because here the boundary from life-to-life is thinnest, and they sense their own mortality without any adult resources. Sensing that Antonio is full of what he has seen, Ultima says, "The strengthening of a soul, the growing up of a boy is part of his destiny, but you have seen too much death. It is time for you to rest, to see growing life. Perhaps your uncles could best teach you about growth—" (244). Both Maria and Ultima sense that it is time for Antonio to go to the farm, where he will learn the cycle of life and death in the natural world and perhaps witness that the seed of hope and renewal continually emerges from the decaying losses and endings of death.

As teachers and parents, we know that children witness the choices and actions that adults take and try to create a life of their own out of these experiences. Some children imitate and absorb their inheritance literally. Other children, for whatever reasons, are more intuitive and creative, attempt to forge a new identity. With the right influence, that creation can be for good and love rather than destruction and hatred. The deeper message is one that many readers who would censor this novel must also believe: no one but God is all-powerful, and the mystery of life cannot be known entirely by human beings. This message might be the common ground to initiate any discussion around this kind of censorship challenge.

If there is any metaphor that embodies the central truth about Antonio's "coming of age" journey, it is the Golden Carp, and the metaphor is one of swallowing whole. The Golden Carp swallows all of man's violent ends and starts the whole drama over again. In the final scenes, as he survives Tenorio's violence gun, he knows that Ultima's has given him the gift of life, but for a price. That price is the powerful owl, her protective totem, and her own physical presence. When he runs to save his spiritual guide, he finds she has had to balance the scales of justice. She gives Antonio her blessing: "I bless you in the name of all that is good and strong and beautiful, Antonio. Always have the strength to live. Love life, and if despair enters your heart, look for me in the evenings when the wind is gentle and the owls sing in the hills. I shall be with you." With that, she becomes his spirit totem. She blesses him and he realizes his meaning is from her and is everlasting. "The tragic consequences of life can be overcome by the magical strength that resides in the human heart" (246-247).

In 2001, many young readers may be drawn to this story because they also experience life as fragmented and destructive. With a clear separation of church and state issues, the kind of healing afforded Antonio by Ultima, if it happens, happens away from school and social community. Yet, the restlessness and destructive activities of many of our students seem to indicate a longing for clear role models, ongoing discussions and critical thinking about ethics, or communal standards for right and wrong. Mixed messages surround them—in school, on the streets, in the media, or within the confines of their own increasingly blended family households. Unlike the Chicano world, the various islands of identity and community remain separate and disconnected. Although they are sophisticated on the material and more superficial social levels, many feel extremely childlike and confused on an internal level. This novel brings that disparity to the surface.

The fact that *Bless Me, Ultima* firmly places Spanish at the center of the novel without explanation or apology further roots it within the Chicano culture. Holding the mainstream white readers at a slight distance, it forces them to experience being outside the cultural experience for brief moments. Within the first two pages, readers encounter words such as curandera, vaquero, llano, llaneros, rancheros, tejanos, brujas, and atole, some of which may be familiar or guessed at from context clues, but a number of which require a Spanish dictionary. Readers, then, are faced with a choice similar to Chicano students coming into the mainstream American culture: find and employ a dictionary, ask a Chicano student or teacher, or remain ostracized from some of the central meanings in the text. It propels the teacher into making these resources available to students and increasing their comfort level with cross-cultural references and words.

As the novel progresses, the challenge intensifies. At key dramatic moments, the dialogue is "Es una mujer que no ha pecado" and "Hechicera, bruja." This shift to Spanish words causes frustration and defensiveness in some readers. By mixing English and Spanish unabashedly within the text, Anaya invites his readers to fully enter the world as he often experienced it as a boy and bring even more resources to the experience. By putting his mixed heritage at the center of the artistic experience, Anaya challenges readers to open their minds and hearts to the language and underlying concepts of another culture.

Novels in American literature that tell the truth about the lives of children have often experienced a journey through the "combat zone" of censorship before becoming accepted canon. Sacred owls that are totems, whose death robs a soul of life energy, the idea of magic in the world for good and for ill, that curses exist and can be removed, the belief that young boys are psychic and can collapse into illness and dreams in order to heal from spirit illness—all indicate a culture that, although not representative of mainstream America, needs to be visible and heard. The intense and provocative conflict between Tenorio and Ultima resides at the heart of Anaya's novel for a purpose: it dramatizes the extreme fear, hope, and potential for transformation that surround sacred powers in life as seen by the Hispanic heart and mind. As teachers, we can only encourage close, accurate reading of this young boy's coming-of-age story, reminding readers that in a troubling, modern world, it emphasizes the importance of spiritual solutions to moral dilemmas. Antonio discovers that although good adults do not always win, the power of goodness within the individual and the community is stronger than the power of evil.

## Works Cited

Anaya, Rudolfo A. *Bless Me, Ultima.* New York: Warner Books. 1972.

Anaya, Rudolfo A. "Take the Tortillas out of Your Poetry." *Censored Books: Critical Viewpoints* 25-37.Metuchen, N.J.: The Scarecrow Press, 1993.

Appleman, Deborah and Margaret Reed, ed. *Braided Lives: An Anthology of Multicultural American Writing.* St. Paul, Minn.: Minnesota Humanities Commission, 1991.

Dick, Bruce, and Silvio Sirias, ed. *Conversations with Rudolfo Anaya.* Jackson: University Press of Mississippi, 1998.

# Protecting Them from What?
# In Praise of *Blubber*

## Faith Sullivan

My friend Cutler Dozier turned thirteen recently and entered the seventh grade at Falcon Ridge Middle School. He likes movies and hanging out with friends. He also likes taking things apart—especially things electronic. He's a whiz at card tricks and as fast with a quip as he is with sleight of hand.

Recently Cutler and I talked about Judy Blume's books, of which he's read a dozen. Currently he's reading *It's Not the End of the World*, in which Blume deals with the effects of divorce on children. Mainly, though, we talked about *Blubber*, one of Blume's most frequently banned books, a story about the nightmare of unchecked peer ridicule. "It was really good," was Cutler's first comment. "It was realistic. I mean, I'm a kid so I would know."

Fifth-grader Jill, *Blubber's* protagonist, fearing rejection by Wendy, the class president, recess captain, and "a very clever person," falls in with Wendy's merciless teasing of the overweight Linda, whom Wendy dubs "Blubber." In fact, most of Miss Minnish's fifth-grade class, no braver than Jill, become Wendy's henchmen in this little war of torment.

Jill does not feel good about being one of the teasers, but neither does she want to become one of the teased, which she surely will if she crosses Wendy. Like many child tyrants, Wendy is clever at exploiting young people's desire to fit in or at least not to stand out.

Does this sort of teasing happen at school, I asked Cutler. Yes. Even in good schools like Falcon Ridge, teasing is an everyday occurrence.

"I've teased," Cutler admits. "Who hasn't? Mostly people tease other people in order to feel better about themselves. The best way to deal with it is to ignore it or laugh at it." The very point that Jill's mother makes later in *Blubber*.

Together, Cutler and I examined reasons why *Blubber* might be banned from some school or community libraries. In a few cases, Cutler thought, it was probably because Jill's friend Tracy, a child of Chinese descent, is called a "chink."

But surely no reasonable person would ban a book on these grounds. After all, children encounter such bigotry in daily life, and the story makes clear that bigotry is reprehensible. Besides all this, Tracy is an admirable and morally grounded character, strong in her loyalty and wise in her counsel, possibly the hero of the book.

Cutler went on to suggest that maybe the book runs afoul of certain censors because several of its adult characters (some of them authority figures) are portrayed as fallible, foolish, or just plain unpleasant.

A couple of teachers are both fallible *and* foolish. And Mr. Machinist, a cranky neighbor of Jill and Tracy's, is an unyielding curmudgeon with a real grudge against young people. It is his mailbox that the two girls stuff with rotten eggs on Halloween night. When they are found out, they're made to rake up all the leaves in Machinist's big yard as a punishment. After all this, quite naturally, the girls still don't like the man. However, they have learned that when dislike leads to unacceptable or illegal behavior, you have to pay the price.

Is this not a message found again and again in classic children's literature? Is it not a message reasonable parents would want their children to absorb? And, as for those teachers—as a former teacher myself, I can attest to the fallibility and occasional foolishness of the breed.

But, yet *another* lesson lies in the aftermath of the Halloween prank. When Mr. Machinist comes looking for Jill and Tracy, the girls ponder who might have betrayed them, since Machinist himself has not seen them stuff his mailbox. Jill fixes on Linda (Blubber), positive that the girl is using this opportunity to get back at Jill for the teasing she's taken from her.

Tracy advises against hasty conclusions: they have no proof, she points out. But Jill persists, heaping even greater ridicule on Linda in the ensuing days and further stirring up Miss Minnish's class against Linda.

However, Jill crosses swords with the bullying Wendy when Wendy insists that Linda does not deserve to be represented by a lawyer in her mock trial for betraying Jill and Tracy. Jill's father is a lawyer, and Jill knows that *everybody* accused of a crime deserves to have a lawyer, even the dreadful snitch, Linda. But, in standing up for Linda at this moment, Jill becomes Wendy's latest victim. Sheeplike and desiring only to stay on the good side of Wendy, the rest of the class fall in behind Wendy, making Jill the new scapegoat. Now Jill knows the cruelty that Linda has endured.

And, by the time the truth emerges, that Wendy was the informer, Linda's dislike of Jill is sealed, probably forever. Rueful, Jill has learned a painful lesson about "innocent until proved guilty."

Ultimately, Jill concludes that she cannot live with herself unless she makes a real stand against Wendy: if she ends up with no friends in Miss Minnish's class, so be it. She still has her loyal and levelheaded friend, Tracy, from the other fifth-grade class, who will stand by her, who indeed has all along counseled Jill against going along with Wendy. Jill sees that one true friend is maybe all a person needs, if she has her self-respect. But, when she makes her stand, Jill discovers an unexpected ally in her own class as well. Courage engenders courage.

Now, surely no reasonable person would ban a book with such valuable lessons about the destructive nature of ridicule and the necessity for standing up to bullies. We parents want our children to learn courage. Don't we? We do not want our children to be sheep, following the pack wherever it may lead. Do we?

Well, then, why *is* this book banned? A further and final reason, Cutler thought, is because Jill's parents, recognizing that they themselves sometimes swear, don't go "ballistic" when Jill and her brother use the occasional bad word. The parents don't encourage bad language but, as Cutler said, "Their attitude is, it's just a word." They save their censure for what they consider more important issues. This made them seem real to Cutler, who did not view their attitude as a general advocacy of bad language by Blume but rather as a single element in the complex make-up of real human beings.

But surely reasonable people do not ban a book filled with valuable lessons over a single small dissatisfaction or even two small dissatisfactions, do they?

## Equating Ignorance with Innocence

Some do. I know that in our communities even now there are people working to ban *Blubber* from our libraries. I know, too, that most of them are conscientious parents trying to protect the innocence of their children, trying to prevent them from growing up too soon, trying to save them from a punishing world.

Their error is equating ignorance with innocence. To understand the existence of evil, to read stories illustrating its existence does not rob children of their innocence. To encounter evil without proper awareness and preparation does rob children of their innocence.

Yet, again and again, the knowledge of pain and evil is represented by the censors as an endorsement of it. We are told that a writer who creates a lying, thieving fictional rascal is somehow advocating lying and thieving or, at the very least, condoning it or turning a blind eye. Would these same censors maintain that knowledge of *disease* or writing about it is an endorsement of it? Evil is a disease.

The censors seem not to understand how fiction works. If the author of contemporary books for children and young adults does not give characters idiosyncrasies, weaknesses, and even iniquities, how is the child to believe in the characters and, by extension, believe in the moral message they may carry?

To believe that perfect people exist, and that it is these folks about whom novelists should write, is to live in a constant state of denial of the real world. And the promulgation of this notion will either drive kids crazy or cause them to mistrust the parents' sanity or integrity.

These same parents may, when pressed, concede, "All right, there are bad people in the world and they do bad things, but I don't want my children reading about them. I can *tell* them about them." However, simply telling a child that certain evils exist is ineffectual. All we're doing is presenting them with intellectual concepts that they often fail to grasp because the concepts lack context and dramatic form. It is for this reason that the great teachers of morality and ethics have always used parables.

The men who wrote the Bible knew of the existence of evil and did not believe that writing about it would cause children who read their stories to become evil or feel that their innocence had been lost in the gaining of this knowledge.

As parents we cannot foresee every dangerous or shocking situation that may confront our children in the world beyond our door, so we cannot prepare them for all the problems they will face. Why *not*, then, share this responsibility with writers of books about hate, jealousy, selfishness, teasing, bigotry, and the other eventualities of children's lives? Why *not* cover as many bases as we can? Don't we owe it to our children?

"Nobody told me it was going to be like this."

How regularly one hears that cry from young adults butting up against the hard, nasty, occasionally criminal facts of modern life.

Why in hell *didn't* somebody tell them it was going to be like this, I want to ask. Where were the parents when these children should have been learning about the real world—about drugs and sex and death and violence? Frequently they were at school board meetings or library board meetings, leading censorship drives against the very books that might have prepared their children.

With the often senseless banning of books, we keep our children not in a state of innocence but in a state of vulnerability. Knowledge is not just power, it is preparation.

Censorship is the fall-back position of parents who will not take personal responsibility for grounding their children early in ethics and morality. A child fully and individually grounded in the values of his family—through example and discussion—is all but immune to the presumed "bad influence" of those children's books that are most frequently banned.

Parents cannot prevent their children from exposure to bigotry or cruelty or even death without locking them away from the real world in which they must eventually make their way, the real world with which they must learn to cope if they're to be effective, interactive citizens.

"There's plenty of time for them to learn about all that later," is the mantra of the censors. By this is meant, "when they're adults." When they're adults it is often too late, because the events, for which they should have been prepared, have already taken place, the influences have been absorbed, and the child has been injured.

Is there a better time or safer way for a person to learn about the sensual delights and lurking dangers of the world than as a child bringing home arm-loads of books from the classroom or library and poring through them where a parent or other adult is present to oversee, to answer questions, and, when necessary, to calm concerns?

The vast majority of books made available to children by schools and libraries are age-appropriate. Five-year-old children are not required to deal with sexual violence, for instance, in the literature provided by trained teachers and librarians. And, if a parent should find reading material in the child's hands that is too mature in content, the parent can explain why and remove the story or book without acting as censor for an entire school system or community.

## Two Readers' Responses

When my three children were small, the oldest and youngest, both girls, learned to read early and found books to be the wonderful friends who were always available for play. The middle child, Ben, a serious little fellow, enjoyed being read to but showed no great desire to read books himself, not even in the first grade when he learned the skills.

As someone who had survived the middle years of childhood only by the grace of books, I was concerned that all of the children develop a love of literature to cheer them through life's lonely or tragic hours.

My husband and I encouraged Ben to check out books from his school's small library; we bought him books and continued reading to him; and though he enjoyed having books in his room and having us read from them, on his own nothing tempted him enough to set him to reading independently. This continued into second grade.

I noticed, however, that when we stood in line at the supermarket, he was enthralled by the headlines on tabloid newspapers: "Three-headed Snake Terrorizes Vacationing Family" or "Aliens Hold Father of Four, Demanding Ransom." One day when the children were at school, I bought a couple of the less lurid tabloids and left them casually lying about the living room. Sure enough, later in the day Ben picked one up and began reading. I continued this practice supplying tabloids, never letting on that they were for him.

After several weeks, I added comic books to the mix, and later, *Mad* magazine. By the time Ben was reading *Mad*, he'd lost interest in the tabloids, and in the third grade he discovered science fiction (on his own), eventually reading all of the Dune books. After Dune came Tolkien and C. S. Lewis and Judy Blume and so on and so on. Did an early diet of tabloids turn the lad into an unwashed recluse, sending out perfume-scented letter bombs to the captains of industry? Not exactly. At thirty-three he's happily married and the managing editor of a high-tech magazine.

If my husband and I had focused our worry entirely on con tent—questionable language, exposed breasts and the like—instead of on a boy learning to enjoy reading, Ben might never have discovered the endless solace, wonder, and enlightenment of books.

Recently I asked my poet daughter, Maggie, about the Judy Blume books which she devoured as a girl. Why was she drawn to them, and what did she derive from them?

"They talked about what I wanted to know. I respected them because they dealt with the way things really were, at least the way things were where I lived. Also, they said that what I was worrying or wondering about was worthy of a writer's time and effort, it was worthy of *respect*. That meant a lot to me.

"I think maybe I myself started writing partly because of that affirmation."

The thing is, children have worries and wonders, some of which they're not comfortable sharing with their parents, no matter how willing the parent is to listen. Judy Blume was a friend Maggie could turn to for some answers or at least the assurance that she wasn't alone in her worries, that other kids had them too.

Isn't it ironic that the children of censorial parents feel *less* inclined to air and share their questions? Sensing the negativity their parents have toward "forbidden" topics, they don't want that same negativity turned on them.

## Two Underlying Reasons for Censorship Attacks

But, when we get down to it, what are the real reasons people feel the need to ban books like *Blubber* from classrooms and libraries? A couple come to mind. The first, mentioned earlier, is an unwillingness to shoulder responsibility for fully grounding their children in the family's value system. If you feel inadequate to the task, it is easier simply to remove everything from their environment that might conflict.

The irony here is that these parents often are religious fundamentalists, who, one would suppose, possess great confidence in themselves as moral exemplars and teachers. When it comes to our children, however, we parents always have fears about our adequacy. The trick is not to use our own sense of inadequacy as occasion for legislating the reading matter of a community.

The second reason individuals engage in censorship is the belief that *their* standards and values or their group's standards and values ought to be the standards and values of all in the community. If the rest of the community won't conform, well, we must legislate their conformity through censorship.

Certain crimes—murder, rape, slavery, theft, for instance—are universally regarded as intolerable, but when we depart from those universals and begin legislating discretionary behavior, we are on a very slippery slope. Once you've departed from the universally intolerable, you find differences between religious groups and even within religious groups about what is acceptable or unacceptable. Whose standards do we adopt?

Why not simply allow for differences and tend our own little kingdom? As Clare Boothe Luce said, "Censorship, like charity, should begin at home; but unlike charity, it should end there."

To presume that Cutler's parents or Maggie's parents lack the intelligence and moral muscle to judge individually whether *Blubber* is appropriate reading for their children is to presume too damned much.

## Works Cited

Blume, Judy. *Blubber*. Scarsdale, N.Y.: Bradbury, 1974.
———. *It's Not the End of the World*. Scarsdale, N.Y.: Bradbury, 1972.

# The Portrayal of Sexuality in Toni Morrison's *The Bluest Eye*

## Steven R. Luebke

Thirty years after its initial publication, Toni Morrison's *The Bluest Eye* appeared on the "*New York Times* Best-Seller List," no doubt the result of being Oprah Winfrey's April, 2000, book club selection. Morrison's novel portrays the deterioration of the Breedlove family, African Americans living in pre-World War II Ohio. At the center of this deterioration is the rape of the tragic character, Pecola, by her father. Pecola's story is a tale of failed initiation; instead of growing into adulthood successfully, becoming an integrated member of the human community, Pecola becomes isolated and takes refuge in a fantasy world. Given the novel's renewed popularity, it will likely become better known and more widely read, and it is therefore important to consider its frank discussion of sexuality.

Morrison's novel includes sexual intercourse, menstruation, rape, and incest. Readers unaccustomed to contemporary fiction may be disturbed by Morrison's openness and directness regarding sexual matters. Indeed, Mac Edwards writes that in a small New York State town, the school board voted to ban the novel from high school juniors and seniors because of its sexual explicitness. As a point of both comparison and contrast, readers may recall that a century ago, *The Awakening*, also a frank, tragic novel about a young woman's defeat by the social standards of her time, aroused great criticism. Kate Chopin only hints at an adulterous love scene and its protagonist grows embarrassed at the mention of the word "pregnancy" in mixed company. The reaction to *The Bluest Eye* that Edwards describes shows that we've come a middling distance since 1899.

In *The Bluest Eye*, explicit sexual description occurs in the section recounting Pauline Breedlove's experiences. Pauline reminisces about her past life, including her first meeting with her husband-to-be, Cholly. It is one of the happier moments in the novel, expressing a joyful, innocent sensuality: "When I first seed Cholly, I want you to know it was like all the bits of

color from that time down home when all us chil'ren went berry picking."
(115). The passage continues by describing the "cool and yellowish"
lemonade "Mama used to make when Pap come in out the fields" and the
"streak of green" on the trees made by June bugs. Later, Pauline's musings
include graphic description of her and Cholly's sexual relationship, with
imagery that recalls their first meeting: "I begin to feel those little bits of
color floating up into me—deep in me. That streak of green from the June-
bug light, the purple from the berries trickling along my thighs, Mama's
lemonade yellow runs sweet in me" (131). These passages unabashedly
celebrate nature and natural fruition in the form of sexual fulfillment. It is
not clear whom Pauline is speaking to in these passages. It may be a friend
or it may be God ("I want you to know"). If it is either, it seems natural
enough for her to speak honestly and without censoring herself.

What is especially noteworthy is the imagery of fruition. Morrison uses
imagery relating to seeds and growth throughout *The Bluest Eye* to develop
the theme of initiation. The novel is structured according to the seasons,
which seems to invoke nature. Moreover, the first time we hear the narrator's (Claudia's) voice, she refers to seeds she and her sister planted and "the
seeds Pecola's father had dropped" in "his own plot of black dirt" (6).
Cholly, at one point rejected by his own father, hides under a pier where "the
dark, the warmth, the quiet enclosed [him] like the skin and flesh of an
elderberry protecting its own seed" (157). Frieda's "tiny breasts" are like
"two fallen acorns" (99).

The description of Pauline's earlier life is contrapuntal to the portrayal
of her later life and the lives of many Southern African American women
(like the character Geraldine) who migrate North. In the South, the women
are like hollyhocks—"their roots are deep, their stalks are firm" (82). Once
in the North, however, they fall prey to what Morrison calls the "Master
Narrative." In an interview with Bill Moyers, Morrison says of Pecola,

> She has surrendered completely to the "Master Narrative": the whole notion of
> what is ugliness, what is worthlessness. She got it from her family; she got it
> from school; she got it from the movies; she got it from everywhere. . . . The
> Master Narrative is whatever ideological script that is being imposed by the
> people in authority on everybody else: The Master Fiction . . . history. It has a
> certain point of view. So when those little girls see that the most prized gift they
> can receive at Christmas time is this little white doll, that's the Master Narrative
> speaking: this is beautiful, this is lovely, and you're not it, so what are you going
> to do about it?

The Master Narrative essentially describes an insidious form of assimilation.
It is reflected in the Dick and Jane primer selections at the beginning of each

section of the novel, which describe the "perfect" white family. As practiced by the characters in *The Bluest Eye*, assimilation involves stifling or denigrating one's natural feelings or characteristics in order to live up to the standards or expectations of mainstream society. In the novel Morrison describes it as getting rid of the "funkiness. The dreadful funkiness of passion, the funkiness of nature, the funkiness of the wide range of human emotions. . . . wherever it drips, *flowers* [emphasis mine], or clings, they find it and fight it until it dies" (83). Thus Pauline's descriptions of her sexual relationship with Cholly are thematically significant; they underscore the fact that at one time the couple was happy but lost that happiness in part because of their surrender to the Master Narrative. The descriptions show Pauline at that stage of her life in a healthy relationship with "the natural" and thus portray her as a foil to the pedophile Soaphead Church, who abhors anything physical.

While Pauline's descriptions are explicit, readers may be more disturbed by the novel's inclusion of an incestuous act between Cholly and Pecola. The act violates one of the strongest taboos in our society and, as J. Brooks Bouson points out, may actually make the reader feel ashamed: "In her strategic public exposure of the incest secret, Morrison breaks the taboo on looking and thus risks shaming her readers. For just as those who are exposed feel shame, so observers of shaming scenes can feel shame" (212). It is not difficult to believe that many readers would feel uncomfortable reading and discussing this part of the novel, but the purpose of literature is not necessarily to make one feel comfortable. The brief, but powerful, scene in Morrison's novel not only shows the extent to which the Breedlove family has deteriorated; more important, it helps delineate the character of Cholly.

Even though Nellie McKay refers to it as "graphic" (3-4), the scene itself does not belabor the action (it is brief—about 2½ pages), and it does not involve a great deal of explicit sexual description. In an interview, Morrison described it as "almost irrelevant" (qtd. in Bouson 224). Some readers may be surprised that the scene is told from Cholly's point of view, but by presenting it that way, Morrison is able to analyze Cholly's character and avoid a sensationalistic, though perhaps objective, description of the event. He comes home drunk, sees Pecola washing dishes, pulls her to the floor, and proceeds to have intercourse with her. Of course the question raised in the reader's mind is, how could this happen? The entire novel, in a sense, is the answer. There is no simple answer, but rather, a series of related explanations.

When Cholly sees Pecola standing by the sink scratching her calf with her toe, he is reminded of the first time he saw Pauline. He feels a "wondering softness" and touches her. His drunkenness, combined with "the confused mixture of his memories of Pauline," and "the doing of a wild and forbidden thing" leads to his actions (Morrison 162).

It is important to note the role played by Cholly's conflicting emotions. Cholly's rape of Pecola originates not out of lust, says Morrison, but "a tenderness, a protectiveness" (162). Thus one critic writes that while Cholly's rape of Pecola is "reprehensible," he does not "rape her mind the way that Pauline and Soaphead [Church] do. Claudia [the novel's narrator] senses that Cholly really loves Pecola: 'He, at any rate, was the one who loved her enough to touch her, envelop her, give something of himself to her'" (cited from the novel 159 in Alexander 301).

Before the act occurs, Morrison presents the reader with Cholly's perception of Pecola:

> Why did she have to look so whipped? She was a child—unburdened—why wasn't she happy? The clear statement of her misery was an accusation. He wanted to break her neck—but tenderly. Guilt and impotence rose in a bilious duet. What could he do for her—ever? What give her? What say to her? What could a burned-out black man say to the hunched back of his eleven-year-old-daughter? . . . How dare she love him? Hadn't she any sense at all? (161)

The description above shows Cholly's act of incest is also an expression of anger and frustration. He is angry at himself, angry, perhaps, at the society he lives in, and he is frustrated by his powerlessness. Cholly displaces his self-hatred, his "guilt and impotence," onto his innocent daughter; by the end of the passage quoted above, he is blaming her. The scene recalls a key experience earlier in his life in which Cholly, having his first sexual experience, is discovered by white men and forced to "perform" for their entertainment. He is unable to direct his anger toward them for making him feel powerless and humiliated, since "hating them would have consumed him, burned him up like a piece of soft coal" (151). Instead, he displaces his anger onto the girl, Darlene. "He hated her" (148), "the one who bore witness to his failure" (151). Darlene and Pecola both bear witness to Cholly's failure.

The same psychological mechanism is apparent in the scene between Junior and Pecola. Junior's mother, Geraldine, who has been hoodwinked by the Master Narrative, makes a distinction between "colored people" and "niggers" and is determined to model herself and her son after the former. She represses all impulses toward physical closeness with others (in this sense she also resembles Soaphead Church), able to share those feelings only with her cat. Understandably, Junior becomes angry; but instead of expressing his feelings toward his mother, he directs his hostility toward Pecola. He invites Pecola over to see the cat, and once she is there, he flings the animal at her, pushes her down and refuses to let her go, and finally throws the cat against a wall. Junior resembles the boys at school who torment Pecola with cries of "Black e mo. Black e mo. Yadaddsleepsnekked"; they are full of "contempt for their own blackness." "They seemed to have taken all of their smoothly cultivated ignorance, their exquisitely learned self-hatred . . . and sucked it all up into a fiery cone of scorn . . . that spilled over lips of outrage, consuming whatever was in its path" (Morrison 65). The fire imagery in both sections illustrates the destructive nature of these characters' anger.

Laurie Vickroy argues that the scene between Cholly and Pecola illustrates another psychological mechanism, projection. "A stressful situation will cause thoughts to travel along the same pathways as those connected to a previous traumatic event, and if immediate stimuli recall this event, the individual will be transported back to that . . . state and react accordingly" (94). The emotions stirred by Cholly seeing Pecola washing dishes reflect those expressed in the scene with Darlene, another time he was unable to protect a helpless female (Bouson 219); it is Cholly, then, not Pecola, who feels "whipped." He fears he has failed her. Vickroy continues, "One way for him to rid himself of his fears is to project them onto Pecola, and in part he tries to destroy those fears by raping her" (95). A traumatized child himself, as Vickroy points out, thrown on the junk heap by his mother and publicly rejected by his father, Cholly's act continues the cycle of victimization.

In addition to displacement and projection, Morrison dramatizes yet another Freudian psychological mechanism through the character Pecola. Maureen Peal asks Pecola if she has ever seen a naked man.

> Pecola blinked, then looked away. "No. Where would I see a naked man?"
> "I don't know. I just asked."
> "I wouldn't even look at him, even if I did see him. That's dirty. Who wants to see a naked man?" Pecola was agitated. "Nobody's father would be naked in front of his own daughter. Not unless he was dirty too."
> "I didn't say 'father.' I just said 'a naked man.'" (71)

This scene begins with what appears to be Maureen Peal's innocent curiosity, but the reader quickly concludes that Pecola is "agitated" because she has experienced a traumatic sexual event. She conflates Maureen's general inquiry with a specific incident and commits what Freud called parapraxis (a "slip"); she reveals a personal secret without intending to.

Immediately following this Morrison has Claudia reflect on the situation in regard to her own experience. One notices a very different attitude:

we had seen our own father naked and didn't care to be reminded of it and feel the shame brought on by the absence of shame. He had been walking down the hall from the bathroom into his bedroom and passed the open door of our room. We had lain there wide-eyed. . . . Apparently he convinced himself that we were sleeping. He moved away, confident that his little girls would not lie open-eyed like that, staring, staring. (71)

Claudia and Frieda exhibit a natural curiosity here, and they are clearly looking at their father without shame. Pecola, on the other hand, feels that merely to look is to be "dirty" and consequently condemns herself along with Cholly. The parapraxis manifests Pecola's anxiety, and the section as a whole allows Morrison to contrast a natural, nonthreatening curiosity about sexuality—clearly a normal aspect of initiation for many people—with fear and shame. It also helps portray the Breedlove and MacTeer families as foils in the novel.[1]

There is a final reason *The Bluest Eye* may be controversial in some classroom settings. Kathryn Earle writes about her experiences as a white person teaching the novel to a class with African American students. Earle describes her feelings of illegitimacy rooted in interpreting and judging characters whose backgrounds are so different from her own. She also mentions some students's beliefs that the novel would be better taught by an African American person. She says that she at first tried to cover up her own emotional response to the novel in order to appear objective, but ultimately discovered it was better to approach the issue of incest and the issue of conflict within the black community openly and honestly.

What is the value of *The Bluest Eye*? In addition to being a well-constructed piece of literature, the novel can help readers appreciate the difficulties faced by the outsider or the powerless, whether it is an individual or a family. One way Morrison accomplishes this is through alternation between first-person and third-person point of view. The former shows Claudia as a youthful participant in the novel's action (and thus subject to the limitations of a child's consciousness), the latter as an older, wiser individual.[2] The older, more understanding Claudia may help readers develop greater empathy for those who in one way or another live on society's periphery and thus increase tolerance and understanding.

The book can also help readers understand the complex nature of a character like Cholly. We read about sexual crimes against children almost every day in the newspaper and probably dismiss the perpetrators as horrible humans, throwaways who have nothing in common with the rest of us. This is not to say that some of them are not, but rather, to suggest that in many cases, there may be more going on than we realize. The character of Cholly is well developed in the novel; Morrison describes his life from his infancy to adulthood as a way to explain and understand his behavior. Earle says that one of the strategies she uses in teaching *The Bluest Eye* is to offer a courtroom-style "professional" defense of Cholly or to ask students to imagine how they would perceive Cholly if he were a friend or person they cared about.

The novel also offers an alternative to the dissolution of the Breedlove family. Our society focuses more attention on the travesty, the dysfunctional rather than the functional, but readers should remember the positive example shown through the MacTeer family. As a foil to the Breedloves, the MacTeers provide a stable, nurturing environment for their children, with "love, thick and dark as Alaga syrup" (12). One part of this family, the narrator Claudia, offers the perspective of one who has grown through witnessing another's suffering. Tirrell writes: "*The Bluest Eye* shows how a moral sensibility may emerge from a text even though no explicit invocations of moral rules or ideals, nor explicit final judgments of moral culpability are made by the narrator . . . even more, the novel portrays a moral sensibility emerging *in the telling of the story*" (122). Tirrell writes that through the process of telling the story, "[Claudia] has something . . . that she didn't have before: she has a different and richer sense of the relations between the individual and the community" (123). As for the rest of us, Laurie Vickroy writes that trauma narratives' greatest value lies in their ability to help "readers empathize with and share the victims' experience . . . and in insisting through their portrayal of narrators that we all must explore our own roles in the victimization, whether our guilt take the form of direct responsibility or complicity" (107). Such self-examination is important for people of all ages and all groups as part of their moral development. We see this exploration in the character Claudia, who plumbs the depth of her own responsibility, and who, in that respect at least, might be the only character whose initiation is a success.

## Notes

1. For a discussion of the symbolic overtones of nakedness, see Vanessa D. Dickerson's "The Naked Father in Toni Morrison's *The Bluest Eye*" in *Refiguring the Father: New Feminist Readings in Patriarchy,* ed. Patricia Yaeger and Beth Kowaleski-Wallace. Carbondale: Southern Illinois University Press, 1989.
2. Lynne Tirrell's "Storytelling and Moral Agency" discusses the novel's complex point of view and argues that the first-person and third-person narrators are the same.

## Works Cited

Alexander, Allen. "The Fourth Face: The Image of God in Toni Morrison's *The Bluest Eye*." *African-American Review* 32:2 (1998): 293-303.

Bouson, J. Brooks. "'Quiet As It's Kept': Shame and Trauma in Toni Morrison's *The Bluest Eye*." *Scenes of Shame: Psychoanalysis, Shame, and Writing*. Ed. Joseph Adamson, Hillary Clark, and Nathan L. Donald (Albany, N.Y.: State University of New York Press, 1999). 207-236.

Earle, Kathryn. "Teaching Controversy: *The Bluest Eye* in the Multicultural Classroom." *Approaches to Teaching the Novels of Toni Morrison*. Ed. Nellie Y. McKay and Kathryn Earle. (New York: Modern Language Association of America, 1997). 27-33.

Edwards, Mac. "From the Editor: The Right to Sexuality Information and Services." *SIECUS Reports: Controversial Issues in Sexuality* 27.1 (2000): n. page. Online. Internet. 5 May 2000. Available: http://www. siecus.org/pubs/srpt/srpt0017.html.

McKay, Nellie Y. "The Novels." McKay and Earle 3-4.

Morrison, Toni. *The Bluest Eye*. New York: Penguin, 1994.

———. Interview with Bill Moyers. *A World of Ideas*. PBS. KTCA, Minneapolis, 1989.

Tirrell, Lynne. "Storytelling and Moral Agency." *Journal of Aesthetics and Art Criticism* 48.2 (1990): 115-126.

Vickroy, Laurie. "The Politics of Abuse: The Traumatized Child in Toni Morrison and Marguerite Duras." *Mosaic* 20.2 (1996): 91-109.

# In Defense of *The Boy Who Lost His Face*

## Jeanne M. McGlinn

Louis Sachar's *The Boy Who Lost His Face* (1989) is a problematic novel for teachers and parents or anyone selecting literature for middle school children. On the one hand, it is an understated but insightful study of peer pressure and moral decision making, and on the other, it presents realistic language and situations that most adults either think children do not know anything about or would prefer that they didn't. However, Sachar, like most realistic novelists, chooses not to whitewash the characters' language or behavior. So selecting this novel presents itself, as in many cases with children's literature, as a difficult choice. Should children read realistic fiction that explores important moral dilemmas that they are facing but in which characters use language with swear words or "adult" behaviors? Or should children be "protected" until they are older from such realities even at the loss of important lessons to be learned?

Sachar is a popular writer, who is also well-known since he won the Newbery Medal in 1999 for *Holes*. But even before the national attention of the Newbery, Sachar was known for the humorous novels he wrote about the lives of middle-grades children, such as *There's a Boy in the Girls' Bathroom*, *Dogs Don't Tell Jokes*, and *Sideways Stories from Wayside School*. His novels match the interests of fourth-through-seventh graders who are usually egocentric and want stories dealing with real situations similar to their own experiences. These readers want to see themselves in the stories they read. At the same time, they like stories that are humorous, poking fun at typical dilemmas, because humor is a powerful antidote to the tendency to take oneself too seriously. Sachar is one of a select group of writers filling this niche for high-quality, insightful books about preadolescent lives that win over readers with humor.

In this novel David, a middle schooler, succumbs to peer pressure to be part of the "cool" in-crowd. He goes along with a prank to steal a cane with a snake-head carved handle from Mrs. Bayfield, an old lady and eccentric artist who lives all alone. Even though he knows what he is doing

95

is wrong and he actually feels sorry for the woman, David adds insult to injury when he "flips her off" to impress the leader of the boys. As he runs off, Mrs. Bayfield hurls a curse at David: "Your Doppelganger will regurgitate on your soul!" (8).

Immediately David is sorry for his actions, rationalizing that perhaps she doesn't even know what the obscene gesture means. He thinks, "What makes the middle finger any worse than any other finger? What if he had just pointed his pinky at her? That wouldn't have been a bad thing to do, would it?" (11). He even experiments giving his mother "the finger," sure that she can't possibly know what it means. If his mother doesn't know what it means, then surely Mrs. Bayfield doesn't, and her ignorance will free him from his guilt. However, his mother does know what it means, so David gets in trouble and has to explain to his father that he was just trying an experiment to see if something can be "bad" if the other person doesn't know that it's bad.

Over the next few days, David experiences a series of minor disasters: he throws a ball through his front window, he falls over backwards in his chair at school, he forgets to zip his pants. He begins to think that these events aren't just random; they are a result of the curse. He thinks, "Everything that happened to her [Mrs. Bayfield] keeps happening to me" (52). At the same time, he knows, in his heart, that no one is causing him to do any of these things. He knows "Mrs. Bayfield didn't do anything to him" (52). But as each new disaster occurs, David finds it easier to rationalize that Mrs. Bayfield's curse is at the root of his problems. He tries to convince his friends and himself that Mrs. Bayfield is a witch and that the series of accidents he has experienced is a result of her curse.

Meanwhile David is the butt of jokes and insults by members of the in-crowd at school. They ridicule and torment him and his new friends whenever they get a chance. Even Scott, his longtime best friend, joins the attack, saying David is too "uncool" and a liability to his newly created image. David tries to ignore the insults or backs down. As his friend Larry sees it, David "loses face" every time he lets the bullies push him around. So David is caught in a dilemma of inaction. He is afraid to act because he "has no face," but at the same time, he dreads the consequences of inaction. For example, he wants to apologize to Mrs. Bayfield but knows he won't because he's a coward and so the curse will continue to haunt him. He also wants to date Tori, the pretty girl with the green eyes whom he has had a crush on for the last several weeks, but he is afraid that the curse will make him do something stupid in front of her. Unable to act, David tries to circumvent the curse by letting his new friends spill lemonade over his head to anticipate the only event that hasn't occurred yet. Thinking this final indignity may have paid off his debt, he decides to take a chance and ask Tori for her phone number: "I might want to call you up sometime to find out about homework, or, you know, ask you out or something" (141). Just at that moment the drawstring on his pants comes untied, and David's pants fall down.

This event finally forces David into action. He runs to Mrs. Bayfield to apologize. But before she will forgive him, Mrs. Bayfield wants David to get the cane from the gang of boys. Challenging Roger, the leader of the in-crowd, to a fight for the cane, David feels all alone. He thinks, "It's me against the world. I have no friends left. My brother hates me. I'm cursed. I can never talk to Tori again" (157). At the same time, he has "a strange feeling of confidence" because he has "nothing left to lose." Standing up to the bullies helps David face his fears and draw on his personal strength, and he realizes things are never as bad as we imagine them to be. Also he sees that his interpretation of the series of coincidences was a result of his own guilt. Because he knew that what he did was wrong, he was punishing himself with his fears. In the end David wonders if we all aren't "cursed" in some way. "We all try to act like we're so important—doctors, lawyers, artists—but really we know that at any moment our pants might fall down." (193). We all suffer from our sense of guilt or inadequacy in some way, and we let it control our actions.

The central theme of the novel is the way in which self-perception affects behavior. David wants to be part of the in-crowd at school and so he goes along with the attack on Mrs. Bayfield even when he feels sorry for her and knows that what they are doing is wrong. Even when the boys reject him, David still knows that if they would include him in their group, he would smile and go along with their cruelties. Part of him realizes that he is willing to do this just to be a part of their crowd. He goes along because he is afraid that he isn't good enough.

David's fear leads to problems in his relationships. When David's younger brother, Ricky, looks up to him, David wonders what he would think of him if he realized that others don't think he is cool. David's lack of confidence is catching, and Ricky turns on him, too, when David fails to stand up for himself. David has a crush on Tori Williams, but he is afraid that she will find out that he's uncool. His fears lead him to give her the silent treatment that actually pushes her away. David is caught by a self-fulfilling prophecy that operates hand-in-hand with peer pressure. Only when David is finally so miserable that he does what he knows is right and what he should have done all along, does he break this cycle. Choosing to do what is right gives him back his true self—his face—and the respect of others. This is the hard lesson that many preteens have to learn and that perhaps some of us never learn.

David has a redeeming character trait that helps him in this dilemma; he cares about people. He sees things from another person's point of view. He tried to suppress this side of himself because it isn't what the boys want, but it's what saves him. Mrs. Bayfield helps David realize that his sensitivity caused his guilt. He kept thinking about the way he had treated her and he felt guilty, so that every time something happened he thought it was connected to the attack. She says, "You probably felt you should have been punished for what you did. . . . And when nobody punished you, you punished yourself" (190). The other boys don't bother to see things from another person's point of view, and so they go on without guilt. David, with "the soul of a poet," feels for others. That may be a "curse in this cold world we live in" (191), but David realizes its value. While he envies Scott his popularity, he realizes he has something more important, his sensitivity. This again is an important truth for preteens to consider; they need to learn the value of character over appearances. In its indictment of peer pressure and how it twists personalities, Sachar's novel has the potential to be useful and instructive to adolescent readers.

Also Sachar's analysis of what makes a "bad" word or gesture "bad" is useful for adolescents to study. David wonders when everyone agreed that certain words are taboo? Do words or gestures mean different things in different cultures? Are the words inherently bad, or does the meaning depend on the interpretation agreed on in a culture? David asks his father, "If you give somebody the finger, and that person doesn't know what it means, then what makes it bad?" (38). In this conversation Sachar explores the semantics of verbal and nonverbal taboo language. The reader is led to understand that the words or gestures do not in themselves contain obscene meanings; meanings come from the people who use them. David's father says, "There's nothing inherently bad about it [the finger]. It is only bad because everyone has agreed it's a bad thing to do" (38). Taboo words get their power from people who use them to insult and curse others.

David also realizes that taboo words and gestures have strong connotations. When David gives Mrs. Bayfield the finger, he is immediately guilty. He thinks that "he'd never given anyone the finger before, at least not for real" (11). He is also embarrassed when Maureen (nicknamed Mo), his shop class partner, uses swear words in self-defense against the guys who tease her about whether she is a boy or a girl. David wishes he could use strong language to defend himself against their attacks, but he can't "imagine those words coming from his mouth" (76). He even blushes when he uses a swear word and thinks that it feels "odd" (120). He only resorts to these words when he is angry or frustrated. He knows that these words aren't appropriate in normal circumstances.

Mo also knows that swear words have the power to attack and insult and should not be used lightly. When David tells about "flipping off" his mother, Mo says, "It's the most horrible thing you can do!" (100). Near the end of the novel when Mo is about to use strong language to describe the in-crowd, she looks at Ricky, David's younger brother, and uses "aardvarks" instead. So she doesn't use swear words lightly, only as a defense mechanism in situations when she doesn't feel she has any choice.

In our day, when many adolescents frequently hear taboo words in film and television, not to mention in their everyday lives, a considered discussion of what gives power to such language and why such words should not be used randomly could actually help kids realize that this isn't the language to use routinely. Just telling kids not to use certain words is clearly not enough. They need to understand the power of words and how that power must be wielded carefully. With this understanding may come the knowledge that there are better ways to solve difficulties than resorting to strong language.

So while some teachers or parents may feel uncomfortable reading every word in Sachar's novel, they should consider its power to help children deal with the peer pressures that affect everything they say and do. Kids need to learn how to distinguish between friendly advice and coercion to do something destructive. David says, "Sometimes you just have to do what your friends want you to do . . . no matter how terrible it is. He had finally learned that. It was the opposite of what everyone had always told him to do. Just say no, he had been told again and again" (130). David realizes that sometimes his *true* friends are giving him good advice in contrast to cool-crowd false friends. It's not enough to follow a maxim—just say no—a person has to think through what is the best way to act.

With humor, Sachar forces kids to look at themselves and realize how complicated the decisions are that they face every day. Like any satire, this novel has the healing power to open and explore behaviors, so kids can think about the ways they choose to act. This type of exploration, in the safe confines of a novel, can help kids to grow. The realism of Sachar's novel will ring true to kids, and they will trust his exploration of the dilemmas they face every day. In the end, David has to do what he knows is right—a good lesson for anyone to learn.

## Work Cited

Sachar, Louis. *The Boy Who Lost His Face*. New York: Knopf, 1989.

# *Bridge to Terabithia:* Too Good to Miss

## Karen Hirsch

One day while meeting a writing group of fourth- and fifth-grade gifted students, I asked the children what their favorite books were. Many responded with *Bridge to Terabithia,* by Katherine Paterson.

"What do you like about *Bridge to Terabithia?*" I asked. Their answers captured some of the central themes of the book.

"It's so sad," one girl said. "It's the saddest book I ever read. I loved it."

"The boy and girl get to be friends," said another student. "Even though that's sort of weird. But I like it that they're friends."

"I liked that one nice teacher," said another boy. "The way she took Jesse to the city and all." The girl who started the discussion spoke up again.

"But that's when Leslie died," she said, and shivered. "Oh, think how terrible it was for her parents."

"And remember, they moved then," added a boy. "Jesse must've felt awful."

"You know what?" a fifth-grade girl said. "When I read a wonderful book like *Bridge to Terabithia* and then I see the book again, like in the library or on somebody's desk, you know what?" I waited, not speaking.

"I just wish I hadn't read it yet so I could read it," she ended in a burst. Some of the others nodded.

We went on then to discuss how Katherine Paterson and others of their favorite authors write and how we might improve our own writing. But I continued to think about the comment of the fifth grader. I understood what she meant. I often look longingly at a book, wishing I had not yet read it. Sometimes, as I did this week with *Bridge to Terabithia,* I reread it. Because I was familiar with this story I savored it in a new way, anticipating each event and noticing details I had missed. And because I'm a writer of juvenile fiction myself, I studied and admired the way Paterson developed her characters, built tension, and used language.

I find *Bridge to Terabithia* an exquisite book. A Newbery Award-winner, (1978) it tells the story of the friendship between two fifth-grade children, Jesse Aarons and Leslie Burke. Jesse, a native rural Virginian, comes from a large and very poor family. Wedged between two older and two younger sisters, Jesse feels frustrated at his parents' expectations of him and by their absence of affectionate gestures. In an effort to gain recognition and admiration, both with his family and with his classmates, Jesse works hard to become the top runner in his class. Though he practices diligently to beat the current lead-runner, a new student's racing skills beat everyone. Her name is Leslie Burke.

Like Jesse, Leslie is a lonely, needy child. Busy with their book-writing endeavors and with their interest in country living, Leslie's parents tend to ignore her need for love and attention. Unlike Jesse, Leslie's family is financially secure and, though living like "hippies," is in a socioeconomic group very different from Jesse's.

Jesse and Leslie are both gifted young people, not unlike the students I teach. These characters and my students share the same kind of curiosity and intensity of very bright people, Jesse in the visual arts and Leslie in writing and in general intellectual ability. Because they live at neighboring farms and because they share a perspective on life that is different from the other kids, Jesse and Leslie become close friends. They spend time together at a woodsy hideout they call Terabithia. To get to their hideout they swing across a dry creek bed from a rope attached to an apple tree.

There, in Terabithia, under Leslie's leadership, they create a richly developed kingdom where they are King and Queen. There they talk endlessly, imagining together and encouraging each other. Sometimes they plot revenge against the school bullies, and other times Leslie tells Jesse Shakespearean stories. Terabithia becomes a second home for them, a safe, secret place for the surrogate family they've become to each other. Their relationship deepens and, though boy-girl friendships are scorned, and certainly rare in my years of elementary teaching experience, Jesse and Leslie are able to openly be friends, even at school.

When a terrible accidental drowning takes Leslie's life, Jesse is shocked and devastated. His profound grief expresses itself though disbelief, rage, and distracted action. He finally accepts Leslie's death through help from her parents and his own, his fifth-grade teacher, and his little sister. The book ends with Jesse's awareness that, although Leslie has died, she has left behind much of her spirit, energy, and optimism with him. As readers, we feel assured that Jesse will carry on, and that Leslie's life will continue through him.

This book is ideal as a classroom novel for late elementary or early middle school students. I have spoken to several teachers of fourth and fifth

graders who find it enormously successful. The issues it raises are meaningful and engaging to this age: friendships, families, school, peer groups, and
death. Discussions, dramatizations, and writing are only a few activities that
a teacher might use to help students explore these issues and the overriding
theme of "building bridges" in one's life. Any child who reads this award-
winning book would necessarily experience personal growth as he/she
identifies with Jesse and Leslie, particularly if offered the framework of a
classroom unit to encourage personal reflection and deeper thinking.

The Newbery Award is given once a year to "the author of the most
distinguished contribution to American literature for children." I read the
winners each year and I encourage my students to try them, too. They are
inevitably well written and deep, and I read them with admiration, respect,
and pangs of envy. Among other definitions, the book must "display respect
for children's understandings, abilities, and appreciations." By "distinguished" the Newbery organization means:

•marked by eminence and distinction: noted for significant achievement
•marked by excellence in quality
•individually distinct

It's easy to see how *Bridge to Terabithia* was chosen.

*Horn Book Magazine* reviewed the book in the year of its publication,
1978. Their review says that the characters in *Bridge to Terabithia* are
magnificent. It also says that the book is rich in descriptive language,
humorous insight on the cultures of different classes, and realistic portrayals
of country school life. The review praises the theme of building bridges as
a particularly powerful symbol in the story.

Since its publication, *Bridge to Terabithia* has been the target of several
censorship challenges. The concerns raised have been about:

•Language: Challengers in Nebraska, Connecticut, California, Pennsylvania,
Texas, and Maine have objected to what they call profanity, vulgar language,
offensive language, or swear words. In the Oskaloosa, Kansas, school
district a challenge "led to the enactment of a new policy that requires
teachers to examine their required material for profanities. Teachers will list
each profanity and the number of times it was used in the book, and forward
the list to parents, who will be asked to give written permission of their
children to read the material."
•Life views or lifestyles: Challenges in Connecticut and Pennsylvania have
said that the book would "give students negative views of life," "make
reference to witchcraft," show "disrespect of adults," and promote an

"elaborate fantasy world that they felt might lead to confusion."

The dominant themes of this book are about learning to know oneself, friendship, and healthy growing up. Jesse and Leslie learn about life from each other, broaden their horizons, and come to appreciate perspectives new to them. Each child offers support to the other and each grows, giving the reader a powerful model of what friendship is. When Jesse gets in trouble over a problem with the school bully, Leslie insists that he stand up for his rights.

"It's the *principle* of the thing, Jess," she says. "That's what you've got to understand. You have to stop people like that. Otherwise they turn into tyrants and dictators." This is new information to the country boy Jesse. But Leslie, and sometimes her family, learn from him, too. Leslie's father, though very intelligent, doesn't have some of the practical knowledge that Jesse has. One time Jesse helps Leslie and Mr. Burke tear out old boards to uncover an ancient fireplace in the Burkes' house. Jessie demonstrates his knowledge of using tools, removing wallpaper, and patching drywall. Mr. Burke looks at him in wonder. "You're amazing," he says. "Where did you learn that, Jess?" And Jesse glows and grows in the praise and respect.

Though my writing-class students didn't articulate specific examples in our discussion of *Bridge to Terabithia*, they seemed to understand the importance of Jesse's and Leslie's friendship, also.

"They were such good *friends*," one boy said wistfully.

"And they didn't pick on each other all the time," said a girl, "the way my best friend always does to me." Teachers who use the novel in fifth grade have told me of the extended, meaningful discussions their students have had during their unit on *Bridge to Terabithia*. Children identify with the characters because Jesse and Leslie are searchers and seekers like all youngsters as they reach for acceptance and maturity in the world. Jesse and Leslie make mistakes, they think and say nasty things sometimes, and they "try out" a variety of experiments to test life.

These children are real and believable people, as are their families, peers, and teachers. The language the characters use is authentic to the setting and to the characters that Paterson creates. They are complex people, and Paterson shows us that in the way the characters behave. Jesse's parents are having financial difficulties, and his dad has to drive a long way in his old truck to get to a backbreaking manual labor job. But things weren't always like that for the Aaronses, and Jesse has a clear memory of those times.

In one early scene, Jesse is practicing his running, pumping hard and imagining how proud his dad would be of him if he could be the fastest runner in his school. Here are his thoughts:

> Maybe Dad would be so proud he'd forget all about how tired he was from the long drive back and forth to Washington and the digging and hauling all day. He would get right down on the floor and wrestle, the way they used to. Old Dad would be surprised at how strong he'd gotten in the last couple of years. (5)

Mr. Aarons ignores Jesse at times or uses language that some may find objectionable. When Jesse, filled with rage and frustration after Leslie's death, throws his paints and paper into water, his dad says, "That was a damn fool thing to do." But not a minute later, his father takes Jesse onto his lap and holds and strokes him with deep tenderness as Jesse cries. "I hate her," Jesse says of his friend. "I wish I'd never seen her in my whole life." And after a long pause, Dad sympathizes, "Hell ain't it?" and continues to hold his grieving son.

These examples of point and counterpoint help the reader know Mr. Aarons for the real person he is. Though a gruff, bitter, resentful man in parts of the story, he frankly and genuinely tells Jesse he's sorry about Leslie, and in his own silent way, he shows his love for his son by doing Jesse's milking chores unasked. He picks Jesse up and carries him, holding him close with tenderness even as Jesse kicks and screams out his anger and grief.

And Leslie's family is complex, too, neither all good nor all bad, but real and believable. It's true that they sometimes ignore her as they pursue their own dreams and fantasies. But they give Leslie a great deal, too. The Burke family seems like several professional families I've known. They so clearly believe in Leslie, in her abilities, in her decision-making skills, and in her high-level thinking. They don't hem her in by some contrived standards of what girls can or cannot do. Leslie scuba dives though their teacher, Mrs. Myers, says that it's "an unusual hobby—for a girl." Leslie has clearly been respected and highly regarded by her parents. She talks about why her family has moved to the country in a way that suggests that she was in on the discussion. When Jesse asks her why she's moved to the country, she says,

> "My parents are reassessing their value structure."
> "Huh?" says Jesse. And Leslie goes on:
> "They decided they were too hooked on money and success, so they bought that old farm and they're going to farm it and think about what's important." (32)

When Jesse objects, she says, "We talked it over. I wanted to come, too" (32).

And the Burkes' grieving when Leslie dies is a measure of how deeply they loved her. One poignant scene is when Leslie's father holds Jesse close. Sobbing and shaking, he tells Jesse, "She loved you, you know." Mr. Burke shows Jesse his grief again when he tries to give Leslie's puppy, a gift from Jesse, to him and can't because the puppy is a connection to his daughter that he can't sever. "'I meant to give you P.T.,' he said. 'But'—he looked at Jesse and his eyes were those of a pleading little boy— 'but I can't seem to give him up'" (127).

Thus, although *Bridge to Terabithia* does have in it the "profanity, vulgar language, and swear words" that some censors offer as reasons to ban, the complex characters and moving story by far transcend the fact that children see those words in print. Even Jesse uses profanity. One time when rain made their excursions to Terabithia miserable and nearly impossible, Leslie makes a fancy speech: "Methinks some evil being has put a curse on our beloved kingdom." Jesse blurts out a baser reasoning: "Damn weather bureau," he says, using language he's bound to have heard every day of his life at home. But one misses the whole person if one defines and dismisses Jesse and his father by their language alone, as the censors are doing.

During Jesse's crisis, Mr. Aarons rises to another stature that is also within him. When Jesse's older sister, Ellie, states what might be the usual "rule" of the culture, "Boys ain't supposed to cry at times like this. Are they, Momma?" (108), both Jesse's father and mother move quickly to squelch her and protect Jesse in his time of pain.

Connecticut and Pennsylvania may have banned *Bridge to Terabithia* because of "disrespect of adults," or "elaborate fantasy." But in real life, which *Bridge to Terabithia* reflects, kids *are* occasionally rude in their talk about adults. Many times I've heard my professor husband talk about one of the nuns in his elementary school whom he particularly disliked. "Sister Banana Nose," he calls her. "Sister Banana Nose could really snap that ruler," he says. "We were all scared of her."

I like the way Katherine Paterson lets us see Jesse as he begins to form a new perspective on his teacher, "Monster Mouth Myers," when she shares a personal life story with him near the end of the story. So, contrary to the Connecticut and Pennsylvania censors, *Bridge to Terabithia*'s more powerful impression is that of Jesse's growth from a kid making fun of his teacher to one who finds a new respect and understanding of another person. Maybe if my husband had gotten to know Sister Banana Nose as a person, he would've felt more compassion for her, too, as Jesse did for Monster Mouth Myers.

As for the "elaborate fantasy" disapproval, any adult who has even the tiniest awareness of what children are like will dismiss it without defense.

Who could watch children play without seeing the pleasure they take in
creating fantasy—the more "elaborate" the better.

The following excerpt from a recent Internet interview with Katherine
Paterson ties the issues together and gives us the unique view of *Bridge to
Terabithia* from the author's perspective. It is, I think, a good way to end
and as convincing a reason as any why this book is worth reading. In the
interview, Paterson is asked why she uses swear words in the book. She
says:

> Jess and his father talk like the people I knew who lived in that area. I believe
> it is my responsibility to create characters who are real, not models of good
> behavior. If Jesse and his dad are to be real, they must speak and act like real
> people. I have a lot of respect for my readers. I do not expect them to imitate my
> characters, but simply to care about them and understand them.

I feel strongly that no child should miss the opportunity to read *Bridge
to Terabithia*, either independently or in a shared inquiry class setting. This
is the kind of profoundly moving and deeply meaningful book that will live
in a reader's memory.

## Works Cited

Doyle, Robert P. *Banned Books*; 2000 Resource Book. Chicago: American
    Library Association, 2000.
*Horn Book Magazine* 54 (Feb. 1978): 48.
Paterson, Katherine. *Bridge to Terabithia*. New York: Thomas Y. Crowell
    Company, 1977.
Website: http://www.terabithia.com/questions.htm.
Website: http://www.ala.org/alsc/newbery-terms.html.

# Stephen King's Cases against Child Abuse: *Carrie* and *The Shining*

## Susan M. Kelley

Stephen King's novels *Carrie* and *The Shining* should not be censored because they explore the complexity of child abuse, from the history of the forces that mold an abuser to the conflicting emotions and the desperate need to please of the abused. Moreover, in painting these psychological portraits, while King may draw sympathy from us for the abuser, he never allows us to excuse the abuser. He shows us the deep innocence of a child being violated by adult selfishness and preoccupation. He shows us the ability of an adult to rationalize his or her behavior so that the fault lies with the child rather than with the adult. In the end, he forces us to condemn all forms of abuse, mental and physical, and to welcome the violent end of the abuser, no matter in what ways we might be tempted not to blame the abuser because of that abuser's childhood history. He shows us what is ripped from the child even when the child, by the end of the novel, is free from the abuser. In other words, King paints a portrait of the complexity of a behavior that does damage to all involved and yet comes down with a firm moral condemnation of the perpetrators and enablers of abuse.

In these two novels, *Carrie* and *The Shining*, Stephen King presents us with situations that are extremely difficult and that are all too common for children. Carrie he paints as an odd child, one the children in her high school feel free to tease and ostracize. As the novel progresses, King reveals the force that molded this child into her role as scapegoat, a mother in a fundamentalist religious sect who punishes her child by locking her into a closet for up to five hours at a time demanding that she pray until she is pure again. The mother dictates the clothes the child wears, how her hair is cut, and her social isolation and daily characterizes Carrie as fallen and evil. Her denial and hatred of sex carries over into her refusal to inform Carrie about developing female bodies so that when Carrie begins her menses in the shower after gym class, she believes she is bleeding to death. This fear is compounded when her mother responds to Carrie's fear and embarrassment by locking her in the closet yet again, fully convinced now of Carrie's irretrievable impurity.

Danny, in *The Shining*, is a normal child in many ways. He loves his father and mother and is unusually bright. His challenge is his father, Jack Torrance, a prep-school English teacher and would-be writer who has recently been fired for losing his temper with a student and beating him nearly to death. Before this incident, there was another temperamental outburst from a drunk Jack Torrance when he discovered that Danny, young enough to be still in diapers, had thrown the papers of his manuscript around his office in a mistaken attempt to organize them. In his anger, Jack bent Danny's arm so far and hard that it broke. While Jack feels remorse and guilt about his actions, he is unable to accept responsibility in a fully aware way. When Jack Torrance suffers the consequences of his behavior, he finds a way for the blame to lie elsewhere.

King understands children's vulnerability in the face of adult tendencies toward narcissistic extremes. He understands the openness of their love that is linked with their need for approval, two forces that drive them to adapt to inappropriate, invasive, selfish, and cruel behavior. He understands that the deck is stacked against them. It is this understanding and the presentation of the psychological sources and ramifications of abuse that argue against censorship of these two novels. Children who are abused need to see that they are not alone and that there is a potential exit from the trap they are in; children who are not abused but who are yet living under adult rule are helped to understand the ramifications of actions adults take and to see how self-involvement and self-obsession can deeply harm others. In a Stephen King novel, particularly in these two novels, the reader learns a basic precept in our culture: to root for the underdog. Stephen King is an author who fights for sanity and normalcy in a world of people driven by their own motivations and desires; he is an author who punishes transgressors; and he is an author who fights for the helpless, for the unjustly excluded, for children.

As a demonstration of how stacked the deck is, King gives Carrie and Danny special gifts that could well provide a way out for each of them. Carrie discovers she has a telekinetic power with which she can move objects. Danny lives with something that is referred to as the ability to "shine"; that is, he can read the feelings others have and can sometimes even know what they are thinking, although he doesn't always understand what it is he "hears." With this gift, Danny can see into the past and the future, but King denies him the ability to change either. Despite these gifts, each of which we readers hope will help these children escape abuse, neither Carrie nor Danny can succeed alone. After she exacts her revenge, Carrie is totally alone and cannot survive. Children, no matter how strong, cannot make it without adult support. It is only Danny, who has help from Dick, the cook at the Overlook Hotel, who survives, but he needs someone who shares his gift and who is a caring and responsible adult to team with his mother to save him. Dick has the qualities Danny's father doesn't. Even though Dick saves Danny, the horror of having to be saved from his own father remains.

*Carrie* opens in the midst of the crisis that initiates Carrie's understanding of the power that has lain latent in her until puberty. Carrie is being teased in the locker room shower after gym class, an occasion we all perhaps dreaded in junior high school and one with which young readers will identify. Just when the teasing reaches its greatest intensity, Carrie begins her menses. The children who do the teasing act with the unconscious cruelty of adolescents. The gym teacher, who should be able to find a way to protect Carrie, as well as to educate and soothe her, instead ends up siding with the group of students, a circumstance that exacerbates the trauma of the sudden flow of blood that marks the start of Carrie's transformation from scapegoat to avenger.

As readers and former adolescents, we understand Carrie's mortification. What we find far more difficult to understand is the motivation and behavior of the adults and fellow adolescents around her. The gym teacher was in a position to help but ended up overwhelmed by the situation and being influenced by the mob mentality of the other girls in the class. Carrie's mother, the most obvious source of support and help, is presented as a zealot who is so involved in her own imaginary world of evil that she cannot attach to her daughter in any but the most condemning way. Even when a fellow student feels appropriate guilt and compunction about the incident and moves to ameliorate the situation by asking her boyfriend to take Carrie to the prom as an act of contrition, the effort backfires and only intensifies Carrie's ingrained cynicism toward kindness and other students' insistence that Carrie remain odd.

Carrie herself shows a surprising inner strength when she accepts the boy's invitation and allows herself to hope for a good time. She defies her mother's irrational arguments against Carrie's going and in the process rediscovers her telekinetic powers, which years ago, after a particularly severe confinement to the closet, she had repressed. Even as King makes us privy to the plan another pair of students has to make the evening hell for Carrie, we find ourselves rooting for her to prevail against her mother, her victimization, and her assignment to the bottom rung of high school society. We want her to beat the odds.

What King calls up in us is all that is decent in humanity. He conveys to us the arbitrary nature of a child falling into an abusive situation, the

efforts of a child to be good enough to evade the abuse, and the internaliza-
tion of the rationalization for that abuse that ultimately defines that child's
sense of self. He shows us how we all participate in the process by not
coming to the defense of abused children and by embracing the rationale of
the abuse. Carrie is strange; Carrie is ugly; Carrie is different. Difference
must be expunged. We have all played into this scenario at some point in our
school, work, and adult lives. We have all regretted our involvement soon
after. It does not hurt us or young readers to be reminded of our obligation
to be decent to other human beings. Nor does it hurt us to understand the
forces beyond a child's control that shape the very oddness to which we
object. King provides the insights and the imperatives about human behavior
that we need in order to maintain civility and tolerance in society.

Stephen King also has a bit of the Old Testament to him. In *Carrie*, he
provides a vengeance that may seem excessive to the crime when all those
even remotely associated with Carrie's isolation and humiliation, as well as
those who are attempting to help her, are killed when she aligns her anger
with her power. Yet if we consider the manifestation of her anger as a
representation of the depth of the hurt, the death of so many students and of
Carrie's mother also indicates the depth of King's sympathy for Carrie. At
the same time, he backs us into a corner by portraying the person she is
when she takes her vengeance as having crossed the line into at least
temporary insanity. While we sympathize, while we understand, while we
want to think well of her, while we cheer her on in her revenge, we also feel
grateful when she, too, dies. The difficulty is gone. We don't have to make
a space for her by accepting her deformity, that is, her crippled soul, into our
group. This is another reason the novel should not be censored. King allows
the complexity of our emotions and judgments to molder at odds with our
decency.

In *The Shining*, Danny Torrance is quite a different character. He is a
regular kid, a five-year-old boy, living with what seems from the outside to
be perfectly regular parents. We meet Danny, as we did Carrie, in the midst
of crisis. His father has lost his job, his mother has thought of divorcing his
father, and Danny himself has begun to see a vision of a child named Tony
who warns Danny about various dangers in his path.

Unlike *Carrie*, however, *The Shining* begins with its focus on Jack
Torrance, the adult, in an interview to be caretaker of a resort hotel over the
winter. The first line of the novel reveals Jack's intolerance of others, his
frustration at his own failures, his sense of comedown, his humiliation, and
his inability to navigate the world: "Jack Torrance thought: *Officious little
prick*" (15). While we start out in Jack's corner, for Mr. Ullman seems just
as Jack describes him, as the novel progresses, we see this expression to be

symptomatic of Jack's problem. He thinks he is superior, he is condemning, he judges, he rages in frustration. At one level, we want Jack to succeed in this job, but as more and more of his past comes clear, we suspect he will not. He can't seem to handle adult responsibility.

Moreover, he reveals this in his language. Adults who are reasonable and responsible in a King novel, particularly in this one, do not use profanity. They have control over their behavior. They have respect for others. Their language reflects their elemental decency. Jack resorts to abusive language as an attempt to injure or destroy those who have more power than he does or those whom he cannot control. Mr. Ullman becomes not just a prick, but a "little" prick; his wife, the woman he has sworn to love and protect, the woman he has been able to control for years, at the first sign of independence is termed a "bitch." That Mr. Ullman remains his boss, despite Jack's internal dialogue, demonstrates the ineffectiveness of Jack's choice of words, suggesting an impotence Jack spends the novel raging against. Rationale for censoring Stephen King's work often focuses on the profanity in his novels. In *The Shining*, Jack's profanity is condemned as strongly as is Jack's behavior. Responsible, decent adults, adults capable of protecting children, control their environment and their language. Responsible adults do not swear.

Jack is anything but responsible. He and a fellow alcoholic, very drunk one night, run into a bicycle that seems to have had a child on it. Because they cannot find the body, they never report the incident. Jack worries about it off and on and swears off alcohol as a result. Nonetheless, he never takes the appropriate adult action. We come to think that perhaps the Tony with whom Danny plays is the soul of the unfound body, for Tony first appears to Danny soon after this incident. Jack's unfinished business, Tony, knows Jack's soul, it seems, and wants to protect Danny. Jack has many opportunities to address his temper and his mistakes; his pride prevents him so that he doesn't grow as an adult or as a character and ends up consumed by his own rationalizations.

Danny is torn in many directions. He loves his mother deeply; he adores his father; he hears Tony's warnings. Even so, Danny is only a child, a very young one at that. He cannot comprehend the complexity of his parents' relationship or personalities, nor can he comprehend the reality of the danger he is in. King reveals Danny's innocence and lack of understanding by putting phrases Danny doesn't understand in capital letters. When he hesitates to tell his mother about his visions, he thinks, "Worse, she might believe him in the wrong way, might think he was LOSING HIS MAR-BLES. He understood a little about LOSING YOUR MARBLES, not as much as he did about GETTING A BABY, which his mommy had explained to him the year before at some length, but not enough" (207). His fears of his parents divorcing outweigh any fears he has of visions or abuse. "The greatest terror of Danny's life was DIVORCE, a word that always appeared in his mind as a sign painted in red letters which were covered with hissing poisonous snakes" (39). He doesn't want to go to the hotel because of the visions he has had, he doesn't want even to get into their rickety car, but he thinks that if he voices his objections, he could cause divorce or worse. He has taken on his parents' problems, a phenomenon not uncommon to young children. In all of Danny's confusion and immense effort to understand, King makes clear to us Danny's essential innocence. This is a child who ultimately cannot defend himself against his father or the manifestation of evil that haunts the Overlook Hotel. He must call on another adult, Dick, the hotel's cook who is spending the winter in Florida, to save him.

Danny and his family meet Dick the day they are given a tour of the hotel, the last day the hotel will have guests and staff. Dick immediately understands Danny's gift, a gift Dick shares. His ability to shine is not nearly as strong as Danny's, but the two of them have that in common. This suggests a surrogate-parental relationship between these two characters, and, by the end of the novel, Dick has become a substitute father. He is willing to fly in from Florida, drive through a snowstorm, and risk his own life to save Danny. Even so, he cannot erase Danny's awareness that his very own father tried to kill him. A substitute is just that, a substitute. Dick is not a replica of Jack and can only hold his place, not take it.

Danny adores his father. He admits he has almost forgotten the broken arm, but he worries about his father doing the BAD THING, drinking, which leads to trouble. His attachment to his father, even his mother recognizes, is far stronger than his attachment to his mother. Those of us who have read about abuse recognize the tendency. A child pays far more attention to an abuser than to a nonabuser. A child tries far harder to please someone whose temper is ungovernable.

Jack fails at the most basic precept of adulthood: to protect his family. He destroys it from within. The first day he tries to fix the roof of the Overlook, he gets stung by a wasp, which leads him to find a nest underneath some shingles of the roof. To Jack, who muses on the event, the nest becomes symbolic of life's tendency to sting him. His musings reveal that "He had not done things; things had been done to him" (121). We discover that when his drunken father abused him, Jack "had come upon a stray dog and kicked it into the gutter" (121). We note that through much of the novel, he continues to kick his wife, the "bitch," until she finally stands up to him. We may feel sorry for Jack, but we resent his blaming his actions on anyone or anything else, and we're shocked that he would kick a stray dog, and we're shocked at his reassurance to himself that "he hadn't *felt* like a son of a bitch" (122). After these musings, Jack goes to get the bug bomb vowing that "They would pay. They would pay for stinging him" (129), a vow that is unsettling in its personal read on what most people would consider a natural event: you disturb a wasp nest, you get stung.

Jack kills the wasps and allows Danny to take the nest to his room. When his wife asks if it's safe, he assures her it is. But we're dealing in symbolic power now, and the nest has come to embody Jack's anger. In the night, the nest comes alive again and the wasps sting Danny repeatedly. Both Danny and Wendy, Danny's mother, turn to Jack with reproving looks, saying that Jack had said all the wasps were dead. Jack has no defense and is mystified by the Lazarus-like reappearance of the wasps. We come to know they represent a force that cannot be killed or contained. Jack will take his resentments and his frustrations out on those closest to him. He will eventually try to kill his family.

The trust Danny has in his father is painful to watch. The difficulty Jack works out in front of his family is equally painful. He is torn in half by his love for Danny and his need to act out his anger. He can rationalize anything he does. He can blame all his behavior on anyone else. At base, he loves his son, but that love does not have the power to outweigh his other faults. This is the truth of abuse that King gives us. Love isn't always all-powerful. Love can't protect those for whom we are responsible. If we can rationalize violence and resentment as fitting motivations for abuse, then we're capable of anything. It is our responsibility as adults to address our past and fix it. If we don't, we are not fit to have children. They will never be safe with us. Therefore, Danny's father must die. And Danny will be left to mourn his father forever, to be confused forever, to love him forever, to be inadequate to save his father forever. King's resolutions are not easy. The ramification of adults not behaving in adult ways is devastating.

King urges us to embrace decency. He demands that we value our children and put them above all else. He declares abuse to be evil and inexcusable for a rational, responsible adult. His moral judgments may strike us as too simple, maybe too black-and-white, but his understanding of the complexity of human behavior negates that assumption. He understands how hard it is to be decent. He can show us all sorts of ways that lead us away from decency that evoke our pity and shame. He insists, though, that there is a moral right and a moral wrong that act as the plumb line in our lives. However obscured that plumb line is by experience and circumstance, it is there to be followed and is seen by those of us who are responsible. It doesn't lead us to happy endings, but it does lead us to strive to be the kind of people we can stand being near our children. This is a conclusion that defies censorship.

## Works Cited

King, Stephen. *Carrie*. Garden City, N.Y.: Doubleday, 1974.
———. *The Shining*. Garden City. N.Y.: Doubleday, 1977.

# Defending Ayla:
# Two Novels about Being Different

## Mary Phillips Manke

Imagine a child in your school who is different from the others. Imagine a child who looks different, who is maturing at a different rate, who seems to learn differently. Imagine a child who likes to do what other children don't like to do, who can't seem to learn the unspoken rules about how to act and who to be. But imagine also a child who clearly is in need of love and care. The child you imagine is a child whose daily life is difficult and sad.

Now imagine a child with all these characteristics but a child born in the Stone Age. This child is Ayla, the young protagonist of Jean Auel's novel *Clan of the Cave Bear*. Ayla is a Cro-Magnon child whose family is killed in an earthquake. She is left alone in a dangerous world. Starving and sick, she is rescued by a clan of Neanderthals. The clan adopts her as their own, or almost their own.

Ayla's rescuers realize at once that she is different from them in skin and hair color, in facial features, in body proportions. But it takes time for them to realize just how different she is. Ayla speaks in words, while the clan members use only a few sounds, communicating primarily through a graceful sign language. Ayla remembers what she experiences and is taught, while the Neanderthals have a deep memory of everything their ancestors have known, something between instinct and access to an encyclopedia of knowledge from a collective unconscious.

The two elders who first rescue Ayla become her family and develop a deep and loving relationship with her. Creb is an aged medicine man, badly crippled. He has never had a real family because of his disability, and he comes to care deeply about Ayla and to cherish the family he is able to form with his sister, Iza, and with Ayla. She reaches out to him for attention and warmth, and he is disarmed. Iza teaches and cares for Ayla. She too is childless, a widow, and thrives on the opportunity to be a mother. She is the clan's healer. She is overjoyed to find that Ayla, though lacking the inbred

115

knowledge that Iza's own child might have, can and wants to learn the craft on which Iza has spent her life.

However, others in the clan are doubtful or hostile. Ayla looks different. She does not know the rules, and when she learns them, she does not always choose to keep them. She looks at people outside the family hearth, invading the privacy needed by those who communicate in sign. She is reluctant to offer total obedience to every male. And when she teaches herself to hunt with a sling, she violates the clan's insistence that men and women follow different paths.

As Ayla grows older, her difference becomes more obvious. The clan members are doubly constrained, by their socialization and by their deep memory of what it is to be a Neanderthal man or woman. Ayla lacks both a large part of that socialization and all the aid of deep memory. As she grows taller than the other girls and matures sexually more slowly than they do, her body is more and more different from theirs.

Ayla is punished for her difference, especially for her violation of rules that the clan members are almost incapable of questioning. When her forbidden hunting becomes known to the clan, she is given what is expected to be a death sentence; she is isolated from the clan and forced to live alone through one month of an Ice Age winter. But her worst grief comes when she becomes the target of Broud, a young man who beats her repeatedly and later rapes her. Her difference enrages him, and he punishes her for it in every way he can imagine. When she becomes pregnant and has a son, the clan comes close to killing the baby. Though he is a child of mixed Neanderthal and Cro-Magnon ancestry, he has some characteristics of his mother's people that the clan identifies as signs of illness. In their harsh world, children born with physical defects are abandoned. Finally, the clan forces Ayla to leave them and her child and find a way to live alone.

Through this abuse, through the pain she feels at being different from the people around her, the people she loves, Ayla remains strong and resilient. She learns skills from the clan, but her ability to go beyond what she is taught, beyond what is in the clan memory, allows her to learn to survive independently. In the clan, the tasks of daily living are clearly divided between male and female, and among those descended from specialists in various tasks. Unlike the members of the clan, Ayla can both hunt for food and prepare it. She can knap flint for tools and weapons and prepare animal skins for use. She can find and prepare herbs for healing and weave waterproof baskets. Clan members are completely dependent on one another; Ayla can survive on her own.

In addition, whether Ayla is unwilling or unable to comply with clan customs, she finds ways to limit or resolve conflict. She loves the man and woman who are her family and does all she can to care for them. Driven into isolation, she uses the skills she has gained—and is not supposed to have—to survive her time of banishment from the clan. For a long time she is able to keep Broud away from her by carefully chosen actions. She becomes a loving mother to her baby son.

A young person who experiences the difference and isolation that are the hallmark of Ayla's life with the clan will find in her a model worth emulating. Strong, dignified, capable, making the best of her life, she can be a talisman for children living outside the comfort of group life—and most children live there at some point in adolescence.

What are the objections to this novel as reading for young people? First, it deals with rape. The description of Broud's first rape of Ayla is both explicit and violent. Some adults would prefer to believe that young people know nothing about such ugly events. The reality is that, from news programs to television and movies, our culture puts forward images of rape that are almost impossible to avoid. Often these images blame women for their own abuse, or imply that men are natural rapists.

However, Auel has written this part of the story with a clear sense that rape is about power, rather than about sex. She shows Broud's actions as outside the norm for the clan, and Ayla as his victim. It is clear that Broud's hatred of Ayla, rather than desire for her or any provocative action on her part, leads to the rape. And there is never any question that Ayla does not want to be raped. At first she is physically and emotionally damaged by it, reduced to silent misery and shame. In time she becomes inured to her abuse, but never does she come to want Broud's attentions, let alone his violence. This depiction helps counteract the images of rape often found in our culture.

A second objection is that the novel blends research-based reconstruction of Stone Age life with its imaginative construction and makes no distinction between the two. Auel has been able to bring careful research to her description of the weather, the geography, the plants and animals, and the tools and techniques of the time. Yet her description of the lives and customs of the Neanderthal people she writes about is primarily imaginative. Such imaginative reconstruction of a period is common in historical fiction, but the remoteness of the time Auel writes about makes it more difficult to see the distinction between what is known and what is imagined. *Clan of the Cave Bear* can be used to raise the question, "How would the author know that? Could that be learned from research, or would she need to make it up?" Such discussion can help young readers understand the difference between history and fiction, as long as adults are themselves clear about the distinction between "fact and fiction."

In thinking about writing this essay, I struggled with what I would say about *Valley of the Horses*, sequel to *Clan of the Cave Bear*. This sequel (actually the second in a series of four) has a great strength in its description of Ayla's triumphant survival in an isolated valley. A reader who has appreciated Ayla's struggles in her years with the clan will want to read about how she uses all her skills and knowledge to overcome the odds so heavily stacked against her.

Another major strength is Auel's treatment of what we would now call racism, felt by other Cro-Magnon toward the Neanderthal clans whose members include both Ayla's persecutor and her beloved adopted family. Ayla knows the Neanderthal clan, and she knows that they are human. The other Cro-Magnon, not knowing them, assume that their different appearance means that they are animals. Ayla is passionate in their defense.

Just as *The Clan of the Cave Bear* strongly opposes sexist images of rape and abuse, *Valley of the Horses* counters images of women as weak and dependent. Ayla, expelled by the clan, travels a long distance alone, caring for her own needs as she travels, until she finds the valley. There she lives successfully. She tames a horse and a cave lion, hunts and gathers what she needs not only for food but also for medicine, clothing, blankets, containers. She builds a plentiful supply of food and artifacts for winter and, during idle times, becomes an artist as she decorates the items she has made. When a Cro-Magnon man, Jondalar, comes to the valley, he is badly wounded and must depend on her for healing and care. As he recovers, their relationship becomes one of equality. Jondalar accepts this quite easily, partly because he is amazed at her achievements and abilities, but partly because the women he has grown up with are also strong and self-sufficient.

The concern that teachers and parents may feel about *Valley of the Horses* is its treatment of Ayla's sexual relationship with Jondalar. Many will see Auel's handling of this relationship as admirable. The image of sexuality she presents is respectful, loving, and healthy. It is also explicit and extensive, though no more so than the content of many romance novels. Teachers using this book in school will want to take into consideration the values and beliefs of their communities in deciding how to use this novel. In addition, Auel presents this positive image of sexuality as characteristic of Stone Age culture, an example of the mixing of what can be known and what cannot be known about this long-ago time.

A last point in defense of these two books is that reading for pleasure is a valuable gift, not just for the enjoyment it provides, but also because of its other benefits. The more people read, the faster and more easily they read. Their ability to read lengthy and difficult texts grows with every hour they spend reading, wrapped up in the pleasure of the word. And the more they read, the more the patterns of written language become available to them, ready to be carried over into their own writing and thinking. Effective readers and writers are made by reading—lots of reading for the joy of it. These two novels are a pleasure to read, hard to put down. They have the appeal of stories like *Robinson Crusoe*, depicting the details and challenges of wilderness survival. And many of the characters, not just Ayla and Jondalar, are well developed and very real.

No one would claim that *Clan of the Cave Bear* and *Valley of the Horses* are great literature. What they are is long, enthralling novels that keep the reader reading, wanting to know more about Ayla, more about her life, so different from ours, more about her next adventure. They offer rich and fascinating information about the Stone Age. They encourage readers to think about sexism and racism in critical ways by setting these dilemmas for our own culture in such a distant place and time. They offer a model of a woman who is strong and resilient, who overcomes obstacles and suffers loss without losing her sense of joy. And they reach out to the hearts of young people who feel lonely and isolated. Both Ayla and these two novels are worth defending.

## Works Cited

Auel, Jean M. *Clan of the Cave Bear*. New York: Crown, 1980.
———. *The Valley of the Horses*. New York: Crown, 1982.

# In Defense of *Crazy Lady*

## Carolyn Reeder

I was taken aback to find Jane Leslie Conly's *Crazy Lady* on a list titled "The 100 Most Frequently Challenged Books of 1990-1999," and when I learned that a challenge is defined as a "formal written complaint filed with a library or school about a book's content or appropriateness," I was baffled. What could anyone find to complain about in *Crazy Lady*, a novel for young people that has won nationwide acclaim?

*Crazy Lady* was chosen by the American Library Association as a Newbery Honor Book, an ALA Notable, and an ALA Best Books for Young Adults. It also received the Hedda Seisler Mason Award and a *Parenting Magazine* "Reading Magic" Certificate of Distinction. It was a *Booklist* Editors' Choice, a *Journal of Adolescent and Adult Literacy* Young Adult Choice, and was listed on both the International Reading Association's Young Adult Choices and the New York Public Library's Books for the Teen Age. In addition, this much-honored book was recognized by the National Conference for Community and Justice.

One of *Crazy Lady's* reviewers wrote, "This book is all heart. A winning story." Another critic tells us, "Its truth reveals that each of us has felt the pain of exclusion and the liberation of acceptance and love."

Besides these formal acknowledgments of Conly's book as an example of excellence in writing and storytelling, teachers and librarians throughout the country have recognized the story's relevance to the lives of today's young people. *Crazy Lady* has appeared on statewide middle school reading lists as well as on the summer reading lists of individual schools and public libraries. How, then, can it possibly be on that other list? And on what grounds was it challenged?

The "crazy lady" in the story is Maxine, who has earned the epithet by her strange appearance and bizarre behavior, but the main character is Vernon, a struggling seventh grader from a rough Baltimore neighborhood. Early in the book, Vernon and his friends taunt Maxine as she lurches down the middle of the street leading her severely retarded son, Ronald. But through a series of believable events, Vernon comes to see Maxine and Ronald as real people—and he comes to care about them.

In spite of his concern that his peers might deride him, Vernon organizes a neighborhood carnival to raise money to buy Ronald the tennis shoes he needs to compete in the Special Olympics. The event is a huge success, but now Ronald's teacher, the beautiful Miss Marlow, seems to be looking for evidence that Maxine is an unfit mother, reasons to have the boy taken away from her.

As I reread the book, I appreciated anew the picture Conly painted of life in this ethnically varied, working-class Baltimore neighborhood. Again I marveled at how she made me feel Vernon's distress about his academic difficulties, his uneasiness about what "the guys" would think of him. Again I felt in awe of a master storyteller. It was hard to remember that I was supposed to be looking for the reason the book had been challenged.

*Crazy Lady* certainly couldn't be faulted for sexually explicit, satanic, or violent content, and the other reasons often cited in challenges seemed just as irrelevant. Could the problem lie with the shoplifting episode? After all, the characters did something patently wrong and didn't get caught. Could it have been all that braggadocio by Vernon's pal about hot-wiring a Toyota—and later actually doing it? Surely it wasn't this reference to "the darn cops," was it? No, but I was getting close. The challenges were for offensive language.

*What* offensive language?

"Well," I was told, "on page 79 Maxine says 'goddamn,' and on page 127 Vernon uses the word 'bitch.'"

In all the times I'd read that book, I never noticed. Why? Because it was such authentic dialogue. Because it was so "in character" for an unstable, out-of-control drunken woman or a seventh-grade boy to use those words in the context of the story. I have the sense that Jane Leslie Conly heard her characters' words in her "mind's ear" and simply recorded them as she wrote the scenes.

I spoke with the author, and she told me that she has received letters from children who ask her why she used those words—and that these usually end "P.S., I loved your book." But she has also received form letters from parents whose children attend Christian schools, letters that cite the words by page number and then ask, "Why should any child read this book?"

My answer to that question would be, "Children should read this book because of its underlying values." As children read to find out what happens, identifying with the main character, they will see that it is possible to withstand peer pressure and do the decent thing. They will see that it is possible to make the enormous effort needed to surmount academic difficulties. Watching Vernon grapple with real-life situations, young readers can't help but absorb some of the tacit lessons he learns in the process. And as they watch him face and cope with significant problems, young readers may find the courage they need to meet the challenges in their own lives.

Conly has no hidden agenda in *Crazy Lady*. She presents no moral lessons in the guise of a story. But as Vernon responds to frustrating situations, the adult characters provide realistic feedback, as when Miss Annie says, "Vernon, don't curse. Cursing is uncouth" (144), or—more important—when his father brings up Vernon's aggressive behavior toward his older brother during a recent argument:

> "You shouldn't have grabbed his neck. He had a great big welt there the next day." Daddy coughed. I kept quiet, hoping it was over. "People go up and down this street with all kinds of bruises, and I know they get drunk or mad and beat up on each other—you've heard them Saturday nights, just like I have. But I always told myself we were different. We might get mad, but we'd settle our arguments without fighting." He looked at me. I turned red. . . . "I know why you did it," he said quietly. "And I'm not saying what you think is wrong. I'm saying you can't fight him." (110)

What I like best about this scene is that Daddy waited until the older kids were out for the evening and the younger ones were in bed before confronting Vernon—and even as he made it clear that fighting would not be tolerated, he acknowledged and accepted the feelings behind the aggressive behavior.

This sense of acceptance is present throughout the book. Family members are accepted as they are—or as they were. Vernon speaks matter-of-factly of his father's illiteracy and his late mother's obesity. Situations that can't be changed are accepted with dignity, too: the family's lack of ready cash, the emptiness left by the mother's death a year before. The book also reflects a sense of community, from the adult who comes out to show his disapproval of the kids harassing Maxine early in the story to the neighborhood's wholehearted participation in the fund-raiser Vernon organizes to outfit Ronald for the Special Olympics.

But that's not all. Conly deals with significant issues in this book, including ageism and racial stereotypes. Miss Annie, the elderly black woman who tutors Vernon, has limited mobility and must use a walker, but she is a powerful force in Vernon's life and in the neighborhood. She's a spokesperson for literacy, too, and for literature ranging from Beverly Cleary's books through the works of Shakespeare.

The most obvious issue raised in Conly's book, of course, is prejudice against those who are different. We see this prejudice in Vernon's initial response to the "crazy lady" and her retarded son, but then we see his attitude change as he begins to see beyond Maxine's "craziness" and to feel more comfortable around Ronald. By the time of the Special Olympics, Vernon has come a long way from the boy who hassled Maxine and thought her son "looked like an ugly animal that got on this earth somehow and really shouldn't have" (42). Here is his description of the crowd waiting for the events to begin:

> There were zillions of people around, and lots of them caught your eye and held it. They had bodies and faces that didn't fit quite right, and some of them had the same expression Ronald did when I first saw him: scared. Maybe they thought you were going to stare, or that you wouldn't like them because of the way they looked or the way they were. Once you smiled, that usually changed. (164-165)

No moralizing, no editorializing. As the story progresses, the reader simply experiences the change in Vernon's perception of the disabled. And perhaps we become aware that Vernon's acceptance of Maxine and her son has had an effect on the attitudes of others in the neighborhood. First we notice that harassing Maxine is no longer a favorite pastime of the other boys, then our eyes widen when Vernon's friend Jerry confides that he has a retarded brother who "lives in a place like a hospital," and finally we share Vernon's satisfaction when all three of his pals turn up at the shoe store to help choose the sneakers for Ronald.

Another strength of this novel is that it puts a human face on some of our society's problems. The effect of job loss on unskilled workers is an abstraction until we learn that Maxine's downhill course began when she was laid off from her factory job because of automation. We know objectively that alcoholism destroys families, but we come to understand the powerlessness of the alcoholic in the grips of addiction when we witness Vernon's confrontation with Maxine after she signs the papers granting custody of Ronald to relatives in North Carolina:

> "You're giving him away."
> "They'd take him otherwise." Her voice was fast and low.
> "If you loved him, you wouldn't do this." I spit the words at her. She started to cry.
> "Ronald's all I have."
> "You could have quit drinking! You could have pulled yourself together!"
> "I tried." The tears rolled down her flabby cheeks. . . .
> "You can't send him away!" I yelled.
> Something moved behind Maxine. Ronald's head appeared over her shoulder.

He grabbed her arm.

"You can't do it," I repeated.

"It's done," she said simply, and she closed the door. (169-170)

*Crazy Lady* shows us that there truly are no easy answers, that sometimes the best choice is simply the lesser (or maybe the least) of the evils. It unobtrusively makes the point that only so much can be done to help others, that in the end we are each responsible for our own destiny and must accept the consequences of our actions.

Though it doesn't have the happy ending most young people expect, *Crazy Lady* has a hopeful ending. The reader is left with a sense of empowerment: An individual—even a young person—can make a difference. People can change.

Imagine finding all this in a book that is a terrific read!

"But what about that offensive language?" The letter-writing parents ask disapprovingly.

Well, what about it? Would these parents forbid their children to leave the house for fear they might see "bad words" scrawled on the sidewalk or hear a teammate break the third commandment? Most children have an excellent sense of what words are off limits in their family, and coming across such words in print is unlikely to prompt a child to use them. But their eyes might widen, and they might ask—as indeed some children have—why the author wrote them.

Conly is not the first writer of children's literature who has been challenged for the language her characters use. In addition to what sometimes appears to be an organized effort to ferret out and object to the occasional *damn* or *hell*, individual parents sometimes make an issue of words they deem politically incorrect. To paraphrase the children's question, why, then, do writers use these words?

I think it's because they have to. Writers of both contemporary and historical fiction create in their books a microcosm of the real world, often choosing to focus on a specific rather than a generic setting. The characters and their speech must be appropriate to this setting—both the place and the time.

We disclose a lot about ourselves the minute we open our mouths. An accent or regional dialect may hint at where we're from. Syntax and vocabulary give a clue to our educational background. Our tone of voice suggests our emotional state. And of course, what we say gives the listener a good indication of our personality, character, and values. It works the same way for the characters a writer creates: The minute they open their mouths, the reader becomes aware of a host of attributes. And before long, the reader senses whether the characters are authentic, whether individually and collectively their words are congruent with their actions.

When Vernon, the narrator, describes the neighbors' surprise that the stingy storekeeper donated half a ham to be raffled off at the carnival, he says, "People's chins just about fell down to their knees." Now, that's authentic. Later, as Vernon walks away from an unpleasant encounter with a neighbor he says, "She's a bitch," and that's authentic, too.

Near the end of the story, Vernon is sure it's his fault Ronald's teacher found out that Maxine is an alcoholic, but Miss Annie quickly straightens him out: "Nonsense. Maxine is an adult, and she's responsible for her own behavior. You have to understand that." Here, you're listening to the authentic voice of a retired schoolteacher.

The storekeeper, after relating what Maxine had said to him that day, asks Vernon, "Can you believe that? She's got a bill as long as history, but she don't mind telling me where to go." I can see him standing there, shaking his head as he turns away.

Drunk and angry, Maxine yells, "Get out of my way, you goddamn busybody!" And then she hollers, "Ronald and I don't need anybody's charity!" Both her behavior and her words are very much in character. (Can you imagine her saying "*doggone* busybody"?) Like the neighbors who witness this scene at the carnival, most readers will focus on the devastating effect Maxine's words have on Vernon, who has worked so hard to make the fund-raiser a success, rather than on the profanity.

I wonder if any of the parents who wrote to Jane Leslie Conly, pointing out the exact location of words they found objectionable, actually read her book? Really *read* it, as opposed to scanning it for words they find unacceptable? My bet is that they didn't. Had they read it, these parents might have decided to remind their children of the family's standards for language, but I doubt that they would have forbidden them to read *Crazy Lady*—much less asked that it be made unavailable to other people's children.

A child who isn't allowed to read *Crazy Lady* will not only miss "a good read" but will also miss the chance to see another young person overcome difficulties and clarify his values. It is hard for me to believe that parents would knowingly and deliberately exclude their children from such an experience.

## Work Cited

Conly, Jane Leslie. *Crazy Lady*. New York: HarperCollins, 1993.

# Keep *Cujo* Unleashed

## John R. Woznicki

Suffering is a part of being human, and the first of three epigrams to Stephen King's *Cujo*, culled from W. H. Auden's poem "Musée des Beaux Arts," makes this point clear:

> About suffering they were never wrong,
> The Old Masters: how well they understood
> Its human position; how it takes place
> While someone is eating or opening a window or just walking dully around. . .

The existence of everyday suffering is obvious. All we have to do is turn on the evening news or open the newspaper and we are confronted with it. It would seem that we no longer need those "Old Masters," those artists who, throughout history, have demonstrated that to be human is to suffer.

Though we may have, perhaps, praised our artists and listened, in a cursory fashion, to what they have had to say, we perhaps haven't paid attention to them as we should have. Perhaps art has been replaced in our culture by other vehicles of communication. We must remember, however, that there *is* a difference between the rendering of an idea through art and an objective depiction of it through, say, the media or, even more objectively, experiencing it firsthand through our own understanding of it. Artists are people who possess special insight to what we all see. They do not merely replicate reality, but they comment on it. Artists are our translators of life, revealing to us what sense to make of what we call reality.

Stephen King is an artist who requires our closer attention. *Cujo* is not mere replication of the reality that we already know; it is not just about the suffering we inevitably face. It is not a book that is gratuitously violent, as it has been claimed to be. *Cujo* concerns our response to suffering and reveals, as many artistic works do, the "beast within us."[1] We are the authors of our own suffering because we choose to remain, struggle to maintain, what Ihab Hassan calls our "radical innocence." Hassan tells us "at bottom,

126

all innocence amounts to a denial of death. . . . it is, therefore, a radical plea for the Self. The plea can be holy or demonic; the self is really the same" (325). We see ourselves as innocent and maintain our sense of self in this innocent state. King recognizes this, and believes our "innocent" pleas for self, whether holy or demonic, to be detrimental. As artist he wishes to make us see that our maintenance of innocence and ignorance of our mortality contribute greatly to our suffering. This is a necessary lesson for the young, those truly innocent, those not yet conditioned to live life ignorant of their mortality. And for the old, the need is for a reinitiation to an idea the "Old Masters" have made known to us. This is why *Cujo* should continue to be published and read by all.

It is in the third epigram of the book that King hints of this important theme of our response to suffering, a quote made by one of the peripheral characters of *Cujo*, the Sharp Cereal Professor; "Nope, nothing wrong here." And that response, one of ignorance, is summed up in the quote. As we have ignored our artists, we humans ignore suffering in every way—the causes of it, the consequences of it. In fact, it is our response to our suffering that plays a part in its continuation. King demonstrates that there are harmful mechanisms that we have in place to keep us ignorant of our suffering, external or social ones such as materialism, internal ones such as our egoism, mechanisms that create and condition us to deal ineffectively with the inevitable suffering and fear that comes with being mortal.

This inevitable suffering in our "fragile world" (King 122) is presented in *Cujo* in many ways. It is present in things outside and within our control: from the cerebral palsy that kills Roger's child to the lead paint on McDonald's giveaway glasses slowly poisoning a nation (35, 97). The manufacturers, advertisers, media members, and government officials are implicated in keeping us unaware of this pain. The Sharp Cereal Company, the "mildly authoritative, big bad wolf" (27, 23), creates suffering, hysteria, and paranoia in the Red Raspberry Zinger red dye scare (31) while Roger and Vic, the advertisers, seek damage control by filling our minds with crud and trivia (194). At novel's end the newspapers and tabloids misreport and sensationalize what happens at Castle Rock while the town officials misinform and fabricate the causes for Cujo's rampage (313). The end result is "fright, pain, and confusion" (78). Ours is a world where our attempt to escape suffering is misguided. We, in turn, become scared of everything: of our relationships, of maintaining physical and mental health, of fitting into and finding a place in society. The world becomes "a crazy quilt of sense and impression" (117), a virtual hell that we must assume responsibility for making sense of.

To make sense of it King employs the figure of Cujo and his disease as a metaphor relating to our situations. Cujo has rabies, a disease of the central nervous system that is fatal if untreated, one that slowly breaks down its victim at the core of its being. It is a disease that is hidden, whose symptoms are often ignored or unrecognized but are yet unmistakable. It is this ignorance of symptoms that eventually leads to death, or at the very least, a painful series of treatments to combat the disease. Cujo's rabies, a disease that is not entirely understood by human physicians, is a metaphor for what may eventually destroy us if they go on unrecognized: our fears and sufferings.

When King tells us that Cujo's "a bright dog, as dogs went" (126), we are meant to confuse Cujo and his human counterparts. King intentionally blurs the division between animal and human. There is much in a name and Cujo is named, though unintentionally, after a real person: William Wolf (in the surname, we find the shaping of this metaphor) who was a member of the Symbionese Liberation Army (Symbionese standing for symbiosis, a coming together, as Cujo melds into the human). Cujo is also a St. Bernard, named after another human, St. Bernard of Clairvaux, a twelfth-century religious figure who sought to restore order in his society through a setting down of a "Rules of Order," contending with, as religions do, the mysteries of life and providing action for confronting them. But as we will come to find in this work, order cannot be had merely by wishing for it or by scripting it because there are too many questions that are left unanswered, questions left as a result of our imperfect methods of understanding life.

These eternal questions involved in what it is to be, questions such as "Who am I?" "Why are we here?" "Why do bad things happen to good people?" are central to the overall theme and summarized in this book's emblem of the question mark. Cujo's maiming by rabid bats left a question mark–shaped scar on his muzzle. This matches Donna Trenton's question mark–shaped birthmark, located above her pubic area, that Donna's lover, Steve Kemp, uses to identify her to Donna's husband, Vic, when Steve reveals to Vic their affair. The shared marks again blur the division between dog and human and, like Cujo's, Donna's mark illustrates our affliction of the hidden disorder. Yet unlike Cujo, we are marked at birth by this hidden "disease," perhaps reflective of that knowledge (supposedly) gained after the fall of humankind, knowledge of our own mortality that we ultimately refuse to face.

The juxtaposition of how Cujo, as animal, deals with his disorder and how we, as humans, deal with ours is made evident. Cujo must learn to deal with pain; but as a lower form of animal, his coping mechanisms involve escape and, ultimately, when escape is not an option, violence. Yet as humans we are not far from how Cujo reacts, creating highly sophisticated forms of those same base responses, escape and violence, instead of using our sophistication to respond in a different, more effective manner. We find, then, as Cujo becomes the monster that we blame as the cause for our problems, that he actually is the manifestation of our problems and our inability to deal with them. And thus, we have a seemingly unending paradox. From the common perspective, Cujo is representative of the bogeyman whose evil causes us misery. Yet we find this representation is one created, psychologically perhaps, as a way to compensate or to transfer our deep-seated intelligence that we are in fact what is evil. People can be monsters too, and this self-perpetuating cycle of misery and suffering and our inability to answer life's questions and cope with our mortality make us forget our humanity and allow what we consider real evil, the bogeymen, to continue to exist. The rest of the book can be seen as a case study to prove this, reflecting the way people are monsters, their reasons for it, and their responses and struggles with this knowledge.

King best demonstrates this through his characters, from major characters such as Vic and Donna Trenton to minor characters such as George Meara. In fact, it is King's range of characters that makes this a most interesting work: each character, faced with some sort of internal and/or external suffering, embodies a particular degree of coping with their "radical innocence," demonstrating the many ways we (mis)manage life's pain. Each of the characters demonstrates this as each ignores Cujo and his exhibited symptoms. The degrees of management/response to the situation involving Cujo express the degrees of our humanity, with some responses more sophisticated and some more base or biological. These responses range from:

Planned ignorance/denial
Relinquishment to fate/luck
"Overt escape" (sex, drugs, alcohol, humor)
"Covert escape" (status, hard work, roles such as masculinity,
    femininity, nostalgia)
Institutional escape (logic/education/religion)
Violence
Scapegoating

These responses are ordered intentionally in this way, as they progress from simple to complex, then back, seemingly, to simple. As some of King's characters are capable only of a simple response, more developed characters such as Vic and Donna progress through a variety of these responses. As each response fails them, they are led further and further away from humanity and back toward a state of being we would consider uncivilized.

George Meara best represents our most base, simple response: our wish to flat-out deny our mortality and ignore our problems. George Meara fears death. His flatulence is a symptom of something wrong deep inside, that which is hidden from our main sense (in this case, sight), but recognizable by other senses (like the monster in Tad's closet that is ignored; it is the smell, like the smell of flatulence, that is passed off by the Trentons as odd but ultimately trivial). Meara's hidden disease, perhaps "the big C" (202), is something so frightening to us, we can't even name it; it is taboo to say the word "cancer." George's reaction is to ignore the symptoms because they might reveal the truth.

Gary Pervier, whose name suggests perversion or distortion from the norm, is a former war hero who has suffered a scrotum injury.[2] Gary's inability to maintain erections suggests his failure to connect and find a place in his society; with the war over, he is no longer any use to anyone. Unable to father children, unappreciated by a society he served in war, and, therefore, uninspired to contribute anything of use, Gary retreats. In his loneliness, without direction or purpose afforded to him by family or work, he suffers, and relinquishes himself to this fate. To escape this suffering, he drinks, creating an alcoholic world of misery filled mostly with hatred, occasions of obscene humor,[3] and indifference, a world inhabited by one.

Steve Kemp is much like Gary; alone, a drifter, denied entry into the larger community. Like Gary, Steve has once had a role in his society, in this case as "artist," but his art is no longer of use. Steve is a poet in an age that has rejected poetry, an age where words are more useful to sell products than to inspire feeling, an age that has ironically forgotten that art is to offer us insight, to make us understand something we have either ignored, forgotten, or have never considered. Rendered artistically impotent, Steve's pen becomes his penis, seeking validation in a world that gives him none. He escapes his identity crisis by having sex (51) while continuing to protect and promote the more socially acceptable role of artist—the traveling poet, the rebel, the do-gooder, the virile, attractive, and charming man, one confident and unquestioned in this ability, the powerful man—a role with its associated images that is at once self-created and aided by society. (Isn't Steve's type that which we find as the leading man in Hollywood and on the cover of *GQ*?)

When Donna threatens this role by denying Steve access to her sexually, he takes this as a personal affront to his ability to fulfill this role. As he loses his substitute path toward establishing identity through sex, as Donna exposes his image as a fraud, Steve's response is violence. He trashes her "home" (208), the place where identity is established and progeny and legacy sustained, and justifies and rationalizes his actions with the logic used to sustain his own role as rebel, as "masculine man" (211).[4] He exerts power by writing Vic a letter about the affair (53), and attempts to use fear to manipulate Donna into reestablishing the relationship. Steve is an impotent artist, but as a regular, "base" human he is potent in his shallowness as he strives, as we all do, to make a mark for himself. As he is denied he becomes violent, contemplating rape (204), and the mark that he makes involves a violent act of masturbation. It is as if this leaving of a "legacy" (his semen on Vic and Donna's bed) is a fragment to shore against the ruins[5] of his suffering, his pain of failing to establish home, place, identity, and his failure to cope with the truth that we are fallible (he hates to lose at tennis) and that eventually we will die. As we usually leave offspring to compensate for this, to attempt to establish a place on this earth, to pass on our genes (as there is a biological imperative to do so), to "endeavor in history" (Hassan 328), Steve cannot, as he is a drifter with no ties to family or no outlet to leave progeny. His seed is spent, unsown.

Joe Camber, however, has progeny to whom to leave his legacy. Camber (meaning bent in the middle, another form of distortion) is a self-described hardworking auto mechanic; his role might be said to be the hardworking, responsible father and husband. Yet for all his hard work, there is dissatisfaction in Joe's life. Joe is frustrated because he feels there is no end to the limit of his responsibilities; he feels as if he can never do enough. His outlet for the frustration he feels (due to his wife Charity's expectations for them to have a "better" life in terms of class status) is violence toward his wife and the occasional alcoholic binge. Mistrust, hatred, and suspicion of others unlike him is the result of this frustration, and he shares Gary's fear of being deemed useless by his society. Joe enjoys the pain he inflicts on Charity,[6] demonstrating how he (we) finds solace for suffering in the pain of others, perhaps giving reason why humans indulge in the macabre and are addicted to violence. Joe attempts to continue Charity's pain and also futilely preserve what little sense of self he has in the form of a legacy, by passing this suspicion of others to his son Brett, who, at age ten, is very impressionable and serves to the reader as a symbol of the future.

Joe's wife Charity attempts to prevent Joe's passing on of his "legacy" by, at first, relying on luck. Charity, beaten into submission by Joe, fears him. She purchases a weekly lottery ticket in order to raise enough money so that she and her son may escape Joe and the life to which he has doomed them.[7] Charity's escape is to her sister Holly's house in Connecticut. Holly has succeeded in escaping Maine and its inherent poverty for those born there (compared with those wealthy who vacation there) by marrying a man who works hard to become a lawyer. Contrasted against Joe's method of "hard work," Charity wishes Brett to see how those with money and status live. Using Holly's family as a model for Brett, she wishes him to absorb strong middle-class values of hard work that will lead to success. Along with those values come "better" ways of living, including inherited social graces (she hates that her husband eats with his hat on). Brett's proposed escape into a better life is one that follows the path of what we would call the American Dream, but we readers see that it is a life that is no better than Joe's. Hatred and mistrust are still a part of this life, as it is directed to those of lower status. So is personal self-absorption that immobilizes and deadens the life of the subject that leads us into addiction; for Joe violence and alcoholism, for Holly ostentatious behavior, greed, and materialism. Products become more important than humans.

Yet Charity believes her escape to Holly's "soundproof" (175) house will give Brett needed "time and perspective" so that he may see the "right" path to take in his future—attending college, finding contentment and happiness in life, alleviating all of the fears that Charity has to suffer in hers. This idea of "time" and "perspective" is one that Vic Trenton has also, as he requires time and perspective to contemplate the state of his marriage after he learns of his wife's affair. Yet we find that time and perspective do not change the subject's mode of thinking; at the end of the story Charity still believes that Brett's best chance to live a misery-free existence is to attend college. Her escape into Holly's world is an escape to a world that is "poor on the inside" (221), one where goods attempt to fill the gaps left by self-knowledge. We understand this as Charity, to protect their trip to Connecticut, becomes responsible for preventing Brett from checking on Cujo in the early stage of his illness. Once there, she ignores Brett's requests to have someone check on Cujo. In her state of obsession to keep Brett in Connecticut, she hides the truth from Brett about Alva, a neighbor, going to see Cujo, completely removing herself and her son, in the name of maternal protection, from the situation at Castle Rock.

Vic Trenton also has a son to protect, Tad Trenton, age four, another impressionable symbol of the future. Vic seemingly has less trouble than Joe Camber fulfilling the role of hardworking, responsible father and husband, but his role is expanded for the reader, that of a solidly middle-class, respected (in a respectable profession) twentieth-century enlightened man whose dependence on knowledge and "efficiency" is highlighted to demonstrate how this dependency is used to quell our fears and relieve our feelings of emptiness. In spite of his success, Vic must suffer nevertheless—first his wife's infidelity and then the death of his son.

When faced with the knowledge of the affair, Vic's first impulse, like

Joe's and Steve's, is that of violence. For Vic, it would have been pleasurable to deal with his anger using violence, an anger that had its source in his futile attempt to understand *why* Donna chose to have an affair. Instead of violence and instead of having the option of losing himself in his pain and relieving it through crying, [8] Vic's role of twentieth-century man who takes it upon himself to figure out all things and provide and produce all answers (the rational man) leads him to figure out Donna's affair and why Steve wrote the note. Of course, he can't; it perplexes him, confuses him, leads him astray, yet he continually adheres to the belief that he "must figure this out" until he is too tired, too impotent to do anything. When he briefly interrupts his quest for the logical truth behind the affair with his question, "d[oes] it make any difference?" (83), he interrupts our analysis of his behavior. This question is meant to be seen as rhetorical by us; for us, the answer is no. Vic's unending pursuit for answers using logic, will never make any difference. It is the same logic that is "God" (278) for Andy Masen, our Andy Griffith–Perry Mason investigator who rises from hometown obscurity and poverty to become a success, yet whose logic has him searching in the wrong place when looking for the missing Donna Trenton. It is this logic that is constructed to actually hide the underlying truth of our mortality, as we therefore ignore that which is meaningful. Logic doesn't solve or account for life's "dead ends" (294-295), the things that we can't make sense of or understand.

It is the same logic perpetuated by the same role of rational man that has Vic ignore his son's pleas that there is something lurking underneath their supposedly happy lives—that there is a monster in the closet. After Donna's attempt at psychology and discipline fails (61), Vic's impulse is to give Tad a panacea, which must be seen as a self-created delusion. He creates what is called "The Monster Catechism" (59-60); he writes words that can be used to wish this latent fear away.[9] It is important to note that in this case these are words of the human and not God—God is dead in the twentieth century and impotent since Tad, perceptive in his uninitiated state, reminds us that "God doesn't believe in monsters, [and] prayers [are] useless" (60). Yet Tad believes in the catechism that his father creates; he carries it around in talismanic fashion. Even when his mother, Donna, yells at Tad, Tad touches this catechism for comfort, as one would fondle rosary beads. Yet when faced with the reality of Cujo and what he represents, the talisman fails. Vic's attempts at logic, as a male, are dumbfounded, providing him with no clue as to the reality of his situation. He becomes too self-absorbed in his own pain from Donna's infidelity and, in his dependency on logic, too tied to his logic to do anything about it, too tied to his responsibilities of his advertising business. This makes him impotent, forcing him to arrive too late to save his son, providing him with ineffective beliefs, generating ineffective catechisms that fail.

Donna Trenton also fails to save her son and is the character who represents a culmination of all of the others' fears and responses to those fears. Donna succumbs to what is called a "fatalistic apathy" (90) much like Gary. As a transplanted New Yorker in Maine, she finds herself suffering a feeling of not fitting in. She is lonely, and those things that give her a sense of self begin to escape her. As a woman her role is vague in her society, and does not provide her ballast in carving out an identity. Donna stood by and watched as she lost those shallow things for which society values her: her looks, her youth. Even the weighty role as mother vanishes as her son gets older and prepares to leave the house for school and, then, for good. To attack this feeling of worthlessness, of female emptiness as she calls it, she has an affair, finding validation in sex, like Steve, turning nostalgically to her youth. She's thrilled by the fear of getting caught (40), and this energizes her for a short period but ultimately does not satisfy her.[10]

When faced with the prospect of defending her son against Cujo, her maternal instinct, like Charity's, succumbs to ineffective strategies. She, too, is ignorant of Cujo's disease, yet like Brett, she intuits something is wrong, though her intuition is misdirected as she attributes this fear to Joe Camber. Like her husband, she also attempts to rationalize the monster in the closet, approaching it logically: "She believed in things that she could see and touch" (213). Donna also is a person of the rational age, college educated, and it is this rationality that provokes her stubborn refusal and leads her to make the wrong decisions. Her decisions to take the car to Camber's, to take Tad along, to exit the car while Cujo lay await, are all amiss and all driven by "*ideé fixe*" (224), the fixed idea of life to which we unwaveringly adhere, therefore debilitating ourselves because we can't escape the fixed idea. We create our own psychological inability to overcome obstacles.

Donna's stoicism, as she represents a modern-day knight templar, fails too. It is only when Donna loses all civility and rationality, becoming the most base of beings, and allows vengeance to spur on a final, violent, anticlimatic attack on a dog whose life and path of destruction had already run its course (301), that she "defeats" Cujo, blaming the dog for Tad's death of heat exhaustion in some sort of a violent form of scapegoating, much as Vic blamed Steve for Donna's disappearance and his inability to save her. Though violence and scapegoating are the final elements of response that we encounter in this book, the result, in the end, is the same: the loss of our humanity and loss of our innocence. There is no more opportunity for Tad's catechism, no more chance for Tad to play his meditation game (128), no more possibility for the automatic response, the constructed ritual, the catechism, no more option to understand or put things in order.

If there were any hope to escape this pattern of behavior, our "*ideé fixe*," it would be represented in the character of Brett Camber, the remaining progeny. Through the novel, Brett is continually caught between Charity and Joe, exhibiting qualities of both parents but, more important, at the end he is a character caught between the mind and body, the mental and physical, learned behavior and base instinct. He is a character at Hassan's stage of initiation, as evidenced by his sleepwalking (189). With Joe gone, a victim of the dog, he will ultimately take on his mother's "perspective" in "time," accepting her advice to attend college and the new mixed-breed puppy as a gift, a dog appropriately named Willie, as in Willie Wolfe, the SLA member for whom Cujo was initially named. The cycle perpetuates, the suffering is constant, and with Brett there is no hope for change; the cave where Cujo developed the disease is never discovered (318).

The only hope there can be is for a complete revolution, the same kind of total change of social thought that the SLA advocated.[11] King, by making Cujo the agent of realization and connecting him by name to SLA, does not call for a violent revolution but for us, through the metaphor of Cujo, to recognize the hidden symptoms of our suffering. We must change our adopted phrase of the Sharp Cereal Professor—"nope, nothing wrong here"—to an apology. To apologize is to recognize our failure, our fragility, and our ultimate fallibility. We must discontinue hiding and escaping this truth, giving our planned, constructed ignorance a decent burial, a daylight burial (70-71)—out in the open where we can see it, acknowledge it, and accept it. This also means discontinuing our hiding behind the veil of censorship—for those people who want to censor this book, censor any or all books, have this same inclination to "bury the b[astard]. . ." (163), or in this case, bury the book. That which we do not confront we will sublimate to our subconscious (in midnight burials, not daylight ones); therefore we will continue to create our own demons and suffer the subsequent nightmares that will escape to the surface.

If King's words, as art, are the "anti-catechism" to which individuals need to be exposed in order to recognize their fallibility, perhaps the individual must choose, not a censorship board bent on hiding things for us, to take the bitter medicine (164) and face his truth. Yes, King's book is a tank that he is driving "right the fuck over us" like Vic and Roger's ad (165); for in novel writing, just as in advertising, "people want to believe . . . people sell themselves" (162). King believes that what he writes is reality, the horror of our reality, not some piece of glamorized fiction; King makes it known in *his* story that the circumstances and responses are not fictionalized: "In a book, someone would have come" (165). This book tells of a "curiously scaled down situation" (215), a microcosm of life, that exposes, in a way much preferred to the SLA's method, the "lie . . . [that] the world was full of monsters and they were all allowed to bite the innocent and unwary" (309). By reading King, we have been initiated. Being exposed to others' perspectives, through literature, we have the ability as individuals to escape the conventions and circumstances that confine us and prevent us from seeing our reality for how it is. No longer do we have to accept the traditional stories and explanations, for they can be lies, illusions; nor do we have to remain ignorant or adopt ideologies just because others have; no longer do we need to have our actions directed or our behavior controlled. We should be in control of the authorship of our own lives. Brett, unfortunately, cannot, freely of his will, act on his brief insight and accepts the traditional, the confined, the censored—what his mother tells him. Learning from Brett's error, we have the unique opportunity to see our way out of this design. Censorship is a crime against insight and against our free will. Keep *Cujo* unleashed.

## Notes

[1]One may be reminded of Henry James's "The Beast in the Jungle," whose character John Marcher comes to realize that the "evil" from which he suffers is within.
[2]á la Jake Barnes of Hemingway's *The Sun Also Rises*.
[3]There is a correlation between Gary's proclivity to obscene humor and the response of the deliverymen after meeting and successfully escaping the rabid Cujo (76); "black" humor is a mechanism to deal with fear.
[4]It is important to note that while he trashes the house, no one hears or notices (211), signifying the ignorance of middle-class suburbia.
[5]See T. S. Eliot's poem "The Waste Land" for artistic treatment of this theme.
[6]Evidenced not only when Joe physically abuses Charity, but also when he initially denies her a visit to her sister, making her beg to obtain permission.
[7]King speaks here, through Charity's remembrance of the Dylan Thomas poem that "had been something about moving through the dooms of love" (119), of another way that we condemn ourselves to suffering, of how our constructed ideas of love doom us to a life of misery.
[8]As Vic admits "at seventeen it was easier to cry, easier to bleed" (80).
[9]King obviously attacks both religion's and our own propensity to alleviate our fears of life by providing easy answers for the mysteries of humanity.
[10]King's use of obscene sexual references is necessary to show how distant

and unattached emotionally the relationship was and how unsatisfying it was to calm her fears of worthlessness.

[11] The SLA wished for an overthrow of adopted bourgeois views for the mutual benefit of all.

## Works Cited

Hassan, Ihab. *Radical Innocence: Studies in the Contemporary American Novel*. Princeton, N.J.: Princeton University Press, 1961.

King, Stephen. *Cujo*. New York: Viking Press, 1981.

# Examining the Power of *Curses, Hexes, & Spells*

## Nicholas J. Karolides

The book "contains satanic themes"; "it is a virtual 'how to' manual on demon worship." It should be removed from elementary school libraries "because witchcraft is a 'religion' and the First Amendment bars the teaching of religion in schools" (Doyle 25); it promotes the "occult and destroy[s] traditional morals and values" (PFAW 53). These are examples of the concerns raised against Daniel Cohen's *Curses, Hexes, & Spells* by challengers.

Censors' requests for the removal of this information text from libraries have met with success and failure. In Claxton, Tennessee, it was placed on restricted access in the elementary school library. It was removed from the libraries—elementary, middle, junior high, or high school,—of Howard County, Maryland; Cleveland; Oklahoma; Wichita Falls, Texas; and Detroit, Michigan, the last in accordance with a directive from a school administrator, who bypassed the district complaint procedure (PFAW 54). In contrast, the book was retained in the Brunswick, Maryland, middle school library as a result of a school review committee's recommendation, which was approved by the superintendent and school board (PFAW 53).

These are some of the challenges and outcomes. What, indeed, are the nature and content of *Curses, Hexes, & Spells*? A cursory examination of it reveals it to be an information book, five of its seven chapters using the word "curse" or "accursed"—"The Old Family Curse" and "Accursed Places"— in their titles. The last two are titled "Black Magic" and "Amulets and Talismans." There are several illustrations: a 1587 woodcut of Adam and Eve, nude, with the Tree of Knowledge represented as Death; a painting of the discovery at sea of the mysteriously abandoned *Mary Celeste*—a true event; an illustration of Macbeth and the three witches from an early eighteenth-century edition of Shakespeare's works; and photographs of Yvonne of the School of Wicca, Salem, Missouri, demonstrating a "cross not my path" spell. The text concludes with "suggestions for Further Reading."

# Curses

Family curses are illustrated against the backdrop of Cohen's opening sentences: "Our love of the weird and horrible is nothing new. Throughout history people have been fascinated by grisly stories—the ghastlier they were the better people seemed to like them" (7). The examples initiate with the "Curse on the House of Atreus," a cycle of mythic stories passed by word of mouth from generation to generation, which became the source of three dramas, the *Oresteia*, written by the fifth-century tragic poet Aeschylus. Atreus is cursed by his brother, Thyestes, who had been deceived by Atreus into eating his own son's flesh (an act of revenge by Atreus because Thyestes had taken his wife as his mistress). Atreus was murdered by his brother's son; Menelaos and Agamemnon, his sons; and then Agamemnon's children, Electra and Orestes, were affected by the curse.

Within the mythological elements, Cohen explains, is the story of a powerful and barbaric family.

> The members of the House of Atreus killed one another regularly, not an uncommon practice in a warrior society, but their arrogance and brutality were so great that they shocked even their violence-prone contemporaries. People must have assumed that they also offended the gods or transgressed the laws of nature and were therefore fated to suffer. (14)

The ancient Greeks, strong believers in fate, assessed the curse as a supernatural or divine force beyond human control.

Two real-world family curses are those associated with the noble Habsburg family, which rose from relative obscurity to 900 years of dominance in pre–World War I Europe, its members being rulers of most of Europe at one time or another. The curse was placed, according to Hans Holzer, author of *The Habsburg Curse*, by a girl who had been raped by a Habsburg duke in the thirteenth century. Among the better-known "victims" are Queen of France Marie Antoinette, beheaded during the French Revolution; Archduke Maximilian, executed in 1867 by rebels after his plans to establish an "empire" in Mexico miscarried; and Crown Prince Franz Ferdinand of the Austro-Hungarian empire, assassinated in Sarajevo by Serbian nationalists.

The Kennedy family of the United States is identified with the family-curse tradition. In addition to the assassination of President John F. Kennedy in 1963 and Senator Robert Kennedy in 1968, their older brother, Joseph, Jr., died during World War II. The youngest Kennedy son, Edward (Ted), broke his back in a plane crash and was involved in a notorious automobile accident on the island of Chappaquiddick that caused the death of his female passenger. (If the book were published today, Cohen would undoubtedly include the deaths of John F. Kennedy, Jr., his wife, and sister-in-law in an airplane crash.)

The possibility of the existence of such family curses is discussed. Cohen indicates that statistics should be able to offer proof that a supposed cursed family had a considerably higher percentage of unfortunate disasters than chance would allow. However, there is no statistical model, and "with so many variables and unknowns in the equation such a model would be a statistician's nightmare, if not a down-right impossibility" (20). The existence of hereditary diseases accounts for some family-curse tales. Another explanation, specific to the Habsburg and Kennedy families, is that both families lived in violent times and places, and persons in high places are likely victims in politically turbulent times. It is also likely, Cohen explains, that commoners also have like and frequent mishaps, but we do not hear about them, so that those that happen to noble and rich families seem to be caused by the supernatural agency of a curse.

The chapters "Accursed Creatures" and "Accursed Places" represent, it seems, studies in contrasts, the former emerging historically out of pagan myths and fears of the unknown, the latter developing out of real events.

> Creatures of one sort or another figure prominently in accounts of super-natural evil. Some species possess reputations for evil and were believed to have been specially cursed. Others, like the fictional hound of the Baskervilles, are agents of curses. Still others like the black cat that crosses your path are omens of evil to come.
>
> Of all the world's creatures, the one that has most universally been regarded with fear and loathing is the snake. The fact that the venom of many snakes is poisonous has not helped their reputation, but mankind's attitude toward the serpent seems more visceral than reasoned. (31)

Cohen traces the history of such creatures: the snake, dragon, apes and monkeys, cats, bats, and goats. Several emerge out of ancient mythology, the snake-dragon for example, which is further viewed in the Old Testament as a "supreme symbol of evil, an undying enemy of the human race" (31) and becomes Satan himself. Cats were worshiped by the ancient Egyptians as divine; living cats were prized by their owners above all other possessions. In contrast, the cat became a Christian demon and was associated with witchcraft since the Middle Ages. "Usually the cat was treated as a familiar. A familiar is a demon or other form of evil spirit sent by Satan to aid the witch in her evil deeds" (37-38).

However, the focus of "Accursed Places" is on real mystery stories about a place, for example, the so-called Bermuda Triangle, and a jinxed ship, the *Mary Celeste*. Their stories are told because they are so well documented, giving us "an unparalleled close-up look at how curse legends might get started and why they are often so widely believed" (49). The disappearances within the triangle of a group of five TBF Avenger torpedo bombers on December 5, 1945, and of a large Martin Mariner flying boat soon thereafter are recounted, these incidents apparently initiating the legend. Cohen cites a dozen other events as early as 1866 and as recent as 1963, involving the inexplicable disappearance of both planes and ships that reinforce the idea of an accursed place. He also identifies several theories that have been promulgated as explanations for the disappearances. His interpretation of this accursed-place legend is revealing: In the mid-1960s popular articles were being published.

> Suddenly what had been a string of strange, but apparently unconnected tragedies were lumped together and given an identifiable title. The mystery which had been attached to each individual case had been fused into the much larger mystery of the place itself. In the latter half of the twentieth century we have created for ourselves a legend of an accursed place as strong as that which medieval peasants attached to gloomy forests or ruined castles. (57)

Hounded by one disaster after another, beginning before her maiden voyage, the *Mary Celeste*, originally named *Amazon*, early on was deemed a jinxed or cursed ship. Her notoriety was assured, however, by her being discovered mid-Atlantic Ocean, six hundred miles off the coast of Portugal, adrift and abandoned.

> The crew had apparently left in the yawl, a small boat carried by the larger ship. There was every indication that they had left in a hurry. All their personal possessions were still on board. The tales of plates still being set on the table and a fire still burning in the galley are exaggerations, but the truth is hardly less surprising. (64)

Cohen surmises that the "bad luck" of the *Amazon-Mary Celeste*, aside from the unexplained disappearance of its captain, his wife and child, and the crew, none of whom were ever found, "might simply be a string of unhappy coincidences" (comparable to hundreds of other ships). He offers several theories that have been proposed to explain the disappearance of the ship's personnel: murder at the hands of the crew, which had reported finding her adrift; murder of the captain by the crew under the influence of the cargo of commercial alcohol; escaping vapors of the alcohol causing a minor explosion that led to the abandonment; eating bread contaminated by fungus ergot that can damage the nervous system, leading to madness and the irrational abandonment; and the surfacing near the ship of a sea monster that had picked off the occupants with its tentacles or had frightened them into abandoning the ship. Current explanations refer to "some sort of mysterious force," (67), including a rumor of flying saucer responsibility.

## Spells and Hexes

The chapter "Black Magic" provides a very brief history of the belief and practices emanating from them.

> During the Middle Ages the Church officially made no distinction between what we now call white magic, or helpful magic, and black magic, or harmful magic. All magic was presumed to be accomplished with the aid of the Devil or lesser demons. Therefore, by definition, all magic was evil, since it involved invoking the powers of evil. In the orthodox view the witch who concocted a potion meant to cure a fever was just as bad as the witch who brewed a potion meant to cause a fever. Indeed, some Church authorities inclined toward the view that good witches were more dangerous than bad ones. Because their real evil—dealing with the Devil—was hidden by their benign magic, they could more easily lead men astray. Thus deceived, a man might endanger his immortal soul. A witch who placed a curse on an individual that caused him to die would only have harmed his body. (95-96)

Despite this official church attitude, Christian elements were added to various spells by medieval Europeans; they believed in magic but were believing Christians. "Adaptation of Christian rituals would seem to make any spell more powerful, even one involving the Devil" (102).

Cohen defines several types of magic—divination: imitative magic; the so-called voodoo doll; and sympathetic magic. He also details several spells, giving only the highlights, and the magician's necessary preparations for conducting spells. (It is doubtless that this segment led to the challenge that the text was a virtual "how to" manual.) Cohen insists on the difficulty of conducting spells and their complicated nature, a point illustrated by the text's details. He asserts, however, that rituals can fail and the magician can find many reasons why, from impure ingredients to a flaw in the performance. If the victim does suffer in any way, then "belief in magic is confirmed. One apparent success can wash away the memory of a thousand failures" (109).

Modern practitioners of magic propose that their focus is on the "psychic" side of the practice, that the chants and materials are methods to invoke "psychic" power. Cohen argues: "This modern explanation, however, lacks conviction. A presumed belief in psychic powers is a slender thread upon which to hang all the elaborate paraphernalia and ritual of the Operation of Grand Bewitchment or any other magical spell" (109).

Cohen does acknowledge the psychological power of suggestion, exemplifying the effects of this power in medical situations—the will to live versus resignation to illness, for example.

> Can one say that suggestion is "magic"? Not really. There is an important qualitative difference between this psychological explanation of why spells sometimes have the intended effect and the explanation offered by believers in magic, even the modern psychically-oriented magicians. The magicians see the power of the spell coming directly from the rituals and the implements or from some force that emanates from the body or mind of the magician. The psychologist views things the other way round. He says that the real power of the spell is not in the magician, but in the mind of the victim, and that if one does not believe in magic no spell, no matter how carefully performed, will have any effect. (110-111)

From these quotes and interpretations it is evident that Cohen does not promote the occult. At every turn, he questions it. He offers explanations, in effect rejecting the notion of family curses, refuting such claims by identifying causal factors and citing insufficient statistics. He discredits, in addition, the so-called "presidential curse" by critically questioning the interpretation of statistics, offering a rational view of the "string of dreadful coincidences" (26). Accursed places, also labeled coincidences, gain notoriety when a series of minor mishaps are attached to a spectacular incident, often magnified by rumors and an imaginative press. Magic spells and hexes are similarly doubted and discredited. Cohen's positions clearly counter the attacks on his text. Indeed, it could be argued that *Curses, Hexes, & Spells* might be recommended reading to dispel the fears of the occult—the fears of curses, hexes, and spells.

## Works Cited

Cohen, Daniel. *Curses, Hexes, & Spells*. Philadelphia: Lippincott, 1974.

Doyle, Robert P. *1999 Banned Books Resource Guide*. Chicago: American Library Association, 1999, 25.

People For The American Way. *Attacks on the Freedom to Learn*. Washington, D.C.: People For the American Way, 1990, 53 and 54.

# Defending Children's Schooltime Reading: *Daddy's Roommate* and Heather's Mommies

## Patrick Finnessy

The presidential election of 2000 brought to the surface many conflicting views in American society. Issues of power and partisanship, the obligation to voice an opinion represented through a vote, and the luxury of having these freedoms by living in a democracy were all revealed. The election also showed that America is torn in its values, bringing to light the shades of gray that now permeate our world. Over two hundred years after its writing, America's Constitution and the Bill of Rights were at work like no other time in its history, starting with the First Amendment.

Freedom of expression is guaranteed in this country; however, the Puritans, our first settlers, introduced censorship through their intolerance of the texts of other religions and cultures. Nevertheless, censorship has been around long before our country's founding, since Ashurbanipal, the king of Assyria, created his reference library thousands of years ago. *The Epic of Gilgamesh*, the oldest work of preserved literature, has appeared on censors' "lists" for hundreds of years. Today, books are censored if they are anti-Christian, anti-Semitic, racist, contain swear words, talk about sex as if people really have it, or if the book "promotes" homosexuality. When it appears, censorship, primarily a form of denial and a fear of new ideas, is usually well-intentioned. Bill Granger, *Chicago Tribune* columnist, once wrote, "Censorship always has a good purpose. [It] is easy because if you ban or delete portions of a book rather than try to understand it, you don't have to explain matters you'd rather not discuss" (9). People For the American Way indicates that these well-intentioned, avoiders-of-sensitive-issues censors succeed in 41 percent of their challenges. "Sex" books are a favorite target and, in particular, those that refer to or mention homosexuality or lesbianism.

Since their publication a decade ago, two seminal works on the subject of parents who are gay have appeared on censors' dockets. Like *Gilgamesh*, these stories deal with such universal themes as friendship, loyalty, sexuality, and love. Of the 100 Most Frequently Challenged Books of 1990-2000, the American Library Association indicates that Michael Willhoite's *Daddy's Roommate* holds the number two slot, and Leslea Newman's *Heather Has Two Mommies* appears at number nine.

When the former school chancellor of the New York City public school system, Joe Fernandez, proposed his multicultural Children of the Rainbow Curriculum in the early 1990s, he included *Daddy's Roommate* and *Heather Has Two Mommies* as recommended/suggested reading. The curriculum was an attempt to recognize the various races, groups, and family situations found in New York. The guide included a 443-page report on families, and three paragraphs of the report referred to Dad's roommate and Heather's Moms. Immediately, word came out that America's schoolchildren would be learning about sodomy, and communities of color suggested that gays and lesbians were ruining their multicultural educational vision. The unrestrained anger over the curriculum played out in debates on *Nightline* and *Larry King Live*, the *New York Times*, and *U.S. News and World Report*. The situation called to mind Anita Bryant's 1977 Florida "Save Our Children" campaign and California's 1978 "Briggs Initiative," which would have terminated all gay and/or pro-gay teachers. In 1994, House Speaker Newt Gingrich criticized programs such as the Children of the Rainbow curriculum, suggesting that anyone who used such books as *Daddy's Roommate* or *Heather Has Two Mommies* was counseling students to consider the gay "lifestyle." In 1994, U.S. Senators Robert Smith and Jesse Helms cosponsored a measure denying the federal funds to schools that "implement or carry out a program that has either the purpose or effect of encouraging or supporting homosexuality as a positive lifestyle alternative." These contentious measures were narrowly defeated.

*Daddy's Roommate* is a thirty-two-page book with single lines of copy beneath full-page illustrations created by Willhoite in 1990. The book reveals a story with a young boy, his father, and his father's lover; the text portrays family activities familiar to all families: cleaning the house, shopping, gardening, going to the beach, playing games, fighting, and reconciling. The book shows natural figures filled with real people. The straightforward story starts out: "My Mommy and Daddy got a divorce last year." With over 50 percent of all marriages ending in divorce, this is a realistic beginning. The story contains effectively realized characters with believable actions and statements. The bright, framed watercolor illustrations complement the text while making such "controversial" statements as "Frank (Daddy's roommate) makes *great* peanut butter-and-jelly sandwiches" or "And in the evenings, we sing at the piano." The story presents, perhaps somewhat unrealistically, an extremely understanding mother who tells her little boy, "Being gay is just one more kind of love. And love is the best kind of happiness." While one might pause at the divorced mother's compassion, the author's intent is clear: to show that a boy in a nontraditional family *can* be content. The mother is supportive because it is clearly in the best interest of her child to be supportive. No one in the family, including the stepparent, neglects the child. These are positive traits for the youngster in his formative years. The story ends, "Daddy and his roommate are very happy together. And I'm happy, too!"

As one father who shared the book with his children said, "The father is very involved with his son. He's depicted as a good role model as is the stepparent." The author makes his point: the child has three affirming role models who care for, love, nurture, and support him. As for the two grown men shown sleeping in the same bed together, this shows the honesty of the situation; these are not platonic roommates. Daddy is in bed with the "roommate" not because he and Mommy no longer love one another, but because Daddy feels love for Frank. America, for better or for worse, has progressed since *I Love Lucy* aired and showed the married couple in separate beds. Children are better off when real-life situations are dealt with honestly, with compassion, integrity, and openness. There is nothing sexual about the two men in bed together. Instead, the author is accurately portraying their level of intimacy for one another. Similar in controversy to the Mesopotamian text, *Gilgamesh*, the strengths of this book are also comparable; this is a book about friendship, loyalty, sexuality, and love.

*Daddy's Roommate* placed second on the list of the 100 most frequently challenged children's books in 1999. Michael Willhoite, in 2000, said of the 10-year anniversary of his work, "To my gratification, the nation's librarians have fought like tigers on the book's behalf." This book has been, as the 10-year edition notes, the target of "censorship, burning, theft, defacement, and a well-orchestrated campaign to remove it from libraries." Willhoite states, "The book is still, triumphantly, what I first intended: a mirror in which children of gay parents can see themselves. Yet it has also been used as a tool to educate children in more traditional families about the gay families in their midst" (book jacket).

Considered one of the first—if not the very first—picture books of a young child living with two lesbian mothers, *Heather Has Two Mommies* was written by Leslea Newman and illustrated in soft shades of black and white by Diana Souza. Newman wrote the book at the request of a lesbian mother who was frustrated by the lack of positive stories about alternative families for her daughter. Initially, Newman submitted the manuscript to over fifty publishers and received an equal number of rejections. Ultimately,

Alyson Wonderland, a subsidiary of Alyson Publications, published it.

The book describes Heather's birth into a family that includes Mama Jane, Mama Kate, Gingersnap, the cat, and Midnight, the dog. Throughout the book, all of the characters are happy—like Willhoite's book—an attempt to be a positive book for children. Three-year-old Heather jumps and runs around throughout almost the entire book. The only time "she feels sad" is when she feels she is the only one without a dad—but this only lasts one page: "Molly [the day-care supervisor] picks up Heather and gives her a hug. 'Not everyone has a daddy,' Molly says. 'You have two mommies. That's pretty special.'" Newman sees to it that Heather is immediately scooped up and lovingly affirmed. It is clear that Newman is focusing not on what Heather does not have but on what she does have.

It is when Heather enters day care that she becomes aware that her parents are different from those of her friends. Yet Heather also realizes that each household is unique and special. To highlight this situation, Newman designs the story so that the children in the day care center draw their different families. The result, as shown by five-year-old Dana Lee Kingsbury's illustrations, reflects America as it really is—pictures of families with two fathers, an adopted brother, a sister in a wheelchair, divorced parents, and stepbrothers and sisters. "Children are an important group to embrace diversity. It's really important for (children) to learn to be respectable human beings" (Wallace 23), says Newman.

*Heather Has Two Mommies*, like *Daddy's Roommate*, reveals a household that is loving, affirming, and nurturing. When Heather asks questions about her home, she is not deceived or given too much information. She is given thoughtful, direct, real explanations about the love the mothers feel for one another and about the process through which she was conceived. Further, there is nothing stereotypical about the two women; there is nothing alarming about their behavior toward the child. Heather sees two human beings who love one another and who keep her safe. The household provides activities that express compassion, support, and trust. These are women who we would want to raise our children because they're good people. Throughout the story, the author makes subtle comments about things like the environment (one character wears a shirt that says "No Nukes") that suggest that these are caring individuals who make a difference in the world; their same-gender status should not be an issue.

While *Heather Has Two Mommies* incited a wave of controversy for having a "gay agenda," it is clear that it is written for educational purposes. Some argue that the book too literally describes Heather's conception and birth. Others suggest that, at 34 pages, it's a little long to sustain the interest of younger readers. This criticism, while perhaps valid, can be dealt with by the instructor in the approach: through discussion and breaking down the reading. *Heather Has Two Mommies* is considered a landmark achievement both culturally and politically. The book is a valuable resource. It is helpful in working with children who need to know that their family composition is healthy. As one professor and gay parent who shared the book with her children wrote, "We have had a copy of *Heather* since the children were born. It is lovingly worn and tattered. It's a frequently requested read at bedtime. Both of our children—a son and a daughter—have a clear idea of how they were conceived and a recognition of lots of different kinds of families" (Cowles).

The author herself cites, "I have gotten a lot of gratitude from lesbian moms" and fan letters from children. The author subsequently wrote other works to educate on issues of parents who are gay. Referring to the Children of the Rainbow curriculum debate, she stated, "The debate left the realm of literature and [became] the defense of lesbian and gay rights to exist on the planet. That's not up for discussion" (Wallace 23).

This is the point of having such books as *Daddy's Roommate* or *Heather Has Two Mommies* in America's schools. Gay parents exist, and this is not up for discussion. Jennings indicates that one out of every three lesbians is a mother, and one out of every five gay men is a father. This is an estimated four to ten million gay parents in the United States, and between six to fourteen million children of gay or lesbian parents are attending America's schools. Sasha Alyson, the founder of Alyson Publications, recognized in the early 1990s the boom in parents who were gay and, thus, saw publishing works such as these as a real boon. Alyson Wonderland became dedicated to providing children of gay and lesbian parents books that reflected the reality of their lives because all children must be taught to acknowledge the positive aspects of each type of household. These books bring validity to many children's lives. David Hawkins suggests, "For every text that comes alive for a child, there must be a live context—both over and above and down underneath the paper and ink. Those sorts of contexts need to come in part, of course, from his experience before he goes to school, and from beyond it, but optimally for all children, and urgently for many, the school itself should provide that context" (5).

To reiterate: these are not books about sex but about families. Children with gay and lesbian parents need to be able to reconcile their love for their mother or father with what they're currently taught in schools and/or in society—that lesbian and gay individuals are evil. These children do not come out of the womb feeling confused; they're taught it through critical condemnations and censorship.

One of the most inane arguments against having these stories went something like this: "Our children will certainly vomit at some point in their lives but is that any reason to teach them about vomit every day and show them pictures of it?" Why do we compare an author's attempt to feature real flesh-and-blood human beings—people who shave, who shop, who share a "little house with the big apple tree in the front yard and the tall grass in the back yard"—with human waste? As the National Council of Teachers of English notes, "Teaching literature to children should be accepted as an integral part of the elementary school curriculum." NCTE asserts that part of teaching involves teaching literature that reveals the presence of gay and lesbian parents, students, and students of gay and lesbian parents because books are to provide students with experiences of real people, places, ideas, and language. Teachers must initiate the habit of connecting words on the page to the world outside (Greenbaum, 17).

These books, criticized for being too didactic and too mature, were written for children ages five and up. While some argue that books with any reference to or suggestion of homosexuality aren't age-appropriate for any school-aged child, Joe, a father who read these books to his two daughters, ages six and nine, thought the books were well suited for his two elementary schoolchildren. "I like the fact that they deal with and talk about the divorce. Some individuals divorce because they're gay, not because they fight or don't like each other." Joe states that this fact provided relief to his daughters, when the books were used to educate them on their real-life situation. He believes that these books are age-appropriate and work *because* of their simplicity, because they're easy to read, and because they don't overload the child with information. When read, both of these books "work" because they present a sense of reality and allow the child to pursue further discussion and ask questions if they're so inclined. It is logical that schools present this type of reading because it isn't always being done in the homes. To educators, it should be clear that a healthy dialogue is important and better than no dialogue at all.

Upon further consideration of the question of age-appropriate discussion of these issues, consider what Greenbaum posits:

> Current common usage of the term appropriate is derived from the concept of 'age-appropriate' behaviors investigated by psychologists, beginning with Jean Piaget. However, recent research refutes the notion that there exists specifically 'age-appropriate' concepts or reading material within a curriculum because a number of teaching experiments have accomplished stage advance by using a variety of instructional methods. Concrete or familiar materials can make very abstract ideas accessible." (16)

Thus, because children of all school ages *are* coming from homes with gay and lesbian parents, children *are* coming from homes where a sibling identifies him/herself as gay or lesbian, children *are* coming from homes where a relative is gay or lesbian, and some children *are* identifying themselves as gay or lesbian, these discussion and readings *are* age-appropriate.

Richard Rodriguez, in his autobiography, notes that a person is not capable of having a "complicated idea" until he has read at least two thousand books because books present individuals with the ability to acquire a point of view. With subtle "selection" of particular works—heterosexual only in nature; with the deliberate exclusion of certain books; with the alteration of books with gay/lesbian/bisexual themes or issues; with the suppression of materials as a result of community pressure, schools distort children's point of view. Certainly, it is the duty of the administrator and the teacher to be aware of the values, feelings, and beliefs of community members, and the community's mores need to be taken into consideration. However, schools also have the responsibility of educating *all* of America's youth and providing them the humanity to understand and accept others, as well as the freedom to weigh ideas and to make their own informed choices. The arbitrary discrimination of excluding works like *Heather Has Two Mommies* and *Daddy's Roommate* is, simply, homophobic.

It is important to create a safer place for children to discuss these sensitive issues. It is also possible to do so without engaging in dialogue about individual, personal beliefs. Children need to have the existence of gay people recognized. They need to hear the vocabulary. They need to be exposed to current events. They need to hear the acknowledgment of authors, historical figures, and others who are gay, lesbian, or bisexual. Why? Because *all* children need to feel safe in schools. Because personal experiences need to be validated. Because teachers do not always know which children have a gay family member or parent. Because teachers do not always know who in their classroom is gay or will grow up to identify him/herself as such. Giving a name to lesbian and gay individuals does not promote homosexuality, nor does it mean teaching about sexual acts. Nor does acknowledging that gay/lesbian/bisexual people exist mean that someone, personally, believes that homosexuality is "okay." It means that you are being honest and open about the world children live in.

President Eisenhower spoke out in the censorship era of the 1950s when he said, "A democracy chronically fearful of new ideas would be a dying democracy." Dealing with sexual orientation in schools is not a new idea, but for many, it is a fearful one. The U.S. Supreme Court has, on numerous occasions, emphasized that "the right to teach, to inquire, to evaluate, and to study is fundamental to a democratic society." Regardless of whether people are comfortable, gays and lesbians comprise part of our democracy. Books have been written to reflect that and to provide greater understanding so that people can inquire, evaluate, and study this fundamental part of our humanity. When the Berlin Wall came down, individuals across the world were excited because East Germany would finally have a voice. The right to argue about an election became critical. In America, each voice should count, no matter whether the voice is female or male, gay, straight, or bisexual. It's part of a democracy. Letters with a stamp are meant to be mailed, food in a refrigerator is meant to be eaten, and books—books like *Daddy's Roommate* and *Heather Has Two Mommies*—are meant to be read. They are our sustenance. They're to be read in our American society because they represent a real and misunderstood part of our American culture. And that's the truth and nothing but the truth, so help me God.

## Works Cited

American Library Association.http//www.ala.org/alaorg/oif/ top100 banned books.html.

Associated Press. "Gingrich Hits Some School Programs on Gay Life." *Boston Globe*. (8 March 1995).

*Censorship: Don't Let It Become An Issue In Your Schools*. Urbana, Ill.: National Council of Teachers of English, 1978.

Cowles, Janelle. Personal electronic communication. 26 September 2000.

Granger, Bill. "Whenever We Censor Books, Do We Not All Bleed?" *Chicago Tribune*. (17 March 1986): 9.

Greenbaum, Vicky. "Censorship and the Myth of Appropriateness: Reflections on Teaching Reading in High School." *English Journal* (February 1997): 16-20.

Hawkins, David. "The Roots of Literacy." *Daedalus* (Spring 1990): 3-15.

Hiss, Tony. "The End of the Rainbow." *The New Yorker* (12 April 1993): 43-54.

Jennings, Kevin. *Teaching Respect For All*. New York: GLSEN, 1996.

Newman, Leslea. *Heather Has Two Mommies*. Northampton, Mass.: In Other Words Publishing, 1989.

People For the American Way. http://www.pfaw.org/.

Rodriguez, Richard. *Hunger of Memory: The Education of Richard Rodriguez*. Boston, Mass.: D. R. Godine, 1981.

Wallace, Elizabeth. "Brightening the Rainbow of Children's Literature." *Windy City Times* (11 August 1994): 23.

Willhoite, Michael. *Daddy's Roommate*. Los Angeles: Alyson Publications., 1990.

# A Defense of *A Day No Pigs Would Die*

## Jim Mulvey

Combine the deadpan humor of Huck Finn, his realistic dialect and uncouth language, his often sad observations of human misery, and his understated accounts of poverty, sin, and death and place this narrator in a *Charlotte's Web*-like world, but without its transcendent, rosy pastoralism, and you will perhaps see why Robert Newton Peck's *A Day No Pigs Would Die* is a major achievement of adolescent literature and one of the most challenged novels in America's schools.

*A Day No Pigs Would Die* recounts a year in the life in Rob Peck, a twelve-year-old Shaker boy, who grows to manhood on a poor Vermont farm in the 1920s. Rob learns important lessons about farming, animal husbandry, self-denial, responsibility, and the necessity of education from his wise but illiterate father, Haven. Like his namesake narrator, Robert Newton Peck was raised as a boy in the Shaker way, a faith that continued long after the sect itself died out and that both tests and strengthens the Peck family as it struggles to eke out a life as tenant farmers. The novel's credibility depends on its autobiographical truth, for as Peck says, "Much of [the book is] autobiography . . . with a garnish or two of fiction thrown in" (Confessions 18). We will probably never know if it's the truth or the garnish that has created the controversy swirling around this realistic novel, but controversial it is.

Between 1988 and 1997 Peck's novel has been reported challenged twenty-three times. The American Library Association notes, however, that for every reported challenge there are probably four or five more. These attacks have occurred in places ranging from Westminister, Colorado, to Burlington, Connecticut; from Anderson, South Carolina, to Utica, Michigan; from Waupaca, Wisconsin, to Melbourne, Florida; and from Baltimore, Maryland, to Pawhuska, Oklahoma (Attacks). *A Day No Pigs Would Die* was the ninth-most-challenged book in 1996 (Attacks) and has the distinction of being the sixteenth-most-attacked book of the 1990s

(ALA). Situated between the fourteenth-and-fifteenth most challenged books, Phyllis Reynolds Naylor's *Alice* series and R. L. Stein's Goosebumps series and the seventeenth-and-eighteenth most challenged books, Alice Walker's *The Color Purple* and Madonna's *Sex, A Day No Pigs Would Die* is attacked for a variety of reasons.

Here is an overview of those challenges: in 1988 the book was challenged in Jefferson County, Colorado, because "it is bigoted against Baptists and women and depicts violence, hatred, animal cruelty, and murder"; it was challenged as suitable curriculum material in the Harrington and Burlington, Connecticut, schools in 1990 because "it contains language and subject matter that set bad examples and give students negative views of life"; in 1993 the Sherwood Elementary School in Melbourne, Florida, was challenged because "the book gave the impression that rape and violence are acceptable." This quote is in reference to a boar and sow mating. And in a challenge to the Payson, Utah, Middle School (1994), parents "had problems with animal breeding, and with a scene that involves infant grave exhumation" (Doyle 75-76).

One significant reason for these censorship attempts is Rob's swearing. The novel opens with Rob, distressed and self-absorbed after being bullied at school. On his way home he sees Apron, a neighbor's ox, suffering and struggling to birth twin calves. Rob stops to help Apron, but his assisting her leads to her injuring him. Having one of the worst days of his life, Rob, in his pain, screams at the ox, "you old bitch" (10); exclaims "ass" and "damn" (10, 18); says "balls" and refers to a cow's "tits" (23, 28); and vents at one point, "It's enough to sell your soul" (18). Such epithets might seem daunting to a defender of an adolescent novel, but if we pay attention to the extenuating circumstances that bring out Rob's language and notice the page numbers of these curses, we see that they are said under duress and early in the novel. I could not find one controversial word after page 28. Why? Because at the beginning of the novel Rob is an angry adolescent, full of confusion and questions. Like many twelve-year-old children, he tests his boundaries. Also, these curses are never directed at others, but are said in frustration and pain. Part of Rob's maturation is his ability to control his mouth, a positive sign, it seems to me.

Another controversial element of the novel is the Pecks' acceptance of the neighbors' behavior. As Shakers, the Pecks refuse to criticize the Widow Bascom for hiring a farmhand, who appears to be her lover. Later, Rob and Haven help the grieving Sebring Hillman get home after he exhumed his dead baby so it could be taken to the Hillman family's cemetery. Sebring conceived the child in an adulterous relationship with Letty Phelps, who killed herself and the baby. For most of the novel, Rob, as are many children, is conflicted over his and his neighbor's different religions. Most people in the community, including Rob's neighbors, the Tanners, are Baptists. Rob feels uneasy about Baptists, primarily because, as a poor Shaker, he is taunted by Baptist kids at school. But Rob overcomes this conflict of religion when he discovers that the neighborly and kindly Tanners, who take him to the county fair, love him (123). These subplots further develop the novel's theme of Rob's development, for he increasingly learns to accept others for who they are and to be nonjudgmental: a good lesson for those who attack the novel.

The most strident criticism is directed, however, at the book's scenes detailing the animal world of the farm.

There is no Wilbur the pig, Templeton the rat, or Charlotte the spider in *A Day No Pigs Would Die*, but there are plenty of animals, creatures who are worked and ignored, bought and sold, and slaughtered and eaten. The small farm is the primal locus of life and death, as it is in both *Charlotte's Web* and *A Day No Pigs Would Die*, but unlike E. B. White's classic children's novel, Peck's realistic adolescent novel directly confronts its readers with birth and death rather than sets them offstage away from the direct perception of its readers.

Yes, Peck's novel does celebrate the glory of birth; for example, while the barn cat Miss Sarah nurses her three new-born kittens:

> Miss Sarah was real happy about it too. She lay there purring and purring and purring, like her motor was running and wouldn't stop. And those three kittens with their wet milky noses all buried into her belly, all sucking away to beat mercy . . . "No matter how many times a barn cat has her kits," Ma said, "it's always a wondrous thing to see." (48-49)

But birth and death appear more often as violent, naturalistic forces. Consider Rob's descriptions of some minor episodes involving the life and death struggles apparent on the farm. Observing a frog in a creek, Rob tells us that

> He plumb forgot about that old black crow that was sitting up above, just watching that game of tag. It didn't take that wise old bird long to see himself a meal. He dropped out of that hickory tree like a big black stone, landed with his feet splashing the water, and took one sharp clear peck at that frog. Hit him dead center. (43-44)

In chapter 7 Rob observes another, much more predatory moment, as he watches a hawk catch a rabbit:

> Whump! The hawk hit only a few rods from where I was standing in the clover. . . . He hit something as big as he was, pretty near. And whatever it was, it was thrashing around on the ground. Seeing his talons were buried in its fur, the hawk was being whipped through the juniper bush for fair. But all he had to do was hang on, and drive his talons into the hearts or lungs.
>
> Then I heard the cry . . . a rabbit's death cry, and it don't forget very easy. Like a newborn baby . . . it's the only cry that a rabbit makes its whole life long, just that one death cry and it's all over. (62)

At one point in the novel, Rob shoots a squirrel so that his mother can use the chewed nuts cut out of the animal's stomach to decorate a cake.

These short scenes, though, are merely punctuation marks between the crises Rob narrates involving the increasingly harrowing and more dire episodes of life and death on the farm. These episodes begin immediately with the Apron birthing scene. Trying to help the ox birth her calves, Rob describes Apron showing him "her swollen rump. . . . Sticking out of her was the head and one hoof of her calf. His head was so covered with blood and birthsop that I had no way of telling he was alive or dead" (8). Rob manages to assist Apron but at a cost. Rob strips to use his clothing to wrench a calf from the ox. Panicked, Apron drags the boy through briars and severely bites his arm: "She bit and bit and never let go. She got to her feet and kept on biting. That devil cow ran down off that ridge with my arm in her mouth, and dragging me half-naked with her. What she didn't do to me with her teeth, she did with her front hoofs" (11-12). Haven, nursing Rob at home later, insinuates that Rob is hurt (punished) for leaving school early that day. But the more compelling lesson Rob learns is that his problems at school seem minor compared to the more painful life-and-death lessons of saving one's farm animals, the very animals that farmers depend upon for their economic survival.

The last third of the novel, chapters 11 through 15, move the reader quickly through three increasingly horrifying accounts of animal mating and death that preface the death of Haven. Each episode, more painful than the one before, demonstrates Peck's control of his material as he realistically presents the often unpleasant duties of farming. In chapter 11 Haven Peck has captured a weasel in the chicken pen and decides to let his neighbor Ira Long train his terrier Hussy to protect the coop. Haven explains to Rob that "once you weasel [a] dog, that dog'll hate weasels until her last breath. She'll always know when there's one around and she'll track it to its hole, dig it out, and tear it up. A man who keeps a hen house got to have a good weasel dog" (101). Unfortunately, Haven puts the dog inside a barrel containing the weasel in order to train it to kill such varmints. Although Hussy destroys the weasel, she is seriously injured in the fight and must be shot by Haven to put her out of her misery. Rob's sensitivity and disgust become apparent as he laments the stupidity of this training: " I hated every second of it. The whole thing seemed senseless to me and I was mad at myself for standing there holding down the barrel lid. I even felt the shame of being a part of it. From the look on Papa's face I could see that he wasn't enjoying it so much either" (103). The chapter concludes with Rob saying "I even got down on my knees and said [Hussy] a prayer. 'Hussy,' I said, 'you got more spunk in you than a lot of us menfolk got brains'" (105).

In chapter 13 Rob once again is confronted with a common but disturbing farm reality, the furrowing of a sow, in particular his pet sow Pinky, a gift to Rob from the Pecks' neighbor Mr. Tanner as a reward for Rob's helping Apron give birth. Thus, again the major life events of mating, birthing, and dying become dominant themes in the novel. Since receiving the piglet in April, Rob has come to love and cherish his pet hog; she and Rob seem at times inseparable. As October arrives and as Pinky has grown to adulthood, Haven and Mr. Tanner have decided to mate her with Mr. Tanner's prize boar, Samson. There is no doubt that Rob graphically describes the mating of Pinky and Samson for the reader, but we have to remember that farm kids witness such events all the time. And though the mating passage doesn't leave much to the imagination, what once again is made very clear is that Rob doesn't treat the mating as some kind of dirty joke; instead, as before, he demonstrates his sensitivity and compassion:

> Butting hard into Pinky's front shoulder with his snout, [Samson] jumped to her rear, pinning her up against the fence. Up on his back legs, he came down hard upon her, his forelegs up on her shoulders. His privates were alert and ready to breed her, and as she tried to move out from under him, he moved with her, and his entire back and body was thrusting again and again. Pinky was squealing from his weight and the hurt of his forcing himself to her.
> As I watched, I hated Samson. I hated him for being so big and mean and heavy. (120)

This scene is pretty brutal, but as Mr. Tanner explains to Rob, who says he has no stomach now for breakfast, " just take Pinky there. She weren't naught but a maiden before this morning. Just a little girl. But from this time on, she's a sow. She know a thing or two. And next time, she'll welcome the big boy" (121). Such a lesson might not be much of a consolation to Rob or for that matter the reader, but it is a fact of farm life, a life that Wilbur the pig certainly would have experienced. Just as Pinky painfully but inevitably grows into a sow, so, too, Rob grows from boyhood to adulthood.

As October turns to December, Haven tells Rob, "let's get it done"(125). The boy understands that "it" refers to the slaughtering of

Pinky, who, because she is barren and therefore an unnecessary expense, must provide the poor family's meat for the winter. Rob once again describes the harsh actualities of death on the farm and his accompanying sadness:

> I saw Papa get a grip on the crowbar, and raise it high over his head. It was then I closed my eyes, and my mouth opened like I wanted to scream for her. I waited. I waited to hear the noise that I finally heard.
>
> It was a strong crushing noise that you only hear when an iron stunner bashes in a pig's skull. I hated papa that moment. I hated him for killing her, and hated him for every pig he ever killed in his lifetime . . . for hundreds and hundreds and hundreds of butchered hogs. (127)

After Haven bleeds Pinky, both son and father break down in tears and share their grief in the most touching scene of the novel, a scene that becomes more gut-wrenching because we know that Haven is dying:

> "Oh, Papa. My heart's broke."
>
> "So is mine," said Papa. "But I'm thankful you're a man."
>
> I just broke down, and papa let me cry it all out. I just sobbed and sobbed with my head up toward the sky and my eyes closed, hoping God would hear it.
>
> "That's what being a man is all about, boy. It's just doing what's got to be done."
>
> I felt his big hand touch my face, and it wasn't like the hand that killed hogs. It was almost as sweet as Momma's. (129)

At the end of chapter 12, Haven tells Rob that "this is my last winter. I got an affection. I know I do. . . . Listen, Rob. Listen, boy. I tell you true. You got to face up to it. You can't be a boy about it" (114). The theme of Rob's growing to manhood continues in this scene and concludes with the father's death in May. Haven's end, though not described (the only death in the novel offstage), becomes even more painful in its understatement, foreshadowing, and dignity.

> Papa lived through the winter. He died in his sleep out in the barn on the third of May.
>
> He was always up before I was, and when I went out to the barn that morning, all was still. He was lying on the straw bed that he rigged for himself, and I knew that before I got to him that he was dead.
>
> "Papa." I said his name just once. "It's all right. You can sleep this morning. No cause to rouse yourself. I'll do the chores. There's no need to work any more. You just rest." (131)

Rob, true to his word, does his dead father's chores, arranges his father's funeral, and at the age of thirteen assumes the responsibilities of manhood—the duties of work and neighborliness taught to Rob by Haven.

At the end of the novel Rob says goodbye to his father: "'Goodnight, Papa,' I said. 'We had thirteen good years.' That was all I could say, so I just turned and walked away from a patch of grassless land" (139). Such unstated, but nevertheless real emotion, as well as the book's lessons and pastoral wisdom, and the picture of family unity and love certainly more than outweigh the problematic nitpicking of those who challenge this novel. Each of the novel's controversies is completely justifiable given the reality of the book's world, the strong family values of the Pecks, the admirable bond between a father and son, and the growth of Rob, who is not only an interesting and sensitive narrator, but a good son. Over the course of a year Rob has learned to look outside himself, to gather the wisdom of nature, to appreciate the tender love of his parents, and to understand the kindness of his supportive Baptist neighbors.

For these reasons, *A Day No Pigs Would Die* is not only an appropriate novel for middle school students; it is a necessary one.

## Works Cited

American Library Association. "The 100 Most Frequently Challenged Books of 1990-1999." http://www.ala.org/a/aorg/oif/top100banned books.html.

*Attacks on the Freedom to Learn: 1987-1996.* Washington, D.C.: People For the American Way, 1987-1996.

Doyle, Robert P. *Banned Books 1999 Resource Guide: Free People Read Freely.* Chicago: American Library Association, 1999.

Peck, Robert Newton. "Confessions of an Ex-Kid." *English Journal* (May 1979): 18-19.

Peck, Robert Newton. *A Day No Pigs Would Die.* New York: Dell, 1974.

# *The Drowning of Stephan Jones* by Bette Greene

## Carolyn Meyer

Several years ago, when I was living in a small Texas town, home to two universities, I was pleased to learn that Bette Greene had been invited by a mall bookstore, part of a national chain, to come to speak in our community. I had read Greene's *Summer of My German Soldier* when it was first published in 1973, and I looked forward to seeing and hearing in person the author of that excellent work.

This was the same pleasant, easygoing college town where my Jewish stepdaughter, recently returned from a year in Israel, had joined the marching band at the local high school, only to discover that the theme of the halftime routine was "Christianity." The band was to march down the field in the form of the Latin cross while playing a medley of Christian hymns. This is not the time or place to describe the viciousness that ensued when we protested, mumbling something about "separation of church and state." The situation quickly escalated with our daughter being demonized in her high school as "the Jew bitch" who was causing all the trouble to the poor, unhappy band members.

"If you don't like the way we do things here, why don't you just leave?" was the recurrent theme in letters to the editor published in the local paper. We were often referred to as "communists," and one letter-writer suggested that our protest somehow heralded the approach of Nazism, right there in Texas.

So I was hardly surprised at the furor that resulted when a number of alert citizens realized that the same Bette Greene who had written so movingly about a Jewish girl's forbidden friendship with a German POW during World War II in *Summer of My German Soldier* had also written *The Drowning of Stephan Jones*, a book that promoted homosexuality!

Perhaps the alert citizens had not actually read *The Drowning of Stephan Jones* but had heard others talk about it and understood that it was about two gay men, Stephan Jones and Frank Montgomery, who move to a small town in Arkansas to open an antique shop. Their very existence

159

infuriates some of the townspeople, particularly a group of high school boys who begin a campaign of harassment and humiliation of the two men that results in the death of one of those men. The boys responsible for Stephan Jones's death are exonerated; indeed, they are celebrated as folk heroes.

A vocal minority in my real Texas town reacted to Bette Greene's novel the way the folks in her fictional town of Rachetville, Arkansas, would have reacted: they wanted no part of the book or its author. The bookstore sponsor of Greene's's visit to our town decided to withdraw the invitation.

I cannot fathom how anyone could read about the tormenting and brutalizing of a couple of gay men and conclude that the book in any way celebrates or promotes homosexuality. If anything, the novel clearly demonstrates that a lifestyle considered sinful by many may come at a high cost of pain and suffering, and even death.

The story is told primarily from the point of view of Carla Wayland, a smart and attractive high school student who is something of an outsider, tainted by the absence of a father and the reputation of her sometimes embarrassingly liberal mother, the town's outspoken librarian. Carla has developed a crush on Andy Harris, the handsome, blue-eyed, popular scion of a prosperous and respected family. This is Carla's first romance, and she can hardly believe her good fortune when her affections seem to be returned. His friends become her friends; at last Carla feels she belongs. But Andy has a wide streak of cruelty in him, the legacy of his thoroughly unpleasant and bigoted father, the owner of a hardware store.

The novel, set at the time of a gay and lesbian rights march in Little Rock, opens just before Christmas when Carla first spots an evidently gay male couple in the Harrises' store and witnesses the first ugly incident of prejudice against them: "*Sodomites!*" hisses a customer, who later continues her diatribe. "'Just because you faggots are ranting and raving and carrying on about your rights outside our statehouse—who do you think you *are*? If God wanted you to have rights, then why would he have gone and invented AIDS!?'"

It doesn't take long for Carla to realize that her handsome boyfriend also hates homosexuals. "'If I were president, first thing I'd do is to make death for homosexuality the law. . . .' Andy tells her. 'Treat queers the same way we treat murderers, let them all fry to a frizzle in the electric chair.'"

Carla attempts to reason with him: "'You can't electrocute someone for *being* something. You can only electrocute people for *doing* something.'" She is shocked and disappointed by Andy's attitude, but she is unprepared to challenge him further. Surely, she believes, this boy for whom she cares so much can't be doing anything really wrong.

The story unfolds throughout the winter with a continuing build-up of tension between the gay men and Andy and his friends. The three boys engage in name-calling, vandalism and graffiti, harassing phone calls, and anonymous letters; their verbal attacks turn physical.

But Carla, in her desire to keep Andy's love and to be part of a group, rarely speaks out. The daughter of the outspoken librarian is too fearful of the consequences—the loss of love and acceptance by her peers—if she speaks her mind.

At times the point of view shifts from Carla to Stephan and Frank, who try to find some way to put a stop to the persecution but who, like Carla, also desire acceptance. Intelligent, decent men, they want nothing more than to live their ordinary lives in peace. One of the subplots involves the efforts of Stephan, a devoutly religious man, to convince his partner to join a church that they both know rejects and condemns them as homosexuals.

The novel reaches a climax on the night of the senior prom. Greene's writing is at its most powerful as she describes the horrifying scene. On their way home from the prom with Carla in the car, Andy and his friends discover Stephan and Frank walking on a lonely road. Frank escapes, but (while Carla remains in the car) Andy and his friends strip, humiliate, and—despite his pleas that he can't swim—throw Stephan into the river. Only when she finally realizes what is happening does Carla take action and run for help. But it's too late to save Stephan.

The dénouement in the courtroom where Andy Harris is on trial and walks away without punishment is certain to rouse the anger of the sympathetic reader, although the grieving Frank Montgomery does in the final pages achieve a kind of justice that the law fails to provide.

I am nearly always surprised by the books that are challenged by adults who seek to keep certain kinds of provocative and disturbing materials out of the hands of impressionable young readers; sometimes I'm not even certain what could be found objectionable. But the fact that *The Drowning of Stephan Jones* has been challenged is no surprise at all. One need only read the daily paper or watch the evening news to realize the extent to which homophobia thrives in this country.

A large number of people are so convinced that homosexuality is a deadly sin that they oppose federal legislation making it easier for prosecutors to try hate crimes based on sexual orientation. What happened to Matthew Shepard, the twenty-one year old homosexual student at the University of Wyoming, who died in 1998 after being beaten and tied to a fence, is not much different from what happens to Stephan Jones in Bette Greene's 1991 novel.

The antigay faction will, without question, continue its efforts to keep this book off the shelves and Bette Greene off the speaker's platform. Bette

Greene does not promote homosexuality, but she does strongly oppose violence against individuals who are deemed "different." After another "disinvitation," this one in Arkansas, Ms. Greene wondered of those who canceled her talk, "Could it be that they did not share my outrage in the unprovoked murder of a young man?" The young man she spoke of was Stephan Jones, the character, but she could have been speaking of Matthew Shepard, the real person.

Stephan Jones is not the only tragic figure in the novel. Tragic in another way is young Carla Wayland, who, faced with overwhelming pressure, kept quiet for much too long. Now, Carla must live with the knowledge that the help she finally offered the suffering Stephan Jones was far too little, and it came much too late. Tragic too, if outspoken opposition to Bette Greene's book were to silence effectively the Carla Waylands among us.

## Works Cited

Greene, Bette. *The Drowning of Stephan Jones*. New York: Bantam, 1991.
———. *Summer of My German Soldier*. New York: Dial, 1973.

# The Invisible Adolescent: Robert Cormier's *Fade*

**Joyce Sweeney**

When asked to participate in this anthology, I was not only quick to agree. I also asked, almost immediately, if I could choose Robert Cormier's *Fade* as my book to defend.

Robert Cormier is a hero and inspiration to many young adult authors, myself included. He has always set the bar very high for the level of literary quality in our genre. His work demands of all of us that we go deeper, tell more of the truth, pull fewer punches with the readers who trust us.

I remember when *Fade* was first published in 1988. I reviewed it for *The Atlanta Constitution*. It was an exciting book for YA authors, because it was dual-published—marketed both as a YA and as mainstream, adult fiction. It confirmed for all of us that the best of what we do could hold up in the "grown-up" literary world. It reminded us again that we should never "write down" to our audience. I remembered it as one of the finest novels I ever read.

When I came to reread it for the purpose of this essay, I could see immediately why the book had been challenged. The protagonist, Paul Moreaux, has a rare genetic condition, transmitted to one male member of his family each generation, that allows him to become invisible, which means he can move freely in and out of the private lives of the adults in his small, French-Canadian community and see the secrets that most 13-year-olds are protected from.

Like any adolescent boy, Paul is excited and curious by this new world that is open to him. But he is also a moral boy and makes a vow to himself he will never use the power of the fade to commit a crime (a vow he will break). He wanders the streets of Frenchtown and almost immediately he discovers that the shopkeeper he works for, Mr. Dondier, is taking sexual advantage of a teenage girl, exploiting her low intelligence and her need for money. Paul is sickened and runs away. He will be running for the rest of the book. His second experience with the fade further erodes his illusions. As a lowly Frenchtown boy, he is thrilled when an upper-class boy from his school befriends him. The boy also has a beautiful sister, and Paul falls in love with her and is dazzled by their beautiful home, affluence, and "golden" life. Of course, he uses his power to return to the home at night and sees the dark underside of the golden brother and sister—they are involved in an incestuous relationship. Once again, Paul is jolted as reality destroys his innocent view of the world.

He sees things—and therefore the reader does, too—that we all wish no child ever had to see. Some of his clean, quiet, respectable neighbors are lustful, scheming, and cruel—even murderous. Paul's innocent world is shattered. We see the child in him literally die before our eyes. But is the fade really to blame? One of the most shattering sights Paul sees is that his father has been demoted and demeaned at work in a way the family never knew, punishment for his union activities. A teacher tells Paul he should stop having aspirations to be a writer because of his nationality and class, dismissing him as a person. Those rude awakenings come when Paul is in plain sight and are meant to be seen as part of what happens to every teenager, as the blinders of childhood wear off. The fade only escalates the process.

This is why young adult books are challenged, banned, and feared. It is painful for parents to see their children grow up and learn how scary and dangerous the real world is. The urge is powerful to shield the children, keep them babies just a little longer, let them live in a cocoon of innocence just one more day.

But young adult authors, and especially Robert Cormier, remember adolescence all too well; we know that—especially these days—innocence begins to crumble in the third grade, and by junior high, the young readers, like it or not, are in the adult world, without a map or compass—in *need* of a book like *Fade* to help them find their way.

Because he is invisible, Paul discovers that the "kindly" grocer he works for is a child molester. Would he be safer if he didn't know? He discovers the rich kids he thought were better than him have more serious problems than he'll ever have. Would he be happier without that knowledge? He finds out the most powerful man in town is a monster who could destroy Paul's father and their whole way of life. Paul's "information" costs him terribly. Knowledge is power; and while Paul's knowledge helps him in many cases, it finally draws him into the adult world of actions and consequences, where he can no longer passively observe. He takes justice into his own hands and in the process, effectively destroys himself.

Cormier makes a strong statement about power in this book. Paul's Uncle Adelard, who passes the fade down to Paul, is not a dashing, exciting "invisible man." He is older than his years, tired, and profoundly sad. He refuses to give Paul much information about the fade clearly because he wants to protect his nephew from the horror ahead. Paul is quickly corrupted by his power. He goes from sexual voyeur to avenger, brutally beating the neighborhood bully.

> Later, in the shed, visible again, I began to tremble as I relived my attack on Omer LaBatt. My attack? It seemed as if the person who had assaulted Omer LaBatt so viciously were someone other than me. I had always avoided violence and confrontations, had fled from Omer LaBatt a hundred times, knowing myself a coward, brave only in my wildest dreams. But the rescue of Joey LeGrande and the attack on Omer LaBatt were not really acts of bravery. What were they, then?

Cormier shows all the powerful figures in the book to be corrupt, from Omer LaBatt to the powerful politician Rodophe Toubert, who victimizes the entire town and tries to destroy Paul's father. Eventually, Paul cannot stand the injustice any more, and he succumbs to the temptation to abuse his power, using his invisibility to murder Toubert.

Uncle Adelard had hinted to Paul that as a sacrifice for the fade, he had somehow lost a beloved brother. The same thing happens to Paul. After he kills, his innocent younger brother dies in his sleep. Not only does every wrong action have a consequence in Cormier's world, the consequence is usually bigger, crueler and more painful that the action. If you sow the wind, you reap the whirlwind.

Any reader of Cormier's collected works will see immediately that Cormier's special contribution to the education of young people is his painful honesty about life. In Cormier's books, as in life, the good guy doesn't always win, the bad guy isn't always punished, and violence usually doesn't solve things—it just leads to more violence. Are these things we don't want our children to know? All teenagers find out the truth about life—it's merely a question of whether a responsible adult prepares them or whether it descends on them unawares and plunges them into depression, or worse, makes them explode in violent frustration. Littleton didn't happen because the two boys involved were too aware of reality; it happened because they had lost touch with reality altogether.

One of Paul's duties as a fader is to find the fader of the next generation and instruct him as his Uncle Adelard instructed him. This turns out to be his nephew Ozzie—an illegitimate "secret" child, who is put up for adoption and raised by a drunken, abusive man. Ozzie learns to fade long before his uncle can find him and warn him of the dangers, and in Ozzie's twisted, troubled psyche, his special power truly makes him a monster. He has none of Paul's compunctions or inhibitions. He is an invisible menace. Yet, we never lose sight of the fact that he is also a wounded, rejected, battered child.

All of us, in this industry, know we are doing a difficult and painful job, helping adolescents get a view of what lies ahead. An image that never leaves me is Holden Caulfield's vision of what he'd like to do with his life—stand at the edge of a big rye field and catch children who are about to run over a cliff. Parents, teachers, librarians, and young adult authors all have to stand at the edge of that cliff, shouting out our warnings to each generation of kids who inevitably run that way. If we try to pretend the cliff isn't there, how can we possibly save them?

The irony of Paul Moreaux is that adolescents are often invisible to us. They don't yet have the experience or words to tell us what they go through. And when they try, we often can't bear to hear it. Somehow we wish they would jump from cuddly ten-year-olds to mature twenty-year-olds and spare us all the mess in between.

I know from my readers' letters and from the response I get when I visit schools that kids are *eager* to talk about the difficult subjects, and they want our input and experience to help them. A novel is often the catalyst that opens the door to that dialogue. If I were willing to write about it, then they feel they can open up and talk about it. It's when children don't get to think issues through that they act out and make bad choices.

Robert Cormier is still a role model to me. It is clear he cares about his young readers enough to never lie to them, never sugar-coat the things they need to know. He has the courage to warn them, in *Fade* and elsewhere, that life will not always be fair, that sometimes they will suffer, and that they have to be brave and stick to their principles—not because life will shower them with rewards, but because, in the end, their own sense of honor and integrity is all they have.

Or we could remove these books from the library because *we* find them disturbing and turn up the stereo to drown out the sound of our kids playing video games, which teach, if you don't like somebody, you can always blow off their head.

The cliff at the edge of the rye field is steeper than it's ever been. We need to keep our best "catchers" on the job.

## Work Cited

Cormier, Robert. *Fade*. New York: Dell, 1988.

# Defending *Fallen Angels* by Walter Dean Myers: Framing—Not Taming—Controversy

## Beth Murray

The plot of *Fallen Angels*, by Walter Dean Myers, is not extraordinary in its skeletal form: a young army soldier from Harlem flies to Vietnam, encounters challenges, builds alliances, sustains injuries, loses comrades, and ultimately returns home; plane to plane. It's a war story, after all. However, Walter Dean Myers's artistic choices in creating this particular story as one soldier's vivid narrative of feelings, thoughts, and observations fleshes out the tale with immediacy and the inevitable controversy that seems to shadow immediacy. In choosing to write a Vietnam War story at all, Walter Dean Myers strode knowingly toward controversy. In choosing to tell the story through Richard Perry, a soldier on the front lines, Myers stood squarely in the complex immediacy of controversy. This is not a "war book" aiming only to clarify military strategy and events, though it does so to some extent. Readers spend a great deal of time inside the mind of Richard Perry, looking out through his eyes, listening through his ears—feeling his feelings. Perspective and depth lean upon each other.

Perry and his comrades refer to their lives and families in the states as being "back in the world." This phrase underscores the enormity of Myers's task as a writer: transporting readers to a different world, in place and time. Today's teen readers categorize a Vietnam War novel as a work of historical fiction. Richard Perry guides the historical journey. Though Perry narrates in the first person, the story relies heavily upon dialogue among multiple characters with varying and often opposing perspectives. The story plays as a movie: episodic, with flashbacks, interior monologues, and a vast cast of characters.

However, the very same narrative element that brings immediacy also brings protection. Myers is careful to cushion the read within Perry's perspective of a pensive young man taking care, questioning, quietly defending, stretching to understand, and learning to live with the emotional paradoxes of war and of life. The most controversial elements are often Perry's observations, not his own actions or words. Perry's perceptions and preconceptions emerge through these observations, on behalf of the reticent reader. In time, the war problematizes many of Perry's prejudgments. As Perry's categorization of his world grows more complex, the reader must wonder past stereotypes as well.

Teaching *Fallen Angels* (or sharing it with teens) invites exploration of censorship issues on multiple levels. In this book, there is something to challenge anyone's thinking. Of course, some readers construe challenges as opportunities to be offended. This book will "offend" almost anyone seeking a reason to be offended. First, it is a war story set largely in Vietnam. Those opposed to that particular conflict or violence in books for young people might oppose this book, despite its acclaimed accuracy. Second, it takes a close look at a multiraced platoon and personifies the "battle within the battle" faced by soldiers of color. Those opposed to plain talk about sometimes divisive racial tension in books for young people might oppose this book. Those opposed to any questioning of the military might oppose this book. Third, this book relies upon an ensemble of characters to spin its story. Most of these characters are soldiers on the front lines of a war. They speak as any range of soldiers might: some formally, some informally, some derogatorily, and some religiously. Characters utter racial slurs, sexual innuendo, homophobic comments, and "cuss" words between their playful banter and professions of solemn support. Those who oppose "offensive" language in books for young people might oppose this book. Those who oppose open prayer might oppose this book. One could choose to view such elements as controversial enough to keep the book available on the shelf, marginally significant enough to entrust it to the hands of a few who could mediate it themselves, or important enough to share it at the center of a broad classroom inquiry into the construction of perspectives and perceptions. Myers lays the groundwork to support such brave inquiry.

In teaching a controversial book, we often anticipate—sometimes tensely—reactions in young readers: the flush of giggles over the allusion to the human anatomy in chapter 10, or the exchanged glances and raised eyebrows as one character blurts out "hell" or "fuck" in the midst of a fiery tirade. Profanity and racial slurs arrest attention as they hope to stereotype, intimate, taunt, and dehumanize. We wait to see if the controversial moment lures or alienates readers. Myers doesn't make us wait in *Fallen Angels*. By page three, the "enemy" Vietnamese are dehumanized and objectified as "Congs." By page 6, the sergeant taunts soldiers with language that would make most people blush. By page 7 the same sergeant has stereotyped and estranged the entire gay population. By page 12, there is a triangle of racial tension involving a Vietnamese cleaning woman, an African American soldier, and a White soldier filled with derogatory labels and knee-jerk bravado, brinking on violence.

So why bother with this book at all? The story is broader and deeper than its necessarily coarse language and imagery. The timeless tensions it explores merit close study. The instructional challenge then becomes gauging comfort levels with explicitness and creating contexts where everything can be interrogated, including discomfort. Myers did not write this book to place readers at ease. The reader is challenged to unpack the battles within battles, the histories and motivations. These tensions are not new nor are they unique to the Vietnam War. They are patterns in human history. Myers tries to help readers find their place in history through Perry's struggles. It is both a war story and a coming-of-age story.

Sometimes the coming-of-age story supersedes the war story. This book is part of a larger mission on Myers's part to share voices formerly unheard and inspire readers formerly unmirrored in literature for young people on their rites of passage. *Scorpions* (1988) and *Monster* (1999) are examples of two other titles working toward that career-long mission. Perry is searching, as are many young people who would be drawn to this text. He just happens to be a soldier. The immediacy of Perry's first-person view pushes the book, through war, toward more universal struggles. Thus the text is doubly rich as the poignant, complex lessons Perry and Peewee, Perry's newfound comrade, and the others learn as they come of age are inextricably bound up with the complex lessons of the Vietnam War. The lines between boyhood and manhood are as blurred as the borders between war and peace. The parallel exploration of personal and global treacherous, unsettled terrain sets this story above other adolescent novels in which the journey is not nearly so plural.

Hostile actions are vital to the authenticity of this tale. However, Myers focuses less on how people die and more on the emotional aftermath, as in the case of Jenkins's death.

> "You know him?"
> "No," I said, "I just met him at the replacement company."
> "Sometimes it goes like that," Monaco said. He started to say something else then shrugged it off, and left.
> I wanted to say more to him. I wanted to say that the only dead person I had seen before had been my grandmother. . . . But Jenkins was different. Jenkins had been walking with me and talking with me only hours before. Seeing him lying there like that, his mouth and eyes open, had grabbed something inside my chest and twisted it hard. (43)

When the platoon commanding officer dies, the aftermath is again more central than the physical demise. Perry has aged over the pages between the deaths. His perspective broadens to collective rather than individual grief.

> Shock. Pain. Nobody wanted to look at anybody else. Nobody wanted to talk. There was nothing to say. Lieutenant Carroll's death was close. It hung around our shoulders and filled the spaces between us. Lieutenant Carroll had sat with us, had been afraid with us, had worried about us. Now he was dead. (120)

As Perry wrote the tragic letter to Mrs. Carroll, Myers broadened the range of perspectives yet again: "I know that it is not much comfort to you that your husband died bravely, or honorably, but he did. All of the guys in the squad who served under him are grateful for his leadership and for having known him"(131).

Other deaths followed, including the loss of comrade and enemy lives—though the line between is increasingly blurred, a hallmark of war, particularly the Vietnamese conflict. Myers wasted not one death as statistic or set dressing. Each was an opportunity to consider another perspective, or deepen the understanding of a familiar one.

> Unlike textbook accounts and television coverage of war, which most often focus on acts of aggression, well-written trade books focus on the results of aggression—the uprooted and ruined lives, the suffering from pain and sadness, and the waste of lives and energy, and resources. If the violence in these stories can convince young people that they must find peaceful ways to settle their differences, then it is justified. (Tomlinson, 45)

Hostile words are also vital for authenticity. No character in this story is simply good or evil, rather an emerging negotiation of perspectives. Take Peewee, for instance, the fast-talking little guy from Chicago whose conversations often turn to verbal boxing matches. Finding a spic-and-span sentence uttered by this character is nearly impossible. However, he is deeper than a foul-mouthed runt. Early in the book, we learn a great deal about Peewee "back in the world" in a few of his own words.

> [T]his is the first place I ever been in my life where I got what everybody else got . . . anything anybody got in the army, I got. You got a gun. I got a gun. You got boots, I got boots. You eat this lousy-ass chip beef on toast, guess what I eat?" (15)

He is a central player in most name-calling volleys. Perry often runs interference for Peewee when he gets too deep with someone too large. In the should-Monaco-marry-the-girl-back-home discussion, Peewee meets our expectations of smart-aleck superficiality by asking: "Is she pregnant?" and "What's she look like?" Then he surprises us as the first romantic in the crowd to say: "I vote for the marriage." When Perry breaks down after a near-death brush with a Vietcong soldier, it's Peewee who comforts him.

Similarly, Peewee internalizes the struggle faced by the young children in their war-torn country. Wanting to help in some way, he starts making a doll with items he finds in the immediate area. As he completes the doll, the platoon watches the smiling woman hand her child—for whom the doll was intended—to an American soldier. The child had been mined. The soldier, the child, and the child's family die instantly. When others check in on Peewee later, clearly shaken and withdrawn, the exterior emerges again.

> "Hey Peewee," I said, "it's okay to feel bad about what's going on over here, man. It's really okay."
> "Me? Feel bad?" Peewee turned over in his bunk and pulled his sheet up around his shoulders. "Never happen."

The words—profane, profound, and mundane—are all part of a larger, more complex context.

The initial categories of censorship concern (war, racial tension, coarse language) pervade the entire book; however, just as Perry and his platoon evolve, so do the categories. War becomes more complicated than "kickin' butt" and being American. Patriotism emerges along a continuum, interpreted variably among characters and situations. Racial lines blur as soldiers lean on each other for platoon survival (though the strongest link is shared between Perry and Peewee, two African Americans). Coarse language begins to sound commonplace for its frequency. The words between carry the memorable meanings. These potentially contentious elements, considered together, mirror the journey of the *Fallen Angels* cast. All are vital to its compelling telling.

This is a valuable book for capable and interested young readers to experience individually. Most teachers and librarians find comfort in an individual approach, given the "lively" language and stark subject matter. However, this book screams for conversation and invites exploration beyond its bindings. What was life for those "back in the world?" What about the Vietnamese perspective? What do veterans, politicians, and protesters think about the event retrospectively? What challenges do we still face? What poetry grew out of this era? What songs? What patterns from this era persist and recur today? What is oppression and who were the oppressors in the Vietnam conflict? What types of oppression does the military fight against? What types of oppression does it support and reward? How do veterans return home? How does a war-torn country adapt to "peace"? Who is this book for? Whom might it offend? Why? How might some story events be described through the eyes of another character, real or imagined, within or beyond *Fallen Angels*?

Imposing this text on young people would do them and the story a disservice. The layers, levels, and perspectives demand committed exploration. The reader needs to be the explorer. Using the text as a vehicle for critical examination of a hotly contested historical period considered from a variety of perspectives would offer all involved a learning experience. The art becomes harnessing the controversy that swirls around this text, framing and naming the subtle levels of controversy, not taming them.

## Works Cited

Myers, Walter Dean. *Monster*. New York: Harper Collins, 1999.

_____. *Fallen Angels*. New York: Scholastic, 1988.

_____. *Scorpions*. New York: Harper Trophy, 1988.

Tomlinson, Carl. (1995). "Justifying Violence in Children's Literature." In *Battling Dragons: Issues and Controversy in Children's Literature*, ed. Susan Lehr. Portsmouth, N.H.: Heinemann, 1995.

# Lois Lowry's *The Giver*

## Avi

In Lois Lowry's *The Giver*, a society is portrayed that exists in the future. Moreover, the society in which the protagonist, Jonas, lives, is depicted in such fashion as to suggest it is the logical outcome of strong tendencies in our own present-day society. That is to say, it is a work of contemporary social criticism presented as a work of fiction. It is a fantasy, even as it is a cautionary tale.

This type of writing is part of a very old, very honored tradition. One can begin with the classic Greek's Aristophanes' *The Frogs*, move on to Erasmus' *The Praise of Folly*, St. Thomas More's *Utopia*, Defoe's *Gulliver's Travels*, Voltaire's *Candide*. More recently, there is Bellamy's *Looking Backward*, Huxley's *Brave New World*, Orwell's *1984* (and *Animal Farm*), Bradbury's *Fahrenheit 451*, and even the recent Hollywood film *The Truman Show*. There are many others. *The Giver* needs to be understood as being part of this literary tradition.

Broadly speaking, what all of these works have in common is that although they are works of fiction, they are critical of contemporary society and contain an implicit warning that if current (whenever that might be) social tendencies persist—the fiction may become real.

*The Giver* is about our own time. It is, briefly, a brilliantly written defense of individualism. In this context it constitutes a critique of the pressures put upon young people for conformity, anti-intellectualism, the drive of mass communication to make everyone look and act alike, the use of drugs as social pacifier, acts of euthanasia. It is against the culture of sameness, of making everything level.

The society that is depicted in *The Giver* is one in which all choice is taken away from individuals. Private and idiosyncratic notions are deeply distrusted, even discouraged. Careers, spouses, children, life and death itself are under the strict control of government. What this society wants—what is required—is absolute conformity, obedience to the authority of the community leadership.

What this book defends is uniqueness, individualism, humanity made wise by the virtue of pain as well as pleasure, the joys and sorrows of the fully developed senses. It is, importantly, a defense of love, too, as perhaps the overwhelming human virtue, love being the quality that enables one to survive and be one's own unique self.

In the portrayal of *The Giver* himself, as the one person in the society who maintains the memory of pain and suffering (because all suffering and pain are removed from the culture) there is a fascinating metaphoric connection to the traditional Passion of Jesus, as the figure who embraces suffering so that others may live in peace.

Indeed, one of the most powerful, loving, and important memories that Jonas receives from *The Giver* is that of a family-centered Christmas.

Having suggested all this, one must wonder why, then, the book has been the subject of such venomous attacks from the religious right. Their claim, broadly speaking, is that *The Giver* promotes the very kind of society that it in fact rejects. Ironically, the criticism of society implicit in *The Giver* often parallels some of the religious right's criticism of America's material culture.

Why, then, the attacks? Perhaps what is most obvious, and perhaps the most difficult to deflect, is that there are those who simply cannot see the work as fictional. As such, it constitutes a failure of imagination, when confronted by a convincingly written work of fantasy. Such readers cannot separate themselves from that which is imaginary, the real from the unreal. A recent letter to Ms. Lowry makes this very clear:

> At first I found your book to be interesting in an odd sort of way. When I got to the end part of the book where the boy Jonas witnesses his father killing a newborn baby boy I was shocked, sickened and highly disappointed in you as a writer Miss Lowry. I was appalled at the manner in which you described the murder of the baby. Have you given any thought to the fact that the way you murdered the boy comes extremely close to the way abortions are performed? Also the way you kill the 'old' in your story sounds closely related to Euthanasia. What is your point? What kind of message are you putting in the innocent minds of young people who read your book? Visions of murder I do not find appropriate for my children or any children—even adults to read. Are we to be entertained by murder which is immoral and sinful?

It's difficult to believe that the author of this letter actually read *The Giver*, given the confusion about the plot and the fact that the letter writer fails to note that the death of the child so horrifies Jonas, he is motivated to *save* a doomed child and flee the controlled society.

Still, the best answer to why the book is attacked is that those who feel threatened by it are *precisely* the kind of people who would create the society portrayed in the book.

But I think there are other issues, perhaps less clear, that need to be addressed. The very plot of the novel puts Jonas in conflict with adult society, and the society that constitutes his so-called family. That's to say, the novel portrays a child as being critical of adult society. Never mind that Jonas's final act of subversion is made in concert with an adult—*The Giver* himself. Here is a story about a child who discovers that the adult world has failed him, lied to him, tricked him as to what life actually is.

This notion, that a child can discover the hypocrisy of adult culture, is often a lightning rod for those who wish to control the lives of young people.

I am reminded of a parent I once met, who proudly informed me that, every time her child wished to see a movie or read a book, she undertook to see that movie or read that book *first* so as to determine its suitability. In so doing, she reserved to herself the widest latitude of contact with movies and books, even while providing the narrowest for her offspring. The issue was—and always is—of control.

As a parent and stepparent of six, I am deeply aware of the struggle that parents face when confronted with the overwhelming pressure children face to conform. It comes from parents, family, other kids, school, the mass media, and perhaps most of all, from the young person's great desire to be accepted, to be a part. But at the same time these young people do wish to be themselves, to be seen as individuals. It is this tension that lies at the core of *The Giver*.

My stepdaughter read the book during sixth grade.

"Did you like it?" I asked her.

"It was my favorite book. I read it in a day."

"Why?"

"Well, you know, I was just learning about feelings, and the book told me how important my feelings were. I loved that."

This from a child who had difficulty expressing her emotions.

Because *The Giver* is addressed to, indeed, is for young people on just these terms, some adults will be nervous. No doubt about it: *The Giver* is a disturbing book. It is meant to be. Indeed, to be disturbed by this tale is a tribute to what the book gives.

## Work Cited

Lowry, Lois. *The Giver*. Boston: Houghton Mifflin Company, 1993.

# Goosebumps by R. L. Stine

## Sandra Soares and Julia Tiede

The Goosebumps books are a series of 63 horror novels for children, written by R. L. Stine between 1993 and 1998. These narratives fall somewhere between "The Twilight Zone," Hitchcock, and the silly spook tales that children make up around the campfire. (I am reminded of the "Lardass" story from the Rob Reiner film "Stand by Me.") The tales all have some elements of the supernatural, most contain some gratuitous slime, there are a number of false scares (usually one kid scaring another, then making fun of the fraidy-cat), and every book puts children in a position of fright, danger, and loss of control. But the Goosebumps books do not contain much in the way of real violence. People do not bleed in these books—though they may occasionally be covered with stinking goo—and it is rare to find threats from human sources, such as kidnappers, burglars, murderers; danger is more likely to come from a mummy, a ventriloquist's dummy, a monster. The stories *are* scary, but the sources of the scares are so patently unreal that they cause more *frisson* than fear.

I can't defend the Goosebumps series on the basis of literary excellence; the books are not terribly well written, the plots are simplistic, the characters are flat, and the special effects are often, as a kid might say, gross. But the books do have redeeming merits. My granddaughter, Julia, nine and a half years old, defends them and explains her reasoning:

> They are fun to read because you don't know what is going to happen next, so you keep reading. The stories move; like you go into this creepy house and down in the basement there's something really scary. The books are a little scary, but I like scary stories, and I know it's fake. Little kids might have bad dreams about them, and they might think that there are monsters under the bed; the books tell about how bad the monsters are. But even little kids should know that the stories are fake.

Kids who don't normally read might read them because they're not like regular stories. Boys don't usually read, but they think these kinds of stories are fun.

Reading is better than no reading. You should always read, because then your reading skills are getting better. And you can read anywhere; you can carry a book in your backpack, but you can't carry around a t.v. Another nice thing about reading is that you can make up what you see.

From an adult standpoint, there are a number of reasons to defend this series. Julia is right when she says that "reading is better than no reading," and Goosebumps actually represents an important transition in reading. One day when Julia and I were in a bookstore, when she was about seven and a half, she asked me to buy her a "chapter book." She felt that she was ready to leave behind books that consisted of a little text and a lot of illustration and move on to books that relied on text for their interest. Goosebumps are clearly "chapter books." Except for the covers, they contain no illustrations, and in fact the descriptions in the books are so vivid that no illustrations are needed. For this reason alone it is worth allowing kids to read Goosebumps. Despite the fact that the main characters of the novels are always twelve years old, the main audience for the series is third and fourth graders (according to a librarian I consulted). I suspect that Goosebumps, and other series like them, are the first nonillustrated books that many children read, preparing them for more serious reading later—and proving to them that words on a page really do have the power to stir the imagination.

Stine seems to prefer first-person narration. Of the seven Goosebumps that I have read, six are told in the first person. This point of view involves the young reader instantly; the narrator pulls in the reader in the same confiding way that Holden Caufield does at the beginning of *The Catcher in the Rye*. "Josh and I hated our new house" (*Welcome to Dead House* 1); "My name is Amy Cramer, and every Thursday night I feel a little dumb. That's because Thursday night is 'Family Sharing' night at my house" (*Night of the Living Dummy II* 1). The younger reader instantly relates to the main character's feelings. Another advantage to first-person narration in a book meant to scare the reader is the reassurance that the main character has lived to tell the story.

In structure, most of the Goosebumps stories are fairly straightforward. *Attack of the Jack-o'-Lanterns*, however, contains two flashbacks at the beginning. In *The Curse of the Mummy's Tomb*, Stine uses prefiguration; the main character repeatedly has trouble keeping one of his shoes tied, and he is ultimately left behind in a dark tunnel as he stoops to tie that shoe. *The Blob That Ate Everyone* is constructed as a modified Chinese box: it begins with a scary episode that turns out to be a story that the narrator has written to frighten his friends. At the end we discover that *the whole book* is a scary story written by a "blob" to scare its blob friends. I believe that for the young person just beginning to read novels these narrative devices are a good introduction to adult literature, which requires keeping track of various episodes and characters. When I first red *Glinda of Oz*, I remember being intrigued by the three plot threads and the switching back and forth between them from chapter to chapter.

The endings of the books bear mentioning as well. In the Goosebumps books I have read, there are two types of endings. One is the happy resolution, generally involving the family. At the end of *Welcome to Dead House*, the family moves out of the town of the "living dead." *The Curse of the Mummy's Tomb*, in which the narrator's parents have been absent throughout the story, ends with a knock at the door: "The sound of ancient, bandaged fingers struggling with the lock. . . . Two shadowy figures lumbered into the room. 'Mom and Dad!' I cried. I'll bet they were surprised at how glad I was to see them" (132). These endings are comforting after all of the anxieties the characters—and the reader—have faced.

The other type of ending is the "endless loop." In both of the *Night of the Living Dummy* books the nasty ventriloquist's dummy is destroyed only to be replaced by another dummy who comes to life. *The Beast from the East* ends with the beginning of another scary game. In *Attack of the Jack-o'-Lanterns*, the narrator discovers that his two young pals, who are aliens, "'only like to eat very plump adults. So you don't have to worry for now'" (113). These endings add a special little scare; they also invite sequels, of course, handy in a long series like this one.

In content, Goosebumps books contain a number of themes that preadolescent children can relate to. Sibling rivalry is often present in the stories, and it is very bitter. Jealousy and competition for recognition from parents is a common plot thread; generally it is happily resolved, even if the ending of the story remains up in the air. When the crisis comes, the competing siblings find themselves finally united against whatever menace threatens them and (often) their family. Parents are generally shown as distant and lacking understanding, and of course they are unbelievers when it comes to the supernatural forces terrifying their kids. Again, these conflicts are usually resolved, and the family stands together in the end. Adults are, however, usually outsiders to the bulk of the plot, which is normal for kids' books for this age; this population is just beginning to spread its wings. The narrator of *The Blob That Ate Everyone* confides to the reader, "My parents are the kind of people who get upset very easily. . . . So I never tell them much. I mean why ruin their day—or mine?" (29).

The most powerful theme of the books is fear, but it is not simply fear of monsters or the supernatural. Over and over the main character of a book, who is generally the narrator, is given bogus scares by another kid (or occasionally an adult), who then unmercifully, and often publicly, teases the frightened child. These episodes cause a great deal of humiliation and, often, anger. Many of the kids admit they are cowards. In *The Blob That Ate Everyone*, Zackie, the twelve-year-old first-person narrator, is afraid of everything—the dark, mice, big dogs, going to the basement when he's alone in the house, "a lot of other things" (48). But he writes scary stories. Why? "I don't know. Maybe I write better stories because I know what being scared feels like" (48). Zackie's schoolmates repeatedly play tricks on him and mock him for his fear. In The *Curse of the Mummy's Tomb* the main character, who gets lost in the Great Pyramid of Egypt, is also afraid of the dark, and he is teased for that by his uncle and his snippy girl cousin. So one of the main fears found in Goosebumps is the fear of being discovered to be a coward. I think, however, that the books contain a certain reassurance that it's really all right to be afraid. Being scared can even be fun; why else read these books?

Another fear prevalent in the Goosebumps I have read is the fear of loss of control. In both *The Night of the Living Dummy* and *The Night of the Living Dummy II*, a ventriloquist's dummy comes to life and is clearly malevolent. In the first *Dummy* novel, the dummy speaks for itself during performances, insulting neighbors and a teacher for being old, fat, ugly (and certainly this is the way that children often see adults); the dummy expresses the inner thoughts of the child. In the second Dummy book the bad dummy repeatedly trashes the room of the narrator's older sister, of whose painting talents the narrator is extremely jealous. The narrator is punished for acts she might have liked to commit but never would have actually committed. We all fear saying what we really think, doing what we wish to—but must not—do.

Loss of control occurs over and over in Goosebumps, and that is a very common fear. In *Attack of the Jack-o'-lanterns*, a group of children are forced to trick-or-treat "forever," also being forced to eat more candy than they want in order to make room in their bags. (This is one of the few books to have any clear moral, a warning against greed and gluttony.) One of the corollaries of loss of control is getting lost, and this happens often, too. In *Welcome to Dead House*, the main characters become lost in their new neighborhood. In *The Beast from the East*, the main characters get lost in the woods, with scary consequences. In this book the lost children are sucked into a strange game, where the monsters make up, and seem to constantly change, the rules. This situation is a real one for children, not only in their own games, but in the game of school, of life.

Darker fears appear, as well. *Welcome to Dead House*, which takes place in a village of the living dead, exploits the fear of death and the dead. *The Curse of the Mummy's Tomb* touches upon the same fear.

The novels work nicely in this way; while children are getting "goosebumps" from the scariness of the plot, they are also working through some of the problems and fears in their everyday lives. And even though some of the fears touched on by the books are far from superficial, the way in which the fears are treated keep them light:

> We both screamed again as the Blob Monster bounced into the room.
>
> [Its] body heaved up and down. The creature panted, its entire body bouncing. White slime puddled on the floor around it.
>
> And then I saw the fat purple tongue leap. It rolled out of the Blob Monster's open belly like a garden hose.
>
> "NOOOOOO!" I opened my mouth in a terrified wail as the tongue stretched across the room. Reached for me. . . .
>
> Reached for me. . . . (*The Blob That Ate Everyone* 104-105).

It's pretty hard, even when you are eight years old, to take a bouncing gooey monster too seriously; the characters are indeed frightened, but the reader really has more the feeling of fear associated with a ride on a roller coaster: screaming is fun. Similarly, it is difficult to construe the few magic spells and incantations found in this book as satanic. They are about as satanic as "abracadabra!"

There is not much overt moralizing in Goosebumps. There are a few lessons—it's not nice to tease, and too much Halloween candy could make you sick—but, basically, it is not didactic children's literature. Really, it's all a game. Goo is more fun than blood, and an evil monster may scare you, but it can never harm you in the way that real people could. I think that the little theme at the end of "The Twilight Zone" is the feeling that most kids must have at the end of a Goosebumps book. And these books do get children to read.

## Works Cited

Stine, R. L. *Attack of the Jack-o'-Lanterns*. New York: Scholastic, 1996.
———. *The Beast from the East*. Scholastic, 1996.
———. *The Blob That Ate Everyone*. Scholastic, 1997.

———. *The Curse of the Mummy's Tomb*. Scholastic, 1993.

———. *Night of the Living Dummy*. Scholastic, 1993.

———. *Night of the Living Dummy II*. Scholastic, 1995.

———. *Welcome to Dead House*. Scholastic, 1992.

# In Defense of *Gilly*

## Connie Russell

*Thanks to the human heart by which we live,*
*Thanks to its tenderness, its joys, and fears,*
*To me the meanest flower that blows can give*
*Thoughts that do often lie too deep for tears.*

Wordsworth's words quoted by Mr. Randolph in *The Great Gilly Hopkins* are a metaphor for Gilly, its feisty protagonist. Katherine Paterson's Newbery Honor Book, written in 1979, features an eleven-year-old foster child who has been shuttled from home to home until she buries her feelings so deeply that no one or nothing can hurt her. Her only love is for her mother, Courtney Rutherford Hopkins, who left Gilly behind a long time ago. Gilly's sure there is some significant reason or mistake, or her mother would have come to get her.

Since her last foster mother has been hospitalized for "her nerves," Gilly's on the move once more with Ms. Ellis, the social worker, who is taking her to meet her new family. She's shocked to see Maime Trotter, a large, unkempt, Bible-thumping woman that Gilly sees as just a "fat, fluff-brained religious fanatic" (13); William Ernest, a small, shy, slow boy of seven who hides behind Trotter's skirt; and Mr. Randolph, an elderly, blind black man who takes his meals with Trotter.

Gilly is determined to alienate her new family. She acts disrespectful toward Trotter, scares William Ernest, and scorns Mr. Randolph. By refusing to accept any love and doing everything she can to keep Trotter, William Ernest, and Mr. Randolph from loving her, Gilly can remain in control. After all, she can't give in to any feelings anymore; she needs to be in power. But Gilly hasn't reckoned with Trotter, whose love is as large as her body and who understands that Gilly fights back to escape being hurt anymore. Gilly's actions eventually lead to a decision that will cause her to confront her emotions and some bitter truths.

*The Great Gilly Hopkins* remains one of the books constantly on challenged lists. Those who challenge this wonderful children's book have traditionally objected to it on the basis of swearing, disrespect for adults, and prejudice. Used in a sixth-grade classroom as required reading, the book in a recent formal complaint was charged as inappropriate, lewd, and prejudiced, and not age appropriate (Library and Information Science News 1). In Albemarle County, Virginia, the book was banned in school libraries because "it contains curse words" and "takes God's name in vain." The parent who filed the complaint hadn't read the book—just had listed the profanities. Although a panel of educators twice recommended the book be kept on the shelves, the school superintendent removed it (Staples 2). In Arvada, Colorado, objections to the book in the elementary school library stated "profanity and disrespect" and "Christians are portrayed as being dumb and stupid" as reasons. (*Attacks on the Freedom to Learn*: The 1987-88 Report 16). In Yuba City, California, a student initiated the complaint because of "offensive language" and references to "witchcraft." (*Attacks on the Freedom to Learn*: The 1989-90 Report 33). In each of these instances, the book was retained.

Perhaps one of the lengthiest and most serious challenges took place in Cheshire, Connecticut. Parents, with support from the Rutherford Institute, voiced complaints at a local school board meeting, citing "profanity, blasphemy, and obscenities" as well as "derogatory remarks toward God and religion." They also charged that *The Great Gilly Hopkins* along with *The Alfred Summer*, by Jan Siepian, were "derogatory against blacks and women, and that the authors dragged God and the church in the mud and slyly endorsed unwholesome values such as stealing, smoking, drinking, and simply rebelling against authority" (*Attacks on the Freedom to Learn*: The 1991-92 Report 47). Petitions, a local priest's Sunday sermon, and the threat of a lawsuit from the Rutherford Institute bolstered the objection. While both books were withheld from the students during the review, the school board eventually upheld a review committee's decision to retain *The Great Gilly Hopkins* in the fifth-grade classroom. This district provides alternative assignments to children whose parents object to *Gilly*. Even though a complaint was filed with the state board of education protesting the school board's handling of the matter, the state Department of Education supported the school board's procedure and decision (*Attacks on the Freedom to Learn*: The 1991-92 Report 47).

Not all challenges have been settled as favorably. In Albemarle County, Virginia, a parent objected to the use of the book because of profanity. The superintendent accepted the review committee's recommendations to retain the book in classrooms but ordered it removed from district libraries, stating "In this case I felt the language in the book was not appropriate for all fifth-grade students who would have access to it on open shelves in the library" (*Attacks on the Freedom to Learn:* The 1993-94 Report 202).

Paterson's reply to these challenges is, "Gilly is a lost child who lies, steals, bullies. . . . She would not be real if her mouth did not match her behavior" (Feldman np). Paterson has shown herself to be a master of writing for children. *The Great Gilly Hopkins* alone has garnered many awards: National Book Award, 1979; Newbery Honor Award, 1979; Honor Book, Jane Addams Children's Book Awards, 1979; Christopher Award, 1979; American Library Association Notable Children's Books, 1978; and *School Library Journal* Best Book of 1978 (Paterson np).

To challenge this book is to ignore the critical work of so many prestigious literary organizations. As important, challenges ignore the tremendous popularity this book and other books by Paterson enjoy with students,—students who want stories about real life and real people.

Over the years I have either read this book to children or many times given it to them to read. I found it to be one of the most loved books and a novel that is, in my mind, a landmark book. Children readily identify with the hurt Gilly suffers and empathize with her while sometimes questioning her actions. Vivid debates occur as students discuss the plot as well as the characters. Readers find that Gilly's actions and spirit change as the story progresses. Gilly learns from Trotter's and William Ernest's acceptance of Mr. Randolph. She finds her black teacher Miss Harris a kindred soul who shares her anger with Gilly after a mean trick. Finally, Trotter teaches Gilly about love and acceptance; although Gilly wants to go back to Trotter at the end of the book, she recognizes the loneliness of her newfound grandmother and realizes she needs to stay with her. Telling Trotter that she loves her, Gilly's final thoughts as she goes to her grandmother are "no clouds of glory, perhaps, but Trotter would be proud" (148).

Gilly's story strikes a chord with students allowing them to talk and write about their own feelings. Gilly teaches us that we often lash out in anger when we are hurt by the words or actions of others. She also teaches us that we have to accept the responsibility for our actions. When Gilly is caught with the money she steals from Mr. Randolph, she's forced to give it back and work to pay the five dollars she has given her friend, Agnes. When Mr. Randolph accepts the money and dispenses no sermon on stealing, Gilly takes his hand to lead him to supper at Trotter's house. Students who haven't read other Paterson books clamor for more. They adopt Paterson's techniques in their own writing. For example, one sixth-grade girl attempted the use of soliloquy in her story.

I find challenges to this book interesting, as many of those who object to this book are the same people fighting for the teaching of values in our schools. I can think of no better book than *Gilly* to teach values. Without preaching, Paterson extols the virtues of compassion, honesty, integrity, and responsibility in this book.

Realistically, however, we will continue to have books challenged by those who feel their values are being eroded. Teachers must be prepared to defend book choices in their classrooms, and administrators must support those choices. If teachers believe that certain books may be challenged, they should be prepared to have reviews of those books available for parents. Districts must have a policy in place that allows them to handle challenges appropriately. However, I believe that guidelines for teachers must accompany a district policy. The Eau Claire Area School District in Eau Claire, Wisconsin, published the following guidelines for teachers several years ago:

> • Listen politely to the parent(s).
> • Ask specifically about the objections and whether or not the parents have read the entire book.
> • Be prepared to offer another meeting where reviews of the books as well as any awards are shared with the parent.
> • If the above steps fail, offer an alternative title for the student.

If alternative selections are allowed, most complaints about certain books never reach the challenge stage. Once a policy and guidelines for teachers are in place, their use results in most books being kept in the classroom or library. Consideration policies and guidelines for teachers also provide teachers with the support they need so that they don't self-censor books that they think they'll have problems with.

Paterson's son and playwright David Paterson turned *The Great Gilly Hopkins* into a play several years ago. He managed to make Gilly's inner voice heard by making the play a musical with the help of composer Steven Liebman. *The New York Times* reviewer wrote "Rewards in abundance await audiences fortunate enough to make their way to the New Victory Theater in Times Square." However, David Paterson tells of the ultimate accolade he received. A large burly man sat in a theater seat hunched over and weeping. His daughter patted him on the back and whispered, "It's okay, she's going to be all right. Gilly's going to be fine" (32). Gilly affects people that way. We care for her and her foster family. What more can we ask of a book than to care for its characters as our own?

If we as educators and parents wish to fight alliteracy (an unwillingness to read) along with illiteracy, we must introduce literary works such as *The Great Gilly Hopkins* to our young readers. Books such as Paterson's create lifelong readers.

## Works Cited

*Attacks on the Freedom to Learn*: Reports from 87-88, 89-90, 91-92, 93-
    94. Washington, D.C.: People For the American Way, 1988, 1990,
    1992, and 1994.
Feldman, Barbara J. "Surfing the Net with Kids." 11 September 2000.
    http://www.surfnetkids.com/banned.htm.
*Library and Information Science News*. "What's New?—One Week View."
    2 January 1990. http://www.lisnews.com/topics/censorship.htm.
Paterson, David. "Gilly Hopkins: From the Page to the Stage." *School
    Library Journal*, July 1998, Vol. 44, Issue 7, p. 32.
Paterson, Katherine. *The Great Gilly Hopkins*. New York: Thomas Y.
    Crowell, 1978.
———. Home Page http://terabithia.com/awards.htm.
Staples, Suzanne Fisher. "What Johnny Can't Read: Censorship in
    American Libraries." *Digital Library and Archives*, Winter 1996.
    http://scholar.lib.vt.edu/ejournals/ALAN/ winter96/pupconn .html

# Things Fade and Alternatives Exclude: Truth and Myth in John Gardner's *Grendel*

## Lynda Durrant

Which came first, truth or the need for truth? Or, which came first, the need for truth or the flattery of myth?

John Gardner's *Grendel* retells the epic poem *Beowulf* but from the monster's point of view. In the original, Beowulf is a Dark Ages Geat, a tribal people, who, along with the Danes, lived on the Danish island of Zealand and in southern Sweden. Beowulf was a real person and took part in a 520 A.D. raid on the Franks made by Hygelac, the king of the Geats. *Beowulf* is a Pan-Northern European poem and continued as oral tradition for hundreds of years before it was written down in eighth-century England.

It is Beowulf who saves the Danes in King Hrothgar's meadhall from the horrible man-eating Grendel.

In John Gardner's version, Beowulf does kill Grendel (or does Grendel kill himself?); but the great epic battle, the central event in the original, is more of an afterthought here. Instead, John Gardner asks the reader to consider truth versus myth. How do we know, instinctively, that life is chaotic at best and brutal at worst? Why do we insist on some sort of shape or pattern to our existence even if we know that shape is just an illusion? Why do we say we want the truth but allow ourselves to be beguiled by and pandered to with myth? Why is truth so much harder to find and even harder to acknowledge?

Gardner uses stunningly beautiful language meant to evoke the ancient cadences of Old Norse languages and Anglo-Saxon English. A rough sea is the whaleroad, a calm sea is the swanroad. Eyes are bright as dragonfire, cliffs are wolfslopes, the forest is the wolfroad, starry skies hurl forward falconswift.

But for all its Old Norse pagan atmosphere, *Grendel*, with its irony, slapstick humor, and bleak existentialism, could only be a modern novel.

In Beowulf's time, the Scandian people, the Danes in particular, lived lives nasty, brutish, and short. Night after night in the meadhalls, thanes plot thuggery and murder against rival tribes.

Gardner draws an unmistakable parallel between the male ego and heroism. Heroism is a violent game of rivalry, pillory, and murder disguised as myth. Robbing, stealing, murder—man's darkest impulses can be transmuted (and justified) as heroism. Without these dark impulses there can be no heroism; thus there can be no justification of the male ego's urge to dominate.

King Hrothgar's people (like people everywhere) look for reasons for their suffering. Some of the Danes blame themselves for their misery. Guilt and humiliating remorse are at least better than admitting that the world is made up of random acts of violent chaos and that we are the helpless victims. Guilt means a measure of control. (If I'm a good person . . . if we are good people . . . surely Grendel won't bother us again.)

But Grendel is neither scapegoat nor illusion. He really is evil. He has the strength to tear open meadhalls as though they were made from Lincoln Logs. He eats people and livestock alike. After his meeting with the world-weary dragon, King Hrothgar's thanes can't even scratch him with their swords, much less kill him.

We see the worst part of Grendel in the beginning of the novel. He has no sense of his own evil. He is infantile, selfish, rotten with self-pity, with no more accountability for his actions than a toddler. He is like men when there are no laws to curb man's darkest and most selfish instincts. Grendel sees his humanness (but not his humanity) reflected in the Danes. They even speak the same language, although Grendel speaks an archaic variety. Interestingly enough, the Danes don't see themselves in Grendel. He's a monster and he needs to be killed.

Grendel has another thing in common with King Hrothgar's people; they all suffer an agonizing separateness from the world around them. Both Grendel and the Danes seek patterns and crave reasons for their existences.

Then the Shaper steps into the meadhall and gives Hrothgar's thanes the spurious gift of myth. He praises another time (the fraud of nostalgia) when men were strong enough, brave enough, *man* enough to quash the evil among them. The challenge is presented as a medieval gauntlet: why can't Hrothgar's thanes be like the thanes of old? Things were so much better in the good old days.

Myth is self-flattering (wise, good King Hrothgar), self-aggrandizing (thanes loyal and true), and future-predicting (some day our redeemer will come and destroy Grendel). The Shaper's myths become more and more boastful and at the same time, more and more soothing to the thanes.

And yet, heroes are myth and mere myth is no match for evil. The more the thanes boast, the more Grendel's power becomes absolute. The strongest thane can't even pierce through his fur.

Grendel engages one especially boastful thane, Unferth, in an apple battle, to show how ridiculous heroic myth is. Unferth is chagrined—who will praise his bravery, in song and tribute—when the weapons at hand are glossy, red apples? Unferth follows Grendel back to his cave determined to seek vengeance or die a hero's death trying. Grendel refuses to kill him because killing Unferth would validate a myth, of a loyal thane dying for his king.

> Lying on the cave floor and waiting for death, Unferth says: "Except in the life of a hero, the whole world's meaningless. The hero sees values beyond what's possible. That's the nature of a hero. It kills him of course, ultimately. But it makes the whole struggle of humanity worthwhile." (89)

Grendel says, "And breaks up the boredom."

A humiliated Unferth is carried back by Grendel to the meadhall forever changed. He sees his own heroism as fraud and is unable to take it seriously again. Grendel tells us: "He (Unferth) lives on, bitter . . . crazy with shame . . . and furiously jealous of the dead. I laugh when I see him. . . . So much for heroism." Who Unferth perceives himself to be, a loyal thane of Hrothgar, has been exposed as mere ego, a little man thrusting his sword at the universe, demanding vengeance.

So if myth is false, what is truth? Why do people claim to want the truth then settle gratefully for myth instead? People settle for myth because truth is so much harder to achieve. Truth requires sacrifice and the putting aside of ego. Truth is gentle—the small, still voice—but it requires much more courage than Hrothgar's thanes possess.

Gardner shows us truth with the queen. Old King Hrothgar's queen is a young woman and the sister of a rival leader. She gives up her home, her family, and her own happiness to maintain the happiness of her people and Hrothgar's people. Night after night, she pours mead into Hrothgar's thanes' cups. She is royalty, and the sister of a rival, and yet she acts as a supplicant, as a servant, to Hrothgar's thanes.

She does not complain. She does not plot revenge: "When drunken men argued, pitting theory against theory, bludgeoning each other's absurdities, she came between them, wordless, uncondemning, pouring out mead like a mother's love." When one thane tells her that it was boastful Unferth who killed his brother, she forgives him ("that's in the past") (104).

Grendel tells us about Unferth's reaction: "The demon was exorcized, I saw his hands unclench, relax" (104). Miracle of miracles, she forgives him. She both forgives *and* forgets.

Grendel compares the queen to a rose blooming in December. (Was Gardner familiar with *Den Yndiste Rose er Funden*, the seventeenth-century Danish hymn in which Jesus is described as a rose blooming in darkest winter?) The analogy is the same. The rose—lovely, seemingly gentle, but strong—is praised for being the exception to the rule.

Grendel can't kill the queen, but not for the same reason he didn't kill Unferth. Unferth was a braggart, and killing him would have meant a hallowed place in the pantheon of meadhall champions. Grendel wanted to deny him that pleasure.

One night everyone is there in the meadhall—Unferth, the queen's brother, King Hrothgar, the drunk-and-spoiling-for-blood thanes. In front of all those witnesses, all-powerful Grendel can't bring himself to kill the queen because of her essential goodness. He *wants* to kill her and fantasizes about a lingering and cruel death. (Surely this scene is the reason why this novel has fallen under the censor's ire.)

This scene is also the crux of the book: Truth is goodness and it is truth that will conquer evil. Myth hasn't a chance.

Despite himself, Grendel sees the unselfish good in her. Grendel even thinks about killing himself, for the sake of the baby Grendel, who surely, he believes, had the same goodness as the queen. He recognizes the queen's goodness, but we know better than to believe his comparison. Except for this one small moment in his life, Grendel isn't anything like the queen and never has been.

He is, however, subtly different from now on. Does he feel guilty for wanting to kill her in such a brutal way? And if he feels guilty, does he then recognize the evil within himself?

Gardner writes, things fade and alternatives exclude. It's only a matter of time before something stronger than Grendel shows up. Grendel can feel the power: Something new is in the air.

That something new is Beowulf who has (finally) come to vanquish Grendel. He's a Geat and not a Dane. Again, myth making: An outsider has to kill the dreaded foe. We insiders are not worthy—not pure enough—to conquer evil. Beowulf overcomes Grendel because his reality is stronger. All things being equal, mind over matter wins.

Grendel's sense of self—his pattern, his shape—is *bete noir* to the Danes. That's what the Shaper's flattering myth has told Grendel about himself. But if Grendel can't be their Big Bad Wolf anymore . . . just who is he? His moment of guilt is his chink in the armor, so to speak. He is not pure evil anymore.

Grendel fades; he hasn't got an alternative, so he excludes himself. Does he let Beowulf win? Maybe. He does try to save face. He claims to have been tricked, to have been in some sort of an accident. To not being himself. Again, who is he now?

*Beowulf* the poem leaves no doubt as to who the victor is. The conquering hero is without a doubt Beowulf, the champion of champions. He's the hero generations of drunken Vikings toasted to endlessly.

We who live in the twenty-first century can only wonder. Our very thoughts are tainted with irony and ambiguity. We carefully sift though the evidence, consider both sides, recognize truth and the root causes of myth making, and prepare our arguments as to battle.

## Works Cited

Gardner, John. *Grendel*. Vintage Books ed. New York: Random House, 1989.

# Communicating Pleasure:
# *Halloween ABC* by Eve Merriam

## Judith Volc

## Summary:

A collection of twenty-six poems, *Halloween ABC*, written by Eve Merriam and illustrated by Lane Smith, follows the traditional alphabet book format and features each letter of the alphabet, one poem per letter. These poems celebrate the themes of Halloween with several references to European folklore. Examples of this include the very first poem, in which a poison apple, like the one offered to Snow White, is described as "Delicious, malicious, one bite and you're dead" and is in direct contrast with the Elf (in the poem for E), which "laughs in secret, hides from sight, can curdle milk, . . . can guard from harm, can bring a charm." Elves are tiny, often mischievous beings who bring good luck (charms) to those who treat them well. People often left food for them or, as in the story of *The Shoemaker and the Elves*, make clothing for them. Some sort of good deed by humans would be rewarded by the elves. Neglect, on the other hand, was often punished by the elves, who left some sort of mess or other mischief for the people to deal with. Perhaps the trick in "trick or treat" comes from these beliefs.

Noted poet Eve Merriam understands and communicates the pleasure that most people of any age get when they are just a little scared—that controlled fright when you know it's mostly in your imagination and there's really nothing scary out there. All Hallow's Eve may be rooted in a practice meant to frighten away evil spirits, but today Halloween is a holiday for dressing up, going to parties, eating too many sweets, and enjoying some momentary fright when someone says "boo." In our culture the consensus seems to be that scary is fun.

## The Alphabet

Merriam incorporates humor as well. The poem for F describes a Fiend as a "friend with fiendish glee as happy as can be, mixing fiendish drinks, stinking up the sinks." The humor is on two levels here. Kids love things that "stink." Stinky is a common nickname and not always derogatory. Holding one's nose and announcing that something stinks is a cue for laughter among many children. Adults, on the other hand, have probably faced a clogged sink with a sigh and a plunger but are willing to laugh about the experience later. Merriam also describes the fiend as "unwinding all the clocks, mismatching all the socks, growing grass upon its head, and never ever going to bed."

Here the humor for adults will again differ from that for children. Children up to about fifth grade will find the most humor in the line about "growing grass upon its head" and "never ever going to bed"—things they may wish on some level to be able to participate in or even accomplish. Adults understand better about clocks stopping and socks never matching because those are realities in their lives.

The variety of types of word play also characterizes this collection. Perhaps one of the best examples is in the poem for M. Here Merriam lists the attributes of Masks.

> Guises, disguises
> all kinds of surprises:
> A peasant's a king,
> a king's a knave,
> a knave's a donkey,
> a donkey's a slave.
> Conceal, conceal,
> peel off and reveal
> the mask that no one detects:
> your face that the mirror reflects.

The play on words in "guises, disguises" sounds fun to children. The different meanings for the same sound, guise which means appearance, how one looks, and disguise which means to change that appearance. Then, older children and most adults might tie the two words to the last line about the face of a person in the mirror. The guise is one that each person presents to the world, something donned every day, while the disguise is assumed and is more open and apparent, something more fun and communal.

The center lines deal simply with the practice around the world of donning masks to pretend to be someone or something else. The intent may be to change status such as the peasant disguised as a king—the poor and often powerless pretending to be rich and powerful, or a child dressed as a superhero. Next the king, a man of power and hopefully of wisdom and humanity, becomes a knave or a cheat, a rogue—someone with no sense of the responsibility that a ruler should display—or a child dressed as a cat or clown.

In our culture the donning of masks is mostly playful, but in other cultures it may have deeper meanings. The masks of the Hopi and of Masaii hold religious and cultural significance. Gail Haley's book *Go Away, Stay Away* deals with a fictional family beset with small nuisances that are driven away when family and friends don masks and engage in a ritual to drive them out. Haley's notes at the end detail the Hobby Horse Dance of central and western Europe and mentions similar practices in Africa, Indonesia, China, the Pacific, and among Native people of both North and South America, including some Arctic peoples.

T for Trap features a play on words with similar sounds and similar meanings.

> Get a trap set a trap
> trap trap trap
> tap you slap you
> try to wriggle free
> coax you hoax you
> snare take care
> catch you latch you
> never get free
> hook you crook you
> can't catch me.

Synonyms for trap included *snare, catch, hoax,* and *hook.* Each is accompanied with rhyming verbs: *trap* is rhymed with *slap,* and here *trap* is used as both a noun and as a verb. Snare is rhymed with care: an interesting choice because caring is not generally connected with snares; so the juxtaposition of these two can generate an interesting discussion about gaining emphasis by using words that enforce meaning sometimes but, at others, by using words that contrast, to draw attention. *Hoax* is rhymed with *coax.* One might be coaxed into a hoax or hoaxed by coaxing. Then *hook* is rhymed with *crook.* Since a crook, historically, is a sort of hook used to capture sheep, the entomology of the word *crook* as someone who takes things might be of interest.

Merriam also manages well the letters Q and X, which are often the bane of ABC books.

Q for Question is spooky because it describes the question "that you dare not ask" after using the wonderful poetic images of writing that question "on the North Wind" or "burying it in a wooden cask." Each reader is left to imagine what he or she personally might be fearful of asking as well as wondering what that might be for another—such as the author herself.

X for Xylophone, not an unusual choice in ABC books, fits the theme because she rhymes *tones* with *bones* while Lane Smith's illustrations of a xylophone completely made up of "leg bones" is slightly macabre. The allusion here is probably to the song enjoyed by many children about "the foot bone connected to the ankle bone" and so on. Whether or not one thinks the song is educational (teaching children the bones of the body from the toes up) or is just silly varies according to the audience. Students see bones in museums in display as educational items. Dinosaur bones are among the most popular exhibits in natural history museums, and Merriam and Smith capitalize on this in both the verse and the illustration.

J for Jack-o-'lantern is, by contrast, straight humor with lines about empty head, missing teeth, and turning to mush or pumpkin pie in the end. Many pumpkins are raised specifically for the making of jack-o-lanterns, and field trips to farms to choose just the right ones for carving are part of the fall season. The type of face chosen may be funny, scary, or highly artistic. There are books published with wide varieties of patterns for faces, safety information about carving, recipes for the seeds and pumpkin flesh, tools for carving, and even candles to illuminate them. Some even include information about composting.

O for Owl uses alliteration of the word "who" as both a question and as the sound owls make. A reading of this poem before children usually elicits a lot of hooting and often recitals of other animal sounds.

The verse with C for Crawlers is rather spooky, but Lane Smith's accompanying drawing of a "crawler" with a human-like head will probably serve to alleviate the scary aspects. While many people find spiders, caterpillars, and worms creepy, others see them as good and necessary elements of the natural world. In the Muslim world, spiders are especially honored. Asthmatics like me had lizards, snakes, and spiders for pets. We're allergic to all the feathered and furry creatures. For us and many who simply see the fascination of the natural world, "crawlers" aren't in the least creepy.

With D for Demon, Merriam ends her poem with the line "the devil with it all!"—a phrase used to toss something aside or to indicate the end of the discussion and which makes light of the fearsome aspects here. This must be read aloud for children to understand it well. The inflection of a voice can convey meaning to an audience who haven't either the experience or background to understand the vocabulary and allusions used by many of our best authors.

On the other hand, the verse for A features a wormy apple, something few children experience because we've eliminated worms from our apples with sprays. They study ecocycles and know that worms are very positive elements in the process of enriching the soil that grows much of the food they eat. This image will work only for those who either understand the reference or who are silly enough to be squeamish about worms.

Bats in the belfry may be another image that most children won't recognize in this day and age when we view bats as highly useful consumers of insects—especially mosquitoes, which most children do know and abhor. The image of a bat today is that of helpful and very positive part of the ecology, and many children will see bats as only beneficial and not frightening at all. Only the connection of bats with the dark and nighttime may resound with children who are afraid of the dark.

Zero ends the whole romp wonderfully when it simply disappears and "no one knows where it came from" or where it goes—at least "No one alive will ever know." That spooky feeling again—the slight shiver to end this foray into the eerie.

The artist, Lane Smith, who received *New York Times Best Illustrated* award for this book in 1987, uses further references to western themes of Halloween, death, and scary monsters.

He uses humor in the illustration for N(ightmare). It shows not only a person in bed with the blankets pulled up to cover the head, but shows a dog cowering beneath the bed. Obviously neither person nor dog is asleep. Equally obvious is the fact that there is nothing there to frighten anyone but the idea of a "something under the bed," because here Smith has put a dog, man's best friend, under that bed.

A fifth-grade teacher annually has students write about how far from the bed they jump each night to avoid what might be under there. And they all know. Some actually measure the distance to tell him, and others write about how they've overcome the impulse. Most of us know someone, even adults, who close the closet door before going to sleep. We laugh about it together in the light, but even those of us who don't have the impulse to do it, do understand it.

When the book is closed and returned to a shelf, it ends this particular exploration of the slightly scary and the reader or listener goes back to the reality of a world of wormless apples and of xylophones with wooden keys but perhaps is left with a better understanding of his or her feelings about scary things, about humor, and about our language. Just as we shrug off the scary movies or plays when we leave the theaters and walk out into the street or turn off the television and leave the room, closing the book and laying it aside cuts us off from whatever was frightening in it.

Merriam's and Smith's take on Halloween in this book is to enjoy the eerie and to laugh at our atavistic fears even while we recognize that they exist. Both allude to basic elements commonly found in a variety of cultures. The exploration of language, its rich meaning, sound, and variety is exemplary. The award-winning art shows humor as well as outstanding design and composition.

## About the Author

The versatile Eve Merriam was an author, poet, copywriter, and playwright. One of her books of poetry for children, *The Inner City Mother Goose*, was made into a musical "Inner City," for which Linda Hopkins, who appeared in it, won a Tony award in 1972. Merriam was recognized for her body of work when she was chosen for the 1981 Award for Excellence in Poetry given to living American poets by the National Council of Teachers of English. She won the Yale Younger Poets Award in 1946 for her first published book, *Family Circle*, poetry for adults.

In her book *There is No Rhyme for Silver*, Merriam writes poetry about poetry and demonstrates the joys and problems of rhyming and not rhyming rather than just talking about it. For slightly older children she wrote *It Doesn't Always Have to Rhyme* with many of the same themes. In *Out Loud* she extols the virtues of reading aloud—especially poetry—and writes poems that make more sense when read aloud than when read silently. Just these few books are outstanding resources for learning about or for teaching about poetry.

## A Few Sources of Further Information about the Author and Her Works

Hopkins, Lee Bennett. *Books Are by People*. New York: Citation Press, 1969.

*Children's Literature Review*, vol. 14. ed. Gerard J. Senick. Farmington Hill, Mich.: Gale Research, 1988.

*Something About the Author*, vol. 40. ed. Anne Commire. Farmington Hill, Mich.: Gale Research, 1985.

*Something About the Author*, vol. 73. ed. Diane Telgen. Farmington Hill, Mich.: Gale Research, 1992.

## Some Notes about Challenges for This Title

*Halloween ABC* is listed number 16 on The Most Frequently Banned Books in the 1990s from Herbert N. Foerstel's *Banned in the USA*.
It is number 31 on the American Library's list "The 100 Most Frequently Challenged Books of 1990-1999, compiled by the Office for Intellectual Freedom of the ALA.

## Some of the Challenges Include

Challenged at the Douglas County Library in Roseburg, Oregon (1989), because the book "encourages devil worshiping."
Challenged at the Howard County, Maryland, School libraries (1991) because "there should be an effort to tone down Halloween and there should not be books about it in the schools."
Challenged in the Wichita, Kansas, public schools (1991) because it is "satanic and disgusting."
Challenged at the Acres Green Elementary School in Douglas County, Colorado (1992), as inappropriate for younger students.
Challenged (but retained) but will be shelved with other works generally available only to older students and won't be used in future Halloween displays at the Federal Way School District in Seattle, Washington (1992). The compromise was for a group of parents who objected to the book's satanic references.
Challenged (but retained) in Othello, Washington, elementary school libraries (1993) because the book "promotes violent criminal and deviant behavior."
Challenged (but retained) at the League City, Texas, Public Library (1993) on the grounds that the book focuses in death, murder, and deception.
Challenged (but retained) in the Cameron Elementary School Library in Rice Lake, Wisconsin (1993), because the "poems promote satanism, murder and suicide."

## Works Cited

Haley, Gail. Go *Away, Stay Away*. Blowing Rock, N.C.: New River Publishing, 1977.
Merriam, Eve. *Halloween ABC*. New York: Alladin Paperbacks, 1995.

# Called to Be a Handmaid:
# Defending Margaret Atwood

## Ruth Wood

I read *The Handmaid's Tale* for the first time riding a tour bus in Europe with my mother. Needling me as I ignored the banks of the Rhine outside our window, she asked, "Why are you reading that trashy book?" I was surprised that my mother, a devoted reader of romances, had any comment to make about this literary novel. "Have you read it?" I asked. "No," she replied, "but you don't have to to see what kind of book it is."

It hadn't occurred to me that the cover of the book and its title might spur the wary to lascivious conclusions, but consider: We typically hear of "handmaids" in archaic or biblical accounts of cloistered and kept women. The solitary handmaid depicted on the 1986 Anchor paperback cover wears a red cloak and a white mitred hat; she carries a straw basket as she walks away from the viewer past an institutional brick wall—Red Riding Hood headed toward an encounter with a wolfish lover?

I indulge this speculation partly to put my mother in common company, but also to help me understand why the bulk of criticisms launched at this novel deal with its "sexually explicit material and profanity," "sexual content," and "obscenity" (People for the American Way, 1991-1992, 1993-1994, 1994-1995, 1996). It's *not* a particularly explicit or sexy book. The premise of the novel is that late-twentieth-century America (called "Gilead") has been so damaged by nuclear fallout, environmental pollution, and international biological warfare that only a small percentage of its men and women remain fertile. Fertile women, now seen as Gilead's key to survival, have been rounded up and secluded from the rest of society to be "hand-maids" who live by rules that will best enhance their chances of getting pregnant. Each handmaid is assigned to a married couple's household and mated once a month by the husband, a ranking member of the ruling order, whose wife has already proven infertile.

The protagonist (a handmaid named Offred) describes her monthly engagement with Fred, "the Commander," crudely rather than sensually:

> *The Ceremony goes as usual.* I lie on my back, fully clothed except for the
> healthy white cotton drawers. . . . Above me, towards the head of the bed,
> Serena Joy [Fred's wife] is arranged, . . . her legs are apart, I lie between them,
> my head on her stomach, her pubic bone under the base of my skull . . . . She
> too is fully clothed. . . . This is supposed to signify that we are one flesh, one
> being. . . . My red skirt is hitched up to my waist, though no higher. Below it the
> Commander is fucking. What he is fucking is the lower part of my body. Do not
> say making love, because this is not what he's doing. (93-94)

The presence of the F-word is of course a red flag for censors, as are the
sensual thoughts that often seem to lurk behind Offred's usually carefully
chosen words. When she informs the reader that "Arousal and orgasm . . .
would be a symptom of frivolity merely " (94), she shows us that real human
sexual responsiveness is only repressed. Indeed, when Serena Joy sends the
yet unpregnant Offred to have sexual intercourse with their chauffeur, Nick,
in hopes that the Commander and she may somehow yet have a child,
Offred's sensual imagination bubbles over: "I can't see his face, and I can
hardly breathe. . . . His mouth is on me, his hands, I can't wait and he's
moving, already, love, it's been so long, I'm alive in my skin . . ." (261).

My mother didn't have to read these passages to "know" that the book
is "trash," nor, I suspect, do censors who want the book banned from high
school reading lists. She merely looked at the cover of a lone woman
departing from a cloistered environment and deftly concluded that the
character ends up sexually compromised—as does Offred. She has been torn
from her husband and five-year-old daughter and virtually compelled to
become a handmaid. Bereft of family and friends with no opportunity for
conversation beyond the managing of daily routines, no reading material, no
television or radio, and nothing but the impersonal touch involved in the
monthly doctors' appointments and "the ceremony," Offred is easily
tempted.

Who can blame censors for making a quick score? On its surface,
Atwood's novel displays a society whose elite women are concubines and
male leaders bigamists; it implies that social sanctions against liberal
sexuality do the opposite of repressing sexual appetites. For most would-be
censors, such content is all that is needed to close the case; a dominant point
of the book *is* that human urges are hard to control.

But just as the novel requires that the protagonist take time to contemplate the series of events and choices that have led her to this virtual prison,
so must a reader work through the novel carefully to get its object
lesson—that indifferent permissiveness coupled with a decreased sense of

social responsibility jeopardizes what Americans like to think of as "inalienable rights" and opens doors to factions that feel justified in controlling women's choices. *The Handmaid's Tale* urges the reader to forego "the privilege of ignoring" and learn to practice judicious self-governance. The novel is almost primly moral—even to the point of being somewhat antifeminist; *Critique* commentator David S. Hogsette noted that Atwood reveals the "absurdity" of "certain extreme radical feminist political views" (262).[1]

Hogsette also notes that the novel exposes the "absurdity" of Christian fundamentalism (262)—though Atwood refrains from giving the moral revolutionaries a specific affiliation. It becomes clear as the list of the regime's enemies expands that *sect* doesn't matter: Catholic priests are often executed; the Quakers are the enemy at one battlefront, Baptists at another; doctors who had practiced abortions before the Gilead takeover are publicly executed; the "Sons of Ham" are exiled into radioactive zones. The *intent* that Atwood abhors is the intent of social critics, purportedly bonded by theological tenets, to regulate and homogenize human behavior so that we do not question authority, so that we accept as natural women's primary function as submissive and selfless childbearers, so that we regard as superfluous women's ability to read, reason, and draw individual conclusions, and so that we accept the premise that governments will fight our enemies better without interference from the multivalent voices of the constituency.

Lois Lowry's popular and oft-censored novel *The Giver*[2] depicts a similarly indoctrinated citizenry. As in Gilead, every citizen in the world of Lowry's novel is assigned by the committee of elders to a role in life that takes best advantage of the "gifts" they're born with. Competition and anxiety are held in check by the equitable distribution of commodities; education and growing up equate with learning and following the vast set of rules by which society maintains harmony and equilibrium. Sexuality is repressed with the compulsory consumption of antiarousal pills (the fabled saltpeter?). Emotional responsiveness has been genetically phased out, environmentally controlled, and governmentally insured by the practice of euthanizing overly sensitive newborns; it is environmentally controlled by the stabilization of weather and the elimination of color and music—a *Brave New World* without soma tablets.

In their stead, the elders obliterate disturbing notions and sensations using the scapegoat model: one member is chosen as "The Receiver"—the sole repository of memories of human emotional experience—from the pain and passion of war to the tender joyousness of family Christmas celebrations.

The protagonist, Jonas, who has become the "Receiver," flees from this dystopian society when he discovers that his heretofore admired parents—and probably every other adult in the society—knowingly perpetuate the illusion that everyone is respected and nurtured, while they quietly exterminate the elderly, the weak, and the genetically inferior. Having realized that human existence is meaningless without shared knowledge, honest communication, and felt feeling, Jonas and the "Giver" (Jonas's mentor, whom he is to succeed), develop a daring plan to redistribute all these stored-up emotional memories among the whole population.

In both these novels, the "freedom not to care" (Hogsette 12) is licensed by leaving dispensable persons nameless and giving the state the power to name (babies are not given names in Lowry's novel until they've proven themselves conformable; worthy newborns are given recycled names—of recently euthanized elderly). As "Offred," Atwood's protagonist is a mere function of Commander Fred's power to impregnate her. Without a *name* or an identity, she has no agency.

Lowry's citizens presumably gave up individual agency voluntarily in order to avoid further horrors of devastating wars, but it is the *failure* to exercise agency among pre-Gilead individuals that enabled the religious regime to seize power in Atwood's novel. Their first step was to merely emboss an "m" for male and an "f" for female on the plastic cards that had become the only form of currency exchange. The next step—a simple command to a national computer network to invalidate money requests to all "f" card transactions—prevented women from going anywhere or doing anything without a male's help.[3]

A confluence of disasters (war rages, earthquakes cause considerable nuclear fallout from damaged reactors built along the San Andreas fault; infertility serums intended for export in Russian caviar somehow get consumed by the America military elite) helped set up the power vacuum that the regime stepped into. "I guess that's how they were able to do it . . . all at once, without anyone knowing beforehand," Offred thinks, "They suspended the Constitution. They said it would be temporary. . . . There wasn't even an enemy you could put your finger on" (174).

In the solitary confinement of her handmaid role, Offred comes to understand and acknowledge that by remaining detached, she had helped to create that vacuum. She remembers, for example, how easily she justified having an affair with a married man: "She [her friend Moira] said I was poaching, on another woman's ground. I said Luke wasn't a fish . . . , he . . . could make his own decisions. She said I was rationalizing. I said I was in love. She said that was no excuse. Moira was always more logical than I am." (171)

Ruefully Offred recalls trivializing her mother's attempts to encourage her political involvement, saying, "'Now, mother . . . let's not get into an argument about nothing.' 'Nothing' [her mother] would say bitterly. . . . 'You're still wet behind the ears, . . . you don't know what we had to go through, just to get you where you are'" (156). Only after she's lost the things her mother had struggled to get can Offred comprehend "how we squandered it"(114)—the right to speak, a life that provided humans with significant choices. "We lived, as usual," she reflects during "Handmaid training," "by ignoring. Ignoring isn't the same as ignorance, you have to work at it. . . . we lived in the blank white space at the edge of print. It gave more freedom" (76). Offred realizes that what she wants is not utter freedom, but the right to choose wisely; she comes to wish she could go back and have a fight with her husband, Luke, over their perceptions of *"important, unimportant"* (200).

Those expected to gorge on Gilead's feast find themselves equally starved by its strictures. Serena Joy's garden, says Offred, gives a "sense of buried things bursting upward" (Howells 40). Offred speculates that Serena Joy, who prior to the revolution had been a performer on Sunday morning religious shows, singing and making speeches "about the sanctity of the home, about how women should stay home," must be furious "now that she's been taken at her word" (45-46). The Aunts—those women who regulate and defend the utterly barren lives that Handmaids must live—realize that the only way to survive such a regimen is to be brainwashed from birth: "*Start them soon* is the policy, *there's not a moment to be lost*—still they'll remember . . . but after [four or five years] they won't. . . . They'll always have been silent" (219).

And while the males seem to suffer less, the most privileged character in the novel—Commander Fred—is "robbed of his choices in the process of robbing others of theirs" (Feuer 3). In spite of having two "wives," he has no lover and no helpmate, for his marriage is made sour and silent by Serena's resentment and jealousy,[4] and the law forbids emotional involvement with his handmaid. Honest conversation is impossible both inside and outside his home. So desperate is he for an even exchange of words that he sneaks Offred into his private room, not for sex, but for a game of Scrabble!

Offred earns her redemption in this book by daring to use words, daring to share an honest thought with a fellow handmaid—an act that reveals to her the existence of an underground resistance network. While walking with Offred on a shopping excursion, a fellow handmaid asks her if she truly believes that God hears the prayers delivered via the prayer machines (something like player pianos). To give her an answer, Offred knows, would be "treason." For a moment she thinks of screaming, running away, or accusing this "blasphemer," but instead she "steels [herself]" and quietly says, "No" (168). This brief interchange is a rite of initiation that eventually buys Offred escape, for the chauffeur Nick is also a member, and he is able to spirit her away to a safe house when her illicit activities with the Commander have been observed by the "Eyes." In effect, she earns her freedom merely by speaking.

"Writing," says Helene Cixous, "is precisely the possibility of change . . . . the precursory movement of a transformation of social and cultural structures" (879). Representing the recorded history of a character who has experienced the transformative power of conversation, *The Handmaid's Tale* is a deeply resonant charge against those in contemporary America who think we can cure the ills of our society by being straightlaced, prohibitive, and conventional in our morality while keeping silent about evils done in the name of free enterprise to our environment, our sense of community, and the poor and ethnically and religiously varied among us.

It's also a charge against the politically, economically, and morally complacent, and the socially and environmentally abusive who don't do their part to preserve what is worth preserving in this democratic society. The novel makes clear that America cannot remain a land of "equal opportunity" with personal freedoms guaranteed by our Constitution, unless we pay more than lip service to those ideals.

"Freedom," said Atwood in an interview, "requires constant vigilance. . . . The choices we make have material consequences; our privileged lives are intertwined with those who suffer elsewhere. . . . Oppression involves a failure to . . . imagine the full humanity of other human beings" (Bryden 53).

For its evenhandedness in condemning the ignorance of huge sections of the American populace, *The Handmaid's Tale* is both a painful and wonderful story—fascinating to read, interesting in its detailed conception of a futuristic society predicated on seeds planted in our time. Except among the "power elite," there are no books and few mirrors in Gilead—no opportunity to see oneself as others see us. The only hope expressed by the narrator is in telling her story to an attentive readership that will realize "why and how the social codes were constructed" and "why an individual accepts them" (Mycak 139-140).

If we take away books that help us look at ourselves for what we are and for what we may become, we foster Gilead. More than just keeping books such as Atwood's novel on our library shelves, we need for them to be taught in our classrooms, for without the dialogue and the deeper looking that classroom engagement affords the reader of *The Handmaid's Tale*, the book may indeed be misconstrued as sensationalism and political diatribe, when in fact it can help us to see the errors of our ways, as long as we reflect upon it rather than merely read it.

## Notes

1. See also Feuer, who says that "Part of Atwood's contribution is to show costs at both ends of the spectrum in the . . . debate" (5); [the Study Guide] "The language is feminist, but the result can be deeply patriarchal" 2; Mycak says that, while Atwood is called a feminist, she really isn't one (127).
2. See Avi's article in this volume.
3. One is tempted to gloss this by saying that Offred got "f_"ed.
4. "I am a reproach to her," Offred realizes (16).

## Works Cited

Atwood, Margaret. *The Handmaid's Tale*. New York: Anchor Books, 1986.

Bryden, Diana. "Beyond Violent Dualities: Atwood in Postcolonial Contexts." In *Approaches to Teaching Atwood's The Handmaid's Tale and Other Works*. Ed. Sharon R. Wilson, et al. New York: MLA Publications, 1996, 49-54.

Cixous, Helene. "The Laugh of the Medusa." Trans. Keith Cohen and Paul Cohen. *Signs* 13.3 (1988): 875-893.

Feuer, Lois. "The Calculus of Love and Nightmare: *The Handmaid's Tale* and the Dystopian Tradition." *Critique* 38 (Winter 1997): 83-95.

Hogsette, David S. "Margaret Atwood's Rhetorical Epilogue in *The Handmaid's Tale*: The Reader's Role in Empowering." *Critique* 38.4 (Summer 1997): 262-279.

Howells, Coral Ann. *Modern Novelists: Margaret Atwood*. New York: St. Martin's Press, 1995.

Lowry, Lois. *The Giver*. Boston: Houghton Mifflin Company, 1993.

Mycak, Sonia. "Psychoanalysis, Phenomenology, and the Novels of Margaret Atwood: A New Critical Approach." In *Margaret Atwood: The Handmaid's Tale/The Power Game*, ed. Jean Michel LaCroix and Jacques LeClaire. Paris: *Presse de la Sorbonne Nouvelle*, 1998, 127-145.

# Defending *Harry Potter*

## Elizabeth A. Poe

For the second year in a row, Harry Potter has topped the International Reading Association's Young Adult's Choices list. In 2000, J. K. Rowling's *Harry Potter and the Sorcerer's Stone* was rated first among the top thirty titles voted on with more than 11,000 ballots cast by seventh- to twelfth-grade students across the United States and its territory Guam. *Harry Potter and the Chamber of Secrets* claimed the lead position on the 2001 list with *Harry Potter and the Prisoner of Azkaban* coming in a close second. Harry's heading the lists comes as no surprise because Rowling's books hold high appeal for readers in this age group. They are, first and foremost, exciting stories about interesting characters told in a compelling manner that draws readers in and enables them to savor the author's words from beginning to end. Creating such stories is not an easy task, given the abundance of reluctant readers among our middle and high school students, and teachers and parents all over the country commend Rowling for giving our young people Harry Potter.

The character Rowling has created is a British orphan who lives rather unhappily with his aunt, uncle, and cousin—the Dursleys—until his eleventh birthday, when he learns he has been accepted at Hogwarts School of Witchcraft and Wizardry because, much to Harry's surprise, his dead parents were a famous witch and wizard. Ashamed and embarrassed that Mrs. Dursley's sister, Lily Potter, was born with magical abilities, Vernon and Petunia Dursley reluctantly take the orphaned Harry in but raise him to believe that his parents were killed in an automobile accident. They tell Harry that the scar on his forehead is a result of this car crash, when in fact it is the mark of the evil wizard Voldemort, who killed Harry's parents because they would not come over to the Dark Side with him. The scar marks the place where Voldemort's curse was deflected by the maternal love protecting Harry. The wizard world believes Voldemort was killed by his own death curse, and Harry is famous because he thwarted Voldemort in his goal to conquer death.

Despite the Dursleys' attempt at hiding his ancestry from him, Harry has inherited his parents' magical powers, and now it is time for him to learn to use them properly at Hogwarts. Thus, Harry learns of the society of magical people and creatures that coexists with the Muggle, or nonmagical, world in which he has been living. His expanded world sports giants, goblins, dragons, ghosts, poltergeists, and unicorns as well as friends Ron Weasley and Hermione Granger. The boarding school Harry and his friends attend is an enchanted castle with talking portraits, secret passageways, and overgrown forests. The students study the art and craft of magic, learning to develop their magical abilities and use them responsibly.

Learning is emphasized at Hogwarts, but age-old struggles between good and evil within the magical world add another layer to Harry's education. Modest, unassuming, and the quintessential reluctant hero, Harry encounters one adventure after another. His adventures may stem from schoolboy pranks—such as sneaking out of the castle at night to visit the village of Hogsmeade, or defending a friend, such as Hagrid the Groundskeeper, against bullying from malcontent students—but they ultimately involve facing the arch-evil Lord Voldemort, the power-hungry wizard who went bad. Although Harry does not really understand it, Voldemort (or He-Who-Must-Not-Be-Named—because he is so fearfully evil) must destroy Harry if he is to gain the power over death he craves. Thus, as Harry's schooling teaches him to cast and unravel spells and otherwise defend himself against the Dark Arts, he is also learning about his place in the scheme of the battle between good and evil raging within the wizard world.

But all Harry's education does not necessarily concern magic. At Hogwarts he quickens his reflexes playing Quidditch, and he develops his sense of loyalty as a member of the Gryffindor House. He learns who his parents were and that when his mother died, her fierce maternal love defended Harry against the evil Voldemort, and her love protects him still. He experiences the warmth of friendship with Ron and Hermione and the affectionate attentiveness of the Weasley family. These nonmagical lessons also prepare him for battle against Voldemort.

Harry is an inspirational character. He is intelligent, hardworking, loyal, resourceful, self-sacrificing, and brave. However, he is not perfect, and far from a goody-goody. He does, as his adult critics point out, lie to adults and break the rules. But Harry is also moral. His seemingly instinctual sense of right and wrong makes him expect and fear consequences for his wrong doings when others might try to argue they were acting for a higher cause that justifies exemption from punishment. Humble and respectful, however, Harry expects to be punished and is surprised by mercy and compassion from authority figures. Often baffled and embarrassed by his fame in the wizard world, he does not believe himself entitled to special treatment; one might say that the significance of Voldemort's lightning bolt scar on his forehead, has *not* gone to Harry's head.

Although Harry possesses many positive qualities, it is his courage that makes him heroically impressive. Time after time Harry stands up for himself and others in terrifying circumstances. He does not give in even when the situation seems hopeless, as it does in *Goblet of Fire* when Voldemort challenges him to a wizards' duel. Surrounded by Voldemort's supporters, the Death Eaters,

> Harry crouched behind the headstone and knew the end had come. There was no hope . . . no help to be had. And as he heard Voldemort draw nearer still, he knew one thing only, and it was beyond fear or reason: He was not going to die crouching here like a child playing hide-and-seek; he was not going to die kneeling at Voldemort's feet. . . . he was going to die upright like his father, and he was going to die trying to defend himself, even if no defense was possible. . . . (662)

Harry clutches his wand and bravely faces his mortal enemy. Such courage in the face of evil not only inspires, it also makes for exciting reading.

The complex plots Rowling weaves throughout the Harry Potter books are another source of reading excitement as well as a means for readers to exercise higher-order thinking skills. Rowling masterfully introduces a multitude of intriguing characters, involves them in intricate plots and subplots, and then skillfully ties up all the loose ends in a way that delights and amazes. Thus, just as Harry and his friends must think both analytically and imaginatively in order to resolve problematic situations in which they find themselves, readers must employ complex thinking skills in order to keep track of the multifaceted characters and unravel intricate plots encountered as they accompany Harry on his adventures. Readers must think analytically as they gain understanding of the rules that govern wizardry and determine whether or not Rowling has created a world that is consistent and believable although completely fantastical. They also exercise their own imaginations as they visualize the settings, characters, and events Rowling so vividly describes. Readers, therefore, experience the importance of thinking on two levels as they participate in Harry's problem-solving efforts, which frequently apply knowledge learned at Hogwarts, and as they use their own minds to envision the world in which Harry lives.

Harry's world and the epic Rowling spins within it are tightly connected to a rich literary tradition. While reading the Potter books, readers will find influences from Greek and Roman mythology as well as glimpses of the

*Cinderella* fairy tale, the *Star Wars* films, Lewis Carroll's *Alice's Adventures in Wonderland* and *Through the Looking Glass*, J. R. R. Tolkien's *Trilogy of the Rings*, Dickens's *Oliver Twist*, Milton's *Paradise Lost*, Dante's *Divine Comedy*, Sir Arthur Conan Doyle's *The Adventures of Sherlock Holmes*, C. S. Lewis's *Chronicles of Narnia*, Oscar Wilde's ghost stories, and tales of Arthur and Merlin, as well as Madeleine L'Engle's *Time Quartet* and John Knowles's *A Separate Peace;* Joseph Campbell's *A Hero with a Thousand Faces*, and images and stories from the Old Testament may also come to mind. By drawing heavily and unabashedly from the literary tradition in which she grew up, Rowling situates her story in literary contexts familiar to many. Her highly creative use of existing literary references, conventions, and motifs may inspire readers to tease out the familiar and explore the unfamiliar literary traditions she uses, thereby providing a layer of intellectual stimulation in the search for intertextual connections. Investigating the creatures, names, and events invented by Rowling can also be an intellectually interesting pursuit.

Some adults have expressed concern over the violence in the Harry Potter books. This question can be addressed in terms of the tradition from which the books stem. High fantasy, the literary category into which the Harry Potter books fall, is inherently concerned with the struggle between good and evil and generally involves magic and other supernatural forces. By making the evil really evil, even violent and scary, Rowling is able to make the good really good, and therefore accentuate its importance. If Harry were not battling pure evil, his victories would be diminished and the story would be weakened. The odds are high for Harry and the risk is great. Thus his triumphs are also great, making him the heroic figure that young readers find so appealing.

Another concern voiced by some adults involves the negative presentation of the Dursleys, Harry's adoptive family, who treat him so dreadfully. Although they spoiled their son Dudley even before Harry arrives, Uncle Vernon and Aunt Petunia flaunt Dudley's most-favored-child status while living in dread that the terrible family secret of Harry's wizardry (they know he has inherited his mother's magical bent even before the letters from Hogwarts arrive) will be discovered, and they will be publicly humiliated. They lie to Harry about his family background, and they lie to their extended family, friends, neighbors, and business associates about where Harry goes to school. Harry in turn deceives them with matters concerning his friends and education at Hogwarts.

Harry and the Dursleys are clearly not a model family, and if they were the only family in the story, there might be justified cause for concern. But fortunately Ron Weasley's family provides a loving surrogate family for

Harry, and Hermione Granger's family (who are Muggles like the Dursleys) exemplifies unconditional parental support. The Weasleys and the Grangers provide a more balanced view of families for both Harry and his readers. Furthermore, the intricate spell Headmaster Albus Dumbledore weaves to protect Harry against Voldemort when he is with his relatives sends a metaphorical message that children are ultimately protected from harm when they are with their families, even though they may not always get what they want.

More problematic for some than the violence or negative portrayal of adult authority figures is the subject matter of wizardry and witchcraft around which the Potter stories revolve. Readers and critics within the Christian community are mixed in their views of Harry Potter as a wizard. Some feel his wizardry is a harmless aspect of a fantasy story, something to be discussed in the family setting to clarify any religious questions it might provoke. Others fear reading Harry Potter will numb youngsters to the evils of witchcraft and perhaps even lure them into the occult, and, therefore, consider it spiritually dangerous reading material. There are also Christians who view the wizardry metaphorically rather than literally. The emphasis in this case would be the battle of good versus evil taking place within the wizard world. It is ultimately not an issue of good wizards against bad wizards, but of good versus evil period. (Dumbledore seems to represent the good that is supporting Harry, but because the series is not complete, we do not know exactly the nature of Dumbledore's goodness and how his powers will play out.) For those open to discussion, Harry Potter can serve as an effective vehicle for examining spiritual beliefs held by individuals or religious groups. Many adolescent readers would welcome such philosophical conversations to clarify their own beliefs and help them understand the beliefs of others. It is important to note, however, that to many young Christian readers the wizards and witches are just part of an imaginative story that affords compelling reading without necessarily raising religious questions.

The Harry Potter books raise other important questions in addition to religious issues. The topic of racism is introduced when pureblooded Malfoy taunts Hermione for being a Muggle and Muggle-mothered Harry for being a Mudblood, while Hagrid is humiliated because his mother was a Giant. The issue of slavery comes into question with Hermione's crusade to free the house elves from their bonds of servitude, even though they do not choose to seek freedom themselves. Concerns about muckraking journalism surface as Rita Skeeter reports illegally begotten information biased against Harry and his participation in the Triwizard Tournament. Encountering these issues in the Harry Potter books may encourage readers to consider them in light of historical or contemporary parallels in their own world. Such thought-provoking subject matter, along with the personally inspiring themes of loyalty, courage, and self-sacrifice threaded throughout the stories, provides food for thought even for readers so caught up in Harry's adventures that they can't turn the pages fast enough.

This fascination with Harry Potter has led to the books' phenomenal popularity around the globe. Record-breaking listings on the *New York Times* Best-Sellers List, spawning the creation of a separate category for juvenile fiction; sales reports of dollars in the double-digit millions; children standing in line for hours to buy the newest Harry Potter release or to meet J. K. Rowling herself have brought unprecedented global attention to a series of books written for children. The attention Harry Potter and J. K. Rowling have received in the media make it impossible to discuss the books themselves without addressing the Harry Potter phenomenon, or as some call it, Pottermania. For with success comes the inevitable criticism, and perhaps the Harry Potter phenomenon is even more controversial than the books themselves. The Harry Potter debate takes place in newspapers, mass market magazines, and professional journals. Some critics object to the hype surrounding the books: the high-powered market strategies, the media honing in on individuals or groups of would-be censors. Others raise their eyebrows at the amount of money Rowling and her publishers are making from books for children. Still, others denounce the literary value of a series so popular, calling it merely faddish.

But critics' concerns pale in the light of preadolescents and adolescents' fervor for reading Harry Potter. Accounts of reluctant readers who devour the Potter stories, of avid readers who have read each of the books four or five times, of families delighting in reading the books together testify to the value of Harry Potter and champion his cause in a way that cannot be dismissed. In addition, J. K. Rowling and Scholastic, Inc., are donating the net proceeds from Rowling's two Harry Potter companion books to Comic Relief, a British charity. Proceeds from *Quidditch Through the Ages* and *Fantastic Beasts & Where to Find Them,* written with Rowling's characteristic wit and cleverness, will go to the Harry's Books fund for the purpose of improving and saving the lives of children around the world.

A good story has far-reaching repercussions, and fortunately readers across the globe are benefiting from Rowling's talent for telling an exceptionally good story. And fortunately as well, those finding themselves in a position requiring them to defend their use of the Harry Potter books will find many willing to help. The American Library Association's Muggles for Harry Potter has over 12,000 members willing to stand up for the bespeckled orphan wizard. Such loyalty is part of the Harry Potter phenome-

# *The Headless Cupid* by Zilpha Keatley Snyder

## Susan Koosmann

There is something eerie occurring in the Stanley family's new home that
becomes apparent shortly after twelve-year-old Amanda arrives dressed in
a strange costume and talking about spirits and spells. It is Amanda who
discovers the legend of the old house and the mysterious ghost that was said
to haunt it in 1896 when it was known as the Westerly house. Unexplained
events occurred then. Rocks fell from above, objects moved, and things were
broken. Particularly disconcerting was the missing head of one of the
ornamental cupids that lined the main stairway. Someone—or something—had severed it from the statue. The head had never been replaced nor
found. Shortly after this incident, the Westerly daughters, twelve-year-old
Mabel and fourteen-year-old Harriet, were sent away to boarding school.
They returned to live in the house as adults, remaining there until their
deaths, after which the house was sold to the Stanleys. Now these strange
events are beginning to reoccur. Rocks and debris fall from nowhere, there
are loud noises at night, and objects break with no apparent reason. The
parents, who are unaware of the legend, are mystified by these events, but
when the children begin to act strangely, they become concerned. Is the
house haunted? Did the family make a mistake moving there? These are
some of the questions that await the reader of Zilpha Keatley Snyder's novel
*The Headless Cupid*, a delightful blend of mystery and suspense spiced with
supernatural suggestion.

   Although the book has received several awards, there are some who
challenge its appropriateness for adolescent readers based on its references
to the occult. Analysis of *The Headless Cupid* reveals that plot references to
the occult are subordinate to the stronger messages conveyed through the
characters, themes, and values presented in the book.

   David Stanley is the eleven-year-old protagonist of *The Headless
Cupid*. The story is told from his viewpoint. When the book opens he is
contemplating the arrival of his new stepsister, Amanda. He has concerns,

one of which is what it will be like having an older "sister" in the house. Since his mother's recent illness and death, it has been just himself, his father, and three siblings: six-year-old, talkative Janie and the four-year-old twins, Esther and Blair. His father's remarriage has brought expected changes. Molly, his stepmother, seems to fit in well with the active, young brood, and the move to the larger, older home was necessary to accommodate the special needs of a blended family. It is Molly's daughter, Amanda, however, who causes the greater concern. David has met her only once before, but he has a premonition that things will be dramatically different after she arrives. This is what David sees when Amanda steps out of the car upon arriving at the Stanley house:

> As soon as David got a look at her, he leaned forward, quickly. . . . "Wow!" He said under his breath. . . . For the first second or two he'd actually thought there were a bunch of springs and wires coming out of Amanda's head, but then he realized it was only her hair. It seemed to be braided in dozens of long tight braids and some of them were looped around and fastened back to her head. The rest of her was almost covered by a huge bright colored shawl with a shaggy fringe, except for down below her knees, where something black with a crooked hem was hanging . . . her mouth moved now and then into what looked like an upside-down smile. . . . The spot in the middle of her forehead . . . seemed to be shaped like a triangle, and when she moved, it caught and reflected the light like a tiny mirror (8).

Amanda's presence makes a profound impact on David, the Stanley family, and the reader of this novel. Her physical appearance, her menagerie consisting of a snake, a lizard, and an ill-tempered crow, coupled with her mysterious and moody personality, intrigue the Stanley children. By claiming to be an expert in occult matters, she piques the children's interest in the spirit world. When she discovers an old newspaper article that details the legend of Westerly house and its proclaimed ghost, Amanda insists that they keep this information—and the plan to contact the ghost—secret from their parents so as not to frighten them. David is uncomfortable keeping secrets, especially when Amanda's required initiation tests prohibit the children from behaving normally around their parents. Rules such as not using silverware, speaking no more than four words at a time, and carrying around live reptiles for a day are acts that seem destined for detection.

David is beginning to have a theory about the situation "which didn't have anything to do with the supernatural" (69). He is becoming suspicious of Amanda's intent. This is fueled by the fact that her interest in the occult is a recent event, she is afraid of the animals in her room, and she seems to be making things up as she goes along. After a disappointing and clumsy seance, David decides the Stanleys do not have much talent for "the kind of magic Amanda was trying to do" (121). Shortly after the seance, the rocks and other unexplained phenomena occur. David becomes more suspicious and eventually discovers that Amanda has been the ghost all along! This information presents him with a dilemma. Should he tell his parents? What will happen to Amanda when they find out? After all, the Westerly girls had been sent away. While David feels empathy for Amanda, he also feels a responsibility to inform his parents.

*The Headless Cupid* is not a book about the occult. Other than references to a few vocabulary words, such as *poltergeist, familiar,* and *seance,* readers will not learn much about occult practices. Activities dealing with this subject are fabricated, and they are revealed as such by the end of the book. This is a novel with a simple plot about complex ideas. It is about family relationships, being accepted, and finding your role in the family. Adolescent readers will learn several valuable lessons by observing the characters in this book: They will learn the importance of being themselves when faced with new situations, to admit mistakes, and to accept responsibility for their actions. They will also learn problem-solving techniques and to look beyond the surface appearance of situations to deeper meanings.

There are three distinct worlds in this book, that of the children, the adults, and the adolescents. The children's world is characterized by make-believe, story telling, games, and magic. Garrulous Janie, shy Esther, and sensitive Blair are memorable characters, delightfully drawn. Open and honest, they add personality, warmth, and humor to the plot. The following conversation is an example of the author's style and tone when dealing with the subject of seances:

> "We're being initiated into the supernatural," [David] looked at Amanda for confirmation.
> Amanda nodded. "Into the world of the occult," she said.
> "Into magic!" Janie said.
> "Oooooh!" Esther said in a now-I-get-it tone of voice, "Dibs on the first rabbit." (62).

This conversation shows three different interpretations of the situation from David's *supernatural* to Amanda's *occult* and Janie's *magic,* but it is Esther's comment that gets the laugh and gives the serious event a less threatening tone.

For the most part, the adults in the story are observant, logical, and practical. Mr. Golanski, the electrician who relates the legend of the headless cupid and the ghost to Amanda and David, notices that Amanda appears to know "too much" about these things. David's father asks him for a rational explanation of why the children are behaving so strangely, and Molly's friend, Ingrid, refuses to believe that ghosts are responsible for the rocks and debris in the house. She believes these are real-world events, and Amanda and David know something about them.

Snyder is sensitive to the sociological and psychological issues facing adolescents. The book introduces emotions surrounding the death of a parent, divorce, remarriage, and the problems facing blended families. It also shows how David and Amanda cope psychologically with these issues.

David is still mourning his mother's death when the book opens. As the oldest, he becomes the caretaker to his younger brother and sisters. He reads to them, guides them, and watches over them when their father is at work. David is the responsible child forced into an adult role. There is no mention of friends his age, and since it is still summer, he has not had an opportunity to make new friends at school. He is probably lonely and curious about having another person his age in the house. He is inquisitive about Amanda's involvement with the spiritual world. There is a brief suggestion that he might be thinking about his mother; however, it is his nature to be skeptical, and circumstances have forced him to be practical, so he is not going to judge the situation on appearances alone. He does, however, question Amanda's unusual behavior.

Amanda is angry. She states that she hates her mother. It is due to her mother's choices that she has to move into these strange surroundings with those annoying children. She states she wants to live with her father because he gives her everything she asks for, but when David tells her that her father *could* make provisions for her to live with him if he wanted to, Amanda explodes. He has probably verbalized her fear of being left out. Amanda is a rebellious child who exploits her mother's fear of reptiles and concerns about her daughter's involvement in the supernatural to get back at her. In the process she is making herself and others unhappy.

Adolescent readers will relate to issues David and Amanda's characters raise about responsibility, rebellion, identity, and family roles. At the beginning of the book Amanda is self-centered, critical, and unsympathetic toward the children. She gets them to weed the garden by playing a slave and master game, but she tells David she does this to practice having power over others. Later, she brags that she and a friend put a spell on one of their teachers to get revenge. She also insists that Esther kill her reptile as part of a ritual, but Esther saves the creature through a thoughtful solution. Perceptive readers might question Amanda's leadership at this point. Is she believable? Is she trustworthy? The children follow her to a certain point, usually finding an acceptable way around her most outlandish requests, and Amanda accepts their alternatives without argument. David suspects a conflict between what she claims to know and what she actually knows early on when Amanda takes him herb hunting. David notices that the exotic plants she is gathering are really anise and Queen Anne's Lace! (49). Whether Amanda is to be believed or not, her initial actions show that she comes into the family demonstrating a disregard for others' feelings.

Another illustration of her callousness toward the children is when she tests their mind-reading ability by having them turn their backs and guess if she is holding a black or red playing card. According to Amanda, most people guess the correct card about fifty percent of the time, and a person correctly guessing fourteen or fifteen cards out of twenty is considered psychic. Amanda claims to have guessed fourteen cards correctly when she did the test. David scores eleven correct guesses, and Janie talks her way up to thirteen, but Esther is crushed when she end up with ten for her score. When she asks Amanda if she has done a good job, Amanda curtly replies, "You did just ordinary. Nothing special" (57). Downcast, Esther goes to David, who reassures her. David then notices that Amanda has not asked Blair to play. When he reminds her that Blair should take a turn, she questions how Blair can do it if he doesn't even talk. She gives in, and Blair takes his position in the chair opposite Amanda. She pulls a card out, looks at it, and asks:

> "Well, what is it?" she said at last. "Is it red or black?"
> "It's valentines," Blair said in a very soft voice. "It's lots of little valentines."
> Amanda threw the cards down. "See," she said to David, "what did I tell you. He just doesn't get it?" (57)

When David looks at the card, he notices that it is the nine of hearts, but the game is over before Blair knows whether he answered correctly. David and the reader now realize that it is Amanda who does not get it, or she does not want to be upstaged. Amanda's insensitivity and sour mood are in contrast to David's supportive attitude and Blair's gentle manner. At this point, Amanda's bossy behavior does not garner much sympathy for her character.

Snyder does not leave Amanda in this static position too long. Her characters model the process by which people can change and grow. The reader gets a glimpse of a different Amanda at the end of the seance scene when the children discover that Janie has offered her mother's ring to the spirit world. David is upset, and Janie is heartbroken when she realizes the ring is gone forever. David insists that they need the ring back. At first Amanda is unsympathetic and stalwart, but seeing David's concern and Janie's remorse, she begins to soften. "Well . . . well," she says. Her hesitation gives readers a split-second view of the empathetic person behind the mask. Before Amanda gives in, however, Blair emerges from Amanda's room with the missing ring.

Amanda has begun to warm up. There are further changes in her personality when she begins to participate with the younger children. At first she competes for their attention by challenging David's story-reading ability. When she discovers the children like her dramatic approach, she begins to see a positive role for herself in the family. The children like her. Perhaps they aren't so bad after all!

Another event that promotes change is when Amanda becomes frightened by the noisy, unexplained appearance of the cupid's head. She had no control over this event and cowers behind David. In an honest exchange with David, she confesses that she was responsible for the other phenomena, using theatrics and scare tactics to frighten the family so they would want to move out. David has known this for a while, but he does not gloat, nor does he show anger. He listens and asks questions about how she created the ghostly activities and, more important, *why* she did it. At this point he is modeling problem-solving behavior. He does not solve her problems for her, however. Amanda takes responsibility for her actions by having private discussions with Molly and her stepfather, which takes the burden for telling off David. For the first time, the Stanleys get to see the real Amanda.

By observing Amanda's behavior, readers learn that it is better to face new, uncomfortable situations by being yourself. Being yourself does not mean having to do everything by yourself. The children demonstrate how even the younger members of the family contribute to creative problem solving. Janie's resourcefulness solves several problems during the Stanley's trial with Amanda's tests, causing David to comment that "every once in awhile Janie used her brains for something besides making a fool of herself" (102). Blair also solves problems. In addition to finding their mother's "lost" ring, he uses kindness to befriend and tame the unruly crow. He also discovers the location of the cupid's head. Even younger readers will see that the Stanley family works together to find solutions to challenging problems.

Not all questions have black-and-white answers at the end of the novel, however. Blair's character is a case in point. If anyone has a sixth sense in this story, it is Blair. He stands apart from the others, frequently ignored, ghostlike, slipping in and out of the plot, but always contributing to it in positive ways. He is perhaps much like his deceased mother, whom David describes as an "unusual person . . . beautiful and gentle and uncertain, and full of strange ideas about things that never happen to ordinary people" (30). She believed in ghosts, talked to animals, and had premonitions. David also notes to the reader that she believed in good omens like rainbows and church bells. Unlike Amanda, Blair has no pretenses, but he does confide to David that he knows Amanda kicks the crow when she is angry and that a ghost girl told him where to find the cupid's head. He also tells David the ghost girl is happy for the cupid to have its head returned. David believes Blair, and he is curious to know more, but unlike his discussion with Amanda, he realizes that "there was no use asking Blair what he was thinking—and besides, with Blair, thinking didn't seem to have a lot to do with understanding, anyway" (201). Perhaps Snyder uses Blair's character to show readers that although there are shams in the world, there are also some things that are not easily explained. Like many good mystery writers, Snyder leaves openings for contemplation suggesting that we need to be critical thinkers, but we also need to save room for the gray areas in life.

Zilpha Keatley Snyder has written a mystery with a message for young adolescents. *The Headless Cupid* is a story about attachment and reattachment; it is about finding your identity and self-worth. The book has received many recognitions and honors including being selected as the U.S. contribution for the international Hans Christian Andersen Honors List, voted the William Allen White Award by schoolchildren in Kansas, Christopher Medals by The Catholic Educators of America, and Newbery Honors. This delightfully written novel is readable and understandable. It deserves to be made accessible for readers of all ages.

## Work Cited

Snyder, Zilpha Keatley. *The Headless Cupid*. New York: Atheneum, 1971.

# In Defense of *Cupid*

## Zilpha Keatley Snyder

On receiving a request from Professor Karolides asking for a defense of my book *The Headless Cupid*, my initial reaction was not entirely one of surprise. I have been aware for some time that at least three of my books have frequently been the subject of serious censorship efforts, most frequently and virulently *The Headless Cupid*. But what did surprise and gratify me was the grand company my Cupid has been keeping. How could I not feel honored to see my small, wooden, headless offspring listed along with the likes of Tom Sawyer, Julie of the Wolves, Gilly Hopkins, and many other widely famed and justly praised creative progeny of so many gifted writers. But putting surprise and gratification aside, and moving on to my attempt to explain and vindicate my story, I believe a brief summary of the plot line might be in order.

*The Headless Cupid* story is seen through the eyes of eleven-year-old David Stanley, the well-meaning and long-suffering older brother of three rather idiosyncratic siblings. David's mother is dead and his father has recently remarried a woman with a twelve-year-old daughter. With David the reader begins to witness his recently acquired stepsister's attempts to use her interest in the occult to get even with the world. Amanda is angry for a number of reasons. For one thing, she is in that early adolescent age group that often displays a certain amount of ambient outrage. More specifically she blames her mother for her parents' divorce and for her mother's remarriage into a family with four annoying younger children. So she decides to torment her mother and stepfather by recruiting her younger stepsiblings into her occult activities, an effort at which she is wildly unsuccessful. Her seance, particularly, is a fiasco. Blair keeps falling asleep, Esther won't stop talking, and Jamie, as always, tries to take over. As Amanda tries to reincarnate the poltergeist that once, according to rumor, haunted their old house in the country, David, the artless and ingenuous protagonist, is at first intrigued by her claims of supernatural powers. But gradually, aided by the instincts of his supersensitive and insightful four-

220

year-old brother, he becomes aware of Amanda's real agenda, as does the careful reader. In the end she is exposed and gets her comeuppance—and loses all interest in the occult. In the subsequent Stanley family stories Amanda is still not the greatest older sister in the world, but she does slowly make some progress toward sibling appreciation.

This might be the place for a few words about the inspirational kickoff for this particular story. When the book was written in the early 1970s there was great public interest in every kind of mystical and/or metapsychical enterprise. Every branch of the media was full of references to such things as astrology, exorcism, poltergeists, telepathy, palmistry, crystal gazing, witchcraft, et cetera. During this time it was brought to my attention that some young people were obviously using their interest in such phenomena mainly as a means to disturb and annoy society in general and, very often, their parents in particular.

So what should I have to say about this situation, as a writer of books for young people? A diatribe against the terrible danger of supernaturalism probably might only serve to make such interests more intriguing. What I tried to do in *Cupid* was to show, in a rather lighthearted way, not only how reprehensible Amanda's actions were but also how ridiculous.

The story has never been criticized for violence, offensive language, or sexual content; implications which, had they been made, could easily have been disproved. But according to its attackers it is guilty of advocating and encouraging supernatural practices. This accusation is understandable in a way since such things as poltergeists, familiar spirits, and seances are indeed alluded to. But the fear that supernatural interests are encouraged and advocated should be allayed by a thorough and careful reading.

A quote from a letter from a young Stanley family fan seems to show that young readers are well able to get the message that Amanda (the would-be witch) is not the hero of the story. The quote: "*Would you please write some more Stanley family stories because they are my favorites. And if you do, will you please have David give Amanda a good crack on the head.*"

So the '70s, with its emphasis on anything and everything mystical, supernatural, spiritual, or simply far-out, did play a part in motivating me to write the story. But times do change, and now again the temper of the times is significant, in that the attempts to censor *Cupid* do seem to attest to the greatly increased fear of the supernatural that seems to have arisen during the last decade. It wasn't until at least fifteen years after the 1972 publication date of *The Headless Cupid* that I first became aware of any attacks on the book. It was about this time that librarians began to inform me that my book apparently had been placed on the list compiled by a group of people who object to any mention of certain subjects in books for children, textbooks as well as trade. This list, which was sent to like-thinking groups all over the country, not only opposed any reference to the supernatural but also any mention or celebration of Halloween. Among their other prohibitions were also such obvious evils as feminism, gun control, evolution, yoga, meditation, one-worldism, vegetarianism, and secular humanism (which apparently is defined as any attempt to encourage ethical behavior without reference to "God's word").

Some of the attacks on my books were personal and even frightening. One of the first occurred when I was being driven to a school in Texas, where I was to give the first of several talks to large groups of children, and was informed that there had been an attempt to get me uninvited and that quite likely a group of protesters would be present at my speech. They were, in fact, but apart from suspicious frowns and avid note taking they remained in the background.

A little later, in Southern California, I was not so fortunate. At the end of a panel on book censorship, a young woman appeared on the stage, grabbed my hand, and put a book of matches in it. Shaking her finger in my face she announced that the matches were a gift and that I was going to repent and burn *all* of my books. Afterward, recalling her glowing eyes and fiery rhetoric, I felt fortunate that she hadn't attempted to set fire to me.

Other critiques are mainly puzzling. Only recently, in their May/June 2000 edition, *Horn Book* published an article by Kimbra Wilder Gish defending the religious right's opposition to any mention of the occult in books for children, in which Ms. Gish stated that in *The Headless Cupid* one child threatens another with occult powers. I was so puzzled by this accusation that I reread *Cupid* from cover to cover, something that I hadn't done for many years, and was unable to discover what Ms. Gish was referring to. The good news is, I really enjoyed the read. I was pleased to find that, in spite of its advanced age, the story holds up pretty well.

And so it goes. Some of the accusations are almost funny. Like the self-appointed critic who asserted that the book teaches "how to relate to a familiar spirit." In the story Amanda does, indeed, have a caged crow that she proclaims to be her familiar spirit. However, the crow obviously doesn't agree. All Amanda ever reaps from her rites and rituals are a lot of pecks and scratches.

The seance has been another bone of contention. There are, it seems, a certain number of people who were terribly offended by the portrayal of a seance attended by children. These people seem to think it quite likely that such an enterprise actually might call up evil spirits or even the devil himself—even a seance run by a fake, and very frustrated, medium and participated in by a rather unruly bunch of attendees.

Perhaps I should admit, at this point, that when my sisters and I were close to the age of the Stanley kids, we had a brief spell of playing seance in a spooky and spiderwebby attic. However, the game didn't last long due to an aversion to spiders and to the apparent disinterest of the ghostly participants we were anticipating. We also played with a Ouija board for a while until arguments, over who was and who wasn't surreptitiously pushing the pointer, put a damper on the proceedings. I can recall a number of confrontations along the lines of "You did too" and "I did not" but no ghostly encounters, other than pretend ones. And our mother, the offspring of many generations of Quakers and a devoted Christian, never seemed worried about our mystical game playing. She had, she said, tried the Ouija board herself as a child and seemed to see it, as we did, as imaginative game playing.

As for the supposition that children might conjure up evil sprits while playing imaginative games, spirits that might encourage immoral and/or antisocial behavior, I feel that such fears are ill-founded. If, for instance, it should happen that a child playing with an Ouija board is inspired to act in an immoral manner, I feel quite certain that the place to look for the underlying motivation is in the realities, the real, everyday needs and fears, of that child's existence. That is what I meant when I had Mrs. Fortune, in *The Witches of Worm*, say that, "We all invite our own demons and we must exorcize our own."

A word about imaginative game playing in general, a theme that occurs in many of my books. I am firmly convinced that such game playing is one of the best ways for children to stretch their imaginations—right up there with reading and a thousand times better than watching TV. And should we encourage our children to develop their imagination? In my opinion a well-developed imagination is necessary not only for any kind of artistic endeavor, but also in many other career areas. Imaginative approaches to problem solving are necessary not only for a successful professional life, but also in the area of personal relationships. And wouldn't it be wonderful if we could develop political leaders who could "imagine" a new and more successful approach to such problems as poverty and war!

But the pendulum continues to swing, and among the changes that passing time has brought are the increasing numerous attack on *Cupid*. That *The Headless Cupid* has not always been seen as a dangerous book is evidenced by the fact that it was a 1972 Newbery Honor Book and soon afterward America's contribution to the Hans Christian Andersen International Honors List. It received the Christopher Medal given by the Catholic Educators of America, was a Junior Literary Guild choice, was on the American Library Association's list of Notable Books, and in 1974 it won the William Allen White award given by the state of Kansas. It has been

# Isabel Allende's *The House of the Spirits*

## Cecilia Bustamante-Marré

*The House of the Spirits*, the first novel written by Chilean author Isabel Allende, is one of the most powerful novels written in exile during the Pinochet era, and the most celebrated novel written by a female Latin American author in the world.

The novel is a powerful account of Chilean history from the beginning of the twentieth century to the first years of the military dictatorship. Though the name of the country is never mentioned, the resemblance is apparent, particularly, in the last three chapters where Allende recreates with intense realism the political struggle that surrounded the election of socialist president Salvador Allende and the military coup that put an end to Chile's democratic tradition.

*The House of the Spirits*, in part autobiographical, can be considered a testimonial novel. Isabel Allende is the niece of former Chilean president Salvador Allende, who was overthrown by a military coup d'état led by General Augusto Pinochet on September 11, 1973. Salvador Allende died during the bloody events of the military intervention, and the Allende family was offered political asylum by the Mexican government. Isabel Allende had never had any political affiliation and thought she had no reason to leave Chile. So she stayed and experienced the first years of the dictatorship. But soon after the coup, Allende has said, she realized that her life could not remain intact. Her work as a journalist kept her in close contact with the changes that were taking place in the country at all levels. She could not stay indifferent so, like Alba in the novel, she got involved in underground activities to help the growing number of victims of the repression. After two years, however, even though her activities were never discovered, she lost her job and was the victim of threats, which made her understand that she had to leave Chile to protect herself and her family. In 1975, Isabel Allende, her husband, and two children left for a voluntary exile in Venezuela where, after six years of nostalgia and silence, she wrote *The House of the Spirits*.

When I left Chile, after the military coup, I lost in one instant my family, my past, my home. I felt like a tree without roots, destined to dry up and die. For many years I was paralyzed by a kind of stupor and by nostalgia, but one day in January 1981, I decided to recover what I had lost. I sat down to write the story of a family similar to mine, the story of a country that could be mine, a continent resembling Latin America . . . it was almost the act of a conjurer. (39)

Rejected by many Latin American editors, the novel was first published in Spain by Plaza y Janés in 1982. That same year it was acclaimed in the Frankfurt Book Fair, and from then on, its success quickly spread throughout Europe and Latin America. In 1985 it was published in the United States, where it immediately topped best-seller lists. Today, almost twenty years later, the novel has sold millions of copies worldwide, has been translated into thirty languages, has received dozens of awards, and continues to be an all-time favorite.

The overwhelming reception of the novel could not be openly celebrated in Chile in 1982, when it appeared. Like many other books, *The House of the Spirits* was banned on political grounds by the military regime. Yet, as is usually the case, that which is forbidden tends to be more appealing—even more so when the book in question had been written in exile by the niece of the overthrown president. The book entered the country clandestinely, hidden in diaper bags and without covers. In Chile, these copies quickly multiplied and circulated in photocopies. Long waiting lists of people would wait patiently to obtain one of these smuggled copies until 1983, when the military government, in an effort to improve its deteriorated image, suspended book censorship.

Soon after its publication in the United States in 1985, *The House of the Spirits* became part of the required reading list of numerous college and university courses on world literature, world history, and, certainly, in specialized courses on Latin America. Even at the high school level, enthusiastic teachers have incorporated the novel into their honors or advanced placement courses.

Three main reasons can justify this inclusion. First, the testimonial value of the novel, which openly denounces the atrocities of the dictatorship. Second, its value as a subversive text that unveils hidden mechanisms of domination that have remained unchallenged for centuries. Third, Isabel Allende's engaging style, which makes it very difficult for the reader to put the book away before reaching the last page. Thus, *The House of the Spirits* has come to be recognized as a pleasurable, as well as effective, tool for teaching critical issues of which our students need to be aware if education's main purpose is to contribute to the creation of a better world.

In spite of its popularity in the United States, *The House of the Spirits* has not gone unchallenged. In fact, several high schools have faced parents' complaints on the charges of violence, sexual explicitness, and anti-Catholicism.

No doubt, violence is everywhere in the novel. Its underlying motive is none other than the denunciation of violence. One of Allende's major merits is, precisely, the way she points a finger at the wide variety of overt as well as veiled forms of violence that have overwhelmed Latin American male-dominated societies for centuries. Many of the sexual scenes in the novel represent the violence of rape, and the only scene that could be labeled anti-Catholic acts as a reminiscence of the most repressive period in the history of the Catholic Church. Through her extraordinary female characters, Allende directs the reader's attention toward these uncontested forms of violence, many of which still prevail as stubborn remnants of colonialism.

The first of these is personified in the colorful portrayal of Father Restrepo, "whose mission in this world was to rouse the conscience of his indolent Creole flock," a mission he would zealously carry on by means of an "unrestrained oratory" destined to "strike the fear of God into the hearts of his parishioners" (4). The vivid representation unavoidably brings to mind the centuries-old violence of inquisitorial practices; the colonial Church and its oppressive power; and most of all, its responsibility in the shaping of Latin America's oligarchic and discriminatory societies, as illustrated in Father Restrepo's sermon, when he points at Nívea del Valle to accuse

> the Pharisees, who had tried to legalize bastards and civil marriage, thereby dismembering the family, the fatherland, private property, and the Church, and putting women on an equal footing with men—this in open defiance of the law of God, which was most explicit on the issue. (5)

With a parodic sense of humor, Allende undermines these tactics of intimidation, traditionally practiced by the Catholic Church in order to control the masses. Father Restrepo's old rhetoric does not have any power over ten-year-old Clara, whose "clairvoyance" allows her to see that his apocalyptic representations of hell cannot be God's idea, but his own.

> They were in one of those long breaks in the sermon that the priest, a connoisseur of unbearable silences, used with frequency and to great effect. His burning eyes glanced over the parishioners one by one. . . . The silence grew thick, and time seemed to stop within the church, but no one dared to cough or shift position, so as not to attract Father Restrepo's attention. His final sentences were still ringing between the columns.
>
> Just at that moment, as Nívea would recall years later, in the midst of all

that anxiety and silence, the voice of little Clara was heard in all its purity.

"Psst! Father Restrepo! If that story about hell is a lie, we're all fucked, aren't we. . . ?" (7-8)

Clara's clairvoyance works in the novel as a symbol of pure, uncontaminated vision, able to see all those aspects of reality that custom has turned invisible to most people. The following example from Millman and Kanter helps to explain the meaning of Clara's clairvoyance in the novel:

> Everyone knows the story about the Emperor and his fine clothes: although the townspeople persuaded themselves that the Emperor was elegantly costumed, a child, possessing an unspoiled vision, showed the citizenry that the Emperor was really naked. The story instructs us about one of our basic sociological premises: that reality is subjective, or rather, subject to social definition. The story also reminds us that collective delusions can be undone by introducing fresh perspectives. (vii)

Nívea, Clara, Blanca, and Alba, as their luminous names imply, are endowed with a clear sense of justice and civic responsibility. They dare to doubt the blind forces of tradition, and work against misconceptions, injustice, and domination.

This episode, the only one in the novel that criticizes the Catholic Church, is not sufficient argument to label the novel anti-Catholic. Father Restrepo represents the old colonial Church, whose sins are well documented. As the text makes very clear, that Church of the 1920s had already begun to be "shaken by the winds of modernism" (4). In fact, as the novel progresses toward the 1970s we are presented with the new roles the Catholic Church gets to play in this increasingly unsettled society. First, through Father José Dulce María's political commitment to social justice and later, during "the terror," we read about the Catholic Church as the sole institution able to help the thousands of victims of the dictatorship, as was the case in real-life Chile.

Another form of violence Allende addresses in the novel—the most fundamental—concerns the privileges of *hacendados* (landowners). Originating in the colonial period, the *hacienda* survived in many Latin American countries late into the twentieth century as an economic and social system that governed those attached to it from the cradle to the grave. *Hacienda* laborers were theoretically free wage earners, but in practice their employers were able to bind them to the land, especially by keeping them in an indebted state. Therefore, this was a system based on a bond of dependency between the *hacendado* and his peasants, which resulted, most of the time, in an authoritarian relationship of master and serf.

Esteban Trueba represents the *hacendado* who, in keeping with tradition, protects and abuses his workers. He considers himself a good *patrón*, and compared to other *hacendados* he may well be. In fact, he does nothing that has not been common practice within the traditional *hacienda*. That is why, narrating in first person, Trueba defends his methods from his granddaughter's disapproval:

> No one's going to convince me that I wasn't a good *patrón*. Anyone who saw Tres Marías in decline and who could see it now, when it's a model estate, would have to agree with me. That's why I can't go along with my granddaughter's story about class struggle. Because when it comes right down to it, those poor peasants are a lot worse off today than they were fifty years ago. I was like a father to them. Agrarian reform ruined things for everyone. (46)

This sort of dialogue between the two narrators is an effective strategy to highlight the weak points of the patriarchal ideology. Trueba narrates the way he recovered the land his father had left abandoned, and how hard he worked to make it produce, as it had never done before. He feels proud of himself. He is respected and admired within his social circle. On the other hand, Alba, as the main narrator, corroborates Trueba's words, but also tells us about those negative aspects of his life that he neglects to mention:

> In the course of the next ten years, Esteban Trueba became the most respected *patrón* in the region. He built brick houses for his workers, hired a teacher for the school, and raised the standard of living of everyone on his land. . . . Trueba's bad temper became a legend, and grew so exaggerated that it even made him uncomfortable. He forbade anyone to talk back to him and could tolerate no opposition; he viewed the slightest disagreement as a provocation. His concupiscence also intensified. Not a girl passed from puberty to adulthood that he did not subject to the woods, the riverbank, or the wrought-iron bed. . . . He did not bother to hide, because he was afraid of no one. Word of his cruelty spread throughout the region, provoking jealous admiration among the men of his class. (55)

In this way, Allende demystifies tradition by exposing the centuries-old violence and social injustice it conceals. In addition to this narrative strategy, Trueba's patriarchal ideology is constantly challenged in the novel by the critical eye of the women in his family. His abusive relationship with his workers, for example, does not escape clairvoyant Clara, when she visits Tres Marías for the first time:

> She was not impressed by the brick houses, the school, and abundant food,

because her ability to see what was invisible immediately detected the workers'
resentment, fear, and distrust; and the almost imperceptible noise that quieted
whenever she turned her head enabled her to guess certain things about her
husband's character and past. (90-91)

Allende's avant-garde women not only see the intrinsic violence and
injustice of the patriarchal world, they also undermined its authority through
concrete actions. Nívea, for example, had a gigantic poplar tree cut down
before her first son was born. That tree had served for generations to initiate
the boys of her family into manhood. She decided to stop the brutal family
tradition to protect her sons. In the same way, Clara undermines Trueba's
authority in Tres Marías, educating the female peasants about their rights.
To her dismay, the embarrassed smiles of the women make Clara realize
that fighting against tradition may not be an easy task:

"Since when has a man not beaten his wife? If he doesn't beat her, it's either
because he doesn't love her or because he isn't a real man. Since when is a
man's paycheck or the fruit of the earth or what the chickens lay shared
between them, when everybody knows he is the one in charge? Since when has
a woman ever done the same things as a man?. . . " they would say. (91)

Trueba's violent reaction when he found out about his wife's harangues
emphasizes the fact that dialogue is not an option in that male-dominated
society, and any attempt at introducing new ideas is rapidly repressed. An
exceptional woman like Clara is not intimidated by her husband's display of
force, but lower-class women know by experience that any rebellious act
may have painful consequences: "The women nudged each other in the ribs
and smiled shyly. . ., knowing full well that if they took into their heads to
put Clara's ideas into practice, their husbands would beat them" (91).

This is a recurring motif in the novel. Nívea had to face it at the turn of
the century when campaigning for women's suffrage, just as Clara confronts
it during the 1920s. And even in the 1940s, Pedro Tercero García finds the
same resistance on the part of the Tres Marías peasants when trying to
convince them to stand up for their rights. His father's response illustrates
very vividly the basic feeling among *hacienda* laborers: "That's the way it's
always been, son. You can't change the law of God" (140). The peasants'
attitude emphasizes the fact that repressive societies sustain their power on
people's ignorance and fear.

In connection with the charge of sexual explicitness, there are many
scenes that are not appropriate for all ages. With the exception of a few
superfluous episodes (that nonetheless spice up the story), the sexual
situations depict either true love or rape. Whatever the case, these scenes

have a purpose.

The rape of Pancha García graphically depicts this tradition of subjugation lower classes have endured for centuries in Latin America. The emphasis here is on the threefold victimization of women: discriminated by sex, by class and, in some cases, also by race. Fifteen-year-old Pancha García is the first victim of Esteban Trueba's concupiscence. He doesn't hide his intentions because he is convinced that he is exercising his right: "He rode his horse slowly. . ., asking after her as he went" (50). No one stops him either because he is the *patrón*. The novel stresses the fact that rape is some sort of inescapable fate for lower-class women:

> Pancha García made no attempt to defend herself. She did not complain, nor did she shut her eyes. She lay on her back, staring at the sky with terror, until she felt the man drop to the ground beside her with a moan. She began to whimper softly. Before her, her mother—and before her, her grandmother—had suffered the same animal fate. (51)

This may explain why Tránsito Soto embraces prostitution with such a passion: "I'm not going to spend my life in the Red Lantern," she confides to Trueba. "I'm going to the capital, because I want to be rich and famous" (60). By assuming this fate voluntarily, and making a "career" out of it, she finds her way out of servitude and gains the possibility of independence and economic success.

Upper-class women in this patriarchal society were not free from limitations either. They were expected to be virtuous, pure, and marry a man approved by their family. Love was not important—it would come with time.

Tradition is challenged, in this case, by Trueba's only daughter, Blanca. She falls in love with a peasant boy, Pedro Tercero García, Pancha García's nephew. Their pure love has grown with them since childhood. At age fifteen they consummate their love on the same riverbank "where, years earlier, Esteban Trueba had stolen Pancha García's humble virginity" (134). The similitudes invite the reader to compare these two episodes, which underscore a hypocritical double standard.

Blanca subverts two patriarchal laws—those of chastity and class. When Trueba finds out, he brutally beats Blanca and blames his wife:

> He accused her of having raised Blanca without morals, without religion, without principles, like a libertine atheist, even worse, without a sense of her own class, because you could understand if she wanted to do it with someone of a decent family, but not with this hick, this simpleton, this hothead, this lazy good-for-nothing son of a bitch. (171)

Clara's response is the blow to Trueba's ideology: "Pedro Tercero García hasn't done a thing you haven't done yourself," Clara said when she could interrupt him. "You also slept with unmarried women not of your own class. The only difference is that he did it for love. And so did Blanca." (171) Once again, Clara makes him see what he does not want to see. But, unable to accept the truth, Trueba strikes her. Many years and much pain would be necessary to make him realize the injustice of his actions.

Patriarchal domination in the household and in the hacienda is the prelude to a much larger form of violence—the authoritarianism of the dictatorship that will take hold of the nation. The final chapters of the novel become a political testimony, which very closely reproduces Chilean history between 1970 and the first years of the military regime. Under the new law, political repression means imprisonment, torture, death, or, in the best of circumstances, exile. Among the many forms of torture, rape is one of the most common. The difference is that now, it has crossed class barriers. A new social class is born in the country—the military. Under them, all civilians are equal. No class privileges are possible anymore—not even for Trueba, now a senator, one of the major instigators of the coup d'état.

Senator Trueba's granddaughter, Alba, is arrested by the political police. She is tortured and repeatedly raped, and there is nothing he can do to save her. He has lost all his power, all his friends, and he is getting a taste of his own medicine for the first time in his long life. Alba's torturer is Colonel Esteban García, Trueba's illegitimate grandson, who, taking advantage of his position, avenges old offenses to himself and his grand-mother, Pancha García.

Having reached the climax of violence, the novel surprises the reader with a message of hope. In prison Alba writes in her mind that one day she will take revenge on Colonel García. But now, when trying to find her hate, she realizes that it has vanished. It is very interesting the way Allende presents the value of writing. Alba's effort to write a testimony that could tell the world about the horror she has experienced in prison allows her to understand that her mission is not to prolong hatred but to break the terrible chain of hate and revenge with forgiveness. It is through the effort of writing, as if piecing together a puzzle, that Alba comes to see the whole picture. It is through the process of reading a novel like this one that our students may acquire a better understanding of their world.

## Works Cited

Agosin, Marjory. "Pirate, Conjurer, Feminist." Trans. Cola Franzen. *Conversations with Isabel Allende*. Ed. John Rodden. Austin: University of Texas Press, 1999. 35-42.

Allende, Isabel. *The House of the Spirits*. Trans. Magda Bogin. New York: Knopf, 1985.

Millman, Marcia, and Rosabeth Moss Kanter, eds. *Another Voice*. Garden City, New York: Anchor Books, 1975.

# Rationale for *How to Eat Fried Worms*

## Lisa A. Spiegel

### Excerpt

"How'd you do it?" said Billy. "What's it called?"

"My word," said his father.

"Gosh, Mrs. Forrester," gasped Tom.

On a silver dish in front of Billy lay an ice-cream cake bathed in fruit syrups—peach, cherry, tutti-frutti, candied orange—topped with whipped cream sprinkled with jelly beans and almond slivers.

"It's called a Whizbang Worm Delight," said Billy's mother proudly. "I made it up."

"Is the worm really in there?" said Billy, poking about with his spoon. And then, scraping away a bit of whipped cream at one end, he glimpsed the worm's snout protruding from the center of the cake.

"Snug as a bug in a rug," said his mother.

"I still wouldn't eat a worm," said Emily, eyeing the Whizbang Worm Delight with envious distaste.

"I would," said Tom. "At least, maybe I would." (77).

### Summary

Billy, Alan, Tom, and Joe are ten-year-olds who have been best friends since kindergarten. When Tom's mother disciplined him for not eating his dinner, the boys idly considered what they would or would not consume.

Alan baited Billy by saying Billy would not eat worms; Billy, unwilling to back down in front of his friends, said he could and thus a bet was born. Alan agreed to pay Billy $50.00 if Billy eats one worm a day for fifteen days.

The boys divided into teams; Tom and Billy versus Alan and Joe. When Billy continued to devour the worms, Alan and Joe deviously schemed to keep them from him; Tom and Billy must counteract their tricks in order to maintain their schedule of one worm a day. This fast-paced story, full of

234

twists and turns, will keep readers guessing as to the winner of the bet, and its surprise ending will delight its audience.

## Relationship of *How to Eat Fried Worms* to NCTE/IRA Standards

*How to Eat Fried Worms* by Thomas Rockwell is a humorous, positive book that is meant for intermediate-grades students but will be enjoyed by readers of all levels, including adults. Although this novel would comply with all of the National Council of Teachers of English/International Reading Association standards (NCTE and IRA, 1996), there are several that would more closely justify classroom use.

Standard two states, "Students read a wide range of literature from many periods in many genres to build an understanding of the many dimensions . . . of human experience" (3). This novel fits well here for several reasons. Most important, it is a genuinely funny book—one where the humor is derived from the *situation*, rather than only the dialogue. Few novels are truly humorous, for many adolescent books designated as humorous are really focusing upon serious problem faced by young readers and relying upon sarcastic speech for humor to lighten the situation.

In this novel, however, everything is funny—watching Billy eating worms in increasingly elaborate ways, witnessing how devious Alan and Joe are regarding preventing Billy from winning the bet, enjoying the good humor of Billy's parents once they discover his situation, and the final laugh of discovering Billy is continuing to eat worms due to his enjoyment of them.

The novel captures exactly the "human experience" of typical ten-year-old boys, thus allowing the reader to witness the world of young males. When idle talk turns into a bet neither boy wants, the wager holds as each is unwilling to be first to back down in front of friends. Because no ten-year-old boy wants to be called "chicken," a high-stakes bet is set with little thought. When Alan realizes he could lose a considerable amount of money, he devises numerous traps to thwart Billy, but Billy is also canny and more than a match for him.

Billy's parents display perfect reactions to their wager, allowing readers to view the boys' actions from another, more mature view. After checking to see if worms are harmful, they decide to let the boys continue their bet and expect them to follow the rules they made. Billy's mother cheerfully assists in cooking some of the worms, and his father oversees the situation to make sure it doesn't get out of hand—he realizes the boys' friendship is more important than the contest. These are actions and attitudes the boys are unable to see, but the reader is able to view all dimensions of the story.

As the wager progresses and both sides become nastier, we see typical ten-year-old behavior taken even further. Never do the boys consider calling the bet off, but even during their most divisive behavior they remember their friendship and admit their actions are wrong, done in the heat of the moment. Each side wishes to win but not hurt the other.

The story's ending is realistic: Billy wins the bet, Alan goes to work to earn the money, the boys are friends again, and there are no hard feelings. The contest is in the past, and the boys are ready to move on to their next adventure—which will probably be as complicated and exciting as their previous one. Again, the reader is witness to typical ten-year-old male behaviors.

This novel is also a good match for Standard three, which reads, "Students apply a wide range of strategies to comprehend, interpret, evaluate, and appreciate texts" (3). Because so much of this novel is in dialogue form and fast paced, students must be able to gather meaning from this writing style as well as follow its textual demands. The book contains illustrations that must be interpreted for a visual understanding of the event depicted.

As the characters are constantly plotting, readers must stay one step ahead of them, forming conclusions about what will happen next and then revising erroneous ones. Students will learn of foreshadowing and predictions (will they be able to foresee the many twists and turns?), and the plot depends on a chain of events that build upon one another, finally ending with a surprise twist.

Because students reading the novel should be about the same age as the characters, they will be able to draw on their personal experiences similar to those faced by the four boys for a greater empathy and understanding of the plot. This novel portrays realistic and common events for this age, and student experiences will add to and highlight understanding of the story as a whole.

The third NCTE/IRA applicable standard is number seven, stating, "Students conduct research on issues and interests by generating ideas and questions, and by posing problems" (3). There is much to question in this novel. Why is it worse to back down rather than making an expensive, hurtful, and potentially harmful bet? Why do both sides become so obsessed with the contest that it consumes their lives to the extent of damaging their friendship, lying, and disobeying their parents? Are the boys as likable at the story's end as the beginning, after their treatment of one another? Should the boys' parents have stopped the bet? Why didn't they? Billy does win the contest, but only by leaving his house without permission; is this right? Is

Billy the true winner? Moreover, he spends the money on a minibike; does he seem responsible enough to own such a vehicle? Why would the boys' parents allow such a purchase for ten-year-old boys? And so on.

The story's end shows the boys as best friends again, but is this realistic after such an intense summer? Would all of them be friends with each other, or would some friendships be lost? Which ones? Why? There is much to question in this book, and students can research other wagers, contests, and feats through such texts as newspapers, almanacs, world record books, and other materials containing this information for continued and related discussion along with other papers and projects.

## Potential Issues with *How to Eat Fried Worms* and Ways to Address Them

This novel's humor is derived from its story line, and readers of all ages should find it both funny and reminiscent of their own lives. Intermediate readers love bets, grossness, pranks, and close same-sex friendships, all of which are in the novel. The novel is rich for discussion as each chapter is short and details the eating of one worm and the events surrounding it. Students will enjoy discussing their opinions of each chapter's events and characters as well as predicting what will happened in successive chapters.

Because the book does not contain inappropriate language or sexual situations, any potential problems would originate from the story line. A central issue is the wager itself (especially as a large sum of money is involved), as betting is not only gambling but illegal for minors, and thus one or both issues might be objectionable to some. However, the boys have the tenacity to follow through on their wager while facing its consequences, and are able to satisfactorily resolve its terms while remaining close friends.

While the contest provides the humor for the story, it also provides the moral lesson for readers: think before you act. Although some readers might try to emulate a wager of some sort with their peers, it is unlikely that they would have the interest and tenacity to continue such a project for any noticeable length of time.

Another issue is the actual worm consumption, for the idea of eating worms will be especially repugnant and fascinating to this age group, and they will be eager to read how each successive worm is eaten. Although Billy grew to enjoy eating worms, this was a device for humor, and the story made it clear that this was an extremely unpalatable action, especially as Billy was unable to eat his worms raw—they had to be cooked or otherwise placed with various ingredients. Some may worry that impressionable students will attempt to consume worms as well, but the reading of an action is not a demand for its performance, and it should be presumed that the average student will not wish to taste-test. The novel also clearly state that consuming earthworms is not harmful, should some intrepid students decide to sample them.

Again, there is room for rich discussion here; for example, why were worms chosen for the bet? How likely is it that Billy would continue eating worms? What would be worse to eat? Who in the class would eat a worm? Has anyone? What nontraditional foods have students eaten? What is eaten in other countries that we would not consider "food" here? What are students' favorite and most disliked traditional dishes? What happens if students don't eat their meals? Are worms better or worse than cafeteria food? And so on.

Another troubling aspect might be the boys' poor sportsmanship during the bet, for after Alan realizes Billy's tenacity, he and Joe begin playing tricks to keep Billy from eating each successive worm. Taken individually, many of their actions are unfair, such as substituting huge night crawlers for the small worms agreed upon in the initial bet, planting the idea that earthworms are harmful if eaten, taking Billy to a sports event and feeding him so much that he would be unable to eat his worm, and so on. Eventually these tricks lead to infighting among the boys, hurt feelings, and eventually parental intervention.

Discussion could include the readers' opinions regarding the characters' sportsmanship. How do they define fair and unfair play, and what real-life examples do they have to share? Do they have better schemes than the characters'? Do they like the characters more or less throughout their reading, and why? Would the characters' parents have intervened earlier, or not at all? What would students say their own parents would have done in this situation, and what would they desire them to do?

However, these characters' actions should be taken in context and are representative of human nature; their exaggeration provides humor and suspense to the plot. Ten-year-old boys are immature; it should be expected that they would engage in such activities to win their bet. It must be remembered that even at their nastiest, the boys had a strong sense of fair play and realized that they were friends first, which was more important to them than their contest. They had no desire to hurt one another or cause damage to their friendship. The topic of friendship would provide for fruitful discussion among readers, as this age group forms close friendships with one another.

Also, Billy and Tom are not innocent victims during the other boys' machinations for they manage to outwit, keep a step ahead, and play a few tricks of their own. While some readers may object to the tricks played, they allow the boys to demonstrate their fair play, friendship, and above all, intelligence. These boys are canny and bright, which outshines their poor actions toward one another.

Do readers think the characters go too far in their quest to win? If so, when should they have stopped? If not, what would readers predict as the boys' breaking point? What would have happened to the boys' friendship had the bet been stopped—or continued—in a more hurtful manner? If readers were in this situation, would they have wanted to continue until the end, or have a parent halt the wager?

Perhaps the novel's most objectionable aspect would be the boys' disobedience to their parents and lying. For example, when Alan invites Billy to a ball game in order to later prevent him from consuming his worm, he lies and says that Tom is unable to go—but Tom was not invited. Alan writes letters stating that earthworms are dangerous if consumed and signs a doctor's name, which is both lying and forgery. Billy's mother enters the bet by fixing delicious dishes to make the worms more palatable, but this is not part of the original agreement and gives Billy an unfair advantage. Moreover, is it wise for Billy's mother to allow him to consume worms and thus continue the bet?

The most blatant example of disobedience comes after the boys' parents demand that the bet be ended and Billy is grounded, told to remain in his room. He has only one more worm to eat, which is smuggled to him by Tom and his younger brother. Upon eating the worm he runs outside with glee; he has won the contest—but it was supposed to be over and he was ordered to stay inside. Billy is then considered the winner, but some may consider Alan the true winner, for the bet was over and Billy was grounded. Billy is not reprimanded for his actions, and the possibility of Alan winning is not considered.

What are the readers' opinions of these events? Which actions are seen as more or less serious than others by readers, and why? Perhaps the richest avenue for discussion is regarding whether or not Billy won the bet fairly; this is a gray area and depends upon the reader's perception. If one believes eating the final worm in the designated time period wins the bet, Billy won; if it is felt that the bet ended with Billy being grounded and unable to leave his house, then Alan won. What would the readers' verdicts be? Do they now see Billy as a heroic winner—or a cheater?

Moreover, another important avenue of discussion here is the relationship between the boys and their parents. Although the boys know the bet is over, Tom disobeys his parents by bringing the worm to Billy, who shows disobedience by not only eating it but leaving the house as well. Why aren't the boys reprimanded by their parents? Are the boys displaying spoiled and disrespectful behavior toward them, or simply caught up in the excitement of the moment after their long wager?

The boys' parents do not appear angry at these final events; should they be? Why aren't they? Is Billy's winning a good decision, or one that will lead the boys into more disturbing or even dangerous behaviors later? Why do the parents find the boys' bet and various disobedient actions amusing?

However, these above events have been taken out of context, exaggerated, and thus sound worse than they appear in the story. The novel itself does not condone the boys' bad behavior; they learn many hard lessons from it and become better friends by the contest's end. The parents are normal, sensible people who first ascertain that earthworms are not harmful and then wisely leave the boys alone to conduct and learn from their bet themselves. Billy is allowed to eat the worms any way he chooses; having his mother prepare them is secondary to the fact that regardless of the dish, he must still eat the worm inside.

The parents keep a close eye on the boys, and when their behavior becomes unacceptable the bet is halted. This occurs immediately before the consumption of the final worm, so Billy's triumphant win will perhaps not be faulted so much as seen as ten-year-old behavior. Allowing the boys to keep the agreement of the bet at this point is a wise move on the parents' part, for now they must deal with its realistic aftermath instead of just the fun and intrigue of eating the worms. Now, real money must be paid and done so in such a way that resentment will not end the boys' friendship. The solution of Alan's father paying Billy then having Alan work to repay the debt is a good one; the boys learn from it.

Here, the class could discuss the benefit—or detriment—of allowing the bet to proceed. Was this the correct decision? What would have happened had the bet been stopped or Billy been declared the loser? Why isn't Alan given more consideration regarding winning the bet?

Billy purchases his minibike, but as all the boys share it, he reinforces and emphasizes their friendship. Had Alan refused to pay or Billy refused the use of the minibike, the goodwill ending would have been very different. Instead, we see that these boys are able to take a bad bet and bad behavior and make it right again—a worthy accomplishment for any age, but especially so for this young age group. Again, we see the power of friendship.

Here, the class could discuss if the boys' remaining friends is realistic. Should Billy, or any of the boys, have been rewarded with a minibike? Is there a more suitable item that could have been purchased for them? Should the boys have been punished for this entire incident by their parents? How would the readers' parents have reacted? Should Alan's money have been put in a savings account, or perhaps donated to charity?

A final problematic issue might be the absence of female characters. However, this story is about ten-year-old boys, and children this age tend not to form opposite sex friendships. Billy's mother provides a female perspective, and this funny book is highly appealing to both boys and girls. Additional female characters would be superfluous.

Interestingly, this absence of females provides one of the richest avenues of discussion among the boys and girls reading the story, for what is the girls' opinion of the boys in the novel and their bet? Do girls make wagers with one another, and if so, what kinds? Do girls care as much about the opinion of their friends as boys do at this age, and is being called "chicken" as much of a tragedy for them as boys? How do females define friendship, and how do their friendships differ from males'? Who won the bet, according to the girls? Would they have disobeyed their parents as the characters' did? and so on. Students will be able, through skillful leadership by their teacher, to examine and evaluate the similarities and differences between the sexes and garner a better understanding and appreciation of each through this story.

## Reviews of *How to Eat Fried Worms*

"Rockwell has an excellent grasp of the language, the thinking, and the Byzantine relationships of 11- to 13-year-olds." *Kirkus Reviews*

"Because of a bet, Billy is in the uncomfortable position of having to eat fifteen worms in fifteen days. A hilarious story that will revolt and delight bumptious, unreachable intermediate grade boys and any other less particular mortals that read or listen to it. . . . Colorful, original writing in a much needed comic vein." *ALA Booklist*

"The clear writing, clever illustrations, and revolting subject matter are sure to make a hit with many middle grade readers." *Library Journal* (starred review).

"Let's hope that we will have more humorous books like this." *Children's Book Review Service*

"Surefire intermediate grade humorous fare." *Instructor Magazine*

*How to Eat Fried Worms* is Thomas Rockwell's most popular novel and has won several awards, including *The Mark Twain Award*, the *California Young Reader Medal*, and the *Sequoyah Award*.

## Works Cited

NCTE/IRA. *Standards for the English Language Arts*. NCTE/IRA, 1996.

Rockwell, Thomas. *How to Eat Fried Worms*. Illustrated by Emily
   McCulley. New York: Franklin Watts, 1973 (hardcover). Bantam
   Doubleday Dell, 1973. Illustrated by Emily McCulley (paperback).

# Journey to Understanding:
## Defending *I Am the Cheese*

## Kristine M. Bjerk

Introducing young people to new books and authors is pure joy for me. Even more exhilarating is watching them share books with each other. Those often-shared books could rarely be found on the shelves of my classroom library. Those books were tattered. Those books got passed from friend to friend. Those books had unofficial waiting lists. *I Am the Cheese* by Robert Cormier is one of those very special books.

One of my eighth-grade students wrote these words in his Reading Response Journal:

> *I Am the Cheese* is a very dramatic book with many unusual twists and turns. I feel that the last few pages were the most dramatic things I have ever read.

Yes, they are indeed dramatic, but also complex, powerful, and beautifully written. Critics seem to agree, as evidenced by the numerous awards *I Am the Cheese* has received: winner of the 1997 Phoenix Award from the Children's Literature Association, an ALA Best Book for Young Adults, an ALA Notable Book, a *Horn Book* Fanfare Honor Book, a *School Library Journal* Best Book of the Year, a *New York Times* Outstanding Book of the Year.

Cormier, in the introduction to the 1997 edition of *I Am the Cheese*, shares his initial doubts about this novel:

> Who would read this complex, ambiguous story? Certainly not young readers. Convinced that I was saying good-bye to my new young adult audience, I sent the manuscript off, with an apology, to Fabio Coen, Publisher of Books for Young Readers at Pantheon and Knopf. He had ushered *The Chocolate War* into print.
> He called a few days later. "No apology necessary," he said. He admitted that the novel would confuse and confound young people. "But why not stretch

their minds? They'll finally love it, and probably read it twice."
Prophetic words.

Twenty years after the publication of *I Am the Cheese*, this new edition
from Knopf reminds me to follow my instincts as a writer, to trust readers, no
matter their ages. But especially if they're young.
And, yes, many of them write to me, saying: "I read it twice."

Many of my eighth-grade students also read it twice, because they loved
it and because they sought a better understanding of it. This desired
understanding was not only for the story itself, but also for the lessons it
offers on thinking for yourself and questioning integrity when it seems
doubtful, even the integrity of large and powerful institutions.

Part of what stretches readers of *I Am the Cheese* is its three different
styles of narration. In the opening chapter we meet a high school–aged boy,
who tells us in a first-person narrative that he is riding an old-fashioned bike
from Monument, Massachusetts, to Rutterburg, Vermont, to see his father
in a hospital there. He tells us he left home that morning without telling
anyone, or calling Amy Hertz, the girl he loves. Hints of the mystery that
will unfold are presented to the reader in passages like this:

> I got up and knew where I was going. But I stalled, I delayed. I didn't leave for
> two hours because I am a coward, really. I am afraid of a thousand things, a
> million. Like, is it possible to be claustrophobic and yet fear open spaces, too?
> . . . And then there are dogs. I sat there in the house, thinking of all the dogs that
> would attack me on my way to Rutterburg, Vermont, and I told myself, This is
> crazy, I'm not going. But at the same time, I knew I would go. I knew I would
> go the way you know a stone will drop to the ground if you release it from your
> hand. (5)

An ominous tone regarding this boy's journey on bicycle continues to
build in later passages such as this:

> I went to the kitchen and took out the bottle of pills from the cabinet and
> decided not to take one. I wanted to do this raw, without crutches, without aid,
> alone. I opened the bottle of pills and turned it over and let the pills fall
> out—they are capsules, actually, green and black—and I watched them
> disappear into the mouth of the garbage disposal. I felt strong and resolute. (7)

The reader is undeniably hooked by the end of this first chapter and
plunges forward in search of answers to the many questions raised: Why is
the boy's father in the hospital? Why doesn't the boy tell anyone he is going
to Rutterburg? Why is he so fearful? Why does he need pills?

The next chapter adds more questions to the list, especially because of the dramatic change in narrative style and content. Chapter 2 begins like this:

TAPE OZK001          0930          date deleted T-A

T:    Good morning. My name is Brint. We shall be spending some time together. (5-second interval.)
A:    Good morning.
T:    Shall we begin immediately? I have been advised that you are ready. The sooner we begin, the better it will be for you.
A:    I'm not sure where to begin.
T:    First, you must relax. And then let your thoughts flow. Take your time—there is no cause for hurry. Go back if you wish—back to your earliest remembrance.
A:    It's hazy—just a series of impressions.
T:    Let the impressions come.
      (5-second interval.)
A:    That night—
T:    Tell me about that night.
A:    It's as if I was born that night. I mean, became a person, a human being in my own right. Before that, nothing. Or those impressions again—lights—smell—perfume, the perfume my mother always wore, lilac. Nothing else. And then that night—
      (12-second interval.)
T:    Tell me about it. (9-10)

The narrative changes yet again in the second chapter to third person—past tense, as "A" tells Brint about that night when he was three and a half years old and lay still in his bed, listening to his parents' voices in the next room. The flashback is interrupted and the interview resumes. In it, we learn that the boy and his parents took a trip together, on a bus. "A" tells Brint, "It was spooky, scary but not in a haunted sort of way. But as if we were being chased, as if we were running away." (13)

Upon finishing Chapter 2, the reader wonders: Why is this interview taped? Who is "A"? Who advised Brint that "A" is ready? Ready for what? Where does this interview take place? Where did "A" and his parents go on the bus trip? Were they being chased? If so, why? How does this interview connect to the boy riding his bike in Chapter 1? In search of answers for this growing list of questions, the reader is propelled forward.

Alternating between the bike ride to Rutterburg, Vermont, and the boy's interview and flashbacks, the ensuing chapters offer information strand by strand. It isn't until the explosive climax near the end, however, that the story of the boy on the bike weaves into the story of the boy being questioned, revealing an intricate design that will answer all the reader's questions if examined carefully.

At the end of the novel, it becomes clear that the boy on the bike and the boy being interviewed are one and the same—Adam Farmer. Adam (formerly Paul Delmonte) and his parents were given a new identity and home by the government as protection from the powerful organization against which Adam's father had testified. Ironically, Adam's father, an investigative reporter, had testified about corruption in government, yet he depended on the government's protection of him and his family.

The novel's ending forces the reader to reexamine Adam's bicycle trip to Rutterburg, Vermont. It must be concluded that Adam did not physically travel there on his bike, but he did indeed make a painful subconscious journey that ended in Rutterburg, to the place where he last saw his parents and where his long-repressed memory comes crashing into consciousness. These memories, of course, are what Brint (T) pressed Adam to recall throughout their interviews, in hopes, we discover, of uncovering some "useful" information:

> T:  I think you reached the point where you cannot stifle the memories, whatever you wish to call them, any longer. In fact, this is what drew you here to this room, tonight, this need to remember. The memories are there—they must come out, they must emerge, they cannot be allowed to fester any longer.
>     (8-second interval.)
> T:  It is not a matter of trust any longer, it is a matter of inevitability. The knowledge must come, you cannot hold it back.
> A:  I know, I know. . .

And he did know. He knew the knowledge was there waiting to come forward, welling up inside him, waiting for him to express it, verbalize it, and in that way make it real. But at the same time, he hesitated. A part of himself resisted.

> T:  What is the matter?
> A:  Let me wait a moment.
> T:  The time is past for waiting.

He knew that but he also knew that Brint, or whoever he was, was sitting across from him, waiting, like a predator, an enemy—he was certain of that now—but he knew also that he had to reveal everything to him, that he could not do it alone.

All he could hope for was that he could find the knowledge about himself without betraying—betraying who? (195-196)

Adam uncovers the horrible truth that the very day after he and his parents had spent the night at a motel in Rutterburg, Vermont, his mother and father were killed. Adam was critically injured and his parents were killed by a car that intentionally struck all three of them as they admired a view by the side of the road. Adam's father seemed to escape the hurtling car, but Adam overhears this exchange among the murderers:

> A voice: "He got away—he's not here!"
> Another voice: "I saw him run. He's hurt."
> Another voice: "They'll get him—they never miss." (220)

Adding to the horror is Adam's recollection of the very familiar Mr. Grey, the Farmers' sole connection to the government and their supposed protector, at the scene of the accident. However, Adam never verbalized his knowledge of Mr. Grey's presence during his interview with Brint. He could not. He would not. Adam completely withdrew when his memory forced him to relive the death of his parents.

Mr. Grey, we learn in the final cryptic chapter, was responsible for the covert transfer of Adam from the scene of his parents' deaths to the facility that contained him during the interviews. This chapter also makes clear that Adam has spent three years in that facility, drugged continually to keep him cooperative. Following Adam's complete withdrawal and the termination of the interview, Brint makes his final recommendation regarding Adam (Subject A):

> Since Subject A is final linkage between Witness #599-6 [Adam's father] and File data 865-0, it is advised that (a) pending revision of Agency Basic Procedures (Refer: Policy 979) Subject A's confinement be continued until termination procedures are approved; or (b) Subject A's condition be sustained until Subject A obliterates.
> END TAPE SERIES OZK016. (232-233)

The implication, though it be fiction, that our government might condone or conspire in "termination procedures" gives would-be censors fuel for challenging this book. In fact, the Panama City, Florida, case (1986-1988) accused *I Am the Cheese* of expressing a "subversive" un-American theme in which government agents are made out to be devious. Furthermore, the accusers added that the novel "slyly cast doubt in the U.S. government, parental authority, and the medical profession" (Karolides 222). While I agree that the idea of such participation by the government and medical professionals is unsettling, it is not cause for censorship.

First of all, even young readers are aware, via the media, of the potential for wrongdoing within professions and institutions. Isn't questioning the integrity of our institutions and professionals, as well as thinking critically about their actions, preferable to blind acceptance? Wasn't it just that sort of questioning that led to the founding of the United States, the Protestant Reformation, the abolition of slavery, the Women's Suffrage Movement, the Civil Rights Movement, and all significant social, political, and religious changes? How then, can we not offer books that give our young people "practice" at questioning the institutions? It seems that this is a necessary skill for responsible citizens.

Second, Cormier's focus is not on the institution of government, but rather on the individual citizen's struggle. Through the characters of Adam and his father, Cormier offers a realistic parallel to many citizens in our country—they trust and mistrust the government at the same time. They depend on it, even though it's not always helpful. Wrestling with such ambiguity, perhaps for the first time, young readers will be primed and ready for meaningful discussion. Do not underestimate the value of these conversations. They encourage young people to view their world more critically, an essential skill for our time.

In addition to the negative portrayal of the government, two other possible objections to *I Am the Cheese* exist. First, the sprinkling of questionable language offends some. "Hell" is used five times (32, 43, 157); "bastard" is used once (43); "crissakes" is used once (42), and "damn" is used once (43). Examined in context, these words are used by the characters in intensely frightening situations. For example, Adam remembers a time he and his father were being attacked by a dog: "'come on you bastard,' his father yelled at the dog. Adam had never heard his father swear like that before, although he said 'hell' and 'damn' once in a while" (43).

These words, though unpleasant, suit the situation and help us better understand the characters. Furthermore, young readers relate to Adam's shock at hearing his father swear and quickly connect it to the seriousness of their situation.

Second, some object to Adam's encounter with the man on the fire escape (153-157). Realizing his bike has been stolen, Adam questions the man on the fire escape and offers him a reward for information about who took it. The scene is disturbing. The man's behavior is lewd and Adam's reaction is painfully shown:

> "There's all kinds of ree-wards, honey," he says. "There's ree-wards and ree-wards." And now, in the dusk, he begins to scratch at himself, scratching his chest where his shirt is open and where curly hair glistens. He scratches with both hands, descending to his stomach. "All kinds. . ." he says, his voice lingering in the twilight.

I am conscious again of the migraine, the throb in my forehead. A wave of nausea crests in my stomach and I taste acid and bile.

"All I want is my bike," I say, my lips trembling, and I'm sad and angry at the same time because I feel like a small boy again, still the coward I always was. There's a whimper in my voice and I hate myself for the whimper and I hate the fat man up there on the fire escape for reducing me to this state. (155)

Cormier causes the reader to experience panic, helplessness, and anger along with Adam. It takes strong, powerful writing to do this. Cormier also reminds us of the unpleasant truth that sometimes adults may behave very inappropriately, a caution most parents give their children at an early age. This theme is introduced early on as Adam receives advice from an old man he encounters in his bike journey: "It's a terrible world out there. Murders and assassinations. Nobody's safe on the streets. And you don't even know who to trust anymore. Do you know who the bad guys are?" (18).

Adam encounters more than his share of bad guys in his journeys, both real and imagined. His solitary struggle is poignantly noted near the end of the book as he sings the last verse of "The Farmer in the Dell," a song his father often sang:

The cheese stands alone,
The cheese stands alone,
Heigh-ho the merry-o,
The cheese stands alone.

Alone, in the institution, Adam thinks to himself, "I am the cheese" (229). These haunting words echo in the reader's mind. Surely we all feel as if we stand alone sometimes, especially when we are young.

Readers of *I Am the Cheese* do not want to do so alone. They want to share it with friends, ponder it, understand it, and discuss it. Seize the marvelous opportunity Robert Cormier has granted. Keep this book on our classroom and library shelves.

## Works Cited

Cormier, Robert. *I Am the Cheese*. New York: Alfred A. Knopf, 1997.
Karolides, Nicholas J. *Banned Books:Literature Suppressed on Political Grounds*. New York: Facts On File, 1998.

# *In the Spirit of Crazy Horse*:
# Censorship and the FBI-AIM Wars of the 1970s

## Maggi Kramm

*In the Spirit of Crazy Horse* was first published in 1983, six years after Leonard Peltier's conviction in the killing of two FBI agents at a shootout near Oglala, South Dakota. The book was soon pulled off the shelves because of two lawsuits for libel, and finally reissued in 1991 after its author, Peter Matthiessen, and publisher, Viking Press, had been exonerated by the United States Supreme Court.

Born in 1927 and educated at Yale, Matthiessen is best known for two nonfiction books set in international locales, *At Play in the Fields of the Lord* and *The Snow Leopard* (which won the National Book Award), and for the controversial *In the Spirit of Crazy Horse*. This last book figures on the reading list of numerous courses on Native American studies and was a bestseller when it was returned to circulation after eight years in legal limbo. It is also largely responsible for kindling mainstream interest in the plight of Peltier and in recent Indian political causes in general.

*In the Spirit* is worth studying on at least three grounds. First, it provides a thoroughly researched account of the "Indian Wars" of the 1970s, when the American Indian Movement (AIM) and other Indian groups clashed repeatedly with the local and federal authorities. Second, the book is a sobering corrective to the notion that the United States, which so ardently defends freedom of speech and human rights in other parts of the world, conducts itself as scrupulously in its own backyard. And third, as the epilogue makes clear, the publication history of the book is itself significant in the history of First Amendment rights.

This is a long book—646 pages, including notes and index—and can easily bog down the casual reader. Its reporting style is heavy on documentation, interviews, reconstruction of events, and lists of participants. Those who are new to this material, or who prefer their investigative journalism to take a neutral stance, will not be reassured by Matthiessen's frequently polemical tone. There is plenty of misbehavior and arrogance on both sides—by AIM members and by the white or white-supported authorities. The weaknesses and contradictions of the latter, though, are typically pounced on, and characters sometimes established through innuendo and *ad hominem* descriptions. The author alludes several times, for instance, to the unproven charge that William Janklow, who as state attorney general in the 1970s was hostile to AIM and who is now in his fourth term as governor of South Dakota, had raped a fifteen-year-old Indian girl in his charge.

Far more sympathetically portrayed are AIM members—many of whom came from the urban Indian ghettoes—and the "traditional" Indians, those who remained on the reservation, often living in crushing poverty but in closer touch with their cultural traditions. The vast majority of quoted interviews derive from Indians or the sympathizers of AIM. Matthiessen remains discreetly laconic about instances of self-serving and corrupt behavior within the ranks of the Indian movement.

One especially disturbing crime during this period, the unsolved murder in 1976 of AIM activist Anna Mae Aquash, puts both AIM and the authorities in a sordid light. Aquash, a Micmac Indian from Nova Scotia, was suspected of being an FBI informant, though possibly the FBI spread the false rumor in order to sow discord in AIM. In any event, many believe that she was killed by members of AIM. Yet there were gross discrepancies in the authorities' handling of the case (for example, the first autopsy said she died of exposure, while the second revealed a bullet in her brain). None of the AIM hierarchy attended her funeral, yet one of the movement's leaders, Dennis Banks, seized on Aquash's violent death to further stoke the animosity between his group and the FBI:

> "Her murder is another example of an FBI cover-up in the attempt to destroy the leadership of the American Indian Movement." Subsequently he [Banks] concluded that no AIM member was guilty of her death. "She wasn't killed by just one person. It was what she represented and what kind of person she was. What happens to a people in four hundred years? Maybe that is the answer. Maybe four hundred years killed Anna Mae." (264)

Matthiessen does not examine Banks's reasons for concluding that his people were innocent. Either the author didn't ask, or he didn't care to report what he found. Instead, he allows rhetoric such as this to pass unchallenged, whereas far less glaring flaws in the government's arguments are rigorously exposed.

Yet in terms of its accuracy of reporting, *In the Spirit of Crazy Horse* has survived the closest and most hostile scrutiny, not only in the press but in several court cases. Through years of tireless research, the author has constructed a convincing case that the FBI and local authorities conspired again and again to crush AIM, through both legal and illegal means.

## "We Are Your Shadows"

As Matthiesen's early chapters narrate succinctly, the violent conflicts between modern Indian warriors and the U.S. government spring from deep and tangled roots. The invading European settlers and Indians couldn't see eye to eye on such basic concepts as whether Mother Earth should be sold. The communal practices of the Lakota and other native tribes made the government's negotiations for land especially vexing. In 1885, Massachusetts senator Henry Dawes declared of the Indians: "There is no selfishness, which is at the bottom of civilization" (17). In turn, the great Lakota chief Sitting Bull observed of the *wasichus*, or "greedy ones": "The love of possessions is a disease with them" (9). The government's history of making and breaking treaties with the Indians has been nothing short of execrable. Yet even then, as now, Indian culture has won the admiration of many non-Indians. The most successful Indian fighter, General George Crook, was moved to remark, "the hardest thing is to go and fight those whom you know are in the right" (11).

The Black Hills in western South Dakota have represented a flashpoint in white/Plains Indian relations from the nineteenth century to the present. Indians long considered the region sacred and would return there periodically for spiritual ceremonies. "These hills are our church," explained one Lakotan. The Fort Laramie Treaty of 1868, meant to safeguard most of western South Dakota for the Indians, giving them "absolute and undisturbed use of the Great Sioux Reservations" in perpetuity, was ignored when gold was discovered seven years later. (A Court of Claims in 1979 would call the federal government's behavior here "the most ripe and rank case of dishonorable dealing in our history" [513].) Sioux resistance was more or less extinguished by 1890, when soldiers opened fire on a band of Lakota at Wounded Knee, not far from the Black Hills. More than 200 of Big Foot's band, many of them women, children, and the elderly, perished. "A people's dream died there," lamented the medicine man Black Elk, whose cousin, Crazy Horse, had been murdered thirteen years earlier while in the custody of the U.S. army. But the Indian problem would not go away. As one Indian observed, "We are your shadows."

Subsequent government policies all but destroyed traditional ways of life, first isolating Indians on reservations, and more recently, relocating many in urban areas. In this century, Indians continue to suffer from the lowest income levels and worst health of all Americans, and those living on the Rosebud and Pine Ridge reservations, near Wounded Knee, are among the poorest of the poor. At least until recently, dispersement of government funds was chronically inequitable, and the tribal councils meant to serve Indians were rife with nepotism and lawlessness.

Matthiessen's book focuses mostly on the protests, skirmishes, and legal and political confrontations of AIM members during the 1970s. These include the protest in Washington, D.C., known as the Trail of Broken Treaties; the siege at Wounded Knee; and the Oglala shootings, which left two federal agents and one Indian dead and led to Leonard Peltier's incarceration for two life terms.

As the author amply documents, the FBI infiltrated AIM and tried to weaken it through counterintelligence, much as they did with the Black Panthers. Among the reasons for the FBI to take a keen interest in political activism in this impoverished region was the importance to local white ranchers of grazing rights on reservation lands, and the mineral value of the Black Hills, which reportedly contain uranium deposits. Also in the 1970s, local tribal council leader Dick Wilson routinely terrorized his opponents on the Pine Ridge reservation—usually the traditionals and "full-bloods"—with a vigilante squad that was funded by the government. Dozens of Indian murders were never solved; few were seriously investigated. Complaints to, and about, the Bureau of Indian Affairs accomplished little.

In frustration, Indians from the reservation joined forces with AIM and descended on the small, mostly white community of Wounded Knee on February 28, 1973. Taking over several buildings, the armed group, about 300 strong, demanded a hearing on their treaty with the government and an investigation into corruption within the BIA. After holding off the FBI, U.S. marshals, and BIA police for 71 days, the Indians finally surrendered. Five hundred people would eventually be indicted in connection with the siege (most of the cases were eventually dismissed or ended in acquittals); the group's demands were not met.

Wounded Knee did, however, bring media attention to the Indians' long-standing grievances. And to those on the reservation, AIM offered some protection against Wilson's goons, as well as a renewed pride in their heritage. But AIM was also belligerent, their sometimes violent principles keeping them at odds with the more peaceful traditionals. Said Ellen Moves Camp, a Lakotan who lived in Pine Ridge, "We decided that we did need the American Indian Movement in here because our men were scared, they hung to the back. It was mostly the women that went forward and spoke out. . . . All of our older people from the reservation helped us make the decision" (65). As she explained, "the AIM people stood up for us until our own men could stand up for themselves. And the West Coast bunch didn't drink, and they didn't fool around; they were hard core, and we knew that we could count on 'em" (527).

Chief Frank Fools Crow, who a year earlier had invited AIM to the reservation, noted in 1976, "The traditionalists do not like violent tactics, so we do not support AIM anymore. But they have accomplished things that our passive methods did not accomplish," and added that even "the questionable attention collected by AIM has given a much-needed boost to the Indians' dignity and self-esteem" (420).

Although there are many characters in Matthiessen's book who strive to behave "in the spirit of Crazy Horse"—that is, with Crazy Horse's selfless dedication to his people, his refusal to compromise with the whites, and his uncanny courage and spiritual strength—none can come close to that great nineteenth-century warrior's competence and integrity. If there is a hero to this book, it is not the higher-profile AIM leaders such as Dennis Banks and Russell Means, but Leonard Peltier.

Born in 1944 of Ojibwa and Sioux heritage, Peltier was raised in the Turtle Mountain reservation of North Dakota and later worked as a mechanic during sojourns in Seattle and other West Coast cities. Bright, given to joking, and well liked, Peltier got into scrapes with the law, as did so many of his peers. From his youth he participated occasionally in sundances, and in 1970 he joined AIM. Thereafter, he mostly traveled around the country from protest to protest or stayed on reservations.

"Leonard was never a troublemaker; he always tried to stop trouble before it got started," said Ellen Moves Camp. "He took a lot of time, and he saw all sides; he was never a vicious man. Leonard is truly big-hearted, kind-hearted" (527). According to his cousin, Steve Robideau, "He was always ready to do *anything*; if he couldn't find no other way to help, he'd go cut their wood!" (521). Sam Moves Camp adds, "There are four qualities very important to the Indian people—bravery, generosity, fortitude, and knowledge—and Leonard had all of 'em" (527).

On June 26, 1975, when Peltier and a few dozen other Indians were camped on the property of Harry and Cecelia Jumping Bull, two FBI agents, Ronald Williams and Jack Coler, drove into the Jumping Bulls' pasture, possibly in pursuit of a vehicle. An exchange of gunfire ensued. By the time the shooting stopped, one Indian, Joe Stuntz, and the two agents, who had been killed at very close range, lay dead. Four suspects were eventually charged for murder, but only Peltier was convicted.

## "They Use the Law to Cheat People"

Did Peltier shoot the agents, as the prosecution successfully argued?

The book does not exonerate him, though it raises certain doubts. In a later appeal, when a judge pressed prosecuting attorney Lynn Crooks to clarify a discrepancy, Crooks retorted, "But we can't prove who shot those agents!" (570). There were other suspects with equally strong claims to being the killer, but they weren't as highly placed in AIM and so, the argument runs, they didn't suit the purposes of FBI, which was to blacken the movement.

As to the question "was Peltier unjustly imprisoned?" the evidence that Matthiessen brings forward is quite compelling. At the very least, Peltier's trial and the government's modus operandi in dealing with AIM exhibit serious flaws.

As in earlier AIM trials, the FBI showed an uncanny knack for producing convenient, often dubious witnesses to fill in gaps in their case. Witnesses for the prosecution later claimed they were coerced by authorities; others were discredited as mentally unstable, including Myrtle Poor Bear. Her highly suspect testimony was instrumental in extraditing Peltier from Canada, where he had fled after the Oglala shootings. As a British Columbia Supreme Court judge later commented on Peltier's case, "It seems clear to me that the conduct of the U.S. government involved misconduct from inception" (319).

Months before Peltier's own trial, two other defendants, Bob Robideau and Dino Butler, had been acquitted in Cedar Rapids, Iowa, for the same murders. The defense had argued that the case cannot be understood except against the backdrop of the chronic violence and racism of the local and federal authorities.

As the foreman in the Cedar Rapids trial explained,

> The jury agreed with the defense contention that an atmosphere of fear and violence exists on the reservation, and that the defendants arguably could have been shooting in self-defense. While it was shown that the defendants were firing guns in the direction of the agents, it was held that this was not excessive in the heat of passion. . . . The government just did not produce sufficient evidence. (313)

One prosecution witness was a prisoner who claimed to have heard Butler's loquacious confession while they shared a jail cell, and later admitted that the FBI was going to cut him a deal in exchange for his testimony. Of this witness the foreman said, "Not one single person believed one single word of what he said" (313).

But Judge Paul Benson, who presided over Peltier's trial in Fargo, North Dakota, cut the defense off at the knees through a series of adverse rulings. He refused to allow much of the evidence that had freed Robideau and Butler and curtailed the defense's presentation of other information, even, as one lawyer observed, "accusing [the defense counsel] in the jury's hearing of wasting the jury's time in its cross-examinations" (360). Writes Matthiessen,

> the suspect affidavits used in Canada, the historical background of Pine Ridge violence, the persecution of AIM by the FBI, the verdict at Cedar Rapids, together with all testimony from that trial, were inadmissible as evidence in his court. The effect of these rulings became clear with the very first prosecution witness: the defense was forbidden to impeach Agent Gary Adams for glaring contradictions in his testimony at the two trials. (323)

One point of considerable confusion was whether or not the bullet casings found near the bodies matched the AR-15 found in the possession of an AIM member. Early FBI lab reports concluded the gun was too damaged to be tested; many months later, when the prosecutors were in need of a smoking gun, another lab report surfaced with more incriminating conclusions. Judge Benson, notes Matthiessen, ruled that "the defense, in its summation, was not to point out the strange timing of all these ballistics reports" (354), and forbad the jurors to take notes or consult the more than 5,000 pages of trial transcript. As a result, "they could not retain pertinent details of the complex and lengthy arguments" (357).

"In the end," Matthiessen concludes, "it was Judge Benson's determination of what the jury should or should not see and hear that became the deciding factor in the trial," which ended in Peltier's conviction (360). A court of appeals would later agree with the defense that much of the suppressed evidence should have been allowed; nonetheless it upheld the conviction. In the nearly twenty-five years since then, Peltier's many supporters have tried, but failed, to win him a new trial or presidential clemency, and he remains in prison.

## The Libel Suits and an Author's Right to Be One-sided

In separate lawsuits in 1983 and 1984, South Dakota Governor William Janklow and FBI Special Agent David Price sued Matthiessen and Viking Press for libel. Price disputed the book's portrayal of him and other FBI agents as racist, corrupt, and vicious, and, like Janklow, attempted to impugn many of Matthiessen's sources as untrustworthy. Janklow charged that the book unfairly portrayed him as morally depraved and racist. He further complained that the accusations by AIM, reported in the book, were factually inaccurate and were "prepared either with a reckless disregard for the truth or with actual malice for the plaintiff" (Karolides 247). After eight years in the courts, and eight legal decisions, the Supreme Court finally ruled that the plaintiffs had not been libeled.

The defense attorney, Martin Garbus, provides an Afterword to the 1991 reissue of *In the Spirit of Crazy Horse*. His seven-page summary of the libel trials and of the legal significance of these decisions provides some of the book's most bracing writing. The republication of *In the Spirit of Crazy Horse*, Garbus asserts, "marks a great victory against a new kind of censorship: the attempt by present and former public officials to suppress books that criticize them or disagree with their policies" and "a defeat for all those who wish to keep this country in the dark about abuses against its citizens in the past and present eras" (593).

Minnesota federal judge Diana E. Murphy, who heard the Price suit, made what Garbus calls "a trail-blazing decision." She cited the importance of protecting an author's right to his or her opinion and "the freedom to develop a thesis, conduct research in an effort to support the thesis, and publish an entirely one-sided view of people and events."

Judge Murphy maintained that, while Price was understandably disturbed by the book, "it is not for this court to balance his distress with the right to freedom of speech vigorously asserted by defendants." Without "clear and convincing evidence of actual malice with respect to a statement of fact concerning plaintiff, the balance tips in favor of free speech" (597). As the *New York Times* commented, the ruling would "encourage greater freedom of authors, less fear and suppression in publishing houses and broader availability of books on controversial subjects" (597).

At the heart of Janklow and Price's cases was a distinction between good sources and bad ones—the latter, Price argued, including "leftists, AIM members, and their sympathizers." In 1989, the U.S. Court of Appeals agreed with the defense's contention that authors should be allowed to repeat as-yet-unproven accusations because "even if a government official could be injured by such reports, to suppress them would unduly inhibit debate on issues of public significance" (599). As the presiding judge, Gerald Heaney, wrote,

> there is a larger injury to be considered, the damage done to every American when a book is pulled from a shelf, as in this case, or when an idea is not circulated. In its entirety, *Crazy Horse* focuses more on public institutions and social forces than it does on any public official. The sentiments it expresses are debatable. We favor letting the debate continue. (600)

Notes Garbus, if the judges had decided otherwise, and Matthiessen and Viking had lost their cases, "Reporters would have been reluctant to rely on sources that judges and juries might find disreputable, and officials would have been encouraged to silence their critics with costly libel suits." *In the*

*Spirit of Crazy Horse*, then, has served not only to bring the injustices committed against Native Americans to a wide audience, but also to preserve a liberal interpretation of the First Amendment.

## Work Cited

Karolides, Nicholas J. *Banned Books: Literature Suppressed on Political Grounds*. New York: Facts On File, 1998.
Matthiessen, Peter. *In the Spirit of Crazy Horse*. New York: Viking Press, 1991.

# Sexual Development:
# Letting Kids Know *It's Perfectly Normal*

## Nancy Bayne

In *Are You There God? It's Me, Margaret*, an often-censored book by Judy Blume, Margaret prays, "Oh, please, God. I just want to be normal" (100). Robie Harris's *It's Perfectly Normal* assures preteens and adolescents that a wide variety of thoughts, feelings and physical changes that occur during puberty and adolescence are, indeed, normal. Through straightforward text and Michael Emberley's engaging watercolors and drawings, children learn about sex according to its dictionary definitions, its historical and social contexts, and its interpersonal and intrapersonal meanings. The narrative is punctuated by interchanges between two cartoon characters, a squeamish bee and a curious bird who reflect two likely reactions that young people may have to the topic.

It is perfectly normal to be curious about sexuality. Children begin exploring their bodies in infancy and ask a myriad of questions as preschoolers. Some children are able to depend on their parents or other caring adults to provide appropriate information in response to their questions and concerns. Others may quickly learn that their questions elicit no informative response and are better not asked. For children in the former group, *It's Perfectly Normal* is an excellent book for parents and children to read and discuss together. Even parents who wish to provide information to their children may not have all the answers, and Harris provides accurate information in sufficient depth for most children. Children in the latter group can read *It's Perfectly Normal* on their own to gain factual information unavailable to them from adults.

Many of the topics discussed in *It's Perfectly Normal*, such as descriptions of the male and female sexual anatomy, physical changes at puberty, and fertilization, are unlikely to be viewed as controversial, and, in fact, this information is available from a variety of sources. It is the relatively unique features of this book that make it both valuable and controversial. These include discussion of gay and lesbian relationships, masturbation, and abortion. Harris takes on these difficult issues in a straightforward, non-apologetic manner that does indeed give the impression that they are perfectly normal behaviors and perfectly normal topics for serious discussion.

While controversial topics in other youth-oriented texts are often hidden away at the end of the book or in a related chapter, Harris brings them out of the closet and into the Table of Contents. The topics are discussed when they fit most logically into the order of the book. They are also grounded in both a social and scientific context. For instance, "Straight or Gay: Heterosexuality and Homosexuality," is part of the first major section, "What Is Sex?" In this chapter, readers learn that the word *lesbian* refers to the Greek island of Lesbos, where the female poet Sappho lived and wrote poetry celebrating love and friendship between women. They also learn that the ancient Greeks actually "hoped that male lovers would be in the same army regiment [because] if a warrior were in the same regiment as his lover, he would fight harder in order to impress him" (17). Harris then briefly describes the major scientific approaches to explaining the development of homosexual and heterosexual identities. More immediately relevant to the reader's life, she also reassures the reader that it is perfectly normal for both gay and straight adolescents to have crushes on members of the same sex or want to see or touch a same-sex friend's body. Harris confronts homophobia by stating that some people dislike, hate, or are afraid of homosexuals, and offering the very reasonable explanation that "people are often afraid of things they know little or nothing about" (18). At the same time she points out that heterosexuals, bisexuals, and homosexuals are really much more alike than different. At the end of many chapters, including this one, the reader is encouraged to talk with trusted adults about the issue.

Masturbation is a common, but guilt-invoking, activity (Baldwin and Baldwin). Harris's title for this chapter, "Perfectly Normal: Masturbation," immediately reassures adolescents that whether or not they choose to engage in this behavior, they are perfectly normal. Kids learn that masturbation is not harmful and that rubbing the clitoris or penis can result in feelings of pleasure. Atypically, the clitoris is also described in the chapters on the female body and on sexual sharing. Sex education materials that focus primarily on the procreative aspects of sexual behavior usually avoid mentioning the clitoris at all, as its sole purpose is providing sexual pleasure. Acknowledging the existence of the clitoris and its function increases the likelihood that young women will be able to experience sexual pleasure and will believe it is normal to do so. While readers are informed that some people believe masturbation is a sin, the overall tone of the chapter clearly implies that "playing with yourself" is okay.

Empirical research shows that children who talk with their parents about sex and birth control are more likely than those who do not to protect themselves against pregnancy, while being no more likely to engage in sexual intercourse (Baker et al.; Milan and Kilmann). While Harris points out the advantages of postponement and abstinence in "Planning Ahead: Postponement, Abstinence, and Birth Control, " she clearly accepts that people, including adolescents, engage in sexual intercourse for pleasure, not just for procreation. She is also realistic about the fact that not all adolescents will choose postponement or abstinence. Approximately 30 percent of adolescents have had intercourse by age 15 and 60 percent by age 17 (Alan Guttmacher Institute). Therefore, the reader can learn about the major forms of birth control including condoms, birth control pills, IUDs, and sterilization. In addition, the title of this chapter and the title of this entire section, "Decisions," send a particularly important message to young women who still believe that their role in sexual encounters is to resist the initiative of the man. It is often difficult for them to consciously choose to be sexually active and make the corresponding choices to avoid pregnancy and STDs because they believe the only acceptable way to engage in sexual intercourse is to *not* choose, but rather get carried away by the moment (Braverman and Strasburger). Once again Harris ends the chapter by advising young readers to talk to parents, doctors, or nurses about planning ahead for sexual encounters.

In "Laws and Rulings: Abortion" Harris describes the many reasons a woman or couple may choose to end a pregnancy. These include dangers to the pregnant woman's health, birth defects in the fetus, the pregnancy being a result of rape, and feeling financially or psychologically unprepared to raise a child. Harris acknowledges that people have strong feelings about abortion and describes the basic positions of pro-choice and pro-life advocates. However, she points out that the Supreme Court, in Roe versus Wade, has ruled that a woman has a right to decide for herself whether she will have an abortion unless it is very late in the pregnancy. The message is clearly that women have a legal right to abortion, though some restrictions may be put on this right by the states.

In addition to the forthright and nonjudgmental presentations on these controversial topics, the inclusion of Michael Emberley's illustrations is bound to raise concern with some individuals or groups. While nearly three of every four human figures in the book are clothed, the one in four that is either naked or partially clothed may at first seem excessive or startling in a society that believes that children should not view naked bodies. Yet, much of the message that the reader is perfectly normal would be lost without these illustrations. One of the most meaningful sections of the book can be found on pages 20 and 21 in "The Human Body: All Kinds of Bodies." Here the reader finds 20 drawings of naked people, young and old, large and small, black, brown, and white, prepubescent and postpubescent. All give the impression of being comfortable in their bodies, whether they come close to the standard American prototype for beauty or are diametrically opposed to it. The message is clearly that bodies of all colors, shapes, and sizes are perfectly normal.

Another critically important drawing is in the chapter on female sexual anatomy, "Outside and Inside: The Female Sex Organs." This drawing shows a girl bending over and viewing her external genitals through a mirror. The accompanying text describes the three openings between the female's legs and these are labeled on the drawing: "anus"; "opening to vagina"; and "opening to urethra." The female reader is encouraged to use a mirror to view her own three openings. Particularly for the female anatomy, it is very important to clearly describe, label, and show the separate vaginal and anal openings as, even today, young women and men may not be aware of the existence of three separate openings.

While the male genitals are more visible and accessible than the female genitals, prohibitions against displaying male full-frontal nudity have been more persistent than those against female full-frontal nudity, most particularly when any degree of sexual arousal is present. Even children who may have had opportunities to observe nudity in art or film are unlikely to see an erect penis. While most boys have direct experience with their own erections, a girl's first experience may come at the time of her first intimate sexual encounter, and the sight of an erect penis may be a surprising or even frightening event that interferes with her ability to take pleasure in this encounter. Thus, the erections illustrated in Harris's book provide important knowledge that is not readily available to most children.

Illustrations of children masturbating reinforce the notion discussed earlier that this behavior is common in children. Two thirds of boys and one third of girls masturbate prior to adolescence (Crooks and Baur). For boys, many of whom learn about masturbation from friends, the illustration of a boy masturbating reinforces the normalcy of this activity and demonstrates that this activity is not limited to his own childhood circle of friends. For girls, most of whom discover masturbation accidentally and rarely speak about it with friends, the illustration of a girl masturbating provides visible knowledge that she is not the only girl who engages in this activity.

Other less graphic, but still controversial, illustrations send equally important messages that reinforce the text's presentation of normal, but nonprocreative, sexuality. As human beings we strive to know and understand the behavior of those around us. We are most comfortable when we can use this knowledge to modify our own behavior as we engage in social interactions. When behavior is new or unusual, both adults and children may stare, trying to assimilate this new information. If they are not allowed to observe this behavior, their discomfort with not knowing or being able to make predictions about this new experience may lead them to dislike the people involved or to trivialize the behavior observed. Thus, the matter-of-fact inclusion of illustrations of same-sex partners with their arms around each other and older couples expressing physical affection in the context of a straightforward and nonjudgmental text allows children the opportunity to safely stare and to assimilate information about gay and lesbian couples and sexuality in older adults in a manner that communicates both the importance and normalcy of these relationships.

In the final chapter, "Staying Healthy: Responsible Choices," Harris says, "A large part of growing up is learning to take care of yourself in a healthy way" (83). She goes on to remind the reader that this means more than taking care of your body; it means taking responsibility for making healthy decisions about your sexuality. *It's Perfectly Normal* gives children the tools they need and the permission to make these healthy choices.

## Works Cited

Alan Guttmacher Institute, *Sex and America's Teenagers*. New York: Alan Guttmacher Institute, 1994.

Baker, Sharon A., Stanton P. Thalberg, and Diane M. Morrison. "Parents' Behavioral Norms as Predictors of Adolescent Sexual Activity and Contraceptive Use." *Adolescence* 23 (1988): 278-281.

Baldwin, J. D., and J. I. Baldwin. "Gender Differences in Sexual Interest." *Archives of Sexual Behavior* 26 (2) (1997): 181-210.

Blume, Judy. *Are You There God? It's Me, Margaret*. Englewood Cliffs, N.J.: Dell, 1972.

Braverman, P., and V. Strasburger. "Sexually Transmitted Diseases." *Clinical Pediatrics* (January 1994): 26-37.

Crooks, Robert, and Karla Baur. *Our Sexuality*. Pacific Grove, Calif.: Books/Cole, 1999.

Harris, Robie H. *It's Perfectly Normal*. Cambridge, Mass.: Candlewick Press, 1994.

Milan, Richard, and Peter R. Kilmann. "Interpersonal Factors in Premarital Conception." *Journal of Sex Research* 23 (1987): 289-321.

# Roald Dahl's *James and the Giant Peach*

## Bill Brittain

From beginning to end—from the devouring of James Henry Trotter's parents in the middle of London by an angry rhinoceros to the impalement of the huge peach on the mast of the Empire State Building and the subsequent happy endings—Roald Dahl's *James and the Giant Peach* is designed to fascinate both children and adults like me who find pleasure in a well-crafted fantasy.

Readers of this essay may raise the point that most of my comments concerning *James and the Giant Peach* involve schools and teachers, while public libraries and librarians are given short shrift. Guilty as charged! I was a public school teacher for thirty-four years, and I'm most familiar with book censorship problems as they pertain to schools. However, I suspect that many of my observations will be germane not only to teachers but to librarians as well.

A review of the plot of *James and the Giant Peach* is unnecessary. Those who haven't yet had the joy of discovering James's adventures can read the entire book in an hour or so. So I'll settle for a few reasons why I personally find the book so delightful.

First of all, the story zips along with incredible velocity. James's change of circumstance from an idyllic childhood to misery and slavery in the home of his Aunt Spiker and Aunt Sponge takes about a page and a half. Is there a need to explain the peach's fantastic growth? Then by all means, let a little man appear out of the shrubbery with a bag of magical green crocodile tongues in his hand. The book abounds with inventive imagery. For example, the rolling of the house-sized peach across the British countryside, threatening lives and property, and finally plunging off the white cliffs of Dover into the sea, with James and his companions inside, summons up mental pictures both comic and fantastic. If ever a story was designed to get children to poke their noses into a book, this is that story.

The peach itself is a remarkable concept, serving James and his friends as a combination living quarters, travel vehicle, and source of nourishment.

Equally remarkable are the friends themselves: Miss Spider, Centipede, Old-Green-Grasshopper, Ladybug, Earthworm, Glow-worm and Silkworm. Not only do the skills of each one play a part in the story, but each has its own unique personality. I particularly like Centipede—he of a hundred boots (or maybe only forty-two) —who not only owns up to being a garden pest but is quite proud of that fact.

From a child's standpoint, perhaps the most important element of the story is that whenever an emergency arises—shark attack, the necessity to fly, or Centipede's fall from the airborne peach, to mention a few—it is seven-year-old James himself who discovers and puts into action a solution to the problems. For example, with the sharks "lashing their tails" and attacking the peach, James determines to lift the peach out of the water; he loops silkworm and spider string, supplied by two companion passengers, around the necks of seagulls—502 of them, tying the other end to the peach stem, until the peach is raised up to the clouds. The formerly powerless child becomes a leader. How could any young reader fail to be delighted by this turn of events?

Equally delightful is the word play Dahl employs. It's clear that here is an author who recognizes the English language as a magnificent toy with which to play. At one point, for example, Old-Green-Grasshopper asks: "Would you be kind enough, Miss Spider, to make the beds?"

Sexist? Not in the least. For Miss Spider does not simply smooth out sheets and blankets. She literally *makes* the beds, spinning out hammock-like resting places so the others will have a place to sleep.

Again, there's the poem in which the evil Aunt Spiker and Aunt Sponge describe themselves and each other. Aunt Sponge believes her destiny lies in Hollywood:

"They'd give me all the leading parts!
The stars would all resign!"

And the reply. . .

"I think you'd make," Aunt Spiker said, "a lovely Frankenstein."

In spite of its many delights, only a few of which I've mentioned, *James and the Giant Peach* has been attacked by some sources. Let's examine some of the reasons for such attacks.

1. *The story is a fantasy. It isn't true to life.*

Very true. And if childhood isn't a time for fantasy, when is? From Shakespeare—*A Midsummer Night's Dream*—to Dr. Seuss—*The Cat in the*

*Hat*, et cetera—fantasy has been a facet of the art of many famous writers throughout the ages. Stretching the imagination of the child and encouraging creativity should be a part of any primary curriculum. This doesn't come about from reading auto repair handbooks or histories of the Civil War. *James and the Giant Peach* fills the bill perfectly.

2. *There's an awful lot of violence in the tale.*

Yes, there is. Before the end of page 1, James's parents are eaten by that rhinoceros. Aunt Spiker and Aunt Sponge are ironed flat by the rolling peach. The peach no sooner reaches the ocean than it is attacked by sharks. Et cetera . . . et cetera . . . et cetera.

But come on! The violence is all of the cartoon variety. We've all seen movies in which Wile E. Coyote, on top of a high cliff, walks out several feet onto thin air. Only when he realizes his plight does he fall, hitting the desert far below with a puff of dust. Moments later, he's back, none the worse for wear.

The violence in *James and the Giant Peach* is of the same ilk. No more do rhinos eat flesh than sharks long to dine on peaches. These aren't real threats, and kids know it instinctively.

A case in point is the deaths of Aunt Spiker and Aunt Sponge. First of all, these two harridans are *so* evil that in spite of their supposed relationship to the title character, they're just begging to be eliminated. Consider this exchange between the two concerning James: "'He probably fell down in the dark and broke his leg,' Aunt Spiker said. 'Or his neck, maybe,' Aunt Sponge said hopefully."

*Hopefully*. That final adverb sums up the comic evil of the two perfectly.

And how do they perish? "The peach rolled on. And behind it, Aunt Sponge and Aunt Spiker lay ironed out upon the grass as flat and thin and lifeless as a couple of paper dolls cut out of a picture book." Haven't you seen the same situation whenever a steamroller appears in a *Popeye* or *Bugs Bunny* cartoon?

Sometimes the comic violence is used to give an ironic twist to an otherwise sickly sweet bit of poetry. Consider this, from among the things Centipede imagines the travelers will encounter on their journey:

> "'We may see the sweet little Biddy-Bright Hen
> So playful, so kind and well-bred.
> And such beautiful eggs! You just boil them and then
> They explode and they blow off your head.'"

In his children's stories, Dahl doesn't linger lovingly over his violence, as is so often the case with adult stories. If you want real, gut-wrenching gore, check out the climactic dinner scene featuring Lecter and Starling in Thomas Harris's *Hannibal.* Or peruse even Dahl's own short story, "Man from the South." But in his stories for children, Dahl uses humorous violence for the sake of surprise, and delight, not for macabre effect.

3. *In the book, all the adults come off as such . . . such jerks!*

Sure they do. The captain of the Queen Mary thinks the peach—held aloft by birds—is a secret weapon. Once the peach is perched on the Empire State building, the heads of the various New York City departments have a rollicking debate over whether the fruit is dangerous and what to do about it. Finally, it is not an adult, but James himself who solves the problem, giving permission for the city's hungry children to eat it all up.

It's essential to the story that James be a wise leader. Therefore, his authority can't be diluted by adults who come up with a solution to every problem. They have to appear ridiculous so that, to the child who's reading the book, James can appear wise. I doubt very much that such playfulness by Dahl will create problems in real life's child/adult relationships.

Still, there are those who will find this delightful and well-told story objectionable. I, therefore, conclude with some comments about those who would censor this or any other book. These comments aren't just theory. They are based on my own experiences as a writer of children's fantasies whose work has been threatened with censorship.

First, in discussions with parents about the suitability of any given story, a teacher should seldom expect to change a parent's mind. Almost always, the parental mind has been made up well before any contact with a teacher is made. This is particularly the case when the objections to the story are based on religious grounds. The object then becomes to win, regardless of the arguments presented.

If the end result comes down to, "Mr./Mrs. Parent, you have your ideas and I (the teacher) have mine. I must respectfully disagree with you and continue with what I think is right," the problem then may get transferred to the principal or superintendent of schools. One can only hope these individuals have the strength of their own convictions and are not excessively swayed by some perceived need to mollify every member of the public.

Second, the parent has the unqualified right to determine which reading material should be withheld from his/her own child. For a teacher to insist, regardless of a parent's objections, that a child be exposed to certain books would be monstrous.

The obverse, however, is equally true. A given parent has no right to dictate what the *rest* of the class will or will not study. If this results in a single child being isolated from the rest of the class for a time, that is the decision of the parent, not of the teacher.

Third and last, in their passion to win (see above), self-appointed censors have become adept at zeroing in on the weak link in any educational chain. Seldom if ever is the teacher with thirty years of experience and a master's plus thirty hours in educational techniques confronted by the guardians of a child's right not to know. It is usually the first- or second-year, nontenured teacher who gets the brunt of the complaints. Here again, it behooves the principal or superintendent to back that teacher to the hilt. To do less is to invite criticism of most of the books in the school library.

The schools and libraries of this nation may be thought of as a vast marketplace, where ideas, theories, and visions of every kind are brought together to be weighted, considered, and tested. We must be forever vigilant so that self-appointed censors, no matter how worthy they consider their causes to be, cannot succeed in closing down the marketplace.

## Work Cited

Dahl, Roald. *James and the Giant Peach*. New York: Knopf, 1961.

# Julie-Miyax: The Emergence of Dual Identity in *Julie of the Wolves* and *Julie*

## Anne Sherrill

When Jean Craighead George's 1973 Newbery Award winner *Julie of the Wolves* appeared, reviewers heralded its success. *The Horn Book Magazine* called it "timeless, perhaps even of classical dimensions" (54). *Best Sellers* said "beautiful literary collages silhouette the intricate mesh of animal-man-earth, an interdependence that draws the best from each contributing member" (45). *Booklist* stated "the well written, empathetic story effectively evokes the nature of wolves and the traditional Eskimo way of life giving way before the relentless onslaught of civilization" (529).

The intriguing story of a thirteen-year-old Eskimo girl surviving on the Arctic tundra has been popular for nearly thirty years. Julie, whose Eskimo name is Miyax, leaves her home in Barrow, Alaska, to escape a twelve-year-old gentle but suddenly abusive husband of an arranged marriage. With Eskimo survival knowledge and basic supplies, she sets out for Point Hope, where she intends to catch a boat and go to the home of her pen pal in San Francisco. However, during her journey she becomes lost on the Arctic tundra and must depend upon her acceptance by a wolf pack for food. She studies the communication patterns of wolves and carefully builds their trust. Her adoption into the pack by the leader, Amaroq, plus her extensive knowledge of nature enable her to survive the harsh life on the tundra. After the cruel and needless death of Amaroq, she finds her way back to civilization and has no choice but to enter Kangik, the town where she has learned her long-absent father now lives.

This award-winning book presents a likeable, brave, and ingenious protagonist; superb detail of the tundra flora and fauna; and fascinating accounts of wolf behavior. Other attractions are the depiction of Eskimo traditions and the cross-cultural struggle posed by the encroachment of the white culture. Just as important, it portrays the growth of a young girl who in the sequel, *Julie*, is finally able to reconcile her identity in both worlds.

Despite its many-sided features, persons have objected to the book for several reasons. The majority address the short scene when Julie's husband attempts to force himself upon her.

*Banned Books: 2000 Resource Book* offers a summary of challenges. Four cited since 1995 deal with this scene. Objectors call it "a rape," "a graphic marital rape scene," "a man forcibly kissing his wife," and "attempted rape of a thirteen year old girl" (Doyle 38). Since the early 1980s People For the American Way has published a survey of censorship and other challenges to public education. Their 1992-93 report lists an objection to the same scene in which a person claims "a young girl is accosted by a mentally disabled boy" (47). Geneva Van Horne states that the scene was a source of frequent complaints in earlier years (342).

The scene is probably of concern to objectors who fail to see it in the context of a larger issue of abuse. To understand what led to the incident and to Julie's subsequent motivation to leave Barrow, one must review earlier events in her life.

Her mother died when Julie was four years old. She and her distraught father, Kapugen, moved from Mekoryuk to a seal camp. She has good memories of these early years, her father, and his friend Naka. It was from Kapugen that she learned Eskimo traditions and a connection to the earth and its creatures. These good times end when Kapugen is forced by law to send Julie to school. That meant her returning to Mekoryuk to live with an aunt. Upon parting, Kapugen tells nine-year-old Julie that if she is unhappy, at thirteen she can leave and marry Naka's son, Daniel. He explains that he will arrange this.

During the years in Mekoryuk, Julie becomes bored and develops an interest in further schooling available in Barrow. When she turns thirteen, she moves there and marries Naka's son in hope of a better life. However, she does not find it. Her friend Pearl senses her unhappiness and assures her that arranged marriages are not taken seriously, that all one has to do is walk away from them and all is forgotten. No one is expected to stay in an unhappy situation.

Two incidents involving abuse move Julie to leave Barrow. One is the physical abuse of Naka toward his wife when he drinks, and the other is Daniel's sudden effort after a year to consummate the marriage to Julie. He does kiss her roughly, tear her dress, and force her to the floor, but nothing else happens. He is as frightened as Julie is. He stomps away, angry with himself.

This one-page scene is not graphic, and as Geneva Van Horne points out, it is necessary to the credibility of the plot. A sensible young girl must have good reason to set off across the Arctic tundra in search of a better life

(342). Nowhere in Eskimo tradition is it taught that abuse of one human being to another should be tolerated.

Some objections imply that Julie's being only thirteen years old makes the incident more shocking. However, by including the early marriage, George is being faithful to Eskimo tradition. In 1978, the elders of the North Slope Borough met at Barrow to record stories about traditions of the Inupiat people in an effort to preserve their heritage for future generations. One section of the subsequent publication relates to family matters. It was common for parents to cause girls to take a spouse while they were still very young because they were taught to practice celibacy before marriage. Marriage was the surest way to resolve potential problems of illegitimate children (254). Advice is also given not to be domineering over a spouse (261). Thus the abuse of Nunan and the attempted sexual attack on Julie are abhorrent to the Eskimo tradition.

According to *Banned Books 2000 Resource Book*, another objection to the book has to do with its themes being "socialist, communist, evolutionary, and anti family" (Doyle 42). Perhaps the objection about its being "anti family" relates in some way to Julie's leaving an abusive situation. The other three labels are indeed elusive; specific dileneation of the first two objections is not available. Perhaps "evolutionary" refers to the survival of the fittest. Certainly the entire ecosystem involving predator and prey mirrors this concept. Wolves hunt young, sick, and old prey. To present survival on the tundra in some other light would be dishonest.

The 1990-91 report from People For the American Way mentions another baffling objection: "some sections might be interpreted as describing an incestuous relationship" (34). Does this imply that some members of a wolf pack are related? Of course they are. Does the objection imply that Julie has an abnormal relationship with wolves? Certainly a girl stranded on the Arctic tundra saved from starvation by a pack of wolves is not an everyday occurrence. However, one of the outstanding qualities of the book is the fascinating interaction between wolf and human. George's detail about wolf behavior is well documented by scientists who have studied wolves.

David Mech, a veteran wolf biologist who studied wolves in the High Arctic, found that in attempting to approach wolves it was effective to lie on his stomach flat and still (*Arctic* 20). This is the strategy Julie uses as she begins her study of wolf communication.

She observes the leader of the pack and names him Amaroq. His mate Silver nips him gently under the chin, crouches before him, and licks his cheek. He responds by wagging his tail vigorously and taking her nose in his mouth. Another wolf tries to take Amaroq's jaw in his mouth, and the leader bites the top of his nose. A third wolf gets down on his belly and rolls on his back. What Julie observes is classic submission and dominance behavior in wolves.

Michael Fox, another prominent wolf scientist, explains the actions of wolves that show submission and dominance. A subordinate approaches a dominant in the low position, tail wagging, and licks the lips of the dominant or prods its mouth corner with the muzzle. It may roll over, exposing its belly. Placing the mouth over another wolf's muzzle or biting the top of its nose is a sign of dominance (59).

Julie learns these lessons well. When she does finally get close to Amaroq, she gazes up at him, then manages to pat him under the chin. By this signal of submission she becomes a member of his pack. This act is certainly within the realm of possibility. Numerous researchers have shown that wolves will come within a few feet of humans with no intent to harm (Mech, *Wolf* 292).

Julie next studies how wolves feed their pups. She needs their cooperation to save herself from starvation. She learns that they regurgitate food for their young. This is signaled by a puppy's nuzzling the adult's mouth. Such behavior is verified by Mech's observations (*Arctic* 60). Later she is able to get food for herself when a friendly pup nudges an adult wolf. Enterprising Julie scoops the regurgitated food into her pot, gathers grass and lichens to use as fuel, and uses one of her precious matches to start a fire.

Van Horne mentions that objectors to the book have called Julie's eating food regurgitated from wolves as "gross" and "unlikely" (342). What such readers fail to see is that the act couples her knowledge of wolf communication with the trust she has gained from the pack, the trust that will make her survival possible. Too, her ingenuity in cooking the regurgitated caribou by using the most primitive methods points to the value of her Eskimo knowledge. Eventually, Amaroq calls her to the den. She sleeps with the pack and shares regularly in their fresh prey, returning to her camp to store and cook food.

Julie's gaining access to the wolf den is a feat in itself but not impossible. It had been David Mech's lifelong dream to get close enough to a wolf den in the High Arctic to study the interaction of adults and pups and how the leader relates to other members of the pack. The opportunity came during two trips in 1986 and 1987 through assignment for *National Geographic Magazine*. On the first trip, he moved closer and closer to the den, being careful not to disturb the pack. Eventually, the wolves trusted him to the point that they left the pups unattended (*Arctic* 45). He observed that the males and females in a pack form a dominance structure and are usually related in some way. Much cooperation in care, feeding, and rearing the pups is evident because they are the center of the pack (*Arctic* 54). A typical day involves sleep, play and social interaction, hunting, and feeding the pups (*Arctic* 58). This is the same pattern Julie observes.

The communication Mech built with the wolf pack on the first trip continued on his return the next year. The wolves recognized him and he again went to the den, setting up a camera within fifty feet of it. A playful pup untied his shoelace much like one of the wolf pups plays with Julie's mitten. At times he lay at the den entrance with pups playing within a foot of him (*Arctic* 99). Although wolves did not feed him and were not responsible for his survival, he was certainly accepted and trusted like a pack member, just as Julie is.

Unfortunately for Julie, one of the wolves that shows strong submission behavior to Amaroq becomes ignored by the pack and a troublemaker for Julie. He steals her food, threatens her, and finally steals her backpack full of survival utensils. Amaroq tracks and kills him. Michael Fox explains that wolves have been known to kill their own kind. Extreme intolerance toward one or more wolves may give way to severe fighting, with the loser being killed or driven away (120). Kapugen had told Julie that some wolves tolerate an unsociable wolf, but if he steals meat from the pups, he is killed. Perhaps Amaroq saw Julie as a pup.

In addition to the fascinating, well-researched detail on wolf behavior and survival skills on the Arctic tundra, there are over twenty Eskimo words in *Julie of the Wolves* and the sequel, *Julie*. Both books provide a tapestry of Eskimo customs. In *Julie of the Wolves* her survival on the tundra is tied to knowledge taught her by her father. As she embarks on her journey to Point Hope, she knows the essentials to carry in her backpack: food, needles, matches, a moosehide sleeping skin, a caribou ground cloth, two knives, and a cooking pot. She knows which plants are edible and how to hunt rabbits, squirrels, and birds. As in the Eskimo tradition, she sings a song as tribute to her prey. She uses all parts of an animal. When wolves leave her some caribou, she makes use of the skin. She knows how to dig a cellar in the permafrost to store food. The clothing she wears is made from animal skin and fur.

The spirits of animals are prominent in Eskimo tradition. Julie makes a totem to Amaroq and asks that his spirit enter it and be with her. R. D. Lawrence has noted the Eskimo affinity between wolves and ravens. Legends often couple the bird and the mammal, both of which were also endowed with spiritual and even godlike qualities. More than a few clans adopted either the wolf or the raven, sometimes both, as their special totems and accepted them as alter egos (194).

Certain customs accompany the killing of animals. Kapugen teaches

Julie about the Bladder Feast, a celebration in which seal bladders are returned to the sea so that the animal's spirit can enter the bodies of newborn seals. The meeting of the elders of the North Slope includes stories about animals to be passed on to younger generations. One custom is to sever the head of any animal killed to allow the spirit to live again. Otherwise, it stays close to the animal's body and mourns and suffers pain. They believe a person's spirit never dies and extend this concept to the animals (53).

In addition to the rich detail on Eskimo traditions, *Julie of the Wolves* and *Julie* present the issue of split identity caused by the pull of two cultures, exemplified by the twentieth-century technological world and the traditional Eskimo culture. In the first novel Julie-Miyax is a poignant example. During her early years at the seal camp she is Miyax, her Inuit name, and she is schooled in Eskimo traditions by her father. With the move to Mekoryuk to attend school, she becomes acclimated to an environment in which more English than Eskimo is spoken and comes closer to being Julie, her gussak name. In Barrow, there is more of the encroachment of the white civilization and its modern gadgets. It is during her time on the tundra that she becomes Miyax once more.

> She had her ulo and needles, her sled and her tent, and the world of her ancestors and she liked the simplicity of that world. . . . Out here she understood how she fitted into the scheme of the moon and stars and the constant rise and fall of life on the earth. Even the snow was part of her. (*Julie of* 130)

She realizes that traditional Eskimos are not outdated and old-fashioned, but wise. Reaching Point Hope becomes unimportant. When Amaroq is shot from an airplane, she cries out her grief in Eskimo. She cannot recall any English.

The several levels to *Julie of the Wolves* have made it attractive to literary scholarship. Jon C. Stott establishes it as a pastoral novel in which the central character withdraws from an urban world to a rural one but inevitably returns to the urban environment. Lessons learned from withdrawal enable the person to better face the human condition (132). With her experience on the tundra, Julie enters into a pure and ideal world followed by an inevitable return to civilization (135).

Theoretically, in the pastoral tradition her experience on the tundra and lessons learned should enable her to cope with the life she left. However, when she finds her way to Kangik, she returns to a father who once represented all that was fine in Eskimo tradition, but who has become corrupted by the influence of the white civilization. He has taken a gussak wife, has modern conveniences, and takes gussaks on hunts from airplanes.

The conclusion of the book does not offer a clear resolution. As Opal

Moore and Donnarae MacCann point out, at the end of the novel when Julie concludes that "the hour of the wolf and the Eskimo is over" (*Julie of* 170) the author appears to consign the culture and any hope of preserving the Arctic ecosystem to dust (28). While on the surface, Julie can be seen as forsaking her Miyax identity, her return to the village corrupted by the white world is the only choice she has. How she will cope is not clear. However, *Julie of the Wolves* is very much the story of a young girl's growth. She is stronger in character upon her return, not only for what she has learned about her Miyax self but because of what she has learned about love.

Her survival on the tundra is linked to a chain of love. There is the love for Kapugen, who taught her the Eskimo traditions and was a loving father; and the love for Amaroq, her adopted father, from whom she learns the love of other creatures for each other and human beings. Her love for Amaroq gives her the feeling she has for Kapu, his puppy, and for Tornait, the bird she shields from the cold. Through Tornait and her wolf family she knows the need for companionship. Her return to Kapugen is in part recognition of that human need. Amaroq's spirit is in her through the totem, and its ritual suggests she will never completely forsake the old ways or her identity as Miyax. What she can bring to the years ahead is a clear self-image and strength of character. She is clearly Miyax-Julie, a different human being from the beginning of her journey.

Her emerging dual identity is best understood by considering both *Julie of the Wolves* and the sequel *Julie*, for it is in the latter that it reaches fruition. She begins her life with Kapugen and his gussak wife, Ellen, in Kangik. The village is a corporation, and one business is that of raising musk oxen. Women knit sweaters and scarves from the underfur and sell them to merchants in Fairbanks. Because there are no caribou in the vicinity, the musk oxen are prey to wolves. Kapugen will kill wolves to protect the herd and, therefore, the livelihood of the village. Julie understands their needs.

However, when she learns that the wolf pack who befriended her in *Julie of the Wolves* is near the village, she is determined to protect them. She once again calls upon her Eskimo knowledge to devise an ingenious plan to rejoin the pack and lead them to a moose herd so they will not attack the musk oxen. The wolf pack recognizes and accepts Julie once more just as Mech's wolves did on his second trip to the High Arctic (*Arctic* 45). Readers of the first book will recognize the hierarchy within the pack and the ritual tributes to Kapu, Amaroq's offspring and now the alpha wolf. In the sequel, the same rich detail on the behavior of wolves exists as in *Julie of the Wolves*. An additional aspect involves how wolf packs stay away from another's territory. David Mech's work reflects good detail on this (*Arctic* 108). Julie's task is to unite two packs so they can share a moose herd. This she cleverly does.

*Julie* offers a tenuous reconciliation of the pull of the two cultures, on the one hand maintenance of many Eskimo traditions and on the other the influences of the white culture. Kapugen's wife, Ellen, wears a long dress called a qaliguuraq. She herself struggles with a split identity, that of her Minnesota upbringing and her life as Kapugen's wife. She introduces the family to apple pie, and they teach her about Eskimo donuts. Children of the village still enjoy blanket tosses, and the whole village joins the celebration of Naluktaq, a whale festival. Julie's love interest, Peter, introduces dances from his native Siberia.

There is also reconciliation on a personal level. When Julie first arrives at Kangik, she speaks only Eskimo. Later she speaks English, partly out of a developing respect for Ellen. Together they birth a musk oxen calf during a blizzard. It is also through Ellen that Julie learns about the possibilities further education can bring. She wants to teach languages, Yupik and Inupiat, to Eskimo children so they will not lose their identity.

Kapugen is reunited with the Eskimo side of himself that he nearly abandoned in the wake of influences from the white world. A critical incident involves allowing only two walruses to be taken because that is what the village needs for food, despite the value of walrus tusks. In this incident, he practices the tradition of throwing the heart back to the sea, thus freeing the animal's spirit. Kapugen returns to valuing the coexistence of all living things. He sets the musk oxen free. The Eskimos can still hunt them and harvest their fur, but the balance of prey and predator will prevail. In recognizing the return of her father's former self, Julie has a sense of reconciliation with him. To Julie, giving the name Amaroq to the son of Kapugen and Amaroq binds her human family and the wild creatures together.

Although *Julie of the Wolves* and *Julie* are works of fiction, both are well grounded in fact. In her acceptance speech for the Newbery Award, George speaks of her own scientific expedition to Alaska to investigate the findings in Adolph Murie's benchmark study, *The Wolves of Mount McKinley*. She spent time on the Arctic tundra to understand permafrost. She observed wolves close up for ten days. In Barrow she saw the conflict of the two cultures (Newbery 337-347).

The many layers, poignant issues, and literary artistry in both books make them outstanding and highly accessible to young readers. It is encouraging that to date there are no recorded objections to *Julie* and a number of the attempts to censor *Julie of the Wolves* have not been successful. Geneva Van Horne suggests numerous ways that *Julie of the Wolves* can be used across school disciplines such as science, social studies, art, music, composition, and drama (340). The same is true for *Julie*. Both books should be staples in the language arts curriculum and reading programs in general. They offer valuable, rich insights into cultural diversity and are best understood when paired.

As important a learning tool as the books can be in traditional disciplines, perhaps they can also instill in young people a dedication to preserving endangered wildlife. Historically, the wolf has been much maligned. One need only reexamine "Little Red Riding Hood," "The Three Little Pigs," or "Peter and the Wolf" for obvious examples. In her acceptance speech for the Newbery Award, George comments on the importance of the continuity and harmony among all forms of nature as necessary for the survival of the earth (340).

Roger Caas pays tribute to the endangered wolf in his introduction to David Mech's book *The Arctic Wolf*:

> One of the most significant species, surely, is the wolf. Humans must learn to understand the wolf, for not only are these few subspecies clinging to the last edge of being, dangling over the void of nothingness forever, but the wolf in its remaining forms is a hallmark animal. If we cannot bring ourselves to understand the wolf, we probably will be able to understand little else. (6)

In *Julie* there is hope that the civilized world and the natural world can coexist. An elder once told Julie: "We are here for each other; the Eskimos, the mammals, the river, the ice, the sun, plants, birds, and fish. Let us celebrate cooperation." Perhaps her emergence as a blend of two selves, Miyax and Julie, can point the way to real-life Eskimos facing the pull of two cultures. Perhaps there is hope after all that the "hour of the wolf and the Eskimo" (*Julie of* 170) is not over.

## Works Cited

*Attacks on Freedom to Learn: 1990-91* Report. Washington, D.C.: People For the American Way, 1991.

———. *1992-93 Report*. Washington, D.C.: People For the American Way, 1993.

Doyle, Robert P. *Banned Books 2000 Resource Book*. Chicago: American Library Association, 2000.

Fox, Michael. *Behavior of Wolves, Dogs and Related Canids*. New York: Harper & Row, 1971.

George, Jean Craighead. *Julie*. New York: Harper Collins Publishers, 1994.

———. *Julie of the Wolves*. New York: Harper Collins Publishers, 1972.

————. "Newbery Award Acceptance." *Horn Book Magazine* 49.4 (1973): 337-347.

Lawrence, R. D. *In Praise of Wolves*. New York: Henry Holt and Company, 1986.

Mech, David L. *The Arctic Wolf: Living With the Pack*. Stillwater, Minnesota: Voyager Press, 1988.

————. *The Wolf: The Ecology and Behavior of an Endangered Species*. Garden City, New York: The Natural History Press, 1970.

Moore, Opal, and Donnarae MacCann. "The Ignoble Savage: Amerind Images in the Mainstream Mind." *Children's Literature Association Quarterly* 13.1 (1988): 26-30.

Murie, Adolph. *The Wolves of Mount McKinley*. Seattle: University of Washington Press, 1985.

*Puiquitkaat the 1978 Elders' Conference*. Transcription by Kisautaq-Leona Okakok. Edited and Photographed by Gary Kean. Barrow, Alaska: North Slope Borough on History and Culture, 1981.

Review of *Julie of the Wolves*. *Best Sellers* (15 April 1973): 45.

Review of *Julie of the Wolves*. *Horn Book Magazine* (February 1973): 54-55.

Review of *Julie of the Wolves*. *Booklist* (1 February 1973): 529.

Stott, Jon C. "Jean George's Arctic Pastoral: A Reading of *Julie of the Wolves*." *Children's Literature: The Great Excluded*. Ed. Francelia Butler and Bennett A. Brockman. Storrs, Conn.: Children's Literature Association, 1974 (131-139).

Van Horne, Geneva T. "*Julie of the Wolves* by Jean Craighead George." *Censored Books: Critical Viewpoints*. Ed. Nicholas J. Karolides et al. Metuchen, N. J.: Scarecrow Press, 1993 (338-342).

# *Kaffir Boy*: A Rationale

## Deborah Brown

Mark Mathabane's *Kaffir Boy* is a powerful firsthand account of life under apartheid in South Africa. In his autobiography, Mathabane recounts his childhood and youth in Alexandra, a Black ghetto of Johannesburg, where he lived until he was eighteen years old. While *Kaffir Boy* is a vivid and realistic account of life under apartheid, it is also an inspiring story about how a young man overcame the hatred and degradation he endured and how he triumphed over racism, poverty, and ignorance. *Kaffir Boy* celebrates the will to succeed and the power of the human spirit.

In recent years *Kaffir Boy* has been challenged because of some strong visual descriptions of abuse and one brief scene depicting sodomy (Brown). The 1-2 page brief scene takes place in a men's compound for migrant workers and describes poor boys prostituting themselves for food. Read out of context, the nonvivid scene would be disturbing. Read in the context of devastating poverty and hunger, however, the brief scene is not a reason to reject the book. When Johannes, the book's narrator, enters the compound with a group of young boys and realizes what is happening, he is horrified and makes a quick escape. He runs toward the gate of the compound "praying that it is open." When he escaped, Johannes "tore down the street, dodging cars, leaping over dongas and fences and puddles" until he reached home (73). Johannes's reaction is a clear rejection of the activity he witnesses.

*Kaffir Boy* can be used in high school English classes for a number of important reasons related to the National Council of Teachers of English/International Reading Association Standards for the English Language Arts including these: (1) Students read a wide range of literature from many periods in many genres to build an understanding of the many dimensions of human experience; (2) Students read a wide range of print and nonprint texts to build an understanding of texts, of themselves, and of the cultures of the United States and the world; to acquire new information; to respond to the needs and demands of society and the workplace; and for personal fulfillment; and (3) Students develop an understanding of and respect for diversity in language use, patterns, and dialects across cultures, ethnic groups, geographic regions, and social roles (Smagorinsky, 1996, viii-ix). Reading *Kaffir Boy* in a high school English class will broaden students' political and world views and provide an opportunity for students to examine a number of important historical, political, and social issues.

The explicit and sometimes horrifying descriptions of poverty, gang wars, and midnight police raids in *Kaffir Boy* will increase students' awareness of oppression and racism. The language, details, and honesty with which Mathabane describes his experiences grab a reader's attention and make accounts of apartheid personal and "real" in a way that discussions of apartheid in history textbooks often do not. He vividly describes the "shacks" in which his family lives in the Alexander ghetto, setting the scenes for the midnight police raids in his home and neighborhood. His family lived in a 15-by-15-foot shack with two bedrooms:

> It had an interior flaked with old whitewash, a leaky ceiling of rusted zinc propped up by a thin wall of crumbling adobe bricks, two tiny windows made of cardboard and pieces of glass, a creaky, termite-eaten door too low for a person of average height to pass through without bending double, and a floor made of patches of cement and earth. It was similar to the dozen or so shacks strewn irregularly, like lumps on a leper, upon the cracked greenless piece of ground named yard number thirty-five. (31)

In a description of a midnight police raid when his father was taken away for two months to do hard labor on a white man's farm, Mathabane writes:

> My sleepy eyes strained to make out objects in the dark, but the darkness was impregnable, ominous; the more I stared into it, the blacker and blacker it became. I felt dizzy. I wanted to scream but my voice was paralyzed. Suddenly flashlights flared through the uncurtained window. Glass shattered somewhere nearby. I yearned to become invisible, to have the ground beneath me open and swallow me until it was all over. (17)

As a victim of discrimination, Johannes often asks complex questions about the various external and internal struggles and issues he faces; when Johannes raises these questions, students have an opportunity to ask and discuss them as well. For instance, when Mathabane was young he assumed that all white South Africans held the same views; he began to learn that was not true when, after a long ordeal of trying to get a birth certificate for Johannes so he could go to school, a white woman listened to his mother's pleas and made sure he got a birth certificate. Johannes's mother said, "You see, child, not all white people are bad; remember that" (119). Johannes encountered other "nice" white people when his grandmother's employers gave him books to read; however, it was primarily through tennis that he learned that not all whites in South Africa were racists. Mathabane writes about meeting Stan Smith, the famous tennis player and his wife, Marjory; he writes about other white South Africans the Smiths introduced him to and how their story reinforced his "belief that among white South Africans there was that small minority that really believe in love, freedom and human dignity for all" (311). Then Mathabane writes that he wondered: "So why should they be lumped into the same foul den as the racists, and made the object of hate and vengeance? Why couldn't the struggle in South Africa be not one of black against white but one that pitted those who believed in freedom, justice and equality against those who didn't?" (311). These are complex questions related to the stereotypes we often grow up being taught either by society, the media, or family—questions that students should discuss. *Kaffir Boy* can be used to help students become aware of their own prejudices and preconceptions and analyze the source of their prejudices.

Although using *Kaffir Boy* to raise student's consciousness about racism and oppression may be the most obvious reason to ask students to read it, several other important and related issues in the book would be good to explore with students as well, depending upon particular students and contexts. For example, the second part of the book focuses on Johannes's mother's and grandmother's insistence that he go to school when he turned seven so that he would "have a future" (133). His mother felt education was the key that would give him a life different from the one they currently lived, and she made great sacrifices to ensure that Johannes went to school. Mathabane skillfully describes how and why he resisted going to school at first; he did not want to give up his freedom and be exposed to the "tyrannous discipline" he had heard about. On the other hand, he "did not want to end up dead in the streets" (130) like many young people did who rejected school and joined gangs. The most compelling argument for school, however, was his mother's insistence that he not grow up to be like his father; Mathabane writes that she said the following:

> "Your father didn't go to school. . . . that's why he's doing some of the bad things he's doing. Things like drinking, gambling and neglecting his family. . . . Lack of education has narrowly focused his life. He sees nothing beyond himself. He still thinks in the old, tribal way, and still believes that things should be as they were back in the old days when he was growing up as a tribal boy in Louis Trichardt." (133)

For Mathabane, getting an education was a struggle, but it "saved [his] life from self-destructing in the ghetto." "The doors that opened" for Mathabane because of education were "the same doors" that led to a tennis scholarship that brought him to America in 1978 (Mathabane, "Some" 25A). In particular classrooms, a discussion about the importance of an education and the value of books to Johannes might be helpful and productive.

The differing views that Johannes's mother and father had toward education illustrate one of the tensions in his family and in his society as well. His father had been taught that a "white man's education was worthless insofar as black people were concerned," while his mother realized that times had changed "somewhat" (133). His father clung to tribal beliefs and resisted societal changes that his mother was open to exploring, including the roles of religion and women in the family and in society. For example, they argued about how the money Johannes's mother made should be used. Jackson, Johannes's father, angrily said to his wife:

> "You seem to forget that I bought you! I own you. Your duty is to look after children, cook for me and do what I say. . . . Instead of putting your energies into cooking and raising children as a good woman should, you put your energies into trying to be the man in this house. What kind of woman are you, heh?" (176)

But Johannes's mother held her ground and insisted that the money she earned was to be used only for the children's education. She replied, "I'm just what a woman should be. . . . A woman who wants the best for her husband and her children." Her fierce determination that her children have a better life and an education illustrates her love for her children, and her love for her children gave her the will to fight for them no matter what role her husband might have expected her to fulfill in the family and even if it meant they would have less money. She also was wise enough to know that someday her husband would be proud of the children when they were successful.

Students might discuss a number of issues related to tensions within a family and between a family and society when a family's traditions and beliefs differ from societal norms and changing perspectives. For example, students could compare the status of women during the 50s and 60s in South Africa (and America) with the status of women now. Also, students might discuss the struggles Johannes experiences between the tribal traditions of his ancestors and more modern social dynamics.

Along with the topical and social/cultural reasons to read *Kaffir Boy* are significant literary reasons as well. The book could be used to introduce students to autobiography and its role in literature and history. Students could discuss how personal accounts may change their views of history and do some research about the use of personal stories by historians. Students might also write their own stories and experiences of feeling discriminated against and what they learned from the experience.

Most important, however, teachers should discuss racism and provide some background information about apartheid in South Africa with students before reading this book to provide a context for some of the book's explicit descriptions. Viewing videos and reading newspaper reports about Nelson Mandela, for example, would help provide background about South Africa. Terms like *apartheid* and *pass laws* should be reviewed also to develop comprehension and understanding of racism on a national scale. Many students seem to have more knowledge about Nazism and the Holocaust in Germany than they do about apartheid in South Africa; thus a teacher might begin a discussion by asking students what they know about Nazism. Mathabane writes in the preface of *Kaffir Boy* that the racial system in South Africa resembles Nazism in many ways and that millions of black children are still "trapped" in the ghettos of Alexandra, where "black children fight for survival from the moment they are born. They take to hating and fearing the police, soldiers and authorities as a baby takes to its mother's breast" (x).

*Kaffir Boy* is an excellent book to use in a larger thematic unit about racism and discrimination in different forms and environments that might include discussing and comparing apartheid in South Africa with the Holocaust in Germany and with racism in the United States. The unit might focus on other firsthand accounts in a variety of literary forms, including *The Diary of Anne Frank*, in play format, autobiographies such as *Alicia: My Story* and *The Autobiography of Malcolm X*, and poems such as "Theme for English B" and "Ballad of the Landlord" by Langston Hughes, "Ballad of Birmingham" by Dudley Randall, and "Come Home from the Movies" by Lucille Clifton. Other novels that might be considered as additional texts or alternative reading selections, if needed, include Alan Paton's *Cry, the Beloved Country* and Andre Brink's *A Dry White Season*.

Teachers might want to be prepared to have alternative reading selections, because *Kaffir Boy* has appeared on several lists of books that have been challenged or banned, including the American Library Association's list of the top 10 banned and challenged books in 1997 and the 100 most frequently challenged books of 1990-1999. *Kaffir Boy* is, however, a well-written and powerful book that has been recommended by the American Library Association and was included on its Reading List for College Bound Students in 2000.

## Works Cited

Brown, Deborah. "Turning Dissension into Discussion." *Wisconsin English Journal* 41 (Fall 1999): 25-28.

Mathabane, Mark. *Kaffir Boy: An Autobiography* [paperback ed.]. New York: Simon & Schuster, 1998.

———. "Some Only Can Dream of School." *USA Today* (13 September 2000): 25A.

Smagorinsky, P. *Standards in Practice Grades 9-12*. Urbana, Ill.: National Council of Teachers of English, 1996.

# In Defense of *Killing Mr. Griffin*

## Susanne L. Johnston

Consider a scenario where violence in the schools escalates to the point that students plot murders of fellow students and against teachers. The scenario is not so far from the truth anymore, as evidenced by recent headlines, but Lois Duncan's *Killing Mr. Griffin* was ahead of its time when it was published in 1978. Students plot to frighten and ridicule their English teacher because they interpret his high expectations and demanding demeanor as mean-spirited vendettas against students. What they don't understand, and what Duncan reveals slowly and expertly throughout the text, is that Mr. Griffin pushes his students to do their best because he has seen wasted lives and wants more for his students. Duncan shows how peer pressure, failures of communication, and ignoring early signs of mental disturbance can lead to unthinkable consequences.

Because of those unthinkable consequences, *Killing Mr. Griffin* is number 64 on the ALA list, *The 100 Most Frequently Challenged Books of 1990-1999*. It is the fourth-most-challenged book of 2000, according to a January 2001 ALA news release, for violence and sexual content. The book is indeed violent: the students do kill their teacher, an old woman and possibly another person are murdered, another murder is attempted, and one incident of animal torture is described. The sexual content includes innuendo and manipulation based on perceived desire. Yet, when placed in context, this seemingly horrific story is not about violence and sex, but about the life-altering consequences of deviant behavior.

One of the fiercest threats that young people face remains peer pressure, as it has for decades and probably centuries. The chance of appearing to be a failure or not being popular in front of peers has driven many people to otherwise unthinkable acts. The teens in *Killing Mr. Griffin* are no different, except that one of them is a psychopath whose charisma charms others into following his destructive lead. Instead of the usual pranks and mischief, Mark convinces his friends to kidnap their English teacher and humiliate him the way Mark feels Mr. Griffin has humiliated him. The others go along,

285

treating it initially like a joke and even manipulating a lonely innocent girl into their scheme because she is someone no one would suspect. Good kids with good grades, potentially bright futures, and loving families are lured into evil. Sounds like something we wouldn't want our young people to read about, but if we look closer we can use this book as a case study of adolescent naivete and ignorance and the accompanying problems.

Early on in the book Duncan shows Mark's seductiveness and treachery. While in seventh grade he invites Jeff, a fellow student he has just met, to watch him set a cat on fire. Jeff watches and, rather than be sickened, he is drawn to Mark's "magnetic" eyes and "a special beauty, something so striking and strange that it stop[s] the heart and cause[s] those near him to catch their breath" (26-27). This "special beauty" in Mark comes to the forefront only when he is planning to manipulate or hurt someone, but it is so striking that those around him are caught off guard and lured in by his charm, rather than repulsed by his plans. Later, in twelfth grade, Mark feels humiliated by Mr. Griffin, who caught Mark plagiarizing a paper and forced him to repeat English. Rather than take the responsibility for cheating and accepting the consequences, Mark blames Mr. Griffin and convinces his friends that they, too, should blame Mr. Griffin for their failures.

An astute reader will recognize Mark's charm for the self-serving manipulation that it is and use it as an example of antisocial behavior to be avoided. Animal torture is often one of the early warning signs of a psychopath who will, given enough time, turn to human targets. Rather than condemning the book for presenting such a disturbing idea, Duncan should be praised for alerting readers to the patterns of such troubled individuals.

As Mark connives to kidnap and denigrate Mr. Griffin, he plays on the weaknesses of his "friends." The cast is carefully drawn and assembled by Duncan to represent the pathos of the typical high school student body and the attitudes they have toward teachers. Jeff is the star of the basketball team but has been drawn to the charismatic Mark ever since that day in seventh grade. Jeff's parents, blind to what is really happening in his life, think the world of their star athlete and believe he is doing Mark a favor by sticking with him for the past five years. Combine this with Jeff's athletic mastery and teachers like Dolly Luna, who make homework exceptions on game nights, Jeff is easily persuaded to despise Mr. Griffin for his high expectations.

Betsy is head cheerleader and Jeff's girlfriend. Though she is cute, not pretty, her personality makes her both attractive and well-known. Her cuteness and ready smile have enabled her to manipulate people all of her life to get everything she's wanted. When people don't respond to her charm, she tries harder to please; when that doesn't work, she strikes out at them.

She can't get Mr. Griffin to give her leeway in English, and although she is attracted to Mark, he is uninterested but always gives her hope—the perfect combination to lure her into the plot against Mr. Griffin.

David is "beautiful, popular, elfin-faced . . . president of the senior class" (8), and dissatisfied with his life. Living with his mother and grandmother, his father having walked out ten years prior, David is tired of overwhelming responsibility. With his mother working long hours to support the family, David's job is to entertain and wait on his grandmother every day after school rather than spend time with friends. He feels his future slipping away with a failing grade in English—not getting a scholarship, so when Mark asks, "[h]ow long has it been—since you've done something wild—just for fun?" (38), David is willing.

Susan is teased constantly by her three brothers about being an old maid, as they remind her that she hasn't yet had her first date. Her thoughts are always on "someday—someday—" (7). She feels that her parents' good looks and spirit have been spent on her brothers, leaving her feeling "homely and . . . lonely and . . . unhappy," but Mark knows that she would give David "the moon" if he "put a little sunshine into her life" (24). When David gives her "sunshine" at Mark's request, Susan is ready.

Mark has lived with his aunt and uncle for five years, since his father died in a fire and his mother turned her back on him. He gets no supervision and does as he pleases, allowing him ample time to discover the neediness of each "friend" and use it to make them willing partners in his vengeance toward Mr. Griffin.

Duncan brings to light the insecurities of her characters, the universal hopes and dreams of teenagers, and then she dashes them with one deed followed by lies, cover-up, and murder. She shows that all students are vulnerable in one way or another, whether they are popular or not, athletic or not, products of stable families or not. Rather than suppress this book as one more text full of gratuitous violence, it should be seen as a starting point for discussions between teachers and students. With violence increasing in our schools, clearly some students are disillusioned with life, with school, with adults. Suppressing their thoughts by allowing them to read only "happy" books with fairy-tale boy-meets-girl-and-they-live-happily-ever-after endings merely drives their angst and frustration underground, where it festers and grows into explosive rage.

Imagine that rage targeted at a teacher like Brian Griffin, who demands promptness, politeness, thoroughness, and responsibility from his students. When students fail to measure up he fails them; when they do, he expects even more because he wants them to realize their full potential, but students interpret this as vindictive. Now contrast that with another teacher, Dolly

Luna, who demands nothing of her students but that they have a good time. Brian Griffin doesn't mind if students hate him, while Dolly Luna tries only to be a friend. Neither teacher is the ideal, because neither is available as an adult mentor who can listen to student concerns and give understanding and guidance.

We have all, at one time or another, felt that Mr. or Miss or Mrs. or Ms. Teacher was either "unfair" or was the greatest person in the world. Some classes we looked forward to each day and some we dreaded or slept through, but rarely, if ever, did we talk to the teachers involved and tell them why. Lois Duncan gives us teachers on the two extremes of expectations, which leaves plenty of room for a discussion in the middle of students' expectations of teachers as well as teachers' expectations of students.

We see ourselves in these characters: the uncertainties, the brash cockiness used to cover up the insecurities; the impulsive acts entered into for the sake of acceptance; the guilt and shame for deeds done and deeds undone. *Killing Mr. Griffin* gives students an outlet for their anthem "Unfair" when teachers assign failing grades to mediocre work, "Unfair" when it seems only the popular are happy, "Unfair" when the most outgoing girls get the cute boys (even when the girls aren't pretty), "Unfair" when teachers demand more than they are willing to give, "Unfair" when it seems that life will never get on with itself because high school lasts an eternity and the world beyond is only "someday."

Yes, the book is violent; yes, the book relies on sexuality to manipulate characters; yes, the book shows us our struggles and our weaknesses. But *Killing Mr. Griffin* can alert us to all these dangers vicariously, as does all good literature, so that we can experience the full range of emotions through characters and better prepare ourselves to face similar challenges in our lives. It can open the dialogue about school violence and be the instrument to make schools havens of intellectual and social growth, rather than institutions of fear and misunderstanding.

Books are guardians of words: words are power, power is control, and control over our emotions is essential. Books that give voice to our ideals and emotions enable us to learn before we make mistakes, to change mistakes that have already occurred. We have in our history a great example of literature changing a country. Many people attribute Harriet Beecher Stowe's *Uncle Tom's Cabin* as a major impetus for raising people's awareness of slavery and the need to abolish it. Lois Duncan's *Killing Mr. Griffin* may be the book that will give us a keener understanding of troubled adolescents and the full gamut of uncertainties they face. Perhaps if we engage our students in frank discussions we can reach them before it is too late. We owe our young people nothing less.

## Work Cited

Duncan, Lois. *Killing Mr. Griffin*. New York: Dell, 1978.

*Harry Potter Series Again Tops List of Most Challenged Books*. ALA News Release. 02 Feb. 2001. 07 Feb. 2001 http://www.ala.org/pio/presskits/midwinterawards2001/challeng-ed.html.

*The 100 Most Frequently Challenged Books of 1990-1999*. 10 Oct. 2000. 29 Oct. 2000 http://www.ala.org/alaorg/oif/top100banned-books. html.

Stowe, Harriet Beecher. *Uncle Tom's Cabin*. 1852. New York: Penguin, 1981.

# Harry Mazer's *The Last Mission*, and More

## Ken Donelson

### A True Story Which May (or May Not) Have a Point

Several thousand years ago when I was teaching English in a western Iowa small town, I was greeted one day by a visitor, a mother of one of my students. Though the exact details are long gone in the mists of time, she was there to complain about a book her son was reading.

She came to me, she said, to learn what I thought of the book and why I had assigned it. When she learned that I had not assigned it and that it was her son's choice, she relaxed a bit. I do not remember the author or the title of the book, but it was a war novel, World War II, I think. The incident that she objected to was near the end of the book. One of the main characters had been hit and was slowly, inevitably dying, drip of blood by drip, as the protagonist watched, unable to do anything to save his best friend.

As the blood seeped out and death entered the door, the protagonist monotonously repeated over and over, "Goddamnit, Goddamnit, God-damnit." The mother was as horrified by the scene as I was and agreed without any urging that scenes like this in a war book were legitimate even if she didn't want the book in her house. I believed her when she added that she wept when she read this scene.

"But," she protests, "wouldn't it be equally effective and just as shocking if something other than blasphemy was used? Wouldn't it have been as good if the author had used . . ." and here she paused for a word. She never found it.

At other times with other parents (censors), I've had them insist that "Oh, darn" or "Oh, heck" or the like, maybe even "Oh, Hell" or even "Oh, damn" would work as well in a similar situation to that in the novel. This parent was a reader, and she had a feel for language, and she recognized that "Goddamnit" was the right word, not because the language pleased her but because she could find no other word or words that worked so honestly.

I had expected a censor, I was ready for a censor, but she was a sincere person and, most important, a reader aware of the complexities of the world and the fact that the horrors of war take us into areas far beyond our usual linguistic abilities.

And so I was congratulating myself on what we had accomplished together when she broke into my reverie, "Couldn't a really fine author have found language that wouldn't be offensive to me, or many other people?"

## Harry Mazer Meets the Censors

Harry Mazer has been no stranger to censorship. *Snowbound*, his second novel, came under attack in Wisconsin for using "four-letter words for bodily wastes" and for using objectionable language like "crazy bitch" and "stupid female." Mazer heard from an editor that a scene in *The Dollar Man*, his third novel, where a young character was taking a shower was thought to be a scene of masturbation.

*The War on Villa Street*, his fifth novel and the first to receive serious attention from critics, had more problems. Officials at Greece School District in Rochester, New York, found "offensive language," and two mothers compiled a list of forty-six dirty words in the book. The term "retard," a disparaging word for a retarded person, came under attack though the word was not used by Mazer but rather a character in the book. In Waltham, Massachusetts, a school committee member reported a complaint about that "vile" book.

Mazer's eighth novel, *I Love You, Stupid*, was happily received by censors since, as Mazer and favorable readers would admit, the book is unashamedly about sex and about the wonders and mostly the problems that sex brings to young people. In a speech Mazer gave to Illinois school librarians on October 16, 1986, he explained why he wrote the book. "It's about sexual curiosity, the need, the frustration. It's about two kids' first sexual relationship. It's also about relationships and how sex and feelings are intertwined. How sex, without friendship, without love, destroys itself." That honest statement did little but arouse the censors, and Mazer has heard from many of them ever since.

## *The Last Mission* and *The Island Keeper*

Mazer's two best books, in my opinion, are *The Last Mission* and *The Island Keeper*. Different as they are in almost every way, both of them have been affected by censorship—*The Last Mission* in obvious ways since it's about young men at war, *The Island Keeper* in perverse ways since it seems a simple but effective feminine Robinson Crusoe book.

*The Last Mission* is one of the finest YA war stories, maybe the best of them all. It's not merely Mazer's telling the story—it's mostly Mazer's life as he lived it. In the novel, Jack Rabe uses his brother's identification and enlists in the Air Corps though he's only fifteen. In the real world, Harry Mazer did not enlist early. Other than that single and important difference, Mazer's life and Mazer's novel walk hand in hand. He became a waist gunner on a bomber in World War II; he endured the alternate boredom and terror of bombing runs over the continent. His closest friend was the radio operator. His plane was shot down only a few weeks before the end of the war, and his friend was killed though not in the way Mazer long believed. Years after the war's end, Mazer learned that his friend bailed out safely only to be killed by a German officer immediately after he landed.

*The Last Mission* is an incredible book. It is honest in its portrait of men, particularly young men, at war and what they face every day, from boredom to frustration to terror and back again in a constant replay of what war does to people. And what does war do? It demeans them, it hardens them, it makes them less than human, and too often, it kills them. It may even degrade them before it kills. Or if it does not kill them physically, at the least it kills them spiritually.

Mazer brilliantly conveys the sense of young men at war, at first filled with purpose and then slowly drained of everything, save the need to continue to exist even when that need seems pointless. And it is precisely Mazer's ability to make us believe in Jack Rabe and his fellow airmen that inevitably led to censorship.

Anyone who's survived a few days in the service learns that the one most functional word in the army or navy or marines or whatever is the word *fucking* followed by a word of your choice, for example, *officers* or *food* or whatever. Jack Rabe learns it and he uses the language as it is used in the service. So does his crew. When his closest friend, Chuckie O'Brien, tells Jack to cut down on his smoking since he's so fucking jumpy, Jack takes no offense. That's the way airmen talk. When Chuckie refers to *shit on a shingle*, Jack knows it means chipped beef on toast, as does anyone who's been in the service since World War II.

Some people did not take kindly to Mazer's honest use of language. Mazer had worried about the overuse of service language, but it was impossible to know what was the right amount and what was too much. An editor had warned Mazer about the language, but as Mazer pointed out, he couldn't pretend to write an honest novel about a war he knew firsthand without using some language that would offend. It was an authorial and editorial battle that could not be won since censors soon proved that too little or too much, neither was acceptable.

A parent in New Jersey announced that *The Last Mission* was "profane, sacrilegious," which was countered by Mazer, who said that he couldn't agree more. The book is about war and there's nothing sacred about war. Another censor charged that the book was full of "gross obscenities" and was degrading and irreverent. A Wisconsin school board member called the book "vulgar" and another member pontificated, "Students shouldn't be subjected to that kind of language." In a sense, but not the censor's, no one should.

But there were defenders who worried about the books that made war seem noble, and no one accused *The Last Mission* of being that. One school board member said, "Having served in Korea, I thought the language very mildly written. An obscenity is used only when the character is under duress. I'd encourage my kids to read it." In Texas, a school voted to ban *The Last Mission* only to rethink its policy a few months later. One parent noted, "War is not heck—it is hell. And I for one want my son to know about it."

One could easily assume from reading the censor's words that Harry Mazer used obscenities repeatedly. That is not the case. The words appear to make a point, and Mazer lets it go at that. What is sad is that the dispute about the obscenities has obscured the fact that Mazer has written an amazing graphic and honest portrait of war and men at war, men we care about, men who care about each other when nothing else seems to matter. Having read it at least ten times, I can testify that the novel holds up well after many rereadings. Having recommended it to many classes and having required its reading several times, I can attest to the popularity of the book. Even readers who wonder about the language—or may question whether the obscenities are necessary—come to admire Jack and his battle with growing up, especially in that time and that place, even if Mazer's language does not win them over.

But the battle over *The Last Mission* had one unforeseen consequence in *The Island Keeper*. In his speech to the Illinois school librarians, Mazer noted that he and his editors wanted more book sales, particularly sales to book clubs. So when he sat down to write *The Island Keeper*, he said to himself, "I'm going to write a book that the book clubs are going to have trouble not accepting, a book without language, without any sex in it."

Mazer did it. *The Island Keeper* is a marvelous book about a young girl, fat and with no self esteem, who forces herself onto an uninhabited island in the middle of a large lake and stays there amidst hunger and cold. She learns to kill to survive. Indeed she learns to do anything and everything needed to survive. And she's alone.

Mazer in that speech to Illinois school librarians admits that the joy of being chosen by the Junior Literary Guild was tempered by the realization that he didn't need censors for *The Island Keeper*. He had already done their work to make the book economically palatable. Since the girl was alone on the island there could be no sex. Since she had no need of language, her language would remain vague, even pure. Essentially, Mazer was his own censor. And he said,

> How easy it was. The censors didn't do it. They didn't even know me, but they touched me. Censorship is a disease that touches us all. I think [the book] is good, it sold well, kids liked it, good reviews, but would it have been a better book if I hadn't censored myself. And if I did it, I wonder how many other writers would do it.

## A Rueful Endnote

I've spent much of my thirteen years of teaching high school English and more than thirty-five teaching English to university students battling the censors. Over the years I've fought to save D. H. Lawrence and J. D. Salinger and Tennessee Williams and Arthur Miller and more. I've written about the evils of censorship. I've spoken about them.

And when I teach I could brag—until late in the 1970s—that I had never lost a battle in the censorial wars. And sometimes I forget, because my sole defeat was so quiet and known only to one other person, and pretend that I never lost a battle. But I did and I lost it over Harry Mazer's *The Last Mission*.

Here's how it happened. Alleen Nilsen and I were preparing the first edition of our text on YA (adolescent) literature. I was enamored of Mazer's book, and since I was doing a section on war novels it seemed obvious that Mazer's book was the answer, particularly the section from chapter 3 when Chuckie and Jack swear at each other. It came time for us to deliver our manuscript, and when it was returned to us, I noticed that the editor was less than rapturous about *The Last Mission*.

I was prepared to battle for the book, but I was stopped short when I read the editor's comment, "Don't forget that some of your readers might be offended by some of the words," presumably *fuck* or *shit*. Someone, I've charitably forgotten just who, worked me over until I began to see the economic logic in not offending anyone for any reason. And, after all, there were some innocents among English teachers and librarians. Just who in hell they were remains as mysterious today as it did then, but convinced I became.

I know now just how wrong I was way back then. But it still doesn't seem funny to me no matter how I rationalize it to myself.

## Works Cited

Mazer, Harry. *The Dollar Man*. New York: Delacourt, 1974.

———. *I Love You, Stupid*. New York: Crowell, 1981.

———. *The Island Keeper: A Tale of Courage and Survival*. New York: Delacorte, 1981.

———. *The Last Mission*. New York: Delacorte, 1979.

———. *Snowbound*. New York: Delacorte, 1973.

———. *The War on Villa Street*. New York: Delacorte, 1978.

———. Speech to Illinois School Librarians, October 16, 1986. Private copy to the author of this article.

# Afraid of the Dark: Censorship, Ray Bradbury, and *The Martian Chronicles*

## Michael Angelotti

> They began by controlling books of cartoons and detective books and, of course, films, one way or another, one group or another, political bias, religious prejudice, union pressures; there was always a minority afraid of something, and a great majority afraid of the dark, afraid of the future, afraid of the past, afraid of the present, afraid of themselves and shadows of themselves.
>
> The Martian Chronicles 105

Ray Bradbury wrote "April 2005: Usher II," one of twenty-six chapters in *The Martian Chronicles* (1950), in the style of Edgar Allan Poe. It is the futuristic story of Mr. William Stendahl, a Poe zealot who "delicately contrived" on Mars the House and atmosphere of Usher to intricately replicate Poe's fictional creation. Stendahl further embellished the House and grounds by adding horrific touches from many of Poe's other works, particularly "Murders in the Rue Morgue," "The Cask of Amontillado," and "The Masque of Red Death." His object was deadly revenge against the government censors and like-minded "Moral Climate" people who had burned all of Poe's works in the "Great Fire" of 1975, and ten years later, Stendahl's entire illegal library of 50,000 books. [Please see Bradbury's *Fahrenheit 451* (1953) for the infernal details.] Specifically, Stendahl invited prominent censors, citizens, and members of the "Society for the Prevention of Fantasy" to a "costume ball" at the House of Usher II, during which he subjected his victims to grotesque deaths perpetrated by Stendahl's mechanical manifestations of Poe's ironic fictional motifs; for example, one killed by a robotoid gorilla, another in a pit by a swinging pendulum, a large group by the red death, and whoever somehow survived to evening's end, by the swift and crushing collapse of the House of Usher II upon itself.

As a reader who also happens to admire the works of Poe, I could relish the ironies and literary allusions to Poe's works. They were abundant and cleverly worked into this story. No doubt, Bradbury had at least as much fun writing this piece as did I reading it; although I must admit that at times I was aghast at the fiendish slaughter of forty-something human beings, fictional or not, censors or not. The very idea! Surely Stendahl was insane. But, then again, that was one of Bradbury's intentions, wasn't it? Nevertheless, I appreciated Bradbury's excellent literary craftsmanship, the interplay of his own style and content with Poe's style and content. Clearly, this story is a quality piece of writing. And I never once confused Bradbury, the author, and Stendahl, the fictional character, nor thought Bradbury a criminal for creating this story nor felt a single impulse to imitate Stendahl's actions in real life. That is, I was not moved to censor the book because of the possible harm it could inflict upon an impressionable reader.

But why was this story written as it was in this book? To make a unique and interesting "chronicle" that in itself engages the reader in story while moving along the larger narrative while restating one of its major themes? Done. Which theme? The politics of government versus human rights? Of government and censorship? At least those. The lead quote to this chapter was spoken by Stendahl near the end of his impassioned recounting of the history of a continuing censorship nightmare born in the second half of the twentieth century as projected by a Ray Bradbury writing in the late forties very much aware of the brutal promise of Senator McCarthy's Un-American Activities Committee to wreak havoc on the U. S. artistic community. Assuming that Stendahl speaks for Bradbury, the author's position on censorship leaves little to the reader's imagination. And given the publication of *Fahrenheit 451* in the midst of the McCarthy paranoia, one cannot help but admire Bradbury's courage under fire (not to pun).

Throughout *The Martian Chronicles* Bradbury questions the ethics, actions, and moral character of governments, I think fairly put, over the history of humankind, but especially those so characterized as "colonial," who conquered, plundered, and arrogantly erased the identities of whole peoples, without conscience, often in the name of pious religious orders.

*The Martian Chronicles* was Bradbury's futuristic story of a Mars inhabited by an ancient, dying civilization, hastened to its extinction, erased, in body and artifact, by Earth "colonizers." Yes, as reader, one can marvel at his writing. Yes, as reader, one can become more aware, become more deeply sensitive to the earthbound issues he so powerfully raises, think differently, even be persuaded to condemn, act against, such action by his or her own government. And yes, Bradbury includes, rather blatantly, the U. S. government of the time of the novel as a primary evildoer. And, yes, extreme acts of censorship and book burning have been part of world history, even United States history. But in this book and others it is the scale of it, the extinction by fire, the bibliocide of all works of fantasy and imagination that raise consciousness.

Again, there is not much of a stretch between the brewing communist witch-hunts of Senator McCarthy's Committee on Government Operations of the Senate of the late 1940s and early 1950s and Bradbury's depictions of extreme acts of censorship in those of his works immediately preceding and following McCarthy's Committee. Nor does he omit callous environmental destruction and crimes against indigenous peoples. Whether extreme literary censorship or suppression of political beliefs, governmental paranoia is governmental paranoia. And usurped individual freedoms is the result. Strong anti-government political statement? Yes. Portrayal of grotestesque acts of violence by human beings upon human beings? Yes. Excellent literary writing worth preserving, fighting for? Yes.

So, how censorable is this story? This book? If history serves, not very to the general public readership to this point in the twenty-first century. Like Shakespeare, its literary value and continuing interest to readers protect it. But the public school arena provides different risks. There, recent and troublesome challenges have occurred. What is their nature? And what can be done to protect accessibility to *The Martian Chronicles* for teachers who may freely choose to teach it and those students who may freely choose to read it?

To address the question of the vulnerability of *The Martian Chronicles* to censorship at this writing, I will discuss it in the context of data provided by the Office for Intellectual Freedom (OIF), the American Library Association's censorship database website, and a recent censorship case illustrating in some detail how one school and teacher responded in all the right ways to a parental challenge of her teaching of *The Martian Chronicles* to her eighth grade students.

The "OIF Censorship Data Base 1990-1999" recently graphed three sets of data on its website depicting challenges to book accessibility, which indicate that (1) in terms of numbers of recorded *challenges by institution being challenged*—schools (2925), school libraries (2013), public libraries (1462), and museums/galleries (43) were the four institutions most challenged during this period; (2) in terms of numbers of recorded *challenges by type*—sexually explicit (1446), offensive language (1262), unsuited to age group (1167), occult/satanism (773), violence (630), homosexuality (497), religious viewpoint (397), nudity (297), and racism (245) were the nine most frequently challenged targets during this period; and (3) in terms of numbers of recorded *challenges by initiator of challenge*—parent (3427), patron (878), administrator (541), board member (206), teacher (169), and pressure group (163) were the six most frequent initiators of challenges during this period. Interestingly, religious organization (107) and clergy (89) taken together represent the fourth most frequent initiator, and there were only ten recorded challenges during this period by elected officials.

Of importance is the statement by the OIF that "Research suggests that for each challenge reported there are as many as four or five which go unreported." Assuming that the relative positions of more to less frequent items in each group would remain the same with unreported challenges factored in, one might conclude from the data taken as a whole that the most likely challenge would come from a parent concerned about sexually explicit content or offensive language or material unsuited to an age group (or some combination of these) and that the challenge would be directed to a school or school library. In fact, that is the nature of a 1998 challenge of the teaching of *The Martian Chronicles* reported by the Edison, New Jersey, *Star-Ledger* in its April 9, 1998, edition.

The article reports that the issue centered on a chapter in *Chronicles*, "June, 2003: Way in the Middle of the Air," which tells the story of a group of southern blacks gathering to fly to Mars to establish their own settlement. They are harassed by a viciously racist southern white man who frequently degrades them individually and as a race and often uses the term "nigger" to accentuate his rancorous language use. The point of the story is to make a strong statement against racism and project a sympathetic, positive image of African Americans.

The students in question were eighth graders, among whom were two African American students. The mother of one of the African American students claimed that the oral reading of the story "humiliated" her daughter and its offensive language was inappropriate for the maturity level of eighth graders. The teacher had carefully prepared herself and the students in advance of the teaching, and the book was among those on the school district's approved list. The mother presented her case to appropriate school and district personnel. Ray Bradbury, in a telephone interview, noted the positive portrayal of African Americans and thought it "ridiculous, at this late date, to criticize the use of the word. It was a different time." University experts strongly defended the book. The district had in place American Library Association Guidelines, was opposed to censorship, and supported the teacher's position. The mother, also opposed to censorship, per se, engaged the press. The district relented, and upon further study and the subsequent recommendation of the middle school English department chair, moved the book from the eighth grade to the tenth grade on the grounds that the story in particular and the book in general required a more mature reader than eighth-grade students.

In a related story, the teacher wrote a letter about the case to the

National Coalition Against Censorship (NCAC), which printed a "shortened version" of the letter in its Censorship News Online, "Issue #70: Censorship and Ray Bradbury's *The Martian Chronicles*, Summer 1998." In the introduction to the letter "excerpts," NCAC notes that the teacher chose *Chronicles* "for its relevance to the science and social studies curriculum" and "In preparation, she read articles on science fiction, critical essays of Bradbury's work, and teaching materials from the Center for Learning for use with the novel." In the version of the letter provided by NCAC the teacher wrote that:

> Because of its use of the word "nigger," I briefly considered skipping the chapter, but I felt that was a cowardly thing to do. . . . I decided . . . to do a guided reading of the chapter. . . . As soon as we started the novel, we were engaged in discussions of social criticism—environmental issues, gender issues, colonization issues, etc. For the controversial chapter, I created a worksheet. . . . I told my students that this was a controversial chapter . . ., that we would meet a character who would use the word "nigger" several times, as well as curses. We then discussed the author's purpose in creating this character. The students correctly concluded that the reader was supposed to hate Teece, and that Bradbury was trying to illustrate the evils of racism, prejudice, and discrimination. . . . I felt that I had established a safe environment in my classroom and that my students were ready for this material. I read the chapter aloud to the class, stopping frequently for discussion. . . . The mother of one of my African-American students objected to my reading of the chapter aloud and especially to my saying "nigger" instead of saying "the n-word" or skipping the word entirely. . . . The mother went to the principal, my department head, and the assistant superintendent of curriculum. All supported my use of the book and teaching methods. She was advised that she could file a complaint against the book. Instead she went to the *Star Ledger*. . . . After much discussion in which using an expurgated version, dropping the book altogether, or shipping it to the high school was debated, the decision was made to move the book to the tenth grade (where Bradbury's *Fahrenheit 451* is also taught). . . . My district wanted the issue to go away, and I knew that although they supported what I did, they would not fight for the book. I was afraid that they would go the expurgated route (I informed my department head that I would not teach that version). . . . But what disturbs me even more is the fact that the far-reaching repercussions of this incident are not being addressed. Teachers in the seventh grade are now reluctant to recommend, much less teach, *Sounder* and *The Autobiography of Miss Jane Pittman* (both Board approved books). Copies of Art Spiegleman's *Maus II* were removed from a Scholastic book fair and students were only permitted to purchase it after they returned a letter signed by their parents acknowledging the "mature content" of this book.

What strikes me first about this case is that the behaviors of teacher and district were admirable, appropriate, and consistent with professional guidelines. First and foremost, they seemed thorough in their readiness for and response to this challenge. If asked, I would advise the teacher and district to do approximately what they did do, except, perhaps, not make the final decision to move the book to the high school. As far as I know, the teacher's employment was never threatened. The issue was the book and its appropriateness for eighth-grade students. Still, this case makes clear that you can do all the right things as a teacher—perform rationally, sensitively, even heroically—and still lose. In sum:

1. She selected a book of solid literary quality characterized by elements integral to the learning potential of her students, her teaching agenda, and her school program of study.
2. She researched the book thoroughly, consulted with colleagues, developed a teaching plan, and prepared her students for the experience well in advance of teaching it.
3. She reacted to the challenge according to the established school and district procedures, which were consistent with the ALA guidelines.
4. She responded according to her sense of personal ethics, even refusing to teach an expurgated version.
5. She published her take on the case to the profession at large.

As I wonder about this case, an absolute conclusion is impossible for me simply because I was not there and do not know the context intimately. Certainly, there may be more here than the relentless drive of a parent for her child. But according to the teacher's letter, five classes of eighth graders apparently engaged in a productive study of the book—a study that had been available to fifteen previous years of eighth graders. The department chair was quoted as making the final decision after further study. Maybe her decision was purely professional and apolitical, although one would think that during that fifteen years *Chronicles* would have been assessed many times for its "appropriateness" for eighth graders. But maybe cases like this also suggest that something more fundamental than avoiding school-community conflict should drive instructional materials selection. And it is a tough place to go. But there is the issue of honest choices in book selection appropriate for the student audience versus book selection to avoid censorship on whatever grounds, which is in itself censorship.

What becomes clear regarding censorship and book selection is that easy, guilt-free, decisions are hard to come by, particularly when one weighs possible consequences. Book selection in a school setting comes before the fact. Any choice of one book for all, de facto, denies all other books for all—at least for the moment. Is it really the literary quality or complexity or reading level or maturity level that is at issue, or is it the chance that the content or language use or point of view might be offensive to someone real or imagined? What of matters of courage, professional integrity, job security, school politics, teacher comfort level with text? That is, is the selection purely driven by personal ethics and pedagogy or not? Most elections, in my experience, have reflected a mix of pedagogic and other influences to arrive at the most contextually appropriate choice. What has not been acceptable to me is that avoiding the best piece of literature available for a particular group of students does not matter—that literature is literature. That attitude insults the needs of student and teacher alike.

I wonder about the student and the parent at the center of the Edison controversy. If the student continues on to the local high school, she likely will encounter *Huckleberry Finn* and *To Kill a Mockingbird*. What then? And what of the teacher who so strongly defended her personal ethic against censorship and her professional privilege to select books for her students? How will she approach the next challenge? Will she unconsciously or consciously precensor to avoid challenge? And what of the effects on other teachers? Students? Where does the censorship of one book end?

In the case of classroom use of *Chronicles*, questions are easy to raise. Answers are slippery and so related to context. In the end, the best answer resides in the heart and judgment of the professional teacher: knowledgeable of students, content, and teaching methodologies; aware of context; confident in abilities. Even then, as the Edison case points out, there is the body politic. So my answer is not one a teacher frustrated by challenges to book selections or the threat of challenges wants to hear. There is no magic formula to solve the problem. There is only doing the best you can do based on the best information available in readiness for and delivery of work with literature and kids. And trusting in self and the continuing effort to engage your students and yourself in the most enjoyable, productive literary experiences possible. If challenges occur, you do like our Edison teacher—the best you can. If you should lose, you go on, strengthened, but not diminished, by the experience. Faith in self and faith in the kids must save the day. Maybe that is the answer you want to hear after all. Maybe that is my rationalization for the way I tell it to myself.

Finally, what has Ray Bradbury, himself, written about censorship? Of course, one could accurately say, everything he writes or has written is a defense of absolute freedom to write what he wants. But what does he think outside of the words he puts inside of the mouths of his characters? Listen to these excerpts from his revised (1979) "Coda," an addendum to *Fahrenheit 451*. Sound familiar?

The point is obvious. There is more than one way to burn a book. And the world is full of people running about with lit matches. Every minority . . . feels it has the will, the right, the duty to douse the kerosene, light the fuse. Every dimwit editor who sees himself as the source of all dreary blanc-mange plain porridge unleavened literature, licks his guillotine and eyes the neck of any author who dares to speak above a whisper or write above a nursery rhyme. . . . In sum, do not insult me with the beheadings, finger-choppings or the lung-deflations you plan for my works. I need my head to shake or nod, my hand to wave or make into a fist, my lungs to shout or whisper with. I will not go gently onto a shelf, degutted, to become a non-book. . . . And no one can help me. Not even you. (175-179)

And so we end, where we began, like the incessant cycles of censorship itself, with a second quote from "April 2005 Usher II" as Stendahl finds retribution in the bricking in of Garrett (as per Poe's "Cask of Amontillado") in the wine cellar of Usher II for his leading role as "Investigator of Moral Climates" in the burning of great literary works, in particular those of Poe:

"Garrett?" Called Stendahl softly. Garrett silenced himself. "Garrett," said Stendahl, "do you know why I've done this to you? Because you burned Mr. Poe's books without really reading them. You took other people's advice that they needed burning. Otherwise you'd have realized what I was going to do to you when we came down here a moment ago. Ignorance is fatal, Mr. Garrett." (118)

And so, once again we confront humankind's greatest literary sin: "ignorance." And the most powerful argument against censorship: to ensure that humankind does not fall to the inexcusable sin of Ignorance. And we confront again the censor's mortal enemy: imagination. Arguably, Ray Bradbury's imaginative works themselves carry within, perhaps, the richest commentary on censorship in literature today. And they are written with honesty and courage (some may say arrogance). To now, censors attacks on Bradbury's works have been relatively modest. At some point, censors may take them more seriously. Then we shall see.

## Works Cited

American Library Association—Office for Intellectual Freedom (OIF). 2000. "OIF Censorship Database 1990-1999: Institution Being Challenged, Challenges by Type, Initiator of Challenge." http://www. ala.org/ala. org/oif/index.html.

Bradbury, Ray. *Fahrenheit 451*. New York: Ballantine, 1953 (Eighty-first printing 1990, with revised "Coda" 1979, and "Afterword" 1982).

——. *The Martian Chronicles*. Bantam: New York, 1950 (Bantam paperback edition, 1979).

National Coalition Against Censorship (NCAC)—CENSORSHIP NEWS ONLINE.2000. "Issue #70: Censorship and Ray Bradbury's *The Martian Chronicles*." Summer, 1998. http://www.ncac. org/cen_news /cn70bradbury.html (Edison case, teacher letter).

The *Star-Ledger* Archive. "Mom wants Edison school to pull sci-fi book." 1998. http://search.starledger.com/cgi-bin/.

——. "Edison ditches old version of classic book." http://search. starledger.com/cgi-bin/.

NOTE: Please see the following sources for extensive assistance and free materials related to censorship and responding to challenges:

American Library Association—Office of Intellectual Freedom publication "Coping with Challenges: Strategies and Tips for Dealing with Challenges to Library Materials" at http://www.ala.org/oif/copinginf.html.

National Council of Teachers of English (NCTE), *Guidelines for Selection of Materials in English Language Arts*. An NCTE Standards Document available at http://www.ncte.org/censorship/guide.shtml.

# *My Brother Sam Is Dead*:
# Embracing the Contradictions and
# Uncertainties of Life and War

## Kathy G. Short

*My Brother Sam Is Dead* consistently appears on recommended reading lists for upper elementary and middle school students. English and language arts educators promote the book because of its high literary quality, particularly in relation to strong character development and use of setting. Social studies educators recommend this historical fiction novel because it offers alternative perspectives on the American Revolution and raises controversial questions and issues for students to consider.

Another type of list on which *My Brother Sam Is Dead* has consistently appeared throughout the years is lists of the most frequently banned books in the United States. Clearly there is something beyond literary merit and historical perspectives that has caught the attention of the public.

So what is it about this historical fiction novel that captures both praise and condemnation? After describing the plot and themes of the book, I will overview the major criticisms that have led to censorship challenges and then discuss the literary and historical qualities that have led to awards and frequent use of the book in English and social studies classrooms.

*My Brother Sam Is Dead* was the first children's book written by James and Christopher Collier, two brothers who have since collaborated on other historical novels for children. In their collaborative writing process, Christopher is primarily responsible for the plot outline and the research needed to verify historical accuracy and authenticity. James crafts this research into a powerful piece of fiction. Written in 1974, the book received immediate acclaim by being named a Newbery Honor book, quite an accomplishment for a first novel.

The novel explores the complexity of the issues surrounding the American Revolution and war in general through the story of a Connecticut family torn apart by divided loyalties. The father is a Tory, a loyalist who wants to maintain his business and protect his family, while older brother Sam has decided to leave college and join the rebel forces. The story is told in first person through the eyes of Tim, the younger brother who must remain at home and deal with conflicting loyalties within his family and community. Tim idolizes Sam but, at the same time, loves and respects his father.

While the American Revolution is often portrayed in history textbooks as a battle between the Americans and the British, the Colliers based their novel on the fact that all people living in America at that time were British subjects. The war was thus between various groups of Americans whose loyalties were different and whose positions were much more complex than simply Tory or Patriot. The Colliers portray the war as a *civil* war which divided families and communities rather than "good guys versus bad guys."

For example, while Tim's father is a Tory, he chooses not to become involved in the war while other neighbors actively support the conflict or join armies for one side or the other. A continuum between the two opposing positions was filled with many individuals, including those whose loyalties were unclear, neutral, or shifted according to whichever side appeared to be winning. The complexity of why various Americans did and did not get involved in the war is reflected through the range of characters that Tim encounters.

The novel begins with Tim witnessing an argument between Sam and his father over Sam's participation in a rebel uprising. Sam has come home to steal his father's gun in order to have the needed credentials to enlist in the rebel forces, an action that leaves the family without protection.

The war comes closer to Tim when he and his father take a trip to sell cattle and get supplies for the family tavern. While he and his father are given safe passage by local protection units sympathetic to the loyalists, on the way home his father is taken captive and only through trickery is Tim able to safely return home. The rebel bands that Tim and his father encounter are criminals who use the excuse of war to rob and kill, and they increase Tim's ambiguity and confusion about who really are the "good guys" in this war.

Tim takes over his father's work in their tavern and is soon so tired he has no time to think about war. The ugly reality of war again invades Tim's life when he sees a neighbor decapitated by loyalist forces and another young boy taken away to prison camp during a local skirmish.

When Sam's company returns to the area to winter, Tim and his mother are able to see Sam more frequently, and Tim becomes troubled by his brother's motivations in joining the rebel forces. Tim realizes that his brother remains in the army, not because of duty, but because he likes the excitement of being part of something big. Ultimately, Tim's family pays a terrible price when Sam and his father both lose their lives in the war. The father dies because of the terrible conditions on a prison ship, and Sam is executed as an "example" to other troops when he is falsely accused of stealing his own family's cattle.

In the epilogue, Tim writes fifty years after the war about the events in his life since that time and reflects on the terrible price his family paid. While he notes that the United States has prospered as an independent nation, he also remembers his father's words, "In war, the dead pay the debts of the living." He ends with this statement, "I keep thinking that there might have been another way, besides war, to achieve the same end" (245).

The Colliers also include a section entitled "How much of this book is true?" where they note which details in the book are factually based on actual individuals and events and which are fictionalized. The historical details and sources provided by the Colliers indicate their commitment to the accurate portrayal of historical events, although telling the story of history always involves interpretation by the historian.

Clearly, *My Brother Sam Is Dead* is a novel that deals with difficult issues through its focus on the devastating effects of war on one particular family, a focus that immediately raises the concern of censors. In particular, censorship challenges have arisen for a number of reasons. One is the use of profanity by several soldiers. Another is the graphic descriptions of physical violence when a neighbor is decapitated and another is shot. When the mother can no longer cope with her problems after losing her husband and realizing that her older son is likely to be executed, she resorts to drinking for a time. Tim uses alcohol at one point to survive the cold when he is trapped alone in a bitter snowstorm. Finally, some critics have noted that the book, written during the height of the Vietnam controversy, takes a general stance against war and specifically questions the American Revolution.

Despite these censorship challenges, English, language arts, and social studies educators have continued to use and recommend this book. For English and language arts educators, the major appeal of the book is its strong literary quality which meets objectives within an English curriculum. This novel is an excellent one for studying character development because Tim, the young narrator, is a dynamic character who undergoes significant, but believable, change through the course of the novel. Sam remains a relatively static character who loses some of his enthusiasm for fighting but still remains dedicated to his army. At the same time, Tim's perspectives and priorities gradually shift in complexity as he lives through difficult life events and matures from a naive young boy to a mature young man. The authenticity of the characterization provided by the Colliers is one reason why profanity is used several times by soldiers involved in battle.

Related to the strong characterization is the authors' effective use of setting to influence character and plot. Tim's ambiguity about the war shifts as he moves from place to place; this is particularly apparent during the supply trip, which parallels his confusion over which side of the war he personally wants to support. Whereas the town where Tim's family lives is primarily Tory sympathizers, Sam encounters strong Patriot views when he is away at college, which leads him to make his life-changing decision to join the rebel forces. Each setting reflects different perspectives on the conflict that shift the plot and influence the characters' actions and views.

The novel also encourages explorations of many different possible themes as well as provides an ending that invites further dialogue about the necessity of war. The authors invite response instead of neatly tying up loose ends. As readers discuss this novel, themes of the realities of war as they affect individuals and communities will likely be raised as well as themes regarding family relationships and responsibilities. Readers are immediately struck by the harsh realities of war through the deaths of the father and brother, and these realities are contrasted thematically with Sam's romantic view of war as heroism and the fight for freedom. The mother's anguish at the loss of her husband and son and Tim's reflections on whether the cause of freedom might have been gained in another manner can support readers in exploring the theme of war in a complex manner. History textbooks accept the necessity of war without question, and this novel asks readers to stop and think about whether war is really always the only way to accomplish our goals as a country. Readers are encouraged to explore this theme from a range of perspectives, including the causes of a war, individual reasons for fighting in a war, and the costs of war at different levels within a country, community, and family.

The book focuses less on details about where and when certain battles were fought and more on the values of family love, responsibility, respect, honest work, and the value of human life. The tensions between father and son, the mother's attempts to hold the family together despite their differences, the necessity of assuming responsibilities for absent family members, and the death of a parent are issues that today's students can relate to in powerful ways. The difficulty of family relationships is especially expressive in the portrayal of how Tim is torn between obeying his father and respecting his brother, particularly given his love for both.

Finally, the novel can be related to a study of historical fiction as a genre that goes beyond facts in order to personalize history and that uses the past to help explain the present. This novel is also an excellent way to connect the study of literature and history and to distinguish between fiction and fact by using the authors' note at the end of the book.

Within a social studies class, the use of novels such as this one serves to bring history alive as a story of the people who lived during a particular time period and made decisions that affect our lives and country today, not just a recounting of dates, people, and battles. Historical fiction brings history to life for today's students. Historical fiction also provides multiple perspectives on historical events that have too frequently been presented unidimensionally in textbooks. History textbooks have typically presented the American Revolution through a singular perspective on the necessity of the war to achieve freedom from England. By using this novel along with other novels set during this time period, teachers can encourage students to explore multiple interpretations of this specific war and of broader issues such as the dilemma of the uncommitted citizen and the necessity of war.

Because the Colliers portray the war as a civil war, the issue of who was patriotic and loyal to the country is challenged, and the oversimplification of these issues in textbooks is raised for debate. Also, because the main character in the book, Tim, is undecided about the war and must weigh various situations and events, the reader is effectively drawn into thinking through these issues alongside Tim. Sam's belief in the cause of freedom, which leads to his death, provides a powerful contrast to Tim's experience of freedom through the rest of his life but his questioning of the means to accomplishing that freedom. The Colliers invite debate—they have not decided the issue for readers—and they invite thoughtful discussion.

While some critics object that this novel encourages debate about war, controversy is the foundation of a social studies education. The valuing of differences and the challenging of ideas remain at the heart of a democracy in a diverse, free society. Teaching about ideas that are controversial has been one of the keystones to education, and novels such as this one open the possibility for dialogue.

While the Colliers do carefully present a range of perspectives on war through their characters, they also deliberately selected events that build toward a strong antiwar message. All authors and historians have a perspective, and so their work should not be criticized for making that perspective explicit for readers. Instead, teachers can use this book to talk about all history as interpretation and the importance of researching the perspective of novelists and historians and the thought collective of the time period in which they write, not just the time period they write about.

By having students read this book alongside other books about this time period as well as the history textbook, teachers can highlight history as interpretation. These comparisons could include comparing "facts" as presented across the books, reading aloud sections of the various texts that relate to the same events, creating alternative endings for any of the novels based on the interpretations offered by other texts, or rewriting the history textbook by using perspectives from historical fiction.

One possible comparison is between *Johnny Tremain* (Forbes, 1943) and *My Brother Sam Is Dead*, both strong literary novels dealing with the American Revolution but with contrasting attitudes toward war. *Johnny Tremain* was written in 1943, when the United States was immersed in a war that was supported with great patriotic fervor by the majority of Americans. The belief that "our side is right" and that war is justified prevailed, and so it is no surprise that Esther Forbes wrote a novel that glorified the American Revolution as necessary and worth the sacrifice of life. In contrast, the Colliers wrote their novel during the Vietnam War era, a time period when American society was questioning the necessity of war for solving political and social problems and focusing on the value of human life. Their decision to portray the American Revolution as a civil war and to focus on its effects through one family's devastating experiences grew out of society's views during the time period in which they wrote. This comment is not meant to question the historical accuracy of this novel. The Colliers did not twist the facts, as they knew them, but made every attempt to verify the events and people included in the novel. However, as writers and historians, they also brought their own interpretations to how they told the story with these facts.

The strength of this novel is not in its factual detail but in its potential for raising questions about what is read in history books and about the problems we all face in our daily lives. The ending reminds us that there are not clear-cut answers to most of life's problems and that we need to face and embrace the contradictions and uncertainties. *My Brother Sam Is Dead* challenges us to think about this complexity and invites us to engage in dialogue with others about these issues. Where the censors see profanity, violence, alcoholism, and a lack of patriotism instead lies an invitation for thoughtfulness about the ways in which we live our lives and the realization that our decisions will affect both our lives and the lives of future generations.

## Works Cited

Collier, James, and Christopher Collier. *My Brother Sam Is Dead*. New York: Four Winds Press, 1974.

Forbes, Esther. *Johnny Tremain*. Boston: Houghton Mifflin, 1943.

# Censored: An Author's Perspective *

## Christopher Collier

Twelve-year-old Timmy Meeker, struggling with his brother's seventeen-year-old girlfriend over an incriminating piece of paper, slammed her as hard as he could on the side of her head. "You little bastard," shouts Betsy (84). This is a line my brother wrote for one of the climactic moments in *My Brother Sam Is Dead*. Can it be that all across America ten-year-old girls are sitting in fifth-grade classrooms reading out loud "You little bastard" to their classmates? Judging from the reaction from outraged parents, one would think so. But I doubt it. I haven't yet met a teacher of any experience who would set things up that way. Nevertheless, the use of *Brother Sam* in classrooms across the country is challenged scores of times every year. In 1996 People For the American Way listed it among America's ten most challenged books—just after Steinbeck's *Of Mice and Men*.

The use of profanity and obscenity was not the only reason for the challenge, however. Parents complained about graphic descriptions of battlefield scenes, the consumption of alcohol, and an "unpatriotic" view of the American Revolution. At one large protest meeting, which I attended unrecognized, one woman objected to the book because one of the authors once wrote for *Playboy* (which is true—but it wasn't me). Although the board of education in this last instance decided to keep the book in the library, often enough the decision is the reverse.

We write these books primarily to teach American history. The bottom line is that students will learn nothing from them unless they read them. They won't read them—and if they do they won't remember what they read—unless the story engages, interests, and excites them. For that to happen we must reach our readers on an emotional level. The scenes we

---

* From *Brother Sam and All That: Historical Context and Literary Analysis of the Novels of James and Christopher Collier* © 1999 by Christoper Collier. Reprinted by permission of the author.

draw must have impact: that means not only intellectual engagement with the ideas we present, but also emotional engagement with the characters we depict. Indeed, though history itself holds unending materials for dramatic narrative, it is difficult to capture the actual emotional content of historical figures' characters. It is a lot more honest and literarily feasible to use fictional characters to personify and imbue with emotion the ideas we want kids to understand and remember. Thus strongly connotative, colorful, and striking words are a major literary tool to create character, context, and their interrelationships, all to bring about real historical understanding.

Dealing with censorship is not new to me. My first encounter with attempts to bar books from classroom use came when I, a new untenured teacher of eighth graders, had a panel of six high-level students read and discuss George Orwell's *1984*. This was in the mid-1950s, Joe McCarthy's heyday. They were spooky times. It was on this occasion that I learned the first of the Six Lessons about Censors that I describe here.

**Lesson One:** The censors have not read the book.
When one of my eighth graders carried home a paperback copy of *1984* with a slightly lurid cover—for 1955—depicting a bosomy young woman wearing a sash across which was emblazoned "Anti-Sex League," my principal heard from my student's mother. To his lasting credit and my lasting gratitude, the principal permitted me to meet in his office with the horrified parent, who also happened to be the reigning president of the PTA. I asked her what she objected to. I was degrading her daughter's taste by giving her communist—remember the era—trash. But what was it in the book that was communist or degrading, I was allowed to persist. I wouldn't read this garbage, said Mrs. PTA.—and she hadn't. Nevertheless, I was told to remove the book from my course, and asked to submit all my future reading lists to the principal. How to squelch young enthusiasm for innovation and excitement in the classroom.

Another episode illustrating Lesson One—censors have not read the book—is much more recent: 1993, in fact. *Jump Ship to Freedom* follows the risky adventures of a young slave who gets mixed up in the writing of the U.S. Constitution in 1787. In the course of the year or so the book covers, Daniel Arabus rejects his view of himself as a stupid nigger and comes to see that he is as brave, smart, honest, and wise as any white person he meets. He grows from "I was black and wasn't as smart as white folks," (2) to "it seems to me that there ain't much difference one way or another. . . . take the skin off of us, and it would be pretty hard to tell which was the white ones and which ones wasn't." (187) A pretty uplifting story, it seems to me. Although readers encounter the word darky as early as page 11, it is not until page 20 that they smash into nigger. One black sixth grader never got past page 2 before complaining to his teacher. The school principal pulled the book from the library shelves; a little tempest brewed and local NAACP officials became involved. In the end, *Jump Ship* was removed from elementary but not middle-school library shelves, though the teachers "all agreed not to use the book in lessons so as not to offend students."

The fracas generated some interesting comment. "Parents argued," a newspaper account explained, "that the book was dangerous because some students will only flip through the beginning of the book and not read it all." This view raises an intriguing question: Must all books for school use be written so that no single page if read alone will not offend anyone? There is no evidence that any of those objecting to the book ever read it; indeed their comments lead pretty clearly to the conclusion that they did not. I will return to "the N word" later.

**Lesson Number Two:** Censors are mindless. We often run into situations where editors of anthologized excerpts from our books want to remove words, phrases, whole episodes for whatever editorial reasons—or nonreasons—they might have. Thus the suggestion of one censor to substitute restaurant for the customary 18th-century tavern in a story about the American Revolution. Restaurant is a French word not used in America for two generations after the Revolution. The same censor was told, apparently, to remove all the gods, damns, god damns, etc. In one scene our narrator "began silently to pray, 'Oh, please God, oh please.'" The censor struck it. That same mindless censor also accepted our substitution of hard cider for wine, apparently wholly unaware that they both have the same alcoholic content. Hard cider is apple wine. The examples of this sort of mindlessness go on and on in uncounted tedium.

**Lesson Number Three:** Censors don't understand the context of the situation. Much that might appear on first glance to be merely simple mindlessness is often an inability to see the offending element in context. This might, for instance, explain a censor's failure to distinguish profanity from prayer. A common basis for censorship is to strike episodes that appear racist or sexist. Often these episodes are included in order to attack the very attitudes they display. The example of Daniel's racist remarks in *Jump Ship to Freedom* cited above is a good example. In *The Clock* we attack raw sexism in the workforce by focusing on a victim of it. We have been challenged for not having Annie stand up to her lecherous supervisor. But that was 1810—which leads me to . . .

**Lesson Number Four:** Censors lack historical perspective—even of their own times. Books have been challenged for the use of the word Japs. But anyone who remembers the era of World War II at all knows that Jap was the universally employed term. Read some of the classic books written about that war. In John Hersey's *Into the Valley* about a battle on Guadalcanal in 1943, not only do the soldiers regularly use the term Jap but Hersey himself uses it in his narrative. Would a battle account of GI dialogue of 1943 ring true if the soldiers referred to their deadly enemies as Japanese? In my other life as a professional historian I work with Indians a good deal. They call themselves Indians. Must we have our frontiersmen in a novel about the expanding west say that the "only good Native American is a dead Native American." Yet I know of a young seventh-grade teacher who says she will not use a book that uses the term Indian. And how do we keep up with what are acceptable terms for Negroes, colored, blacks, African-Americans? Certainly we all agree not to use the word nigger when we can avoid it, but how real would it sound for Confederate troops in 1863 to say Negro—not to mention African-American. Would Huckleberry Finn be the same story if his companion was referred to as African-American Jim?

The lack of historical perspective, however, goes way beyond the use of historically acceptable terms. We have been informally challenged as sexist for having Willy in *War Comes to Willy Freeman* dress as a boy in order to be able to make her way from place to place through revolutionary era society. Apparently, many parents of young teenagers have so little understanding of the past that they fail to see how difficult—indeed nearly impossible—it would be for a fourteen-year-old black girl to travel alone through New York and Connecticut in 1782. On one occasion we had an editor change a statement made by a Revolutionary Era bandit from "You're acting like a couple of old women" to You're acting like cowards." I think the dialogue loses a lot in that translation. How can youngsters of today ever understand the progress of women over the past generation if they don't know the situation of women in America in the past—indeed the traditional situation of women everywhere?

**Lesson Number Five:** The concerns of censors change over time. In the 1970s we were not made aware of objections—if there were any—to damns, god damns, even son of a bitches. Objections to profanity (there is virtually no obscenity in our books) rose during the late 1970s and into the 80s. This fits the upward curve of the popularity of fundamentalist Protestantism. In the earlier era, the wake of the Vietnam peace movement, concerns centered on violence as depicted in our battle scenes. More recently, we have encountered objections to depictions of alcohol drinking—indeed, even the word tavern as I have already noted. And even more recently there have been the alleged violations of sex and racial sensitivities. Sometime, if you just wait long enough, the censors will lose interest, though you can be sure that new ones—or the same old ones—will appear with new concerns. They are always there.

**Lesson Six:** I have met the enemy and I am them.
Historians, of course, study change over time, and Lesson Six is one that time—not any censor—taught me. If an author is lucky enough to see his books still in print and selling briskly a generation after he wrote them, he must confront the very real possibility of a disjuncture between the audience he wrote the books for and the audience that is now reading them. The publishers of the Hardy Boys, Nancy Drew, and Tom Swift routinely update their old tales. It is especially true of the past thirty years that social change has been profound and rapid. The connotations expressed by certain words are not the same in 1998 as they were in 1974.

In 1939 Clark Gable's famous *Gone With the Wind* "damn!" was a shocker; to today's audiences it doesn't mean a thing. What I have seen over the past decade or so, however, is the reverse of the loss of shock value in certain words. Where damns, god damns, hells, and Jesus Christ were strong shockers for fifth graders, but to their parents quite unexceptionable in 1974, this is no longer the case.

About ten or twelve years ago we began to hear from our middle-school readers complaints about the "swears" in our books. Why did we have to use them? I have already responded to that question. The one I want to deal with now, is what do you do when the social and intellectual climate changes so much that words have a different effect on readers—indeed even mean something quite different to them?

Same words—different meaning. Similarly, in the verbal context of the early 1970s, the full and steamy wake of the free speech movement of the previous decade, it took a damn or a hell to carry any emotional weight. *The Bloody Country*, for example, is full of them, even on occasion in the mouths of nine-year-olds.

But the free speech waters rose to flood tide and beyond. The filth of speech on television and in films today has become so outrageous that a backwash was sure to come, and the tide ebbed with a rush. Parents are so disgusted with obscenities in the media that they are now much more aware and concerned about their kids' verbal encounters at school. Indeed, even some of the kids are concerned.

Thus a goddamn in 1998 carries a much heavier impact, believe it or not, than it did in 1974—or so, at least, our letters and conversations with

# The Atlanta Journal
## THE ATLANTA CONSTITUTION

PAGE 2-B, SATURDAY, JULY 16, 1983

# *Trying to kill reason itself*

It is a tale of conflict, moral ambiguity and history.

A Tory father is pitted against his patriotic son during the American Revolution. Both believe they are right and both suffer. The story poses few easy questions and offers fewer easy answers. It is designed to make young minds consider in some depth the price of liberty.

Judging from the hullabaloo in Gwinnett County over the book, "My Brother Sam Is Dead," some older minds, as well, could use a refresher course on this subject. A group of parents wanted to ban the book from school library shelves, but, wisely, the school board said no. (The board did agree to place an edition abridged by the publisher in elementary schools.)

What's so objectionable? Well, it seems, "My Brother Sam Is Dead," contains a bit of salty language. Accordingly, some parents claim the book is "garbage" and predict it will lead to "moral decay."

The book is sprinkled with passages like this: " 'Damn it, that's rebellion,' one of the farmers said. 'They'll have us in war yet.' "

Or this: "He told Mr. Beach to go to hell and galloped his horse at Mr. Beach."

And at one point, we have this: " 'God, can't you do anything right, Tim?'

'Don't curse,' I said. 'It's a sin.' "

There are other bits of profanity, but it's hardly the stuff to scandalize young ears. In fact, it's talk that most students encounter daily on network television, in movies, on public sidewalks and, undoubtedly, on Gwinnett County school grounds.

In the book, such profanity adds dramatic emphasis and realism. It is not gratuitous. In any case, "My Brother Sam Is Dead" is not required reading in Gwinnett; it simply graces the system's supplemental reading lists.

Garbage? The American Library Association lauded the book as "a sobering tale that will leave readers with a more mature view of history and war." It was named a Newberry Honor Book and was nominated for a National Book Award in 1974, the year it was published.

In its narrative, the price of liberty is bloodshed, death and anguish within families. Its protagonist pays the ultimate price so that future generations may live in a republic of diverse views, cultures, religions and values.

Living in such a republic, of course, presents some challenges. In Gwinnett County, as elsewhere, our system demands a continuing sacrifice: We must tolerate diversity. We cannot define the world in our personal terms and force that definition on others. There are other points of view to consider, other values that must be allowed. We have the freedom to choose among them.

As John Milton observed three centuries ago: He who "kills a man kills a reasonable creature, God's image; but he who destroys a good book kills reason itself."

In 1885, The Committee of the Public Library of Concord, Mass., banned Mark Twain's "Huckleberry Finn" as "trash suitable only for the slums." Twain considered this "a rattling tiptop puff . . . (which) will sell 25,000 copies for us sure." Maybe the would-be censors of Gwinnett have ensured that "My Brother Sam Is Dead" will get an avid perusal by schoolchildren from Norcross to Buford. Maybe they have performed a public service.

young teenagers and their parents tell us. Indeed, that is the Lesson Six that I learned. I recently reread *The Bloody Country*, and found many of the curse words and especially the use of nigger, unnecessary, even grating on occasion. The lesson, of course, is that if the intellectual or cultural perspective of the readership changes, there can be actual changes in the received meaning of certain words. Thus what is not censorable in one era might certainly well be in another. The great question is, what should an author of a frequently reprinted book do about it? If the words on the page no longer get the intended response—one which they once did, should an author, given a chance, alter the words in his original? Should he, in other words, censor himself?

This gets me to the central authorial question. If you know certain elements of a situation are liable to offend some influential readers, why don't you just omit or change them? Let me tell you a story.

I earlier described the wrestling bout of Timmy and Betsy in *My Brother Sam Is Dead* over a note Timmy was carrying to Loyalist spies. In this scene Timmy fails in his effort to participate in the war and becomes thereafter an increasingly confused and distressed onlooker. In his political development it is a climactic moment. We had to give it some emotional impact. When the first draft came to me with Betsy's "You little bastard," (84), I called my brother to tell him that the teenage daughter of the town's most respectable family would not have used that word. Not that folks in the olden days didn't—they used every word we do today, not excluding the f—one. But Betsy wouldn't. "OK," says James, "what would she say?" "You little viper; you snake," I suggested. "Oh, come on; we're writing for teenagers in 1974. Those words carry no force at all." I had to agree; the literary needs outweighed the historical ones.

Over the years, I have asked hundreds of middle-school kids to suggest a phrase that their mothers would accept, but that would pack the same wallop. The best they have come up with so far goes like this:

## Original Version

Then she jumped me. She caught me completely by surprise. She just leaped onto me and I fell down backwards and she was lying on top of me, trying to wrestle her hands down inside of my shirt. "Goddamn you, Betsy," I shouted. I grabbed her by her hair and tried to pull her head back, but she jerked it away from me. I began kicking around with my feet trying to catch her someplace where it would hurt, but she kept wriggling from side to side on top of me and I couldn't get in a good kick. I hit her on the back but in that position I couldn't get much force. "Get off me, Betsy."

"Not until I get that letter," she said. She jerked at my shirt, trying to pull it up. I grabbed at her hands and twisted my body underneath her to turn over so I would be on top, but she pushed her whole weight down on me, grunting. So I slammed her as hard as I could on the side of the head.

"You little bastard," she shouted. She let go of my shirt with one hand and slapped me as hard as she could across my face. My nose went numb and my eyes stung and tears began to come.

## Sanitized Version

Then she jumped me. She caught me completely by surprise. She just leaped onto me and I fell down backwards and she was lying on top of me, trying to wrestle her hands down inside of my shirt. "Curse you, Betsy," I shouted. I grabbed her by her hair and tried to pull her head back, but she jerked it away from me. I began kicking around with my feet trying to catch her someplace where it would hurt, but she kept wriggling from side to side on top of me and I couldn't get in a good kick. I hit her on the back but in that position I couldn't get much force. "Get off me, Betsy."

"Not until I get that letter," she said. She jerked at my shirt, trying to pull it up. I grabbed at her hands and twisted my body underneath her to turn over so I would be on top, but she pushed her whole weight down on me, grunting. So I slammed her as hard as I could on the side of the head.

"You bloody skunk," she shouted. She let go of my shirt with one hand and slapped me as hard as she could across my face. My nose went numb and my eyes stung and tears began to come.

A third version of the same episode was presented in an expurgated edition of the book that Scholastic put out (without consulting us) for its club distribution. I goes like this (96-97):

The she jumped me. She caught me completely by surprise. She just leaped onto me and I fell down backwards and she was lying on top of me, trying to wrestle her hands down inside of my shirt. I grabbed her by her hair and tried to pull her head back, but she jerked it away from me. I began kicking around with my feet trying to catch her someplace where it would hurt, but she kept wriggling from side to side on top of me and I couldn't get in a good kick. I hit her on the back but in that position I couldn't get much force. "Get off me, Betsy."

"Not until I get that letter," she said. She jerked at my shirt, trying to pull it up. I grabbed at her hands and twisted my body underneath her to turn over so I would be on top, but she pushed her whole weight down on me, grunting. So I slammed her as hard as I could on the side of the head.

She let go of my shirt with one hand and slapped me as hard as she could across my face. My nose went numb and my eyes stung and tears began to come.

Perhaps opinion will differ as to which version makes the most memorable impression. My brother and I often disagree. But on this one, we do not.

When kids ask why we use all the "swears" in our books, I try to explain that you just can't have soldiers in battle saying "Goll ding it, I've been hit," or "I'm shot, good gracious." Readers know that is not what they said; the story would lose credibility and we would lose readers. Look again, for instance at John Hersey's 1943 battle account I mentioned earlier. The much lesser public tolerance for profanity at mid century forced writers into pallid representations of dialogue.

Hersey's battle hardened GIs use phrases like "You can bet your shirt." One Marine captain, in rallying his scattering troops in the heat of deadly combat, says "Gosh, and they call you marines." Now we know he didn't say "gosh," and the use of the word in this context fails utterly to capture the spirit and emotion of the moment and casts an aura of unbelievability over the whole account.

Finally, let's confront the N word. *The Bloody Country*—on one level about interstate relations during the Confederation years—is on another level about the relative balance of property values and human values in the formative era of United States history. Ben Buck is the son of a mill owner—property values obviously symbolized by both the mill and the name Buck. His closest friend is the family slave, Joe Mountain. In the course of the story Ben realizes that if he loses the mill, he will end up a wage slave working for someone else and with little freedom of action or independent control over his life. Joe, on the other hand, learns that the only way he can gain his freedom is to get away from the mill. Ultimately he runs away.

We first encounter the N word on page 3. Joe was half Mohegan, and Ben says, "You're an Indian yourself." "Hell, I'm not an Indian," Joe Mountain says, "I'm a nigger." "Besides, if I'm not a nigger, how come I belong to your father? Indians can't be slaves, only niggers." (4) This begins the development of our theme of the universal need for individual freedom. In the era of American slavery from the mid-17th century to 1865, whites—North and South—did not like to use the word slave. Note, for instance, that the U.S. Constitution written in 1787 condones the institution by referring to slaves as "persons. . . held to service or labor" and "persons imported." Nigger was a less embarrassing euphemism for slave. It was universally used that way. But let's try our dialogue again. Ben says "You're an Indian yourself." "Hell, I'm not an Indian," Joe Mountain says, "I'm a Negro." "Besides, if I'm not a Negro, how come I belong to your father? Indians can't be slaves, only Negroes." Try it again substituting African-American for Negro. Do you see what I mean?

Our use of the N word is intended to deepen the depiction of the misery of slavery and of the degraded status of free blacks as well. Most of our readers are white. It is our effort to convey to them the trials of people of African ancestry in North America. We want youngsters to understand the difficulties of growing up black in America. We think this is necessary for them to think knowledgeably and wisely about contemporary conditions about which they, as adult citizens, will have to make decisions affecting their own and others' lives. Without knowledge of the horrors and misery of the black—especially, slave—experience that has embarrassed America for centuries, future citizens cannot confront intelligently the racism that so degrades the nation. And without confronting it, they cannot rectify it.

This is our fundamental objective in the Arabus Trilogy. In *War Comes to Willy Freeman* we try to show the problems faced by the most powerless people—young, black, female, and slave. But in the end Willy struggles through, not happily, but free, at least. In *Jump Ship to Freedom*, Daniel learns firsthand the searing ambiguity of a Constitution for white freedom and black slavery. And in *Who Is Carrie?* our little black girl faces the awful future of never knowing if she is slave or free. In all of these novels the word nigger is unavoidable if anything close to historical verisimilitude is to be drawn. But beyond that, the word is necessary in order to portray the horrible condition of enslaved African-Americans in a way that evokes an emotional response that draws the reader into the story.

We know that our approach to the historical roots of the nation's race problem works. These books are used in largely black-populated inner city schools. We get approving fan letters from students there. One eighth grader wrote from New Jersey, "This week I picked up the book *Jump Ship to Freedom* and I could not put it down. I am a black girl who of course has heard many things about the black situation but I've never really got into it. When I read this book, a whole new world opened up to me. My mother is buying the other two volumes today.

"Thank you for writing these books. Sometimes children my age with all the things I have and my beautiful home need to experience other things." Indeed, an eighth-grade teacher wrote from Austin, Texas, after having read *Willy* and *Jump Ship* asking for a photo: "I really do think that many of my students will be surprised to discover that you are of African-American des-

December 7, 1996

The Star
Chicago Heights, IL.

To the Editors:

We have recently become aware of the controversy in your area over our book, "War Comes to Willy Freeman." While we regret that it caused some discomfort to one student, we still believe that the book ought to be used in your schools.

"War Comes to Willy Freeman" is part of a trilogy about a black family during the American Revolution. It was designed specifically to heighten awareness among school children to the suffering endured by blacks under slavery. The book has won many awards, and has been read by millions of children in thousands of American schools. It is routinely assigned in inner city schools, where students, teachers, and administrators are largely black.

We did not introduce the offending word lightly, but only after long discussions between ourselves and with our editor. We ultimately concluded that no other word would present black history truthfully. That we do not condone casual use of the word is made clear in the epilogue to the book. While it is true that in rare instances there have been objections to the word "nigger" in the dialogue, by far the majority of black parents and educators believe that their students ought to be given a realistic view of the horrors of slavery. We will do nothing to ameliorate conditions for blacks if we pretend that those conditions do not exist. Surely nobody would want us to present slave owners as speaking courteously to their slaves.

In assigning "War Comes to Willy Freeman," Ms. Comandella was only doing what thousands of other American teachers with black students in their classrooms have been doing for fifteen years. We hope that concerned parents will take the time to read "War Comes to Willy Freeman" to see if they really think, it is "racially insensitive."

Cordially,

*James Lincoln Collier*

cent." After seeing my picture, she wrote, "I still plan to use your books during Black History month"

It should be clear by now that as we write we use neither curse words nor racial slurs without giving them thorough consideration. We do not use nigger when some other term will do as well. Nor do we say goddamn when we could say gosh with just as great an effect. As a matter of fact, the number of complaints we received from middle schoolers about "swears" in our books caused us to write our last two books with almost none. It was not easy. A partial solution was to make the two fourteen- or fifteen-year-old protagonists in *With Every Drop of Blood* old-fashioned fundamental Christians, given to quoting the Bible rather than spouting profanity. In that book we got rid of much of the profanity that would have been standard among soldiers, and we tried to use the N word only when absolutely necessary. In this scene fourteen-year-old Johnny has just been captured by a black Union soldier, Cush, and wrestles with his world turned upside down. "Taking orders from a darky was another shock, especially one my own age. It was just the strangest thing, for I'd never heard a darky even speak back to a white person, much less give them orders." This works, but wouldn't the sense of shock and role reversal be a lot more intense if the N word was used instead of darky? And, in any event, are 20th-century African-Americans any less offended by darky than nigger?

The American Library Association Office for Intellectual Freedom has all sorts of guides and other materials to help deal with efforts at school and library censorship—more especially how to head it off at the pass before it erupts into a major community battle. But I have a few suggestions that might help avoid even the thought of challenging the books you choose to use in class. Make sure your books are grade level appropriate. Consider carefully whether you should read them to students, have students read out loud in class, silently in class, or at home. Communities differ radically in their tolerance for obscenity, profanity, and racial and gender slurs. Be sensitive to those levels of tolerance. But in the end, the choice of classroom materials belongs to the professional, not the parents. Parents may know what is best for their own children, but teachers are better judges of what's best for the whole class.

## Works Cited

Collier, James L. and Christopher Collier. *The Bloody Country*. New York: Macmillan. 1976.

———. *The Clock*. New York: Delacourt, 1992.

———. *Jump Ship to Freedom*. New York: Dell, 1981.

————. *My Brother Sam Is Dead*. New York: Four Winds Press, 1974.
————. *War Comes to Willy Freeman*. New York: Dell, 1987.
Hersey, John. *Into the Valley*. New York: Knopf, 1943.
Orwell, George. *1984*. New York: Harcourt Brace, 1949.
Steinbeck, John. *Of Mice and Men*. New York: Viking, 1963.

# Literature, History, and Social Value: In Defense of *Native Son*

## Nellie Y. McKay and Dave Junker

Published in 1940 to great critical acclaim, Richard Wright's *Native Son* was the first African American novel to be a Book-of-the-Month Club selection. This was a signal breakthrough for the field: black literature had entered the mass American public reading space. Whether one judges it subsequently by the assessment of literary critics, or for its impact on writers, or its continued use in the classroom, the novel's place in history is undeniable. The deluge of scholarship and commentary that has followed it through time, laudatory and controversial, even as we turned into the twenty-first century, prolongs the unabated critical and general interest in this text. Its frequent comparison with *The Grapes of Wrath* (Steinbeck) and *Crime and Punishment* (Dostoyevsky) underscores the magnitude of the respect in which it is held by many experts in literary history.

Writers in the African American tradition openly acknowledge the novel's importance to the development of African American writing. In 1941, Ralph Ellison, a friendly but stern critic of Wright's naturalism, credited the novel for moving African American fiction toward a "grasp of American reality" through its improvement and modernization of technique and enlargement of theme. (Ellison 22). Decades later, Henry Louis Gates Jr. surmises that "if one had to identify the single most influential shaping force in modern Black literary history, one would probably have to point to Wright and the publication of *Native Son*" (Gates xi).

Yet, for all this high praise, skeptics of its literary and/or social values have, since its appearance, done everything they could to discredit the merits of *Native Son*. Some have even sought to remove it from public access in certain venues like schools and public libraries. They object to the raw violence, the level of rage and anger that the protagonist projects toward white liberals, and Wright's open indictment of American racism. They often use his brief membership in the Communist Party as evidence of his anti-Americanism, thus casting aspersions of his fitness to be a respected citizen of this country.

For all of the negative arguments against it, *Native Son* is not a book (not that any book should be) that should be removed from public access. For even in 2001, when some would say that significant advancements have been made in race relations in this nation, it is difficult to deny that many of the ugly realities of racial and sexual power that the novel lays bare manifest themselves almost daily in our society. To ban *Native Son* from the opportunity for exposure to continued debate and discussion at all levels of its readership is to effect an evasion of some of the most critical issues the U.S. needs to resolve in this century. It would suggest our willingness to concede that today our level of public discourse on race has not come very far since Gunnar Myrdal wrote in 1944, four years after the publication of *Native Son*, of our tendency to keep the problems of race relations "below the level of consciousness" (30). The novel merits a place in the public sphere, not for the brutality in the text, but because of its honest reflection on the violence that Wright felt "life had made . . . over and over again" for millions of black Americans ("Bigger" 455). Those who attempt to silence *Native Son* for its concerns with oppression and rage would do well to consider their part in the denial of this history. In addition, while the novel provides a mirror of American race relations during the Great Depression, it also offers a vivid and complexly drawn context for students to examine "patterns of responsibility" between individuals and their society (Hall 81). In short, the historical, sociological, and literary value of *Native Son* make it vital to the interests of American society and culture.

Based on the reactions of most readers, Wright succeeded in his attempt to create an African American novel that no one could "weep over," but one they "would have to face . . . without the consolation of tears" ("Bigger" 454). Doubtless, his statement contributed to the text's inclusion among books most often censored in America. But thoughtful readers understand that neither Wright's purpose nor the results were gratuitous or intended to be sensational, nor were they without serious social or artistic value. On the contrary, *Native Son* records a great artist's reactions in his representation of the "horror of Negro life in the United States" ("Bigger" 461) in that time. It was the vehicle through which the author confronted an apathetic, uncaring public with the stark realities of American racism, drawing from the many examples of racial terror he witnessed while growing up in the South, and the degree of racial fear that enforced and justified the small humiliations and large atrocities of Jim Crow segregation.

Accordingly, Wright's novel thrives on swift action and a palpable sense of danger, which take shape through its protagonist, Bigger Thomas, a twenty-year-old black male living with his impoverished family on Chicago's segregated South Side, known as the "black belt." Bigger is a composite of several images of black males Wright felt whites feared most, those "who consistently violate the Jim Crow laws of the South" ("Bigger" 437). The novel has three parts. In the first, "Fear," readers meet Bigger's inarticulate rage and his awareness of the limitations that his surroundings place on him, limitations that lead him into a course of petty crime and idle degeneracy. As if to sound an alarm to readers, and to America, the novel begins with the ringing of an alarm clock in the "dark and silent room" in which the Thomases—a mother, two boys, and a girl—awaken (4). Evidence of the starkness of their environment increases as they take turns averting their eyes to enable each other to dress in dignity. But soon the small one-room apartment is "galvanized into action" as Mrs. Thomas screams and the girl, Vera, leaps atop the bed, both calling for Bigger to kill the enormous rat that has returned as if to stalk them (4). In a flurry of angry curses and wild commotion, Bigger succeeds in battering the rat to death with a heavy skillet.

Through the brilliance of Wright's symbolism, this opening scene foregrounds the presence of violence in Bigger's black life and triggers a sociological interest in ideas on the influence of environment on the individual versus individual responsibility. While the image of the rat, with its "black beady eyes," in an ironic way anticipates the image of Bigger as the threatening black intruder pursued by a frightened and angry mob that occurs later in the novel, this scene also suggests to us that Bigger's role as a protagonist is endowed with a degree of agency which we are left to later evaluate.

From this scene on, when we include ourselves, the narrative encompasses four competing perspectives on Bigger's action: ours, his brother's, his sister's, and his mother's, which together create criteria by which to judge his future actions. First, Bigger elicits our sympathies because of the dehumanizing environment and the conditions of fear and anger it forces on him. Second, flanked by his admiring younger brother, Buddy, he assumes the role of the masculine chivalric hero as he comes to the aid of his mother and sister to slay the metaphorical dragon: "The two brothers stood over the dead rat and spoke in tones of awed admiration" for the size of their defeated enemy (6). When Buddy alerts Bigger to the "three-inch rip" in his "pant-leg," to call attention to the reality of the danger he faced, Bigger responds with a sense of masculine pride, "Yeah; he was after me all right" (7). The exchange is one of shared satisfaction in Bigger's ability to execute the symbolic rites of manhood and, in their youthful innocence, the young man's potential to act as a positive role model for his younger brother. In the absence of a father in the home, Bigger fills the vacant role of protector of his family.

However, Wright complicates the image of a protective Bigger by emphasizing his capacity for violence in the way that he redirects his aggression from the rat to his sister, Vera. This third view of him suggests his potential to distort and misapply qualities of masculine aggression, and signifies his potential danger to women. When Vera desperately implores him to get rid of the dead rat, "Bigger laughed and approached the bed with the dangling rat, swinging it to and fro like a pendulum, enjoying his sister's fear" (7). Angered by his apparent inability to fully understand his action, his mother reprimands her older son for causing Vera to faint. From her point of view, Bigger exhibits no communal values through which to share responsibility for making better the conditions of their lives. "If you had any manhood in you," she scolds, "we wouldn't have to live in this garbage dump. . . . All you ever care about is your own pleasure! Even when the relief offers you a job you won't take it till they threaten to cut off your food and starve you! Bigger, honest, you the most no-countest man I even seen in all my life" (8,9). His mother's severe criticism of him suggests that his joblessness arises from his apathy and degeneracy, which results in low self-esteem.

These multiple and often conflicting perspectives on Bigger Thomas throughout the narrative underline the literary complexity of *Native Son* and encourage our critical investigation of the social factors in the novel, but yield no easy resolutions. Environmental pressures appear as motifs throughout, specifically in the form of both natural forces and racist social forces: in the oppressive cold and the "white snow" falling everywhere; in the dichotomy between the Thomases' squalid one-room apartment and the Daltons' luxurious mansion; in the images of glamour, wealth, and beauty that mock the aspirations of Bigger and his friends as they watch the movies in their local theater; in the violence whites inflict on the black community in retaliation for Bigger's crime; in the overwhelming power of the white media to incite and control public opinion; and the court's predetermination of what is justice.

Issues relative to Bigger's lack of agency surface throughout the text in conjunction with the forces that oppress this antihero, reinforcing a process of interpretive dialogue between them. For example, although it may appear as positive action on his part when he accepts the job at the Daltons', he does so only to silence his mother's berating of him and to serve some short-term relief for the family's insolvent situation. What he knows, but cannot articulate, is that the jobs that are open to him will never change the basic conditions of his social and economic status in the world. This knowledge, along with his sense of entrapment in the circumstances he must tolerate, are concerns that destroy him from within.

Thus, Bigger's new job as chauffeur to the politically liberal, rich, white Dalton family, which on the surface suggests his compliance with his mother's wishes to "make something" out of himself "instead" of continuing to be "just a tramp" (9), turns out to be the worst thing for him. His first assignment, to drive daughter Mary to a lecture at her college, goes shockingly awry because Mary and her boyfriend Jan decide to skip the lecture and end upon a drunken binge. At the end of the evening, Bigger has to carry an unconscious Mary to her bedroom. Before he can escape that chamber undetected, old and blind Mrs. Dalton wanders into the darkened room calling Mary's name. Immediately, feeling "hysterical terror," Bigger attempts to silence the unconscious Mary's incoherent mumblings by covering her face with a pillow and inadvertently stifles her. Then, in even greater fear of discovery, Bigger subsequently decapitates Mary and disposes of her body by incinerating it in the Daltons' furnace. The vivid description of Mary's death ends the first section of the book. In the second section, "Flight," Wright follows the police investigation into Mary's death alongside Bigger's deliberate rape and even more brutal murder of his girlfriend, Bessie, for equally hysterical reasons as those leading to Mary's death and the manner of his disposal of her body. He is desperate to escape, but the police capture him. The final section of the novel, "Fate," covers his court trial and the judge's pronouncement of the death sentence on him.

In *Native Son*'s literary rendering of social history, this plot also offers a shocking dramatization of the role that sexual violence plays in enforcing racial dominance in America. Specifically, *Native Son* responds to the crime of the lynching of black men that marked the nation's history in the late-nineteenth and first third of the twentieth centuries. For while the text portrays Bigger as a delinquent with violent impulses, the forces that drive him to murder are rooted in the specter of the lynch mob that hovers over him in the symbol of Mrs. Dalton. Described as a "white blur" standing "silent" and "ghostlike" at the door of Mary's bedroom, had she been sighted when she discovered Bigger and Mary alone in Mary's bedroom, she would have instantly convicted Bigger of rape and murder (85), and for her "to hint that he had committed a sex crime was to pronounce the death sentence" on him (243). Bigger's impulsive fear of being caught in Mary's room suggests his full awareness of the racial codes that punished black men for the slightest suggestion of sexual relations with white women. Here the novel provides symbolic commentary on the "panoply of rules, taboos, and penalties" through which white supremacy has historically ensured its dominance over blacks ("Bigger" 438).

That the rape of a white woman by a black man provides the central point of dramatic action in the novel speaks to America's centuries-old racist practices to ameliorate white anxiety about interracial sex and racial mixing. Following a familiar pattern during Bigger's trial, the prosection's insistence on the charge of rape generates the hysteria that reveals the psychology of the lynch mob. Most lynching of blacks involved the torture and hanging of the accused, who had no access to the judicial system. In the 1930s there was a "marked increase in the frequency of lynchings" (Shapiro 205); and highly publicized cases, like that of the famous Scottsboro Boys, which went into the courts, often involved trumped-up rape charges that often led to lynch mob hysteria (Shapiro 205-213). Biased newspaper accounts of the case of Robert Nixon, a young black Chicago man charged with the murder of a white woman, gave Wright the material for his novel. Modern readers, skeptical that an ostensibly objective press would portray Bigger as a "jungle beast" in the "grip of a brain-numbing sex passion" (279), need only refer to the *Chicago Tribune*'s portrayal of Nixon as a Negro whose "characteristics suggest an earlier link in [that] species" for proof that Wright hardly stretched the truth (Leavelle sec. 1, p. 6). In addition, the speed at which the case was hurried through the courts and the quick judgments rendered are examples of the process known as "legal lynchings" and the white public's desperate thirst for black execution.

While the central action of the novel turns on Bigger's reaction to the symbolic danger of white femininity for black men, the incidental treatment of Bessie's rape and murder by the public reinforces the disparity between the social values according to white versus black women. For while Wright's text reveals how the murder and alleged sexual violation of Mary incited mass public hysteria, the prosecutor used the murder and actual sexual violation of Bessie only to illustrate to the jury Bigger's capacity to rape and kill Mary:

> [t]hey were using his having killed Bessie to kill him for his having killed Mary, to cast him in a light that would sanction any action taken to destroy him. Though he had killed a black girl and a white girl, he knew that it would be for the death of the white girl that he would be punished. The black girl was merely "evidence." (331)

Wright fully understood that "white people never searched for Negroes who killed other Negroes. . . . crime for a Negro was only when he harmed whites, took other white lives, or injured white property" (331). As such the novel reveals the impunity with which the criminal justice system treated the victimization of black women and men. Because unequal justice and race and gender oppression still persist, *Native Son* remains not only a monument to a blot on U.S. history, but relevant to particular challenges American democracy still faces today.

For while the text captures and memorializes the violent reality of race relations in Depression-era Chicago, its visceral power compels emotional reactions that serve a larger end by engaging us all in questions of individual and societal responsibility. In a stroke of genius, Wright's Bigger gains a degree of our sympathy because of the environment he was given, the accidental nature of Mary's death, and the racist hostility the dominant culture had toward him, at the same time that the author forbids interpretation of him as an unequivocal victim by emphasizing the irreducibility of his individual responsibility. Building on the motifs introduced by the rat scene at the beginning, the text invites our consideration of this aspect of the situation through its tripartite structure.

The first two divisions of the narrative, "Fear" and "Flight," foreground the circumstances of Bigger's crimes to force us, like members of the jury in the third and final section, "Fate," to sort through the nexus of variables that determine the degree of his guilt. Unlike the jury, however, the reader of *Native Son* knows more about the conditions under which the crime occurred than either the prosecution or defense. From our third-party positions we are privy to Bigger's consciousness, the events that lead up to the crimes, and the discrepancies between the court's reconstruction of those events. We know, for example, that Bigger's denial of raping Mary is truthful. Thus, the reader, it would appear, is the ultimate determiner of justice in this case.

But Wright does not make our job easy, either. As readers we confront ambiguous tensions between the culpability of the environment and the degree of Bigger's individual agency that force us even more deeply into philosophical questions about selfhood and existence. Ethically, we can agree with Bigger's lawyer, Max, who elicits sympathy for Bigger by emphasizing his "powerless" victimization at the hands of "blind social forces" (390). Yet, as persuasive as Max is, Bigger as ultimate victim comes into conflict with our knowledge of his cold self-interest and bemused contempt for his friends, family, and perhaps most of all, his girlfriend, Bessie, whom he cold-bloodedly murders. So while Max's defense of his client contains the most grandiose rhetoric in the novel, his well-meaning attempt to save Bigger reduces him to a symbol for an ideological agenda that falls short of the possibility to achieve justice in this case. Max does not ever fully comprehend the truth of Bigger's deepest existential crisis. At the novel's close, the white lawyer, like Mrs. Dalton, remains symbolically "blind": the black Bigger obscures his vision of Bigger the human individual. At the same time, for himself, Bigger constructed the meanings of his murders as acts of "creation" for their ability to confer power onto black subjectivity in open defiance of the codes of white supremacy. They answered his need for individual affirmation and a form of redemption beyond his racial self that the world had denied him. The primacy of the individual, Wright's text insists, contravenes any ideological or purely sociological claims on reality.

Essential to the democratic requirements of civic engagement, *Native Son* requires deep and careful analysis of what it has meant to be black and white throughout American history. While the novel reaffirms the need for balance between America's desire for both individual freedom and national unity, it draws attention to how racism compromises and distorts these ideals; how gender and sexuality function to perpetuate racial divisions; and how failing to adequately address hatred, fear, and violence can only ensure and magnify their destructive power. As long as these fault lines exist in our system, *Native Son* is a complex all-important book in American literary history, especially accessible to the young who are willing to explore its painful truths and yet unanswered questions in their search for an American democracy that serves equally all of the nation's peoples.

## Works Cited

Ellison, Ralph. "Recent Negro Fiction." Review of *Native Son*, by Richard Wright. *New Masses* (5 August 1941): 22-26.

Gates, Henry Louis Jr. Preface. *Richard Wright: Critical Perspectives Past and Present*. Ed.Henry Louis Gates, Jr., and K. A. Appiah. New York: Amistad, 1993. xi-xvi.

Hall, James C. "Teaching Interculturalism: Symbiosis, Interpretation, and *Native Son*." *Approaches to Teaching Native Son*. Ed. James A. Miller. New York: The Modern Language Association of America, 1997. 81-88.

Leavelle, Charles. "Brick Slayer Is Likened to Jungle Beast." *Chicago Sunday Tribune* (5 June 1938): Sec. 1,p. 6.

Myrdal, Gunnar. *An American Dilemma: The Negro Problem and Modern Democracy*. New York: Harper and Row, 1944.

Shapiro, Herbert. *White Violence and Black Response: From Reconstruction to Montgomery*. Amherst: University of Massachusetts Press, 1988.

Wright, Richard. *Native Son*. 1940. The restored text established by the Library of America. New York: Perennial Classics, Harper & Row, 1998.

———. "How Bigger Was Born." *Native Son*. 1940. The restored text established by the Library of America. New York: Perennial Classics, Harper & Row, 1998. 431-461.

# Sweet Dreams: In Support of *Nightmares*

## Margaret Yatsevitch Phinney

When I heard Jack Prelutsky speak at a conference in 1986, I snapped up *Nightmares: Poems to Trouble Your Sleep* to add to my growing collection of books by this imaginative and creative children's poet. When I heard that the book had been targeted for banning, my first reaction was, "But why?"

It is usually a parent who object to *Nightmares*, and the grounds, almost invariably, are that the poems will terrify children who read or hear them. On the book-marketing website amazon.com, there were four reviews of *Nightmares*. The one dissenting and anonymous, but nevertheless vociferous, reviewer provides us with a colorful summary of the objections that have been voiced by parents in Wisconsin (Attacks 1993-1994, 231), Nevada (Attacks 1987-88, 33), Washington (Attacks 1989-90, 85), Iowa (Attacks 1993-94, 96-97), and other places around the country. He (or she) writes:

> What is wrong with you people? Since when is bodily mutilation and consumption of children by nightmarish ghouls appropriate reading for ANYONE, let alone elementary-school aged children? This man (Prelutsky) has a gift for the english [sic] language and for vivid prose. It is a shame that it was wasted on this garbage. I have no problem with spooky stories. I am an Annie Rice fan, for god's [sic] sake. This crosses the line into territory that should NEVER be explored by small children! (Jeffrey)

To avoid the suggestion of downplaying the ghoulish elements in the collection, let me acknowledge the most fiendish of the lot before I go any further. It is "The Ghoul," the eleventh of the twelve poems in the collection, that seems to cause the most consternation. This poem, buried at the back of the collection, is, indeed, grisly: the creature, who quietly waits outside the school, "lunges fiercely through the air / as they come out to play, / then grabs a couple by the hair / and drags them far away." Then "He cracks their bones and snaps their backs / and squeezes out their lungs, / he chews their

333

thumbs like candy snacks / and pulls apart their tongues." Yes, this *is* potentially frightful fodder for children when encountered too young or in an insecure context. One parent (*Attacks* 1994, 188) was concerned that children would be afraid to walk home from school after hearing or reading the poem. The other poems are not quite so ghoulish, but their protagonists also exist to capture you in one way or another: to haunt your souls, to drink your blood, to trap you under a spell, or just "to get you" for some indeterminate purpose.

Why then, we might ask, should such fare be within reach of children? For the rest of this chapter, I offer reasons—from the perspective of a parent, a teacher, and a former child (with a long memory)—for keeping this book on the shelves of our school and community libraries.

## The Issue of Fear: To Be Human Is to Risk

Since our beginnings we have lived with the anxiety that we may come to harm from natural disaster or at the hands of imagined creatures or fellow humans driven by ill-intent. Such fear is a natural protection, having built a keen awareness and acute wariness into our genetic makeup. We would not have survived tiger, typhoon, and tribal warfare had we not developed that healthy vigilance.

Fear's counterpart in the human spirit is an insatiable curiosity about our physical, social, and psychic worlds. Driven first, perhaps, by our need for food and living space and then by our need to know the earth and its secrets, we risked incredible danger to spread our species from Africa through Eurasia and across the land bridge to the "New World." We met ourselves coming and going, joining our genes with those who went before, by crossing the great oceans. In order to prevent ourselves from becoming immobilized by our fear of the unknown, we had to learn ways of coping with that fear. There is a myth that the Devil does not reveal his name, for, by so doing, he loses power. By assigning names and attributes to "the things that go bump in the night"—the feelings that have the potential to freeze us in our tracks—we are better able to know those feelings and develop strategies for dealing with them. In the prescientifc era, we wore talismans, submitted ourselves to spells, drank protective potions, or practiced safeguarding rituals. We created stories that told us what would save us from various creatures—a stake through the heart of the vampire, a silver bullet for the werewolf, a dish of milk for the tomten. These were strategies that allowed us to believe we could conquer—or at least manage—the unknown, and keep moving on.

As science taught us rationality, we let go of bogeymen, but we now realize that we actually *enjoy* the thrill and satisfaction of turning anxiety into constructive energy. Not only do we want to *know*, but we want to challenge ourselves to *feel* what we know. It isn't enough merely to map the Antarctic or the central African jungle, we must also challenge ourselves to ski that frigid continent and transect on foot that nearly impenetrable, viper-infested forest. Our challenges must be personal, kinesthetic, and visceral. We actually *relish* the prickle on the back of the neck when our senses or our imaginations confront the fearful unknown.

## Child Appeal

How then might this risk taking and self-invitation to face fear head-on translate for children? I would start by returning to my own childhood memories. Are any of you, dear readers, old enough to have heard this one?

Someone came knocking
At my wee, small door;
Someone came knocking,
I'm sure—sure—sure;
I listened, I opened,
I looked to left and right,
But nought there was a-stirring
In the still dark night.
Only the busy beetle
Tap-tapping in the wall,
Only from the forest
The screech-owl's call,
Only the cricket whistling
While the dew drops fall,
So I know not who came knocking,
At all, at all, at all.

The deliciously shivery memory of hearing my mother read Walter de la Mare's "Someone" when I was barely school-age—a poem written even before her own birth—has stayed imprinted in my psyche for upwards of half a century. I grew up deep in hill country, where natural sounds from the animal, plant, and mineral worlds could be heard by those who stood still a moment. There was always something both unnerving and invigorating about the sounds that I couldn't identify. This poem acknowledged and validated the ambivalence and emotional complexity of my own real experiences. I asked to hear it over and over, and when I could read, I read it to myself. It is not so far removed, in either its suspense or it's wording, from this excerpt from Prelutsky"s first *Nightmares* poem, "The Haunted

House":

> Filmy visions, ever flocking,
> dart through chambers, crudely mocking,
> rudely rapping, tapping, knocking
> on the crumbling doors.

So too, I remember the crawly image of

> Snip, snip, the scissors go,
> And Conrad cries out: Oh!
> Snip, snip they go so fast,
> And Conrad's thumbs are off at last!

from Dr. Heinrich Hoffmann's 1845 poem "Snip Snip—The Story of Little Suck-a-Thumb," Little Suck-a-Thumb was *warned* to stop sucking his thumb and suffered the grisly consequences when he disobeyed. When, at seven or eight, I heard Hoffmann's poems, I found them horrifying and funny at the same time. Even as a child, I realized that the ideas were preposterous, for it was totally outside my life experience that anyone or anything would do such a thing as cutting off the thumbs of a thumb sucker. I could imagine the child-eating maniacs in "Hansel and Gretel," "Baba Yaga," "Little Red Riding Hood," and "Snow White" with a kind of ambivalent detachment, a nervous amusement that such *ideas* could exist, balanced by the surety that they were total fantasy.

I did not suffer from unwarranted fears as a result of hearing such scary and violent words, nor did I think all grownups were evil, nor did I believe that "That great, long legg'd scissor man" would suddenly appear to snip off my soggy thumbs. Why so? I believe, even as the back of my neck prickled, I knew I was safe. Because my parents smiled as they read or recited, because I knew they loved me and looked out for my safety, because they had always clearly distinguished between fantasy and reality, I was free to enjoy the thrill of being *safely* scared. Even as my primal brain said, "Flee," my intellectual mind inwardly laughed, knowing that it was all just imagination at play. I could suspend disbelief and allow terrible images to surface, while simultaneously remaining secure in the comfort of a parent's lap. Furthermore, I could regulate the intensity simply by closing the book and going to dinner. The *ownership* of my anxiety belonged to *me* and was within *my* control . That gave me pride and confidence about my ability to handle my own emotional state. What a gift this array of stories and poems gave me!

I also look at children from the outside in through my years of experience as an elementary teacher. One of our biggest problems as teachers is finding material that interests children—that keeps them coming back for more. The way children become competent readers is through extended practice, practice based on their own choices. Many children get this practice when they discover reading material that they find emotionally appealing, material that is built around favorite characters, themes, or plot structures. Some prefer "tame" stories like those about Clifford, the big red dog, or Curious George the mischievous monkey, or *The American Girl* series. Others only want to read imaginative, high-action fantasies like the Harry Potter stories, C. S. Lewis's *Chronicles of Narnia*, or Tolkien's Hobbit books. But for some, the scarier the books are, the better. These children voraciously read the Goosebumps books and the irreverent words of poets like Prelutsky, Silverstein, and Dahl. They seek out the forbidden and the profane, as much to give themselves relief from rigid institutional constraints as to fire their thirsty imaginations. When they are in the company of friends, in the safety of a supportive home or classroom environment, and are given time to talk and wonder and otherwise explore their feelings about a spooky poem or story, they engage with enthusiasm and humor. They come back to the well-written, emotionally appealing poems and stories over and over again. It is a teacher's dream when children become "hooked" on reading for pleasure.

As Paula Fox pointed out in an earlier volume (Karolides 319), we have the legal right in this country to express ourselves, and to choose what we wish to read. Although I support the notion that parents have the right to make decisions about what they feel is and isn't appropriate for their *own* children, they do not have the right to tell the rest of us what is tolerable for *our* children. Just because a parent's intuition tells her that *Nightmares* is inappropriate for *her* child does not mean it is inappropriate for *all* children. I loved poems and stories like these. They drew me ever further into reading. They helped develop that tolerance for uncertainty that all good readers need to develop in order to continue reading a mystery story or a suspenseful drama. *And my parents and teachers taught me how to keep such stories in perspective.*

Rather than preventing contact with provocative literature, we must help children understand and analyze the wide variety of material to which they are constantly exposed. Otherwise, when they are away from the safety of the protective bubble their parents have tried to create and they stumble across something truly frightening on the Internet, or see a Freddy Krueger movie during a sleepover at a neighbor's house, they will, indeed, be afraid to walk home from school. How can young people develop critical thinking skills if someone else has narrowed the choice of materials available for analysis and comparison? If we do not teach children from an early age—when we still have the opportunity to help them develop balanced perspectives—that they have the legal right to express their ideas and to make personal choices, how will they even *become* critical thinkers?

## Inaccessibility

Another argument to counter the assertion that this book will scare small children is that it really isn't *accessible* to young children because of the density of the vocabulary and the complexity of the poetic structures. It would be the rare six-year-old, indeed, who could read

> Shapeless wraiths devoid of feeling
> hover blindly by the ceiling
> ranting, chanting, shrieking, squealing
> promises of dread.

Even if seven-year-olds were able to attempt pronunciation of the words, what meaning would they make of it? My expertise in early literacy development tells me that most primary children would neither know the meaning of at least six key words in this sentence (*wraiths, devoid, hover, ranting, chanting,* and *dread*), nor would they have enough experience with syntax to be able to sort out the structure of the last two lines. I confirmed this by unemotionally reading these lines to a bright, literate-for-her-age, worldly, TV-wise seven-year-old acquaintance. I asked her to listen and tell me what the poem meant. When I was done she looked at me blankly and shrugged, slightly embarrassed that she didn't have an answer for me. Young children are immunized from the impact of poetry like this by their lack of experience. And any young child who pulled this book off the shelf by happenstance while casually browsing and who did not like scary material, would quickly return it because the skeleton illustrating the cover signals the reader that this is a scary book.

## Cultural Heritage

Another element that takes the fearful edge off this collection is that there are no "new" creatures in Prelutsky's poems. These poems extend a long cultural genealogy of imaginary creatures: the participants in this collection—ghosts, will o' the wisps, bogeymen, vampires, dragons, trolls, witches, ogres, werewolves, wizards, ghouls, and skeletons—have all been around a very long time in (mostly) Western European folklore. They are the protagonists in oral tales, written stories, nursery rhymes, movies, TV programs, and theater. Their names and descriptors are part of our everyday language: will o' the wisp is a synonym for elusiveness; songs of longing are "haunting"; an anorexic person is described as "skeletal"; a mean woman is "a witch"; an unscrupulous lawyer is a "bloodsucking vampire." By the time children are in the intermediate grades and are experienced enough with language to handle the complexity of the poetic structures and the density of the vocabulary, they will have heard of all these creatures in multiple contexts. In fact, it is *necessary* that young people know these creatures and what they stand for if they are to understand the cultural nuances of the English language. The poems simply describe and elaborate upon the cultural perception of these spooky creatures that we have inherited through the eons.

Fear of fear, then, is not a valid argument for banning this book.

## The Quality of the Writing

I have left the most important issue until last in a shameless effort to have this the point that stays with you as you leave my arguments for keeping *Nightmares* on the shelves. The most relevant of all questions is whether or not there is literary value in Prelutsky's poems. If there is none, if, as the critic claims, this work is merely unholy trash, then the point is moot: why spend our library funds on trash? Q.E.D. But if, on the other hand, the work has literary merit, then it *must* be available for enjoyment and study. The value is there, in spades.

In the absence of a television when I was growing up, I was immersed in literature from earliest childhood, and rhythmical, rhyming poetry was my favorite genre. I loved the beat of metered poems like "The Wreck of the Hesperus" and "The Cremation of Sam McGee." It felt like my mother was singing when she read such poems aloud. Later, when I could take over the reading myself, and in the absence of the ability to carry a tune, I entertained myself by reciting these musical poems endlessly to myself. When I picked up *Nightmares* I turned first to the poem about the dragon, my favorite imaginary creature. Only four lines told me this was perfect meter, a poem one could sway to.

> In a faraway, faraway forest
> lies a treasure of infinite worth,
> but guarding it closely forever
> looms a being as old as the earth.

I know firsthand how hard it is to combine ideas, vocabulary, rhyme, and rhythm and still come up with perfection, but here is perfection. Prelutsky has a master's ear for creating traditional rhyming poetry, and all of the poems in this collection are beautifully metered, with rhymes that never feel contrived.

And oh! The imagery! Prelutsky is so generous with figurative language. Imagine a creature "as old as the earth," "It's body is big as a boulder," and "It's teeth are far sharper than daggers" all describing this ancient and perennial "Dragon of Death." Metaphors like "steely sharp claws," "His eyes are pools of fire/his skin is icy white," and fingers that are "ten bony sticks" are woven throughout the collection to enhance the images of the creatures he describes. Rich pickings for a teacher who is helping middle school children understand literary imagery!

Prelutsky is also a master at incorporating the sounds of language into his poems. Nearly every poem, for example, has at least one alliterative line. The hiss of "In that sulfurous, sunless and sinister place" put us directly into the fiery depths where the Bogeyman lives. The hard "Bs" and "Gs" combined with the assonance of the "Os" emphasize the hardness of the troll: "His blood is black and boiling hot, he gurgles ghastly groans." Ono-matopoeia, too, gives sound to his creature. You can *hear* his skeletons dance on the page:

> And they'll dance in their bones,
> in their bare bare bones,
> with the click and the clack
> and the chitter and the chack
> and the clatter and the chatter
> of their bare bare bones.

Children love the sounds of words that fit well together. Many's the time I have read an onomatopoeic or alliterative poem to my students, then listened to them repeating the "soundful" phrases as they run out to recess. Creating good sound combinations in poetry is one way to build appreciation in children.

And finally, Prelutsky offers us the richest of vocabulary! In my experiences as a reading teacher, one of the gaps between good readers in upper elementary school and those who struggle is lack of exposure to more advanced vocabulary. Often the material that is used to teach reading in the primary grades contains very controlled, sterile words designed to support an artificial sequence of reading skills rather than develop breadth of language. When children move into the intermediate grades and middle school, they start to encounter less common words in their reading material.

Those who have not had extensive literary exposure outside school find themselves missing meaning because they are unfamiliar with so many of the words. Consider the vocabulary in this verse from "The Haunted House":

> Revenants on misty perches
> taunt the ghost that lunges, lurches
> as it desperately searches
> for its vanished head.
> Shapeless wraiths devoid of feeling
> hover blindly by the ceiling
> ranting, changing, shrieking, squealing
> promises of dread.

I know more sixth graders than I care to count who would be unfamiliar with seven or eight of the words in this verse alone. Although this poem has, perhaps, the heaviest vocabulary load of all the poems in the collection, the kinds of words he uses here are found throughout the work. Prelutsky offers us invitations to try out and explore richly descriptive words, words that give us more language tools with which to talk and think about our world. And—for those who care—knowledge of such words raise verbal scores on those ubiquitous achievement, aptitude, and verbal I.Q. tests!

I quoted an anonymous critic earlier as saying that Prelutsky "has a gift for the english [sic] language and for vivid prose. It is a shame that it was wasted on this garbage." To me that says that children who want to take the risk of safely exploring their emotional courage should not have well-written material through which to make that journey. However, children will find the material that interests them, one way or another. Let it be good.

## Acknowledgment: Understanding the Concerns

"But," you might say, "you are a grown-up. You can distinguish between fantasy and reality. You know the ideas and images are products of a fertile imagination applied to cultural legacies. Children don't have that maturity or background." Yes, let me acknowledge the fearful parents' view for a moment, for I agree that there is a time and place for literature, any literature, but especially provocative literature.

One part of that timing and placement is knowing the listeners, respecting their sensibilities, and providing outlets for exploration of their fears or misunderstandings. This includes knowing their developmental levels (as Scot Smith has discussed elsewhere in this volume) as well as knowing each individual's interests and tolerances. When the anonymous

critic said, "This crosses the line into territory that should NEVER be
explored by small children!" I would be inclined to agree, where the
emphasis is on "*small* children."

Very young children, through about age six or seven, need time to learn
to distinguish fantasy from reality. If they still believe in Santa Claus, the
Easter Bunny, and the Tooth Fairy, they don't have enough life experience
yet to realize that certain things aren't physically possible or intellectually
logical, nor have they developed the self-confidence that allows them to
control and conquer their fears. Belief comes easily in the absence of
practical experience. Children still living in fantasy worlds *are* vulnerable
to being frightened by fantasy stories and images. I have witnessed this
vulnerability toward imaginative literature a number of times. A friend read
Sendak's *Where the Wild Things Are* to her four-year-old son one evening,
an only child who slept in his own room in a large old Victorian house. The
story terrified him because he believed the walls in his room would turn into
the place where the wild things live. He refused to sleep there: his parents
had to move his bed into their own room. It was a full year before he was
developmentally ready to see that the book was fantasy and could move back
to his own (redecorated) room.

As a teacher, I would not read the poems in *Nightmares* to children in
the primary (K-2) grades. I would want to be sure that *all* the children are
very clear on the difference between fantasy and reality before I deliberately
introduced the collection at any grade. However, I would want the collection
available in the library for children to choose if they are interested. Their
interest will draw them, unwittingly, into an appreciation for quality writing
while supporting their need to explore the dark side of human nature through
clearly fictional creatures.

## Solution: Common Sense

Isn't this a matter of common sense among thinking, observant parents
and teachers? The fact that a parent reads Prelutsky's "Ghoul" and
recognizes that it would truly frighten her six-year-old son is an indication
that the parent knows her child—knowledge that would guide her not to read
the poem to him. But the parent of a six-year-old child down the street might
recognize that his child, who is confident in her understanding that ghouls
are make-believe, finds humor in such nonsense. He might not hesitate to
settle securely with his daughter in a soft chair and laugh with her over the
grisly humor, spiced richly with descriptive words and images as the ghoul
"swallows their toes like toasted tarts/and gobbles down their heads." *Both*
parents must have access to the book to make the appropriate decision.

Q.E.D.

# Works Cited

*Attacks on the Freedom to Learn.* Washington, D.C., People For the American Way, 1987-1988, 1989-1990, 1993-1994 Reports, 1988, 1990, 1994.

Dahl, Roald, *Revolting Rhymes.* Illustrated by Quentin Blake. New York: Alfred A. Knopf, Publisher, 1983.

de La Mare, Walter. "Someone" in *Poems Children Will Sit Still For: A Selection for the Primary Grades,* edited by Beatrice Schenck de Regniers, Eva Moore, & Mary Michales White. New York: Scholastic Books Services, 1969.

Hoffmann, Heinrich. *The Ultimate Shockheaded Peter or Horrible Stories and Noisy Pictures: A Junk Opera.* Adapted by Martyn Jacquies, edited and translated by Lammchen Kralle. Berlin: Autoenhaus-Verlag Plinke, 1999.

"Jeffrey Dahmer Meets Shel Silverstein." http://www.amazon.com./exec/obidos/tg/stores/detail/-/books/0688045898/customer. reviews/ref=pm _dp_in_6_7/107-3454476-7440555. October 17, 2000.

Karolides, Nicholas J., Lee Burress, and John M. Kean. *Censored Books: Critical Viewpoints.* Metuchen, N.J.: Scarecrow Press, 1993.

Prelutsky, Jack. *Nightmares: Poems to Trouble Your Sleep.* Illustrated by Arnold Lobel. New York: Greenwillow Books, 1976.

Silverstein, Shel. *Where the Sidewalk Ends.* New York: Harper & Row, 1974.

Tolkien, J. R. R. *The Two Towers.* Boston: Houghton Mifflin, 1954/1994.

# The Pigman's Story:
# Teaching Paul Zindel in the 21st Century

## Grant T. Smith

There is much *not* to like about John Conlan and Lorraine Jensen, the principal protagonists in Paul Zindel's classic novel, *The Pigman*. John is clearly the instigator of much of the mayhem that follows in their wake; Lorraine passively acquiesces to John's mischief. But both are liars. They swear (or at least John says 3@#$% when he gets angry). They abuse drugs. Beer, wine, and cigarettes seem to be their staple diet. They label all adult authority figures as morons. Even a pet store clerk is labeled "this nasty floorwalker" when he tells them not to feed the animals (77). They destroy public and private property. Neither urinals nor a friend's home is safe when they are around. They whine endlessly about the "phoniness" of others while never recognizing their own flaws. John laments the absence of affection from his parents; yet, when he has the chance to show genuine affection to Lorraine, he becomes a sexist bore. A fellow classmate is called a "four-eyed dimwit" (3), and according to John, each of their friends "had a problem all his own" (119). They are extraordinarily egocentric teenagers. Quite frankly, adult readers may find it difficult to connect with them as real characters, much less like them.

Would I want to have either of them as a son or a daughter? Would I want my own children to associate with them? Would I want to teach them in a ninth-grade English class? Well, probably not. Even though they are obviously sensitive youngsters and very good writers, when I go into the men's room, I want to be reasonably sure that the urinal is not going to explode beneath me. And I do not want to be in the middle of a spelling quiz when twenty-five apples start rolling down the aisles toward me. Such juvenile mean-spiritedness doesn't appeal to me. However, my fourteen-year-old son told me after he finished the book that he would very much like to know John and Lorraine, and he certainly saw them with much more sympathy and compassion than I. Ultimately, this "perceptive" view of teenagers is what saves *The Pigman* as a *bildungsroman* novel. And this is why I have even taught *The Pigman* in a sophomore English class.

These two deplorable characters may distort the world they see, but this distortion resonates with many teenagers who feel disenfranchised from the world around them and vulnerable to any charismatic figure who promises excitement and attention. John and Lorraine live in dysfunctional families, but their families reflect the fragmentation of modern society that teenagers deal with every day. John remains emotionally distant from Lorraine and Pignati, the lonely, old man they "befriend," but this distance mirrors his mother's and father's emotional unavailability to him when he most needs it. Lorraine, whose views of sex have been warped by her mother's sexual paranoia, yearns for an emotional connection to any male teen. Teen readers can thus connect with John and Lorraine because these characters signify much of what teenagers know as "reality."

To my son, John and Lorraine were not indefensible. John and Lorraine may tag Miss Reillen as the "Cricket" because she is overweight, yet they do befriend a lonely widower who needs desperately some companionship in his life. These teenagers skip school and miss completely why they (more than anyone else) should pay attention to the amendments to the Constitution that guarantee their freedom of expression. Yet, they ponder in a poignant way various meanings of life: *carpe diem*, influential adults, relationship with others, premature death, respect, and responsibility. And any young adult reader who has experienced divorce in his or her family will read the irony and complexity in Lorraine's conclusion: "It makes me think that love between a man and a woman must be the strongest thing in the world."

Every adolescent who pleads with his or her parents to be "treated as an adult" and to be given "adult" privileges will live John and Lorraine's fantasy evening in the Pigman's home wistfully and romantically. And those readers will come crashing to earth when only a few pages later they live John and Lorraine's "morning after" that is filled with harsh words and hard glares. John and Lorraine learn that being an adult is easy when you wear costumes and a fake mustache. It is much more difficult when the toast burns and the garbage needs to be taken out. Teen readers who have strained relationships with "The Old Lady" and the "Bore" may identify with John and Lorraine who understandably rebel against sexually repressed, abusive, compulsive, and dishonest parents. However, those same readers will take note when John and Lorraine (literally looking at life through new glasses) finally admit their complicity in the Pigman's death and their role in building their own cages. "There was no one else to blame anymore," says John. "Our life would be what we made of it—nothing more, nothing less" (148–149). As many readers have noted, they feel they know John and Lorraine very well because of all that the author reveals about them (Mertz 28).

When I taught *The Pigman* to a class of tenth graders in Las Vegas, Nevada, I taught the novel as a classical *bildungsroman* novel, a story that deals with the development of a young person from adolescence to maturity. It satisfies all of the elements of a "rite of passage" tale or an "education novel." It is autobiographical. The protagonists grow up in a setting that they feel constrains them socially and intellectually. Their parents are hostile to their creative instincts and antagonistic to their ambitions or new ideas. Lorraine and John don't actually flee this repressive atmosphere—they are stuck at home and at school—but they do find a refuge in Pignati's home, where their real education begins. They have one "near sex" experience that initiates them to adulthood. They do some serious soul searching when their friends trash Pignati's home and, of course, when Pignati dies, and this soul searching leads to a new vision of life for them. Zindel claims that John and Lorraine experience an epiphany of sorts at the end of the novel (*Teacher's Guides* 1).

I followed *The Pigman* with the classic film *Rebel Without a Cause*. The students had little difficulty seeing the parallels between the book and the movie: the anti-hero protagonists who have redeeming qualities, the conflict with authority figures, the musings on the meaning of life, the attempt to playact adult roles, the flirtation with death, and the loss of innocence which (at least for Jim Start) leads to wisdom and reconciliation. The students also had little difficulty identifying the parallels between Judy in *Rebel* and Lorraine in *The Pigman*—both girls played supportive roles to the more dynamic boys.

After viewing and discussing *Rebel Without a Cause*, the class next read *The Catcher in the Rye*. Again the students were quick to recognize the conventions of a rite of passage novel in *Catcher,* and they saw many parallels between Holden and John, not the least of which that both boys are counseled to see a therapist! But at this point I asked the students to revisit *The Pigman* and *Catcher* from two different points of view—an adult point of view and (if the student was a male) from a girl's point of view. Some of the girls in my class felt that John remained immature throughout the novel, even after the death of Mr. Pignati, a death for which he never fully accepts responsibility.

If you are fifteen years old and struggling with all of the pains of puberty, it is about as difficult to read *The Pigman* from an adult point of view as it is for a parent, struggling with the pains of raising that fifteen-year-old, to read *The Pigman* from an adolescent's point of view. But as Wayne C. Booth argues in "Censorship and the Values of Fiction," teenage readers often overlook Holden's deficiencies and Salinger's subtle contrasts between what Holden says and what Holden does. Teenagers tend to see only Holden's sensitivity, compassion, generosity, and struggle for a pure world (Booth 162-163). They tend to overlook Holden's deficiencies: his habitual exaggerations, his nonstop criticism of everything, his inability to shed his Peter Pan persona and live a mature life. The same can be said of John Conlan (and to a lesser extent of Lorraine Jensen). Teen readers may tend to overlook John's and Lorraine's deficiencies, focusing instead on their vulnerability and supposed victimization. These two characters are "role models" for teenage readers primarily in their representation of the consequences a person suffers when he or she makes a dumb decision. To them life is a series of games played at the expense of those unfortunate enough to get in their way. Is this readily apparent to a young adult reader? Probably not, and so this is where English teachers enter the picture.

The first questions I ask my students are, "Can we trust these narrators? Why or why not?" John is an admitted liar, and Lorraine is so filled with psychoanalytic garble that their role as reliable narrators is severely tested. In many ways, John and Lorraine's confessions are dramatic monologues where, speaking from a moment of crisis, they disclose much more about their own "true" nature than they do about the phony world around them. Also, because the reader only knows the story from John and Lorraine's point of view, the reader must either take their account as truth, or consider the possibility that there are other "true stories" out there. These stories may either contradict John and Lorraine's story or, at the very least, add a dimension that the protagonists have (for whatever reason) omitted or changed. This is a profound concept for young adult readers to consider: Whom do we trust? How do we determine what is true? How do I shape truth in my own narratives?

Huck Finn and Holden Caulfield are often classified as unreliable narrators or "naive narrators" because they lack a sophisticated comprehension of the events they describe. Given their admitted tendency to exaggerate and distort events, John and Lorraine may be placed in this same classification, and the reader must be wary of anything they report. The reader must consider the narrators' motives, alternative points of view, and alternative judgments. If John and Lorraine are fallible in their narrative, can we believe their descriptions of their parents? Can we trust their account of the party at Pignati's house? An adolescent who begins to read and question with this frame of mind quickly becomes a mature, sophisticated reader, a reader capable of understanding the complexity of narratology in fiction. Readers of *The Pigman* cannot rely solely upon the narrators to provide insights of the human condition, or relationships, or the society in which John and Lorraine reside; the readers must glean those insights themselves.

Because *The Pigman* is narrated in alternate chapters by a boy and a girl, the novel also offers readers a wonderful opportunity to study gender differences. I challenged my students to examine carefully the voice of each narrator. What did John include in his narrative that Lorraine left out or modified? When did they contradict one another? What motivated each narrator? How did each narrator respond to the same conflict? How did John perceive himself? How did Lorraine perceive herself? How did each narrator perceive others? Who is beautiful? Who is not? How do both characters perceive relationships? John writes the last chapter. What would Lorraine have written? There are any number of questions that can be raised about gender differences and similarities in this novel.

As I stated above, *The Pigman* is a *bildungsroman* novel. But the *bildungsroman* is generally interpreted as the male rite of passage. The male experience is the universal experience. But today we have read enough of Carol Gilligan, Nancy Chodorow, and Jean Baker Miller to know that Freud, Piaget, and Kohlberg may not have been speaking for everyone when they defined the individuation process. Today we know that there are certain assumptions in this "universal" individuation process that may be appropriate of a boy's experience but not necessarily for a girl's experience. For example, one assumption in the *bildungsroman* is that there are choices and opportunities that wait the protagonist, and that the protagonist has the independence and mobility to make those choices and take advantage of those opportunities. This is not necessarily a given for a girl. Even today, a girl knows that her "independence" or destiny involves not only the decisions that she freely makes, but the dialectic of history, social structures, politics, and the behaviors of others around her. Lorraine learns this quickly enough when John yells at her to take out the garbage . . . after all, she made it.

John Conlan may reasonably expect that the sexual experience traditionally present in a *bildungsroman* will ultimately be a positive experience; the same cannot be said for Lorraine, and her "sexually repressed" mother knows this. In a male rite of passage there is the symbolic rebirth, a symbolic acceptance by society of the "new autonomous man" who has much wisdom and experience to contribute to others. But even though we have enjoyed thirty years of the second wave of feminism, many girls still suspect that life does not offer the limitless possibilities that it apparently offers boys. Indeed, until recently, many female protagonists in rite-of-passage novels ended up married, mad, or dead! One of my students in Las Vegas suggested that John's mother was all three! And finally, Gilligan suggests that this "privileged" image of the separate, independent, autonomous self may not even fit the image of a girl who finds her identity in connection with others. I found that my students responded with enthusiasm and maturity as we discussed gender issues in *The Pigman*.

Paul Zindel wrote *The Pigman* in 1968. I was surprised to read that the novel is on any censor's hit list. Paul Zindel is a Pulitzer Prize–winning author. It is true that Zindel has characters who drink, smoke, swear, steal, lie, trash another person's home, and generally distrust any authority figure more than thirty years old! Indeed, from John and Lorraine's description of their teachers and parents, I'm not sure I would trust them either! But ultimately, the novel is an excellent example of ethical fiction because it places opposites side by side. John and Lorraine are next to Pignati, and this confrontation with difference forces the teens to learn from a stranger. This is what strangers do for us. Strangers make us see beyond ourselves and our narrow immature definitions of morality or reality. Strangers force us to confront our fears, prejudices, weaknesses, ignorance, and desires. Alive, Pignati forces John and Lorraine to reexamine how they want to live. Life is what you make of it, says John (159). Dead, Pignati forces John and Lorraine to discard their cavalier attitude toward death and accept its finality. This is what ethical literature does. We should teach it.

John and Lorraine may not have many values that adults can admire—but they ultimately realize that they cannot continue to live by their own rules if they hope to participate fully in society. John and Lorraine learn from Pignati that "love" is not playacting in another's clothes. Love is sharing with another everything that is important in one's life. "Love between a man and a woman must be the strongest thing in the world," says Lorraine, who has experienced blessedly little love in her life.

John and Lorraine learn that being an adult means more than the freedom to skip school and bomb urinals. Being an adult means taking the time to have fun and sharing that fun with someone who means everything to you. But being an adult also means that sometimes that fun and sharing leads to disaster, and you can't always make amends for those mistakes. Being an adult means accepting responsibility for being stupid. John and Lorraine learn they can no longer blame their parents or the cops or the teachers or even their friends for the cages they build around themselves. John and Lorraine learn that a loss of innocence comes at a painful cost to themselves, but it may come at a far greater cost to another. These are valuable lessons to learn when you are a sophomore in high school.

Flannery O'Connor said that only people with hope and courage read novels. Those are the people who dare to take long looks at themselves and dare to live others' experiences (78). John and Lorraine take a long look at themselves. They dare to share in Pignati's experiences and thereby gain what this stranger had to give. We should all have the courage to take that same look ourselves.

# Keeping Their Parents Happy:
## Roald Dahl's *Revolting Rhymes*

**David Furniss**

> I guess you think you know this story.
> You don't. The real one's much more gory.
> The phoney one, the one you know,
> Was cooked up years and years ago,
> And made to sound all soft and sappy
> Just to keep the children happy.

So begins Roald Dahl's "revolting" retelling of "Cinderella," but in fact, I'd say that these lines are an appropriate introduction to all of *Revolting Rhymes*, Dahl's satiric take on six classic stories for children: "Cinderella," "Jack and the Beanstalk," "Snow White," "Goldilocks and the Three Bears," "Little Red Riding Hood," and "The Three Little Pigs." While not all of the tales are as "gory" as the first one, in which the Prince chops off the heads of Cinderella's two stepsisters, all echo the sentiment expressed in the six lines above: there's more to these stories than the little-kid versions will tell us. As I will argue later, I believe that Dahl had in mind an audience in the later primary grades and above, still young but ready to move beyond simple and "safe" nursery rhymes and Disney-treated fairy tales, readers discovering the delights of irony and parody, of poking fun. And while the clear intent of the book is to entertain, the tales portray courageous and resourceful young people, not victims of wolves or evil witches.

We know, of course, that nursery rhymes and fairy tales are not really "safe"; at least earlier versions of them would not have earned the Disney seal of approval. In the Grimm telling of "Cinderella," for example, the evil stepsisters chop off their toes in order to slip into Cinderella's glass slippers, and later, birds pick out their eyes as they ride to Cinderella's wedding. A child in the eighteenth century might have heard about a girl in red who meets a wolf in the woods and then encounters him again at her grandmother's house, dressed in Grandmother's clothing. The climax is more

"gory" and suggestive than in later retellings, including Dahl's: the girl
removes her clothes at the wolf's request, whereupon the wolf eats her up.
The French writer Charles Perrault is often credited or blamed for revising
the Red Riding Hood story, along with other familiar tales such as
"Cinderella" and "Sleeping Beauty," at the end of the seventeenth century.
Disney's *Cinderella* drew on Perrault and gave us safe magic in the phrase
"Bibbidy-bobbidy-boo."

While I doubt anyone would be troubled by Disney's fairy godmother,
many have been outraged by Dahl's *Witches*, which was one of the ten most
censored books between 1982 and 1994, according to the People For the
American Way. While *Witches* is clearly the most controversial of Dahl's
books, a quick look at the American Library Association's *1999 Banned
Books Resource Guide* shows several others have also been attacked: The
*BFG* [Big Friendly Giant], *Charlie and the Chocolate Factory*, *The
Enormous Crocodile*, *George's Marvelous Machine*, *James and the Giant
Peach*, *Matilda*, *The Minipins*, *Rhyme Stew*, and of course, *Revolting
Rhymes*. Dahl has been the particular target of censors in Stafford County,
Virginia, who have repeatedly cited the author's work for "encouraging
children to disobey their parents."

In the 1990s, *Revolting Rhymes* was attacked three times, according to
the guide to banned books I cited above. Objections were raised to violence
in the tales, the presence of witches, and the word "slut" in "Cinderella." A
parent in Massachusetts claimed that the book was "offensive and inappropriate for children," which led to its removal in that community's elementary
schools. The objectors in Stafford County apparently found no incitements
to disobedience in this particular case, but still attacked the *Revolting
Rhymes* for "spoofing" nursery rhymes.

Of course, the six tales in *Revolting Rhymes* are not nursery rhymes at
all, nor are they the sort of stories that would appeal to the very young
audience that reads nursery rhymes. As a matter of fact, children don't
usually *read* nursery rhymes. To the charge that *Revolting Rhymes* are
"spoofs," however, they must stand guilty: Dahl's purpose is quite obviously
to satirize these folk tales. Each of them has one or more humorous twists on
the familiar story. For example, Cinderella in the beginning is spoiled and
demanding, not sweet and innocent. To the fairy she cries,

> I want a dress! I want a coach!
> And earrings and a diamond brooch!
> And silver slippers, two of those!
> And lovely nylon panty-hose!
> Done up like that I'll guarantee
> The handsome prince will fall for me!

Her ugly, evil stepsisters find her glass slipper on a case of beer after the ball and manage to switch one of their oversized shoes for it before the Prince comes along. When the Prince sees whom the shoe fits, he chops off her head and also that of the other stepsister. Cinderella experiences a change of heart: "How could I marry anyone who does that sort of thing for fun?" She asks the fairy to find her a "decent man," and is awarded a "lovely feller" who makes marmalade. The ending of this tale is familiar, not twisted: "Their house was filled with smiles and laughter. And they were happy ever after."

The twist in the Goldilocks story is that Goldilocks is the villain. Dahl tweaks both the tale and protective parents in the opening lines:

> This famous wicked little tale
> Should never have been put on sale.
> It is a mystery to me
> Why loving parents cannot see
> That this is actually a book
> About a brazen little crook.
> Had I the chance I wouldn't fail
> To clap young Goldilocks in jail.

After devouring the three bears' breakfast, breaking Baby Bear's chair (a precious antique), and soiling the sheets of their beds, Goldilocks gets hers:

> ". . . go upstairs," the Big Bear said,
> "Your porridge is upon the bed.
> But as it's inside mademoiselle,
> You'll have to eat her up as well."

In the Snow White story, the dwarfs are really ex-jockeys who have "one shocking vice": betting on horses. Snow White steals the magic mirror and asks it to reveal a secret, not who is fairest, but which horse will win the steeplechase. The mirror makes Snow White and the dwarfs rich:

> Thereafter, every single day,
> The mirror made the bookies pay.
> Each Dwarf and Snow White got a share,
> And each was soon a millionaire,
> Which shows that gambling's not a sin
> Provided that you always win.

It's perhaps surprising that no one has objected to the message in the last two lines, but then older readers may have to admit that Dahl has a point there.

Red Riding Hood appears in two of the tales. In the story that bears her name, she remains fully clothed, and rather than being eaten, she coolly shoots the wolf herself, changing her hood for a wolfskin coat. In the next tale, she receives a phone call for help from one of the Little Pigs, whose brothers have been eaten by a second big bad wolf. She obligingly shoots this one as well, but the story doesn't end there.

> Ah, Piglet, you must never trust
> Young ladies from the upper crust.
> For now, Miss Riding Hood, one notes,
> Not only has *two* wolfskin coats,
> But when she goes from place to place,
> She has a PIGSKIN TRAVELING CASE.

As for the story of Jack and his beanstalk, Jack's mean and abusive mother is the first to climb it. The Giant uses his nose to locate her (he smells the blood of an English mum, I suppose) and quickly gobbles her up. This doesn't sadden Jack particularly, but it does demonstrate to him the virtues of bathing.

> "By Christopher!" Jack cried. "By gum!
> The Giant's eaten up my mum!
> He smelled her out! She's in his belly!
> I had a hunch that she was smelly."

Fully scrubbed, he avoids detection and steals the Giant's treasure. "'A bath,' he said, 'does seem to pay. I'm to have one every day.'"

I described these tales and quoted from them in some detail to do more than show the clever ways Dahl twists and "spoofs" these six children's stories. I also hoped to give a sampling of the sophisticated language in the poems. All are written in the same, singsong rhythm that echoes "Twinkle, Twinkle, Little Star" and so many other children's rhymes. Yet, as I stated earlier, the reader he has in mind is not a small child. These tales are designed to appeal to older children raised on the other stories, but who now want to see themselves as more than children. Dahl's language speaks to them, as when he replaces "Once upon a time" with "The animal I really dig/Above all others is the pig," calls Goldilocks "that little toad, that nosey thieving little louse," or reflects on the evil queen eating a beef heart she thinks is Snow White's: "I only hope she cooked it well. Boiled heart can be as tough as hell." The objectors in Virginia may be right in assuming that some three-year-olds wouldn't appreciate someone tinkering with Mary and her lamb, but Dahl wants to tell his readers that they're smart and sophisticated. We can hear this when he takes on the protective parent role, winking all the while, in quoting his evil Goldilocks:

> She bellows, "What a lousy chair!"
> And uses *one* disgusting word
> That luckily you've never heard.
> (I dare not write it, even hint it.
> Nobody would ever print it.)

Dahl also reaches out to these older young readers in the way he portrays his young protagonists. The young people in these tales are much stronger, not to mention more interesting, than their counterparts in the traditional stories. The only main character who isn't admirable in some ways is Dahl's uncivilized Goldilocks, who is truly a bad kid. The others are quite different. Snow White is not a victim awaiting rescue. Cinderella is at first a spoiled brat, and Dahl's readers certainly would see this and also recognize that in the end, she's no longer greedy or grasping, and thus more deserving of her happy-ever-after life. As for Red Riding Hood, she is in control from the start. One of my daughters was so delighted with the way Red turns the tables on everyone that she memorized the poem and recited it during her school's Poetry Week. It would be far too much of a stretch, of course, to say that these characters "empower" young readers. The stories are mainly in the service of fun. But I think it's important to note that, while occasionally violent (in the way cartoons have been for decades), the young people in Dahl's tales are not the victims of violence, as is so often the case in the traditional tales. I might even suggest, with perhaps a bit of exaggeration, that these young characters choose Hamlet's second option when faced with adversity: they "take arms against a sea of troubles, and by opposing, end them."

There remains the matter of language, specifically, the occasional vulgarism in *Revolting Rhymes*. When I began working on this piece, I asked my daughters, now teenagers who still return to Dahl from time to time, to reread *Revolting Rhymes* and consider what parts or features of them might be objectionable to parents. As I said, both have been fans of Dahl's books for years: the oldest estimates she has read *Matilda* twenty times and considers Matilda one of her childhood heroes. They may have been surprised at first to learn that *Revolting Rhymes* had raised parental objections, since they had read Dahl without hearing any objections from anyone. However, after reading the book again, they noted the word "slut" in the Cinderella story—the word that led to a challenge in Iowa—and also a number of places where "hell" appears, including the line from "Snow White" I quoted earlier.

Troublesome words can indeed leap off of a page, especially if one is looking for them. Because "crude" appears as a descriptor of Dahl's language several times in the guide to banned books, I surmise that his pages are often trolled for offensive words. It's certainly true that one can hardly fail to miss "slut" in "Cinderella," as it appears at the end of a line and is uttered by none other than the less-than-charming Prince: "The Prince cried, 'Who's this dirty slut? Off with her nut! Off with her nut.'" It's also true that "slut" is a vulgar word, the most vulgar word in the book. I think the question to ask is, does Dahl use it gratuitously, simply for shock value? I would argue that he doesn't. Dahl wants the word to strike his readers, yes, and it may well surprise many of them to find it in a book. I would note first of all that the word is presented in a very broad sense; I can see no suggestions that it's meant to characterize Cinderella as sexually promiscuous. But the key point is that it is spoken by the Prince, the putative ideal match for our Cinderella, and this effectively lifts the tale from the realm of convention with one strong yank.

It would be naive to think that *Revolting Rhymes* would likely be the first place a fifth or sixth grader might come across that word, not when "sucks" has replaced "stinks" in the hallways. This may not convince every parent that *Revolting Rhymes* is appropriate for children, and I have stated before that the book is not aimed at children of all ages. I don't imagine children younger than 10 or 11 would see the humor in the book, any more than they would be able to decipher a word like "mademoiselle" when it's applied to Goldilocks. This is for children who don't just want to be *told* they're no longer "little kids"; they want someone to talk to them as Dahl does: as people who have been around the block a few times, as readers who can go beyond fairy-tale endings and "bibbidy-bobbidy-boo" to find delight in an author's insouciance, and yes, irreverence. And now that they know how to read and choose books on their own, I believe they also want to read poetry and stories written skillfully and full of surprises, written in their language, poems and stories that they might want to memorize and share with others, that they might even imagine themselves writing.

## Work Cited

Dahl, Roald. *Revolting Rhymes*. New York: Penguin Books, 1982.

# Running with, Not from, *Running Loose*

## Chris Crowe

I've been using Chris Crutcher's first novel, *Running Loose* (1983), in my young adult literature courses for almost ten years. Though Crutcher has produced several fine novels since his debut work, I continue to teach *Running Loose* because it's basic Crutcher: its characters, plot, and style preview his later work, and I know that students who like *Running Loose* are sure to enjoy Crutcher's other books. I also continue to use this novel because it, like all the rest of his YA books, was named a "Best Book for Young Adults" by the American Library Association (ALA), and because Crutcher is someone any student of YA literature and any teacher of teenagers needs to know. He's one of the most popular YA authors of our time, having earned praise from critics, teachers, and teenagers and having received the Assembly on Literature for Adolescents ALAN Award in 1994 and the 2000 Margaret A. Edwards Award for Lifetime Achievement from the ALA. In addition to the critical acclaim, popularity, and awards, as a former high school jock myself, I teach the novel because I like the realism of Crutcher's tale about a high school athlete.

*Running Loose* is the story of Louie Banks, a high school senior in the tiny town of Trout, Idaho. Despite the threatening presence of the local redneck, bully, and team fullback, Boomer Cowans, Louie tries out for and earns a starting position on the football team. His season begins well—in addition to becoming a key player on a team bound for its third consecutive state championship, he also lands the most popular girl in school, Becky Sanders, as his girlfriend—but Louie's good life begins to unravel when his team is preparing for their toughest game of the season. In a team meeting, Coach Lednecky suggests that the only way for Louie's team to win is for them to take out the opposing team's star quarterback, Kevin Washington, an African American. "I don't want to sound prejudiced," says Lednecky, "but I played with blacks up at the U, and there's only one way you can stop them. That's to hurt 'em. And I'm telling you now, and I don't want it to leave this room, I want that Washington kid out of the game! Early!" (49).

When Boomer Cowans's cheap shot takes Washington out of the game, Louie's wild and indignant protests to the referees and coaches alienate him from the local school society and introduce him to adult hypocrisy. After meeting with the principal, a former football coach himself, and Lednecky, Louie is kicked off the team and suspended from school. "We can't have Louie running loose in our school with that kind of attitude" (95), explains the principal. Louie's action is supported by his parents, his girlfriend, and Dakota, owner of the local tavern and one of Louie's mentors, and it is their support and advice that calm him down and prevent him from taking more drastic action against the principal and coach.

In time, Louie's romance with Becky blossoms, and with permission from his father, Louie and Becky spend a night together in her family's cabin in the mountains. Although Louie has looked forward to having sex with Becky, when they're alone together in bed, he tells her he cannot go through with it. Her mature response teaches him something about sex. "It's a funny thing about things like sex, things we're supposedly not supposed to do. Once it's okay to do it, it's okay not to. . . . Sex is a scary business, and it's probably best to wait until you're really ready" (117).

Soon after their romantic getaway, Louie faces the most difficult situation of his life when she is killed in a car accident. He makes a scene at her funeral, railing against the preacher, God, and feckless attempts to explain tragedy and soothe grief. Louie's mood settles later when Dakota helps him understand that tragedies happen because "this life ain't partial" (140), and Louie apologizes to those he offended at the funeral and begins a period of solitude that helps him work his way through the grieving process.

In early spring, Louie's life finally takes a turn for the better when Coach Madison invites him to join the track team as a long-distance runner. In addition to giving Louie something productive to do, his long training runs provide him plenty of time to sort out his emotions and the tragic events of the previous fall and winter. His season ends on a high note when he follows Coach Madison's advice to "Run your race. Run loose like always" (185) and ends up winning the district championship in the two-mile.

Though Louie still resents the hypocritical actions of his football coach and principal, by the end of the novel, he has learned some important lessons about life.

> I learned some about friendship and a whole lot about love and that there's no use being honorable with dishonorable men. There's nothing they can do to you when you don't care anymore. I learned to accept myself even though I'm not Clint Eastwood or Joe Montana or Carter Samson, and that you can get through almost anything if you have people around you who care about you. And I

> learned that when all is said and done, you're responsible for every damn thing
> you do. (189-190)

By his own admission, Louie has changed, but even after the novel's many
life-changing events, when confronted with adult hypocrisy, he remains as
wisecracking and rebellious as he ever was.

Crutcher has put his own spin on the effect of his story on his narrator:

> Louie Banks in *Running Loose* has grown up believing that life is fair, that
> adults don't lie, that if you work hard you get what you deserve, that good
> intentions count, that disappointments can be overcome by hard work, that his
> parents and teachers and coaches have his best interest at heart. Then his coach
> asks him to play dirty football and, though Louie refuses, he sees that cheaters
> do win—at least in the sense he has always considered winning. Lies work.
> When he loses his girlfriend senselessly in an automobile accident, he learns that
> not only are people not fair, life is not fair. ("Healing" 36).

Though it was first published in 1983, Crutcher's novel continued to be
read and objected to throughout the 1990s. It appears on the ALA's "100
Most Frequently Challenged Books of 1990–1999," and several articles like
the ones by Betty Greenway and Sara Boose describe challenges to the
novel. For readers looking to be offended, *Running Loose* offers plenty to
object to, including material that generates the three most common
challenges to books. According to the ALA's Office for Intellectual
Freedom, 67 percent of the reported challenges to books in the 1990s
focused on three areas: "sexually explicit" material (25 percent), "offensive
language" (22 percent), or books that were "unsuited to age group" (20
percent) ("100 Most").

In addition to some references to masturbation, Crutcher's novel has
two scenes that might be called "sexually explicit." The most notorious part
of *Running Loose* is the "popcorn scene." In it, Boomer Cowans claims an
urban myth as his own when he brags how he cut a hole in the bottom of a
popcorn box, inserted "Old Norton," his nickname for his penis, and drove
his movie date into a frenzy of passion when she reached for a handful of
popcorn. The other scene that might be considered sexually explicit is Louie
and Becky's night at her cabin. In the first scene, some readers will find
Boomer's prurient tone, his sexist attitude, and the references to his penis
offensive. In the second scene, nothing sexual is made explicit, and Louie's
courage to turn down an opportunity for sex can actually be seen as an
admirable stand for abstinence.

Not surprisingly, the popcorn scene has drawn by far the most
complaints, and Crutcher has defended it on more than one occasion. In

"Taking a Hit from the Censors," he addresses a school board in Pennsylvania that, because of objections about the popcorn scene, has removed *Running Loose* from the school. In his letter, he explains why he included that scene in his novel:

> I heard that story when I was in fifth grade. I was eleven years old. I was told it was a true story and believed that. It was told to me by a high school kid who worked in my father's service station. Looking back I recognize him as a person whose self-esteem depended on putting others down, but at the time I looked up to him because he played football and talked tough. And he was a high school kid; something of a hero to me.
>
> No young person who has read *Running Loose* will ever believe that is a true story. For those of you who haven't read the book, know that the story is told by a bully, and the narrator calls game on it in the next paragraph. Is it a pornographic story? Of course it is—it denigrates women. Is it called pornographic? Yes it is; Louie Banks plays it up as exactly that. . . .
>
> *Running Loose* is not a book about popcorn and penises. It is a book about injustice and it is a book about loss. It is a book about standing up for oneself and it is a book about learning who to listen to. (26)

Crutcher goes on to say, "I believe the truth is best told in its native tongue. I cannot tell stories about people approaching adulthood without presenting them in the light in which I know them. The Boomer Cowans of the world and the silly urban myths will not go away because I refuse to write about them" (27).

The popcorn scene occupies less than half of page twelve, and, as Crutcher points out, is only a small part of a section that serves to characterize Boomer Cowans as the kind of low-thinking, small-minded bully who would be more than willing to carry out his coach's request to intentionally injure another player. It is essential that Boomer's character be established early in the novel because later his assault on Kevin Washington serves as the catalyst for the story's first major conflict.

As mentioned earlier, the second most common objection to books in general is offensive language, and although the novel doesn't use the "F-word," *Running Loose* is sprinkled with lighter profanity that is commonly used in modern society, including the use of "God" as an exclamation. None of the profanity in the story is gratuitous, excessive, or distracting; it comes naturally from Louie and other characters and, in addition to characterizing them, adds to the realism of the story and its characters.

Crutcher uses occasional profanity in his stories because he believes in presenting life as realistically and unvarnished as he can. In an interview with Teri Lesene, he explains why his straightforward presentation of contemporary language and social situations is so important.

> You have to tell the truth and you have to be protective about your characters. Truth is best told in its native tongue, so I let my characters speak for themselves. To take any words away because someone finds them objectionable would be denying someone the right to free speech. Not to acknowledge sex and language is to deny kids' life. It is okay to say to kids, 'Not in my house.' But it is not okay to condemn kids for using the language in the first place. (62)

Crutcher's truthful presentation of profanity certainly gives his characters a realistic and honest voice, but readers who have zero tolerance for profanity will probably be offended by the language regardless of Crutcher's intent.

In an e-mail to one of my YA literature students, Crutcher suggested an approach to dealing with readers or parents who object to his use of realistic language.

> About language: What I do is ignore people's worries about that. In discussions I always say, "Look, *tell* kids you don't like that language. *Tell* them why it bothers you. Initiate *discussion* about it. That way instead of making it a mystery and getting into power struggles over words, you can let them see your values and give them the freedom to develop their own." In the best of worlds, people would understand that it isn't the author using that language, but the character he or she creates. There is an important distinction there. So in answer to your question, I justify myself that way to the censors, and in the long run, don't feel I *have* to justify anything I write. I am the first to tell somebody how the back cover on a book works. Slamming it shut is the same as pushing the on/off knob on your TV. And we all have *that* choice.

Crutcher believes that rather than avoid profanity or ignore that it exists, it is ultimately better for young people to see the world as it really is. "[I]n an effort to keep children from the pain of living," he says, "and in an effort to control them, we tell them lies" ("Healing" 35). He says that lies work immediately to shield children from some of the pain of life, but in the long run they fail in their purpose because "everyone invariably runs into situations in which what they've been told for the sake of expedience simply doesn't hold up in the real world" ("Healing" 35-36).

The third most common objection to books is that they're not age appropriate, and this general complaint has also been directed at *Running Loose*. This complaint is less the fault of Crutcher or his novel than it is the fault of what I call the "trickle-down effect of good books." When teachers or other adults discover a book they like, they often recommend it widely without much thought to the level of the book or the level of the readers to which they're recommending it, and thus good books for older or more mature readers end up being read by kids who aren't ready for them. *Running Loose* is a fine story that will find a sympathetic readership among readers who, like Louie, are on what Crutcher calls "the edge of having to live their lives themselves" (Carter 44). The themes and issues at the heart of this novel might be inappropriate for readers who are not yet old or experienced enough to appreciate them. The novel is written simply enough that even middle school readers could read and comprehend it, but their ability to appreciate its real strengths would likely be limited, and some immature readers would be distracted by the language and sexual references that occasionally crop up in the story.

In my YA literature courses, my students read Crutcher cold with no prefaces or warnings from me. Nearly all my students are English majors and also members of the Church of Jesus Christ of Latter-Day Saints, a religion that embraces conservative, traditional Christian values. They typically enjoy their introduction to Chris Crutcher, and I can always count on *Running Loose* to stimulate lively class discussion. They are quick to recognize the literary strengths of the novel. Most often mentioned is Crutcher's lively, authentic YA voice. Louie Banks's narration is clever and realistic; he sounds like a smart teenager, not like an adult trying to sound like a teenager. They also like the character of Louie because he's moral without being stuffy, because he's able to make fun of himself, and because he learns important lessons about life. My students also point out that, unlike many YA authors, Crutcher is not afraid to include adults in positive roles who help Louie through his coming-of-age experiences by offering support, understanding, and plain old good advice. And, of course, my students like Crutcher's lean, fast-paced plot. *Running Loose* is not slowed by digressions, nonessential description, dead-end subplots, or extraneous characters. The fast read appeals to my busy readers; they also realize that, because of its tight plot, *Running Loose* is likely to appeal to teenagers who resist reading.

Perhaps more important than their appreciation for Crutcher's craft is my students' favorable response to the beneficial impact the story will have on YA readers. In a paper comparing Crutcher to Robert Cormier, one student wrote, "Robert Cormier's stories suggest that you can't trust *any*one; Crutcher's books teach that you can't trust *every*one." Indeed, reading about Louie's experiences in *Running Loose* will help teenagers realize that not all adults deserve their trust. As readers follow Louie through his story, they will learn with him how to distinguish truth from hypocrisy, reasoned action from irrational action, and good adults from bad adults. And, by "listening" to Louie's friends and mentors, especially Coach Madison, Dakota, Becky, and Carter, teenage readers will realize that despite the fact that young people lack adult status and authority, teenagers do have the power—and the responsibility—to resist adult hypocrisy and unethical behavior. Fortunately, *Running Loose* doesn't encourage unreasoned or immature resistance to unrighteous adult authority; Louie's experiences and Dakota's advice present the benefits alongside the risks and consequences involved with standing up for one's own beliefs.

Despite their overall praise of *Running Loose*, some students are bothered by certain aspects of the novel (but only one student has ever reacted to it so strongly that she refused to finish it). Generally, a few students feel the story is too romantic, that it lacks realism. Some don't like its paperback cover (at least three versions that I know of). A handful agree with Betty Greenway and other critics that the plot is contrived, and some students, especially those who never participated in high school athletics, find the story boring. Others point out that Louie's emotional outbursts are unrealistic and distracting and that the novel covers too many topics and themes.

Three of my students' four most common criticisms of *Running Loose* parallel the aforementioned objections raised by others: references to masturbation, sexual situations, and the use of vulgar language. Ironically, my students' most common complaint is perhaps the most trivial: Louie calls his parents by their first names. When I question them about this, they explain that Louie's use of his parents' first names annoyed them as they read because, in their experience, kids don't address their parents that way. Invariably, one or two other students will then admit that in their families, children *always* use their parents' first names. Our discussion then turns to the underlying cause of the students' annoyance: a perceived disrespect of adults. Certainly, Louie delivers boatloads of disrespect to a few adults in *Running Loose*, but many students are quick to remind the class that several adults in the story are presented positively and receive plenty of respect from Louie.

I'm always pleased when our conversation turns back to the strengths of the novel and when my students recognize an aspect of Crutcher's novel that critics like Susannah Sheffer have repeatedly praised. "Crutcher makes his 'good adult' characters as persuasive as the evil ones. There's no 'kids are true friends but adults are unreliable' message here; and, although Crutcher is clearly scornful of adults whose rules are arbitrary and who exist only to exercise power over kids, he lets the authentic, caring, courageous adults be the ones who make a difference" (11). In *Running Loose*, Louie benefits enormously from the wisdom and kindness of several authentic, caring, courageous adults, including Dakota, Coach Madison, Becky's father, and, of course, his own father. This is an aspect of *Running Loose* that my students, most of whom have benefited from a number of benevolent adult mentors, come to appreciate very much.

Louie's actions in *Running Loose* almost always provoke some class discussion on ethics and moral courage. Standing up to Lednecky and the school principal the way he did required a bit of rebelliousness and a lot of courage. Unlike his teammates and many of the townspeople who stood by and watched Boomer Cowans intentionally injure another player, Louie did not hesitate to speak out even though he knew his actions would surely have unpleasant consequences. Throughout the novel, Louie continued to confront injustice and hypocrisy wherever he saw it, and although my students don't always agree with his methods for dealing with injustices, they do admire Louie's courage and willingness to take a stand. Their reaction would certainly please Crutcher, who prides himself on the recurring theme of having a character stand up for himself. In an interview he said, "There is no act of heroism which does not include standing up for oneself. That is usually the hardest thing to do because it is embarrassing for one thing. Heroes stand up when it is easier to sit down. They are visible when it is easier to be invisible" (Lesene 62). That certainly describes Louie Banks.

Our class discussions about *Running Loose* always include mention of elements of the story that might result in challenges by parents or citizens groups, but my students, conservative and traditional as most of them are, aren't interested in discussing those aspects of the novel. Instead, they want to talk about what they liked about the story: the characters, Crutcher's narrative voice, the fast-paced plot, and the ethical and moral issues raised by the book. By the end of our work with *Running Loose*, all my students recognize the books's merits and Crutcher's overriding good intentions. His novel makes it clear that he not only knows and understands real teenagers but also that he cares deeply about them. Like the great majority of YA authors, Crutcher wants to use his writing talent not to make the lives of teenagers worse but to help them make their own lives better. As he has mentioned in many interviews, troubled teenaged readers often tell him what a positive impact his stories have had on them, and this only reinforces his belief that good stories can make a difference in reader's lives.

> Stories can help teenagers look at their feelings, or come to emotional resolution, from a safe distance. If, as an author, I can make an emotional connection with my reader, I have already started to help him or her heal. I have never met a depressed person, or an anxious person, or a fearful person who was not encouraged by the knowledge that others feel the same way they do. *I am not alone* is a powerful medicine. If others feel this way, and they have survived, then I can survive too.

As an adolescent, I would rather have hot tar poured up my nostrils than talk about my pain. But if I can consider someone else's pain and it is the same as mine, I can begin to work things out. If I can cry at a movie or reading a book when I can't cry about my own life, I will begin to get in touch with ways to deal with the losses, which is what this is all about. ("Healing" 39)

When my students, or anyone who has a bone to pick with *Running Loose*, recognize that Chris Crutcher is both an experienced therapist and a fine storyteller who has only the best interests of young people at heart, it becomes very difficult for them to worry at all about the aspects of the novel that might provoke challenges to it.

## Works Cited

"100 Most Frequently Challenged Books of 1990–1999." American Library Association. 31 July 2000. http://www.ala.org/bbooks/top100 banned books.html.

Boose, Sarah. "Will I 'Run Loose'?" *Voices from the Middle* 6.3 (March 1999): 18-22.

Carter, Betty. "Eyes Wide Open." *School Library Journal* (June 5, 2000): 42-45.

Crutcher, Chris. "Fathers and Sons." E-mail to Nathan C. Phillips. 8 Feb. 2000.

———. "Healing through Literature," *Authors' Insights: Turning Teenagers into Readers & Writers.* Ed. Donald R. Gallo. Portsmouth, N.H.: Boynton/Cook Publishers Heinemann, 1992: 33-40.

———. *Running Loose.* New York: Dell, 1983.

———. "Taking a Hit from the Censors." *SIGNAL* 19.1 (Fall 1994): 25-27.

Davis, Terry. "A Healing Vision." *English Journal* 85.3 (March 1996): 36-41.

———. *Presenting Chris Crutcher.* New York: Twayne Publishers, 1997.

Greenway, Betty. "Chris Crutcher— Hero or Villain? Responses of Parents, Students, Critics, Teachers." *The ALAN Review* 22.1 (Fall 1994): 19-21.

Lesene, Teri. "Banned in Berlin: An Interview with Chris Crutcher." *Emergency Librarian* 23 (May/June 1996): 61-63.

Sheffer, Susannah. "An Adult Reads Chris Crutcher." *The ALAN Review* 24.3 (Spring 1997): 10-11.

Smith, Louisa. "Limitations on Young Adult Fiction: An Interview with Chris Crutcher." *The Lion and the Unicorn* 16 (1992): 66-74.

# Conquering Our Fears:
# Alvin Schwartz's *Scary Stories* Series

## Caroline G. Majak

Scary stories have been part of both oral and written literacy for a long time. They are not mere fads of the TV generation or the creations of R. L. Stine. As I think back to my own childhood, many of the stories I heard were scary stories. In the version of *Little Red Riding Hood* that I was told, the wolf ate Grandma and Little Red Riding Hood and, then, the woodcutter chopped the wolf open to save Grandma and Little Red Riding Hood. Other stories, such as *The Three Little Pigs* or *Hansel and Gretel*, were also enjoyed by my classmates and me. Spooky stories, such as "Little Orphan Annie," captured our imaginations and kept us listening. We couldn't wait to help with the refrain, "And the goblins will get you if you don't watch out." Although these stories were scary, I remember wanting to hear them over and over again. I am also pretty sure that I understood that these were "just" stories.

Stories about ghosts, goblins, and other creepy creatures are centuries old. Alvin Schwartz continues this tradition in his collections of scary stories. In 1981, Schwartz and Caldecott Award winning-illustrator Stephen Gammell combined their talents to create *Scary Stories to Tell in the Dark*. Later, they produced two other books together: *More Scary Stories to Tell in the Dark* (1984) and *Scary Stories 3: More Tales to Chill Your Bones* (1991). While these books are generally recommended for children ages 9 and older, parents and teachers will want to consider the children's interests and reading levels before introducing these stories to their children. This assortment of spooky stories, songs, poems, and rhymes appeals to a wide range of ages, interests, and tastes. For additional pleasure, Schwartz also includes one spooky game in this series.

Attempts to ban or censor children's literature have been on a steady increase each decade of the past forty years (Huck 106). *Scary Stories to Tell in the Dark* (1981) by Alvin Schwartz "remains among the most popular for children and the most challenged." (Pistolis 39). There are important reasons

366

that parents, teachers, librarians, and other adults in the lives of children should resist efforts to censor these books. This chapter provides a few specific reasons for making sure the *Scary Stories* series remains available and accessible to all children.

## Enjoyment

There is no denying that many children enjoy reading books that are suspenseful and mysterious. "Children chose to read scary books without encouragement from adults and sometimes against adult directives" (Richards 831). Researchers are not exactly sure why children read these books, but they do have some clues. Some children like to read these stories because they enjoy talking about them to their friends. They also like the suspense and the mystery of the stories. They find them entertaining. One child reported, "I like to get scared" (Richards 831). Children need many opportunities to select the books they want to read. If we want to instill in them the desire to read, children must be encouraged to find books they enjoy.

Enjoyment of reading is especially critical to the engagement of reluctant readers. Typically, reluctant readers receive little or no satisfaction from reading. They are not interested or motivated to read. Yet, when given a chance to select their own stories, reluctant readers will read. They especially enjoy reading scary stories. These appeal to reluctant readers for a variety of reasons. The stories are short. The brief text, consisting of interesting characterizations, settings, and plots, invites the reluctant readers to find satisfaction, success, and enjoyment in their reading, a task that many have consciously set out to avoid (Worthy 484-485).

## Confronting Their Fears

Some believe that scary stories will terrorize or traumatize children who read them. In fact, they are more likely to produce the opposite effect. Rather than being horrified by these stories, most children gain a sense of control over their lives as they challenge and confront their fears vicariously through these suspenseful stories. These stories allow children to examine, discuss, and confront their fears in the safety of their homes, classrooms, and libraries.

Children, like many adults, fear the unknown; therefore, captivating stories about ghosts, death, or haunted houses become vehicles for exploring and discussing these topics. For example, "The Thing" is a story about two good friends, Ted Martin and Sam Miller, who while sitting on a fence notice something move in the field across the road. They can't be sure what it is.

Each time the thing appears it gets closer and closer. By now Ted and Sam are getting scared. They start running but soon decide this is foolish. So they return to take a better look. What they see is something wearing black pants, a white shirt, and black suspenders. It looks pretty much like a skeleton. Sam decides to touch it. Ted takes one look, screams, and they both run. A year later Ted gets sick and dies. Upon his death, Sam thinks that Ted looks very much like the thing: the skeleton. After reading "The Thing," children might want to discuss ghosts and death. They might ask, "Are ghosts real?" "What kind of courage does it take to confront a ghost?" "Would you touch a ghost?" "Why?" "Why not?"

## Control

It is important to remember that while these stories may be spooky, discomforting, or even frightening, children control what happens as they read them. They determine whether they are ready for a particular story. They even decide how they will deal with the illustrations. Some of the children will examine the illustrations very carefully, while other children will just take a peek at them. Other children will ignore them completely. Exercising control over things that might be a bit intimidating empowers children and encourages them to be risk takers.

## Using Their Imaginations

These exciting stories encourage children to use their imaginations. While all of these stories are likely to stir the children's imaginations, I believe that the only game that Schwartz includes in the series, found in *Scary Stories to Tell in the Dark*, provides an excellent example of how children use their imaginations as they listen to them. "Dead Man's Brains" is just the type of game children will enjoy telling in a dark room right around Halloween, although this game can be played any time. The story begins, "Once in this town there lived a man named Brown. It was years ago, on this night, that he was murdered out of spite. We have here his remains." As the story is told, children get to touch various items on a plate, which represent the parts of a dead man. There is a squishy tomato for the brain, peeled grapes for the eyes, a chicken bone for the nose, a dried apricot for the ear, etc. All of the key elements of the game are foods that children can recognize. After such an engaging story, imagine what kind of stories children might be able to create themselves!

## Great Variety

One of the strengths of Schwartz's series is the variety that can be found in each of the books. Some of the stories are spooky, bone-chilling, and quite eerie, while others are hilariously funny or just plain silly. Some of the stories are just weird. There are also songs, rhymes, chants, and poems. Alvin Schwartz's *Scary Stories* series are suspenseful and mysterious. They are also quite entertaining.

When we think of spooky stories, the images that we often conjure up are haunting, eerie, or macabre. Rarely do we think of these stories as being funny. Each of Schwartz's books contains a section that is guaranteed to make children laugh out loud. "The Viper" is a funny story about a widow who received a phone call from a man who said, "This is the viper. I'm coming up." When the man called again announcing that he was the viper and that he was coming up, the woman decided to call the police. Thinking it was the police at the door, the woman opened it. There stood a man, who said, "I am the viper. I vish to vash the vindows." There stories poke fun at our fears of ghosts, death, the afterlife, consequences, or meanness.

Some of the stories are just weird. Children, especially intermediate-grade children, like "weird" stories (Richards 832). "Sam's New Pet" is likely to have great appeal for these children. In this story, Sam's parents go to Mexico. On their return they bring Sam a pet. The pet goes everywhere with Sam. One day when the pet becomes ill, he takes the pet to the veterinarian. The veterinarian promptly tells Sam that what he has is not a pet but a sewer rat with rabies. Weird. Weird. Weird.

## Models for Writing

Because of this variety, teachers will find numerous ways to incorporate these books into their curricula. Language arts teachers might want to use stories, poems, and chants in the books as models for writing. These can serve as examples for writing in a succinct, compelling, and precise fashion. Teachers can also discuss plots, settings, and characterizations. The rather limited texts could be studied for methods used to quickly establish mood with words such as "dark," "alone," "creaky," and "creature."

## Storytelling

Exemplary storytelling permeates this collection. The jump stories "beg" to be retold, rather than just read. "The Walk" from *Scary Stories to Tell in the Dark* is perfect for getting others to jump. An unidentified narrator tells the story about two men (one of them the narrator's uncle) who just happen to run into each other and end up walking down the same lonely dirt road. Although both men are really scared of each other, they just keep walking. As it gets darker, their fear of each other intensifies. But, they just keep walking. They continue to walk deeper into the woods without saying a word to each other. The punch line for the story comes when the narrator says, "The man was terrible scared of my uncle, and my uncle was terrible scared of—(Now SCREAM!)" (11). Of course, the person, who is grabbed at just the right moment, will jump.

Causing others to jump is so much fun for the storyteller. For some children, reading the stories provides enough satisfaction for their tastes; however, other children delight in retelling the stories themselves. A motivated storyteller needs only to remember a few details to deliver the surprise endings of these stories, and the recognition of success (and fright) is immediate.

## Discussions

Children also want to discuss the stories they read. Urban legends are especially important venues for discussion. Urban legends are contemporary oral stories that are often repeated from one person to the other as if they were factual events. Rarely is the authenticity of these stories challenged when they are shared. In reality, there is little evidence that these stories ever occurred.

Schwartz includes several urban legends in each of the books. For example, "High Beams" is a story about a girl who notices that she is being followed by a truck as she drives her car home. Even though she tries to lose the truck, she can't. When she finally pulls into her driveway, she learns that the truck driver has been trying to protect her from the man crouched down in the back seat of her car with a knife.

Disturbing? Yes. However, children should be encouraged to discuss what problem-solving skills the girl used. They might be encouraged to discuss other things the girl might have done to avoid the situation. Many of the children will actually be relieved to learn that some of the stories they thought were true are really made-up stories that have been shared as if they were factual.

## Concluding Statements

From the scary illustrations on the front of the books throughout the entire series, Schwartz and Gammell have provided a collection of stories to satisfy the tastes of most children. Yes, the stories are spooky, eerie, and frightening. They are also engaging, entertaining, and enjoyable. While no single book is right for all children, children should have access to books in the Alvin Schwartz's *Scary Series* because children enjoy them. Reluctant readers actually read them. They also contain considerable variety. This variety opens many possibilities for teaching and learning.

## Works Cited

Huck, Charlotte S., and Susan Hepler, Janet Hickman, and Barbara Z. Kiefer. *Children's Literature in the Elementary School.* Seventh edition (revised by Barbara Z. Kiefer). Boston: McGraw Hill, 2001.

Pistolis, Donna Reidy, ed. *Hit List: Frequently Challenged Books for Children.* Chicago: American Library Association/Office of Intellectual Freedom, 1996.

Richards, Patricia O., Debra H. Thatcher, and Michelle Shreeves. "Don't Let a Good Scare Frighten You: Choosing and Using Quality Chillers to Promote Reading." *The Reading Teacher* 52, 8 (May 1999): 830-840.

Schwartz, Alvin. *More Scary Stories to Tell in the Dark.* New York: HarperCollins, 1984.

———. *Scary Stories 3: More Stories to Chill Your Bones.* New York: HarperCollins, 1991.

———. *Scary Stories to Tell in the Dark.* New York: HarperCollins, 1981.

Worthy, Jo. "Removing Barriers to Voluntary Reading for Reluctant Readers: The Role of School and Classroom Libraries." *Language Arts,* 73 (November 1995): 483-492.

# Will McBride's *Show Me!*

## Marc Talbert

Sexual behavior is intensely personal and honest, yet something all of us share. Fittingly, *Show Me!* is intensely personal, yet something honest and powerful to share with children concerning the pleasures of our individual and common sexuality.

All of us should be blessed with a healthy and joyful attitude toward sex. For me, as for many of us, striving for this kind of attitude has been a lifelong struggle. I wish *Show Me!* had been part of the early years of my sexual awareness. It would have saved me decades of sexual misunderstandings, doubts, and fears.

Where was *Show Me!* when I was growing up? It wasn't even a gleam in Will McBride's eye. When *Show Me!* entered my life, I was in my midtwenties. It provided for me the bold honesty and psychological soundness I needed to begin healing my sexual self. If such a statement seems too personal for you, as if I am exposing too much of myself to you, perhaps you should flip to the next essay. Getting personal is not something I am prone to doing—except in fictional settings, with characters of my own invention. But I believe *Show Me!* is an important book to champion, and I do not believe it is possible to write a strong defense of *Show Me!* without getting personal.

If *Show Me!* is the powerful and appropriate book I believe it is, it should challenge each of us, including me, to come out from that emotionally comfortable hiding place of psychological theory and jargon. It should challenge us to do more than denounce the sorry state of our culture's sexual attitudes—the giggly, arrested-development sexploitation of sitcoms, for example. *Show Me!* should inspire each of us to transform theory into practice, to bring intellect and body together, to practice mature, healthy sexuality in our daily lives—in other words, to do our individual parts to improve the state of our culture's collective sexual attitudes.

As a child of the 1960s and 1970s, it is curious for me to look back and realize that I somehow missed out on the sexual revolution. I was always too inhibited to explore sex with anybody but myself, and even then with the most excruciating sense of modesty and guilt. Being naked in my family was limited to showers, baths, the doctor, and changing diapers.

I am the eldest of four children. When the first of my two little sisters arrived, I was finally old enough to help my mother with the diaper-changing chore. Being introduced to female anatomy on the changing table is anything but erotic to a young boy—interesting, yes; exotic, yes; smelly, yes; erotic, no. After the first couple diaper-changing sessions, I remember being afraid that my oldest younger sister was an anatomical freak. The pictures I'd seen of naked women were from paintings of old European masters, who never showed labia (or pubic hair, for that matter). Little pixies or nymphs, both male and female, in such animated movies as "Fantasia," never had genitals, either. The combined effects of Rembrandt and Walt Disney (an unlikely but powerful combination) caused me to worry that the vertical folds of skin between my sister's legs over time might not grow together (or, to my mind, would not heal)—that their "privates" might not become more horizontal and less visible. This worry was reinforced by the arrival of a second sister.

Where was *Show Me!* when I needed it?

It was only when I was old enough to babysit children from other families, part of which unavoidably involved changing the diapers of girls, that I discovered all girls were designed like my sisters. Discovering this was a great relief.

My sexual ignorance was not limited to female anatomy. Even the female protagonist in one of my own novels was more observant of male genitalia than I was before the age of ten. For many years Bernie skinny-dipped with her older brother in her ranching family's stock tanks without feeling awkward or self-conscious. And then, one day, lying naked near him, drying off in the sun:

> With his face covered he didn't look like Carlton. He looked like a strange boy lying naked next to her. . . . [His body] looked hard and muscled and dangerous and it gave Bernie the creeps. His arms were sprawled, palms up, by his sides and his legs were spread slightly apart, his feet spraddling outward. From his feet, her eyes followed his legs up to where they tied together in a jumbled knot of saggy, lumpy, wrinkly skin. A dark end stuck out of the knot, looking like the wrapped tip of a worn rope. This end was flopped over, pointing in her direction, nesting in a thin crop of blond, curly hair that glowed golden in the sun.

from *Rabbit in the Rock* by Marc Talbert

Until I was eight or nine I didn't realize that some boys' penises were different from my circumcised penis. The boy babies I had changed while babysitting were small versions of my own. Pictures of the Michelangelo statue "David" displayed for the entire world a tubular penis, quite elegant, which I assumed was modified by the sculptor for the sake of modesty.

One day, in the mildew/ammonia atmosphere of a swimming pool locker room, I was startled to discover that my best friend had a penis similar to Michelangelo's "David." I might have thought he was a freak, but his type of penis wasn't the only one I saw in the locker room—now allowing myself to look furtively from the corners of my eyes. That shocking discovery, in itself, shows how sexually modest I was as a child, and how sheltered and modest my best friend was, as well as the other boys I palled around with.

Was such modesty healthy? I don't think so. Where was *Show Me!* when we needed it? To be curious about how other naked boys look, after all, is not necessarily to invite homosexuality into one's life. It is to invite masculinity into one's life—homosexual or heterosexual or, in my case, confused (which I have since learned is common).

My sense of modesty was not changed by my first brush with sex education in seventh grade. It was taught by an elderly woman with a canned set of worksheets, accompanied by the boys' film (shown only to the boys) and the girls' film (shown only to the girls). In the canned worksheets, we learned names for sexual organs, shown in diagrams that sliced them in half to expose their innards. A sadist couldn't have presented penises and uteruses in a more clinically horrific way. I remember thinking: So *that's* what I look like, sliced in half! Looking at those bloodless cross sections took all the excitement and glamor from sex organs and what they were capable of doing. Perhaps that was the intent of my teacher.

Where was *Show Me!* when we seventh graders needed it?

Now, as the happily married (for nineteen years!) father of two daughters (six and nine!), I want my children to be proud of their bodies—to be unashamed of them, to be unafraid of them, to be in charge of them. After all, their bodies—all our bodies, male and female—are a profound part of what make us human. I want my daughters to celebrate being human—and female—in a healthy, positive manner.

In the culture in which we live, aiming for this ideal is difficult. In the media and in popular culture, "enhanced" nakedness—nakedness turbocharged in inappropriate ways—often is a tool to economically seduce children and adults—to tap insecurities and to transform these insecurities into the need for certain clothes, makeup, a certain cola or beer, certain music, and certain TV shows or movies.

*Show Me!* is not a panacea for the sexual perversity that is so much part of our culture, but it could be a powerfully healthy start.

> Benito had thrown off his covers in the night and Eloy assumed that, once more, his brother had come home late after partying with his *vatos* and fallen into bed with his clothes on. Eloy smiled. If Benito's jeans get any tighter, he thought, there won't be any room for what makes him a man. Every little thing he's got will tuck tail, crawl inside . . . and my brother will become a girl!
>
> from *A Sunburned Prayer,* by Marc Talbert

I went through my adolescence suitably addled but with my senses pretty much untouched. I kissed my date at the junior prom the same way I kissed my aunts—on the cheek. My gropings were limited to accidentally touching a bra strap when I hugged a cousin goodbye.

College was much the same, except that I sometimes agonized over the sex drive I was apparently missing. Weren't men supposed to reach their sexual peak in the early twenties?

All kinds of questions began to plague me. Were the differences between men and women more than skin deep, more than different clothes and hairstyles? Were the similarities between men and women more profound than the differences? Such questions wouldn't let go and were disturbing. Why was being a man so complicated? Why were women so mysterious?

Where was *Show Me!* when I needed it?

> A couple of weeks ago, Toby and Harold's fifth grade class began studying "Human Growth and Development." That was Miss Follensby's way of not having to say "sex." All the girls tried not to snigger when Miss Follensby said *penis* out loud—which she did seventeen times in two weeks—everybody counted—and the boys would try not to smirk. And the boys would look at their desk tops when Miss Follensby said *vagina*—which she did thirteen times—and the girls would try not to blush.
>
> Miss Follensby acted as if nobody had any feelings when she said *penis* and *vagina.* Toby thought that was stupid. Every *knows* that boys walk around with penises. . . . He could feel his, scrunched up in his too-small jeans. And every girl has a vagina. And *everybody* has breasts that are pretty much the same in fifth grade—except for Robin. . . . You just didn't *say* so . . . It's embarrassing.
>
> from *Toby,* by Marc Talbert

Upon graduating from college, with my degree in elementary education,

I began teaching fifth grade and, like Miss Follensby, part of what I taught was "Human Growth and Development." The kids knew what that meant, and they expected it to be the highlight of their year. That may be why it was traditionally taught toward the end of the year, as leverage to control attitude and behavior during the rest of the year. Personally, I was relieved to have a whole year to prepare for something with which I had very limited personal experience.

So, striving to be an excellent teacher, I went to the library to find books that would help me teach the basics of healthy sexual attitudes to fifth graders.

Unfortunately, the library was not much help. So I went to one of those dying breed, a good, independent bookstore. I found trendy stuff that was actually helpful—remember, this was at the tail end of the sexual revolution I had missed. Among the books I found that I eventually used in my classroom were: *Are You There God? It's Me, Margaret* and *Then Again, Maybe I Won't* (both by Judy Blume, an author I was too old to have grown up with), John Neufeld's *Freddy's Book* (which I highly recommend for its humor and empathy), and *The Facts of Love* by Alex and Jane Comfort (solid and safe and informative).

*Show Me!* was the most controversial of the books I found—shelved high, out of browsing range. I flipped through it and, still in shock, surprised myself when I bought it. I took it home and, from cover to cover, let it work its magic. From that first day, *Show Me!* shook me up—helped me to see human sexuality differently than I had before and to think about sex in more healthy, unabashed, and, finally, joyful ways.

Having said this, I can't say that I felt comfortable with all of *Show Me!* It shocked me in many ways, and still does. It flew in the face of most everything I grew up with. But after shock wore off, I began to see the wisdom of its approach.

*Show Me!* contains beautifully composed black and white photographs of boys and girls, all of them naked, and a few parents, men and women, also naked with their naked children, apparently comfortable in their bodies and with the young bodies around them. They are obviously not ashamed of their bodies. There are photos of erect penises, one boy's with a sleeveless t-shirt hanging from its crook. This photo, in particular, poses the question, for both boys and girls: can one's sex organs be funny (and fun), ridiculous, silly? Of course they can. Laughter is one way of expressing the joy of being a boy and a girl, of being playfully sexual.

There are photos of a girl pointing to her labia, of older girls touching each others' breasts. There is a photo of a girl touching a boy's penis, and one of a boy touching a girl's nipple, his penis becoming erect. There is a photo showing, side by side, the difference between a circumcised and an uncircumcised penis. There is a series of photos of a young man and a young woman making love (which invites the question: is making love more than having sex?)—culminating in intercourse.

None of the photographs are meant to be erotic. They are beautifully composed and sexual . . . and personal. They are matter-of-fact without being jaded and, unlike most print or television ads, without an ulterior agenda. They celebrate human sexuality in a dignified and (remarkably) private way.

Accompanying these photographs are the words and perceptions of real, living children—commenting on what the photos show, with humor and down-to-earth honesty—in contrast to the perceptions of a cranky pair of adults that occasionally interrupt to express outrage and disgust.

I am still uncomfortable with the part of the text that begins: "One time I watched him [my brother] and his girlfriend making love." To my way of thinking, making love is not a spectator sport. But even this part of the book provides valuable material for discussion. Were the young man and young woman shocked and angry—or unconcerned—to discover they'd been watched? Did the boy who caught his brother "doing it" sneak off before being discovered? What do these imagined scenarios say about the one who imagines them? How would each of us feel in a similar situation—as older brother or younger sibling?

To McBride's credit, this part of *Show Me!* doesn't preach but, rather, sets the stage for what follows, a very personal and quite beautiful portrayal of sexual play and intercourse between a young man and a young woman. The book then culminates in the birth of a child.

Lonely as it can be to find validation in the business of becoming a whole, and therefore sexual, human being, I dream that each child who explores *Show Me!* will find emotional company. For the lucky teachers, parents, grandparents, and other relatives and caring adults who can share this book with children, the well-considered explanatory text at the end, by Dr. Helga Fleischhauer-Hardt, is most helpful. Not only is it a wonderfully open, challenging, and healthy defense of Will McBride's photographs and the accompanying commentary of the children, it gently leads adults, step by step, through the unfolding of human sexuality, from infancy to adulthood. While providing this wealth of information, she takes the time to gently recognize the sexual insecurities each of us may have brought with us from childhood into adulthood. Importantly, *Show Me!* is a book not only for children but for adults in their lives.

Over and over, and in many different ways, Dr. Fleischhauer-Hardt emphasizes: Guilt and sex should not be as inextricably linked as they are in our culture. As she writes: "We hope this book will serve parents and children as a source of information and guide them toward a happy sexuality marked by love, tenderness, and responsibility."

> Matt lay in bed, listening to his heart beating. Without thinking he reached toward his crotch and felt himself as he sometimes did when he was lonely or sad. He felt oddly small and cold. A warm feeling grew as he touched himself. It felt good.
>
> Matt closed his eyes as he fondled himself. Suddenly a vivid picture of the [car] accident—and the face of his mother and sister—flashed across his mind. His hand froze where it was.
>
> Matt's mind was alive with thoughts, thoughts flopping around in his head. If my mother is dead, Matt thought frantically, she must be in heaven. If she's in heaven she must be looking down at me. If she's looking down at me, she must see what I'm doing to myself.
>
> Breathlessly, these thoughts repeated themselves over and over. He drew his hand from his crotch and held it against the sling.
>
> *Can she see me?* Matt was horrified. *Or worse, can she hear my thoughts?*

from *Dead Birds Singing*, by Marc Talbert

Where was *Show Me!* when Matt needed it!

I hope that every child and young adult will engage in honest, non-exploitive, joyful sexual exploration, with themselves and others—without worrying that someone, dead or alive, is watching and disapproving. I hope that every child engages in sexual play after having been provided by their parents with a healthy and loving attitude concerning their own bodies and the bodies of others. *Show Me!* can help foster such attitudes.

To ban *Show Me!* says more about the censor's sexual insecurities and unhealthy sexual attitudes than it does about the book itself.

Where is *Show Me!* for the sexually insecure, the sexually wounded? Right here among us. Thank goodness.

## Works Cited

Blume, Judy. *Are You There God? It's Me, Margaret*. New York: Bradbury Press, 1970.

———. *Then Again, Maybe I Won't*. New York: Bantam, 1971.

Comfort, Alex, and Jane Comfort. *The Facts of Love*. New York: Crown, 1979.

McBride, Will. *Show Me*. New York: St. Martin's, 1975.

Newfeld, John. *Freddy's Book*. New York: Random House, 1973.

Talbert, Marc. *Dead Birds Singing*. Boston: Little, Brown, 1985.

————. *A Sunburned Prayer*. New York: Simon & Schuster, 1985.

————. *Toby*. New York: Dell, 1987.

————. *Rabbit in the Rock*. New York: Dial, 1989.

# Not So Loathsome After All:
# A Defense for Hastings and Wijngaard's
# *Sir Gawain and the Loathly Lady*

## Scot Smith

When Selina Hastings paired up with the Greenaway-winning illustrator Juan Wijngaard to retell the Arthurian legend of The Wedding of Sir Gawain and Dame Ragnelle, the result was simply stunning. In 1985, *Sir Gawain and the Loathly Lady* garnered the prestigious Kate Greenaway Medal, the award given to the best illustrations found in a British book for children. Since then, it has achieved near classic status. One finds their book on reading lists throughout the English-speaking world. While there is so much to admire in these twenty-nine pages, there is also much to be concerned about—from profanity to sexual innuendo. Wijngaard's depiction of the gruesome Dame Ragnelle alone is enough to distress very young children, not to mention parents and educators. Furthermore, its explicit feminist theme is bound to offend some conservatives. Thus, I am left with this question, a dilemma faced almost daily by practicing librarians like me: do the merits of this book outweigh the controversy it will create? My answer is an unequivocal yes.

I first encountered Hastings and Wijngaard's *Sir Gawain and the Loathly Lady* while in library school and have not stopped using it since. I booktalk it to help introduce a unit on traditional literature and folklore. I have incorporated Wijngaard's brilliant but at times bizarre illustrations into a lesson on art history and styles in art. *Sir Gawain and the Loathly Lady* remains the centerpiece for my annual multimedia storytelling project.

Then again, I am a high school librarian. The students who make up my audience and who check the book out from the shelves are not horrified by the ghastly portrayal of the nightmarish Loathly Lady. Nor does the abusive language of the Black Knight fall upon innocent and sensitive ears. These kids have heard it all and repeated most; foul language is not a concern. As for the sexual themes, let's be realistic. In today's sex-charged teen environment, the sexual consummation of a marriage is a mild topic indeed. I figure teenaged males, as devoted fans of misogynistic rap music, could use a strong dose of feminism. Again, I work with teenagers, and technically speaking, *Sir Gawain and the Loathly Lady* is a picture storybook for children. If I were a librarian in an elementary school or even in a middle school, I would have to ask myself, is this book age appropriate?

Depending upon which bibliographic source one uses, *Sir Gawain and the Loathly Lady* is recommended as appropriate from anywhere from first grade to fifth grade, from age nine to adult. I tend to agree with the latter. At this point, we must recognize some of the inherent differences between the aforementioned British Greenaway Medal and its American counterpart, the Caldecott Medal. Librarians and educators often rely upon awards for justification of a challenged book. If a book has won a major award, then that award alone speaks for the merit of the book. However, that argument does not necessarily prove effective in the case of *Sir Gawain and the Loathly Lady*. One can argue that the British define "children" and "children's books" more liberally than Americans do. After all, Richard Adams's classic *Watership Down* was published in the United Kingdon as a children's book. While American picture storybooks are typically designed for the primary grades of kindergarten through third grade, British picture books are marketed toward a broader audience. Past winners of the Greenaway Medal include Charles Keeping's illustrations for Alfred Noyes's epic poem *The Highwayman*, Michael Foreman's biography *War Boy: A Country Childhood*, and Alan Lee and Rosemary Sutcliff's *Black Ships Before Troy*. Few American educators would argue that these books—with their mature themes and extensive text—are age appropriate for children in the primary grades.

The same holds true for *Sir Gawain and the Loathly Lady*. The vocabulary alone would make the book difficult even as a read-aloud for first and second graders. Indeed, the library vendor Follett lists it with a reading level of 4.0. Based upon the Fry Readability Index, the vast majority of American picture storybooks have a reading level between 2.0 and 3.0. The reading level alone should give us an indication for which audience *Sir Gawain and the Loathly Lady* is best suited. Only the star readers below fourth grade could easily handle many of Hastings's polysyllabic phrases. *Melancholy, grotesque, rheumy, hideousness*, and *penitent* represent but a few of the words bound to be unfamiliar to the primary reader. My point here is simple; that in some books, but certainly not all, there exists a correlation between the Readability Index and age appropriateness. Not only might the vocabulary of the book be confusing to the primary reader but so also might be the story's complex plot and mature themes. Yet that which only so few students could read might easily be read to them. For that reason, I see this book as a perfect read-aloud for those intermediate grades. Having established the readability of the book does little to help us determine its appropriateness. For that, more detailed analysis is needed.

The legend itself is simple enough. While hunting in the forest, the unarmed King Arthur becomes separated from his party and must make his way back to Carlisle Castle alone. As he treks through this foreboding forest, he comes to a pond. On the other side of the pond stands the Black Knight, armored and ready for battle. Without his mystical sword Excalibur, the king is helpless. Realizing that there would be little glory in killing a defenseless opponent, the Black Knight gives Arthur a riddle to solve. If the king cannot answer the question of what do women most desire, then he will be killed and his kingdom will fall into the hands of the Black Knight. For the next three days, Arthur queries every woman he sees, from high ladies of the court to the goose girls in the market, without finding a sufficient answer. On the third day, Arthur, having resigned himself to defeat, returns to the forest to meet his certain death. He has no answer for the Black Knight.

Along the way, he hears a voice from the forest, a voice that is calling him by name. At the edge of the forest, he spies a creature so hideous it takes his breath away. Hastings describes the Loathly Lady as:

> Her nose was like a pig snout's; from a misshapen mouth stuck out two rows of yellowing horse's teeth; her cheeks were covered in sores; she had only one eye, rheumy and red-rimmed, and from a naked scalp hung a few lank strands of hair. Her whole body was swollen and bent out of shape, and her fingers, on which were several fine rings, were as gnarled and twisted as the roots of an old oak. (13)

Wijngaard's portrait of the Loathly Lady is, however, what brings this disgusting monster to life. One would be hard-pressed to find a more frightening portrait anywhere in the pages of children's literature. Even the most gruesome portrayal of Baba Yaga pales in comparison to Wijngaard's eerie Loathly Lady. Though abominable in appearance, she appears to have a good heart, for she offers Arthur an exchange. If he as a king will grant her one wish, then she will give him the solution to the Black Knight's riddle. Desperate beyond measure, Arthur agrees. The Black Knight had asked what do women truly desire, and the Loathly Lady whispers the answer in his ear. She then asks for her end of the bargain—a husband from one of the knights of the Round Table. Arthur is naturally appalled; how can he ever ask one of his knights, loyal as he might be, to make such an incredible sacrifice and marry this hag? At first, he refuses, stating that the hag has asked for the impossible, but she reminds him of the honor of kings to keep their word. Though deeply troubled, Arthur agrees. He then bids the creature farewell and rides to meet his adversary, the Black Knight.

Arthur quickly thwarts his rival by correctly answering his question. Having been bested by Arthur once again, the Black Knight shouts "God damn you, Arthur. May you roast in Hell!" (16). If the word "hell" does not scare many teachers away from this book, then "God damn" surely will. What does one expect the Black Knight, as dastardly and malevolent an opponent as one can face, to say? As the profanity is completely in keeping with his character, then it is justifiable. A similar example is Katherine Paterson's controversial and often challenged *The Great Gilly Hopkins*. Gilly, as an unruly foster child, curses like a sailor, but her language is consistent with her character. The same holds true for the Black Knight. The language issue here differs substantially from that issue we occasionally encounter in films for children—where certain characters blurt out profanities for the sole purpose of obtaining a "PG" rating, a move designed to broaden the audience of the movie and eliminate the "G" rating stigma associated with films for kids. The Black Knight curses Arthur not for the sake of cursing but rather because that is what Black Knights do. Would Arthur, Guinevere, or Lancelot use such profanity? Perhaps, but we must expect a character as malicious as the Black Knight to be as vile as possible. The fact that he curses makes him just that—the antithesis of the honorable and noble Arthur.

That Arthur is honorable brings us to the next issue in the story. He had promised the Loathly Lady a husband from one of Knights of the Round Table. Although his knights have sworn fealty to him, even the medieval codes of chivalry have their boundaries. Arthur is deeply troubled; he owes his life and his honor to the hideous creature in the forest, but how can he ask even his most loyal of knights to make such a humiliating sacrifice so as to marry this hag? Distressed to the point of tears, Arthur consults Guinevere. He asks her how he might save his honor. Arthur does not have to wait for her answer, for Sir Gawain, sitting nearby, has overheard their conversation. To save his king's honor, Gawain eagerly volunteers, thereby condemning himself to wed this monster of monsters rather than a beautiful maiden of the court.

Herein lie several of the significant themes of the book—that a man must be true to his word, that honor should come before glory, and that personal sacrifices must be made for the good of the whole. Educators should always ask several questions of a controversial book. One of those questions is whether or not the book contains a worthwhile theme. Ask that question of *Sir Gawain and the Loathly Lady*, and the answer is self-evident. We are only halfway through the book and have already encountered not less than three critical thematic issues, those of honesty, honor, and self-sacrifice. Arthur and especially Gawain display those personal traits and prove the merits of the story's themes.

Having agreed to marry the Loathly Lady, Gawain goes with Arthur into the forest to bring the bride-to-be back to the castle for the wedding ceremony. What a dismal affair the wedding is—no dancing, no drinking, no festivity at all. Indeed, the mood seems more like a funeral than a wedding. If there is a wedding, then there must naturally follow a consummation of the marriage. Thus, the scene shifts from the banquet hall to the bedroom. At this point, we have reasons for reservations once again. The sexuality in *Sir Gawain and the Loathly Lady* is very subtle. We as adults know what Gawain must do, but sexual intercourse is never mentioned in the book. Indeed, sex is scarcely implied by Hastings. Thus, parents and teachers need not be overly concerned with the sexuality of the book.

Nor should they be overly concerned with what happens next. As Gawain is a character in an Arthurian legend, we know that his loyalty to his king will be rewarded. His act of marrying Dame Ragnelle alone has broken half of a horrible curse. When he turns around in his bedroom, he sees not the deformed Loathly Lady but a stunningly beautiful young woman. Yet, he is immediately faced with a dilemma. The young maiden tells him that she can take her current form only for half the day. Which would he prefer—that she be beautiful during the day but hideous at night or beautiful in the evening and hideous during day? Again, we encounter some implied sexuality. More powerful than the subtle sexual innuendo at work here is the strong feminist one. Essentially, she is asking Gawain to choose between a "trophy wife" to parade around the castle during the day or a magnificent woman to be his lover at night. Dame Ragnelle challenges him on both accounts, pointing out the flaws in either choice. Frustrated and unable to decide, Gawain gives up; he asks her to choose. Inadvertently, Gawain has broken the other half of the spell. He has given his wife what she most desires. A woman most desires the right to have her own way. That is the answer to the Black Knight's question and perhaps the root of more controversy.

The theme that a woman deserves the right to have her own way is stated so explicitly and at such a critical juncture in the narrative that it cannot help having a powerful impact on its audience. Again, we must ask ourselves if this theme is a worthy one. While few would deny that women should have the right to freely choose what they want, such overt feminism—especially in a picture storybook for children—may offend some conservatives. Here we must remember that the story is set in the Middle Ages, a time in history when the everyday lives of women were truly "dark." If the no-longer-Loathly Lady and her husband can agree that a woman has the right to make empowered choices, then what does that say to us in our more enlightened times? I do not wish to delve into the issues of pro-choice and Affirmative Action, but few would disagree that women still are not always entitled to have their own way. Because the women of today are still constrained by the rigors of a male-dominated culture, *Sir Gawain and the Loathly Lady* could be used in the classroom to stimulate critical thought on a sensitive issue.

In the introduction of this essay, I asked myself if the merits of *Sir Gawain and the Loathly Lady* outweigh the controversy it might create. Whether or not concerned parents, teachers, and administrators will buy into my rationale is uncertain. Indeed, any defense of a challenged book puts the defendant in a precarious position. When I teach censorship to my students in my children's literature class, I always stress the significance of community standards. That *Sir Gawain and the Loathly Lady* has won awards in the United Kingdom and appears on reading lists in Canada, Australia, and New York state would be a weak justification on my part if I were defending the book in rural East Tennessee, where I grew up. To religious fundamentalists, international awards do not amount to merit. Medals alone will not vindicate this book. Nor will reading lists. The true measure of the worth of this book can best be determined by what appears between its covers.

*Sir Gawain and the Loathly Lady* possesses a quality I shall call—for lack of a better term—universal intrinsic value. In essence, I am saying that this is a good book. Period. End of debate. And what constitutes a good book? By using the word intrinsic, I am stating that the book is valued solely on what it is and not what awards it has won or where and how it has been used. If nothing less, the book contains Juan Wijngaard's stunning illustrations, illustrations so well crafted that *Sir Gawain and the Loathly Lady* could stand alone as an art book. Add to those illustrations Selina Hastings's masterful retelling of this well-known Arthurian Legend, and one has the makings of a classic picture storybook. Hastings's style turns a good tale into a great one. What makes this book so successful is that it combines a work of literature—Hastings's retelling—with a work of art, Wijngaard's illustrations.

If a book is to have near universal appeal, then it naturally follows that its themes should possess a universal appeal. I can safely say that the story's feminist theme will not appeal to everyone. However, that theme is only one of four. Let us not forget that: (a) Arthur kept his word to the Black Knight and the Loathly Lady, both honorable and noble deeds, (b) Gawain chose humility over personal glory, and (c) Gawain was willing to make an incredible sacrifice for the good of the whole. When I ask my students to evaluate a work of literature, I urge them to consider whether or not the book has more than one idea. Great stories have multiple themes and layers, all ripe for analysis and discussion; the mediocre one represent "one-idea wonders." Because a picture storybook contains four integral themes, I realize its value, not only as a piece of quality literature but also a tool to teach students to think critically.

Finally, my last rationale comes from the students who have experienced this book. After my students, be they the high schoolers who check the book out from my library or the future teachers in my children's literature class, have read *Sir Gawain and the Loathly Lady*, I know they will say, "This is a good book." For me, that is rationale enough.

## Work Cited

Hastings, Selina. *Sir Gawain and the Loathly Lady*. Illustrated by Juan Wijngaard. New York: Lothrop, Lee, & Shepherd Books, 1985.

# Toni Morrison's *Song of Solomon*:
# An African American Epic

## Suzanne Elizabeth Reid

Reading Toni Morrison's *Song of Solomon* is an experience that moves most readers deeply, impacting the visceral, intellectual, and emotional parts of ourselves. From the beginning paragraph, where Robert Smith announces that he will fly from the top of Mercy Hospital at 3:00 p.m. and then jumps to his bloody death, the book steps on the average reader's sense of decorum, comfort, and sentimental hope for an easy end. That is the point of Morrison's writing and the power of her book. It teaches valuable lessons about humanity, history, and the effects of racism—not just by appealing to the reader's logical understanding of the vocabulary, plot outline, and character development, but also by shocking the reader into responding emotionally, by breaking through the "willing suspension of disbelief" that Coleridge assigns to all educated readers.

The beginning scene is a riot of color, noise, and event. The orderly world of Mercy Hospital with its all-white clientele, its three-story mass hushed by falling snow, is interrupted when Mr. Smith emerges on the roof with his blue silk wings; he has promised to fly from the height of Mercy. The crowd of about fifty black-skinned onlookers is focused by a tall black woman wrapped in an old quilt who raises her voice to sing out a major theme of the book: "O Sugarman done fly away/ Sugarman done gone/ Sugarman cut across the sky/ Sugarman gone home" (6). The only middle-class figures in the crowd wear appropriate coats for winter weather, but even they erupt in a shower of spilt velvet rose petals and the moans of inconvenient childbirth. Thus, Macon Dead III is born, the grandson of the only black doctor in the city, the son of a successful businessman, but the first black child allowed to be born within the sanctuary of Mercy Hospital, and then only grudgingly. The tall black singer is his Aunt Pilate, whose economic poverty and spiritual richness contrast with his childhood world full of physical comforts but empty of emotional conviction.

And so Morrison begins her insistence that readers feel and experience the disrupting clashes within African American history. On the one hand, the African American heritage brings with it the rich stark colors of bloodshed in the raw experiences of birth, sex, and death, unmuted by technology and wealth. Its comforting sounds of song and speech bloom forth from deep roots of memory composted into myth and poetry by time and travel. On the other hand, the middle-class ethos of the white world, as observed and understood by blacks striving to attain social recognition and material security, both marginalizes and smothers African Americans, muting the vibrance and vitality of their roots and, ironically, severing them from the very security and safety they seek.

Although *Song of Solomon* contains no major character who is white, the influence of racism pervades the novel; Morrison forces the reader to acknowledge its pernicious effect on men who strive to overcome its limits and women who try to ignore its presence. She offers several stories of spoiled lives. Macon Dead I and Macon Dead II have followed the rules and amassed material comfort; one loses his life and the other sacrifices his ability to live in friendship. Guitar and Porter have never enjoyed such wealth; their lives have been marred by accident and the careless response of whites to their plight.

Macon Dead III, nicknamed Milkman, begins as the book's thoughtless, feckless protagonist, the end product of two families who have tried, by following the rules set out by the dominant society, to escape the scourge of poverty passed down from slavery. Milkman's father, Macon Dead II, has worked hard to acquire property and to isolate his family from the dirt and the poverty of his community—necessarily the African American community since, as a black man, he is ignored by any other community. His own father had achieved the American dream; he had bought and developed with his own sweat and vision a beautiful tract of land in Pennsylvania, "Lincoln's Heaven," a farm with a future, an inspiration for other men in that African American community. But, when members of the white community grew jealous and greedy for the land, Macon II saw his father shot in the back while he sat on his own fence. The American dream proved to be unsustainable for black men, especially anyone smart and ambitious enough to reach beyond the marginal realm of poverty and social invisibility established for them by their contemporary white American society. What Macon II chose to learn from this experience was that loving and trusting people is not safe and that success depends on the acquisitive ruthless ways of those in power. Thus he becomes a landlord, merciless, who cuts his low-income black tenants no slack.

Macon Dead II makes his way to Detroit and marries the daughter of a doctor, educated and materially successful but barred from practicing at Mercy Hospital because of his black skin. While Macon Dead II appreciates with great finesse the physical gifts of his wife, he fails to relate to her or his three children except as symbols of his material success. He isolates his two girls from any contact with other children, caring more for the cleanliness of their expensive clothes than any friendships they might develop. The two girls never marry, although Corinthians finally does burst into a relationship with Henry Porter late in life, a relationship her father tries to destroy. The girls are trained to mimic the manners of the white upper-middle class but are barred from consorting with their economic and educational equals by the overriding poverty of their neighborhood. In the middle of the twentieth century, the African American middle class was tiny, and few eligible bachelors of the same status were available. Morrison portrays Macon Dead II as equally lonely, drawn to the easy warmth and song of his sister's house but lacking in understanding about how to form a personal relationship. He senses that he is the object of scorn and laughter in the community, but he doesn't know enough about people to figure out why. His narrow vision is focused on obtaining more and more wealth and property rather than on learning why and how to live. Any core of warmth and trust has been destroyed first by the shocking murder of his father and then by his fear that his sister Pilate has stolen the gold they had seen in the cave where they hid afterward.

If Macon's vision is narrowed by fear of poverty, the vision of Guitar, Milkman's older friend and mentor, is narrowed by hate. When Guitar was very young, his father was sawed in half in an industrial accident, the body tossed so carelessly in the coffin, with no attempt to reflect its human origin, that the two halves were buried facing each other. The white mill owner brought candy to the children and a token fee to the mother instead of offering any real sustenance, so the family was doomed to the endless struggle of poverty. During his teenage friendship with Milkman, Guitar's sensitive intelligence becomes focused on rebellion against racial injustice. In the wake of the racist violence that was finally made public knowledge in the 1950s and 1960s, especially the brutal murder of Emmett Till, who whistled at a white woman, Guitar joins a highly disciplined group whose purpose is to avenge these random murders of African Americans by white Americans. These men, who name themselves the Seven Days, are dedicated to balancing the scales; each selects a day of the week and vows that when any black person is murdered on that day, he will commit a similar deed to a white person. Thus, their lives are devoted to waiting in hate to prove their love for their race. Guitar's mind dissolves into obsessive suspicion even of his best friend, and his hatred turns personal. Other members of the Seven

Days waste their lives in loneliness and self-destruction. Robert Smith, who leaps to his death at the beginning of the book, has been a member, and so has Henry Porter, who drinks himself into a pitiful stupor, peeing on his neighbors and begging for sex. Morrison implicitly asks if vengeance is the only possible response for loyal men with a sense of honor.

Morrison explores one answer in the character of Pilate, the sister of Macon Dead II. After witnessing her father's murder by white men and after being hidden in the house of a white woman, Pilate's life is virtually untouched by the white world; inadvertently, she avoids racism by avoiding civilization. Instinctive and natural, almost like an earth goddess who has given birth to herself, she has no navel, making her seem unconnected to the civilized history of humanity. Pilate discovers sex almost accidentally, and she bears her daughter Reba the same way. But "natural" is not without discipline or reason; she leaves the home of a preacher when he begins to fondle her, and she has learned to read and fend for herself.

Insulted by repeated rejections when friends and lovers discover her lack of a navel, Pilate "tackled the problem of trying to decide how she wanted to live and what was valuable to her." She confronts values at the simplest and most important level, asking herself the questions that every self-motivated and psychologically healthy adult must ask: "When am I happy and when am I sad and what is the difference? What do I need to know to stay alive? What is true in the world?" (149). With profound intelligence and strength of character, Pilate solves the problem of poverty and isolation by caring more for people than things and by respecting her own instincts and experience more than social opinion or status.

The invention of Pilate is generally regarded as one of Morrison's finest achievements. Pilate prevails with dignity, wisdom, and compassion over the obstacles of witnessing the murder of her father and the loss of his Eden-like farm, the hardships of migrant work, and the physical difference that made her the object of suspicion. Pilate's character provides one of the most compelling models for human growth and fulfillment in all literature. Part of Morrison's genius, however, is that she does not simplify nor sentimentalize this portrait. While Pilate has conquered her own difficulties, she is ultimately unable to convey her strength to her daughter. Reba is simpleminded and lets people, especially men, take advantage of her easy generosity. She is lucky at winning things and cares for people only superficially without asking for personal respect. She survives from day to day, drifting between momentary pleasures without thinking or planning.

Nor is Pilate able to pass on her self-possession to her granddaughter Hagar, who is loved too easily, permitted to ask for anything she fancies, and never made to take responsibility for her own livelihood. She fancies her younger cousin Milkman and the titillating games of teaching him about sex. Their relationship is too easy to last, for both of them lack the mental stamina or discipline to consider the implications of their relationship. When Milkman ends their relationship with cruel indifference, Hagar threatens to kill him, playing out her anger in a most adolescent fashion without the guile or mental presence to change her words into action. After months of this drama, she collapses and dies.

During Hagar's funeral, Pilate insists that her granddaughter was loved. But in Hagar's tragedy, Morrison has demonstrated that merely appeasing and indulging a child's whims are not enough. Children, especially girls, need the kind of attention that teaches them to cope with life rather than to submit to it. Guitar, wise in the ways of death and life, recognizes Hagar as a "pretty little black-skinned . . . doormat woman" who had needed instead "what most colored girls needed: a chorus of mamas, grandmamas, aunts, cousins, sisters, neighbors, Sunday school teachers, best girl friends, and what all to give her the strength life demanded of her—and the humor with which to live it" (306-307). Girls need advice, caution, and direction. The tragedy of Hagar teaches an important lesson about promiscuity, materialism, and selfishness, but most of all about the need to experience the challenges and responsibilities that force a young girl to shape her life with meaningful values that don't depend on the superficial affirmations of romantic play. Hagar's complete despair forces Pilate to cope with the ultimate suffering, the needless death of a beloved child.

Milkman's life is so easy, thanks to his father's wealth and the undemanding devotion of the women in his life, that he is not forced to make a choice until after he is thirty. Milkman is the male counterpoint of Hagar, another child who has been spoiled rather than taught. He is the long-awaited male, insulated from the rigors of poverty and other realities of African American life in the twentieth century by his father's wealth and his mother's innocence. Ruth had grown up on a pedestal, placed there by her father's reputation as the only black doctor in the city, without real friends or mentors who connected her to normality. Now also separated from her husband's affection and trust because of a misunderstanding, she dotes on her son with the same thoughtless sentiment and dependence with which she has raised her older daughters. Unlike Pilate, she has never made her own decisions about how to live and how to bring happiness to her home. Passive-aggressive, she rebels with silly ineffectual gestures, unaware of how to become a capable mother, and neglecting to share her thoughts and secrets with her daughters. Her home has become sterile, dry, and awkward. Milkman is attracted to the more authentic and responsive affection in Pilate's home. Pilate has survived on her own by working, by exploring, and by seeking the kinds of adventures usually possible only for males.

It is this kind of adventure that Milkman finally begins, after the Christmas when he realizes that the lightheartedness of first love has disappeared from his relationship with Hagar, and in fact, that his own heart is vacant. Guitar has warned Hagar against belonging to anybody, against giving her life away: "It's a bad word, 'belong.' Especially when you put it with somebody you love" (306). The message is also pertinent to Milkman, who has let himself belong to whoever would claim him, working for his father, minding his mother, letting his sisters serve him, letting Hagar devote herself to him. He has failed to take ownership of his life and give it direction. While Hagar tries to refine her image with the surface values of corporate America, in cosmetics and clothes, Milkman takes a trip that begins with similarly superficial aims but evolves into a more authentic quest. He leaves home to find the gold he thinks Pilate has hidden in a cave. Tracing his roots back to rural Virginia, Milkman finds that he is capable of more than he knew. He learns to listen to the natural vicissitudes of life; he learns the give-and-take of a loving relationship; he learns the sly humor of human intelligence, and he learns the wastefulness of greed and hate. Like Pilate, he is beginning to learn to "fly"; he is learning to accept the accidents of life without bitterness, but to own the map for one's life, to take as much control as is possible, to value oneself as well as others.

In the end, he is victorious in bringing the beginnings of peace to his family, but also in the end he and Pilate are destroyed by the corruption of what could have been good in Guitar. As wise, as sensitive, and as intelligent as is the nature of Guitar, his experiences of poverty, racist oppression, and the random senseless murders of Americans who are black have warped his mind. Guitar becomes paranoid and greedy. Like the white man, he tries to take by force what doesn't belong to him. In the end, Milkman "flies" to grapple with Guitar, the embittered former friend who has just killed Pilate. Perhaps Guitar represents Milkman's shadow self, what Milkman might have become without the privilege of an extended adolescence, isolated from the wounds of such harsh reality. Perhaps Pilate has represented the virtues of an African American sensibility unsullied by racism, hatred, and materialism. Perhaps Milkman is joining Guitar in flying from a life that has become hopeless.

In exploring the options normally available to African American males and females in the mid-twentieth century, Morrison's epic implies that the strength to love, even in the face of racism, comes from openly and generously exploring the world, learning its geography, and making decisions about one's life based on individual experience. Ignore excess materialism; settle for survival and comfort. Demand respect for yourself, and pay attention to those whom you love. Appreciate the sounds, textures, and colors of the natural world. These are only a few of the lessons woven into Morrison's story.

Although not on the American Library Association's "Ten Most Challenged Books for 1999, " Toni Morrison's *Song of Solomon* is listed as the 84th of the "100 Most Frequently Challenged Books of 1990–1999" as determined by the 5,718 challenges reported to or recorded by the ALA's Office for Intellectual Freedom. In a relatively recent case with a high profile in the news, *Song of Solomon* was removed from the required Advanced Placement reading list of Maryland's St. Mary's County Public Schools by a small group of parents and other citizens who protested the book's descriptions of incest, explicit sex, implied sex, promiscuous sex, public urination, and the liberal use of foul language. While the superintendent ruled that it was inappropriate as a text for high school students, it could remain available in the school library. One parent indicated that the book is "mired in humanity's muck and generally void of intellectual depth"; but the fact that *Song of Solomon* received the National Book Critic's Circle Award in 1978 and that author Toni Morrison received the Nobel Prize for Literature in 1990 indicates a quite contrary opinion among literary experts.

Morrison's book is intricately crafted, its scope and mythic incidents rooted in Homer's *Odyssey*, European traditional folk literature, and Christianity. The imagery is stunningly precise, and the psychologically authentic dialogue creates unforgettable scenes and characters. The plot lines circle around each other like the lives of a close community; each reading reveals another subtle relationship. So carefully designed is Morrison's book that each verb and noun of the opening paragraph can be connected with an event or theme in the ensuing pages. Morrison's use of strong language and imagery is neither accidental nor cheap; it is highly authentic to the diverse cultural groups whose quests and struggles it realistically evokes. The incestuous relationship of Milkman and Hagar emphasizes their similarities. Their failures to thrive as whole people are rooted in their isolation from a wider community, spoiled by parents trying to compensate for racist crimes against their ancestors. The descriptions of sex emphasize genuinely complex human relationships; no gratuitous description titillates the reader. The two most graphic sex scenes portray sensual discipline and mutual generosity. When Macon Dead II makes love to his wife, Ruth, he spends the time and exercises the control to appreciate and pleasure her; when Macon Dead III and his new friend, Sweet, make love, they are sharing the same kinds of generosity. Morrison's descriptions of sex are healthy antidotes to the self-centered and abusive sex often portrayed in modern film and television. Likewise, the use of expletives seems necessary to express how close to the core of each person is the anger or frustration or, in the hunting scene, the celebration of male energy. Morrison uses strong language and provocative imagery to make us feel as well as understand how deeply her characters have suffered for generations, how tragically so many lives have been ruined and wasted. Wrongs have been committed. We need to know this with our hearts, bodies, and minds if we are to change. *Song of Solomon* is an anthem to the resilience of African Americans, their ability to soar above a reality too harsh to bear, to search for connections and love in the face of racist hate, to begin again after a wasted life. Its music contains rhythms that fascinate, melodies that haunt, and motifs that persist in the mind long after the first hearing. The novel's lesson is an important one for all students who would learn about the whole American experience.

## Works Cited

American Library Association, "100 Most Frequently Challenged Books of 1990–1999," http:www.ala.org/oif/top100bannedbooks.html, 2000.

American Library Association, "Ten Most Challenged Books for 1999," http:www.ala.org/news/archives/v55n12/99bookchallenges.html, 2000.

Morrison, Toni. *Song of Solomon*. New York: Penguin, 1977.

Samuels, Wilfred D., and Clenora Hudson-Weems. *Toni Morrison*. New York: Twayne Publishers, 1990.

Smith, Valerie, ed. *New Essays on Song of Solomon*. New York: Cambridge University Press, 1995.

# Clorox the Dishes and Hide the Books:
## A Defense of *Snow Falling on Cedars*

**Jenny Brantley**

Life is hard. It can also be deeply and richly satisfying and rewarding. This is one of the lessons of the novel *Snow Falling on Cedars* by David Guterson. If we journey with the main character Ishmael Chambers through love, war, and hate, we, too, can learn that even though life can be cold, that even though grief can "attach itself with permanence," we can, with Ishmael, watch his mother (who has suffered the loss of husband, estrangement of son, and division of community) and learn to take "pleasure in life," watch her standing at a stove "ladling soup with the calm ease of one who feels there is certainly such a thing as grace. She took pleasure in the soup's smell, in the heat of the woodstove, in the shadow of herself the candlelight now cast against the kitchen wall" (346).

*Snow Falling on Cedars* is a beautifully written, multifaceted novel, a novel of interracial romance, of courtroom drama in a modern *To Kill a Mockingbird*, of high-seas adventure, of the shameful historical fact and details of the imprisonment of Japanese Americans during WWII. Mostly the novel explores the mistakes of a rush to judgment, a judgment based on race and skin instead of deeper values.

In September of 1999, an English teacher in a high school twenty-five miles northwest of San Antonio, Texas, faced disciplinary action for assigning the book to seniors. The principal banned the book from classroom use, citing its "graphic violence, racial bigotry and honeymoon sex" ("'Snow' Generates Heat at High School" 31). In October of that same year, the teacher tendered her resignation ("Boerne Teacher Resigns Over Book-Banning" 22).

Those who wish to ban this book from high school classrooms are also guilty of a rush to judgment. Herein lies the paradoxical question: How can we learn about the abysmal moral failures of a rush to judgment based on surface values and appearances if we are unwilling to read and learn the lessons of these failures?

The novel asks deep and abiding questions: Who are we? What causes our actions? How do we face the consequences of our actions? Motivation and consequence—these are the essence of our humanity.

In the novel, unlike in life, we can break down characters into motivation and consequence because they are stationary, unchanging inside the pages. In analyzing each character, we can then see more clearly into our own motivations, looking at our own abilities to face the consequences of our actions. Are we brave enough, smart enough, careful enough? Perhaps if we ask ourselves these questions *before* we act, then we become capable of greater humanity. If, when reading *Snow Falling on Cedars*, we ask ourselves *why* Ishmael calls Hatsue *"that fucking goddamn Jap bitch"* (251), then perhaps we can grow to understand the deeper levels of racism, of the rush to judgment. If we never attempt to understand racism, to bring it to light, then it lies hidden and festering until we lose a part of ourselves.

Ishmael loses a part of himself, literally and figuratively. In the war, he loses his arm and he loses his ability to see past the surface of skin. In fighting the Japanese, he learns to hate Japanese. After the war, he comes home and sees Hatsue in the grocery store. Hatsue says "with detached formality" that she is sorry to hear about his arm (331). Ishmael sees her, in her incredible beauty, hold the child of Kabuo, and says, "The Japs did it. . . . They shot my arm off. *Japs*" (332). He is overwhelmed by his loss and seeks to hurt those he loves. During this period of difficult homecoming, he also sees her on the beach, the place where their innocent prewar love began. He says to Hatsue, "I'm not asking you to try and love me. But as one human being to another, just because I am miserable and don't know where to turn, I just need to be in your arms" (334). Hatsue refuses him, saying, "I hurt for you, I honestly do, I feel terrible for your misery. . . . You're going to have to live without holding me" (334). Frozen in this love-hate relationship, Ishmael is crippled, and only through a deep and careful look into his history, into his motivation, his actions, and the consequences, can he come to terms with his loss. By later saving Hatsue's Japanese husband, a difficult, initially rejected, and powerful *choice*, Ishmael has saved himself. Now he is only missing an arm instead of missing both his arm and his ability to feel love and pain. Instead of becoming an incomplete war veteran, missing his humanity and his arm, he becomes a complete man who fought in a war. He is healed from the John Wayne paradigm set up in some segments of American society. He can acknowledge both his fear and his hatred; he can move on.

As young people, Hatsue and Ishmael fall in love, a secret love since he is white and she is Japanese. Then World War II comes. Hatsue is sent to an internment camp for Japanese Americans; Ishmael is sent to the Tarawa Atoll. Both lose their innocence and their love; both lose a part of their humanity. Before she leaves for the camp, Hatsue mulls over the question of identity—is it blood or geography? Through some hard lessons, she will learn it is both.

Hatsue serves as a counterpoint to the rush to judgment. She thinks before she acts; she is willing to make the difficult decisions and to stand by her decisions with grace and courage. Before she and her family are sent to the internment camp, her mother confronts her about the secret love she and Ishmael have shared, saying "You must live in this world, of course you must, and this world is the world of the *hakujin* (whites)—you must learn to live in it, you must go to school. But don't allow living *among* the *hakujin* to become living *intertwined* with them. Your soul will decay. Something fundamental will rot and go sour" (202). Her mother's rush to judgment, her racism, is caused in part by the rush to judgment of the American society in sending the Japanese Americans to internment camps. Her motivation, like many of the other characters, is clearly caused by the war. Hatsue, in her uneasy position as a first-generation Japanese American, knows that it is too late to honor her mother's request. Hatsue is "intertwined" with America—its land and its people. She thinks to herself:

> She had one foot in her parents' home, and from there it was not far at all to the Japan they had left behind years before. She could feel how this country far across the ocean pulled on her and lived inside her despite her wishes to the contrary. . . . And at the same time her feet were planted on San Piedro Island, and she wanted only her own strawberry farm, the fragrance of the fields and the cedar trees, and to live simply in this place forever. (205).

In the spite of the racism she faces and the indignities of the internment camp, Hatsue decides to call the island her home.

This clarity of visions, this careful and considerate look at the world, carries her through the trial of her husband. She speaks to Ishmael, asking him to address the unfairness in his newspaper: "The trial, Kabuo's trial, is unfair. . . . You should talk about that in your newspaper." Ishmael, in his coldness, asks her to tell him what is unfair. He says, "But sometimes I wonder if unfairness isn't . . . part of things. I wonder if we should even expect fairness, if we should assume we have some right to it" (325). Hatsue, in spite of her time in the internment camp, in spite of the losses she and her family have faced, in spite of her husband's unjust imprisonment, believes in fairness. She says,

> I'm not talking about the whole universe. . . . I'm talking about people—the

sheriff, that prosecutor, the judge, you. People who can do things because they run newspapers or arrest people or convict them or decide about their lives. People don't have to be unfair, do they? That isn't just *part of things*, when people are unfair to somebody? (326)

In this quote, Hatsue calls into question those who have rushed into unfair judgments—the precise doctor/coroner who tells the sheriff to look for a Japanese martial artist, the judge, the jury, even her own community. Hatsue also addresses the spirit of democracy—the belief in fairness, the belief that we can rise above traditional hatreds, that we can avoid the rush to judgment, that those in authority in our society—the juries, the police, the lawyers, the school boards—can see beyond the silences, injustices, and racist beliefs which cloak themselves in platitudes ("the world just isn't fair") and assumptions of authority. Hatsue believes in fairness, in part, because she must, because these are the people of her beloved home.

This place she so loves, the setting of this novel, is a remote island off the coast of Washington state, a place, one might assume, far from the reaches of racism and war, far from the "graphic violence" and "racial bigotry" which so bothered the administrators near San Antonio, Texas. The time is pre– and post–World War II. The main players, in addition to Ishmael and Hatsue, are Kabuo, the man Hatsue meets at the camp and later marries; and Carl, the German American fisherman who Kabuo is accused of killing, who was also Kabuo's childhood friend. This soup of cultures, skins, and colors is changed with the coming of the war.

Kabuo and Carl, Japanese American and German American, are more alike than different. Friends in youth, fishing together and sharing their lives, at the advent of war, Kabuo is sent to kill Germans and Carl is sent to kill Japanese. Through exact and careful details of war (the graphic violence), a reader is made to see the *motivations* for their hatreds.

During the war, Carl survives the sinking of the *Canton*. After the war, he returns home a man who "couldn't speak. Even his old friends were included in this, so that now Carl was a lonely man who understood land and work, boat and sea, his own hands, better than his mouth and heart" (297). He becomes a man who needs land, "room, far more room than his boat could offer, and . . . in order to put his war behind him—the *Canton* going down, men drowning while he watched—he would have to leave his boat for good and grow strawberries like his father" (297).

Kabuo, also a war veteran, is taught to hate the German Nazis he is asked to kill; when Carl tries to explain the disagreement over ownership of land (cited in the trial as the motivation for the murder), Carl says, "I was out at sea, fighting you goddamn Jap sons a—" (404). Kabuo stops him, saying, "I'm an American. . . . Just like you or anybody. Am I calling you a Nazi, you big Nazi bastard? I killed men who looked just like you—pig-fed German bastards. I've got their blood on my soul, Carl, and it doesn't wash off very easily" (404). This meeting takes place on a fishing boat, out on the sea, the fog symbolically and literally encasing the two men. (I won't reveal the outcome since the book turns in part upon this scene.)

Like Carl, Kabuo finds horror in the war, horror that remains with him. He becomes a silent man, plagued by inner torment. Guterson describes a darkly passionate scene of war, with Kabuo killing a young German boy-soldier who lies dying, begging for his life. Kabuo, "after he'd killed four Germans," learns his warrior side, his "dark ferocity . . . passed down in the blood" (168). Guterson writes, Kabuo "saw only darkness after the war, in the world and in his own soul, everywhere but in the smell of strawberries, in the good scent of his wife and of his three children." (168).

Both Carl and Kabuo come home to the land, to find salvation in farming and family. Their actions in war have consequences, but like many of the characters in the novel, Carl and Kabuo can control their own behaviors, behaviors which reach a climax in the meeting in the fog. They finally confront each other with honesty, the rush subsides, and the reader is left with the possible hope that a friendship can be rekindled.

This novel gave me insight into motivations and consequences of my youth. I, too, grew up in a time of war when it was easy to lose sight of humanity, easy to judge based on skin color, easy to hate, easy to rush to a judgment.

I began the first grade in rural North Carolina in the fall of 1965. My country was in the midst of the Vietnam War, schools were being integrated, bras and draft cards were being burned. I knew that blacks and whites never ate together, never married; they just worked together. I rode the school bus with two very distinct groups—the kids from the Freewill Baptist Children's home and the black kids. The children from the Home had been abandoned by parents and grandparents; some had been beaten and abused, some arrived at the Home covered in cigarette burns and bruises. They were tough kids, survivors, and all white.

The black kids were the experimental group, the first kids to be integrated into the white public schools. Many were poor and smelled of wood smoke and fried foods. They were probably afraid, but they were angry too. They were tough kids, survivors.

It was a volatile mix. I remember huddling beneath the school bus seat as switchblade knives flashed above my head. I remember fistfights and blood. I remember name-calling—nigger, bastard, orphan, ofay son of a bitch. The white kids did not want the black kids at "their" school, but the white kids were not wanted by their parents.

During this time of my youth, college-age boys were beaten and spit upon for wanting hamburgers and fries at a Woolworth's café in Greensboro, North Carolina. The simple act of ordering a meal evoked visceral hatred and violence from white men sitting and drinking sweet ice tea.

A rush to judgment, a rush to anger, without thought of consequence. I never talked about these events with my parents because I thought life was just this way.

The popular culture of nightly news and slick magazines of my youth often only served to fuel the anger, fear, and frustration. Not only was my own country torn across lines of race and gender, but thousands of miles away, another country, a small place of farmers and green jungles, was torn across lines of geography and ideologies. What in the world could this place of "graphic violence" have to do with a young girl living in rural North Carolina?

When I was eleven, two of my cousins left for Vietnam as boy-Marines, coming home quiet and haunted. I remember seeing a picture on the cover of *Life* magazine—a soldier holding his bleeding buddy, his eyes a line with his helmet, staring out at his country. My aunt saw the picture and wept; she thought the soldier was her son. I think she was right. He was the son of all the mothers.

I remember watching the nightly news and seeing a naked young girl, about my age, covered with napalm, burning, running down an open path—a human torch, her mouth an O of anguish. That path, I remember thinking, looked very much like the path by our cow pasture, a place where I, too, liked to run. Who had done such a terrible thing to her, to this girl my age running down a path like my own? I never talked about this with my parents because I thought life was just this way.

I think many of us living in the South at that time, poor and white, poor and black, learned to hate someone, something. We were powerless to hate the people who made us poor, powerless to hate the men who sent our boys away, so we just hated each other. I knew I wasn't supposed to say the word "nigger" in public; it just wasn't polite, but politeness has little to do with racist thoughts. We could be polite in public, but in our homes, where the first lessons of life are learned, we used Clorox on our dishes after the blacks who worked in our fields had eaten on them. In our homes, just after supper, watching the nightly news, we were learning to hate the Vietnamese for killing our boys.

Just because you don't say the word in public, just because you ban the book with the word in it from the classroom, you do not cure the problem. What does? Education.

I was twelve when I discovered Harper Lee's *To Kill a Mockingbird*.

Scout was so much the story of my life, or at least how I wanted my life to be. Scout and I both had watched our fathers kill rabid dogs; we both wore food costumes on Halloween. (Scout was a ham and I was a pumpkin.) But more than anything, through the words and actions of Atticus Finch, I learned I could rise above racism and hatred.

Much of our society is even more segregated and divided than ever. Popular songs sing of hatred toward women, blacks, whites. Internet sites are devoted to bomb building and racial superiority. People kill each other for trying to merge onto an interstate. A simpleminded, enraged war veteran assassinates children in Oklahoma City. Boys at a school in Colorado swagger into a library wearing trench coats and carrying automatic weapons. Just as many of us carry the images of Vietnam and Greensboro, North Carolina, as our touchstones, our students carry in their heads images of war and civil unrest, of Oklahoma City and Colombine. Our society now shouts all the "impolite" words in public, but for some reason, many still want to "protect" our children from learning the history of these words, the motivation and consequences of using such words, the results of our rush to judgment. We are still putting on faces of moral superiority while Cloroxing our dishes, bleaching them into an artificial whiteness—just in case lips of color have touched them. It is nothing less than hypocritical.

*Snow Falling on Cedars*, like *To Kill a Mockingbird*, is a book with the possibility of causing social and moral change. At the end of Guterson's novel, Ishmael confronts the motivation for his hatred and his rush to judgment; he comes to realize the consequences:

> But the war, his arm, the course of things—it had all made his heart much smaller. He had not moved on at all. He had not done anything great in the world. . . . He had coasted along for years now, filling the pages of his newspaper with words, burying himself in whatever was safe. (442)

In this epiphany of soul and self, Ishmael is now ready for an act of grace. He is deciding to move beyond his hatred, to attempt to be fair, an act of greatness of which we are all capable.

Now, more than ever, we need to put this book into the hands of our high school students. Through reading this book, students can learn about motivation and consequences, about the failures of a rush to judgment. Through reading this book, we all can learn about what we can control—our own behaviors. As Ishmael realizes at the end of the novel, "accident ruled every corner of the universe except the chambers of the human heart" (460).

## Works Cited

"Boerne Teacher Resigns over Book-banning." *Houston Chronicle* (27 Oct. 1999), STAR ed.: 22. UMI-Proquest. 6 July 2000.

Guterson, David. *Snow Falling on Cedars*. New York: Vintage, 1995.

"'Snow' Generates Heat at High School." *Houston Chronicle* (10 Sept. 1999), STAR ed.: 31. UMI-Proquest. 6 July 2000.

# Defending *The Stupids*

## Gail Munde

Are you surprised to find that two monuments of children's humor, *The Stupids Step Out* (1974) and *The Stupids Have a Ball* (1978), have compiled substantial histories as objectionable material for children? These books seem incongruous beside their companion titles in familiar lists of challenged works, more frequently populated by realistic fiction for older children and adolescents that cross the frontiers of sexuality, race, drugs, violence, and religious beliefs. What content, language, or thematic treatment could adults find threatening in these enduringly popular picture books? At first glance, it may border on the absurd to take such challenges seriously.

Be assured, however, that some adults have found these books not only unsuitable, but dangerous for young children. Their offenses include encouraging childhood defiance of authority, using the derogatory term "stupid," and planting the notion that no one, especially an adult family member, is above ridicule. Objections to ridicule and defiance of authority will endure as one of the central reasons for book challenges as reader age increases, so it is useful to examine challenged reading material for the early-age child.

*The Stupids Step Out* and *The Stupids Have a Ball* were the first two books in a series of four, followed by *The Stupids Die* (1981) and *The Stupids Take Off* (1989). The books are the products of the author-illustrator team of Harry Allard and James Marshall. Both have impeccable credentials and long, distinguished careers in children's publishing. Allard authored the now-classic Miss Nelson books (*Miss Nelson is Missing, Miss Nelson Is Back, Miss Nelson Has a Field Day*), which Marshall also illustrated. Marshall wrote and illustrated the enduring George and Martha series (*George and Martha, George and Martha Encore, George and Martha: The Complete Stories of Two Best Friends*), the *Cut-Ups* books, and many humorous renditions of fairy tales. Most "best books" lists and core collection bibliographies published during the late 1970s and the 1980s are replete with titles by Allard and Marshall, including those in *The Stupids* series. Books in the series were widely reviewed at publication in standard sources such as *Booklist, Horn Book, School Library Journal,* and the *Bulletin of the Center for Children's Books.* More recently, Allard and Marshall's titles have shown up in accelerated reader lists around the country, *The Stupids* books generally at second- and third-grade reading levels. Other than Allard's *Bumps in the Night,* lists of frequently challenged books are untouched by Allard's or Marshall's other works, and include only the first two titles in *The Stupids* series.

The Stupid family consists of Mr. Stanley Q., the Mrs., and their children, Buster and Petunia, along with their "wonderful dog Kitty," their "superb cat Xylophone," and lots of cousins, uncles, and other relatives. Allard's deadpan text ("One day, Stanley Q. Stupid had an idea. This was unusual.") is the perfect foil for Marshall's slapstick drawings (framed paintings adorn the walls, always preposterously mislabeled; dog Kitty inexplicably wears an Indian headdress, and the Mrs. often sports the cat as a chapeau).

The nature of the complaints includes the books' use of the word "stupid"; for example, "How can people give praise to a story that makes fun of stupid people. Stupid is a very hateful word. Kids shouldn't use the term STUPID at all."[1] "[The book] encourages disrespectful language," "describe(s) families in a derogatory manner and might encourage children to disobey their parents," and "makes parents look like 'boobs' and undermines authority" (Pistolis 1996).

Research has consistently indicated that humor is children's strongest preference for reading material. Studies by Wendelin, Greenlaw, and Fisher have traced this finding as far back as 1925, across hundreds of books and thousands of children. Children's preferences for certain types of humor and humorous devices appear to follow closely the stages of cognitive development, and the match between joke and reader is the central appeal of the *Stupids* series. The books' joke content and presentation are exactly what children three to six years of age are able to grasp and appreciate intellectually, and therefore, to find funny.

The three-year-old enters the concept formation period, which continues until about age six. These years are part of Piaget's preoperational stage, which spans ages two through seven. Concept formation is the ability to distinguish incongruities of class or category and to understand violations of concept norms. Although appearance norms are the earliest to fix in memory, other examples of concept norm violations also include nonsense words, rhymes, puns, and unexpected word pronunciations.

Concept formation means that a child is developing a burgeoning set of expectations regarding what is realistic and unrealistic, between what is normal and not normal, and between what is socially acceptable and unacceptable. The child begins to catalog and classify situations, behaviors, and events based on their congruence with his or her life experiences. This ability to identify incongruities is essential to the appreciation of humor. Indeed, incongruity is generally recognized as the cornerstone of humor, for without the correct set of expectations, the unexpected is neither surprising nor funny. *The Stupids* are funny to children and adults because they violate so many of the concept norms children have acquired during the toddler and preschool years. Adults don't wear socks on their ears, or cats on their heads, or let the dog drive the car, and "mashed potato sundaes with butterscotch syrup" are not delicious. In fact, these incongruities are funny to children because it is the adults who violate the norms in these books and not the child characters.

Children recognize the implicit threat of punishment for violating some behavioral and social norms and the double standards that may be applied in such situations. They are conscious that what might be considered funny if done by an adult could result in punishment if done by a child. Objecting that the books "make parents look like 'boobs'" is a misunderstanding of both the creators' intent and the child's pleasure. The child readers' release from anxiety that accompanies violation of an expected norm could not happen if it were Buster and Petunia who instigated the stupidities.

Many of the sight gags devised by Marshall involve wearing ridiculous clothing. In *The Stupids Have a Ball*, the family throws a costume party for all the relatives to celebrate Buster and Petunia's bad grades ("Hooray!" cried Mrs. Stupid. "This time Buster and Petunia flunked *everything!*"). The guests parade in rabbit suits, Napoleon outfits, and wear candelabra and hens on their heads. Mr. Stupid dresses as General George Washing Machine. It is not until the last guest departs that Mrs. Stupid realizes she has forgotten to inform her guests that the party was a costume ball.

In *The Stupids Step Out*, the family jumps into the tub with their clothes on (no water of course, for "If we fill up the tub, our clothes will get wet"). Stanley Q. wears his new stockings on his ears, and when the family visits Grandmother and Grandfather, Grandpa is wearing a boy's Victorian outfit backwards. The day out ends with the family dressing in their pajamas—matching clown outfits, complete with pointed dunce caps. During the period that preschoolers and first graders are learning to select appropriate clothing and dress themselves in the morning, the Stupids' complete misunderstanding of dress conventions is hilarious to those children *precisely* because they have developed the correct set of expectations about what people are supposed to wear.

As children grow and learn, they rapidly develop a "catalog" of expectations that will serve as a basis for what is funny or not funny. At numerous points along the way, they have a need to recognize their learnings through cognitive "self-congratulation" or, more simply put, a satisfying sense of superiority because they "get" the joke and the joke is not on them. Mastery over the foolishness and nonsense presented in *The Stupids* is one aspect of the books that makes them so funny to children. Only when children have established for themselves the reliability of a concept do they enjoy distorting that concept in the guise of a joke. Children do not normally find humor in physical or intellectual challenges that they have not yet mastered; for example, bathroom humor is not funny to children until they are confident about their own toileting.

Adults who object to *The Stupids* may believe that making fun of stupid people is cruel and unworthy, particularly when the object of the joke is parents and other adults. Their point is not to be denied, for even Plato had moral reservations about the justice of laughing at a fool. He argues in the *Philebus* that laughter presupposes an ill will, a rejoicing at the spectacle of another's foolishness. However, in the case of the *Stupids*, I do not believe that Plato's argument can be applied, for he bases the charge of cruelty on an assumption: that in order for us to enjoy the weakness or ignorance of another, the other must be in a subordinate position. Our pleasure is cruel only when the object of the joke can exact no revenge for the mockery. This proposition does not apply when children laugh at the foolishness of adults, particularly the outlandish nonsense of the Stupid family, for children recognize their subordinate position and the potential for correction and discipline. If the positions were reversed, however, then the joke would be cruel indeed, for it is reprehensible for an adult to make fun of a child's weakness or ignorance.

Would these books be as funny to children if the title family were named "The Sillies"? Probably not, because "silly" implies an intention to amuse that "stupid" does not. One reviewer of *The Stupids Have a Ball* comments, "It isn't just that the Stupids are stupid, but that they are so happy in their stupidity that makes them appealing." The Stupids are completely oblivious to their own nonsense while child readers and listeners find enjoyment in the superior knowledge, the "knowing better" that allows them to get the jokes in the text and images.

Child readers and listeners who are too early in the concept formation stage will not find the books humorous because they lack the cognitive capacity required to understand the specific forms of humor in the books. For instance, one of Allard's and Marshall's running gags through the series is to show framed pictures hanging on the wall, always absurdly mislabeled. If the child reader/listener has not developed an image-based representational capacity, then a picture of a fish labeled as a "dog" is not funny. So, if the incongruities in Marshall's illustrations have to be pointed out by an adult, or Allard's text explained, then the child is more likely to be confused than amused by *The Stupids*, and I would not recommend the books for these children. If the child does not understand the incongruities in full, she or he may fix only upon how much fun it is to say *stoo-pid* and apply it to every noun in his or her vocabulary on a regular basis.

According to research on the development of children's sense of humor, by age five (Kappas) they are provoked to humor by the slapstick, exaggeration, and nonsense employed in *The Stupids* books. Children at ages four through six can replicate these joke conventions in their own attempts at humor and can draw and appreciate funny pictures. The humor of *The Stupids* can be accessible to children as early as ages three/four, but would begin to fade at age six/seven. At age seven, children enter Piaget's concrete operations stage, which ushers in the "age of realism" in humor development. Perhaps because of this, and perhaps as a response to school, children may refuse to suspend disbelief and find the simple incongruity of *The Stupids* no longer funny because "things couldn't happen that way." This, and a general refusal to engage in playful behavior, fades as the child develops further into the middle years and the sense of humor returns, this time to focus on more complex intellectual word plays, puns, and riddles.

The Stupids, both the characters and their ridiculous behavior, are such a perfect match for the intellectual and social capacities of the three- to-six-year-old that they have enjoyed broad appreciation by this age group. The Stupids invite the child reader's ridicule only because the child recognizes and understands the multiple conventions violated on every page and the absurdity of the propositions. Like older children, adults may not be willing or able momentarily to suspend their sense of the normal order, which is a basis for appreciating the absurdity in *The Stupids* books. They may take the jokes to be at their expense and be offended by them. They may fear that children, encouraged by their ridicule of the Stupids, will generalize this disparagement to all adults. But a child is *not* an adult and does not take any of this into account, unless of course the adult happens to be wearing a chicken tied to her head.

## Works Cited

Allard, Harry, and James Marshall. *The Stupids Have a Ball*. Boston: Houghton-Mifflin, 1978.

————. *The Stupids Step Out*. Boston: Houghton-Mifflin, 1974.

Fisher, Peter J. L. "The Reading Preferences of Third, Fourth, and Fifth Graders." *Reading Horizons* 29.1 (1988): 63-70.

Greenlaw, M. Jean. "Reading Interest Research and Children's Choices." *Children's Choices: Teaching With Books Children Like*. Ed. Nancy Roser and Margaret Frith. Newark: International Reading Association, 1983. 90-92.

Kappas, Katherine H. "A Developmental Analysis of Children's Responses to Humor." *The Library Quarterly* 37 (1967): 67-78.

Pistolis, Donna Reidy, ed. *Hit List: Frequently Challenged Books for Children*. Chicago: Office for Intellectual Freedom of the American Library Association, 1996, 1-2.

Plato. *Philebus*. Trans. J. C. B. Gosling. Oxford: Clarendon Press, 1975. 47-49.

"The Stupids Have a Ball" (unsigned review). *Bulletin of the Center for Children's Books* 32 (1978): 32, 21.

Wendelin, Karla Hawkins. "Taking Stock of Children's Preferences in Humorous Literature." 2.1 *Reading Psychology* (1980): 24-42.

## Selected Book Reviews

*The Stupids Step Out*

*Booklist* 70 (July 15, 1974): 1251.
*Bulletin of the Center for Children's Books* 28 (November 1974): 37.
*Library Journal* 99 (April 15, 1974): 1210.
*Teacher* 92 (October 1974): 110.

*The Stupids Have a Ball*

*Booklist* 74 (March 15, 1978): 1185.
*Bulletin of the Center for Children's Books* 32 (October 1978): 21.
*Hornbook* 60 (September 1984): 611.
*School Library Journal* 24 (April 1978): 65.

## NOTES

[1] Amazon customer review of *The Stupids Step Out*, written by Anne, a parent, on April 29, 2000, referring to the audio cassette edition of the book. Review posted at *www.amazon.com*.

# Bette Greene's *Summer of My German Soldier*: The War within the Human Heart

## Rosalie Benoit Weaver

As a Jewish girl growing up in a predominantly Christian fundamentalist small Southern town during and immediately after the years of World War II, Bette Greene is able to draw on her unique childhood experience in her fiction. One major theme in her work, the ugly effect that fear and intolerance of difference can wreak on human lives, pervades her first and most well-known novel, *Summer of My German Soldier*. In this novel Greene effectively and creatively transfers the hatred and anti-Semitism of World War II Europe to the small, Southern town where her main character lives.

Greene depicts the growing friendship between Patty Bergen, a twelve-year-old Jewish girl living in Jenkinsville, Arkansas, and Anton, a young German escapee from a POW camp outside of town. By bringing the reality of World War II to the postwar small-town South, Greene highlights the effects of racial and religious bigotry within the United States, within a small Southern town, within the family of Patty Bergen, and ultimately within Patty herself. Greene skillfully sets World War II, a war waged for racial, religious, and political dominance, as the backdrop to the war waged within Patty for love and acceptance.

The novel opens with the townspeople turning out to watch the arrival of a trainload of Nazi prisoners of war, young German soldiers, whose appearance strikes Patty as neither threatening nor shameful: "the only thing I sensed was a kind of relief at finally having arrived at their destination" (3). Nevertheless, it soon becomes evident that both Patty and Anton (one labeled Jewish and one a Nazi) are seen as outsiders, and they both struggle to escape the fear and hatred generated by their perceived difference.

Perhaps it is this fear of difference that causes some readers of Bette Greene's novel to see it as too disturbing for its young adult audience. Various criticisms of the novel take exception to Greene's treatment of domestic violence in her graphic depiction of the brutal beatings Patty takes at the hands of a father who cannot love her or himself. Other critics see anti-Semitism in Greene's contrast of the dark figure of the Jewish father against the dignity and goodness of the young German POW. Another view is that Greene is too hard on the social mores of small towns in the Bible Belt. Like Patty, Greene challenges the status quo by questioning the injustice of long-held beliefs and social conventions. Although Patty pays a large price for her questioning, in the end she transforms her self-hatred into a self-awareness that gives her the courage to move beyond the limits set by her town and her family, and to continue speaking out against injustice.

The opening line of the novel reveals the extreme pressure Patty feels to fit in and be pleasing in the eyes of others: "When I saw the crowd gathering at the train station, I worried what President Roosevelt would think" (1). Patty worries that her townspeople's public display of curiosity about the German prisoners of war might be seen as a danger to national security and ultimately as unpatriotic. She is quick to defend her community, "[w]e're as patriotic as anybody" (1). In this first scene, Greene introduces the general sense of patriotism that is often called on to cover up the realities of intolerance and hatred. As the novel progresses, Greene slowly unravels this widespread notion to reveal what lies beneath. When Patty reports to her family's black housekeeper, Ruth, that she has been watching the arrival of the prisoners of war, Ruth sees through the convention of patriotism to the truth about war: "Well I don't care nothing about no wars and no medals, I just care about my boy coming back safe" (6). For Ruth, the patriotic message that war is honorable and glorious rings false. The truth is that her son, who fights to defend freedom, is treated unjustly by his own country, discriminated against at home, and segregated from whites in the army. From the start, Greene challenges her readers to dig beneath the surface of conventional beliefs to find the real truth.

This challenge continues throughout the novel but not in a "preachy," didactic way; rather, Bette Greene dramatizes without comment, human conflict which, in turn, evokes reader response. From this initial reaction, adolescent and postadolescent readers can then begin to examine their own preconceived attitudes and feelings, and often gain new insights into the mysteries of the human heart. One such mystery is that of child abuse. Her father's anger and violence toward Patty are deeply disturbing to readers:

> At his temple a vein was pulsating like a neon sign. . . . Only one foot advanced before a hand tore across my face, sending me into total blackness. But then against the blackness came a brilliant explosion of Fourth-of-July stars. . . . The pain was almost tolerable when a second blow crashed against my cheek, continuing down with deflection force to my shoulder. . . . Knees came unbuckled. I gave myself to the sidewalk. Between blows I knew I could

withstand anything he could give out, but once they came, I knew I couldn't. (58)

This explosion of hatred, so graphically described, evokes from Greene's readers intense feelings: anger and disgust. In their initial reaction to the father's cruelty, readers often label him as evil, while they see Anton as all-good. Greene will not allow such easy answers. While Anton equates Patty's father to Hitler, "Cruelty is after all cruelty, and the difference between the two men may have more to do with their degrees of power than their degrees of cruelty," he admits that he has no right to judge anyone because of his role in the Nazi army, which he describes as "two years of being as inconspicuous a coward as possible" (119).

Bette Greene instinctively knows what all the best young adult writers have learned: that the move from adolescence to adulthood is a continuum that is marked by the development of critical thinking skills, and that reading is one major way to hone these skills. Nilsen and Donelson, authors of the foremost textbook on teaching young adult literature, compare the "stages of literary appreciation" to steps to self-awareness, from "finding oneself in a story," to moving beyond this egocentric view. As adults-in-progress, these readers move to the stage Nilsen and Donelson describe as "venturing beyond themselves" to "look at the larger circle of society," and they choose literature that "raise[s] questions about conformity, social pressures, justice, and other aspects of human frailties and strengths" (40).

*Summer of My German Soldier* provides the opportunity for developing readers to move beyond simple labels and stereotypes to gaining insight into complex issues. Even Patty, in extreme physical and emotional pain, refuses to see her father solely as evil. She explains, "other times I think he's beating out from my body all his own bad" (115). Anton reinforces her insight when he tells Patty what her father did after the beating: "He stood watching the housekeeper help you into the house. Then he came into the garage and talked to himself. Over and over he kept repeating, 'Nobody loves me. In my whole life nobody has loved me'" (116). Patty's response to this revelation raises a difficult question about the human heart: "I don't understand. Why? How could he be so mean and then worry that he isn't loved?" (116).

Into this already complicated issue, Greene mixes racism. Mr. Bergen's experience of anti-Semitism in a small southern town has caused him to internalize the hatred he has felt and to turn that hatred on his own daughter. Discerning readers will find a balance to Patty's father in her grandfather and grandmother, who refuse to use anti-Semitism as an excuse for blaming others for one's victimization. Her grandparents credit the press for telling the true story of Patty and Anton: "tonight people throughout the world will be reading about how a Jewish girl befriended a German boy" (169).

Greene's novel exposes young adult readers to the origins of self-hatred: in Patty's case her father's hatred and cruel abuse, the emotional distance and constant criticism of her mother, and the rejection of her peers. It reveals, further, the results of self-hatred and shows that she does not have to accept self-hatred as her legacy; she is determined to pursue the truth about society as a reporter.

Bette Greene's exploration of the dynamics of racism provides important insight to young adult readers about their own experiences with hatred and intolerance. As the tragedy at Columbine High School has shown us all too brutally, hatred and intolerance occur in our schools every day. This is a topic that touches the immediate world of today's young people, and educators and parents must help them to confront and deconstruct the underlying assumptions that contribute to their self-destructive behavior.

Bette Greene's on going analogy between Patty and Anton, with Patty as a kind of prisoner of war within her family and community, is a concept that is attractive to young adult readers. As Patty's friendship with Anton develops into a love story, her courageous attempt to help Anton escape parallels her own impending break from her father's oppression and the townspeople's scorn. Both Anton's and Patty's status as outsiders brings about their individual persecution and adds complexity to the theme of doomed young love.

Ultimately, the value of this novel lies in its presentation of the complexity of hatred. The backdrop of World War II anti-Semitism combined with postwar Southern racism provides rich texture for Greene's study of one young woman's struggle with self-hatred. Her father transfers his self-hatred to his daughter: "I saw the hate that gnarled and snarled his face like a dog gone rabid. He's going to find out someday I can hate too—" (58). The townspeople find her actions incomprehensible: "'Jew Nazi-lover!' screamed the minister's wife" (164). Even upstanding Jewish citizens like the lawyer Mr. Kishner, attack Patty: "Young lady, you have embarrassed Jews everywhere. Because your loyalty is questionable, then every Jew's loyalty is in question" (177). Ironically, the two people who show Patty the way out of her war within herself are a young German soldier and an old black housekeeper. The only "family member" who visits Patty in reform school is Ruth, who has worked for Patty's family for years, and who loves Patty dearly: "And from that first day I walked into your house I loved you the most, and I love you the most today. . . . Why, I ain't even the only one. He loved you. Anton did" (191). As Patty is left to examine her relationship to herself, her family, and to society, the reader must move through these same issues.

By exploring hatred from various angles, some of them very uncomfortable ones, Bette Greene refuses easy answers to complex questions. Her refusal is what attracts so many young adult readers to her novel and makes it worthwhile reading almost thirty years after its first appearance. For teachers trying to provide students with every opportunity for honing their critical thinking skills, Bette Greene's *Summer of My German Soldier* is a wonderful tool.

## Works Cited

Greene, Bette. *Summer of My German Soldier*. New York: Dial, 1973.

Nilsen, Alleen Pace, and Kenneth J. Donelson. *Literature for Today's Young Adults*. Sixth edition. New York: Longman, 2001.

# Judy Blume's *Tiger Eyes*:
# A Perspective on Fear and Death

## Charles R. Duke

No one would ever accuse Judy Blume of shying away from controversial topics. In fact, her works show up consistently on various lists of most-censored books. In spite of this, or even perhaps because of this, adolescents find what Blume writes related to a variety of issues in their lives to be meaningful and readable. *Tiger Eyes*, a novel written in 1981, is no exception.

Although many events in an adolescent's life loom large and often appear insurmountable, death is one that can be expected to have a lasting impact. Few young people have sufficient experience to draw upon when a parent, sister, brother, or other close relative dies to be able to cope with the loss, much less find some kind of rational explanation for the fears associated with the continued absence of a loved one in their lives. Few adults do either. Yet little discussion occurs in most families or in school settings that might assist young people in finding ways to cope with such fears.

Adam Wexler operates a 7-Eleven store in Atlantic City. One night while tending the store, he is robbed and shot. *Tiger Eyes* traces the impact of this event upon his daughter, Davey, Jason, a younger son, and Adam's wife, Gwen. No one fares too well in this story when it comes to dealing with death, and Blume traces the responses of the various family members with candor and often a bluntness that probably causes adult readers to squirm a bit, especially since the adult role models in the story, good intentions included, don't necessarily supply the support or answers that the family needs.

Blume is particularly effective in capturing the emotional roller coaster that Davey experiences. Initially, relatives and friends arrive to offer sympathy to the family and to provide assistance around the house. We see these efforts through the eyes of Davey, and although on one level she understands what they are trying to do, on another level she rejects their attempts and wishes them gone from her life. Predictably, Davey withdraws from just about everyone, including her boyfriend; she doesn't eat, she loses weight, and she won't clean herself. When she goes to school, she suffers anxiety attacks, hyperventilates, and passes out. In the meantime, her mother tries to hold the family together but, fearful of an unknown future, can't bring herself to deal with the decision of whether to reopen or sell the store. Finally, the family doctor prescribes a change of scene, and the whole family travels to New Mexico to spend some time with Adam Wexler's sister, Bitsy, and her husband, Walter.

Having dealt with the initial reactions of the family—mainly in terms of various forms of denial about Adam's death—Blume then moves on to examine the next phase—reestablishing the family unit. At this point, Blume paints a tidy picture of Bitsy and Walter's life, one that is heavy on routine and restriction, short on creativity and spontaneity. Davey and her family might expect to find security in such a routinized and restricted world, and for a time they do. Bitsy assumes the mothering role as Davey's mother finally succumbs to her own grief and withdraws from her responsibilities as a parent for almost a year, leaving Davey, basically, to fend for herself. It's a neat juxtaposition; first Davey could not deal with her life and the mother held the pieces together; then Bitsy and Walter offer an apparent safe haven and attention to the two children, leaving the mother now to wrestle with her own demons and loss.

Davey finds she has to escape from the highly structured and restrictive world of Bitsy and Walter, which has been designed to minimize any dangers or changes in life. She goes rock climbing and in the process becomes acquainted with Wolf, a college student. The appearance of Wolf is a welcome distraction and offers Davey a completely new focus for her thoughts and actions. It is Wolf who gives Davey the name Tiger Eyes, and gives her hope to believe that she can once again build relationships with others. Within this new world, however, Blume offers some intriguing counterpoints related to fears of violence and death; there is Walter's insistence, for example, of carrying a rifle with him in his car every time he leaves his house; there is his work at the Los Alamos lab where the atomic bomb was designed and where he continues to work as a weapons expert. There is the racism exhibited between the inhabitants who live in the government compound at Los Alamos and the natives who live outside it. And then there is Davey's work as a candy striper in the local hospital, where unknowingly she befriends Wolf's father, who is slowly dying of cancer. And finally there is Davey's friend Jane who, fearful of what her future may hold, resorts to alcohol to numb her fears.

Blume reminds readers subtly but powerfully that death and violence are never far from us and that the world, in general, can be, at times, a fearful place. Such ideas, of course, are not calculated to win approval from adults who would wish to keep such news from their children as long as possible. Books that address such topics draw adult censors like a magnet. But Blume also has another message in this book that undoubtedly causes alarm among some adults. In various ways, Blume suggests that we all, young and old, have our fears and that we have to make difficult choices about how we deal with them in our lives. Some people decide to let others make the choices for them, choices that at the time, at least, seem safe and attractive but later may turn out not to be so suitable after all. This is certainly the case when Davey's mother brings her family to stay with Bitsy and Walter at their urging, only to discover that if she really wants to be a parent to her children, she has to face her fears, work through them, and make a life for the children independent of well-meaning but parochial-minded relatives.

Others make their own choices and have to learn to live with the consequences of such actions. Jane, for example, is well on her way to becoming an alcoholic, choosing to drink to avoid her fears of never finding her place in the world. Readers will find alcohol abuse described rather graphically, ranging from Jane's getting drunk because she is socially insecure around boys to her showing up drunk at an audition for the school play. Even though Davey tries to help by suggesting counseling and providing Jane with materials that pinpoint the dangers of alcohol, it is still Jane who has to make the final choice to seek help.

Often, in making choices, it is important to have someone whom you can trust, someone with whom you can talk about your fears. Davey tries to the best of her ability to be that person for Jane, but also recognizes that sometimes a person has to seek professional help. Both Davey and her mother benefit from their sessions with Miriam, a family counselor, as they try to come to grips with their fears. Davey also is helped by her association with Wolf, who is mature beyond his years; she is even helped by Wolf's father, who, while knowing he is dying from cancer, faces it with dignity and calmness. In any case, making choices in an uncertain world is pretty scary stuff for anyone, but particularly so for young people who haven't had much practice yet. Yet Blume lets adolescents know through Davey's experiences that they can be responsible and that they don't necessarily have to make all the tough decisions by themselves.

Missing from this book is any attention to nonsecular responses to death. At no time does Blume have her characters enter into any discussion about the role of religion and faith in facing death and related fears. Only once does Davey raise the issue of an afterlife, for example, and then only in a letter to Wolf, when she decides to tell him about the death of her father and her own fear of dying. She writes, "Sometimes I think about dying and it scares me, because it is so permanent. I mean, once it's over, it's over. Unless there is something that comes after. I like the idea of an afterlife, but I can't really bring myself to believe in it" (170).

The fact that Blume chooses to omit any discussion of this perspective on death no doubt incenses the far right. In dealing with the aftereffects of Adam Wexler's life, his wife turns to a therapist and even encourages her daughter to do so as well, rather than turning to a minister or some form of organized religion. Davey explains why this may have occurred. She reveals that she once read that organized religion is based on guilt and fear. She further reveals that each of her parents was half-Jewish and that, although they had tried going to several different churches, they ultimately ended up going to none. Clearly such a choice would not set well with many critics. Blume's stance toward religion in this book and her choice of actions for her characters undoubtedly have been the primary reasons why *Tiger Eyes* has remained on most censorship lists for so long.

Blume makes it clear that Davey's family individually and collectively have to decide what choices they will make. No one else can make the choices for them. They can try to insulate themselves from the world and live within a highly protected environment such as Bitsy and Walter have created or they can opt to strike out on their own and create a new life, one based on their own choices. These choices are both scary and exhilarating because it means that whatever they do, they are taking responsibility for their actions. The real message of *Tiger Eyes*, however, may be captured in the letter Davey writes to Wolf, where she admits for the first time to someone else her fears. This excerpt, which Davey gets from a magazine, is particularly telling:

> Each of us must confront our own fears, must come face to face with them. How we handle our fears will determine where we go with the rest of our lives. To experience adventure or to be limited by the fear of it. (170)

Until Davey confronts her greatest fear, one attached to her father's death, she cannot move on with her life. We learn that Davey arrived in the store shortly after her father was shot and, as he lay wounded in her arms, he kept asking her to help him. Although there was nothing she could have done for him, she has lived with the fear that somehow she failed him. Afraid she would forget this, she has carried with her in a brown paper parcel the clothes she was wearing that night, which are soaked with her father's blood. And she always has a bread knife close by when she sleeps in the fear that she will not be prepared to fend off any attacks that might be made on her. She does not want to be like her father and be unprepared. With the help of her mother's therapist, Davey finally is able to tap into the emotions and fear she has carried with her ever since her father died and is able to put them aside. Symbolically, she carries the clothes and knife to a cave and buries them. As she does so, she says,

> "Goodbye, Daddy. I love you. I'll always love you. This doesn't mean that I'm not going to think about you anymore. This doesn't mean that I'm never going to think about that night, either. . . . But from now on I'm going to remember the good times." (200)

Regardless of how censors may view *Tiger Eyes*, the novel, for all of its realism, is not depressing, nor is it likely to have a negative effect on its adolescent readers. Blume shows us, through Davey and her mother, in particular, that people can survive some very traumatic events, can learn to face their fears, and still can find ways to move on with their lives in productive and meaningful ways. For Davey and her family, that choice means leaving the structured and protective world of Bitsy and Walter and returning to Atlantic City, where fears still reside but where the future and its opportunities hold great promise and adventure.

No author ever can hope to address in just one book all the fears or the uncertainties that adolescents feel, but books such as *Tiger Eyes* can offer both a sympathetic and realistic perspective on what it's like to deal with the fear of death and the unknown, and emerge stronger and better prepared at the other side of the experience. As Davey says to her friend Jane as they part, "*La vida es una buena aventura.*"

## Work Cited

Blume, Judy. *Tiger Eyes*. New York: Bantam Doubleday Dell Book for Young Readers edition, 1991.

# Sex, Swearing, and Sacrilege:
## A Rationale for *Vision Quest*

**Wendy J. Glenn**

Terry Davis's *Vision Quest* describes two weeks in the life of Louden Swain, an eighteen-year-old high school senior who is about to face the biggest wrestling match of his career. Louden lives with his father, a liberal-minded car dealer, and his girlfriend, Carla, a worldly young woman who hitches her way into town after leaving home due to pregnancy. Louden's mother lives in nearby Seattle with her new husband and family. To wrestle in the number-one slot in the 147-pound weight class, Louden must lose seven pounds before the big event. He spends his time training and living on Nutrament and spinach. As the match grows near, Louden becomes reflective, and the novel addresses his insights and newfound awareness as he prepares to enter the world after high school. Although only two weeks elapse in the duration of the novel, flashbacks and revelatory passages present a complex young man who is inspiring in his honesty and thoughtfulness. This honesty, however, may be too much for some audiences, especially those quick to censor nontraditional values. The most likely aspects of the novel to be attacked deal with Davis's treatment of sexuality, profanity, and religion. Despite criticism, this novel is powerfully and skillfully written with characters that we come to know and a sense of perspective that is motivational and worth knowing.

Teenage sexuality is often controversial in novels and elsewhere, and this story does indeed contain much reference to the physical act. As a result, censors are likely to make this their first target. This is a sexy book. References to pubic hair, the clitoris, and pudenda, among others, are included that may serve to surprise and appall some readers. However, we must consider the protagonist to assess whether or not these terms are used for shock value or in a way that is revealing and appropriate. We hear this story from the perspective of an eighteen-year-old male. That explains Davis's choice of language. More important, young Louden is intrigued by the human body, so much so that he reads medical texts, including Gray's *Anatomy*, *Pathology*, and *Obstetrics and Gynecology*, in his free time and hopes someday to become a physician. His precision of language shows his knowledge rather than an attempt to be vulgar and crude.

In addition, several fully developed and explicit sexual passages in the novel take place between Louden and Carla. Not only do these young people live in the same home, they share the same bed. For some readers, the graphic detail will be too much. These young people are very much drawn to one another physically and hold a modern view of sexuality; anything goes. In their first encounter, raw passion is evident. As Louden describes,

> Carla . . . pulled my hair and bit me little hard ones and dug her fingers into me all over. Thank Christ she keeps her fingernails short. I squeezed her till her vertebrae cracked and drove into her with all my abdominal strength, which is a lot even in the off-season. Carla laid her head back and made beautiful animal sounds. . . . [I] twitched like a freshly killed snake and gasped like a victim of cardiac collapse. I had never experienced any feeling like that before. It was several universes beyond any pleasure I'd even imagined. (83)

This is honest writing and a true reflection of adolescent male sexual thought; Davis refuses to resort to sentimentality and sappiness.

Yet these young people are not in the relationship for the physical element alone; there is a gentleness and intimacy that goes beyond adolescent lust. They, in fact, have earned what Louden calls semimarital status. In one sexual interlude, Louden says, "We make slow love, lying on our sides, tummy to tummy, like old people probably do. We touch and kiss lightly, practicing our tenderness" (114). Louden takes his relationship very seriously and loves Carla deeply. He notes that Carla

> had the best things I like about girls and the best things I liked about guys. She was soft and beautiful and made up little animals and could be kind and tender. But she also swore creatively and worked hard at stuff besides her appearance and did what moved her—like leaving home or peeing with the door open or going with a black guy or banging on the steering wheel. Maybe when you get older you begin to appreciate many of the same qualities in the opposite sex that you do in your own. It would be pretty hard to live closely with somebody if you couldn't like her or him at least for the same reasons you liked all your other friends. (64)

Their relationship, although sexual, is perhaps more mature and emotionally intimate than that of many adults.

Censors may also criticize the profanity Davis has chosen to employ in the novel. Questionable terms range from the not-too-offensive "damns" and "asses" to the most shocking "f-word." Personally, the overuse of profane language among people in general indicates to me a lack of creative thinking and limited vocabulary. However, we are dealing with teenage males as our primary characters (and probably audience, as well). As a high school teacher, I can attest to the rampant use of such words and phrases among young people; a walk down the hall reveals a cacophony of lewdness. If Davis is striving for reality, as he claims he is, the voices of his characters must shadow the world he is attempting to emulate, profanity and all. Portraying the world as it is does not necessarily condone that which is being shown. Whether or not we want to admit that some young people speak this way doesn't change the fact that they indeed do.

One of the most interesting elements of Davis's novel concerns his discussion of Christian religion, a topic sure to raise the eyebrows of those concerned with banning any book that undermines this stronghold of conservative thought. Louden is not a believer, plain and simple, and he is not afraid to admit such. At one point, for instance, Louden describes Christ as a man "with all those wasted dreams, all those deluded souls on his back" (121). This lack of faith has roots in an illness his mother suffered as a result of her giving birth to Loudon; she endured pain for the next fifteen years. In terms of treatment, her doctor encourages her to skip the hysterectomy as she "wouldn't be a woman anymore" if she underwent the surgery (19). Instead, he prescribes "vibrating machines, hot and cold towels, and . . . capsulated herbs. . . . He also told her that God was the greatest healer" (19). When both medical and spiritual methods fail and her condition does not improve, however, Louden shows his skepticism in the claim, "I don't know what God treated her with" (19).

Yet, despite this seeming criticism of Christianity, this novel is one of the most spiritually inspiring that I have read. Ironically, Louden's favorite film is *Jesus Christ Superstar*, one that he makes certain to view every Christmas Eve. He claims he has "always wanted to believe that story, and this movie version concentrates on some believable aspects" (133). He goes on to explain, "Christ is a guy who has committed himself to a goal none of his people clearly understands. He is disciplined and calculating in pursuit of the goal. He defines his whole reality as though the goal—eternal life for himself and everybody who believes in him—were really possible. He lives fierce and proud and then he dies" (133). The connection to his own quest for wrestling success is obvious. Louden is about to wrestle a young man he himself has difficulty believing he can beat. Nevertheless, he perseveres, doing all he can to prepare for the bout both physically and mentally. Christ's film character serves as an inspiration in his own life.

Louden also addresses why conventional religion doesn't appeal to him despite the fact that the film version of the same story does. He tells us,

> I *know* the characters in that movie. They're real. In all my younger days in Sunday school I never heard one biblical story about characters I figured I knew. I didn't even believe the living people in Mom's church were real. But in the movie everybody yells and fights and cries and sweats and farts and probably fucks, and Judas has some noble qualities, and Simon is an archfreak and dancin' fool who slobbers like the Sausage Man [a fellow wrestler], and Jesus warns God he'd best take him soon before he changes his mind, and that poor fucking Pilate just wants to let Jesus off, but he can't because it's not part of the way things are defined. (133-134)

What I particularly like about Davis's treatment of religion is that Louden truly thinks about what it all means. There are few things that scare me more than individuals who blindly accept what they are told without question; Louden typifies the thinkers I admire. He neither fully accepts nor rejects Christian theology but is critical in the formation of his spiritual views. He claims,

> There are certain points in the movie—like when Jesus is yelling at God about why he has to die—that set me free from my normal consciousness, that disrupt my competitive relationship with life. I mean when Jesus lets blast at God with that shrieking falsetto of his, I get shudders and my eyes tear. I want to jump up and scream some primal sound. What I feel is that I'm a human being and one of my human being teammates has just done a wonderful, beautiful, transcendent fucking thing with our limited human ability. And I'm proud. (135)

Despite controversy over any of the above criticisms, readers of *Vision Quest* will have to agree that it is a well-written novel. Davis is a master storyteller who weaves together past, present, and presumed future in a complex and tightly bound tapestry. There are a rhythm and pacing that keep the novel engaging and interesting; we want to know how this will turn out. Davis's use of reflective passages and flashbacks as described by Louden is revealing and essential in the development of both complex plot and characterization. One night, for example, Louden is in a half-asleep, half-awake state and begins dreaming of a childhood event that left a powerful impression upon him. He begins, "I lie here and think about Shute [his competitor], about Mom and Dad, about Carla, and about the short time I've got left to be a kid. And finally I drift into a reverie about the river, about the first time I saw it" (39). The remainder of this scene contains a description of Louden's visit as a "fat little Cub Scout" with his Mom and Dad to Lake Roosevelt. Because a new turbine is being installed in Grand Coulee Dam, most of the lake water has been drained. As a result, the water is low enough for Louden and his family to see his great-grandfather's old homestead, "the stone foundations of buildings, fence posts dripping rusty barbed wire, a rusted-through water trough sticking out of the mud" (42). Louden, in particular, remembers his grandfather's reaction to what used to be the cemetery, home to the grave sites of the original homesteaders. "I turn and see my great-aunt holding my grandfather and patting his head like he's a little kid," Louden recalls. "Soft-hued in their cotton and flannel, fat good old people, they stand in my memory, clinging and shaking, sinking imperceptibly into the mud of Lake Roosevelt" (42). This passage reveals Louden's sensitivity and genuine concern for connection. He states, "Even though it's a sad memory and has the power to depress me bad sometimes, I still like remembering. It's the only look I've ever gotten into my family history" (43). Later in the novel, he brings Carla to this same place, sharing with her a site that holds powerful emotions for him and allowing her to connect as well.

One of the greatest strengths of this novel is seen in the character of Louden. Simply put, he is a decent human being, one who is proud without pretension and kind without sickening sweetness. As a real character, he possesses both good and bad traits, but the good make him worth knowing despite the bad. Sure, he cusses and has premarital sex with the woman he loves, but if this is the worst we can say of him, we have little ammunition for his persecution. And if we can also remember his concern for others, passion for life, and dedication to his sport, he has much going for him.

As an athlete, Louden makes great sacrifices to become the best performer he can be. In addition to hours of daily training, from practice sessions with his teammates to lonely runs each evening, he closely monitors his diet. A few episodes in which he describes his nutritional intake are not only insightful as to his character but humorous, as well. When his coach asks him one day, for example, "Did you have any breakfast?" Louden replies, "A veritable feast, Gene. A big bowl of Carla's yogurt with some giant chunks of fresh pineapple" (85). Quite a spread. Later, Louden refuses, despite great temptation, to partake in some candy his father and Carla are eating with pleasure. He controls his desire, noting, "Eating trash food after all this time would spoil the pattern. It would upset the rhythm I've got going with my body and break the deal I made with my spirit" (160). This young man's willpower is impressive.

As a student, Louden is admirable. He is graduating early and has already completed enough college courses by mail to have earned sophomore status (31-32). Due to his family's lack of financial resources, he wants to spend the spring working full-time to cover college expenses for the next year. He has also opted to write a senior thesis, not because he must but because his topic intrigues him. He wants to explore the answer to the question "What gives life meaning?"—rather weighty for one of any age. Over the course of the novel, various mediums, from *A Christmas Carol* to the writings of Carlos Castaneda and James Agee, enter into his thinking and reveal a mature and thoughtful young man. His concept of life and death, for example, shows the depth of his ponderings: "[An] awareness and acceptance of death sets up an almost contradictory way of looking at life. On the one hand, you know your time is short, so you use it preciously. Then on the other hand, you know it all comes to dust anyway, so you don't value anything too highly. You have things in a perspective that allows you to live in equilibrium with the universe" (162). His musings encourage us to think.

This insight sets up Louden's later reaction to a fatal car accident he and his team members witness on the way to a match, further revealing the complexity of his character. Louden literally sees one of the victims go up in flames; he is not able to rid his mind of this image. He claims, "I didn't wrestle well at all. I had a real hard time shaking the whole scene from my mind, especially the head lolling back as if to scream. To this day I can see it. On the way home we felt the bus dip when we drove over the site of the wreck. The fire had melted the asphalt and left a low place the county hasn't filled to this day" (173-174). Louden is a sensitive young man, strongly affected by an event about which his teammates laugh and joke. His kindness is also shown in a passage he shares from his youth. As a child, Louden struggles to make sense of his mother's illness and, as a young adult, remembers little. One day, however, remains vivid for him. After returning from a victorious Pop Warner football game in which he was voted most valuable player, Louden finds his mother in her bed "with her curtains all drawn up tight, curled up like a little animal in her bed, holding her pelvis and crying" (20). He tells us,

> I burst into tears. . . . I ran up and jumped on her bed and probably half crushed her. I just hugged her and cried like a little kid. All I said was, "I'm sorry you don't feel good, Mom." I just kept saying that. . . . Then I went downstairs and cried by the furnace. . . . I fell on the floor like I was having a fit. I remember the concrete was cold at first but got really warm. If that doctor were alive today I'd kill the cocksucker with my bare hands. (20-21)

Louden obviously cares about those who are close to him and possesses humanity and passion that drive him both on and off the wrestling mat.

If nothing else, this novel is motivational and inspirational, not only from an athletic perspective but as a guide for daily living as well. Louden has the uncanny knack for celebrating humanity in all that he sees. He recognizes the power of average people to do amazing things. The same pride he feels after watching *Jesus Christ Superstar* arises on other occasions. When his friend Otto, for example, is named Prep Lineman of the Year at a pep assembly, Louden cries openly with pride. He also experiences overwhelming emotion when he witnesses soccer player Pelé in action during a televised match:

> Pelé whips off his jersey and starts to jog around the stadium. . . . [H]e was waving his jersey high and flashing his ivories wide and crying like a baby. . . . [M]y eyes filled with tears for him and all his great days of playing. I wish every human being in the world sometime in his life could know the glory of tears like Pelé's. . . . A person sure doesn't have to be a great athlete or politician or doctor or artist or entrepreneur or performer of any type or degree of greatness to find challenge in life. About half the time I think it's a great victory just to be able to smile semiregularly, to keep your head up, to keep from giving in and getting mean. I'm not ashamed to admit I need regular transfusions of confidence to keep me going. I need some examples that remind me, by God, it can be done. (137)

Louden is more than a sterotypical jock; he embraces his experiences, allowing them to touch and shape him as a human being.

One of Davis's concerns in writing this novel is to encourage individuals to be strong and persevere, to cope with the struggles of the everyday world rather than "give in to the challenges . . . , get bitter or give up their responsibilities" (215). Louden embodies this idea and gives it voice in his senior thesis. He reads Tom Robbins's book *Another Roadside Attraction* and appreciates how "these Robbins people create their own meaning in the way they live. They live as though certain things were important, so those things become important. . . . That's something I believe in. It's the same thing Castaneda means when he says that by the power of our will we can stop the world and remake it" (179-180). He firmly believes in the myth of self-discovery and that the idea of a person "finding himself" is ludicrous and escapist. He claims,

> What really happens among the few people who make it happen is not that they find themselves but that they "define" themselves. I used [in his thesis] the example of Bob Dylan. Dylan wanted to be a folk-hero-singer, so he made up a history, went on the road and followed the tradition, worked hard, and by the power of his will and imagination became his dream and probably more. I talked about how, even if you define yourself as a Christian and believe in eternal life, you've got to realize your time on earth is incredibly short. And I explained further that along with this has to go the realization that we not only die alone, but that, really, we live alone, too. That no matter how we love our families and

friends, we can't breathe for each other when our alveoli clog up with cigarette smoke and car exhaust, that we can't pee for each other when our kidneys stop working, and that we can't really comfort each other once we know these things. This is the real reason . . . why we've got to love the people who deserve it as fiercely as we love our own lives. (189-190)

I must admit, I was a bit concerned about defending this particular novel after hearing the comments of colleagues and friends who had already read the work. My professor and mentor warned, "Oh, that's a sexy book," when she learned of my choice. A friend informed me that the novel was the source for her first exposure to the word, "clitoris." Having read the novel, however, I have no regrets. *Vision Quest* offers a powerful story written with skill and style, one that I would not recommend to every young reader but to any who is searching for meaning, insight, and inspiration.

## Work Cited

Davis, Terry. *Vision Quest*. New York: Dell, 1979 (Laurel Leaf 1991).

# The Avenger Strikes Again: *We All Fall Down*

## John S. Simmons

## Introduction

Over the past quarter-century, Robert Cormier has been spinning tales about young people involved in one problematic circumstance or another emblematic of present-day Americana. Unlike many young adult (YA) novelists of an earlier time, the young people depicted are not athletic heroes, nor are they sweet young things successfully guarding their virtue. And the America these youngsters inhabit is not the Leave-It-to-Beaver or Andy Griffith's Mayberry locale either. The kids are complex individuals and not always the types you'd like to have as next-door neighbors. Such teenagers appear in all of Cormier's texts, and those found in *We All Fall Down* (1991) are no exception.

## Why It's Good

The creation of intertwined plots that reach a credible climax is signature Cormier. In *We All Fall Down*, these strands include two white, upper-middle-class, small-town families living in a relatively uneventful locale. Three other teenagers and one middle-aged, mentally challenged resident round out the cast. From this *dramatis personae*, Cormier has constructed four subplots that he manipulates with characteristic adroitness, bringing them together in a totally credible climax at the drama's final curtain.

Because the plot does involve violence, subterfuge, and unexpected twists, suspense emerges as one of the text's features. Cormier has demonstrated the ability to create suspenseful stories in most of his earlier novels. *The Chocolate War* (1974) and its sequel, *Beyond the Chocolate War* (1986), *After the First Death* (1979), *I Am the Cheese* (1977), and *Fade* (1988) all provide fast-paced, gripping action, often accompanied by

427

a sense of foreboding. All of the above can be found in *We All Fall Down*. Throughout his fiction, Cormier employs his journalist's sense of detail to offer graphic images of events as they transpire—images often redolent of painful, frightening, and disgusting elements that rivet the reader's attention, although many may well "skip over those parts." Add to this ingredient the author's distinctive ability to cloak action with a sinister overtone that frightens even as it entices readers.

"Sinister" is an appropriate term for denoting the character of Harry Flowers, one of the two evil geniuses in the novel. As Jonathan Swift portrays the Lilliputians as cute little people who disguise malevolent, sociopathic traits in their actions, Cormier is able to invest well-dressed, well-mannered, intelligent white teenage males with capacities to commit cruel, diabolically destructive acts that Harry, their leader, labels "funtime." In this capacity, Harry Flowers takes his place with Archie Costello, Brother Leon, Brint, and Artkin (to name a few) in the author's gallery of near-sociopathic malefactors whose cunning, cynical acts wreak pain and suffering, both physical and psychological, on several innocent, undeserving characters—ones with whom most readers sympathize.

Before leaving the critique of Cormier's character presentation, a word of praise for the characterization of another member of the novel's cast is in order. Mickey Looney, who is, in fact, "The Avenger," represents an example of the author's penchant for experimentation. Mickey, a middle-aged retardate, is bent on violent retribution to Harry Flowers and his house trashers. Having witnessed their destructive caper, he vows to make them pay. This decision is based on his quixotic/malevolent view of his role in society. In flashbacks, the reader learns that Mickey has already committed two acts of premeditated murder but has done so as an eleven-year-old. Cormier, with characteristic subtlety, leads his reader to the realization that Mickey reflects a multiple personality. As he plots to do away with Harry and his trashers, he reverts to his identity as a preteen crusader for justice. It is in this state that he threatens the life of Jane Jerome, and his ultimate confusion over his true self leads to his violent suicide. As in the epiphany of where Adam Farmer truly exists in *I Am the Cheese*, the author withholds this awareness until very late in the text.

Through the interplay of his characters, teenage and adult, Cormier addresses a number of important social issues in turn-of-the-century Americana. One is the problem of adjustment caused by the mobility of families whose breadwinners climb the ladder of prosperity and heightened social status. The Jeromes move to Burnside, a rather posh community, causing their three teen/preteen children to search for a new comfort zone in unfamiliar surroundings. The issue of divorce and its effects on an upscale

Burnside family drives one teenage offspring to seek escape in alcohol and participation in the "funtime" destructive ventures of Harry Flowers's small high school contingent. Also included is the presence of a violence-prone, middle-aged retardate whose behavior almost results in the brutal murder of the young female protagonist.

In a thematic sense, there is no more important message in *We All Fall Down* than the presence of random violence as perpetrated by young adults in the United States of America in the decade just completed. Harry Flowers is the son of a successful, affluent architect. As stated earlier, he is the picture of the teenager most popular, most likely to succeed in his gleaming suburban high school. He is in no way a marginalized gangbanger from the depths of an urban ghetto. He doesn't need to steal for survival or to sustain a nonexistent drug habit; in fact, the issue of drugs or deadly weapons among the novel's young people is never mentioned. Yet Harry's social *raison d'être* is to create mischief, mischief that runs the gamut from making disruptive noise in a local movie theater to the virtual demolition of a lovely home, the occupants of which are unknown to the assailants. Harry recruits three cohorts for his "funtime" mission, plying them with alcohol and exploiting their boredome and (in the case of Buddy Walker, the novel's male protagonist) unhappiness. Harry's callousness, shrewdness, and opportunism can be seen in sharp focus toward the novel's end. He phones Jane Jerome, who has just escaped death at the hands of the mentally challenged Mickey Looney and has also broken up with Buddy Walker, the love of her life (also, in reality, one of the housewreckers). Cormier presents the scene in this manner:

> "Listen, you don't know me. But you know my name. My name is Harry Flowers." Then quickly, at her intake of breath: "Wait, don't hang up, please don't do anything. Just listen, that's all, a minute, two minutes. Just let me say what I have to say. . . . What I have to say is this: You've got Buddy Walker all wrong. Sure, he was with me and the others that night at your house. But he was drunk, didn't really know what he was doing. He didn't touch your sister. What happened to your sister was an accident whether you believe it or not, but Buddy had no part in it. . . ."
> "Why are you telling me this?" she asked, surprised at how calm and reasonable she sounded. How cool.
> "I owe him this call. Look, I don't even like him. He's the kind of guy that I can't stand. Thinks he's better than other people, including yours truly. But he's sorry about what he did that night. His father and mother were getting divorced and I took advantage of his crappy life. That's why he got drunk and came with us to your house. . . .
> "Buddy's in trouble. He's drinking again. He stopped for a while but now he's drinking more than ever."

> She heard him take a deep breath.
> "I was thinking," he said, his voice becoming intimate, like a caress in her ear. "Maybe we could get together sometime." Smooth, sly. "You know, to talk about all this. Just you and me. . . ."
> The telephone was suddenly like a snake in her hand. She dropped it to the floor and let it lie there for a moment before slamming it down on the receiver. (196-197)[1]

Frighteningly, the reader must come to the realization that this could be the boy next door.

Many literary observers espouse the belief that art imitates life. In his focus on the theme of random violence among seemingly happy, well-adjusted young people, Cormier could well be considered a prophet in his own time. A few years after *We All Fall Down* was first published in 1991, the following calamities took place:

- 1996—a lone white teenager guns down classmates at Frontier High School, Moses Lake, Washington. No apparent motive.
- 1997—a high-achieving, white male high school student takes the lives of classmates at Pearl High School, Pearl, Mississipppi. No apparent motive.
- 1997—a lone white male high school student shoots and kills classmates at West Paducah High School, Paducah, Kentucky. No apparent motive.
- 1998—two white male high school students shoot to death classmates at West Side Middle School, Jonesboro, Arkansas. No apparent motive.
- 1998—a lone white male high school student shoots and kills classmates at Thurston High School, Springfield, Oregon. No apparent motive.
- 1999—two white male high school students shoot at large number of classmates at Columbine High School, Littleton, Colorado, killing eleven classmates and one teacher. They then turn their weapons on themselves. No apparent motive.

"No apparent motive" applies to Harry Flowers as well. While his actions were not lethal (although he does inflict serious injury on Jane Jerome's fourteen-year-old sister), his intentions were destructive in the extreme. In searching for answers to Harry's behavior, readers may well return to *The Chocolate War* (1975) in which the villainous Archie Costello, when questioned about his demeanor by his right-hand man, Obie, replies, "Life is shit." The motives of the Archie Costellos and Harry Flowerses? Go figure.

All of the above are disturbing to countless citizens as we begin a new millennium. The problem of random violence among our youthful popula-tion, however, is one we shove under the rug at our peril. Robert Cormier's

*We All Fall Down* represents an artistic effort to deal with it. On the cover of the Bantam paperback edition of the novel, the following excerpted quote from *The Washington Post Book World* appears: "Engrossing, Disturbing, and Furiously Paced. . . ." [2]Author Robert Cormier sent a personal letter to the writer of this essay in May 1985. In this document, he stated, "I do write to disturb—I think indifference would be the worst reaction."[3] It is reassuring that Cormier continues to write disturbingly about matters that *should* disturb us.

## Why It's Censorable

Throughout his tenure as a YA novelist, Robert Cormier has demonstrated a willingness to ignore several of the taboos that had been respected by the great majority of his predecessors. In *The Chocolate War*, he creates evil in the person of Brother Leon and in the presence of a sinister group called "The Vigils" in a traditionally conservative Catholic high school. In the same text, he describes masturbation on a number of occasions. The plot of *I Am the Cheese* is built around the cold, often homicidal behavior of a U.S. government agency extremely similar to the Central Intelligence Agency (CIA). In *After the First Death*, he includes a no-no in the extreme: the brutal murder of small children. To that, he adds a graphic description of foreplay between two adolescents. The setting of *The Bumblebee Flies Anyway* (1983) is an experimental hospital whose patients are terminally ill young adults. It should come as no surprise, therefore, that he assaults yet another citadel of orthodox mainstream American life in *We All Fall Down*.

Before dealing with the "Big One" in *this* novel, it seems appropriate to catalogue the taboos ignored therein. In a ten-year review of incidents reported by People For the American Way's highly useful annual report *Attacks on the Freedom to Learn* (1988-1997), the author of this essay found that use of inappropriate language and explicit treatment of sexual activity still ranked at numbers 1 and 2 among topics for complaints and challenges.[4]

In terms of bad words, this Cormier novel does contain a sprinkling. None of the teenage male characters use them very often, and the females almost never. The f-word never appears, although a synonym ("screw") is used once or twice in dialogues of Harry's group. Compared to the majority of YA novels written in the past thirty-five years, the language is tame indeed. (As a matter of plain fact, if the bad words inclusion becomes a criterion, very few of recently written YA novels would be acceptable for either classroom study or library acquisition.) They are there, however, for those parents, citizens, and "concerned groups" who worry about such matters.

Within the past twenty years or so, another set of criteria, that which falls under the rubric of "Political Correctness" (PC), has become a contentious matter to those members of American society who are committed to that issue. Once again, *We All Fall Down* can plead innocent of such heresies. The N-word is *never* used; in fact, racial, religious, or ethnic minorities are never the focus of attention of characters in the novel—although Harry Flowers does occasionally use a mild black dialect imitation in the donning of one of his many masques. It could be argued that the mentally challenged Mickey Looney is on a couple of occasions the butt of derision, but these incidents do not figure in the progress of the narrative to any appreciable extent.

The sexual intimacy element of Cormier's text is tame indeed and would probably cause little distress among would-be censors. Let's face it: compared to Judy Blume's novels, especially *Forever*, or some of Paul Zindel's earlier ones, or a few of Gary Paulsen's tales, *We All Fall Down* is Victorian in its treatment of boy-girl involvements. There is a love relationship, and it *does* involve a few episodes of intense petting, but the lovers are two sixteen-year-olds, both virginal, both engaged in their first romantic encounter, both obviously inhibited in their foreplay moves. Buddy, the male lover, does experience what Dr. Ruth Westheimer used to label "premature ejaculation" in her TV nightclub act of yore. Notice how Cormier presents it:

> They could not get enough of each other, which made it necessary for them to have rules. Unspoken rules but rules all the same, declaring boundaries, how far they could go, by some mutual instinct. How long kisses should be, how far touching and caressing could proceed. Cupping her breast drove him wild, thick juices in his mouth, the threat of a sudden embarrassing eruption. But never both breasts and never inside her sweater. They embraced lovingly in a sweet tumble of bodies. Buddy never pushed beyond those silent limits, although one night he stiffened in the middle of the longest kiss they ever had, their mouths meshed, tongues wrapped around each other, his hand kneading her breast, and he fell away from her, shuddering, then became silent. She reached out in the dark—they were in the backseat of his mother's car—and touched his cheek, felt moisture there, realized that tears had spilled from his eyes. And took him in her arms, tenderly, delicately, loving him for those tears as she had never loved him before. (130-131)

By most contemporary standards, pretty tame, *n'est-ce pas*?

The senseless destruction, cruelty, violent impulses, and intimidations have been discussed previously. Some parents and/or concerned citizens may find them objectionable, but certainly they do not compare with the recent novels of writers such as Walter Dean Myers, Todd Strasser, Robert Newton Peck, Alice Childress, and Lois Duncan. And when compared to Cormier's earlier texts, especially *The Chocolate War* and *After the First Death*, violence in *We All Fall Down* is relatively minor.

It is in the area of "family values" that this novel is most vulnerable to attack. Alarm may be felt particularly by those who think the traditional, nuclear family of an earlier time has deteriorated, to some extent, because teenagers read books in school that seem to mock or question the Norman Rockwell image of the family at prayer around a Thanksgiving dinner table. In the early 1990s, former Vice President Dan Quayle created a popular debate when he criticized the Murphy Brown TV series, particularly the way in which the series's protagonist first prepared for, then happily delivered, a child out of wedlock. The vice president's tirade was red meat for the several special interest groups already deeply involved in confrontation with all whom they suspected of New Age skullduggery. By then, Dr. James Dobson's Focus on the Family group was crusading against Murphy Brown and her ilk. So was Donald Wildmon's American Family Association, Phyllis Schlafly's Eagle Forum, Tim and Beverly LaHaye's Concerned Women for America. Pat Robertson's Christian Coalition, and Gary Bauer's Family Research Council, to name the more visible ones. It goes without saying that books on that subject, particularly those introduced into public school classrooms and libraries, quickly came within their field of vision. In *We All Fall Down*, they have a likely target.

The fate of two families is featured in this novel. First, there are the Jeromes. They are newly arrived in the small, upscale community of Burnside. (Cormier is quite familiar with such communities from his lifelong residence in east central Massachusetts.) They, father, mother, two teenage daughters, and one preteen son, go their separate ways until their house is assailed and younger daughter becomes comatose through her injuries. For most of the novel, they tiptoe around each other unable to function until, near the story's end, one daughter recovers and the other is rescued from near catastrophe. It takes the shock of these events to bring them back together as a functional family unit.

More distressing is the Walker family, which undergoes virtual dissolution as the narrative progresses. The father admits to infidelity and then announces his plan to move out, probably to move in with his considerably younger secretary. This unexpected decision throws the remaining family members—an attractive, well-educated, gainfully employed mother; a sixteen-year-old son who is socially sensitive, scholastically successful, and physically attractive; and a younger daughter who is popular, heavily involved in high school activities, and also attractive—into a tailspin.

The centrality of the divorce to the dissolution of the Walker family would be ample cause for this text to be challenged by the "family values" advocates. Such a reaction should be exacerbated by the fact that it was precipitated by a husband's extramarital affair. Furthermore, the separated couple remains apart at the story's end, failing to provide the fairy-tale ending so cherished by many American adults.

The issue of divorce has become an extremely sensitive one to many American parents over the past couple of decades. This concern gained the national spotlight during the adjudication of the Hazelwood (Missouri) decision finally settled by the U.S. Supreme Court in January 1989. Two eleventh grade school newspaper editors in Hazelwood East High School (an affluent, largely white St. Louis suburb) okayed, among others, an editorial on the effects on children of parental divorce. When the school principal quashed the editorial (actually, there were two), the students' parents sued under the First Amendment. Four and a half years later, the Rehnquist court voted in favor of the principal; writing for the majority, Associate Justice Byron White stated, in effect, that student freedom of expression could be removed when such expression was inconsistent with the educational mission of the school. It has been inferred that the building principal shall be the ultimate arbiter in all such cases. Since then, censorship challenges have used this precedent often in raising their objections.

In any event, the dissolution of the Walker family won't sit well with a great many "interested parties." Those same people will not be gratified by the picture of the adults involved: a father who turns his back on his children and a mother who becomes virtually inert in her inability to face the bitter reality of the moment. Probably most vexing would be the impact of the rupture on sixteen-year-old Buddy, who seeks escape in alcohol and later in the "fun" offered by the Mephistophelian Harry Flowers. The animosity between Buddy and his distracted sister, Addy, only intensifies the unpleasant picture of family life Cormier has created.

A less well-developed but added element of criticism of The Family can be found in yet another Harry Flowers ploy. Faced with compelling evidence of his involvement in the Jerome house trashing, Harry admits his guilt but claims to the authorities that he was acting alone and that Jane Jerome gave him the house key. The police are skeptical but not Mr. Flowers, devoted father and upstanding citizen. When asked by Buddy why he took all the blame, Harry replies:

> "Is it so hard to understand?" Harry asked. "Am I supposed to be a bad guy or something? Sure, I like to raise a little hell, have a good time, smoke a little pot, drink a little booze. Does that make me a prize heel? Hey, Buddy, I'm

good to my mother and don't hassle my father. I make the honor roll. My folks appreciate all that. And when I got into trouble, my father helped out. My father loves me. He wrote the check and asked no questions." (105)

Thus the reader is provided another example of Harry's cynicism and manipulative acumen but, more important, the willingness of Mr. Flowers to buy his son's way out of trouble.

In summary, it's hard to find illustrations of good family life in *We All Fall Down*. Those parents and citizens who expect, in fact demand, that school programs of study reflect *their* brand of morality are often less than enthusiastic when they learn that their kids are assigned, read critically, and respond unequivocally to such literary selections. The same Jonathan Swift mentioned earlier also once stated, "Man loves the lie." When young people read and internalize literary texts that provide glimpses of life as it sometimes can be, their insights may be expanded, but to many adults, that's *not a good thing*. With characteristic candor, the author speaks in such direct, honest, unequivocal terms that readers, both adult and YA, will find the mirror he holds up of ordinary people (with apologies to Judith Guest) most disturbing. Cormier reaches behind surface appearances to the intimate complexities of family life, U.S.A., circa Century 21. These, when revealed, can be troubling. At the same time, they can provide teachable moments. That's the two-edged sword that can be found in *We All Fall Down*.

## Works Cited

Cormier, front cover.

Cormier, Robert. Personal letter sent to John S. Simmons, Leominster, Mass., May 25, 1985.

Cormier, Robert. *We All Fall Down*. New York: Bantam Doubleday Dell, 1993. 196-197 are from this text.

Simmons, John S. "Middle Schoolers and the Right to Read." ALAN Review. 27, no. 3. Urbana, Ill.: NCTE, Spring/Summer 2000 45-49.

# Understanding Sexuality Education: Two Books by Lynda Madaras

## Faye J. Perkins

Sex education! The mere mention of this subject can elicit a multitude of reactions; it is almost synonymous with controversy. Call it what you may—human growth and development, family life, reproductive health, value clarification, or character development—disguising the name does little to protect a teacher or administrator from the wrath of a minority of parents who vocally protest the inclusion of sexuality education into the school curriculum. Parents opposed to sexuality education generally believe that (1) sexuality education will lead to sexual experimentation, (2) sexuality education should be taught only by parents and has no place in the school curriculum, or (3) if human sexuality curricula is taught that it should focus on abstinence only and not include information on contraception and sexually transmitted diseases (STDs). Parents opposed to sexuality education would most likely support censorship of two sexual-development books written for adolescents and their parents by Lynda Madaras.

In 1983, Newmarket Press published Lynda Madaras's book, *What's Happening to My Body? A Growing Up Guide for Mothers and Daughters*. Chapter titles in this book are:

    I.    Puberty
    II.   Changing Size and Shape
   III.  Body Hair, Perspiration, and Pimples
  IV.  Boobs, Boobies, Knockers, Melons, Jugs, Tits, and Titties: Your Breasts
    V.  Changes in the Vulva
  VI.  Changes in the Reproductive Organs
 VII.  The Monthly Miracle: The Menstrual Cycle
VIII.  Puberty in Boys
  IX.  Sexuality

In 1984, Madaras followed the success of the book for girls with a complementary book for boys titled *The What's Happening to My Body? Book for Boys: A Growing Up Guide for Parents and Sons*, also published by Newmarket Press. Chapter titles in this book are:

I.　Puberty
II.　The Stages of Puberty
III.　Changing Size and Shape
IV.　Body Hair, Whiskers, Beards, Mustaches, Perspiration, Pimples, and Other Puberty Changes
V.　Ejaculation, Orgasms, Erections, Masturbation, and Wet Dreams
VI.　Girls and Puberty
VII.　Sexuality
VIII.　A Few Final Words

The majority of these two books provide the basic physiological information about what's happening to the bodies of boys and girls as they go through puberty. Madaras encourages adolescents to explore, understand, and accept their bodies and the changes that they are going through during puberty. She wants to answer the question "Are these changes I'm experiencing during puberty normal?" She includes actual questions and stories that she has collected from years of teaching sexuality education to adolescents. Simple line drawings are used to convey information related to topics including ovulation, the stages of pregnancy, the stages of pubic hair growth, and the five stages of male/female genital development. Inclusion of slang terms is used to help the reader understand the technical, yet correct, terms.

These books, however, go beyond the "nuts and bolts" of adolescent sexual development and *briefly* deal with issues such as feelings about changes one goes through during puberty, making decisions about sex, birth control, sexually transmitted diseases, homosexuality, and sexual crimes. She tackles these issues, which many parents and children may feel are embarrassing, directly and by using correct and specific language. Yet, her books are written in a "readable" style to reach the target audience of the prepubescent nine- to thirteen-year-old.

In the introduction, Madaras encourages parents and children to read the book together or at least discuss the topics covered in the book. She realizes that some readers may be offended by particular information and may disagree with the some of the values reflected in the book. She addresses this concern in her introduction to *What's Happening to My Body? A Growing Up Guide for Mothers and Daughters* by writing,

This book, and those I mention in the bibliography, may reflect values that are not the same as yours. This doesn't mean that you can't use them. You don't have to throw out the baby with the bathwater. Instead, you can use these books as an opportunity to explain your own point of view. For example, the topic of masturbation comes up in Chapter 5 of this book. The discussion of masturbation reflects my attitude—that masturbation is a perfectly fine, perfectly healthy thing to do. This attitude may conflict with your moral or religious views. If that's the case, you can read this section with your child, explaining how and why you feel the way you do. (16)

Dr. Ralph Lopez writes in the foreword to the same book, "I have finally found a book that is clear and concise and that takes a no-holds-barred approach on so extraordinary a topic as your body. It is frank and may well offend some people who would prefer to keep youngsters in the dark ages about sexual information."

Even though we are all sexual beings, there are centuries of tradition—both cultural and religious—that prohibit or censor any frank, open, and honest discussion dealing with issues related to sexuality. In the late 1970s and early 1980s, about the time these two books were published, this censorship took on new force with the election of Ronald Reagan and other conservatives. Reverend Jerry Falwell launched a new phase of his "Clean Up America" campaign and stated, "In school textbooks, pornography, obscenity, vulgarity and profanity are destroying our children's moral values in the guise of 'value clarification' and 'sex education.' Our children are being trained to deny their 200-year heritage" (Jenkinson 58). Conservative textbook critics Mel and Norma Gabler, founders of the Education Research Analysts, had sex education as one of their many targets. The Gablers and their organization acted as consultants to pro-censorship groups and provided thorough analyses of textbooks that could be used to support changes or complete exclusion of books found to be anti-Christian and anti-American. Madaras's two books were on their "hit" list.

After compiling hundreds of reports of censorship, Edward Jenkinson listed sex education as the number-one target of protesting organizations (62). In 1978, a library in Eldon, Missouri, and local school districts banned the *American Heritage Dictionary* because it contained thirty-nine objectionable words dealing with sexual definitions. The state of Texas took Webster's *New World Dictionary of the American Language* off the state's purchase list since it included sex-oriented words such as bed, fag, horny, hot, knock, queer, rubber, shack, and slut. Henry Reichman warned school districts that "virtually every available textbook and library resource material treating human sexuality is likely to be found objectionable by someone in the community, even if the sex education class is entirely elective" (35).

Madaras's two books were no exception to Reichman's warning.

What is the basis of objections to educational material dealing with human sexuality? There are a variety of issues. For some parents, it is the belief that discussion on sexuality belongs in the home and not in the school. Ideally, if all parents were properly prepared to assume this responsibility and did so, human sexuality would not be needed in the school curricula. However, many parents do not feel comfortable discussing these issues with their children and appreciate the school including sexuality education in the curriculum. A survey completed in Wisconsin in 1996 found that virtually all parents wanted their children to learn about AIDS at school; that over nine of ten parents wanted schools to teach about abstinence; and over eight of ten parents wanted their children to learn about birth control at school (Bogenshneider 39). The position taken by Wisconsin's Department of Public Instruction supports the role of the parent by stating, "The primary responsibility for education about sexuality as one area of total human growth and development rests with the parents, guardians, or other persons responsible for minor-aged children. However, the school certainly has an opportunity to supplement and complement those standards and programs established at home and within the community" (153). In writing her two books, Madaras was not intending to *replace* the parents in teaching their children about puberty, but was providing sexuality information in a way to *help* parents discuss these issues with their children. As stated previously, Madaras encouraged parents and children to read the book together and hoped that it would provide a springboard for discussing topics covered in the book.

Another objection to sexuality education in the schools and written material dealing with sexuality is the belief that the mere discussion of sexual behavior is thought to be synonymous with advocating that behavior—the "If you talk about it, they will do it" mentality. Research does not support this belief. As reported by Berne and Huberman, "In studies of seven abstinence-plus programs that were followed by lessons on contraception, students surveyed one and two years after the program *maintained abstinent behaviors longer than a control group*" (230). In countries such as Canada, England, France, the Netherlands, and Sweden, age at first intercourse is similar to that of the United States. However, those countries have teen pregnancy rates that are at least less than half the U.S. rate (Dryfoos 1). In these countries, sexuality education is infused throughout the educational curricula, government policies explicitly favor sex education, there is much more openness about sex, and contraception is readily accessible. Rather than promoting sexual behavior, sexuality education can help students postpone sexual initiation; once sexually active, it helps promote increased use of contraceptives to help decrease the rates of unintended pregnancy and sexually transmitted diseases (STDs).

One must realize that even if books like Madaras's are censored and sexuality education is eliminated from the schools and only taught by the parents, children will still be bombarded with sexual messages via the media. According to John Davies, "By age 18 a young person will have seen 350,000 commercials and spent more time being entertained by the media than any other activity except sleeping" (28). In a study by Strasburger, it was found that out of approximately 14,000 sexual references on TV annually, only 165 of them dealt with sex education, contraception, abortion, or sexually transmitted diseases (747). Popular teen magazines, music lyrics, music videos, advertisements, the Internet, and television contain an abundance of sexual content that may communicate potentially harmful health messages. Providing factual information on sexuality by using correct and specific language, Madaras's books can help combat the plethora of misinformation that is generated via the media.

Other objections to Madaras's books may be related to differing religious beliefs. In both books, Madaras discusses homosexuality (a little more than one page in both books), contraception (a little over a page in the girls' book and seven pages in the boys' book), and masturbation (two pages in the girls' book and seven pages in the boys' book). These are three topics that some would argue as inappropriate material based upon religious convictions. However, Madaras feels that even in disagreement, there is value to the information and that parents could use these books as an opportunity to explain their own point of view regarding these and any other controversial issues.

Madaras handles the topic of contraception very differently in the two books. In the book for girls, Madaras does not even mention specific names of contraceptives but addresses some common adolescent myths regarding getting pregnant: you can't get pregnant the first time you have sexual intercourse; it can't happen to me; you can't get pregnant during your menstrual cycle; and you can't get pregnant if a male pulls his penis out of the vagina before he ejaculates. For more specific information on contraceptives, Madaras refers the reader to her list of resources in the "For Further Reading" section of the book. In the boys' book, however, the section on contraception provides brief descriptions of the IUD, diaphragm, birth control pills, condoms, contraceptive foam and spermacides, contraceptive sponges, natural family planning, and sterilization. The information is not a "how-to" guide on contraceptive use but a basic introduction to the options that are available to those couples who choose to be sexually active but don't want a pregnancy.

In both books, abstinence is not mentioned as a form of contraception. This omission may be a primary target of censors. Again, it should be the role of the parent to discuss their beliefs on abstinence and contraception to supplement the information given by Madaras. The fact that abstinence is not covered doesn't mean that she believes that adolescents should not be abstinent.

Some parents believe that discussion of contraceptives gives their child a mixed message. On one hand, they are told to be abstinent, but on the other hand, they are told that if they are sexually active they should be responsible and use some form of contraception to protect themselves from pregnancy and STDs. Some parents favor an abstinence-only curriculum that would eliminate the concern of "mixed messages," focus only on abstinence, and not include information about contraceptive use. The majority of parents, however, want a comprehensive, abstinence-plus sexuality program that covers more than what students report is being taught in today's sex education programs (Henry 10). With teenagers having the highest rates of STDs of any age group (one in four young people contracting an STD by the age of twenty-one), and with the highest teenage pregnancy rate of any western industrialized country, it seems ludicrous not to discuss contraceptive methods with our adolescents—whether or not they are sexually active. As Madaras states, "Even if you're not having sexual intercourse yet, it's a good idea to learn about birth control" (Daughters 175).

Madaras's no-holds-barred approach is evident in the section on masturbation. She states that "masturbation is not harmful in any way" (Boys 124) and that "masturbating is a way of rehearsing for your adult sex life. By learning how to give yourself pleasure sexually, you are taking the first step in learning how to have sexual pleasure with someone else" (Daughters 86; Boys 126-127). In her straightforward way, Madaras answers questions such as do most boys and girls masturbate; is masturbating harmful; is it all right to imagine things when you masturbate; can masturbation affect your athletic performance; and will masturbating a lot when you're young affect your sex life when you're older. In the boys' book, she addresses the question "Is masturbation 'sinful' or morally wrong?" She concludes that each person must make an individual decision on this matter and if you're confused by the different messages you hear that you should talk with an adult or religious leader about this issue.

Once again, we must realize that even if information on masturbation is censored, children are exposed to the topic through playground jokes, locker room discussions, and the media. Boys and girls basing their beliefs on jokes and locker room talk is likely to be the blind leading the blind. Wouldn't it be better to address the issue openly and honestly rather than hide behind the cloak of sin and immorality? As Henry Reichman states,

> Scientific truths should not be kept hidden out of deference to the religious or
> moral beliefs of community members, no matter how widespread and sincerely
> held those beliefs may be. Some parents, for instance, believe that masturbation
> is harmful and sinful and discourage their adolescent children from touching
> their sex organs. That is their parental right, which the school must respect. But
> this can in no way justify keeping from students the scientific truth that
> masturbation causes no physical harm, and that most experts believe its
> psychological consequences are, for the most part, benign. (36)

The discussion on homosexuality in Madaras's books is also another
"lightening rod" for censors. First, Madaras offers a definition of homosexuality as "having sexual thoughts, feelings, fantasies, or activities that involve
someone who is the same sex as you are" (Boys 163). She also explains the
range of feelings among people by stating that "very, very few people are
strictly heterosexual or strictly homosexual. Most of us, regardless of
whether we're mostly homosexual or mostly heterosexual, have at least
some feelings in the other direction at some time in our life" (Boys 164). In
the boys' book, she points to the fact that "almost one-third of the heterosexual men in this country have had at least one homosexual experience with
another man to the point of orgasm at some point in their lives" (163). This
one experience, however, does not define a person as homosexual or
heterosexual.

In the two books, Madaras answers the question "Is homosexuality
wrong?" in very different ways. In the book for girls, Madaras simply states,
"If you have homosexual thoughts, feelings, or homosexual experiences at
times, it helps to know that this is natural and normal" (178). In the boys'
book, she answers the question much more ambiguously by stating,

> Different people have different ideas about what is morally wrong or sinful.
> Some people consider homosexuality morally wrong or sinful; others don't.
> Some people view homosexuality as a mental sickness and feel that homosexu-
> als need psychological help to "cure" them. Still others don't feel that homosex-
> uality is either wrong or a sign of sickness. They feel that some people just
> happen to be homosexuals, that it's a personal matter, and that there's nothing
> wrong or sick about it. (164-165)

This seems like neither an endorsement for or against homosexuality but an
indication that there is a wide spectrum of opinions regarding homosexuality. This answer by Madaras would be a great segue for a parent to discuss
their personal beliefs regarding homosexuality.

Again, we must realize that adolescents will be discussing the issue of homosexuality whether or not it is dealt with at home or in the school. Generally, among peers, it is dealt with in a very harsh, degrading, and hateful fashion. Young children, even though they may not understand the concept of homosexuality, learn that calling someone queer, gay, dyke, or fag is as demeaning as you can get. As reported by the Massachusetts Governor's Commission on Gay and Lesbian Youth, 97 percent of students in public high schools report regularly hearing homophobic remarks from their peers, and 53 percent of the students report hearing homophobic comments made by school faculty and staff. In 1996, twenty-one homosexuals were murdered, and 2,529 homosexuals were injured by assailants who did not agree with their sexual orientation (Southern). These statistics probably represent the tip of the iceberg since the majority of assaults may go unreported or the law enforcement agencies may not register the crime as a hate crime. Because of the harassment, violence, and isolation that many gay students experience in the schools, they often become substance abusers, drop out of school, or turn to suicide as a last resort.

Madaras's inclusion of homosexuality in her two books is at least an attempt to help develop a better understanding of homosexuality. Homophobia is an irrational fear generally based on a lack of information and understanding. As stated by Giorgis, et. al., "This homophobia or extreme hostility and fear of homosexuality results in prejudice and discrimination that must be countered by comprehensive educational programs that dispel myths and teach that ignorance, intolerance, and hatred toward gay and lesbian classmates is unacceptable and will not be tolerated" (31). In a report by the Henry J. Kaiser Foundation, 76 percent of parents want their child to be taught about homosexuality and sexual orientation in school, and 74 percent of parents want topics such as homosexuality to be "discussed in a way that provides a fair and balanced presentation of the facts and different views in society" (10). Not only should homosexuality be included in the comprehensive educational programs, it also needs to be discussed in the home. Madaras's book can help initiate that discussion between parent and child.

Madaras recognizes the fact that we are all sexual beings and that adolescents have many questions and concerns about their sexuality. Sexual health is one dimension of a healthy, balanced lifestyle. To ignore the issue of sexuality, to hide information from our children related to sexuality, or to let them learn vicariously through their peers and media is to neglect our responsibility as parents and educators. We may disagree about the appropriateness of the content or the specific values that are presented in Madaras's two books. We can, however, agree that we want happy, successful, healthy, and resilient children who understand and accept their bodies and the changes that they are going through during puberty. As Peter Scales states, "Democracy is a messy business, and it is right that we argue about what values sexuality education ought to reflect and what content it ought to include. But, as we go about equipping young people for success, let us draw strength from the happy conclusion that, in our most basic beliefs, there is more that unites us than divides us" (121).

## Works Cited

Berne, Linda A., and Barbara K. Huberman. "Sexuality Education: Sorting Fact from Fiction." *Phi Delta Kappan* (1995): 229-232.

Bogenschneider, K., J. Tsay, C. Wu. *Wisconsin Parents Speak Out: Report of the Findings from the Tapping Into Parenting (TIP) Surveys in 12 Wisconsin Communities.* Madison, Wis.: University of Wisconsin–Madison/Extension, 1996.

Davies, John. "The Impact of the Mass Media Upon the Health of Early Adolescents." *Journal of Health Education* (1993): November/December, supplement, S28-S35.

Dryfoos, J. "What the United States Can Learn About Prevention of Teenage Pregnancy from Other Developed Countries." *DIECUS Reports* 14 (1985): 1-7.

Giorgis, Cyndi, Kyle Higgins, and Warren L. McNab. Health Issues of Gay and Lesbian Youth: Implications for Schools. *Journal of Health Education* 31 (2000): 28-36.

Henry J. Kaiser Foundation. *Sex Education in America, A Series of National Surveys of Students, Parents, Teachers, and Principals: A View From Inside the Nation's Classrooms.* http://www.kff.org/content/ 2000/3048.

Jenkinson, Edward B. "Protest Groups Exert Strong Impact." *Censorship and Education.* Ed. Eli M. Oboler. New York: The H. W. Wilson Company, 1981.

Madaras, Lynda, and Area Madaras. *What's Happening to My Body? A Growing Up Guide for Mothers and Daughters.* New York: Newmarket Press, 1983.

———, and Dane Saavedra. The *What's Happening to My Body? Book for Boys: A Growing Up Guide for Parents and Sons.* New York: Newmarket Press, 1984.

Massachusetts Governor's Commission on Gay and Lesbian Youth. *Making Schools Safe for Gay and Lesbian Youth: Education Report.* Boston: Commonwealth of Massachusetts, 1993.

Reichman, Henry. *Censorship and Selection: Issues and Answers for*

*Schools.* Chicago: American Library Association; and Arlington, Va.: American Association of School Administrators, 1988.

Scales, Peter C. "Sexuality Education in Schools: Let's Focus on What Unites Us." *Journal of Health Education* 24 (1993): 121.

Southern Poverty Law Center. "Anti-homosexual Crime: The Severity of the Violence Shows the Hatred." *Intelligence Report.* Montgomery, Ala.: Southern Poverty Law Center, 1997.

Strasburger, V. C. "Adolescent Sexuality and the Media." *Pediatric Clinics of North America.* 36.3 (1989): 747-773.

Wisconsin Department of Public Instruction. *Curriculum Guide for Instruction in Health Education,* Madison, Wis.: Wisconsin Department of Public Instruction, 1985.

# The Subversive Quality of Respect: In Defense of *The Witches*

## Amanda Bergson-Shilcock

There is no shortage of reasons that Roald Dahl's *The Witches* came in at #9 on a list of most frequently challenged books of the 1990s (Forstel). Would-be censors have objected to the book's tone, its characters, its plot, and its supposed values. Feminists object to the book's contention that all witches are women. Wiccans object to the witches' evil natures. Others object to the book's irreverent tone, bathroom humor, incompetent adult characters, and so-called bad influence.

Yet *Witches* remains vastly popular, selling thousands of copies and remaining internationally in print nearly two decades after its original publication. No doubt its staying power is spiced by the aura of prohibition, but what else—besides Dahl's generally high status among young readers—prompts such endurance?

Ironically, the book's fundamental appeal is every bit as seductive as adults fear, but in a manner they have yet to perceive. *Witches* is beloved, and dangerous, for one simple reason: It takes children seriously.

A late offering from Dahl, the book was published years after *Charlie and the Chocolate Factory*, his best-known work. Written for eight- to twelve-year-olds, *Witches* concerns the adventures of a small boy, orphaned by a car accident, who is being raised by his Norwegian grandmother. A self-proclaimed expert on the topic of witches, she provides her grandson with the tools to recognize and protect himself from the malevolent creatures, who disguise themselves as ordinary women.

Although society scoffs at the notion of witches, the enormously fat, cigar-smoking Grandmamma is intent on preparing her charge for the day when he might be faced with a member of this horrifying, child-hating sorority. And well she might worry: at the tender age of eight, he will be confronted with not one witch, but the entire annual gathering of two hundred English witches—and they will turn him into a mouse.

*Witches* has some familiar Dahl themes—the youthful protagonist benefits from the love and care of an elder figure; there is an obnoxious little boy (this one named Bruno Jenkins) who gets what's coming to him. There are autobiographical echoes of Dahl's unhappy war experiences in the boy's litany of reasons that it is better to be a mouse than a man.

Most characteristic of all, there is a trademark, yet deliciously fresh, conspiracy of children against evil. Like nearly every classic fantasy, the book sets up a dichotomy and leaves its hero almost alone against the dark side. With only the eighty-six-year-old Grandmamma as an ally, Dahl's nameless boy must face a world that is by turns indifferent and cruel. Yet, although sobering, the challenges he faces are not unique. Indeed, his youth and inexperience render him a natural heir to the long folk tradition of unlikely saviors.

Dahl's sure-handed storytelling carries the plot along at such a clip that it's easy to overlook the trust he is placing in the reader. Far more than simply entertaining his youthful audience, Dahl writes to their fierce intelligence and passion: their wish to save the world, their unhesitating belief that they can.

In this light, *Witches'* silly, posturing adults are merely a backdrop of annoying static that interferes with the meaningful characters and action at the forefront. The boy's cheerful first-person narrative is at once endearing and intriguing: how will he manage to get out of this situation? Certainly there is an element of wish fulfillment. With Grandmamma's ever-present support, he engages in gleeful subversion of most forms of authority, such as outwitting the hotel maid intent on drowning his (forbidden) pet mice. Even when they do obey the doctor and journey to the seaside for her health, the decision is portrayed as their magnanimous agreement.

Yet the fantasy is not complete. Like children everywhere, Dahl's boy and his grandmother are prey to the uncaring whims of fate and the establishment: legal requirements of the boy's guardianship mean that they must move from Norway to England. Still, they cope marvelously. Whether charming their waiter at the seaside resort, or fast-talking her way out of a tight situation with the Grand High Witch of All the World, Grandmamma is an endless source of practical creativity. There is no problem she cannot solve, and yet she gives her grandson the ultimate form of respect: she asks for his opinions, she listens to his suggestions, she uses his ideas.

This is fairly radical behavior for an adult in a children's book. Intriguingly, however, it is not what has energized opponents of *Witches*. Rather, objections to the book center on the relatively narrow categories outlined above: that it is sexist; that it propagates harmful stereotypes about witches; that it is vulgar; that is unrealistic; and that it is a bad influence that, among other concerns, encourages children to be disrespectful and bathe infrequently.

The "Dahl is antiwoman" arguments are based primarily on selective quotation. The line in question reads: "A witch is always a woman" (9). Because Dahl's witches are so thoroughly savage, this line has been interpreted as evidence of his supposed bias against women generally. However, it is important to note that immediately following it is the statement "On the other hand, a ghoul is always a male" (9). In fact, many of the protesters *don't* mention this inconvenient fact. As a result, those who haven't read the text themselves may not know that Dahl's offensiveness is evenhanded.

Further, the suggestion that *Witches* is antifemale flies utterly in the face of the story's center of gravity: the strong and redeeming bond between the boy and his grandmother. Grandmamma is a powerful, reassuring anchor in his eventful world. Her unstinting affection and his absolute reciprocation are essential elements of the story. Indeed, without such a plausible ally, the boy's quest would be far lonelier and much less appealing.

The second class of objections is slightly more complex. Some readers who hold Wiccan beliefs (often called witches or white witches) wrote to Dahl complaining about his portrayal of witches. And indeed, they might have legitimate grounds for protest. *Witches'* witches are irredeemably evil; there is no suggestion that they can be otherwise. Yet although the question of prejudice is a valid one, it's hard to imagine that the deliberately exaggerated, outrageous *Witches* could really affect ordinary perceptions of Wiccans. In reality, Dahl's bald, toeless witches—blue saliva and all—no more defame Wiccans than the evil Siamese duo from Disney's *Lady and the Tramp* defame cats.

On the question of vulgarity, *Witches* is undoubtedly guilty of bathroom humor. This is hardly accidental; Dahl himself noted that "children regard bodily functions as being both mysterious and funny" (quoted in West, 84). Whether Dahl's canny recognition of his audience's amusement threshold is grounds for condemning the entire book is debatable.

Additional charges accuse the book of being cruel and unrealistic. Indeed, the boy's parents are killed early in the story, via an offstage car crash. However, this is little more than a plot device that allows the elder and younger generations to team up. Dahl's brief, distant handling of the event speaks more to a desire to continue storytelling than a hatred for parents. And although not dwelled upon, the event is hardly depicted as fun or funny.

The final group of objections combines a host of complaints under a single umbrella that might best be named "bad influence." There is no misquotation or selective interpretation in this case. It is perfectly true that

Dahl's boy hero is opposed to bathing. Grandmamma is in full agreement, as (she explains) witches find it harder to detect children when their natural scent is masked by a good layer of dirt. While this attitude may be gratifyingly amusing to any child who dreads bathtime, it's hard to imagine intelligent parents having difficulty drawing a line between the mores of *Witches* and those of their own household.

The question of disrespect is more complicated. It is certainly true that *Witches* encourages the questioning of authority. But it invariably does so from a stacked deck. The authority in question is never wise, and often not even well-intentioned. Thus, instead of fostering knee-jerk rebellion among his youthful readers, Dahl seems to be endorsing something more like a healthy skepticism.

Grandmamma and her grandson are not portrayed as mini-anarchists, running rampant over social convention for the sheer thrill of it. Rather, they are courageous visionaries who are endangered as much as elevated by their actions, as when Grandmamma boldly lowers the boy off the hotel balcony in a half-knit sock, then calmly bluffs her way through the unexpectedly early return of the Grand High Witch. Later, the two conspirators create a daring plot to slip mouse-maker potion into the witches' food, a plot that can work only if both boy and elder carry out their tasks with split-second timing. To this end, *Witches* is dangerous in that it ridicules blind obedience and glorifies independent thinking. Parents' fear of the book's so-called bad influence may simply reflect their own discomfort with a story that pulls no punches in illustrating the foibles, failures, and plain human frailty of its adult characters.

Erica Jong, reviewing the book for the *New York Times* when it was initially released, called *Witches* "a curious sort of tale, but an honest one, which deals with matters of crucial importance to children: smallness, the existence of evil in the world, mourning, separation, death" (45). Yes, it's fantasy, but quite a tempered one. The insane risks taken by its protagonist nearly always result in disaster—not just when his disobedience results in being trapped in the witches' meeting and turned into a mouse, but also later when he is dashing through the hotel kitchen and has half his tail sliced off. Most movingly, at the end of the book there is a frank discussion of how long both he and his grandmother are likely to live—a child's natural question, honored with a straightforward, believable answer.

And contrary to protesters' charges of unreality, the wild, ludicrous dream of a story is constantly punctured by the reality of mundane consequences. Dahl is practical enough to know that if fancy is allowed to spiral upward endlessly, even the dreamiest reader will eventually tire of the giddiness. To sustain the delicate tightrope of fantasy, the writer must allow it to bend and dip, and he does: veering from campy ridicule (Bruno's parents are so pathetically dreadful as to almost be unfunny) to blithe acceptance (so you're a mouse, big deal) to businesslike planning: how can a newly minted mouse and an aging granny facing a three-hour deadline get hold of some Formula 86 Delayed-Action Mouse Maker potion?

Censoring *Witches* on account of vulgarity is, ironically, Dahl's own argument in a different cloak. Where some parents want to shield their children from coarse language and scary images, the nurturers in Dahl's work want to protect their charges from the more serious threats of physical harm and death.

There is nothing wrong with wanting to protect children from having to cope with more than they're ready to handle, and a great deal to be gained from teaching them to read with a skeptical eye. But to remove *Witches* on grounds of vulgarity and defamation misses the point: it is a rollicking adventure story with a not-inconsequential message. True, it can't resist gleefully thumbing its nose at the mainstream, but Dahl is generally an equal-opportunity offender. For every hysterical, carelessly cruel Mrs. Jenkins, there is a silly, witless Mr. Jenkins.

The marvelous irony is that for all of the battles being waged against it, *Witches* isn't being censored for its genuinely revolutionary position. Indeed, its radical respect for young people does not even register with protesters, as evidenced by their claims that the book is "derogatory toward children" (Schulerbooks).

Thus, attempts to ban *Witches* are more about the medium than the message, and perhaps about adults' unease with a world that refuses to grant automatic respect on the basis of sheer longevity and instead gives superior status to a precocious boy-mouse and his cigar-chomping grandmother.

Buried one thin layer beneath the surface sass is a very potent philosophy: that children are every bit as thoughtful, creative, and brave as the best adults around them, and that things go wrong when their intelligence and humanity *aren't* respected. In that light, *The Witches* isn't an attack or a diatribe. It's a manifesto.

## Works Cited

Dahl, Roald. *The Witches*. New York: Puffin Books, 1985.

Forstel, Herbert. "The Most Frequently Banned Books in the 1990s." In *Banned in the U.S.A.: A Reference Guide to Book Censorship in Schools and Public Libraries*. Westport: Greenwood Press, 1994. Online. Internet. 2 January 2001. Citation available at: http://www. cs.cmu.edu/People/spok/most-banned.html.

Jong, Erica. "The Boy Who Became a Mouse." *New York Times*. (13 November 1983): Sec. 7, 45.

Schulerbooks.com includes the "Derogatory toward children" citation in its section on banned books. Online. Internet. 16 April 2001. Citation available at: http://www.schulerbooks.com/homepage/bannedbooks. titles.html.

West, Mark I. *Roald Dahl*. New York: Twayne Publishers, 1992.

# Breaking the Rules: A Defense of
# *A Wrinkle in Time*

## Susannah Sheffer

"People underestimate children's ability to understand big concepts," Madeleine L'Engle said in a magazine interview in 1999. Censoring books because they contain ideas that children aren't supposed to think about is, above all, a cruel underestimation of both the children and the ideas. *Writing* good books for children, on the other hand, is all about respecting young readers and daring to speak with them about big ideas. Authors of beloved children's books tend to be people who remember their own child selves well enough not to underestimate their readers or stay cloistered within the narrow confines of controlled vocabulary and safe topics.

I mentioned to two children I know that some adults don't think kids should read *A Wrinkle in Time*, and they looked at me, baffled. It was the same bafflement I felt when I was in fourth grade, and there was controversy about books by Judy Blume and other authors who wrote openly about growing up. My friends and I were already reading those books avidly, and I didn't understand what the parents thought they were shielding us from. Was it necessary to protect us from a representation of our own feelings and experiences? Did they think we didn't know or think about the things in these books? Had they so little memory or understanding?

The fact is that kids, more often than not, find a way to read what has been cut from an assigned list or even removed from a school library's shelves. If it's good, and maybe *because* it has been the subject of such fuss, kids will tell each other about it. Censorship is an attempt to silence the words of an author, but what really gets silenced is the chance for authentic and meaningful conversation between adults and children. Forbidding books that children love and find resonant just adds to their growing list of things that adults don't understand and that have to be discussed only with other kids.

In such cases, authors remain among the few adults who *do* understand

and remember, which is probably why they are so cherished (and why they get so many letters from their young readers). For me and my friends, books were so often where our thoughts, feelings, and experiences got confirmed. Good books also took our feelings and transformed them, as art does—gave them back to us as something new, something that enlarged our understanding of the world and of ourselves. Books became points of reference; in that sense, they became experience.

One day in eighth grade, I stood on a street corner talking with my best friend about the fact that what teachers and rulebooks said about writing didn't always match what was true of the good writing we knew.

"Like that thing 'don't use one-sentence paragraphs,'" my friend said.

"Right!" I agreed, suddenly remembering something. "What about that dramatic moment at the end of *A Wrinkle in Time*, when Meg is desperately trying to figure out what she has that IT doesn't have, and suddenly she realizes the answer? That's done with one-sentence paragraphs and it's obviously right to do it that way."

Meg, you see, had by then become someone we knew, and the book—including its language and paragraphing—was a touchstone, something we could look to as an example.

That climactic scene seems right to me still, all these years later. There is Meg, the book's heroine, trying with all her strength to resist the powerful, controlling brain called IT, which has her beloved baby brother in its clutches. Figuring out what she has that IT doesn't have seems an impossible task, but then it hits her:

> . . . as Meg said, automatically, "Mrs. Whatsit loves me; that's what she told me, that she loves me," suddenly she knew.
> She knew!
> Love.
> That was what she had that IT did not have. (207)

And so by concentrating intently on her love for her brother, Meg is able to wrest him from the control of this huge, diabolical brain.

*A Wrinkle in Time* has always been a book that breaks rules. That's why it took so long for a publisher to accept it originally, why so many children have treasured it for the nearly forty years it's been in print, and probably why so many people have objected to it.

When I say that *Wrinkle* breaks rules, I don't even remotely mean to suggest that it is a careless or irresponsible book. Quite the contrary. The rules it breaks—that children can't handle big ideas or complex language, that children's books shouldn't take on the problem of good and evil, that books should fall clearly into categories, and, of course, that writers shouldn't use one-sentences paragraphs—are rules that are mostly better broken. I remember *Wrinkle* as a book that put words to what I believed and cared about and blasted my mind open to new ideas, both at the same time.

It's a hard book to summarize. It's an adventure story, as Meg Murry, her younger brother, Charles Wallace, and their new friend, Calvin, search the galaxies for the Murrys' missing father, who has been sent on some kind of secret mission and has not been heard from in years. It's a book of physics and mathematics, because Meg's father has been involved in experimental research on tessering, a way of travel that, though it sounds fantastical, actually draws upon theories of the fifth dimension and relativity. It's a book that challenges totalitarianism and mind control, not unlike *Brave New World* and *1984* and Lois Lowry's *The Giver* (which are also frequently censored). It's a book about children who don't fit the norm and how they struggle with the rejection and pain that causes. It's a book about a strong family whose members respect each other's individuality and love each other in spite of their faults and imperfections. It's a book about the heroine's self-discovery, and it is, ultimately, a book of triumph and praise.

Many of the challenges to *A Wrinkle in Time* over the years have been on religious grounds—that it celebrates mysticism and the occult and that the theology embedded in the story is unorthodox. It's hard to defend the book against these charges because it feels as if critics who make these claims are speaking an entirely different language, or are simply scanning every children's book for certain key words without taking context or essence into account. The characters accused by some readers of being witches are not truly witches in any sense of the term. They are extraterrestrial beings, probably closer to angels than to anything else in our own lexicon, and in any case hardly corrupting of children's morals (on the contrary, they are clearly on the side of the good and clearly love and care for the children). The book is indeed fantastical, in that it posits ideas like time travel. But like most good fantasy, it is grounded in a solid human reality as well. Above all, the book is not a theological tract but a novel, albeit one that clearly comes from the author's deep beliefs and values (but where else should a novel come from?). Anyone who reads Madeleine L'Engle's nonfiction knows how important her Christian faith is to her, so it must have been a strange surprise to her when people of that same faith were among the book's most vocal critics. In any case, I'm not in a position to argue the book's merits from a theological perspective, nor do I think that it makes sense to do so. *A Wrinkle in Time* surely won the Newbery award and became a treasured favorite of so many young readers because it is a great tale, a powerful tale, one that returns us to ourselves with greater awareness. It surely won the award because of kids like the 10-year-olds in the writing workshop I teach, who, the moment they heard me mention the title, exclaimed, "Oh! I loved that book! It was so interesting!"

Here are some specific reasons that the book is of value:

It often leaves kids excited about physics and math and astronomy. Once, in the middle of a ninth-grade class, a few of my friends and I leapt up excitedly to demonstrate a concept from *A Wrinkle in Time*, to our teacher's amused delight. Some of the big concepts that Madeleine L'Engle dares to offer her readers are concepts of Einsteinian physics. The universe is interesting, L'Engle continually seems to be saying. Troubled and full of struggle, but so wondrous too, both in its vastness and in the details.

Then, on the other hand, there is the part of the book that will be familiar to many readers—Meg's feelings as an awkward adolescent and her steadfast defense of both herself and her younger brother, despite their failure to fit with others their age. Stories in which an unhappy heroine discovers her own value and discovers that she doesn't have to become like everybody else in order to be loved are always welcome, and as a story of this type, *Wrinkle* is first class. Meg chafes against her faults—her stubbornness, her impatience—but in the end it is her faults that save her and Charles Wallace. Combined with her fierce loyalty, Meg's supposed faults give her the determination to resist being controlled and to love her brother for who he truly is, not who others would have him be.

It's ironic that one parent challenging *A Wrinkle in Time* objected to it on the grounds that it indoctrinates readers, because the book stands profoundly *against* indoctrination. The evil of the planet Camazotz, which houses the central brain IT and has imprisoned the children's father, is that it is entirely about conformity. Everyone is controlled by IT and everyone thinks and behaves alike. When one of the planet's inhabitants nervously protests, "All my papers are in order," anyone familiar with totalitarian regimes on our own planet can recognize the allusion. Camazotz is a totalitarian regime in the extreme, and what Meg discovers there—that *like* and *equal* are not the same, that removing difference and individuality is not and cannot ever be the solution—is an idea that bears discovering again and again. Adults talk to kids about tolerating difference; *Wrinkle* acknowledges how painful difference often is and how hard tolerating it can be. Yet the book shows very clearly that the alternative is worse. It seems to me that kids instinctively recoil at the idea of Camazotz because they *don't* want to be bouncing their balls in perfect unison or thinking someone else's thoughts. People joke about teenagers' drive to look and act like everyone else, but those are coping strategies more than anything else, and adolescence is at least as much about discovering your true self as it is about trying to join the crowd. Meg wishes she could fit in, too, since she suffers each day in school for being different. But she doesn't want to fit in at the expense of her own true self, and she doesn't want to rule out the possibility of being loved for her true self. The book is, among other things, about holding out for those two ideals.

Before the group sets out on its intergalactic travels, an ordinary scene in the Murrys' kitchen, with Calvin visiting the family for the first time, shows that even conventionally successful (popular, good at sports) Calvin delights in Meg's idiosyncracies and reveals that he too has never felt that he fits in. When Calvin enthusiastically exclaims, "I'm not alone any more! Do you realize what that means to me?" Meg is skeptical at first. She's sure that she is the alone one; Calvin is the one who knows how to be accepted. "But you're good at basketball and things," she protests. "You're good in school. Everybody likes you" (44).

"For all the most unimportant reasons," Calvin says. "There hasn't been anybody, anybody in the world I could talk to. Sure, I can function on the same level as everybody else, I can hold myself down, but it isn't me" (44). And so the idea is introduced early on in the story that trying to blend in and become exactly like everyone else isn't worth the destruction of one's own identity.

Ultimately, Meg neither betrays herself nor ends up alone. She saves her brother and resists IT's mind control herself, *and* she finds real and sustaining love from Calvin, her peer, not by muting the parts of herself that are most essentially Meg, but rather by holding on to those essential parts. It's wonderful to let young people know that this is possible.

Like any coming-of-age novel, *Wrinkle* is about the loss of various kinds of innocence. The children see how pervasive evil can be (though one suspects that they had a visceral sense of it already), they see what people are capable of doing to one another, and Meg learns—with a thud of realization that many young people will identify with—that parents cannot, in fact, always make everything all right. Meg definitely does come of age with this realization, but the growth includes a recognition of her own strengths and an ability to love her parents as they have always loved her—with full awareness of their faults and imperfections.

Despite its direct look at the power of evil, *Wrinkle* is ultimately about the value of persevering. "Do you think we would have brought you here if there were no hope?" one of the guides asks the children early on, and that feels like the essence of what L'Engle is saying too: do you think I would have written a book about darkness if I didn't think human beings, in all our fallible, impatient, stubborn glory, didn't still have hope of fighting it? And so *A Wrinkle in Time* tells us that it is not only superheroes who triumph. It is regular children, regular people, who hold on to what they most clearly know and value, who gather courage to act, who don't necessarily end up more beautiful than when they began, but who do, nonetheless, end the book with someone's hand in theirs, because it is possible to be loved anyway, to triumph anyway.

*A Wrinkle in Time* is about not underestimating ourselves. Of course, caring adults want to protect children from danger, but *A Wrinkle in Time* insists that we shouldn't protect simply by closing our eyes or demanding that children close theirs. We protect, as the guides in *Wrinkle* do, by offering what love and strength we can, and by figuring out ways for children to recognize the value of what they know, what they have, what they are. There is nothing to be gained by banning a book that talks about darkness. What helps children are books that acknowledge darkness and then show that it is possible to make light, to make a difference as we set out on our own travels.

## Works Cited

L'Engle, Madeleine. *A Wrinkle in Time*. New York: Farrar, Straus, and Giroux, 1962.

Sheffer, Susannah. "A Conversation with Madeleine L'Engle." *Growing Without Schooling*, 126, vol. 21, no. 5, Jan./Feb. 1999.

# *Yellow Raft in Blue Water*

## Minfong Ho

Like a thick plait, the separate strands of three women's lives are braided into an intricately interwoven story by Michael Dorris in his novel *Yellow Raft in Blue Water*. Set in an unspecified Plains Indian reservation in Montana, this narrative history is told through the voices of first Rayona, then her mother Christine, and finally her grandmother, Aunt Ida. With each telling, the missing gaps and long-hidden secrets of the intriguing saga are woven in, until we have at the end a multilayered account of the family history and a deeper understanding of the family dynamics among the women. Each of their voices is distinctive and totally convincing—15-year-old Rayona, vulnerable in her studied, deadpan cynicism; hard-drinking Christine, frank yet fatalistic in her sexuality; and old Aunt Ida, stoic and proud to the end. Yet, braided together, their overlapping memories reveal them to have more than a family resemblance: they are, all three of them, fiercely proud and independent women.

The story begins with Rayona at the bedside of her hospitalized mother, having her hair braided. Although we do not know it until much later, Christine has just been told by a doctor that she does not have much longer to live (cirrhosis of the liver is intimated). This impending sense of mortality galvanizes Christine—to make sure that her daughter has a stable home, and to leave her with a legacy. With a haphazard sense of urgency, their belongings stuffed into trash bags, mother and daughter set off on a road trip back to Christine's childhood home on the reservation, where she must confront the unresolved tension with Aunt Ida, the woman who raised her, and where Rayona struggles to understand her own place in the complex family tapestry.

Set as it is in contemporary America, the Indians in Dorris's novel are thoroughly modern, as comfortable with country-western songs and soap operas on television as they are with ceremonial tribal dances. Caught in that fragile nexus between losing their traditional culture and being absorbed into modern "white" culture, they grapple with a sense of loss while still determined to transmit a worthwhile legacy.

It is in fact a rich, compelling book. With deft artistry, Dorris handles the universal themes of family relations, the search for identity, and rites of passage, within the context, specific to contemporary Native Americans, of concerns over tribal tradition, a sensitivity to the natural environment, and racism. Published to widespread acclaim in 1987, *Yellow Raft in Blue Water* garnered a *Booklist* Editor's Choice in both the Adult and Young Adult categories. The *Boston Globe* pronounced it "eloquent"; the *New York Times* praised the book for its "remarkable psychological density"; the *Los Angeles Times* called it "energetic, understated and seductive."

It was Michael Dorris's first novel, but his credentials were impeccable. Descended on his father's side from the Modoc tribe, Dorris grew up on the Fort Belknap reservation in Montana for part of his life, going to school there. He later attended Georgetown University (B.A. in 1967) and then Yale (M.A., 1970), after which he founded and chaired the Native American Studies Program at Dartmouth from 1972 until 1989. Among his many books are *The Broken Cord*, a nonfiction account, which won the National Book Critics Award, on fetal alcohol syndrome and its debilitating effect on his adopted son, and *The Crown of Columbus*, which he coauthored with his wife, Louise Erdrich. He has won numerous prizes and awards, including fellowships from the Guggenheim Foundation (1978), the Rockefeller Foundation (1985) and the National Endowment for the Arts (1989).

Why then has his first novel become a target for censorship?

It isn't hard, knowing the proclivities of organizations like the Moral Majority and the ProFamily Forum, to make some educated guesses as to why some readers of *Yellow Raft in Blue Water* might find it objectionable.

There are a few passages that are, if not sexually explicit, at least unabashedly erotic. In the scene that takes place the "morning after" Christine and Elgin first make love, for instance, there is no embarrassment or coyness, much less guilt or shame. We have here only a strong woman who knows who she is and what she wants, and has no qualms about saying it.

> I woke before dawn, dazed and stiff, my body flowing as if he were still touching it. My tips of my breasts stung and my mouth tingled. My hair had straightened and hung loose and heavy. Next to me. . . . Elgin sprawled on his stomach. I had seen plenty of men but he blotted them out. His legs and feet were long and slim, his back was deep with muscle. He gave off heat, and I moved to feel it against me. He raised his head, his eyes half-closed, his mouth warm honey. I said to him what I had never said to anyone before. I said I need him. (180)

There are also other passages that describe childbirth in graphic, unapologetic detail. Here is the scene when Rayona is born:

> There was nothing but my pain. I gave myself to it, drowned in it. . . . My
> muscles obeyed their own will. I fell back, my body collapsing against empty
> space as the baby slipped from me. . . . She was a long dark shape, smeared with
> white cream. . . . The clamped cord, which had joined us, stuck from her
> stomach, and below that, her legs were thin, as if made out of rubber. . . . I
> guided her mouth to the hard nipple of my left breast, and she knew what to do,
> drew me into her, took what she needed. (196)

Unless censors are all celibate and childless, or unless they belong to
some anachronistically prudish subset of people who believe that "doing it
is all right, but writing about it isn't"—there really is nothing to object to in
this book. No violence, no rape, no incest, no torture—only simple
descriptions of simple, natural acts.

Yet there is something else at work here that might have provoked calls
for censorship. *Yellow Raft in Blue Water* has, and I think the censors sensed
this on some level or another, a deeply subversive subtext.

An instance of this subversiveness takes place early on in the book, in
a conversation between Rayona and the white Catholic priest who tries to
recruit her for his God Squad on the reservation. "'I hear you speak your
native tongue, Rayona,' he says one day after I've arranged the altar for his
morning Mass" (47). When she admits to it, Father Tom tries to show off his
mastery of the language himself, and says something that a Tribal Council
member had taught him was a greeting. "'I smell like dogshit!'" Father Tom
booms out at me in Indian. The church echoes with his force" (47).

It is a trick, of course—the ultimate trick that the linguistically
powerless can play on those who have forced them to learn the dominant, the
foreign, language. Rayona immediately saw that and understood it for what
it was, but chooses not to laugh at him. "Just say hello," she says mildly, and
gives him "the ordinary word" for the greeting (48).

Still, the point has been made. The mighty English speaker has been
toppled from his accustomed position of superiority, to become the butt of
an insidious communal joke. (No wonder that the early colonists, be they
French, English, or Spanish, preferred to rely on translators rather than
venture to learn any "native" languages themselves—it was not because they
felt too superior to try, but because they dared not expose their vulnerability
linguistically.)

Similarly, in a brief interchange when Rayona was only seven and
Christine was trying to explain to her what to expect of Aunt Ida just before
she was about to visit them in their Seattle apartment, Christine said,

"She doesn't talk much. She'll speak to you in nothing but Indian."
"Doesn't she know English?"
"Not unless she wants to." (223)

These incidents, minor as they may be in the general context of the book, illustrate a premise that is inherently subversive. Indians choose to speak English only when they want to; the monolingual whites have no such choice. Pointing this out effectively reverses the established hierarchy of the dominant language (English) over the minority (Indian) one.

This attitude extends beyond the linguistic realm to underlie the rest of ordinary life. It is the last, bittersweet triumph of the subjugated. Drastically simplified, it goes like this: We can talk (and act, and think) like you do when we choose to, but you cannot talk (and act, and think) like we do. We have been forced to mimic you, and yes, it is a source of humiliation and grief, *but*—we have a choice that you do not. Precisely because we have been thus subjugated, we are now bilingual, bicultural, and so we can choose *not* to talk (and act and think) like you. We will play your game when we want, but ultimately, it is your game—and we can take it or leave it. And when that happens, it is not so much an act of rebellion on our part as it is of simple rejection. We have something else, another language, another set of beliefs, another system of behavior, that is valid and viable to us. . . . You don't.

Of course Dorris says nothing nearly this blatantly, but I contend that the basic premise is there, and it is what the censors, those self-appointed guardians of conventional morality, might have felt most threatened by. That there are alternative systems of belief and behavior that render their own irrelevant must have made them feel very uncomfortable.

In very much the same way that the three women can slip back and forth between speaking English and "Indian" at will, they can also choose to adopt or discard other trappings of the dominant white culture. Thus, Christian sacraments like marriage (and monogamy) are observed, then shed; blind faith in the Virgin Mary is upheld, then abandoned; a high school diploma is within reach, then left unpursued. Jobs, apartments, cars, friends and lovers are all taken on, then left off. These women have none of the accouterments of bourgeois society—no Wealth, no Husband, no Career. But—and this is what is so truly subversive—they have no need of any of these things.

What they have retained, fiercely, stubbornly, admirably, is an indomitable spirit and a sense of self, and this they weave together to form a strong, matrilineal sense of family.

This is revealed only gradually, when we look closely at the complex kinship relations between the three women. What emerges with each woman carrying the narrative history backward in time are the hidden details, the missing links. And so we learn only at the very end that Aunt Ida is not in fact Christine's mother at all, but her first cousin as well as her half-sister (Christine being the product of an affair between Aunt Ida's father and her mother's sister). As a teenager not yet out of high school, Aunt Ida in effect adopts and raises this illegitimate baby as her own and is fiercely possessive of her. Aunt Ida also reveals—in the third and final portion of this story—that her other child, a son named Lee, was fathered by a handsome classmate after he returned grotesquely disfigured from the Korean War. Both of her children, then, born out of wedlock as they are, fall outside of the strictures of conventional (read Christian) morality. Only Aunt Ida knows who the fathers of these children are, and if she has not shared this information with anyone else, it is not because it is a source of guilt or shame, but simply because—in the de facto matrilineal family that she has formed—it has become virtually irrelevant. What matters to her is that she has single-handedly raised them; with grim determination she has devoted her whole life to nurturing them. It doesn't matter who fathered them—she has mothered them. When one of these children dies and the other one leaves, she spends her time in a kind of solitary limbo, in effect mourning the one and waiting for the other to return.

Her "daughter" Christine's mothering style is different, but no more constrained by the boundaries of conventional morality than hers was. Lured by the call of the wide world outside the reservation, Christine has a series of casual liaisons with (usually married) men, then goes off to the big city, Seattle, to try her wings (almost literally, in a job making the "black boxes" for airplanes). She falls in love with Elgin, a black man, and soon becomes pregnant by him. They eventually get married at his suggestion, and it becomes, sure enough, virtually irrelevant. They live separately, and each has other lovers without really bothering to hide the fact from the other. Yet in her own way, she remains intensely loyal and loving to him.

And as with Aunt Ida, mothering became a role that was crucial to Christine. She says, laconically, "I am nobody's regular daughter, nobody's sister, usually nobody's wife, but I was her mother full time" (222). As such, Christine saves the early morning as times for a quiet togetherness with her daughter, and (the censors would say "but") she also brings the baby along with her when she goes barhopping, and introduces her lovers to Rayona, despite being legally married to Rayona's father. It is this kind of openness that allows Rayona to say, with real nonchalance: "I don't know what she sees in him (Elgin). She has other boyfriends who call when they promise, pay the check at restaurants, and want to live with us" (6).

Conservatives might condemn Rayona's offhand attitude toward her mother's lovers as amoral, the result of a depraved upbringing; liberals might applaud it for being unhypocritical and healthy. But the really subversive subtext is that it really doesn't matter to Christine or Rayona what other people think. They have developed between them a closed system of ethics that make the opinions of the larger society of only peripheral importance. Their actions are guided not by what others might want and expect them to do, but by what they themselves want to do. On some deeply instinctual level, they have a sense of rightness and wrongness that works for them, and they trust that.

Thus, when Christine abruptly abandons her daughter at Aunt Ida's doorstep rather than have to humbly ask Aunt Ida to take her in, it may seem like an irresponsible and impulsive act, but we understand later that she was acting in a way consistent with her own integrity ("If I said I had been wrong to defy her, that I was sorry for the grief I had caused, if I shamed myself there in front of Rayona, Aunt Ida would, . . . make a home for my daughter . . . [but] I saw Rayona watching and it came to me that nothing, nothing was worth her witnessing me laid low"). So, instead of mouthing the abject apology that she was expected to, Christine held onto her last shred of pride and said to Aunt Ida, "Go fuck yourself anyway" (253).

This kind of fierce, defiant pride must have been familiar to Aunt Ida. After all, she was sparked by a similar kind of defiance when, years earlier, she rejected the offer of her lover, Willard Pretty Dog, to live with her because she realized that this offer was based on pity and a sense of duty rather than genuine love.

> I watched his stiff new mouth open and close, saw the flash of teeth and tongue, the eyes that didn't see me, that couldn't, that never would. He finished his proud declaration and looked to me for gratitude. I heard my words as much as thought them, "Your mother's right. It's better you go. . . . There won't be room for you.". . . I didn't hate Willard, but I no longer wanted him. And I never let myself again (351).

The portrayals of these Native American women seem to me compelling and convincing, although, on a personal note, I must admit that I know very little about Native American history and culture. There is nothing in my background as a Chinese woman who grew up in Thailand that has prepared me to understand Native Americans in general, or the Native American women in *Yellow Raft* in particular. Yet something in Michael Dorris's portrayal of them moved me deeply. Perhaps it was because I had cringed at the countless renditions of Chinese stereotypes in Western culture, of the Charlie Chans and Suzi Wongs that are in essence characters dressed in "cultural drag" to entertain literary tourists come to gawk at the exotic. I have become sensitized to portrayals of "ethnic" characters who have been, either deliberately or unconsciously, defamiliarized and demeaned at the hands of their creators. In contrast, however, Dorris writes with none of the sly condescension that comes with being a voyeur beckoning his readers to peep in some freak show. All three of the women he portrays are real people, strong willed and self-confident, if proud to a fault.

Could it be that the strong family resemblance in their personality traits might be characteristic of the Indian culture in general? Rash as it might be to extrapolate from these three women—Ida, Christine and Rayona—in particular to Native Americans in general, yet the recent history experienced by Native Americans after the arrival of the Europeans on the North American continent is nevertheless similar enough and painful enough that such an extrapolation would not seem farfetched.

Even a cursory glimpse into the history of the Modoc tribe, for instance, with which Dorris had a tribal affiliation, is enough to suggest that the Modocs had endured so much oppression and suffering that it is no wonder that its survivors turned out as stoic and strong willed, as defiant and proud as the women in *Yellow Raft*.

What happened to the Modocs is similar to what happened to many other Indian tribes of early America. As more white emigrants settled onto Modoc territory of the Pacific Northwest, conflict between the two groups escalated as well, reaching a peak in 1864, when the U.S. government stepped in and forced the Modocs onto a reservation over a thousand miles north of their tribal land.

Increasingly dissatisfied with the confined life there, an insurgent band of about eighty Modocs and their families, led by Kintpuash (a.k.a. "Captain Jack" to the whites), broke free from the reservation and returned to their original homeland, where they roamed free for two years. When the U.S. military tried to force them back north, the Modocs made their last stronghold in the California lava beds, where they conducted a protracted guerrilla war in the ravines of the hardened lava against over a thousand U.S. soldiers.

Eventually, inevitably, in June 1873, they were forced to surrender, and the Modoc leaders put on trial for murder. Without any legal counsel, and with only a very basic knowledge of English, the Modoc leaders were found guilty and sentenced to hang. After the hanging, Captain Jack's head was pickled and exhibited in a sideshow in Washington, D.C. His family and other followers were forced into boxcars and shipped back into the reservation that they had so briefly and futilely broken free from.

With an ancestral history like that, is it any wonder that Michael Dorris would be highly sensitized, on the one hand, to the stubborn strength of contemporary Native Americans, and on the other, to their vulnerability? The three women in *Yellow Raft*, like their tribal ancestors, had been systematically stripped of their land, their culture, their language. And yet, against all odds, some of them have survived, and in the process have managed to braid together the remnants of their values and their culture, so that these shared memories form a strongly interwoven whole. In this way, with this kind of patient recounting of their personal experiences, Ida and Christine and Rayona have braided an intricate history of their own making. And through them, and through his book *Yellow Raft in Blue Water*, Michael Dorris has bequeathed a form of legacy not only to those descended from his tribe but to all of us.

Should the censors have the power to take that away too?

## Works Cited

Artful Dodge. "A Conversation with Michael Dorris." http://www.wooster. edu /artful dodge/dorris.html.

Brayard, Anatule. "Eccentricity Was All They Could Afford." *New York Times* (7 Jun 1987): VII 17. http.//www.nytimes.com/books [book archive search: "Yellow Raft in Blue Water"].

Charles, Jim. "The Young Adult Novels of Michael Dorris." *Alan Review* 25.3 (1998): 21-23. http://scholar.lib.vt.edu/ejournals/alan/spring98 /charles.html.

Dorris, Michael. *Yellow Raft in Blue Water*. New York: Henry Holt, 1987.

Kakutani, Michiko. "Multiple Perspectives." *New York Times* (9 May 1987):17. http//www.nytimes.com/books[book archive search: "Yellow Raft in Blue Water"].

# Index of Authors and Titles

# About the Contributors

## Robin M. Boles, Compiler

MICHAEL ANGELOTTI is Chair of the English Education department at the University of Oklahoma, Norman, where he also teaches Instructional Leadership and Academic Curriculum, Special Topics in Literacy, and Theory and Research in Education, among other courses. A professional writer with articles published in several scholarly journals, he is director of the Oklahoma Writing Project and formerly the editor of *English International*.

AVI has published some fifty titles, ranging from picture books and early readers, to chapter books for middle school readers to novels and short stories for young adults. The founder of Breakfast Serials, he is credited with restoring children's book serialization to our nation's newspapers. He is the winner of many awards, including two Newbery Honor Books—*True Confessions of Charlotte Doyle* (1991) and *Nothing But the Truth* (1992)—and two *Boston Globe/Horn Books* awards.

NANCY E. BAYNE has taught university courses and presented to parents, community members, and professionals on sexual behavior for over twenty years. She is a professor of psychology at the University of Wisconsin-Stevens Point.

AMANDA BERGSON-SHILCOCK is a lifelong advocate for children's literature. Her background includes eight years spent working in a large public library and four years providing "Booktalks" at schools before their annual book fairs. Her essays have been published in the *Christian Science Monitor* and *Growing Without Schooling* magazine.

KRISTINE BJERK taught eighth-grade Language Arts in Hudson, Wisconsin, for six years and is currently a full-time mom (and private tutor) for her two young sons.

JENNY BRANTLEY, a native of North Carolina, lives and works in Wisconsin, where she is the editor of *Literary Magazine Review*. Her poetry has been published in *Room of One's Own, North American Review, 13th Moon, Hurricane Alice, Women and Language, Genre,* and other magazines. Her most recent scholarly work is an article on Gloria Naylor in *Everything Got Four Sides: The Early Novels of Gloria Naylor*. Presently, she is coediting an anthology of women's literature.

BILL BRITTAIN taught English and remedial reading at the junior high level for 34 years. He is the author of *The Wish Giver*, a 1984 Newbery Honor Book, and 12 other books, including *The Mystery of the Several Sevens* (1994), *The Fantastic Freshman* (1988), and *All the Money in the World* (1979).

DEBORAH BROWN, Assistant Professor of English at the University of Central Oklahoma, teaches graduate and undergraduate courses in English education, composition, and young adult literature. Her articles have been published in such journals as *Journal of Adolescent and Adult Literacy* and *Wisconsin English Journal*. She is a former president of the Southeastern Ohio Council of Teachers of English and coeditor of its journal, *FOCUS: Teaching English Language Arts*.

KATHERINE T. BUCHER is an associate professor, Graduate Program Director of Elementary/Middle School Education, and coordinator of library science in the Department of Educational Curriculum and Instruction at Old Dominion University, Virginia. Her major interests include children's and young adult literature, school libraries, and middle school education. Dr. Bucher has published articles on children's and young adult literature in a number of journals, including *English Journal* and *The ALAN Review*.

CECELIA BUSTAMANTE-MARRÉ wrote her doctoral dissertation on Isabel Allende's *The House of the Spirits*. She is an assistant professor of Spanish at the University of Wisconsin-River Falls, where she teaches courses on Latin American and Spanish literature and Latin American Civilization.

CHRISTOPHER COLLIER, Professor of History at the University of Connecticut and the official Connecticut State Historian, is the coauthor (with his brother James Lincoln Collier) of several books, including *Jump Ship to Freedom* (1981), *War Comes to Willy Freeman* (1983), and *My*

*Brother Sam Is Dead* (1989), and numerous scholarly and popular articles about the history of Connecticut.

CHRIS CROWE is a professor of English at Brigham Young University, where he teaches courses in YA literature, English education, and creative writing. Currently, he serves as editor of the YA literature column for *English Journal* and as president-elect of ALAN. He is the author of *Presenting Mildred D. Taylor* (1999) and of a forthcoming YA novel, *Mississippi Trial, 1955* (2002).

KENNETH DONELSON has been a professor in the English department at Arizona State University since 1965. He has written over 20 books and scholarly articles on censorship and young adult literature, including *The Students' Right to Read* (1972), *Teaching English Today* (1975), *Literature for Today's Young Adults* (1st edition 1980), "Fifty Years of Literature for Young Adults," (1990), and "'Filth' and 'Pure Filth' in our schools—Censorship of Classroom Books" (1986). He has been coeditor of *English Journal.*

CHARLES R. DUKE, a former high school English teacher and curriculum coordinator, has authored books on the teaching of English, including *Creative Drama and The Teaching of English* and *Teaching Literature Today*; he has edited others, including *Reading and Writing Poetry: Successful Approaches for the Student and Teacher* and *Poets' Perspectives: Reading, Writing, and Teaching Poetry.* Currently he serves as the Dean of the Reich College of Education at Appalachian State University, North Carolina.

LYNDA DURRANT is the author of *Echohawk*, its sequel, *Turtle Clan Journey, The Beaded Moccasins: The Story of Mary Campbell*, and *Betsy Zane: The Rose of Fort Henry.* She teaches remedial reading to children.

PATRICK FINNESSY, an educator for fourteen years, has taught English, speech, and theatre in Iowa and Illinois. He created a curriculum guide for the anthology *Growing Up Gay/Growing Up Lesbian.* A presenter of workshops at local, state, and national conventions, he is currently the Director of the Office of Gay, Lesbian, Bisexual, and Transgender Concerns at the University of Illinois at Chicago.

BRIAN FITCH teaches in the Department of English and Philosophy at the University of Wisconsin-Stout. His work has appeared in *ArtWord Quarterly, Helsinki Review, The North American Review, Prairie Schooner, Sewanee Review,* and others.

DAVID FURNISS, Professor of English at the University of Wisconsin-River Falls, teaches courses in literature, ranging from American literature to literature for adolescents, and freshman English. He directs the university's Writing Center and teaches the practicum for tutors. He has written about Vietnam War literature, baseball literature, and composition pedagogy.

WENDY J. GLENN taught in the public schools for six years. Currently she is a faculty member at Northern Arizona State University, where she teaches methods courses in literature and language and supervises student teachers. Other publications related to issues in adolescent literature have appeared in *The ALAN Review* and *Arizona English Bulletin.*

NAT HENTOFF, one of the foremost authorities on the First Amendment, explores our freedoms under the Bill of Rights and the 14th Amendment by showing how Supreme Court and local legislative decisions affect ordinary Americans every day. He also looks into the health of the Constitution on the streets, in schools, in police precinct houses, and in newspaper coverage. In 1995, he received the National Press Foundation Award for Distinguished Contributions to Journalism, and in 1999, he was a Pulitzer finalist for commentary. In 1983, he was awarded the American Library Association Intellectual Freedom Round Table Imroth Memorial Award. A Jazz expert, Hentoff writes on music for *The Wall Street Journal* and *Jazz Times* and has written numerous books, including *The First Freedom: The Tumultuous History of Free Speech in America* (1980), *Free Speech for Me But Not for Thee: How the Left and the Right Continually Censor Each Other* (1992), and his most recent book, *Living the Bill of Rights* (1998). News-paper Enterprise Association has distributed Hentoff's column since 1992.

KAREN HIRSCH is a Resources Teacher for Gifted and Talented in the Eau Claire, Wisconsin, schools. She is also a writer of books for children and young adults. Her novel *Ellen Anders on Her Own* (1994) received the Arthur Tofte Award, the highest award for Juvenile Fiction, from the Council for Wisconsin Writers, and the "Outstanding Achievement for Books Published in 1994" from the Wisconsin Library Association.

TIM HIRSCH is a veteran teacher of American Literature at the University of Wisconsin-Eau Claire, where he teaches a course on Mark Twain, including *The Adventures of Tom Sawyer*. In all of his teaching, he seeks to connect literary works to their cultural contexts—the conflicts they reflect, the attitudes of the characters and the author, and the public's responses to the book. He promotes the study of regional writers, and he founded the Waldemar Ager Association to promote and preserve the writings of this important Norwegian-American writer.

MINFONG HO is the author of several books for children and young adults, among them *The Clay Marble, Rice without Rain, Hush! A Thai Lullabye* (1996 Caldecott Honor Medal), and *Maples in the Mist*. She has received numerous awards and citations for her work. She learned English only after Chinese and Thai and, therefore, thinks of it as her third language.

SUSANNE L. JOHNSTON has been a Senior Lecturer in English at the University of Wisconsin-Stout since 1991 and reviewer for *The ALAN Review* since 1993. She is the author of *Focus on Relationships* and contributor to *Twentieth Century Young Adult Writers* and *Reading Their World: The Young Adult Novel in the Classroom* (2nd edition).

DAVE JUNKER, a Ph.D. candidate at the University of Wisconsin, Madison, received his M.A. in Afro-American Studies. He currently working in 19th and 20th century American literature with a focus on satire, humor, and the relationship between music and literature.

NICHOLAS J. KAROLIDES, Professor of English and Associate Dean, College of Arts and Sciences at the University of Wisconsin-River Falls, has served as editor of the *Wisconsin English Journal*. His censorship publications include: *Censored Books: Critical Viewpoints I* (coeditor), *Banned Books: Literature Suppressed on Political Grounds*, and *100 Banned Books* (coauthor). Other major works include: *The Pioneer in the American Novel (1900-1950), Reader Response in Elementary Classrooms: Quest and Discovery*, and *Reader Response in Secondary and College Classrooms*. He has been honored with the UW-RF Distinguished Professor Award and the Regents Teaching Excellence Award for the University of Wisconsin system.

SUSAN M. KELLY is a professor of English at Fairmont State College, West Virginia. She has written broadly on contemporary film and literature; currently, she is interested in the South African author J. M. Coetzee.

SUSAN KOOSMANN, who has taught English in grades seven through twelve, presently teaches English at an alternative high school in Little Canada, Minnesota.

MAGGI KRAMM teaches English at the University of St. Thomas in St. Paul, Minnesota.

STEVEN R. LUEBKE, associate professor in the Department of English at the University of Wisconsin-River Falls, has published numerous articles on contemporary American literature and on teaching.

CAROLINE G. MAJAK is a professor in the Department of Curriculum and Instruction at the University of Wisconsin-Eau Claire, where she currently teaches language arts methods courses to undergraduates. Dr. Majak has written many articles and presented at local, state, national, and international conferences, primarily to acquaint school personnel and parents with quality literature and to encourage them to make this literature accessible to all children and youth.

MARY PHILLIPS MANKE, associate dean of the College of Education & Professional Studies at the University of Wisconsin-River Falls, has been a professor of Foundations of Education and Women's Studies. She has published articles in such journals as *Educational Studies, Educational Foundations,* and the *Journal of Research in Rural Education.* Her book *Power in Classrooms* is used in teacher education classes in the United States and Canada.

M. LEE MANNING is a professor in the Department of Educational Curriculum and Instruction at Old Dominion University, Virginia. His major interests include young adult literature, middle school education, and multicultural education. Dr. Manning has published articles on children's and young adult literature in a number of journals, including *English Journal* and *The ALAN Review.*

JEANNE M. McGLINN, associate professor of education at the University of North Carolina at Asheville, teaches children's and adolescent literature and supervises students preparing to teach English and language arts. She is the coordinator of the Classroom Materials column of the *Journal of Adolescent and Adult Literacy* and frequently reviews books for this journal, *The ALAN Review*, and *Voice of Youth Advocates*.

NELLIE Y. McKAY is professor of American and African American literature at the University of Wisconsin, Madison. She is coeditor of the *Norton Anthology of African American Literature* and writes extensively on African American women's writings.

CAROLYN MEYER published her first book for children in 1969. Since then, she has written more than 45 books of fiction and nonfiction for children and young adults. Many of her books have been named by the American Library Association to their annual list of "Best Books for Young Adults," as well as named and chosen as selections by the Junior Library Guild. Recent titles include *Mary, Bloody Mary* (1999), *Anastasia, The Last Grand Duchess* (2000), and *Beware, Princess Elizabeth* (2001).

PETER E. MORGAN, associate professor of English at the University of West Georgia, teaches literature and cultural studies. He has spoken and published nationwide on issues of multiethnic young adult literature and the student's right to read.

JIM MULVEY is a professor of English at the University of Wisconsin-River Falls. His presentations and publications deal with Ernest Hemingway, modern American fiction, composition theory, children's literature, and censorship.

GAIL MUNDE is associate dean of libraries at the University of Nevada, Las Vegas. She has worked in academic libraries for 15 years and was most recently the associate director of Joyner Library at East Carolina University, North Carolina. She has authored several articles on children's and young adult literature and is particularly interested in humor development and children's reading interests.

BETH MURRAY is an assistant professor of Language Arts at the University of Wisconsin-Milwaukee in the Department of Curriculum and Instruction.

FAYE J. PERKINS is a professor and assistant chair in the Department of Health and Human Performance at the University of Wisconsin-River

Falls.  Her teaching responsibilities include "Methods and Materials in Health Education," "Teaching Family Life and Sex Education," and "Health and Fitness for Life."  In 1994, Dr. Perkins was named "Outstanding Faculty Member of the Year" by the College of Education.

MARGARET YATSEVITCH PHINNEY, associate professor and director of the reading program at the University of Wisconsin-River Falls, taught elementary school for 12 years and now teaches graduate and undergraduate courses in elementary literacy education.  Her publications include a teacher resource, *Reading with the Troubled Reader*, book chapters, articles in several journals, including *Language Arts* and *Linguistics and Education*, and six children's books; recent titles include *Exploring Underground Habits* (1999) and *Loose Tooth* (2000).

ELIZABETH A. POE, a high school English teacher for 13 years, is assistant professor of English education at West Virginia University, where she teaches courses in instructional methods and young adult literature.  A former president of the Assembly on Literature for Adolescents of NCTE (ALAN) and book review editor for *The ALAN Review*, she currently serves as editor for *SIGNAL Journal*, the young adult literature publication of the International Reading Association (IRA).  She is the author of *Focus on Sexuality, Focus on Relationships*, and *Presenting Barbara Wersba*.

CAROLYN REEDER, a former teacher, writes historical fiction for young people.  Her novels include *Shades of Gray*, set in the aftermath of the Civil War; *Moonshiner's Son*, set in the Virginia Blue Ridge during the prohibition era; and *Foster's War*, a World War II home-front story set in San Diego.  Ms. Reeder is also coauthor of three adult nonfiction books about the history and people of the Shenandoah National Park area.

SUZANNE ELIZABETH REID teaches at Emory & Henry College in southwestern Virginia.  One of her favorite classes is Great Books, in which she and nine other faculty teach *Song of Solomon* by Toni Morrison.  Dr. Reid has written several books and articles about literature for young adults, particularly about Cynthia Voigt, Ursula K. Le Guin, science fiction, and using literature to teach English as second language.

CONNIE RUSSELL, a retired K-12 reading/language arts coordinator, is currently consulting and doing workshops.  She has published several articles on reading and writing as well as chapters for two books.  She was president of the Wisconsin Council of Teachers of English and received the Chisholm Award for Distinguished Service to the English Language Arts profession in Wisconsin.

SHARON M. SCAPPLE, an associate professor of English at Minnesota State University-Moorhead, teaches courses in adolescent literature and English education. She has written on literature for young people and has featured a course on censorship and young adult literature at the University of Minnesota.

SUSANNAH SHEFFER's books include *Writing Because We Love To* and *A Sense of Self: Listening to Homeschooled Adolescent Girls*. For many years she edited *Growing Without Schooling* magazine and now serves as an adviser to that publication and as a writing mentor to homeschoolers. She edits Heinemann's Innovators in Education series and writes a regular column for New Moon Network.

ANNE SHERRILL, Professor of English at East Tennessee State University, teaches courses in literature for adolescents and composition theory and practice. She has delivered and published numerous professional papers and is coauthor (with G. Robert Carlsen) of *Voices of Readers: How We Come to Love Books*. Other books include *Four Elements: A Creative Approach to the Short Story* (with Paula Robertson Rose) and *Literature IS: Collected Essays of G. Robert Carlsen* (with Terry C. Ley).

KATHY G. SHORT is a professor of Language, Reading, and Culture at the University of Arizona and has worked extensively with teachers to develop curricula that actively involve students as readers, writers, and inquirers. She has coauthored many books, including *Creating Classrooms for Authors and Inquirers, Learning Together through Inquiry, Literature as a Way of Knowing,* and *Teacher Study Groups*. She is currently coeditor of *Language Arts*.

JOHN S. SIMMONS, Professor Emeritus of English Education and Reading at Florida State University, in the past has served as the Chair to the Standing Committee Against Censorship, NCTE, and a member of the Task Force, NCTE/IRA on Intellectual Freedom. He is the author of 16 texts and 110 articles and essays on teaching English and reading to grades six through twelve, and censorship in the schools.

JANE SMILEY is the author of many novels and stories; recent titles include *Horse Heaven* (2000), and *The All-True Travels and Adventures of Lidie Newton: A Novel.* (1999). She received the Pulitzer Prize in 1992 for her novel *A Thousand Acres* and was inducted into the American Academy of Arts and Letters in 2001.

GRANT T. SMITH taught high school English in Las Vegas, Nevada, for ten years. Currently, Smith is an associate professor of English at Viterbo University in La Crosse, Wisconsin, where he teaches Young Adult Literature and Methods of Teaching English in the English Education Department.

SCOT SMITH works as a librarian media specialist at Central High School in Knoxville, Tennessee. He also teaches children's literature at the University of Tennessee. He has published and presented several papers on young adult literature.

ZILPHA KEATLEY SNYDER published her first book for children in 1964; her 38th book came out in the spring of 2001. Her books have received three Newbery Honor awards, two Christopher Medals, a William Allen White award, a Hans Christian Andersen International Honors listing, several American Library Association Notable Book listings, a George C. Stone Recognition of Merit award, and a Beatty award given by the California Library Association. They have been published in eleven languages.

SANDRA SOARES is a professor of French at the University of Wisconsin-River Falls, where she also chairs the Modern Language Department. Dr. Soares taught French, Spanish, and English for two years in the Chicago public schools. The rest of her teaching career has been spent at the University of Wisconsin-River Falls, where she is finishing her 27th (and final) year.

LISA A. SPIEGEL an associate professor of secondary education at the University of South Dakota, teaches courses in young adult literature and middle/secondary education. Her publications and presentations focus on her special interests—gender issues, rural education, and middle grades students—as they relate to language arts instruction.

FAITH SULLIVAN is the author of six published novels: *Repent, Lanny Merkel, Watchdog, Mrs. Demming and the Mythical Beast, The Cape Ann, The Empress of One*, and *What a Woman Must Do*.

JOYCE SWEENEY published her first short story in *New Writers* magazine at the age of eighteen. Her first novel, *Center Line*, won the Delacorte Press Prize for Outstanding Young Adult Novel in 1984. She has published eight more novels, which have won numerous awards, including the Nevada Young Readers Award, the ALA Best Books list and the New York Public Library Best Books list. Her most recent novel is a sports thriller called *Players*. She has also published short stories, articles, and poems.

MARC TALBERT taught fifth and sixth grades for four years and is currently a full-time novelist working on his 14th book, scheduled to come out in the spring of 2002. Titles include *Dead Birds Singing* (1985), *Pillow of Clouds* (1991), and *Small Change* (2000). His novels are realistic fiction, three of which are historical, for middle readers or young adults. Many of them have been published in foreign countries such as Japan, Britain, Germany, Norway, Spain, Columbia, and France.

JULIA TIEDE was born in June of 1991 and is now in the fifth grade. Julia likes to play soccer, read, play football, and write. Her favorite subject in school is math. Julia's ambition in life is to become a teacher.

MARSHALL TOMAN is the chair of the English Department at the University of Wisconsin-River Falls, where he teaches courses in film, writing, and the humanities. As a Fulbright Senior Lecturer in 1997-98, he taught American literature, particularly American ethnic literature, in the Czech Republic. He has published articles on *Powwow Highway*, Joseph Heller, Eudora Welty, and Upton Sinclair. In 1999 he coauthored a grant to establish a University reading group "Toni Morrison: Cultural Critique through Narrative," devoted to examining Morrison's *Beloved, Paradise*, and nonfiction writing.

LINDA VARVEL has taught English in public high schools in Minnesota for nine years, in addition to teaching acting and directing plays at Henry Sibley High School and at the Perpich Center for Arts Education. Currently she is an instructor of English composition and reading at Anoka Ramsey Community College, Minnesota, and is working on a collection of essays and two plays.

JUDITH VOLC has served as a children's librarian, and coordinator of children's and young adult services and is currently Children's Literature Specialist at the Boulder Public Library over the past forty years. She has also taught children's literature at several Colorado universities, and she has spoken at many organizational conferences including NCTE, ALA, and IRA. Volc has served on several book award committees, including the Newbery Committee for ALSC.

ROSALIE BENOIT WEAVER is an associate professor of English at Bemidji State University and is chair of the English department. Among the classes she teaches are Young Adult Literature and Literary Criticism, both helpful in addressing censoring challenges of *Summer of My German Soldier*.

DAVE WOOD is a book reviewer, freelance writer, and past vice president of the National Book Critics Circle. After many years of teaching college, he served for fifteen years as book review editor of the *Minneapolis Star Tribune*. He is the author of six books, the most recent of which is *The Anderson Chronicles* (2000), an informal history of Augsburg College, where he and coauthor Richard Nelson taught.

RUTH WOOD, associate professor of English at the University of Wisconsin-River Falls, is the author of *"Lolita" in "Peyton Place": A Study of Highbrow, Middlebrow, and Lowbrow American Fiction of the Fifties* and has done scholarly work on censorship, television sitcoms, and assessment in the composition classroom. She has also been a secondary school English teacher.

JOHN R. WOZNICKI is an assistant professor of English at Fairmont State College, West Virginia, where he teaches courses in modern and contemporary American literature. Dr. Woznicki 's book *Ideological Content and Political Significance of Twentieth Century American Poetry*, will be published in 2002. He has also contributed articles to *Moira: A Poetry Journal, The Robert Frost Encyclopedia*, and *The Explicator*.